W9-BVG-936

Second Thoughts

Critical Thinking for a Diverse Society

FOURTH EDITION

Wanda Teays

Mount St. Mary's College

 **Higher Education**

Boston   Burr Ridge, IL   Dubuque, IA   New York   San Francisco   St. Louis
Bangkok   Bogotá   Caracas   Kuala Lumpur   Lisbon   London   Madrid   Mexico City
Milan   Montreal   New Delhi   Santiago   Seoul   Singapore   Sydney   Taipei   Toronto

The McGraw·Hill Companies

Higher Education

A DIVISION OF THE MCGRAW-HILL COMPANIES

Published by McGraw-Hill, an imprint of The McGraw-Hill Companies, Inc., 1221 Avenue of the Americas, New York, NY 10020. Copyright © 2010, 2006, 2003, 1996. All rights reserved. No part of this publication may be reproduced or distributed in any form or by any means, or stored in a database or retrieval system, without the prior written consent of The McGraw-Hill Companies, Inc., including, but not limited to, in any network or other electronic storage or transmission, or broadcast for distance learning.

This book is printed on acid-free paper.

1 2 3 4 5 6 7 8 9 0 DOC/DOC 0 9

ISBN: 978-0-07-338670-6
MHID: 0-07-338670-7

Editor in Chief: *Michael Ryan*
Editorial Director: *Beth Mejia*
Sponsoring Editor: *Mark Georgiev*
Marketing Manager: *Pamela Cooper*
Developmental Editor: *Phillip Butcher*
Production Editor: *Regina Ernst*
Manuscript Editor: *Thomas Briggs*
Design Manager: *Allister Fein*
Production Supervisor: *Louis Swaim*
Lead Digital Project Manager: *Ron Nelms*
Composition: *10/12 Sabon by Macmillan Inc.*
Printing: *45# New Era Matte Plus, R. R. Donnelley & Sons/Crawfordsville, IN*

Library of Congress Cataloging-in-Publication Data

Teays, Wanda.
  Second thoughts : critical thinking for a diverse society/Wanda Teays.—4th ed.
      p. cm.
  Includes bibliographical references and index.
  ISBN-13: 978-0-07-338670-6 (alk. paper)
  ISBN-10: 0-07-338670-7 (alk. paper)
  1. Critical thinking—Textbooks. I. Title.
  B809.2.T43 2009
  160—dc22

                                   2009008599

The Internet addresses listed in the text were accurate at the time of publication. The inclusion of a Web site does not indicate an endorsement by the authors or McGraw-Hill, and McGraw-Hill does not guarantee the accuracy of the information presented at these sites.

www.mhhe.com

To Rahma

I planned on you arriving on time.

You were late.

Who could blame you,

Things take time.

And besides, this was your entrance,

Not mine.

But there, by the sidelines,

I could see

That we would all be transformed.

And we were.

We couldn't have predicted

Your impact.

It was like a force of nature,

Cataclysmic,

With everything, every tiny thing

Changing.

We see the world with new eyes,

Your eyes.

You celebrate it all, each stone

Each leaf.

Your joy in being alive,

That joy,

Spreads like the dawn

Unstoppable.

Contents

PART THREE
Going Out into the World   431

Preface

Yes, there were times when I forgot not only who I was, but what I was, forgot to be.
Then I was no longer that sealed jar to which I owed my being so well preserved,
but a wall gave way and I filled with roots and tame stems for example, stakes long since
dead and ready for burning, the recess of night and the imminence of dawn...

SAMUEL BECKETT, *Molloy*

In my garden, away from the rest of the world, it is quiet. I forget who I am, and the pressures of life recede. I leave my garden renewed, ready to return to the busy life of teaching and learning, meeting with my students, working with colleagues, serving on committees, and trying to make a difference as an educator.

It's wonderful to get another opportunity to reshape, revitalize, and update *Second Thoughts*. So much has happened in the world since I worked on the previous edition. It is crucial that we help our students develop critical thinking skills to confront the societal issues we face, as well as reach their own academic and personal goals. We can lay that foundation in our classes and in modeling clear, defensible reasoning. A major concern throughout this text is showing students how to apply what they've learned, so the concepts and techniques are tools—not abstractions. Instructors using this text see the hallmark elements as follows:

- **Balance of skills and techniques with practice and applications.** Students develop their analytical and reasoning skills while learning how to transfer them to a wide variety of applications.
- **Relevant and lively case studies and timely exercises.** The text contains an extensive range of in-class exercises of varying degrees of difficulty and examples and cases that are current—not archaic or canned.
- **User-friendly structure.** The clear writing style helps students grasp ideas and concepts easily; the checklists and step-by-step explanations make the text accessible and interesting; and the sense of humor adds to the quality of the text.
- **Diverse perspectives.** Widening the playing field strengthens problem-solving skills, enlarges students' understanding of the world, and helps them see the value of different frames of reference in their thinking and writing.

- **Sensitivity to ethical components of critical thinking.** The material in the text encourages students to become critically engaged with social issues and to think about what ends are worth achieving. Students acquire tools for social and ethical decision making.
- **Flexibility of use.** Instructors find it easy to customize the text for their classes by focusing upon particular sections in the skills and applications chapters.

In this fourth edition, I have tried to retain those qualities and strengthen the text. I have always stressed diverse perspectives and the value of approaching problem solving from different frames of reference. Those "second thoughts" often bring fruitful results. So, encouraging students to take the time to reflect and to be open to diverse points of view will help them become more adept as critical thinkers. You don't have to look very far in *Second Thoughts* to find examples, group topics, and exercises that incorporate diverse perspectives and provide techniques, strategies, and checklists for building critical thinking and logic skills.

Critical thinking textbooks play different roles, depending on how the instructor approaches the course. What I do in *Second Thoughts* is lay a strong foundation in analytical skills, giving students a footing in both critical reasoning and logic—and then present ways for them to apply what they've learned. This is found both within individual chapters and in more in-depth and extensive applications in the last part. The text is structured with flexibility in mind—so instructors can arrange the material in the order that works best with their course objectives. Chapters are cross-referenced to make it easy to locate and review key material.

Throughout the text are exercises of varying degrees of difficulty. They are drawn from current events, legal rulings, moral dilemmas, statistical studies, bioethics, science, politics, the news media, film, and popular culture. I've included cases that are timely and thought provoking. Many are also fun for students (and faculty) and spark interesting discussion. These are structured so that they can be used during class or assigned as homework or as a group project.

You'll also find some inspiring and insightful pieces—for example, articles by bioethicists Gregg M. Bloche and Jonathan Moreno, and writers Maria Vargas Lhosa and Thich Nhat Hanh, as well as speeches by Nobel Prize winners Eli Wiesel and the Dalai Lama. Our lives are richer because we can read and reflect upon such works. Students come to see that critical thinking and criticism are *not* synonymous—that deconstructing arguments is but one aspect of analytical reasoning. Being able to analyze and reflect, as well as construct arguments, is also vital. And seeing beautifully written and well-reasoned arguments helps further that goal.

In *Second Thoughts,* concepts, techniques, and applications are integrated as we proceed. As a result, group topics and exercises are placed throughout the chapters. In this way, students can get feedback as they go—rather than waiting until the end of the chapter. Students then have many opportunities to apply what they learn and to practice, practice, practice.

⊞ Organization and Revisions

There are three parts in *Second Thoughts:*

Part 1, "Acquiring Critical Thinking Skills," focuses on the basics of critical thinking. The language chapter (Chapter 2 in the previous edition) has been moved to Part 3.

Part 2, "Sharpening the Tools," focuses on key aspects of logic, such as analogies, fallacies, cause-and-effect and statistical reasoning, syllogisms, validity and soundness, and rules of inference.

Part 3, "Going Out into the World," consists of applications—on language, advertising, the Internet, media and popular culture, and a new chapter on legal reasoning and LSAT prep.

These three parts work together to offer a solid foundation for developing fundamental critical thinking techniques and skills. The key revisions to this edition are as follows:

- **Reorganization of the text to emphasize and strengthen skill building before turning to application.** The result is that the first and second parts focus on critical thinking and logic and the third part consists of the five applications chapters.
- **Updated examples.** Material is updated and longer articles have been added for in-class discussions or group or individual analysis. I also added more material on scientific and hypothetical reasoning, and added "quick quizzes" for students to easily test their progress.
- **Expanded coverage in key sections.** In order to help students develop their skills (e. g., in constructing and deconstructing arguments), more discussion and examples have been added. Both Chapters 2 and 3 (on argumentation and analysis, respectively) have been beefed up, so students will get a solid grounding in these areas.
- **New (consolidated) chapter "Voices and Visions: The Media" that merges the chapters on the news media and on film/popular culture.** The first half is on the news media (e.g., tabloidism, analysis of newspapers, watchdog role of the media, professional standards, freedom of the press, ownership and control, and the sports media). The second half is on film and popular culture (e.g., analyzing popular culture, drawing inferences, assessing music and film reviews, and constructing arguments). This chapter works particularly well with Part 1 (the critical thinking section).
- **New chapter on legal reasoning and LSAT prep.** This provides more opportunity for strengthening deductive and inductive reasoning. The first half of the chapter focuses on legal reasoning (e.g., legal precedent, assumptions, and controversial cases in the law, such as same-sex marriage and detainees' rights). The second half focuses on LSAT prep (with hints on reading comprehension, analytical reasoning, logical reasoning, and writing, as well as logic

puzzles to practice deductive thinking skills). This chapter works particularly well with Part 2 (the logic section).

Goals of This Text

As a result of my work with students from different backgrounds, I wanted to create a textbook that would provide a solid foundation in critical thinking and logic—and have lots of applications to put their knowledge to work. Skills and techniques are best seen in action, rather than in the abstract. That's why one-third of this book consists of applications (language, the Internet, advertising, the media, and legal reasoning). The tools of the first two parts are then put to use in wide-reaching ways in the third part.

Another goal was to provide a channel for different ideas, different frames of reference, and different points of view. Given the diversity of our society, it is important to broaden the playing field. This is why there are many voices, not just one, in this textbook. It also gives students opportunities to examine the ways their own perspectives influence what is examined and how problems are solved.

The chapters work together to help students develop their capacity to think carefully, constructively, and systematically. With the tools they acquire, they will be able to tackle issues, ideas, policies, and decision making and apply what they have learned. I often include references to current events, popular culture, and moral and legal dilemmas, as well as global issues. Many of my students can connect with such illustrations and examples—and they appreciate the range of topics. I want students to see how much critical reasoning can help us, whatever the discipline.

There are important social problems that we need to examine in a thoughtful way. Students want to see the relevance of what they learn in terms of the lives they lead. Instructors need to relate what we teach to the world we live in and to reshape curricula and pedagogy to recognize and reach a wider audience. I am heartened by all the instructors I see who strive to do just that.

In most colleges and universities, critical thinking is considered a foundation course—one aimed at first- and second-year students. This highlights how important it is to be doing this work. Once the scaffolding is in place, we can begin to see how valuable it is to think and write clearly and defensibly. There is a lot of satisfaction faculty can derive from helping students acquire the skills and techniques set out in this book and put to action in our courses. There's really nothing like teaching and learning—the link we have together as faculty and with our students is powerful and deeply fulfilling. I wish you all the best in this journey. And I thank you for letting me play a part by using this textbook.

Acknowledgments

There was so much we saw
And never knew.

LOUISE ERDRICH, *Tracks*

I am grateful for the enthusiasm for learning and the generosity of spirit I see in my students. There is a great satisfaction in seeing students develop the skill and confidence to take risks with their own thinking and writing—and to demonstrate how imaginative and insightful they can be. Such moments remind me why I love to teach. It is clear that there is work to be done, that we need to think more deeply about issues such as human rights and justice. Critical thinking is a crucial step in reaching that goal. Looking at all the gifts in my students and their deep sense of fairness, there is reason for hope.

I am grateful to all those philosophers, lawyers, college administrators, bioethicists, writers, Nobel Prize winners(!), reporters, artists, illustrators, and cartoonists who allowed me to reprint their work. Thanks also to the companies and ad agencies that so generously allowed me to use their ads in this text. That these voices come from people all over the world reinforces our common humanity and brings in a richness of ideas, voices, and perspectives.

Thanks also to friends Mary Anne Warren and Michael Scrivens for all their encouragement. Colleagues and my fellow philosophers at Mount St. Mary's College gave me ongoing moral support. And my family helped me keep everything in perspective.

I appreciate the thoughtful criticism and insights of the reviewers who gave their time and effort to help polish this work:

- Anne D'Arcy—CSU Chico
- Eric Kostiuk—Chaffey College
- Kate Norlock—St. Mary's College of Maryland
- Tim Snead—East Los Angeles College

Their constructive criticism helped me shape this new edition. Thanks also to all those instructors who used *Second Thoughts* and who share similar ideas about what we can accomplish as educators. I want also to thank my editor, Phil Butler, for being such a helpful guide and kind person. Thanks also to Regina Ernst, Tom Briggs and all those at McGraw-Hill who helped in production and showed such care in their work. There is so much to be grateful for.

Something happens when others believe in us and support our attempts to make dreams reality. It makes all the difference in the world.

Acquiring Critical Thinking Skills

CHAPTER ONE

Out of the Fog: The Pathway to Critical Thinking

Nothing was clear to lonesome Quoyle. His thoughts churned like the amorphous thing that ancient sailors, drifting into arctic half-light, called the Sea Lung; a heaving sludge of ice under fog where air blurred into water, where liquid was solid, where solids dissolved, where the sky froze and light and dark muddled.

E. ANNIE PROULX, *The Shipping News*

We can't always see clearly as we navigate through the shifting terrain of our lives. Critical thinking is vital for finding our way out of the fog. Issues jump out at every turn—as when you read a news article about a Canadian mother who froze her eggs for future use by her 7-year-old daughter. Evidently, the child is likely to become infertile due to Turner's syndrome. This means that the daughter could give birth to her own sister or brother, with her mother becoming the grandmother of her own child ("Girl Could Give Birth to Sibling," *BBC News*, 3 Jul 2007). It's a bit like the song "I'm My Own Grandpa." Let's listen in as the pundits register opinions:

- **Dr. Richard Kennedy, of the British Fertility Society:** "This altruistic (generous) behavior [on the part of the mother] is not dissimilar to the scenario where a parent donates a kidney to a child."
- **Josephine Quintavalle, of Comment on Reproductive Ethics:** "The psychological welfare of the baby itself has to be the principal concern. Such a baby would be a sibling of the birth mother at the same time as the direct genetic offspring of the grandmother donor."
- **Melanie Bolvin, mother of the seven-year-old Flavie:** "I told myself if she had needed another organ like a kidney I would volunteer without any hesitation and it is the same kind of thought process for this."

- **Quintavalle:** "In psychiatry we are hearing more and more of children suffering from identity problems, and specifically a condition called 'genealogical bewilderment.' Could it possibly get more bewildering than this?"

It *is* bewildering. The skills we learn in critical thinking lay the foundation for dealing with such dilemmas. Notice how both Dr. Richard Kennedy and Melanie Bolvin compared donating a human egg to donating a kidney. Kennedy insists that they are "not dissimilar," but his *saying* so does not make it true. For one thing, donating a kidney does not result in another human life! We would need to look at the analogy and see if it holds (this we'll do in Chapter 6). However, donating eggs, not kidneys, leads to the possibility of her becoming both a mother and grandmother of the same child. Ethicist Josephine Quintavalle raises the issue of the frame of reference: Do we look at the issue from the standpoint of the mother? The daughter? The child? The perspective can change everything. There's a reason this situation has been labeled "genealogical bewilderment."

The ability to think critically and to articulate ideas is powerful and compelling. Without these skills, we'd struggle to sort out thorny cases we read about—and face in our own lives.

Critical thinking is a form of *mental gymnastics:* It helps us solve problems, ask questions, organize our thoughts, and express ourselves clearly and defensibly. It helps us navigate our way through life. Think of it this way: If you can't solve the problem of how to change a flat tire, you could be sitting by the roadside for an awfully long time. If you can't find the right question to ask your doctor when he tells you that you've torn a ligament from trying to change the tire yourself, you may not know your prognosis. And if you can't write a letter to the tire manufacturer about your brand new tire having a blowout for no apparent reason, you may not be able to get redress as soon as you'd like. Our world expands with our abilities; things that were once unattainable come within reach.

Our analytical skills help us separate opinions ("Wow! That was the best movie I've seen in years!") from arguments ("That was the best movie I've seen in years. It had great acting. The story was so good, I didn't dare leave to buy more popcorn for fear I'd miss something. Plus, the special effects left *The Matrix* in the dust!"). Stating a preference falls into the category of an opinion ("I don't like wallets. I prefer to put money in my pocket or carry everything in a bag"). This is also the case when someone states an impression or feeling ("Bruce seems reluctant to go bungie-jumping").

We need good critical thinking skills to be able to construct and dismantle arguments. Developing those skills will be a central goal of this text. In this chapter, we will get an introduction to the territory, examine frames of reference, compare critical thinking and logic, examine description versus inference versus argument, look at building blocks of as well as obstacles to critical thinking, examine the role of diverse perspectives, and look at problem-solving skills.

▦ Introduction to the Territory

Critical thinking entails many levels of thinking; some are called "higher order," while others are "lower order." Lower-order thinking skills—alias *basic skills*—include memorizing, summarizing, labeling, observing, and sorting into assigned categories. Higher-order skills—alias *comprehension skills*—include application, synthesis, drawing inferences, comparison/contrast, justification, analysis, evaluation, moral reasoning, and inductive and deductive reasoning. Both orders have their place.

Knowing how to think clearly helps us separate well-reasoned from weak arguments, sift out unwarranted assumptions, and spot opinions camouflaged as evidence. When analytical skills are missing or in disrepair, you can't think straight and you miss the obvious—not to mention the subtle or hidden.

It is not easy to examine our own assumptions or see how values color our perceptions. **Perspective** is the point of view or frame of reference a person takes in approaching an issue or situation. Filmmaker Errol Morris says, "The only thing I do that's different from other people is I call attention to the fact that I have a point of view. I call attention to the fact that how we see, what we see, is constructed, and that looking at how it's constructed is often a useful exercise" (*The New York Times*, 20 Apr 2008).

When someone is partial to one thing or another, they exhibit a **prejudice.** Prejudice can be positive or negative. The more assured we feel, the better we can "think on our feet," recognize prejudice and bias, and unravel convoluted reasoning. There is power in this. We grow as individuals when we are able to subject our own systems of thought to scrutiny. Our lives change when we can think clearly.

▦ Frame of Reference

Comedian Elayne Boosler reportedly said, "I'm just a person trapped in a woman's body." If you were to tell the story of your life, certain things would jump out at you as most significant. But if your mother or father or your best friend were to tell *your* life story, it would differ from your version. No one is an entirely dispassionate observer.

Each of us has a particular vantage point from which events are seen and understood. This is what is known as our **frame of reference.** It is shaped by our prior knowledge, assumptions, values, traditions, and language, among other things. Recorded history tends to be imprinted by the most powerful members of society. The events, the definitions, and the very terms of the inquiry may reflect the interests of the dominant class. And these terms may work to preserve the status quo. Our view of the world is not value-free. We are influenced by different contexts and by different frameworks. These contexts can be temporal (1980s, 1990s, 2000s), sociocultural (Tex-Mex, Boston Irish, Amish), linguistic (urban slang, formal English, text messaging), and so on.

Be aware of the frame of reference. Consider who or what is most affected and what would likely change with a shift of perspective. And when you speak from personal experience, try to recognize what is unique and what is common with the experiences of others. Be careful not to presume any more than can be supported.

▦ A Solid Foundation

An educated citizenry is at the heart of a true democracy. People who can think critically cannot be manipulated into believing lies are truths. Our system of governance rests on voters being informed and caring enough to act on their convictions. The entire jury system depends on people being able to tell the difference between opinion versus fact and between weak versus well-supported reasoning. "Misinformation campaigns" work only when we fall for them, when we accept unsupported claims and tolerate sloppy thinking.

To determine the truth or falsity of claims, we must subject them to careful scrutiny. This is also true with any claims made by a credible source.

We should base our knowledge on solid ground. We may discover there is no one "truth" to be found, such as when we are choosing between two worthwhile options. It is important that the groundwork be in place for us to examine, analyze, criticize, and reflect. We want to eliminate possible obstacles that may trip us up and cause our reasoning to veer off in the wrong direction.

Critical thinking is rooted in a **social context:** that slice of time, location, culture, politics, and community that shapes our identity and places us on a historical spectrum. We are unique but we are not separate; we are part of a community. This fact of our connectedness affects everything we do. Through our actions we demonstrate our ways of thinking. One of our tasks is to give each side a hearing, so we can fairly assess the evidence in light of the relevant considerations.

Group or Individual Exercise

The Barstow Beauty Queen

In May 2001, just weeks after being named "Miss Barstow" in the town's beauty contest, Emily Arnold, a high school senior, was celebrating winning the crown, her 18th birthday, her pending graduation, and her acceptance to the University of Arizona when she pulled a prank, never imagining the consequences. Read the excerpt below and decide what *you* think should have been done to address the misdeed:

> At a rival classmate's house, she impulsively grabbed a piece of chalk and scrawled the words "NOT NICE" and "MEAN" on a car windshield. The schoolmate's father [Stan Clair], a California Highway Patrol (CHP) sergeant, caught her in the act, called for backup—three squad cars showed up—and had her and six friends arrested. The father wants the district attorney to file charges of vandalism.
>
> Tonight, Emily Arnold—cheerleader, honor student and class treasurer, so long the beneficiary of small-town life, now the victim of it—will give back her crown. The

sudden controversy has left Barstow divided. "There are some people who felt that she should be asked to leave [the position], and others who felt that she should not," said Kris Watson, director of the Miss Barstow contest for the last 12 years. (Scott Gold, "The Short, Sad Reign of Miss Barstow," *Los Angeles Times*, 28 Jun 2001)

Answer the following:

1. Do you agree with Mr. Clair's response to the incident? Set out three pros and cons of his action in light of *his* own daughter's behavior:

   But [the CHP officer] Stan Clair, a member of the school board, insisted on pressing charges of vandalism, a crime that can bring a $1,000 fine and a year in jail. Some criticize him for that, pointing out his own daughter had been accused of shooting a neighbor's house and car with a paint-ball gun only hours before the notorious chalk incident. That situation, they say, was resolved without need for law enforcement. (Gold, "The Short, Sad Reign of Miss Barstow")

2. What three to four thoughts or suggestions would you share with Kris Watson, director of the Miss Barstow contest?

3. As you might expect, the public responded. Set out your thoughts on the comments about the case printed in letters to the editor of the *Los Angeles Times*:

   RESPONSE 1, WALLY ROBERTS: "Any reasonable father in such circumstances would have made the errant teens clean up the mess and apologize . . . in the circumstances, he grossly overreacted and used his authority as a CHP officer to do so."

   RESPONSE 2, MARK HERDER: "I want to commend Sgt. Clair and the CHP for their courageous takedown of Miss Barstow. Few people know or even care about the growing epidemic of teenage beauty queens run amok. Just yesterday I caught one scribbling 'wash me' with her finger on the dusty windshield of my car. Sgt. Clair, where were you and your three squad cars of brave highway patrolmen when I needed you?"

   RESPONSE 3, MARK ESPENSCHIED: "Shame on Clair, shame on the Kiwanis Club and shame on half the citizens of Barstow. . . . In a perfect world, Clair would be reprimanded by the CHP and kicked off the school board. By all means, get out of town, Emily Arnold. Go to where you can continue to excel."

▦ Overview of Critical Thinking

Arguments: The Common Ground of Logic and Critical Thinking

You arrive home and turn on the TV. On comes an ad: "More people prefer Sammy's to Pizza House pizza." Ready to place your order for a BBQ chicken pizza, you glance at the TV screen. "In a study of 300 people, 154 preferred

Sammy's." The ad agency for Sammy's underestimates you, however, as your brain cells are on standby for action! Fortunately, you are able to figure out that of the 300 people studied, 154 preferred Sammy's and 146 preferred Pizza House pizza. This is a difference of only 8 people, or 2.6 percent. Allowing for a margin of error of 2 to 3 percent, the study actually revealed very little, other than that the contest was virtually a draw.

When studying critical thinking, we acquire skills and tools to construct or dismantle arguments, examine data, weigh evidence, read more carefully, subject our own reasoning to assessment, reflect on our beliefs, and articulate our own ideas clearly and defensibly. We each start to feel like a mental acrobat, no more the fool.

Propositions are the building blocks of arguments. A **proposition** is an assertion that is either true or false. The form of a proposition is that something is being predicated of some subject, such as "Some moviegoers [subject] are popcorn-eaters [predicate]." Propositions can function together as a body of evidence offered in support of a particular claim. This forms an argument.

Argumentation is central to both critical thinking and logic. An **argument** has two major parts: the conclusion and the premises. This means arguments consist of a set of propositions, at least one of which (called a **premise**) is offered as evidence for accepting another proposition (called the **conclusion** or **thesis**). Our main concern is to assess the quality of the evidence as support for the conclusion. That relationship between the premises and the conclusion is pivotal. Dismantling and assessing arguments is the bread and butter of critical thinking.

We meet arguments everywhere—in advertisements, newspapers, TV, radio, political campaigns, and classroom discussions. Some arguments are of little importance. Others have changed the world. In a *strong argument,* the premises provide sufficient support for the conclusion (thesis). The conclusion should follow from the premises, so if each premise were presumed to be true, the conclusion would be true as well—or highly likely in an inductive argument (like one using statistical reasoning).

Here's a strong argument: "All race-car drivers take risks. Some race-car drivers are killed in accidents at professional auto races. Therefore, some risk-takers are killed in accidents at professional auto races." If the two premises are true, the conclusion must be true. Unfortunately, many arguments fall short of this goal. The premises may offer some support but do not make as strong a case as we'd like. There may be **missing pieces,** so that the overall picture is twisted and the argument is deficient. Here's an example: "Many accidents of drivers under 20 years old involve drivers who are using cell phones. Carlos regularly uses his cell phone and is only 19 years old. Therefore, he'll probably get in an accident some time this year." What's missing here? You probably saw it—those in accidents using cell phones are generally not "hands-free," Carlos may have a speaker system or use a Bluetooth device, or perhaps he turns his cell phone off while driving. For that matter, Carlos may not drive at all! These crucial missing pieces mean the argument is not very strong. Or the argument may be poorly worded or badly constructed. On the other hand, the evidence could present an airtight case. Our task is to figure this out.

Comparison of Logic and Critical Thinking

Being a good critical thinker and being a good logician are similar yet different. The key similarity is that both emphasize analysis and careful reasoning. The key difference is that logic is more narrowly focused, whereas critical thinking has a broader scope. **Logic** focuses upon argumentation; the task of the logician is to determine the strength of the evidence as support for the conclusion.

The logician makes *three key distinctions:* What kind of argument is this? How convincing is it? Does it rest on evidence we know (or can determine) to be true? Each question lays the foundation for all further steps the logician will take, as we'll see below:

Three Key Questions in Logic

- **What kind of argument is it?** Logicians divide arguments into two categories: deductive and inductive. With **deductive arguments,** it is claimed or implied that the premises completely support the conclusion. With **inductive arguments,** the evidence is not sufficient for the conclusion to follow with certainty. The *difference* between these two categories of reasoning is analogous to playing with a full deck of cards versus a deck in which there are missing cards.
- **How convincing is the argument on its face value?** With deductive arguments, we seek to determine if the conclusion will *certainly* be true if we assume the premises are all true. With inductive arguments, we decide how *probable* the conclusion is if we assume the premises are all true. The focus is basically on *structure*. In the case of deductive arguments, these are called logically **valid arguments.**
- **Does the argument pass the truth test?** Are the premises in fact true—is the evidence cited really the case? **Sound arguments** have two characteristics: They are valid arguments *and* they have true premises. When there's doubt, we don't know if the argument will pass the truth test. When there's a false premise, the argument cannot be considered sound, even if it is well structured. An unsound argument could be invalid, have false premises, or both.

One of the tasks of the logician is to decide if the evidence really offers the quality of support for the conclusion. This corresponds to the standard of proof in criminal trials *("beyond a reasonable doubt")*. Classically, logicians studied only deductive arguments, the model was mathematics, and the objective was certainty.

Here's an example of a valid deductive argument: "All Chihuahuas are dogs. No dog is a reptile. Therefore, no Chihuahua is a reptile." If the first two premises are assumed to be true, then the conclusion will certainly be true as well—it could not be false. The conclusion follows beyond any doubt. Of course, the evidence cited may not fully support the conclusion. Often the evidence is just not strong enough, even if it helps make the case.

Many arguments rest on probability or unproven assumptions, corresponding to the standard of proof in civil trials: a *"preponderance of the evidence"* (where a simple majority of the evidence must point to the conclusion). Whichever standard of proof we seek, logic gives us the means to examine arguments.

One aspect of developing critical thinking skills is making sure we have a footing in logic. For that reason, the first and second parts of this book help develop both critical thinking and logic skills. The last part focuses on different applications of those skills.

Critical Thinking: A Broader Scope

Critical thinking encompasses much more than argumentation, and so it is a broader discipline than logic. It includes skills of observation, description, inference, language analysis, assessment of the role of frame of reference, and examination of unwarranted assumptions or other obstacles to clear thinking. To be good thinkers, we need to be observant. We need to watch carefully and have our antennae out.

Be attentive to details while not losing sight of the larger framework. Take nothing for granted. We do not want to be oblivious, to be "asleep at the switch," or to overlook something that could break the case. Here's an unfortunate oversight: In 1999 the CIA provided incorrect targeting data that led U.S. warplanes to bomb the Chinese Embassy in Yugoslavia during a NATO air strike. Evidently, "The CIA had not noticed the embassy's new address in the Belgrade [Yugoslavia] telephone directory" (Bob Drogin, "School for New Brand of Spooks," *Los Angeles Times*, 21 Jul 2000). Duh!

Examining the Evidence

An important aspect of critical thinking centers on examining the evidence. This involves surveying the situation, clarifying goals, looking at the process by which evidence is obtained, watching for problems, and weighing the evidence. Weighing evidence involves separating evidence from background information, deciding on a set of criteria to sort it into categories or evaluate it, and then seeing how well it supports the conclusion. We will look at this in Chapters 2 and 3.

For example, if the criteria for a scholarship centered on academic merit, then financial need would not be a factor. If the sole requirements for an ideal mate were that the person be attractive and rich, then traits like integrity, generosity, and sense of humor would be of little relevance. If your criteria for a good movie included lots of special effects, then you probably would be drawn to action films over dramas.

The Global Dimension

Bilinguals and the Brain

The *BBC News* reported on a language study by a York (Canada) University researcher that suggests a link between bilingualism and brain-power. Read about it, keeping your mind open to alternative explanations. Answer the questions that follow.

This latest study appears to back up the theory that language skills also have a protective effect. Dr. Ellen Bialystok and colleagues at York University assessed the cognitive skills of all those involved in the study using a variety of widely recognised tests. They tested their vocabulary skills, their non-verbal reasoning ability and their reaction time. Half of the volunteers came from Canada and spoke only English. The other half came from India and were fluent in both English and Tamil. The volunteers had similar backgrounds in the sense that they were all educated to degree level and were all middle class.

The researchers found that the people who were fluent in English and Tamil responded faster than those who were fluent in just English. This applied to all age groups. The researchers also found that the bilingual volunteers were much less likely to suffer from the mental decline associated with old age. "The bilinguals were more efficient at all ages tested and showed a slower rate of decline for some processes with aging," they said. "It appears . . . that bilingualism helps to offset age-related losses." (See "Being Bilingual Protects Brain," *BBC News World Edition,* news.bbc.co.uk, 15 Jun 2004.)

Answer the following:

1. What assumptions do the researchers make in using sample groups from different countries (and, possibly, different backgrounds)?
2. Offer at least two alternative explanations for the research subjects from India having superior cognitive abilities besides their language skills.
3. Research the studies done on turmeric and Alzheimer's disease. As you may know, the spice turmeric is in curry—which is often used in Indian cooking (e.g., see "Curry 'May Slow Alzheimer's,'" *BBC News,* news.bbc.co.uk, 21 Nov 2001). Studies indicate that turmeric may be a reason that Alzheimer's disease is rarely found in India. If diet may be a factor in Alzheimer's, should it be factored in when assessing this study on bilingualism's supposed benefits? Share your thoughts.

Sorting for Relevance

Being able to pinpoint **relevant evidence** is crucial to problem solving. The more relevant the evidence, the greater its role or impact. Consider how each piece of evidence links to the thesis. Determine if it functions independently (on its own) or dependently (in collaboration with other pieces of evidence). Frequently, the so-called evidence is way off the mark—irrelevant to the thesis. People can be gullible (e.g., regarding celebrity endorsements or negative political campaigns). They may ignore relevant evidence, and fall instead for an emotional appeal.

We often face a glut of information, such as from Internet searches. The information may be off topic, out of date, or misleading. Or it could be focused on persuasion, as we see in a lot of advertising, where the "evidence" may be lacking or omitted.

Let's look at advertisements, one for yogurt and one for cigarettes. The ad for Yoplait berry banana and kiwi daiquiri yogurt has a photo of three pretty young women who are laughing and appear to be having fun. In the top left corner is written, *"It's Like . . . Girls' Night Out,"* and in the lower right in large letters is *"Good!"* Nothing in the ad addresses the virtues of the yogurt—the "girls" are not even eating yogurt. In the second example, a cigarette ad, we see a photo of a building (nightclub?) in midnight blue. In the center of the ad is written, *"There are no strangers here. Only friends we haven't met."* These last words are positioned so we connect the idea of meeting these new "friends" with smoking Marlboros.

The evidence for concluding that we should buy this yogurt or that cigarette centers on an imagined experience, not the product in question. This overlooks more relevant factors—such as the nutritional value of the yogurt or the health concerns of smoking. As we will see, that's when critical thinking tools can come to the rescue.

Individual or Group Exercise

Grade Quotas

With 46 percent of Princeton students getting grades in the "A" range (counting plus and minus), the administration is cracking down and instituting quotas. As of the academic year 2004–05, Princeton University's new policy is setting a cap of 35 percent on A's in all courses, except for independent studies (which will cap at 55 percent). The dean argues that grade inflation could no longer be ignored: "Our feeling then was that we could just let it go, and over the next 25 years every-one would be getting all A's," says Nancy Weiss Malkiel. "But would that really be responsible in terms of the way we educated our students?" Update: The number of A's in all Princeton undergraduate classes went from 47% in 2004 to 40.7% in 2008. (Teresa Mendez, "Deflating the Easy A," *Christian Science Monitor,* 4 May 2004).

Answer the following:

1. What assumptions did the dean of Princeton make regarding the high number of A's?

2. What is the most relevant support cited for concluding that Princeton has grade inflation?

3. What is the least relevant support cited for concluding that Princeton has grade inflation?

4. Syracuse University professor William Coplin argues that students learn in the classroom less than half of what they need to know for real life. Distributing higher grades gives them room to explore other areas of interest and to develop as people. "Most students do not see college as a

place to develop skills. They see it as a place to get a degree and have a high GPA," he says. "The truth is, skills are more important than GPA." He worries that attempting to stamp out grade inflation will simply make students even crazier about grades (Mendez, "Deflating the Easy A"). Do you think he's right? Share your thoughts.

▦ Descriptions versus Inferences

When we describe, we try to objectively state a set of facts. A good description provides us with the essential features of the thing by listing its qualities or characteristics. An inference is an answer to the question, "What's it about? What story does this tell?"

Descriptions, like a set of facts, are statements about what is or is not the case. A description is usually most helpful if it is as straight forward and impartial as possible. Generally, each item in a description is verifiable by examination. For example, we might describe a friend by giving her height, weight, eye color, hair color and style, and the like. Occasionally, an inference sneaks in as a description. For example, suppose someone says, "He's tall, slim, and a real hunk!" One person's "hunk" is another person's wallflower, so such value-laden judgments have to be pulled out and placed in the inference category, as they can be quite problematic.

We have to watch what is included in the description. Descriptions often act as support—the foundation—for inferences. An inference may or may not be well supported by the evidence behind it. For example, a description of a player who falls on the court might include the following: "He fell after being hit, he was lying down, but now he is bent over, holding his leg and moaning." An inference might be, "He seems to be in discomfort, he looks like he's in pain, it's probably pretty serious, and the coach looks worried."

Descriptions and inferences often get intertwined, and our own values or points of view can influence the description, as we see in this discussion of golfer Tiger Woods:

> Tiger Woods has risen above mere human status and become an embodiment of immortal excellence, [an] exemplar of mental discipline. The coverage of him often centers upon this question: How did this creature come about? Woods seems able to mute the chatter that normal people have in their heads and build a tunnel of focused attention. Writers get rhapsodic over this facility. "Woods's concentration often seems to be made of the same stuff as the liquid-metal cyborg in *Terminator 2:* If you break it, it reforms," David Owen wrote in *Men's Vogue.* Then they get spiritual. In *Slate,* Robert Wright only semi-facetiously compared Woods to Gandhi, for his ability to live in the present and achieve transcendent awareness. (David Brooks, "The Frozen Gaze," *The New York Times,* 17 Jun 2008)

Inferences are not necessarily impartial, for they often involve an attempt to make sense of the evidence, not just report on what is seen or heard.

An **inference** is a conclusion drawn on the basis of a description or other sorts of evidence. Inferences are not necessarily impartial, for they often involve an attempt to make sense of the evidence, not just to report what they see or hear. An example may help. Julie Salamon writes about a year in the life of Maimonides Medical Centre in Brooklyn (*The Economist,* 8 May 2008). She describes the chaotic emergency room, with patients waiting in holding patterns like aircraft at a busy airport, and the "frequent flyers," as the staff call those they send away with prescriptions for medicines these patients cannot afford, knowing they will soon be back in a bad way once more. Salamon paints a compelling—and damning—portrait of a dysfunctional health-care system. From her *description* of all that chaos, Salamon *infers* that the system is dysfunctional.

Exercises

1. How would you *describe* the photos in Figures 1.1 and 1.2? What would you *infer* is going on? Give your description and draw at least two different inferences for each photograph.
2. Look at the photograph of the signs in Figure 1.3. Draw some inferences from the smaller sign (placed on a street in West Hollywood).

FIGURE 1.1
Describe what you see.
What can you infer?

Photograph by Wanda Teays. Copyright 2008.

Photograph from Operation Cue (Office of Civil and Defense Mobilization, 5 May 1955, from the National Archives, ARC identifier 541789). Reprinted with the permission of the National Archives, Still Pictures Unit.

FIGURE 1.2
How would you describe this? What can we infer from this photo?

Photograph by Wanda Teays. Copyright 2004.

FIGURE 1.3
What can you infer about the reason for posting this sign? Do you think drivers obey it?

3. Draw two inferences about the Alabama prison system from the following:

BIRMINGHAM—Back in the day of chain gangs, Alabama passed a law that gave sheriffs $1.75 a day to feed each prisoner in their jails, and the sheriffs got to pocket anything that was left over. More than 80 years later, most Alabama counties still operate under this system, with the same $1.75-a-day allowance, and some sheriffs are actually making money on top of their salaries. The menu on a recent day in the Limestone County [Alabama] Jail was two pancakes and syrup, sausage and milk for breakfast; peanut butter sandwiches, chips and Kool-Aid for lunch; and white beans, turnip greens, fried squash, cornbread and sweet tea for dinner. (Yahoo News, 16 May 2008)

4. Draw two inferences about math whizzes from the following:

Some people probably suspected the math whiz from grade school wasn't in his right mind. Apparently he wasn't—he was in his right *and* his left mind. A recent study of adolescents with above-average math abilities found the right and left halves of their brains are apparently better able to interact and share information than the brains of average students.
   "Giftedness in math, music or art may be the by-product of a brain that has functionally organized itself in a different way," said Michael O'Boyle, psychologist at the University of Melbourne and one of the study's co-authors. ("Your Health: A Smarter Brain," www.forbes.com, 13 Apr 2004)

When we offer a description, we should try to be aware of our own frame of reference. Note any potential for bias or for interference in giving a fair and detailed description. Background knowledge is not necessary—and may even get in the way. When you drew your inferences from looking at the photograph in Figure 1.2, did you think about nuclear explosions? The photo is of mannequins used in overground nuclear testing. You can look at others taken (they are mind-boggling!) at the National Archives website (www.archives.gov).

Exercises

Directions: Look at the photographs in Figures 1.4 and 1.5. Answer the following for each photograph:

1. Describe what you see in the photo. (Draw up a list of descriptive items for each photo).
2. What do you think the photo is about? Draw some inferences on the basis of what you see. What is going on here?
3. Look over both your description list and list of inferences:
   a. What is different about the two lists?
   b. What assumptions came into play when you made your inferences?

FIGURE 1.4
What do you
observe? What
do you infer?

Security/Pacific Collection/Los Angeles Public Library.
Reprinted with permission.

FIGURE 1.5
What do you
observe? What do
you infer?

Security/Pacific Collection/Los Angeles Public Library. Reprinted with permission.

Group or Individual Exercise

Directions: Let's look at the marriage of Al and Milly. Read the letter Al sent Milly, and consider what the letter reveals.

Al's Demand Letter to Milly

"You *will* see to it: That my clothes and linens are kept in order, That I am served three regular meals a day *in my room*, That my bedroom and study are always kept in good order And that *my desk is not touched by anyone other than me.*

"You *will* renounce all personal relations with me, except when these are required to keep up social appearances. In particular you will not request: That I sit with you at home. That I go out with you or travel with you.

"You *will* promise explicitly to observe the following points in any contact with me. You will expect no affection from me and you will not reproach me for this. You must answer me at once when I speak to you. You must leave my bedroom or study at once without protesting when I ask you to go.

"You *will* promise not to denigrate me in the eyes of the children, either by word or deed." (See "His Head in the Ether, He Was among a 'Sorry Herd of Humans,'" *The New York Times,* 10 Nov 1996.)

Answer the following:

1. What do *you* think about this man?
2. What sort of marriage is this? These two questions ask you to draw inferences.
3. What supports your assessment? This is an issue of *evidence.*

Perhaps the fact that this letter was written in 1914 may affect how you see the man and the marriage. This is an issue of *context.* Perhaps the fact that Al was famous may affect your assessment. Or the fact that he was a scientist (as opposed to an artist, surgeon, or truck mechanic) may color your interpretation. Would your inference be different if you knew that "Al" is Albert Einstein, renowned scientist, and "Milly" is Mileva Maric, who met Einstein while a student (she was the only female there studying physics)?

Descriptions versus Arguments

Arguments take many forms, but they differ from descriptions *and* inferences. When we describe, we try to objectively state a set of facts. A good description provides us with the essential features of the thing by listing its key qualities or

You Tell Me Department

Mad Cow Disease

USA has had thousands of "downer" cows (dying mysteriously) since 1981. If the bug entered U.S. beef 15 years ago and has been multiplying ever since, a million cows could be infected. Mad-Cow mortality figures hide behind the skirts of Alzheimer's. Some U.S. doctors know the truth, yet haven't blown whistles. Pittsburgh Veterans hospital autopsied 53 sequential Alzheimer's victims. Sampling 1 showed 5.5 percent had died of Mad-Cow, sampling 2 that 6.3 percent died of Mad-Cow. Alzheimer's death tolls are doubling and tripling, not characteristic of a genetic disease *ergo* the shadowy presence of another *probable cause*.

Since beef and sheep farmers have been sending "downer" livestock to rendering factories to be made into "protein powder" for livestock for the last 26 years, Mad-Cow prions could be in every ounce of meat, milk, pork, chicken, egg, cheese, or butter you have eaten since 1970 and in every bite you eat today and in gelatin caps, animal glandular supplements and in the glue on the postage stamp you will use. . . . Mad-Cow is the most prevalent, virulent disease to hit this planet since the plague. Conceivably it could represent the end of all human life here. . . . It is certain that we will see many more cases associated with CJD (Creutzfeldt-Jacob disease, the human version of Mad-Cow disease) than we have ever seen with AIDS as Mad Cow infection has been found all over Europe. ("What Is Prion and How Does It Affect Us?" *The Open Line,* 26 Feb 2005)

You tell me: What can you infer about the author's point of view in the above passage? Which claims most warrant backup support? State them.

---

characteristics. If you draw an inference on the basis of a description, then you have a conclusion to an argument. The combination of the description and the inference forms an argument. Compare this description to the inferences that follow:

> **Description:** The kitchen had dirty dishes stacked in the sink. There was a pan on the stove with dried-up beans stuck to the bottom. A bag of flour was lying on the floor, with its contents spilled out, leaving a white powder covering half the room. Grandma was not to be seen.

> **Possible inferences:** "Clearly, someone broke in while Grandma was working in the kitchen and they've abducted her." Or: "Clearly, Grandma was fed up with cleaning up after Uncle Joe and his four fishing buddies. She obviously wanted to make a statement!" And so on.

A description is different from an argument because it *lacks a conclusion.* A description is like a careful observation. For example, here's a *description* of Jasper: "Jasper is a cockatoo, three years old, with white and peach-colored feathers." If we add the conclusion, "Therefore, Jasper will not be easy to sneak into the movie theater," we now have an *argument.*

Drawing Inferences

People regularly conclude one thing or another on the basis of what they see or hear. They are *drawing inferences.* An inference is the same as a conclusion. Sometimes the inferences we draw are well founded; sometimes they are not. Think of those stories about someone who shoots a family member in the middle of the night. The person is awakened by a noise, grabs a shotgun, and when the door opens, lets the suspect have it. Unfortunately, they just killed Uncle Roy, who dropped by to give them a surprise present.

Drawing inferences is a part of our lives. It pays to be careful, however. Consider this example: In July 2001, Kevin Pullum, convicted of attempted murder, strolled out of the Los Angeles Twin Towers jail wearing a badge with a photo of actor Eddie Murphy from *Dr. Doolittle 2*. Although the escapee is black, he does not resemble Murphy. Apparently no one checked Pullum's fake badge as he passed by the security booth. As Bill Cunningham of the Cook County Sheriff's Department in Chicago put it: "He's walking around with a picture of Eddie Murphy on an ID and no one noticed? That's bad. One small mistake can compromise security for the entire jail" (Beth Shuster and Kenneth Reichs, "Jail Escapee Is a No-Show at Surrender," *Los Angeles Times,* 17 Jul 2001).

Not all inferences have the sort of fallout as the case above. We draw inferences as part of our work as students and faculty. But we also draw inferences in relationships. And so on.

Exercises

Part One

1. Assume you would like to model sandals for a magazine ad. The agent has asked you to send a *description* of your feet. Try to be precise as you can (assume also that he has no way of seeing a photograph of your feet). After you set down your description, draw an inference about the likelihood of your getting the modeling job.

2. What can you infer from the comments of W. D. Richter, director of *Slither, Dracula,* and *Invasion of the Body Snatchers:*

When I was a kid, I liked horror and science fiction films as much as I liked anything. I actually probably watched them a little more religiously. I'd go to the movies by myself to see *The Day of the Triffids* [1963] and *The Blob* [1958] and all that stuff. It's just a wonderful release of the human imagination. I think that's its ultimate appeal: it takes you somewhere out there and makes you picture a universe that's just far more fantastic than the little town you're living in, or whatever your particular arena is at that time. (Matthew R. Bradley, "An Interview with W. D. Richter," in Kevin McCarthy and Ed Gorman, eds., *"They're Here . . ." Invasion of the Body Snatchers: A Tribute,* Boulevard Books, 1999)

3. Here is a description of two robbery suspects in Sarnia, Ontario, Canada. Note any parts of the "descriptions" that are less than certain and/or involve inference(s) on the part of the police:

City police have released detailed descriptions of two people wanted in connection with an armed robbery in downtown Sarnia Sunday morning. Police are looking for a native woman in her early 30s who is described as having dark eyes, long, straight dark hair to the small of her back, a large mouth, straight yellow teeth and pock marks or scars on the sides of her face. She was wearing light blue jeans, a black leather jacket and white shoes when she walked into the Drawbridge Inn around 8 a.m. brandishing a kitchen knife.

Her accomplice is described as a male who appeared to be over the age of 40. He was about six-foot-four, thin and lanky, with short, dark brown, messy hair, sunken cheeks and what a police press release refers to as "buggy eyes." He was wearing a dark brown sweater and dark blue jeans. . . . (Dan McCaffery, "Police Describe Robbery Suspects; Kitchen Knife Was Used, No Injuries," *The (Sarnia) Observer*, 19 Mar 2008)

4. State what you can infer about those who detest bad punctuation from the following:

While we look in horror at a badly punctuated sign, the world carries on around us, blind to our plight. We are like the little boy in *The Sixth Sense* who can see dead people, except that we can see dead punctuation. Whisper it in petrified little-boy tones: dead punctuation is invisible to everyone else—yet we see it *all the time*. No one understands us seventh-sense people. They regard us as freaks. When we point out illiterate mistakes we are often aggressively instructed to "get a life" by people who, interestingly, display no evidence of having lives themselves. Naturally we become timid about making our insights known, in such inhospitable conditions. Being burned as a witch is not safely enough off the agenda. (Lynne Truss, *Eats, Shoots & Leaves*, Penguin Books, 2003)

5. Do two rounds of describing someone (in writing preferably, or verbally if in group activity—draw from a list of athletes, singers, models, actors, politicians, or the like). For example, you could select a model in a print ad to use as the basis of your description.

   Round 1: Describe the person in as much detail as you can without mentioning race or ethnicity. After you finish, add a paragraph of reflections on the ease or difficulty of omitting race/ethnicity from the description.

   Round 2: Describe the person in as much detail as you can, including race or ethnicity. After you finish, compare the two descriptions and note to what degree this additional element added to or detracted from the quality of your description.

Part Two

Directions: Below is a list of descriptions of a student's dorm room. State three *different* inferences you could draw about what sort of person she is, citing the evidence to back up your inference.

1. There are empty potato chip bags and chocolate wrappers under the bed.
2. There is a half-eaten cheese sandwich in the sink, along with a pile of dirty dishes.
3. There are five posters on the walls—all cartoon characters.
4. There are five empty milk cartons stacked neatly by the door.

5. There are piles of chemistry books strewn on the desk and floor.

6. There are four kinds of perfume bottles sitting on the side table, still in their packages, unopened.

7. There is a huge Mickey Mouse pillow on the bed.

8. Two ticket stubs for last week's Sonics' basketball game are on the desk.

9. The bed is neatly made and has a bright orange comforter on it.

10. The windows are all open, with the blinds pulled up.

11. A speeding ticket, ripped into tiny pieces, lies next to the perfume bottles on the side table.

12. There is a neat stack of sci-fi and action film DVDs on the floor by the TV.

Quick Quiz

1. *True or false:* A description is an argument focused on traits or characteristics.

2. Is this an *argument (yes or no)?* "The burglar who crawled through the kitchen window might have been a big brute. You could tell by the fact that the window was completely broken—glass was everywhere. Plus, there were very large footprints on the freshly washed floor."

3. *True or false:* An inference functions the same as a conclusion of an argument.

4. Can an argument have a description as one or more of its premises (*yes or no*)?

5. *True or false:* A description is the answer to the question "What's it about? What story does it tell?"

6. Is this an *argument (yes or no)?* "The big brute of a burglar was caught. He'd gotten stuck trying to crawl out through the dog door. Sure enough, he was big—he must have weighed 300 pounds and was over six-foot-five. He didn't get much though—he only had $50 in his pocket, a nice wood chopping board, and three knives for chopping vegetables."

7. *True or false:* An inference functions the same as a description in an argument.

8. *True or false:* You can use the term *inference* interchangeably with "conclusion."

The Role of Ideas in Analysis

Without the ability to analyze effectively, we would flounder. In situations that require us to dismantle reasoning or solve a problem, our analytical skills are crucial. Another aspect of analysis is the ability to work on the level of ideas.

Through ideas and insights, we are able to move forward, solve problems, break deadlocks, and overcome mental paralysis.

There are two key aspects to the role of ideas in critical thinking. One is *having ideas,* and the other is *applying and examining ideas.* This includes assessing the various parameters that may act as constraints, such as time, money, and available resources.

Consider this breakthrough idea: With 100 million land mines worldwide, finding and eliminating them is a must. The Gambian giant pouched rat may one day replace dogs for sniffing them out. Evidently, dogs are hard to keep healthy, especially in tropical Africa. Also, they bond with their trainers, making it hard to switch them to a different handler. The rats have the advantage of smaller size—they weigh around 3 pounds, so they don't trip the land mine charges. Furthermore:

> **First:** In their little red, black and blue harnesses, they look like miniature sniffer dogs. But their trainers at Sokoine University of Agriculture say the African pouched rats can do a much better job than dogs—and they do it for a bit of banana. "Rats are good, clever to learn, small, like performing repeated tasks and have a better sense of smell than dogs," said Christophe Cox, the Belgian coordinator of a project that is training 300 rats to locate mines by recognizing the smell of dynamite and TNT. ("Rats Nose Knows Best," www.landmines.org)

> **Second:** "Throw a stick for a dog to fetch, and after 10 times the dog will say, 'Get it yourself, buddy,'" Mr. [Frank] Weetjens said. "Rats will keep working as long as they want food." . . . "Rats 'don't give a fig about people,'" says Harvard Bach of the Geneva demining center. "They're almost mechanical in the way they work," he says. (Michael Wines, "For Sniffing Out Land Mines a Platoon of Twitching Noses," *The New York Times,* 18 May 2004)

Exercises

Part One

1. As we can see from the above report, the need for trained Gambian rats seems obvious. But they require a human trainer to work with them and, after locating a land mine, to hand them a piece of banana or other tasty morsel. Once trained, the rats sniff out a mine, then sit and scratch at the spot until they are rewarded with food. A human explosive expert then destroys the mine—obviously a risky proposition. Assume *your* help is needed to attract the people to work out in the field: What do you think should be included in a job ad for handlers of the land mine–sniffing rats? List them (or write the job ad that'll be placed in the newspaper!).

2. The thought of freezing to death—or being frozen after death—gets a chilly reception. Nevertheless, answer any *two* of the following questions:
   a. What inferences can you draw from the fact that at 35 degrees, bleeding virtually stops and the brain can survive for hours (reported in *Wired,* May 2004)?

   b. Can you think of an idea for putting this fact to commercial use—how could it be used in furthering cryogenics (freezing bodies for eventual revival)?

   c. State two to three concerns that this assertion raises: "As far as anyone knows, there's nothing physically impossible about reviving a frozen head" (Wil McCarthy, *Wired,* May 2004).

Part Two

1. A jewelry firm called American Design sells a "Fat-Be-Gone" ring. The online ad was said to claim that "when worn on the little finger, the ring slims the thighs. The ring finger is for the stomach, thumb for the face and so on—all with 'no drugs, no starving, no sweating.'" Lynn McAfee, director of the Council on Size and Weight Discrimination, observes, "I don't think it's unreasonable that we want to have a miracle." She evidently has a Fat-Be-Gone ring, saying, "In the back of my mind, I say, 'Well, maybe it will work'" (Greg Winter, "Fraudulent Marketers Capitalize on Demand for Sweat-Free Diets," *The New York Times,* 29 Oct 2000).

Answer the following:

   a. Is there any harm (and maybe even good) in wearing a Fat-Be-Gone ring?

   b. What concerns should be raised about allowing a company to market a Fat-Be-Gone ring?

   c. What elements of being a good critical thinker will help you in deciding whether there is any merit to such a diet cure as this?

2. What's wrong with this reasoning?

KEITH: Hey, Shakir, what's up?

SHAKIR: You may not want to know, Keith! I just read an article about this weird disease in New York and New Jersey called MRSA that starts like a rash and goes to skin abscesses or amputation. Get a load of this *[reading out loud]:*

"The Department of Health is tracking the outbreak here but declined to provide the number of cases it has found. Last month, Steven, who asked that his last name not be published, developed what he thought was a pimple on his leg, but it soon grew painful and larger. Doctors lanced the boil that formed and began antibiotics, but the infection failed to respond and starting growing toward Steven's groin. 'The fact it wasn't responding [to drugs] and it was moving up that way was terrifying,' he said. 'It was eating up tissue.' After a lengthy hospital stay and five antibiotics—some administered intravenously and one, Zyvox, administered orally at $100 per tablet—the infection started to abate. Doctors told Steven they believed he contracted it at the gym." (Sam Smith, "Killer Rash Breaks Out," *New York Post,* www.nypost.com, 30 May 2004)

KEITH: Wow! That's awful, man. It's another reason not to go to a gym! I'm staying away from them, that much I know.

SHAKIR: Yeah, you just don't know what disease you'll get when you hang out at a gym. That's why I work out with weights at home and jog—you won't find me catching infections like this.

Diverse Perspectives in Critical Thinking

In assessing arguments, it helps to be aware of whose interests prevail, whose history has priority, whose frame of reference determines the norm, and who sets the criteria for decision making. These are all aspects of the **perspective** taken on ideas and events and the framework of assessing them. People know when they are being valued or devalued. Those who witness even subtle demonstrations of prejudice have a sense of injustice.

It may be hard not to laugh at jokes we are the butt of. It may be hard not to buy into a mentality that is ultimately degrading and destructive. We are all affected by justice and by injustice. We ignore this at our peril.

To look at ethical and political decision making as clearly separate from culture, class, gender, and ethnicity is to effectively assume a mistaken sense of neutrality. For example, Martin Luther King Jr., the Dalai Lama, Mahatma Gandhi, and Cesar Chavez are often cited as heroes. But if we fail to examine their concern for human cruelty, injustice, and systemic racism, we turn them into caricatures instead of sources of spiritual strength, leadership, and guidance.

One source of strength is the knowledge that we affect each other's lives. We have an impact on the course of events and on the public consciousness.

Advantages of Diverse Perspectives

Critical thinking gives us such techniques as analysis, observation, and reflection. These are powerful tools. Our knowledge grows when we recognize diverse perspectives, when we go beyond routine (narrow) interpretations and look at the broader picture. We can then see how stereotypical modes of thought have shaped our values, laws, and policies.

We never know when our tolerance will be put to the test.

Nik Scott artist, Curious Productions, Australia. Copyright 2008. Used with permission.

I hope you've got nothing against sausages

Take oppression, for instance. People complain that oppression goes both ways. Some say that the oppressed are unjust to members of the dominant class if given the chance, that nothing much changes when the tables are turned. The oppressed can be as vicious as the oppressor. But that's no reason not to reflect on the human condition, not to study the interplay of culture and morality, not to raise questions about how we treat one another.

That members of disadvantaged groups seem ungrateful or angry should prod us to reflection—and action. Being raised on gospel, or Kentucky hill music, or rap, or rock and roll plays a role in our identity. So do family barbecues and traditions around religious holidays. Our task is to see what those influences have been and determine their effects. See the illustration on page 24 for a humorous.

The Seven Key Dimensions of Diversity

1. **Frame of reference:** Look at the point of view presented—its strengths, weaknesses, and omissions. Consider alternative points of view and any new concerns and questions that could be raised.
2. **Power dimensions:** Look at the ways power is manifested and who the authority or power figures are. Consider possible shifts in the balance of power.
3. **Values and beliefs:** Look at the set of values that predominate. Consider alternative systems of belief that could be used. Watch for the major assumptions of the author (warranted or unwarranted).
4. **Race and ethnicity:** Look at the race/ethnicity of the key players and the ways in which race affects how the problem is defined and what solutions are offered. Consider the likely results of a shift of perspective.
5. **Class:** Look at the dominant perspective in terms of economic class. Watch for values linked to social class and any assumptions that indicate a class bias.
6. **Personal parameters:** Look to see if the gender, age, sexual orientation, or other personal parameters of the author and intended audience affect the focus or methodology.
7. **Language:** Look for biased or prejudicial uses of language and the ways in which the use of language evokes images or expresses a set of values.

It's not always easy to "get out of the box," to open up our minds to other ways of thinking and explore unfamiliar territory. Yet, as all travelers know, something happens when we turn things over, when we let go of the entrenched ways of doing things.

Sharpening the Inquiry: Incorporating Diverse Perspectives

- Try to determine how the intended audience shapes the dialogue or affects the presentation. *Ask yourself:* Who is this aimed at? Why this, rather than some other, audience?
- Try to determine the points of view being presented. *Ask yourself:* From whose point of view is this article written, this story told, this song sung, this version of events made public?

- Try to determine what would change with a shift of perspective. *Ask yourself:* What would be added or omitted if this were presented through a different set of eyes or in a different voice?
- Try to determine where the power rests, what forces are setting the agenda. *Ask yourself:* Who stands to gain or lose? Who is most powerful and most vulnerable?
- Try to determine the set of priorities and underlying values. *Ask yourself:* What set of values and beliefs are being subscribed to, and where might conflicts arise?
- Try to determine the extent to which you see diversity. *Ask yourself:* Is there enough diversity in terms of critical factors like race, ethnicity, class, gender, and underrepresented groups?
- Try to determine the extent to which economic factors, like class, shape the discourse. *Ask yourself:* Does the perspective of a particular class dominate or shape the presentation?
- Try to determine the extent to which gender and sexual orientation slant the inquiry. *Ask yourself:* Do gender and sexual orientation affect the content and values being expressed?
- Try to determine the ways in which language is used to create an effect. *Ask yourself:* How does the use of words, quotes, and other sorts of expression reveal a set of values or way of seeing the world?
- Try to determine how factors such as age, religion, nationality, and ability versus disability shape the inquiry. *Ask yourself:* What assumptions and values are at work in terms of the participants or the audience?

Think about teams and committees. In 2008, the president of MIT, Susan Hockfield, gave a speech on diversity and inclusion. She observed, "When we listen only to people who agree with us, we cease to grow. Fortunately, the reverse is equally true." Diverse teams are better at solving complex problems. With homogeneous teams, unquestioned assumptions remain unquestioned, and everyone gets stuck in the same place. Hockfield noted, "When our ideas are challenged and amplified from different directions, they get stronger and better, and we do, too" ("Diversity and Inclusion: Building a Solution Worthy of MIT," Speeches, web.mit.edu).

Diversity can be a powerful tool. Look at juries. The best juries do *not* consist of people who are similar in terms of background, age, gender, religion, and the like. The less diverse the makeup of the jury, the more likely members are to be uncritical. As trial consultants observe, "Active participation by all panel members and the critical evaluation of a wide range of perspectives is the hallmark of an effective jury." In contrast, the ineffective jury may be caught up in a drive for consensus and a reluctance to disagree, resulting in a hung jury (Andre T. Cavagnaro and Elise G. Devecchio-Cavagnaro, "Jury Diversity Prevents Dreaded 'Groupthink,'" *The Los Angeles Daily [Law] Journal,* 14 Mar 2002).

Exercises

1. Your college newspaper, *The Oracle,* wants to run a story on faculty members dating students. How would the issue be seen if you were (pick two and set out each perspective) a 30-year-old single professor, a happily married student, a 19-year-old student who is single and lonely, a 22-year-old student, an administrator, or the parent of an 18-year-old student attending the college.

2. Read the following and state two key observations pop singer Madonna makes about what she learned from her religion and one piece of advice she offers. Then offer one idea, concern, or criticism about Madonna's remarks?

   "One is that we are all responsible for our actions, our behavior, and our words, and we must take responsibility for everything we say and do. When you get your head wrapped around that, you can no longer think of life as a series of random events—you participate in life in a way you didn't previously. I am the architect of my destiny. I am in charge. I bring that to me, or I push that away. You can no longer blame other people for things that happened to you.

   "The other is that there is order in the universe, even though it looks like chaos. We separate the world into categories: this is good and this is bad. But life is set up to trick us. It's a series of illusions we invest in. And ultimately those investments don't serve our understanding, because physicality is always going to let you down, because physicality doesn't last. . . . You just have to keep doing your work, and hope and pray somebody's dialing into your frequency." (Rich Cohen, "Madonnarama," *Vanity Fair,* May 2008)

3. Discuss the frame of reference (perspective) of the author and any biases or values evident:

   To say he was paralysed by the tension would be an over-statement, but nerves were dragging him ever down towards an exceedingly murky pit of despond [British tennis player Tim]. Henman perennially talks of his love for Wimbledon, and all its advantages. But it comes at a cost. The public expectations—and this year they were further raised by his success in Paris—reach a level disproportionate to anything he experiences during the rest of the year. To be sure, he can feed off the support and raise his game. But he is also aware that every missed shot is greeted like a death in the family. He has talked at length about the fact that tennis is more than winning and losing; of the necessity of playing to his own strengths. In Paris he had little or no outside pressure; at Wimbledon this pressure is continuous and unrelenting. ("Henman Sets Off for Heaven via Day in Hell," *The Guardian (UK),* sport.guardian.co.uk, 23 Jun 2004)

4. The state of Florida has gotten rid of computers and typewriters in its prison law libraries. As a result, Florida prisoners who wish to appeal their case now have to draw up their legal appeal by longhand. Read about the situation and answer the questions that follow:

   The Corrections Department removed computers and typewriters in May 2001, arguing that they had to do so to save money. Florida has 71,000 inmates, the 5th largest prison system in the U.S. Florida has executed 51 prisoners since 1979 (behind only Texas and Virginia) and has 371 people on death row. Prisoners' Rights groups argue that removing the computers and typewriters limits what prisoners can do. Kara Gotsch of the ACLU says, "When it's handwritten, it's not as effective for them." Rebecca Trammell of the American Association of Law Libraries says most state prisons provide typewriters to prisoners. Allen Overstreet of the Florida Corrections Department said only around 5% of prisoners use the law libraries and it would save $50,000 a year (on repairs and upkeep) to get rid of the typewriters. (Jackie Halifax, "Florida Prisoners Lose Access to Typewriters," in *Los Angeles Daily [Law] Journal*, 25 Jun 2001)

Answer any two *of the following:*

a. Set out the concerns from the perspective of prisoners in Florida.
b. Set out the concerns from the perspective of prisoners in states that currently have computers and typewriters available for inmate use.
c. Set out the concerns from the perspective of Florida officials, pressured by taxpayers to cut costs.

Obstacles to Clear Thinking

All sorts of things can trip us up—for instance when we rush into decisions without thinking about the consequences. Sometimes we are impulsive; other times we are obedient or submissive, letting others think for us. Do you listen to yourself and sometimes hear the voice of your mother or father or a friend, like a tape playing in your head? Do you detect in yourself patterns of behavior that are unhealthy or destructive? Each of us has failings, cultural baggage, and blind spots. These need to be overcome if we are to attain clarity and quickness of mind. Let us examine some key obstacles to clear thinking.

Survival Issues

We tend to assume that others' basic needs are being met, so they have the ability to focus, learn, and reason. But this may not be the case. Some people struggle with physical or emotional survival issues. These include an abusive environment, substance abuse, poverty, hunger, eating disorders, depression, rage, and a stress-inducing lifestyle. Take responsibility to reach out to such individuals. If you yourself are dealing with survival issues like these, get help. A person's ability to think clearly may turn on survival issues.

Prejudice, Bias, and Oppression

Prejudice comes in many forms, including racial or ethnic prejudice, gender bias, ageism or speciesism, and hatred of fascists, right-wingers, leftists, conservatives, or liberals. It may be directed toward one or many individuals or groups. It can be so internalized that it functions seamlessly and invisibly. Some types of prejudice are viewed as healthy (such as prejudice against knife-wielding murderers); others are not. It's these potentially harmful prejudices that merit attention.

Bias functions as a kind of blinder or filter, slanting our thinking one way or another. It must be set aside if we want to formulate strong arguments, and act out of a sense of justice. Whereas prejudice and bias have to do with attitudes and states of mind, **oppression** involves action. All three are rooted in a set of values and beliefs that we need to examine.

Some deplorable acts and policies were once thought to be justifiable, such as whites-only laws, Japanese internment camps in World War II (see Figure 1.6), anti-gay ordinances, and the forced relocation of Native-Americans. **Racism** is prejudice aimed at members of a racial or ethnic group. It can be manifested in subtle ways but often involves treating others as inferior or alien.

Racial profiling is no less controversial now than it was in the past. For example, in 2008, a United Nations panel urged the United States to end racial profiling of Americans of Arab, Muslim, and South Asian descent. This practice has been widespread since the terrorist attacks of 9/11 (*China View News*, 8 Mar 2008).

National Archives Still Pictures Unit (ARC Identifier 536854). Reprinted with the permission of the National Archives, Still Pictures Unit.

FIGURE 1.6
Relocation of Japanese-Americans to Manzanar, California, in April 1942. This is one instance of racism in U.S. history—the internment camps of World War II.

People may harbor suspicions of others who look different or who have different values and beliefs. Such suspicions have fueled racism and a rise in hate crimes. **Hate crimes** are one of the most odious expressions of prejudice. The American Psychological Association says of hate crime that not only is it an attack on one's physical self, but it is also an attack on one's very identity. Only recently has our society given it a name and begun to monitor it, study it, and legislate against it ("Hate Crime," FBI Uniform Crime Reports, www.fbi.gov).

It is a short distance from racist or biased ways of thinking to actions and policies, which underlines how vital it is to watch for this obstacle to clear thinking.

Unreflective Acceptance of Cultural and Societal Attitudes

Cultural traditions and societal attitudes help shape our lives. However, traditions may have negative aspects, such as the materialistic dimensions of Christmas, weddings, and birthday celebrations. Cultural attitudes can act as blinders. Think of a jury exhibiting culturally biased attitudes toward people of different cultures, races, genders, economic classes, religions, or employment status. In such cases, a young Latino or African-American male might be more likely viewed as a gang member than a teenager who is white or Asian. And so-called white-collar crime is rarely taken as seriously as other types of crime.

Societal assumptions can also block clear thinking. For instance, if we assume children cannot tell the difference between fantasy and reality, it may be hard to evaluate their claims of molestation or abuse. We think children are vulnerable to manipulation. We assume children often exaggerate or lie. As a result, children's claims about violence, incest, or inappropriate behavior could be ignored.

Outmoded views can leach onto our thinking about other societies (we are "civilized"; they are "primitive"). We need to watch the assumptions we make, for they may lead us astray.

Falling Prey to Stereotypes

Stereotypes are generalizations made on the basis of little or no evidence. They are oversimplified concepts or images—for example, men are stronger than women, women have more stamina than men, men are better leaders, women are better parents, boys are better in math, girls are better at reading, elderly people are easily confused, young people aren't politically savvy, rich people know how to manipulate the system, or poor people are lazy. They are not necessarily negative; a stereotype can reinforce conventional ways of thinking. Watch also for multiple stereotypes for the same trait. They can be either positive or negative (e.g., thin = disciplined *or* anorexic, old = wise *or* infirm, wealthy = snotty *or* sophisticated, and gay = stylish *or* abnormal).

Fortunately, there has been movement in this area. Think of the stereotype-busting that has occurred in the recent past: Tiger Woods changed stereotypes about golfers; Venus and Serena Williams changed stereotypes about tennis players; Andre Agassi, Bruce Willis, and Montel Williams changed our view of bald men. Mira Nair, Queen Latifah, Halle Berry, and Salma Hayek changed stereotypes about women in film. Once we are able to watch and listen more carefully, we can avoid succumbing to negative stereotypes.

Blind Obedience and Unquestioning Deference to Authority

It's easy to be influenced by celebrities and authority figures. Blindly following a politician or a religious leader can be as bad as the unquestioning acceptance of a movie star's endorsement. A little detachment can be an asset.

There are plenty of leaders who took their followers down paths of destruction and moral decay. Look at the examples of Jim Jones (who led 900 of his cult members to commit mass suicide), Pol Pot (who led the Khmer Rouge on a reign of terror and genocide in Cambodia), and David Koresh (who was killed with his cult followers at Waco, Texas).

In less dramatic ways, we may defer to family, friends, or social groups. We are vulnerable to the forces of conformity and to those who pressure us to think in one way or another. We need to be reflective and ask questions. Basically, our rule of thumb should be this: Not all authorities are credible. Look carefully and think about the evidence. We can make use of the advice of an authority, but we should not be manipulated by that individual.

Habit and Conformity

To the extent that we are victims of habitual ways of doing things, we dull our skills at observation and description. There is a reason people describe habits as "traps." As writer Samuel Beckett said, "Habit is the great deadener."

We go on autopilot at times. Some of us go to the same restaurants, order the same things, hang out with the same people, vacation in the same spots, and generally favor the familiar over the unknown. Some of us vote along party lines without considering the candidate or the issues. In doing so, we may overlook issues or potential consequences for the political party or for society. And just because "we've always done it this way" doesn't mean that it is the best, or only, way.

Just look at security alerts about terrorist threats (color coded as red, yellow, etc.). The fact that such alerts started to become fairly routine has *not* made people vigilant and on the lookout for terrorists. Hardly.

> Repeated warnings, intended to heighten Americans' awareness of the possibility of a terrorist act, appear to have had the opposite effect, especially since so far, they have not been followed by attacks. Results from polls by the Pew Research Center suggest that since the first terror alert was issued in 2002, people's anxiety level has decreased with each successive warning. People living in tornado country, researchers find, usually ignore storm watches altogether, unless their town or area is specifically named. Even then, few take any action to avoid the storm unless they see the sky darkening, the wind come up or some other real evidence. (Benedict Carey and

Anahad O'Connor, "As Public Adjust to Threat, Alerts Cause Less Unease," *The New York Times,* 3 Aug 2004)

Routine warnings seem to get filed away with other routines and habits.

Be careful not to assume the **deadly triad** of the *status quo* + *habit* + *stereotypical thinking.* This triad is formed by the mind-set of the dominant culture, habitual ways of doing things, and belief systems that lock attitudes and stereotypical thinking into place. Think of this deadly triad as conceptual snow goggles. We stare through them, seeing the world through tiny slits. We can focus on this or that but have only a narrow range of vision. To get a clearer view, we need to yank the goggles off. We will then get a broader perspective.

Limited Access to Information or Evidence

Rep. Romano Mazzoli says, "Access is it. Access is power. Access is clout. That's how this thing works" (www.democracymatters.org). We are not always able to see the big picture because of limited access to information. Others may control access, as in the case of a teacher, supervisor, doctor, family member, or friend. But at times we are limited by physical conditions or by the ravages of time. For example, documents are lost, people die, and artifacts disintegrate.

This is the case with the only audio recording of the assassination of President John F. Kennedy. The recording was made through an open microphone on a police motorcade and then recorded onto a Dictaphone belt at police headquarters in Dallas, Texas. Scientific analyses over the decades since 1963 have been inconclusive. The Dictaphone belt has become worn and damaged by the constant replay—so it is unclear if there were three shots (the official version—Oswald shot Kennedy) or four (Oswald was *not* the lone gunman). Thanks to technology, scientists may soon be able to get a digital image of the sound patterns. This might then settle the question of the number of shots fired. (See Michael Janofsky, "Salvage Work Is Begun on Kennedy-Killing Tape," *The New York Times,* 3 Aug 2004.)

Sometimes information has been censored or edited. Without access, the door may be hard to pry open. Look at the FBI discovery of "misplaced" boxes of 4,500 documents in the case of Timothy McVeigh, who was convicted of killing 168 people in the Oklahoma City bombing.

Later evidence suggests that McVeigh and Terry Nichols, who was also convicted, did not act alone—at least 10 Aryan Nation bank robbers were also involved. However, evidence has been lost or destroyed that might put some theories to rest. "FBI agents were so suspicious of a link [that] they analyzed video footage of the robbery to see whether McVeigh participated (inconclusive). That video was destroyed in 1999 by the FBI despite rules to the contrary." (Associated Press, "FBI Suspected McVeigh Part of Conspiracy," 25 Feb 2004)

Whenever access is limited or controlled, critical thinking is handicapped. We must then seek other sources of information. Become adept at piecing together puzzles and drawing inferences from nuggets of details. Also note that there may be other routes—such as international news sources, church documents, handwritten notes, letters, e-mails, and photographs—to knowledge and awareness.

Exercises

Directions: For each of the following, draw three possible inferences. Note that all the quotes below are from *David Thomson on the Alien Quartet*, Bloomsbury Movie Guide No. 4:

1. "I am not sure that—and I am not saying that—*Alien* is a great film. It is 'only' something I have never been able to get out of my head—just as there are somethings that, once admitted, can never be removed from the body."

2. "'We're going to blow up the ship,' says Ripley. She, Parker and Lambert will then have to make their escape in the shuttle. As the trio pull themselves together, Parker turns his flame-thrower on Ash's discarded head. In two bursts, we see the 'skin' come off like thick paint, exposing the hard plastic skull."

3. "We meet Drake, a raw-faced crew cut man . . . a joker named Hudson . . . and Vasquez . . . a sultry, muscled Latina [not in real life] who is doing body-building exercises within a few minutes of waking. 'Hey, Vasquez,' asks the joker, 'have you ever been mistaken for a man?' 'No,' growls Vasquez, 'have you?' And Drake gives her a handshake, grinning in delight, and tells her she's bad. No matter how far in the future we go, it seems, Marines are Marines."

4. "Viewers of *Alien* films often feel the need to shower away the gluey mucous of the creatures afterwards. The surge of power in the pulse rifles and the flame-throwers is enough to enlist the most insistent pacifist. For combat on film *is* like sex: it is a joining rhythm and the chance of crescendo. And as we participate in the blazing away of it all, even fear lifts a little. We are close here to some inner secret about weapons, about how they appeal to the id while putting away idiot consequences."

Psychological Blocks

Have you ever been so anxious you couldn't think straight? Have you ever stuck your foot in your mouth just when you hoped to say something impressive? The perfect mate approaches and—Blap! We lose it. Then there is the nightmare job interview when the mind goes completely blank. Such **psychological blocks** as anxiety, depression, and fear can suck the neurons right out of our skulls!

Professor Debra Moon observes that self-esteem problems can get in the way of good reasoning. She's right. When individuals suffer very low self-esteem or have a vastly inflated view of themselves, their perceptions can get twisted.

Some think that these extremes operate on societal levels as well. Those from "developed" countries like the United States, Canada, and European nations may not always understand the problems facing Third World countries. Similarly, there may be imbalances within a "developed" country—for example, when those with power and wealth have opportunities unavailable to those in the lower classes. In addition, rampant consumerism—"I want, I want, I need"—can distort our vision so we put our own desires far above the needs of others. We need to be aware of this potential obstacle and watch for emotional and mental roadblocks.

One-Sided Thinking

A narrow frame of reference may help us zero in on a problem, but we have to use it like a tool. **One-sided thinking** can function like blinders, blocking us from a clearer understanding of what's going on. Each person who tells a story looks at the topic through a particular filter. That filter is made up of values, beliefs, assumptions, experiences, knowledge or ignorance, and, at times, even desire.

With one-sided thinking, a narrow angle, limited perspective, or skewed presentation of evidence throws things off balance and creates a bias. This bias can slant the inquiry and result in a limited grasp of the situation. We need to watch for this in our own reasoning, as well as that of others. Our angle of approach and our worldview shape what we see and how we think.

It helps to see how a particular frame of reference affects how stories are told, problems are formulated, and arguments are structured. Once we notice this crucial dimension, we can give a more accurate analysis.

Exercises

1. Brown University junior Abdullah Alsharekh came from Kuwait on a student visa. Read about his situation and share your response:

    Abdullah, currently in his junior year, now takes every precaution to avoid looking suspicious, since he knows he is automatically suspect in the eyes of American officials. He used to head home for breaks without preregistering for classes, but now he makes sure to preregister so he can carry the confirmation sheet—along with his student ID, his grades from the previous semester, and a copy of his paid tuition bill—to the airport as evidence that his intentions are purely academic. Even armed with such proof, Abdullah says the interrogations put him on edge. "It's weird," he says. "I know I haven't done anything wrong, but I always feel guilty. Even if you're not guilty, you look it. It's very, very uncomfortable." (As quoted by Lizzie Seidlin-Bernstein. "The Usual Suspects," *Anthology of Creative Nonfiction* 2002–2003, www.seg.brown.edu/projects)

2. The movie *Shawshank Redemption* contains an exchange about Brooks, the librarian. Brooks gets notice of his parole but does *not* want to be released from the prison he's known for so long. Read the exchange and then discuss the issue of becoming so accustomed to a situation or way of life—even an unpleasant one—that it is hard to even imagine, much less desire, what it

would be like if things changed. Would you say this is another form of the debilitating effects of habit?

RED: Man's been here fifty years [referring to Brooks]. This place is all he knows. In here, he's an important man, an educated man. A librarian. Out there, he's nothing but a used-up old con with arthritis in both hands. Couldn't even get a library card if he applied. You see what I'm saying?

FLOYD: Red, I do believe you're talking out of your ass.

RED: Believe what you want. These walls are funny. First you hate 'em, then you get used to 'em. After long enough, you get so you depend on 'em. That's "institutionalized."

JIGGER: Shit. I could never get that way.

ERNIE (SOFTLY): Say that when you been inside as long as Brooks has.

RED: Goddamn right. They send you here for life, and that's just what they take. Part that counts, anyway.

3. List three ways to either substantiate or disprove the claim that "children in this culture grow up knowing that you can never be thin enough and that being fat is one of the worst things one can be" (Susan Bordo, *Twilight Zones*, University of California Press, 1997).

4. Read the following excerpt and then answer the questions below.

In a 1995 survey, nearly 200 aspiring American Olympians were asked if they would take a banned substance that would guarantee victory in every competition for five years and would then cause death; more than half answered yes. A recent seminar on teenage steroid use, held in New York City, revealed these desperate efforts to boost athletic performance: A female basketball player asked a doctor to break her arms and reset them in a way that might make them longer; pediatricians were being pressured by parents to give their children human growth hormone to make them taller and perhaps more athletic; doctors were being asked by the parents of football players to provide steroids so their sons might gain college scholarships.

A molecular scientist, speaking on condition of anonymity, said in an interview that a foreign exchange student staying with the scientist's family was approached at a swimming pool by a stranger and was told, "You are absolutely beautiful; I'll give you $35,000 for one of your eggs." The student accepted the offer. . . . (Jere Longman, "Pushing the Limits," *The New York Times*, 11 May 2001)

Answer the following:

a. State the major obstacles to clear thinking in the quest for a more perfect body (e.g., by using performance-enhancing drugs or nutritional supplements) in both amateur and professional athletes.

b. Assuming we don't want young athletes to find doctors who will break their arms so they might have an athletic advantage and black markets in genetically engineered human eggs, what sorts of steps could be taken to address this situation?

c. Was the beautiful foreign exchange student thinking clearly when she agreed to sell her genetic material for $35,000?

Quick Quiz

1. *True or false:* The frame of reference is the point of view from which something is presented.

2. All of the following are aspects of sharpening the inquiry—incorporating diverse perspectives—*except:*
   a. Who this is aimed at (audience)
   b. Who stands to gain or lose (power balance)
   c. Whether there are any fallacies of reasoning (clarity of logic)
   d. What set of values and beliefs are at work (values)

3. The *social context* refers to (a) the slice of time, location, culture, politics, and community that shapes our identity or (b) the substance of what is written, taking into account the concepts and ideas raised.

4. *True or false:* An example of an obstacle to critical thinking is deductive reasoning.

5. The term *bias* refers to (a) an argument made by an opponent or (b) a filter or blinder, slanting our thinking one way or another.

6. An example of *unreflective* acceptance of cultural and societal attitudes is:
   a. Hate crimes against ethnic minorities and gays
   b. Quota systems in educational institutions
   c. The idea that white-collar crime is less serious than other crimes
   d. Acting out of habit

7. *True or false:* Loaded language creates an inherent bias in the very terms used.

8. That Jim Jones led 900 members of his cult to commit mass suicide is an example of (a) blind obedience to authority or (b) hate crime.

9. An example of limited access to information is:
   a. David Koresh and his followers being killed at Waco, Texas
   b. The public's ignoring security alerts as signified by colors (orange, red, etc.)
   c. Racist speech in political tirades such as that of the Aryan Nation
   d. The inability to determine how many shots were fired at President Kennedy due to the worn Dictaphone

10. *True or false:* Psychological blocks include anxiety, depression, and fear.

▦ Problem Solving

Some social conflicts and problems are ongoing; others are resolved fairly quickly. For instance, how near can someone get to a political rally to hand out protest literature? Someone had to figure that out. If we don't know where we are going, it is hard to get off the ground. If we don't know what tools we plan to use along the journey, we could be spinning our wheels in the sand.

Subjecting even a messy moral dilemma to the problem-solving model may be useful for generating ideas or insights and leading us to viable options. The model provides a structure for approaching a wide range of problems that we may face.

Stages of the Problem-Solving Model

Stage 1:   Define the problem.
Stage 2:   Set out the criteria for decision making.
Stage 3:   Lay the groundwork.
　　　　　Generate ideas, look for analogies, and consider diverse perspectives.
Stage 4:   Sort and weigh evidence.
　　　　　Evaluate what you have and formulate a workable hypothesis.
Stage 5:   Survey and shape what you have.
　　　　　Fill in holes with further information, examples, or discussion.
Stage 6:   Set out your decision or plan of action.

Exercises

Directions: Select one of the cases below or do all that are assigned by your instructor. Run through the problem-solving model for each of the cases, setting out the stages.

1. The case of genetic hybrids:

    About 150 goats that have been bred with a spider gene are to be housed on 60 acres of a former Air Force base in Plattsburgh, N.Y. Montreal-based Nexia Biotechnologies, Inc., said up to 1,500 genetically altered goats may eventually live at the facility. The goats have been bred with a spider gene so their milk provides a unique protein. The company plans to extract the protein from the milk to produce fibers called "Bio-Steel" for bulletproof vests, aerospace and medical supplies. Spider silk has a unique combination of strength and elasticity with an ultra-lightweight fiber. The agreement included an up-front payment for the university, funding for research and development expenses plus royalties on the sale of silk-based products. ("Biotech Company to Produce 'BioSteel' Milk," *Associated Press,* 18 Jun 2000)

2. The case of the narcotic lollipop—should the FDA ban it?

    Abbott laboratories developed a narcotic lollipop intended to calm down children before surgery. A group of doctors asked the federal government to bar the narcotic lollipop. They argue that the narcotic, *fentanyl,* is too dangerous for children and that the lollipop could create new problems for doctors. Some doctors suggest that a tranquilizer would be preferable, since it doesn't have the same risks as the narcotic. The FDA asked Abbott to set up a training program to insure anyone using the lollipop will be familiar with its dangers and its proper use. They said that doctors now make up their own, unregulated, sedatives to calm children and the FDA prefers one that can be given in controlled doses and under federal control. (Mike Goodkind, "Help Your Child Relax to Reduce Pain and Recover More Easily after Surgery, Says Anesthesiologist," www.med.stanford.edu)

3. The case of the sperm donor:

A man who donated sperm to a lesbian couple is being made to pay maintenance by the Child Support Agency (CSA). Andy Bathie, 37, from Enfield, North London, claims he was assured by the couple he would have no personal or financial involvement with the children. He donated his sperm as a friend rather than go through a fertility clinic. Only anonymous donors at licensed centres are exempt from being treated as the legal father of a child born as a result of their donation. Mr. Bathie, a firefighter, said he cannot afford to have children with his own wife due to the financial implications. . . . A spokesman for Human Fertilisation and Embryology Authority (HFEA) said: "The law says that men donating sperm through licensed fertility clinics are not the legal father of any child born through that donation. Men giving out their sperm in any other way—such as via internet arrangements—are legally the father of any children born with all the responsibilities that carries." ("Sperm Donor to Pay Child Support," *BBC News*, 3 Dec 2007)

4. The case of the deaf couple and deaf embryo:

Is it wrong for a deaf couple to select a deaf embryo? For the most part, concerns around genetic testing of embryos centered on whether people were trying to create a "brave new world" of super-humans. However, a recent case raises a different set of concerns. Now a deaf couple have turned [genetic testing] on its head: far from wanting a flawless child they actively want a baby which suffers the same hearing difficulties as they themselves. The couple have become icons in a deaf movement which sees this impairment not as a disability but as the key to a rich culture which has its own language, history and traditions: a world deaf parents would naturally want to share with any offspring. (Clare Murphy, "Is It Wrong to Select a Deaf Embryo?" *BBC News*, 10 Mar 2008)

5. The case of infertility risks due to cooking oil:

Families in Mali that regularly eat the traditional (fried) dishes may be running the risk of becoming infertile. This is because as Mali is sub-Saharan Africa's biggest cotton producer, cotton oil is the oil of choice for most cooks, mostly because of its lower price. A health scare has arisen because many of the country's oil factories lack the refining equipment to remove the toxin gossypol from cottonseed. It is gossypol, according to the Malian Consumer's Association (Ascoma), that can cause infertility. "Gossypol is responsible for azoospermia—that's an absence of sperm in the semen," Ascoma's Ibrahima Sangare says. "It's also responsible for interrupting the menstrual cycle and pregnancy and can also affect the liver and the heart," he says. Attempts to discourage consumers and sellers have yet to be successful. As long as cotton oil sells for almost half the price of the imported cooking oils, most large families do not feel they have a better choice. (Celeste Hicks, "Mali's Infertility Cooking Oil," *BBC News*, 12 Mar 2008)

CHAPTER TWO

Nuts and Bolts:
The Basics of Argument

A nephew of mine—he was about five or six at the time—used to tell me his dreams each morning. One day, . . . he told me: "Last night I dreamed that I was lost in the forest. I was scared, but I came to a clearing, and there was a white house, made of wood, with a staircase that turned around, with steps with runners, and then a door, and out of this door you came out." He suddenly stopped: "But what were you doing in that house?"

JORGE LUIS BORGES, "Nightmares," *Everything and Nothing*

We never know when our lives may radically change course because of events we could never have foreseen. Take the case of Ascension Franco Gonzales. Wednesday, August 29, 2001, was a big day for Gonzales, a dishwasher from Hidalgo, Mexico, now living in Los Angeles. While sitting at a bus stop, Gonzales saw an armored truck coming along the street. As the truck drove by, the doors flew open and out fell a plastic bag containing $203,000. Gonzales picked it up and, fearing for his life, hid the loot. After spending an evening trying to figure out what to do, he called the police and handed in the money. Think about it: What would you have done if the $203,000 had landed in front of you?

Gonzales could have snuck back to Hidalgo with his $203,000 and lived off his riches. But he didn't. While listening to the radio, he heard the DJ wonder if there was anyone honest enough to hand in the missing money. Gonzales affirmed that he was such a man. Plenty of others thought he blew the chance of a lifetime. When asked what they would have done with a bag of money landing at their feet, they said:

RESPONSE 1: Reyna Hernandez, store employee, said, "I wouldn't have turned it in. I would have started a business."

RESPONSE 2: David Widom, social worker, said, "I think I would have turned it in. It's the honorable thing to do."

RESPONSE 3: John Snell, janitor, said, "I wouldn't let the temptation get me. I would resist."

RESPONSE 4: Johnny Shabaz, who thought Gonzales a fool not to take the cash, said, "He's crazy—the man's as crazy as a Betsy bug" (Jocelyn Y. Stewart and Hector Beccerra, "Many Say They Would Have Kept Bag of Loot," *Los Angeles Times,* 30 Aug 2001).

As we can see, each respondent has a different perspective revealing a range of possible responses. Our task as critical thinkers is to be able to follow their reasoning and assess its strength. To do this, we need to have some tools at our command. In this chapter, we will look into the fundamentals of argumentation. This includes examining the building blocks of an argument and discussing how to dismantle an argument and how to put one together. This requires that we learn how to distinguish descriptions from inferences, how to sort facts from opinions and ideas, and how to recognize the different forms of argumentation. We encounter arguments all the time and in all kinds of settings (even, as with Gonzales, sitting at a bus stop!). This means we have a great deal to gain by developing our skills in this area.

We can avoid fights, but we cannot avoid arguments. Every day we are confronted with arguments for this or against that. An argument presents us with a claim (called a **thesis** or a **conclusion**) drawn on the basis of a body of evidence (called the **premises**). When making an argument, we want it to be convincing. In the best-case scenario, the premises are *sufficient* for the conclusion; that is, we need nothing else by way of support for the conclusion to follow. Ideally, the conclusion comes right out of the premises, so we don't need to make some imaginative leaps over glaring gaps. We construct arguments as part of our lives.

It is useful to see how the mind works and to study what goes into decision making. Consider the case at hand—contrast the chain of reasoning that Gonzales went through with that of Johnny Shabaz. Gonzales's thought process can be set out like so:

I now have a bag with $203,000 in it.

I heard a disc jockey challenge the one who found the bag of money to be honest.

I was the one who found the bag of money.

I'm going to take his challenge.

I know being honest means calling the police and turning in the money.

Therefore, I'll call the police and turn in the money.

If we were to gaze into Johnny Shabaz's head, we'd see this:

Gonzales found a bag with $203,000 in it.

Anyone who finds money and doesn't keep it for himself is crazy as a Betsy bug.

Therefore, he's crazy—the man's as crazy as a Betsy bug.

In both cases, we started with the same two facts: (1) The bag of money landed at Gonzales's feet, and (2) he had the chance to keep it. Both Gonzales and Shabaz acknowledge that reality. However, the arguments then go in entirely different directions. This happens all the time. People regularly start from the same place and end up at polar extremes. This diversity of opinion and lack of predictability should be kept in mind as we observe those around us and examine arguments.

Ascension Gonzales shows us how one person thinks through a most unexpected opportunity to become wealthy. As we saw, people often react differently to events. To put this in perspective, we need to grasp the reasons they think as they do. Being able to dismantle arguments is crucial for making sense of what we read and hear. And being able to articulate our own thoughts is just as important.

Opinion versus Reasoned Argument

Suppose you have just finished your shift, and you stop by the cafeteria for coffee. The people at your table are discussing whether a man on a hunger strike should be force-fed if he slips into unconsciousness. Here's what they have to say:

ALISHA: Anyone stupid enough to go on a hunger strike deserves to die! Forget him!

JESS: What's wrong with you, Alisha? Either you die for a noble cause or your life has no meaning!

ANDY: I don't know why you two are fighting. Didn't you study history? Mahatma Gandhi went on hunger strikes for what he believed in, so hunger strikes must be a good thing.

FRANCESCA: Gandhi went on hunger strikes when he was competent to decide what was worth dying for. I'm not sure anyone on a hunger strike is competent to make an informed decision. When in doubt, choose what's best for the person's health. Therefore, we should intervene when lives are at stake, whether it's for a hunger strike or anything else. The guy should be force-fed.

ERIN: Francesca, why should we listen to you? You're no expert on hunger strikes—or much else for that matter. In fact, you barely made it through high school and had to go to a community college for your degree!

As you can see, not all of the reasoning rests on a solid foundation. Let's look at this more closely and see just what's going on:

- **Dismissing with a wave of the hand:** Alisha dismisses people on hunger strikes ("stupid") but offers no reasons for her judgment. Such name-calling does not count as reasoned argument. We need evidence!
- **Presenting false either/or choices:** Jess's either/or argument ignores the fact that there are more than two options. Therefore, Jess's reasoning is flawed.
- **Appealing to famous figures as evidence:** Andy turns to history, but he fails to explain why, if Gandhi did it, then it must be right. A few words of explanation would make all the difference.

- **Making a reasoned argument:** Francesca sets out reasons for saving the life of a person on a hunger strike. Those reasons can be assessed to see if they are convincing, so her argument gives us something to work with.
- **Launching a personal attack:** Erin tries to take down Francesca's argument by a personal attack. However, whether Francesca went to public school is irrelevant to the issue being argued. The question is, "Does Francesca offer good reasons for her conclusion?"

We encounter arguments all the time. Arguments come in all shapes and sizes. Some are funny, others serious. Some are short and pointed, others long and involved. We need to be able to examine the structure of an argument, set out the evidence, and evaluate it. Once we understand the nuts and bolts of argumentation, we can incorporate them into our own thought processes.

Argumentation

An argument is one of the more significant means of persuasion. There are two components to an argument: (1) the thesis (conclusion) and (2) the evidence (premises). An author's thesis (conclusion) rests on a set of reasons offered as support. These reasons are called **premises**. An **argument** consists of *only one* conclusion and *at least one* premise:

$$\text{Premise(s)} + \text{Conclusion} = \text{Argument}$$

A thesis (conclusion) rests on a set of reasons (premises) offered as support. You need *at least one* premise to have an argument. If the same set of evidence is used to support two propositions, treat it as two separate arguments and analyze each one separately.

Here's an example of an argument: "Cutting a pet bird's wings is cruel because it limits or eliminates its ability to fly. Birds that can't fly are like guinea pigs with feathers. Only someone who is cruel would turn their bird into the equivalent of a guinea pig." Notice the two components: (1) the thesis (the conclusion: "Cutting a pet bird's wings is cruel") and (2) the premises (the evidence: "It limits its ability to fly. Birds that can't fly are like guinea pigs with feathers. [and] Only someone who is cruel would turn their bird into the equivalent of a guinea pig"). Without both components, there is no argument. You *could* have an opinion ("You're cruel for cutting Buddy's wings"), you *could* have an idea ("You ought to train Buddy to fly only around the yard"), and you *could* have a description ("Buddy weighs 56 ounces and has beautiful blue feathers and an orange tail"). But if you don't have the two components—at least one premise and an inference drawn on the basis of that premise (e.g., your observation or idea)—you don't have an argument.

With all this in mind, let us return to the argument that it is cruel to cut a pet bird's wings. Start by locating the conclusion. Then group together all the reasons (the premises) supporting the conclusion. This sets out the argument in a tidy way. Number each premise P_1, P_2, and so on, to designate premise 1, premise 2, and so

Arguments versus Nonarguments

Examples of Arguments	Examples of Nonarguments
• Jody cooked the eggs for 5 minutes. The eggs looked okay, but tasted like rubber. So Jody cooked them too long. • The waffles were nice and golden. Ninety-nine percent of nice, golden waffles are delicious. Therefore, the waffles will probably be delicious.	• Chickens that aren't caged sure lay tastier eggs! • Jody ought to buy a cookbook. • The topping for the waffles contained blueberries that Vicky and Ben picked yesterday. They picked a lot of berries, even though they got sunburned.

on, and use C for the conclusion. Don't worry about the order at this stage—we can rearrange the premises later if necessary. We get:

P_1: Cutting a pet bird's wings limits or eliminates the bird's ability to fly.

P_2: Birds that can't fly are like guinea pigs with feathers.

P_3: Only someone who is cruel would turn the bird into the equivalent of a guinea pig.

C: Therefore, cutting a pet bird's wings is cruel.

Ask yourself if there are any assumptions associated with the argument. An **assumption** is treated as a "given"—no proof is usually offered. Assumptions can be **warranted** (defensible) or **unwarranted** (not defensible) and thus merit our consideration.

In the case of our pet bird argument, the author assumes that there are no good reasons for cutting a pet bird's wings (such as to protect it from crashing into a window or flying into a ceiling fan). Also, they assume that the life of a pet bird with cut wings is inferior to that of a bird that can fly. Stating reasons for that view would strengthen the argument.

Sometimes people throw in things that are superfluous to the argument itself, such as personal commentary ("Can you believe Nicola told Dr. Tan this? It's really ridiculous, but here's what she said!") or background information ("Do you know what I read in *The Chicago Tribune*? Listen to this!"). Set that aside; focus on what evidence is presented and how it supports the conclusion.

Let's look at another argument. In a December 4, 2006, letter to the editor of *The New York Times*, Alka Agrawal discusses the treatment of a suspected terrorist, Jose Padilla. He argues:

America is a wonderful country, and I say this particularly as the child of immigrants who have lived the American dream. We are supposed to stand for liberty and human rights. Could any of us be declared enemies of the government, like Jose Padilla, and be locked up for years without charge and under such inhumane conditions? What has our country come to in the name of security? How will history judge all of us who stood by and allowed our government to act this way? We should be holding demonstrations around the country to show Washington and the world that America's people do not believe that this is what America stands for.

Remember, we first locate the conclusion. It is the last sentence. Converting the rhetorical questions to assertions and numbering the premises (P_1, P_2, P_3, etc.), we get:

P_1: America is a wonderful country.

P_2: We are supposed to stand for liberty and human rights.

P_3: Any of us could be declared enemies of the government, like Jose Padilla, and be locked up for years without charge and under such inhumane conditions.

P_4: Look what our country has come to in the name of security.

P_5: History will judge all of us who stood by and allowed our government to act this way.

C: Therefore, we should be holding demonstrations around the country to show Washington and the world that America's people do not believe that this is what America stands for.

Keep in mind that a strong case means the evidence presented (the set of premises) gives solid support for the conclusion. That is different from creating a *persuasive* argument, given that we might be persuaded by a threat ("Agree with me or I'll step on your sore toe"), by a celebrity's testimonial (e.g., Bozo likes red balloons, why don't you?), by appeal to patriotism, and so on. The use of irrelevant premises, devious or deceptive reasoning, or other trickery does not constitute good thinking. We'll see how this is done. Let's start with the case of Kate Crisp, who jumped to conclusions and was a long time realizing her error.

CASE STUDY

Dissing Ken Wilber

Read Kate Crisp's letter to the editor of Shambhala Sun *magazine and then answer the questions that follow. Note that Ken Wilber writes in the area of spirituality and consciousness studies and has published over a dozen books.*

For the past two years I have been dissing Ken Wilber all over town. I just hate the guy. Years ago I was at an art event and a gangly man flailing his arms about knocked me down and didn't apologize. I asked my cohorts who he was and got the reply: "Oh, that's Ken Wilber."

After that rude encounter I saw Mr. Ken all around town. I always gave him a surly look and he always ignored me. He would always somehow end up in a line near me, at the post office, at Kinko's, wherever, and he would always be giving a grand, boring discourse to someone. He frequently was with a girl who gazed at him with reverential rapture. Nausea was my m.o. when I saw this "great mind of the western hemisphere."

But the thing that really bugged me about Ken Wilber was the photos. When I saw that photo of him on the cover of the September *Shambhala Sun,* I just knew I had his number . . . on top of all his faults, he was VAIN! I mean really, Ken Wilber does NOT look like that picture at all. Well, maybe a little bit, but obviously the picture was 20 years old or majorly retouched. He looks ancient in real life and his head is about 40 times bigger than that photo reveals.

Well, wouldn't you know it, last week I strolled into Business Express and standing right in front of me was the REAL Ken Wilber, the one on the *Sun* cover. Not MY Ken Wilber, not the person I had been seeing and loathing for years, but someone else. This WAS the person on the magazine cover. I felt totally deflated. Here I had spent all this mental energy hating Ken Wilber and it wasn't even HIM!

Now who the hell was this fake Ken? At least ten people have told me that fake Ken IS Ken. "Look, there is Ken Wilber!" someone always said, much to my annoyance. One of my friends even went up to fake Ken and had a conversation with him and excitedly reported to me "Ken's" words of wisdom.

I am sorry to say that real Ken Wilber just does NOT work as an object of my aggression. True, he does look kind of "LA" in his brand new white Range Rover. And true, he does wear little tank tops and swoopy down jeans that show off his buff physique. True, he kind of waltzes through space as if to say, "Hey there everybody, I'm smart AND I'm sexy!" but real Ken just doesn't cut it for me. There just isn't enough material for me to work with. The show is over. And the worst part is NOW I've lost another object for all my pent-up aggression.

Answer the following:

1. What is Crisp's main argument about the fake Ken Wilber? Set out her evidence for concluding that she "hates" (is bugged by) the man she thinks is Ken Wilber.
2. What does she conclude, after she realizes this was not the real Ken Wilber?
3. State the strongest claims supporting her statement "And the worst part is NOW I've lost another object for all my pent-up aggression."

Source: Letter to the editor, *Shambhala Sun,* March 1997. Reprinted with the permission of the *Shambhala Sun.*

Facts, Opinions, and Ideas

In the course of our daily activities, we often come across someone citing a fact, expressing an opinion, or offering an idea. Any of these may play a role in a person's reasoning and decision making, and so merit our attention.

When we think of facts, we think of things or events known to be true. This covers actual occurrences and actions. It also includes concepts that can be proven true, as seen in science and mathematics. **Facts** are actually the case, known by observation or authentic testimony (as with a credible source), as opposed to what is inferred, conjectured, or invented.

Generally, we think of facts as empirically verifiable, true by definition or by mathematical proof. Empirically based facts can be proven by means of our five senses—sight, smell, touch, taste, and hearing: "Carrots are vegetables" and "Water freezes at 32° Fahrenheit." Mathematical definitions, axioms, and proven theorems operate as facts—treated as true by definition or derivation (derived from theorems and postulates).

We tend not to question that which is presented as fact—especially by those regarded as trustworthy. That is not always wise, as we have seen with the cases of journalists (e.g., Jayson Blair of *The New York Times*) who fabricated details in news articles.

Factual judgments are often treated as facts, as we see with "Smog is bad for your lungs." These are inferences drawn from earlier observations—for example, about the sorts of ingredients in smog and the studies that show the effects of those ingredients on the respiratory system. The rule of thumb is this: A factual judgment is not normally as strong as a fact, as it is at least one step away. Consequently, an inference drawn on the basis of the fact cannot be assumed to be true, but must be scrutinized.

Opinions fall into three major categories: (1) conjecture, (2) reasoned speculation, and (3) legal opinion. Statements of **conjecture** can be seen in the following: "The best music is rhythm and blues" and "Practicing verb drills is a drag." Opinions are often based on perception, individual taste, or emotion, relative to the point of view of the person(s) voicing the opinion. This gives rise to the refrain, "Well, that's just a matter of opinion." Public opinion is a synthesis or shared view of the people, the collective. This is usually obtained by statistical studies or polls.

The second category of opinion is the **reasoned speculation** of someone well versed in the area in question. Here are some examples: "Mad cow disease must have jumped to other species, like sheep, because of the animal feed" and "Those who thought Lenin had syphilis must have been on to something, given the reported symptoms he showed." The difference between this category and the first one is that here evidence *could be cited* and some agreement might then be reached with the listener. In contrast, there is no such expectation in those opinions that are relative to taste or perception.

The third category is **legal opinion.** In a legal context, opinions may be expressed as a formal statement, a ruling, or considered advice. Court opinions, for example, function as an explanation for a decision that becomes law. Court opinions have legal force, so in high-profile or controversial cases, such opinions are widely studied for their significance and likely consequences for future cases. The reasoning of the judge(s) or justices can guide future policies and decision making and may act as a precedent for years to come.

Facts and Opinions

Fact, analysis, and opinion are often linked, though opinions may or may not have a factual basis. It is a fact that we utter words. What they signify requires analysis, and whether the speaker thinks they make sense is a matter of opinion. When people set out the reasons for an opinion, we now have an argument. The issue of what is fact versus what is opinion should not be taken lightly.

It helps to see why clarifying facts and opinions matters. Think of criminal law. The fate of a defendant could rest on how credible we consider the testimony concerning the fingerprints found on the weapon or at the scene of the crime in determining guilt or innocence. Court challenges are calling for a reassessment:

> Edward J. Imwinkelried, a leading expert on forensic science who has worked with prosecutors and defense lawyers, said there was a "very good possibility" that the challenges would lead judges to instruct juries that a fingerprint analyst was not a scientist offering exact conclusions but an expert giving an opinion.
>
> That, said Mr. Imwinkelried, a law professor at the University of California at Davis, "could conceivably be an important weapon in the hands of defense counsel, because you've got a widespread public perception that fingerprint testimony is infallible." (Andy Newman, "Fingerprinting's Reliability Draws Growing Court Challenges," www.law-forensic.com)

The issue is not moot. Consider the case of poor Brandon Mayfield, an Oregon attorney whose fingerprints were a partial match to one print on a plastic bag found in a van driven by Madrid terrorist-bombérs (causing the deaths of 191 people and injuring hundreds more). The FBI reportedly looked only at the scanned fingerprints and not the original print. Acting on their suspicion of Mayfield, the FBI froze his bank accounts and assets. They detained Mayfield in jail for 17 days before realizing their error. They issued an apology and explanation:

> The FBI identification was based on an image of substandard quality, which was particularly problematic because of the remarkable number of points of similarity between Mayfield's prints and the print details in the images submitted to the FBI. The FBI's Latent Fingerprint Unit will be reviewing its current practices and will give consideration to adopting new guidelines for all examiners receiving latent print images when the original evidence is not included. . . . The FBI apologizes to Mr. Mayfield and his family for the hardships that this matter has caused. (FBI press release, www.fbi.gov)

You might find it interesting to research the case of Brandon Mayfield and get a broader sense of what was set in motion once the FBI noticed the partial match in the fingerprints. As we see by what followed, facts and opinions can take on a life of their own.

Speculation

Speculation is a form of guesswork. We normally use the term *speculation* to apply to either (1) hypotheses that have little, if any, evidence to back them up or (2) unsupported claims. However, as noted in the section on opinions, reasoned speculation can be a powerful tool in medicine and the sciences, as when researchers put a hypothesis to the test.

People speculate all the time—for example, when they offer their theory as to why their dog bit your ankle or when they speculate about intelligent life in other galaxies. There may be a kernel of evidence, but not enough to draw a solid conclusion. Some speculation borders on the ludicrous, such as that born of unfounded assumptions. For example, you see your best friend hugging *your* date and your speculation goes wild!

When we fail to scrutinize evidence or jump to a conclusion, we may end up far from the truth. Consider the 2004 outbreak of monkeypox—a relative of smallpox, a deadly contagious disease—in Illinois, Indiana, and Wisconsin. Infected pet prairie dogs that bit their owners were mostly to blame. The symptoms were ghastly: chills, fever, and pus-filled sores, among others. Of course, some people speculated that it was the result of a terrorist act. "Nowadays, any time there's an outbreak of a strange disease, some people will probably think bioterrorism," Donald Henderson said. "There was no evidence whatsoever of that in this case. But I imagine people thought about it, especially if they believed it might be smallpox" (Gretchen Reynolds, "Why Were Doctors Afraid to Treat Rebecca McLester?" *New York Times Magazine,* 18 Apr 2004).

Some speculation, however, can act as a catalyst in problem solving. The person speculating may be well versed on the topic but be missing pieces of the puzzle. Take, for instance, Dr. Susan Solomon's historical reconstruction of an expedition in Antarctica in 1912 that resulted in the death of explorer Robert F. Scott and four other men. She had weather reports of the region and diaries as the main evidence to work with, but needed more information. Trying to fill in the holes about why they died only 11 miles from a cache of food and heating oil, she speculated

> that Scott, who was now suffering from frostbite, could not go farther and that Wilson and Bowers decided not to leave him. Since they were still able to leave the tent, . . . they may have told Scott that there was a blizzard so he would not know they had chosen to follow their leader into death. (Kenneth Chang, "How Bad Luck Tipped the Scales to Disaster," *The New York Times,* 28 Aug 2001)

Solomon's speculation may not be entirely correct. Perhaps Wilson and Bowers told Scott the truth. Maybe they wanted to abandon the frostbitten chap to save their own hides, but Scott implored them to die with dignity, all together. Perhaps they all just gave up, worn out. And so on.

When we don't have all the pieces but want to offer an explanation or a theory, we often speculate. But remember: Speculation is guesswork, however informed it may be. Keep that in mind as you offer your own tentative explanations—or examine those of others.

Ideas and Hypotheses

Fact and opinions often lead to ideas. **Ideas** take the form of possible solutions, hypotheses, intentions, plans of action, and theories. The ancient roots of the word relate to a general or ideal form, pattern, vision, or standard by which things are measured. More commonly now, we use the term to refer to insights, purposes, or recommendations. Here is an example from Barack Obama's speech at Wesleyan's 2008 graduation ceremony: "At a time of war, we need you to work for peace," Obama told the graduates. "At a time of inequality, we need you to work for opportunity. At a time of so much cynicism and so much doubt, we need you to make us believe again. That's your task, class of 2008" (www.wesleyan .edu/newsrel/announcements/rc_2008). Some ideas are creative leaps, springing from visions or mental images, connected by the finest of threads. Other ideas are mental constructs we generate from our observations or from factual data. Some ideas are narrowly focused; others are broad and sweeping.

Ideas may strike like lightning, unexpected and piercing. Some ideas appear in dreams, or daydreams, with no clear stimulus. Others come in the course of addressing a particular problem, as if part of an organic process. *The Oxford English Dictionary* mentions the "idea man" in Hollywood—someone paid to dream up plots or give new life to old stories, myths, and movies.

Ideas sometimes come through a side door, when our attention is focused elsewhere. Have you ever tried to write a paper and just stared fruitlessly at the computer screen? You give up and are in the middle of doing dishes or talking on the phone when an idea springs forth from the top of your head. That's the creative dimension of ideas formation that cannot be forced or programmed. Anyone can have an opinion. But not everyone can have an idea—much less a good idea.

Exercises

Part One

1. Indicate whether each of the following are facts, opinions, or ideas:
   a. Big Bertha weighs 374 pounds.
   b. Bertha is a sexy woman, even if she's large.
   c. Bertha was born in Wichita, Kansas.
   d. We should build a shrine in honor of Bertha.
   e. Bertha has a lot of silly notions about how to attract men.
   f. Anyone who wants to attract men ought to learn how to bake chocolate cakes.
   g. Chocolate cake is better than brownies any day of the week!

2. Mark the following for facts, opinions, and ideas:

   EDDIE: Tuesday is a drag. Tuesday follows Monday. Sure Monday is an exciting day, but there's no "Tuesday Night Football"! True, it is between Monday and Wednesday. But that's it!! Everything else about Tuesday is a drag. It's three days from Friday, another good day. But that's it!!

   RALPH: You should get your head examined, Eddie! Tuesday is a great day.

   EDDIE: People who hate Tuesday should be able to have a vacation day every Tuesday. This would build self-esteem. It'd also be good for folks to sleep in one day during the week. Mental health problems account for a big portion of lost dollars from employers. Last year thousands of people took medication for depression and more skipped work because they just needed a break. In addition to time off, people should get free movie passes for Tuesday. You can bet that'd be popular!

   RALPH: You are crazy as a loon, Eddie. I recommend a good therapist to solve your problems! Call me tonight for the phone number.

3. Identify the facts (or statements of fact), opinions, and ideas in the following:
   a. The Lakers won game 3 of the playoffs.
   b. The Celtics weren't as good on the court as in game 2.
   c. The Celtics' coach ought to try meditation—it could really make him calmer.
   d. There were thousands of people on the street dancing in front of Staples Center.
   e. The series was covered by TV stations around the world and translated into many languages.
   f. The sportswriter from the *Times* should have had more faith in the Lakers.
   g. The Lakers seemed off their game, even though they won.
   h. The coach was right on to yell at the referees for some of their calls.
   i. Toby ought to watch a few more Celtics games.
   j. The Lakers ought to draft that new guy—Jaguar LeJoune—he's dynamite!
   k. Jaguar is 6'11".

4. Indicate what is fact, opinion, or idea in Cindy Rodriguez's views on dating ("Getting Real in Today's Fantasyland," *Denver Post,* www.denverpost.com, 7 Jun 2004):
   a. If you acknowledge that you want someone who is a few notches above you, then you suffer from low self-esteem or delusion.
   b. I have a solution: Date sideways—Find someone who is real, who makes you laugh and who—this is the most important part—wants you, too.
   c. In June 2004 *Maxim* magazine had an article titled, "Out of Your League and in the Bag."
   d. Let's just admit this up front: A book on dating down won't sell.

5. *The New York Times* published an article that focused on the last meals of condemned prisoners in the state of Texas. We were told some salient details, such as these:

   Twenty-two men chose double cheese burgers, 15 opted for single cheeseburgers, 9 for hamburgers. Next most popular were steaks, typically T-bones, with 27 requests, and eggs (10 requests, most for scrambled). Most desired overall is a side of French fries (56 requests). Ice cream is the most popular dessert (21 requests), Coca Cola the most popular beverage (13, just edging out 12 requests for iced tea). And 24 inmates declined any last meal at all. ("For the Condemned in Texas, Cheeseburgers without Mercy," *The New York Times,* 4 Jan 1998)

   Answer the following:
   a. State one *fact* noted above.
   b. State one *opinion* about this situation, and explain what kind of opinion it is.
   c. State one *idea* about this situation

Part Two

1. An ad on a sign outside an ARCO gas station in Bakersfield, California, read "One in three body builders pumps ARCO gas." Offer some ideas about how you might substantiate the claim being made.

2. Scientist Bette Korber of Los Alamos used the world's fastest computer to compare the genetic material of the many strains of HIV, searching for a common origin. Her statistical study resulted in her estimate that HIV first appeared in the human population around 1930. Researchers suspect that it happened as a result of trapping or eating chimpanzees. What more would you want to know to call this "reasoned speculation" and not just an opinion? (What two or three questions would you like answered?)

3. What suggests that Jeffrey Platt, director of the Mayo Clinic Transplantation Biology Program, is speculating in the following? Explain why.

"Perhaps HIV managed to jump from primates to humans through infected blood from a bite, which allowed the stem cells from the two species to fuse," Platt suggested. "When the genes recombined, perhaps the virus was reawakened" ("Pig-Human Chimeras Contain Cell Surprise," *The New Scientist,* 13 Jan 2004).

Part Three

1. Here are some facts about the U.S. prison system noted by *The New York Times* on March 10, 2008:
   a. One in nine black men, ages 20 to 34, are serving time, as are 1 in 36 Hispanic men.
   b. Nationwide, the prison population hovers at almost 1.6 million, which surpasses all other countries for which there are reliable figures.
   c. The 50 states last year spent about $44 billion in tax dollars on corrections, up from nearly $11 billion in 1987.
   d. Vermont, Connecticut, Delaware, Michigan, and Oregon devote as much money or more to corrections as they do to higher education.
   e. Incarceration rates have continued to rise while crime rates have fallen.

Answer the following:
   a. Given these facts, draw two or three inferences.
   b. State your opinion of *The New York Times* inferring that the United States is a "prison nation."
   c. The *Times* voiced the opinion that "these statistics, contained in a new report from the Pew Research Center on the States, point to a terrible waste of money and lives." Do you know enough from the facts above to agree or disagree with that opinion?
   d. The *Times* expressed this idea: "The key, as some states are learning, is getting smarter about distinguishing between violent criminals and dangerous repeat offenders, who need a prison cell, and low-risk offenders, who can be handled with effective community supervision, electronic monitoring and mandatory drug treatment programs, combined in some cases with shorter sentences." State two other ideas for addressing the high incarceration rate.

2. The following factual claims were made on the TV show *60 Minutes* ("Fingerprints: Infallible Evidence?" *60 Minutes*, 6 Jun 2004). Read them and offer several ideas about what we ought to do when using fingerprint evidence in trials.

   a. There's complete disagreement among fingerprint examiners themselves as to what they need to see in order to declare a match.

   b. In Italy, for example, examiners say they have to see 16 or 17 points of similarity.

   c. In Brazil, it's 30; in Sweden, it's 7 points; and in Australia, it's 12.

   d. Most examiners in the United States, including those at the FBI, don't even use a point system in testing for a match.

   e. Over the last 100 years, there have been only a handful of cases where convictions have been reversed because of faulty fingerprint identification, but that doesn't mean examiners don't make mistakes.

   f. Judges don't require that fingerprint experts who testify be certified.

3. One recommendation to ward off insect bites is to use repellents that contain DEET. However, research raises concerns that DEET might have been a factor in Gulf War syndrome. Read about the study and then answer the questions below:

   A study done at Duke University and published in the November 2001 *Journal of Experimental Neurology* showed that frequent and prolonged applications of DEET (in an average human dose adjusted to rat size) caused neurons to die in regions of rat brains that control muscle movement, learning, memory, and concentration.

   "The rats didn't look any different," says lead researcher Mohamed Abou-Donia, PhD, professor of pharmacology and cancer biology at Duke, "but when we challenged them with a task, they failed." Abou-Donia became interested in this subject while studying veterans who used DEET in concentrations of 70% and in concert with permethrin (not recommended, by the way). "We think part of the problem experienced by some vets may be due to DEET," says Abou-Donia, referring to Gulf War veterans' illness. (Star Lawrence, "How to Be Repellent—to Bugs," Msn.health, content.health.msn.com, 28 May 2004)

Answer the following:

   a. What *facts* were stated in this report? List them.

   b. What *questions* do you have after reading the report?

   c. State three to four *inferences* that could be drawn from the report.

   d. Is it safe to conclude that DEET is a key factor in Gulf War syndrome?

   e. Is your conclusion affected by the knowledge that in Canada, DEET concentrations cannot exceed 30 percent, whereas in the United States, hundreds of products, some with concentrations of 100 percent DEET, are sold over the counter?

The Global Dimension

Fingerprinting Travelers to the United States

In another fingerprinting case, Italian philosopher Giorgio Agamben opted out of teaching the Spring 2004 semester at New York University in protest against the fingerprinting of arriving visitors and employees from other countries. Read the passage below and then list his key points. Note what you consider his strongest point (and why).

> Prof. Agamben says he is deeply opposed to using biological methods to track citizens, including finger and retina prints and subcutaneous tattooing for political purposes. By applying these techniques and devices invented for the dangerous classes to individual citizens, governments have made humanity itself the dangerous class. He views fingerprinting as a kind of tattooing reminiscent of that done during the Holocaust, when Jews and others had numbers tattooed on their inner arms. Agamben says:

> "A few years ago I wrote that the political model of the west is not the city but the concentration camp, not Athens but Auschwitz. That was, of course, a philosophical, not a historical thesis. This is not about mixing phenomena that must be separated. I only want to remind readers that the tattooing in Auschwitz possibly appeared as 'normal' and economic in order to regulate the admission of the deportees to the camp. The bio-political tattooing, which we are forced to undergo today in order to enter the United States, is a relay race to what we could tomorrow accept as the normal registration of the identity of the good citizen considering the mechanisms and machinery of the state." (As quoted by Standard Schaefer, "Italian Philosopher Giorgio Agamben Protests US Travel Policies," *Counterpunch*, www.counterpunch.org, 23 Jan 2003)

Good Arguments, Bad Arguments

Arguments are all around us; the question is what to make of them. Arguments consist of **propositions**. A proposition is an assertion that predicates some characteristic of the subject. It is true or false. Here's an example: "All zoo animals are creatures fond of looking at people." The *subject* is "zoo animals," and the *predicate* is "creatures fond of looking at people." In an argument, we have one proposition that is the conclusion and at least one other that is a premise. It's crucial that we be able to recognize these two components in the argument.

If you are the author, you usually start with a thesis and then proceed to make your case by laying out your evidence. (The terms "thesis" and "conclusion" will be used interchangeably here.) The collection of your evidence constitutes the set of premises. When you stand back and look at your argument, you can see the premises working together to support the thesis. The conclusion of your argument is the thesis that rests on those premises.

The *first step* in dismantling an argument is to locate the conclusion (thesis). If we don't know where the argument is headed, we're lost in a fog. Once the conclusion is clear, we can see how the argument is structured. This entails setting out the premises—the evidence offered as support of the thesis. So, after pinpointing the author's thesis, we list the premises. Before we proceed to weigh the evidence, it is generally advisable to consider any assumptions that factor into the equation.

You Tell Me Department

The Birth of Octuplets

Just when you thought we'd seen the upper bound on multiple births, Nadya Suleman, an unemployed single mother in Whittier, CA gave birth to eight babies. Only one other time in U.S. history has a woman had octuplets. The initial astonishment gave way to consternation, as experts opined about the implantation of so many embryos, the dangers of such a pregnancy, and a host of ethical issues. Higher-order multiple births put both mother and children at risk. Risks for the babies include bleeding in the brain, intestinal problems, developmental delays and lifelong learning disabilities (Elizabeth Landau, "Octuplets Eight Times the Ethical Questions," CNN.com, 30 Jan 2009).

It is unclear how the woman ended up with eight embryos in the first place. Her mother said Suleman was obsessed with children and that she had received fertility treatment using a sperm donor and had embryos implanted. (Jessica Garrison and Kimi Yoshino," Octuplets' Mom Was Hoping For 'Just One More Girl,' Grandmother Says," *Los Angeles Times,* 31 Jan 2009). Doctors gave her the option of selectively reducing the number of embryos, and she refused. The fact the 33-year old woman already had six children, a history of financial woes, and lived with her parents only added to the controversy.

Directions: Read the experts' responses to the birth of the octuplets from CNN.com and from *The Los Angeles Times* (30-31 Jan 2009). Answer the questions that follow.

M. Sara Rosenthal, Bioethicist: If she went to a fertility clinic, there's wide consensus from every single ethicist and fertility specialist that this was irresponsible and unethical to implant that many embryos. This is an outrageous situation that should not happen. The situation raises the issue of whether a doctor ought to override a patient's wishes for the sake of saving lives.

Robert George, Law Professor: In certain European countries, particularly Italy and Germany, the limit on the number of embryos allowed to be implanted at once is three. What you need are professional norms and legal regulations that restrict practices that are inherently very dangerous.

Scott Slayden, MD, Reproductive Endocrinologist: Even with triplets, a doctor would be remiss if [he] didn't tell a woman with triplets about selective fetal reduction. It would be extremely unusual, very strange and hard to believe that somebody who is a professional would put that many embryos into a woman who is 33 years old who has children.

R. Dale McClure, MD, President of The American Society for Reproductive Medicine: If this resulted from an IVF treatment, we can say that transferring eight embryos in an IVF cycle is well beyond our guidelines. The guidelines state that patients under the age of 35 would not have more than two embryos implanted in the absence of extraordinary circumstances.

Arthur Wisot, Fertility Doctor: I cannot see circumstances where any reasonable physician would transfer eight embryos into a woman under the age of 35 under any circumstance. I cannot imagine that any of the mainstream practices in the Los Angeles area were involved in this. I would guess—and it's a pure guess—that she either went out of the country or went to a practice that flies below the radar.

The Nanny: The nanny who works with the octuplets' siblings said Friday that the woman "adores her babies" and is "a perfect mom."

Answer the following:

1. What facts are asserted about the case?
2. What opinions are expressed? Discuss what the range of the opinions tells us about the controversy.
3. What ideas were raised to address the various concerns? Share your own thoughts and ideas about whether this is an area in need of more oversight.

Assumptions

Assumptions may be a factor in an argument. An **assumption** is something that is taken for granted or supposed to be the case without proof. Occasionally they are made explicit; but they are often unstated. Of course, the fact that we assume something does not, in itself, make it true. An assumption generally functions like a hypothesis, *not* like a fact. You would not say, for instance, "Let us assume that $15 \times 3 = 45$," because we *know* that this is true. However, we might assume some common knowledge (e.g., that the listener knows how to multiply).

We also see assumptions when there is doubt, uncertainty, or hypothetical conditions. Here's an example: "Let us *assume* the victim was murdered in the kitchen and carried out to the patio." We treat the assumption *as if* it were true and then see what might follow. In this case, assumptions act like a set of ground rules. However, some assumptions turn out to be completely unfounded or even ludicrous. We saw this in previous centuries in the assumptions that animals were not capable of feeling pain or that certain racial/ethnic groups had smaller brains than Caucasians. Here are some examples of assumptions:

Argument 1: Chong will not be happy that her parents gave her the biggest SUV they could find for her graduation present. She made it clear to anyone who would listen that she wants to be eco-conscious and not own any more gas-guzzling, energy hogs!

Assumption: The SUV Chong's parents gave her is a gas guzzler and an energy hog.

Argument 2: To keep the temperature of the stuffing closer to that of the turkey, I tried just about everything I could think of: filling a cold turkey with hot stuffing, cooking the stuffed turkey in an oven bag for more even heat, shielding the turkey breast with foil, and on and on. None of these tricks worked. The stuffing just wasn't coming up to the temperature as soon as the meat. Consequently, I had to come up with an alternative plan.

Assumption: The stuffing should be at a high-enough temperature to cook thoroughly.

Argument 3: Dozens of teenage smokers as young as 14 had their brains studied with high-tech scans. Vervet monkeys were fed liquid nicotine, and at least six of them were killed so their brains could be examined. In October 2007, activists opposed to animal testing flooded UCLA professor Edythe London's West Side home with her garden hose, causing more than $20,000 in damage. And later, an incendiary device was placed by her front door and was discovered by the gardener. Therefore, the activists thought London needed to be sent a message.

Assumptions: Edythe London was directly involved in the use and killing of the vervet monkeys. Activists also assumed that the damage to her home would send her a message about the use of animals in drug testing.

Warranted and Unwarranted Assumptions

Most people operate most of the time with a set of assumptions. These assumptions shape how they see the world and how they think. One of our tasks is to recognize and make explicit any assumptions. We can then decide whether they rest on solid footing (i.e., are warranted) or whether they are questionable or without merit (i.e., are unwarranted).

If there is evidence to support the assumption, it is a *warranted* assumption and, if not, it is *unwarranted*. This evidence should be stated in the argument itself. For instance, the assumptions in arguments 1 and 2 about SUVs and turkey stuffing, respectively, are both warranted. The assumptions in argument 3, however, are not clearly warranted without more evidence about the case. Watch for assumptions and see if they are warranted. For example, it would be *warranted* to assume that American musicians know what a Grammy is, but *unwarranted* to assume that they could list the Grammy winners of the past decade.

It is easier to examine assumptions that are stated (e.g., "Assume that women have a higher pain threshold than do men" and "Assume that men can lift more weight than women") than those that are unstated. Nevertheless, assumptions may be unstated, so we need to make them explicit. We can then see if they are warranted and decide if the argument holds.

For example, Joyce Trebilcot sets out her assumptions in her article "Sex Roles: The Argument from Nature" (1975). Consider how the argument would be weakened if her assumptions did not hold up.

> For the purpose of this discussion, *let us accept the claim that* natural psychological differences are inevitable. *We assume that* there are such differences and ignore the possibility of their being altered, for example, by evolutionary change or direct biological intervention. *Let us also accept* the second claim that biological differences are inevitable. Behavioral differences could perhaps be eliminated *even given the assumption* of natural differences in disposition (for example, those with no natural inclination to a certain kind of behavior might nonetheless learn it), *but let us waive this point. We assume then* that behavioral differences, *and hence also* role differences, between the sexes are inevitable. Does it follow that there must be sex roles, that is, that the institutions and practices of society must enforce correlation between roles and sex?
>
> Surely not. Indeed, such sanctions would be pointless. Why bother to direct women into some roles and men into others if the pattern occurs regardless of the nature of society? Mill makes the point elegantly in *The Subjection of Women*: "The anxiety of mankind to interfere in behalf of nature, for fear lest nature should not succeed in effecting its purpose, is an altogether unnecessary solicitude." (emphasis added).

Trebilcot makes her assumptions explicit—which helps us analyze her reasoning. If she had not spelled them out, then we would have had to do so in assessing her argument.

Group or Individual Exercise

Directions: Read the following and then answer the questions that follow.

In a provocative hypothesis that has startled AIDS experts, an Oxford University researcher has proposed that AIDS might have entered the human population in a bizarre series of malaria experiments. The researcher, Dr. Charles Gilks of Oxford

University and the Kenya Medical Research Institute, has discovered reports of a series of little-known malaria experiments in which people were inoculated with fresh blood from monkeys and chimpanzees. He suggests that this blood may have infected humans with primate viruses that were the ancestors of the AIDS virus. . . .

Many AIDS researchers have suggested that the human AIDS virus originated in monkeys and chimpanzees. It has been well established that a type of West African monkey called the sooty mangabey is often infected with a virus that is extremely similar to HIV 2, a virus that causes AIDS in West Africa. . . . In his paper, Dr. Gilks described published studies, dating to 1922 and continuing into the 1950's, in which researchers inoculated themselves or others, including prisoners, with fresh blood from chimpanzees or mangabeys. They did this, in most cases, to see whether malaria parasites that are transmitted to primates by mosquitoes can also infect people.

These studies involved 34 people who were given injections of blood from 17 chimpanzees and an additional 33 who were given blood from people who received chimpanzee blood. In addition, two people were inoculated with blood from mangabeys and three others were injected with blood from macaques that had been injected with blood from mangabeys. These experiments, which continued into the 1950's, were the only way scientists knew to learn whether the malaria parasite could be transmitted from monkeys or chimpanzees to humans. (Gina Kolata, "Theory Links AIDS to Malaria Experiments," *The New York Times,* 28 Nov 1991)

Answer the following:

1. What is Dr. Gilks' hypothesis?
2. What evidence did he offer in support?
3. What did the researchers assume when injecting themselves and others with the chimpanzee and mangabey blood?
4. Is there enough evidence to conclude that Gilks's hypothesis has merit?

Missing Premises and Unstated Assumptions

Arguments often have unstated assumptions or missing premises. If so, we must decide what has been omitted because this is an area where prejudice, bias, or questionable beliefs can be hidden. Even if the missing premises are legitimate, it is important to state them. Normally, this evidence should be stated in the argument itself, so the reasoning is clear. Each piece of evidence can then be examined for its role in offering support for the conclusion. If there is evidence to support the assumption, it is a warranted assumption. If not, it is unwarranted. For instance, look at this argument: "Because baggy clothes can be mistaken for gang attire, they should be outlawed." The *premise* is: "Baggy clothes can be mistaken for gang attire" (note the "because" premise-indicator). The *conclusion,* then, is "Baggy clothes should be outlawed." The conclusion does not directly follow from the premise. There is a missing premise, and that is the unstated assumption "Clothes that can be mistaken for gang attire should be outlawed." It is this claim that reveals what is problematic about the argument, as merely restricting clothing won't likely stop gang activity. The issue is not simply the clothes; it is how to stop gang violence or other objectionable behavior.

Checklist for Assessing Arguments

- Locate the conclusion (author's thesis).
- Set out the premises.
- Be sure the premises provide a clear link to the conclusion.
- Watch for omissions and questionable claims.
- Make sure the case is as strong as possible.
- If it seems like a strong case, see how the evidence supports the conclusion.
- Determine the weakest link in case you need to bolster it.
- If the argument is not convincing, find the weaknesses in the reasoning.
- Treat any questionable or unwarranted assumptions like premises, and analyze them accordingly.

Some arguments are strong. If the support is strong and clearly supports the conclusion if we assume it were true, we'd say we have a good argument.

Some ideas are better than others, even for extra cash!

Cartoon by Ted Rall. ©2001 Ted Rall, All Rights Reserved. Reprinted with permission of Ted Rall.

Exercises

Part One

Directions: Find the *conclusion* in the arguments below.

1. "Sleep all day. Party all night. Never grow old. Never die. It's fun to be a vampire" (movie poster for *The Lost Boys*).

2. Vampires are scarier than cyborgs, even though cyborgs seem to be physically stronger. As a result, there won't be many more *Terminator* sequels, unlike the endless vampire films that we never seem to tire of.

3. They say vampires have no reflection. This is based on the traditional view that mirrors reflect your soul. Evil demons have no soul, and we certainly know vampires are evil.

4. Dracula's commands have to be obeyed—otherwise he would lose his temper. Therefore, it was no joking matter when Dracula told the merchant to leave his valuable belongings on the street (adapted from McNally and Florescu, *In Search of Dracula*).

5. Many people may be "iffy" in the face of death, but everyone fears the loss of blood and infections such as AIDS. *Nosferatu* compares the bubonic plague with the spread of the vampire disease. Vampire movies by Coppola and Rice draw similarities between the prolonged effects of vampire attacks and AIDS. The element of danger, mystery, and even death associated with sex is thus re-created in a contemporary context (adapted from McNally and Florescu, *In Search of Dracula*, 1994).

6. Some film critics thought the werewolf scenes were second-rate in *Prisoner of Azkaban* and should have been cut. However, the werewolf had children in the audience wailing—especially when it chased Harry and Hermione. This suggests that the critics simply underestimated the power of the werewolf mythology.

7. Neither robots nor cyborgs are as scary as vampires. This could be due to the fact that they don't suck your blood or need to be killed with a stake through the heart. For that matter, vampires have no heart.

8. As viewers become more savvy about horror films, they get harder to fool—or to scare. Violence in film is starting to numb the audience, and maybe even bore them. Because of that, directors might consider more mind games, as in *The Eye* or *Vanishing*, and less blood and gore.

9. In early zombie films, like *Night of the Living Dead*, zombies moved in slow motion, plodding along like Frankenstein. It was the anticipation that they'd eventually catch up to the humans that was so horrifying. Recent films have dispensed with that idea, as zombies now race along like Olympic sprinters. These newer zombies, like those in *28 Days/Weeks Later* and *I Am Legend*,

certainly run like the dickens, but they also willingly splat their heads into windows while chasing their prey. Zombies may be getting faster, but they are getting dumber, too.

10. The three agents in *The Matrix*—Agents Smith, Jones, and Brown—were more frightening when there were just three of them. When they multiply like cockroaches in *Matrix Reloaded* and *Matrix Revolutions,* they become no different than those armies of robots that heroes must tirelessly overcome in one action movie after another. Consequently, *The Matrix* is higher on the scare-scale than the sequels.

11. Dante had it right all along. It's the one who betrays us that we fear the most, not the one who beats the pulp out of us. Look at the evidence: The one who betrays us cuts to the quick, deep into the soul. Think of Cypher in *The Matrix* or Darth Vader in *Star Wars* or even the Gollum in *Lord of the Rings.* The loss of trust leaves a wound much slower to heal than a physical blow.

12. *Will Smith:* "I don't have much of a secret life. There's probably a more aggressive side that I haven't really played in a movie, but for the most part, the characters I've played in the big summer movies have had a piece of me. And if it's not a piece of who I am, it's a piece of who I wish I was. This goes to show that I'm an open book kind of dude" (quoted in *Wired,* Jul 2004).

Part Two

1. Discuss any assumptions in the following argument: "High school women runners should not be allowed to wear short shorts in running a race. Short shorts may help them run faster, but they are unacceptable clothing for a public event. Short shorts distract the male viewer. Many people who attend track meets are males. It is not a good thing for men to be distracted or offended." We can set out the argument like this:

P_1: Short shorts may help high school women run faster, but they are unacceptable clothing for a public event.
P_2: Short shorts are distracting for the male viewer.
P_3: Many people who attend track meets are males.
P_4: <u>It is not a good thing for men to be distracted or offended.</u>
C: High school women should not be allowed to wear short shorts in running a race.

2. Here is a comparison offered by Ignacio Hernandez, president of MexGrocer .com, a bilingual online grocery store for authentic Mexican food—one of Mexican salsas, the other of American salsas. Pull out the two or three key points.

Says Hernandez, "If you look at the list of ingredients in imported Mexican food brands, it's shorter. They use more fresh ingredients. An example is Herdez Salsa Casera. It probably has only five ingredients: tomatoes, onions, serrano peppers, cilantro, and salt. But if you look at salsas made in the U.S., they have a very long list of ingredients. Maybe they use diced tomatoes, maybe they use dried onions. They're not as fresh, except for a few regional, organic, or smaller type brands."

"Anglo salsas also have a different heat level than the Mexican brands," he continues. "Mild, medium, and hot. The Mexican salsas do not use that terminology. People know that *salsa casera* is hot or medium hot. With salsas from the American Southwest, you can see that many people like a mild salsa. Probably in sales of Southwest salsas, the number one flavor will be mild. If you look at the more authentic salsas, the number one flavor will be the hot. People who like authentic flavors like hot salsas. But the Southwest flavors are interesting and creative. They involve combinations of flavors such as apricot salsa, peach salsa, or raspberry. They are more creative than the originals." ("Why Branding Salsa Is about Roots and Culture," Brand.channel.com, 31 Dec 2007)

3. Stuart Elliot of *The New York Times* writes about the decision to change the 3 Musketeers (characters associated with the candy bar). Set out the main argument for this decision. You don't have to include any background information.

Mr. Whipple has always been white. Uncle Ben has always been black. The Jolly Green Giant has always been, well, green. But there has been an unusual color change for another advertising character, which may be symbolic of the changing face of American consumers. The makeover involves [the] 3 Musketeers, the candy brand sold since 1932. . . . Traditionally, all the musketeers have been white. Now, though, one of the three actors who portray the characters in TV and print ads is black. "We look at the addition of an African-American musketeer as reflective of the diverse society in which we live and the diverse world to which we market," said Alvin Gay, of ad agency Uniworld. "It would be gratuitous [uncalled for] if it wasn't strategically sound," he added. "It comes about from trying to understand the consumer." The more contemporary look in advertising is visible in ads featuring consumers who may be of black, Asian or other ancestry; speak Spanish or another language; cohabit with a same-sex partner; or live in nontraditional families. Even interracial couples, once taboo, are seen.

"It wouldn't surprise me if you told me one of the musketeers is a woman," said Kenneth J. Roberts, corporate identity consultant. The black musketeer "simply reflects the times." ("The New Campaign for 3 Musketeers Adds Diversity to Portray Contemporary America," 12 Feb 1997)

Quick Quiz

1. An argument has two components—state them.

2. Is this an argument (*yes or no*)? Louis is short for an athlete. In fact, he's only 5'10" and weighs in at 168 pounds. He works out three to four hours a day and can be seen running laps just about every morning around 6:00 A.M.

3. *True or false:* You don't have to worry about stating the assumptions when examining an argument, since they are rarely important.

4. The set of all the evidence that is said to support the conclusion is called what? (State the term used.)

5. *True or false:* The author's *thesis* is the same thing as the *conclusion* being drawn on the basis of the support offered.

6. If an assumption has no basis in fact or theoretical foundation (is not defensible), would you consider it (a) warranted or (b) unwarranted?

7. Which one of the following is a *proposition*: (a) No brown trout has feathers; (b) Is that Otis Redding playing on the jukebox? (c) Ouch!

8. *True or false:* An argument can have two or more conclusions.

9. State the *conclusion* of this argument: Tom was feeling adventurous after such a restful sleep. He was glad to have all his finals over and a break before the next term started up. Tom figured he had the time to make a nice big breakfast. Pancakes! Yes, pancakes. He decided to add blueberries to his pancake batter. He added one half cup of berries for each cup of flour. He was careful to turn the pancakes over before the berries burned on the griddle. As a result, Tom's pancakes came out perfectly.

Premise-Indicators and Conclusion-Indicators

All too often, we struggle to figure out an author's thesis as we plow through words and more words. Do you ever have a voice in your head saying, "Yeah, but what's your *point?*" It is not always clear what is the conclusion and what are the premises.

For example, what if someone says to you, "Asbestos is dangerous. It poisons the atmosphere. It is a known carcinogen." If you clutch your head in confusion, you can appreciate signposts that help locate the terms of the argument. **Indicator words** such as "because" and "therefore" function as signposts, eliminating the need for guessing at the premises and the conclusion. These words and phrases signify that a premise or conclusion immediately follows.

Premise-Indicators. A **premise-indicator** is a word or phrase that indicates a premise in an argument. When you see a premise-indicator, know that a premise is being flagged. Whatever follows the premise indicator is a premise—so these indicators help us locate the evidence! Any term that can be replaced with "because" is a premise-indicator. Arguments often contain premise-indicators and/or conclusion-indicators.

> **Premise-indicators:** Because, Whereas, In light of, For, Given that, For the Reason that, Since*

*Be careful: If "since" can be replaced by "because"—for example, "Since I love ice cream, I'll get a sundae"—then it functions as a premise-indicator. Sometimes "since" is a temporal indicator, as in "Since I dyed my hair purple, men have found me attractive." If "since" can be replaced by "from the moment," then it is a temporal indicator, *not* a premise-indicator. Here are some examples:

PREMISE-INDICATOR	PREMISE	CONCLUSION-INDICATOR
Because	you have yanked out clumps of hair,	*you need a vacation.*
Given that	you only like cheese on your eggs,	*I'll put the ketchup in the fridge.*
Whereas	you insist on dyeing your hair green,	*perhaps you could get a role in Elf 2.*
Since	you prefer café latte without marshmallows,	*you won't ruin your diet having another one.*

ALTERNATIVE FORMAT

CONCLUSION	PREMISE-INDICATOR	PREMISE
You need a new car	in light of the fact that	your car is a wreck.
We could use more ketchup	since	grandma put it on her eggs.

Conclusion-Indicators.   A **conclusion-indicator** is a word or phrase that introduces a conclusion in an argument. If you can replace the term with "therefore" without changing the argument, the term is a conclusion-indicator and the conclusion should immediately follow. A conclusion-indicator acts like a red flag, allowing us to spot the conclusion.

> **Conclusion-Indicators:** In conclusion, Accordingly, So, As a result, Therefore, Consequently, Hence, It follows that, Subsequently, Thus

PREMISE	CONCLUSION-INDICATOR	CONCLUSION
Cockatoos are very affectionate.	therefore,	a cockatoo is a great choice for a pet bird.
Birds make great companions.	hence,	birds should be allowed in rest homes.
Guinea pigs are very gentle creatures.	consequently,	they are wonderful pets for children.
Some prairie dogs have monkeypox.	as a result,	it is unwise to grab a wild prairie dog.

Remember: Premises don't always appear before the conclusion—they could follow it. Alternatively, the conclusion could be sandwiched between premises. That's where indicators help!

Transition Words

Transition words indicate an introduction, amplification, clarification, emphasis, illustration, or contrast. They do not function as premise- or conclusion-indicators, *unless clearly shown in the context*—for example, when a list of premises or several conclusions are listed in sequence. Transition words can be located anywhere—in premises, in conclusions, or in a sentence not part of an argument. That means we can't assume that they indicate *either* a premise or a conclusion.

FUNCTION	TRANSITION WORDS
Introduction	In order to, Primarily, The first reason, Initially, In the first place, To begin, In general
Amplification	Moreover, Furthermore, In addition, Provided that, Similarly, Also, Likewise, First, second, third,
Clarification	That is, To restate, In other words, In simpler terms, Briefly, To repeat, To put it in another light, To put it differently, As seen by
Emphasis	In fact, Notably, Nonetheless, Nevertheless, In effect, Above all, Indeed, And rightly so, As such
Illustration	To illustrate, For example, For instance, Specifically, Namely, A case in point
Contrast	However, Alternatively, On the other hand, Notwithstanding, In opposition to, And yet, Conversely, At the same time, In spite of, Despite

Be careful: These words could appear anywhere—in a list of data, a premise, a conclusion, or a sentence outside of an argument.

- Example of a transition word in a proposition and *not* in an argument: "Chicken tamales are difficult to make, but delicious. *In other words,* tamales are not easy to whip up, but they sure are good." (*Note:* The transition word clues us that the first point is being expanded upon—but no argument is being made.)
- Example of transition words functioning as premise-indicators in an argument: "Miso soup is about the best thing to eat if you are recovering from food poisoning. *In general,* you don't want anything too hard to digest if your tummy is turbulent. *However,* meat such as chicken is not so easily digested and is harder on the intestines. Therefore, you'd be crazy to order a chicken tamale so soon after your food poisoning!" (*Note:* The transition words indicate elaboration and contrast of the first premise, effectively introducing premises 2 and 3.)
- Example of a transition word that acts as a conclusion-indicator in an argument: "It's hard to find any dessert that's more tasty than a lemon meringue pie. Consequently, you should rethink making chocolate brownies for the party. *Likewise,* forget cooking up bread pudding, too!" (*Note:* The

transition word amplifies on the conclusions, indicating that another point is being concluded as well. This leaves us with two separate conclusions for the one premise.)

Setting Out Arguments

If we have no evidence to cite as support for the conclusion (thesis), we have no argument. There has to be at least one premise and only one conclusion in an argument. The claim "Elvis impersonators need to get a life" is not an argument; it is merely a proposition. For an argument, you need both "Elvis impersonators need to get a life" and evidence to support the claim. For instance, this would act as support: "Elvis impersonators live in the shadow of Elvis," "People who live in anyone else's shadow need to get a life," and so on. Only the combination of premises (evidence) and conclusion (thesis) can form an argument. We can then see how strong the argument actually is. It helps to be organized. Here's the strategy to take:

Strategy for Setting Out Arguments

- State the conclusion (thesis/hypothesis). This gives you a sense of where you're headed. If you don't know the conclusion, you cannot analyze the argument.
- List the premises (reasons/evidence) one by one.
- Examine the premises to see if they are sufficient to support the conclusion. Look for any holes, such as missing premises, unwarranted assumptions, biased language, or fallacious reasoning.
- List the premises one by one (P_1, P_2, P_3, etc.) above the conclusion to provide order to the argument and make it easier to read.

You then have the premises and conclusion clearly set out, so you can examine the relationship between them, and you are less likely to overlook a piece of evidence.

Example: "All small children should be given a warm bowl of oatmeal every morning. That means Lulu should be given a bowl of oatmeal, since she is a small child."

Put in standard form: First, we locate the conclusion. Do you see it? It is "Lulu should be given a warm bowl of oatmeal." That leaves the premises to be "All small children should be given a warm bowl of oatmeal" and "Lulu is a small child." Let's now number and stack the premises and draw the line above the conclusion. We then get:

P_1: All small children should be given a warm bowl of oatmeal.

P_2: <u>Lulu is a small child.</u>

C: Lulu should be given a warm bowl of oatmeal.

The argument is now in standard form.

Exercises

Part One

1. Circle all the <u>premise-indicators</u> below:

However	Since	Because	Although
Therefore	Whereas	If	Subsequently
Despite	Unless	Given that	Hence
Moreover	Conversely	Accordingly	For the reason that

2. Circle all the <u>conclusion-indicators</u> below:

Conversely	Yet	Whereas	Consequently
As a result	Since	Because	In light of the fact that
Thus	In fact	Given that	In conclusion
Indeed	To restate	Hence	Accordingly

3. Circle all the <u>transition words</u> below:

However	Given that	Therefore	Although
In fact	Since	Accordingly	For the reason that
Above all	Specifically	Hence	Furthermore
Thus	Because	Despite	Initially

Part Two

Directions: Identify any premise-indicators or conclusion-indicators in the following:

1. The mountain lion came into Janet's backyard and jumped in her swimming pool. It was 90 degrees that day, and the air was muggy. Consequently, it was not surprising that a wild animal would try to cool off like that.

2. Because Nik couldn't stop drawing cartoons, he figured that he might as well go into it for a living. Plus, people kept telling him he had artistic talent.

3. Jasper decided to investigate what was going on in the kitchen before the philosophy department party. In light of the fact that Jasper jumped into the cheesecake, we better come up with a plan for an alternative dessert.

4. Adam watched the same YouTube video five times in a row. Everyone else had moved to the kitchen for ice cream and brownies. Adam, however, insisted on watching the show one more time. It follows that Adam was more interested in the video than eating.

5. Given that Julia keeps running down the hall, it is getting awfully hard to pay attention to the history chapter. Julia is just too distracting. And the chapter would be hard to read even if it wasn't so noisy.

6. Rahma prefers blueberries to apples. There are a number of good reasons for this. First, blueberries are small and easy to eat. Second, blueberries are

soft and chewy. They have a nice texture, too. Finally, blueberries are a bit sweeter than apples.

7. Because the electricity is out, we might as well light some candles. The last time the electricity was out, it took hours until the lights came back on. Plus, it's not much fun to sit around in pitch dark.

8. Jasper was not happy with the toys on top of his cage. He kept pushing them around. He really did not like all that clutter. Because of all that, he tossed all the toys overboard, onto the floor.

9. Rahma does not seem to like shredded beef all that much. However, she loves nice little chunks of chicken that are easy to pop in her mouth. She thinks they taste good, too. Therefore, she will definitely want chicken instead of beef for dinner. Also, she finds it easier to stab her fork into the chicken chunks than into shredded beef.

10. Amanda phoned her neighbor when the electricity went out the other day. She wanted to make sure it wasn't just at her house. Also, she was upset and needed to make contact with someone else about the electrical outage. Because she found out the electricity was down on the block, she decided to go on a drive instead of sitting in her dark house.

Dismantling Longer Arguments

The process here is basically the same as for setting our arguments. We want to first locate the thesis (conclusion) and then list the support. Look at this example. Zoe Williams argues that Botox, a drug generally used for cosmetic purposes, such as reducing facial wrinkles, is potentially dangerous. She says:

> Finally, there is proof, or at least the beginnings of proof, that Botox is not as innocuous as it claims to be: indeed, that it is un-innocuous to the point of being (rarely, but [possibly]) fatal.
>
> It works by temporarily paralyzing the muscles. It looks good from a distance, but dodgy up close. It is a great favorite among actors. When you see an actor, photographed off-guard, with a look of shiny, dead neutrality, you somehow know that it is the result of too many injections.
>
> But beyond this instinct, there is the medical fact that it is a poison, injected into the face, and good sense would dictate that this has ramifications. Experience now suggests as much—the US Food and Drug Administration (FDA) has had reports of 16 fatalities linked to injections of Botox and a similar product. The problem seems to occur when the botulinum toxin [= Botox] spreads beyond the injection sites to other areas of the body. The reports detailed cases of muscle weakness, difficulty swallowing and aspiration pneumonia, which occurs when you breathe alien material into your lungs.
>
> It would be foolish to overstate the danger of the treatment, when the more compelling argument against it is still that it is stupid and it makes you look weird. But still, it is worth bearing in mind that it could also kill you. (Zoe Williams, "Shortcuts: We All Know Botox Is Stupid. Now It Looks Like It Can Kill Too," *The Guardian (UK)*, 4 Feb 2008)

If we locate her conclusion and set out and number the premises, we get this:

P$_1$: Botox works by temporarily paralyzing the muscles.

P$_2$: The medical fact is that it is a poison, injected into the face.

P$_3$: It is a great favorite among actors; when you see an actor with a look of shiny, dead neutrality, you somehow know that it is the result of too many injections.

P$_4$: Injecting Botox has ramifications: The U.S. Food and Drug Administration (FDA) has had reports of 16 fatalities linked to injections of Botox and a similar product.

P$_5$: The problem seems to occur when the botulinum toxin [= Botox] spreads beyond the injection sites to other areas of the body.

P$_6$: The reports detailed cases of muscle weakness, difficulty swallowing, and aspiration pneumonia, which occurs when you breathe alien material into your lungs.

P$_7$: Using Botox is stupid and makes you look weird.

P$_8$: <u>It could also kill you.</u>

C: Botox is dangerous.

Looking at the premises, we can see that P$_3$ and P$_7$ are best viewed as a separate argument, so pull them out. We now have two arguments, one stronger than the other. The first one (A$_1$) rests on claims of fact; the second (A$_2$) rests on perception and opinion. Here are the two arguments:

Argument 1

P$_1$: Botox works by temporarily paralyzing the muscles.

P$_2$: The medical fact is that it is a poison, injected into the face.

P$_3$: Injecting Botox has ramifications: The U.S. Food and Drug Administration (FDA) has had reports of 16 fatalities linked to injections of Botox and a similar product.

P$_4$: The problem seems to occur when the botulinum toxin [= Botox] spreads beyond the injection sites to other areas of the body.

P$_5$: The reports detailed cases of muscle weakness, difficulty swallowing, and aspiration pneumonia, which occurs when you breathe alien material into your lungs.

P$_6$: <u>Botox could kill you.</u>

C: Therefore, Botox is dangerous.

Argument 2

P$_1$: Botox is a great favorite among actors.

P$_2$: When you see an actor with a look of shiny, dead neutrality, you somehow <u>know that it is the result of too many injections.</u>

C: Therefore, using Botox is stupid and makes you look weird.

Constructing Arguments

In constructing arguments, we want to make as strong a case as possible, with the premises directly supporting the conclusion. A preliminary step is to set out the pros and cons of your thesis. This has a number of benefits. First, it helps you get organized, so you can see what you have to work with. Second, it helps you consider the opposing side and formulate a response. Third, it gives you an overview, so you can see if your side needs bolstering.

Take the case of Arizona state Senator Karen S. Johnson. In March 2008, she sponsored a bill to allow anyone to carry firearms to public colleges or universities, so long as he or she had a concealed weapons permit and was at least 21 years old. Would you favor it?

Proposed Bill to Allow Guns on Campuses

Pros: Students and faculty would be able to carry weapons to fight off attackers and have some means of defending themselves against well-armed perpetrators; this would allow a quicker remedy/response, given that police cannot respond as quickly as someone at the scene; this would provide some sense of insurance and security in the case of school violence/shootings; it would reassure parents that their children could at least stand a chance if a shooter comes into a classroom or on the campus; Arizona is not alone in seeking such a law—15 states have pending legislation that would make it easier to carry guns on campuses.

Cons: There are more likely to be incidents on campuses if students and faculty can carry weapons, as they will have the means to use a weapon to "let off steam"—the fact that someone carries a gun doesn't mean they can use it under pressure; innocent people may be shot in error as students and faculty fire weapons when reacting to a perceived threat; the fact that 15 states are considering legislation to allow guns on campuses does not mean it is well reasoned—this could be an overreaction and not necessarily a path to safer campuses; this would allow potential killers to easily carry their weapons too; finally, it deflects attention away from trying to help those who are unstable.

Now that we've laid out key pros and cons, we get a wider view. We can then proceed with our argument. Try not to go further than the evidence supports.

Exercises

Part One

Directions: State the conclusion and number the premises (P_1, P_2, P_3, etc.) in the following arguments. If there is more than one argument, state them.

1. Sylvester and Tweetie are not best friends by any stretch of the imagination. For one thing, Sylvester is a cat and Tweetie is a bird. Also, Sylvester would

like to eat Tweetie—which is not something a true friend would do! Plus, Tweetie likes to pester Sylvester, and that isn't very friendly behavior!

2. Snow White is a little irritated with those dwarfs. They follow her around, making a lot of racket with all that singing and clapping. They pester her all the time, asking her to do domestic chores and cook for them. She emailed her best friend Cinderella that she was positively sick of cleaning up after those dwarfs! Consequently, it's not surprising she started to read the "Want Ads" in the newspaper in hopes of finding a job.

3. Snoopy said Lucy is nicer than Linus. He rested his argument on the fact that she gave him more dog biscuits and has a nicer temperament. Plus, Lucy said he had the softest dog fur she ever felt, and this made Snoopy feel good.

4. Look at the way children are presented in fairy tales. Jack and Jill were clumsy and couldn't even take care of a simple chore like fetching water. Goldilocks had no qualms about breaking into the bears' house and eating up their porridge. Little Red Riding Hood mistook a wolf for her grandmother. As a result, it looks like children in fairy tales have no critical thinking skills whatsoever. This is further supported by the fact that Snow White was duped by a haggardly woman with a poisoned apple.

5. Wolves have a bad reputation in fairy tales. They are presented as perpetually hungry. They always seem to be stalking some charming child, gobbling up grandmothers, or threatening nice pigs. They are usually big and ugly and have huge fangs. Given all this, animal lovers need to speak up in defense of the badly maligned wolf.

6. Hansel wasn't a very smart boy, given that he used bread crumbs to mark his way through the woods. He should have known that all sorts of animals eat bread crumbs. Only someone who wasn't thinking clearly would go deep into a forest without some assurance that they could find their way out. A smart person would have done more than drop bread.

7. The Wizard of Oz craze just won't stop. People are obsessed with Dorothy and her sidekicks. There's something about the innocent child overcoming obstacles that wins over the coldest heart. Plus, there is humor and adventure, especially with those flying monkeys and all. And don't forget, the Wicked Witch of the West is one of the greatest villains of all time.

8. Little Red Riding Hood is a lot like Goldilocks. She is a small girl with big eyes. She is very curious about houses. She doesn't always mind her mother, and she has no qualms about walking through a forest. Since Goldilocks never had any problems with animals other than bears, Little Red Riding Hood has nothing to worry about from a wolf following her.

9. Cinderella had two mean stepsisters, who made her life miserable. Her father was negligent, leaving her alone a great deal. Consequently, it is no wonder that Cinderella married a man she just met—particularly if you also consider how pathetic and cruel her stepmother was. Cinderella may have been

an abused child, but she was no wimp. She managed to get a dress to go to the ball. She showed courage in going out so late at night. She knew the importance of getting home before curfew. This goes to show that Cinderella deserves more recognition than just being the pretty girl who woos a prince.

10. Sleeping Beauty now has trouble with insomnia. This is due to her child-hood being cut short by that witch's curse. After a hundred-year-long sleep, it's hard to want to lie down and even take a nap! She must be terrified she won't wake up again.

11. Even though Ursula was an octopus, she developed her feminine charms. She wore bright red lipstick to flaunt her sexuality and had no qualms about wearing a low-cut dress. Thus, Ursula could be viewed as a kind of sea-goddess, not a witch. This is especially the case if we consider how generously she gave Ariel advice about men.

12. Rumpelstiltskin is a bit of a toad. As a result, it's no wonder he never appeared in any Disney cartoons. Just think about it: He was willing to take a baby from an exploited young woman. He could not care less about the devastating effect it'd have on her life. Granted, she made the deal with him in exchange for spun gold. But her stupidity and greed should not hide the fact that that nasty little Rumpelstiltskin deserved a fast trip to the underworld!

13. Cinderella's father is a bit of a disappointment if you think about it. First—and most obviously—he married a mean-spirited woman. Plus, he seems to travel an awful lot—leaving poor Cindy alone to fare for herself. And, finally, why did Cinderella have to rely on a fairy godmother instead of her own father? He dropped the ball on that one!

Part Two

Directions: Set out the arguments by listing the premises and then stating the conclusion (locate the conclusion first). If there is no argument, say so.

1. People who only watch TV news must have a very different view of the world from those who read a newspaper. For one thing, they hear about all the murders, drive-by shootings, gang activity, and neglected children as soon as the news starts. Also, they must think the police put car chases as a top priority, since newscasts are often interrupted so viewers can watch police chasing someone on the freeway and city streets. And, finally, they must think people talk very little, since interviews rarely exceed 15 seconds.

2. Televised executions are suggested from time to time. This is because some people think seeing murderers die will be a powerful deterrent to potential criminals. Furthermore, people like the idea of "an eye for an eye." Watching public executions could also give satisfaction to the victims' families.

3. Children who watch TV before breakfast are less likely to eat a nutritious meal than children who run and play. The reason for this is that watching

TV fills the young brain with far more signals than it can handle before they are fully awake. Also, children watching morning TV want to eat and watch at the same time. When that happens, they just don't pay attention to their meal.

4. It's amazing how much junk accumulates. It seems like, while you sleep, paper multiplies and more magazines creep in, as if little elves were making deposits. Plus, books you surely closed up before tucking in for the night manage to open and rearrange themselves into a mess.

5. Lemon meringue pie smells awfully nice. When my mother makes one, I always admire the nice peaks of meringue before diving in! She never makes it too sweet, either. In fact, it is both sweet and tart at the same time—and the right balance of sweet and tart is crucial for the ideal pie. Therefore, there's no dessert on earth like lemon meringue pie, even though I crave fudge brownies when I wake up in the middle of the night.

6. Argument against California Proposition 8 banning same-sex marriage: "I'm going to vote NO on Prop. 8. I know how I feel, and I'm not that comfortable with gay marriage. But making gay marriage illegal? That's a much tougher question. For me, it's about the people I know. It's about my niece. It's about my co-worker. It's about the gay couple that lives next door. . . . I don't want to use our law to eliminate their chance to take care of and take full responsibility for each other" (Vote "No" on Proposition 8, flyer, Oct 2008).

7. There's not much positive about the price of gas increasing, except for two things. One, bicycles are looking a heck of a lot more attractive these days. Two, those with the technical savvy might be prodded into finding alternative sources of energy. Just think of solar-driven cars or cars with little windmills attached to the roof! Or how about cars that have pedals in them so we can lower gas use by pedaling as we go?

8. Chong persuaded her parents to trade the SUV they gave her for a hybrid. With the money she'll save on gas, she plans to send money to a family in Kenya so they can buy a goat. Being a global citizen is important to Chong, and she is trying to turn her values into action. Therefore, she is much happier now that she doesn't have to spend half her salary on gas.

9. "In seeking to identify and disrupt possible terrorist threats, U.S. intelligence will rely on a suspect's circle of associates and his religious beliefs. But the First Amendment prevents authorities from prosecuting people solely on the basis of association or ideology. In addition, holding radical beliefs is not in itself a criminal act. The Department of Justice is now in a situation where they say, 'If they could be a terrorist, then they are guilty.' But we don't have laws that say, 'If you *could* be then you are.' The risks of this are immense. Subsequently, if we want to move there, then we have to think long and hard" (adapted from Patrick Radden Keefe, "State Secrets," *The New Yorker,* 28 Apr 2008).

10. Even prior to debates about homeland security, surveillance was something we experienced on a daily basis. For example, Washington Square is under 24-hour surveillance. One doesn't know when one is being watched from any particular part of the park. Police network surveillance systems like this one are just the tip of the iceberg. Think of the numerous cameras that capture your image every day at ATM machines, supermarkets, and just about every other business or institution you walk into. Consider how many times your driver's license, work or student ID card, passport, or bank card is scanned. And consider the tracking devices on our cars. As a result, that we live in a surveillance society should be no surprise to us (adapted from Andrew Light, *Reel Arguments,* Westview Press, 2003).

Part Three

Directions: State the conclusion and the premises in the following arguments.

1. "If you believe, as I do, that one important measure of our humanity is our regard for other living beings, then the grisly practices of industrial ranching are immoral. I'm speaking of what is hidden from sight: such horrors as the butchering of live steers, the periodic starving of chickens to stimulate greater egg production and the rigid confinement of animals in cages where they can hardly move for the entirety of their lives" (John Balzar, "Cruel Slaughter of Food Hits a Nerve," *Los Angeles Times,* 13 Jul 2001).

2. "A flag is a unique symbol, one which has no parallel in the values it represents or the emotions it stirs. The flag has played a central role in our nation's historical development, a perpetual reminder of our democratic tenets. . . . The government's interest in preserving the flag's integrity far outweighs any minimal burden on free expression occasioned by requiring people to engage in alternative modes of communication. For those Americans who feel compelled to denigrate their own country (but who nevertheless choose to remain here and enjoy its freedoms), there are many avenues of negative expression available, including verbal denunciation or burning other symbols of the government. Hence, the flag amendment is an appropriate vehicle for preserving that minimal amount of patriotism and respect which any nation needs to ensure its continued vitality" (James R. Bozajian, "Make Flag-Burning Unconstitutional," *Los Angeles Daily Journal,* 25 Jun 2004).

3. "Thomson points out that there is a great range of activities in which it is justifiably assumed that parents have a legitimate right to determine their children's participation. There is no general reason to suppose that childbirth is different; there are no compelling grounds (such as the expectation of great harm) to justify overriding the parent's prerogative. Hence insofar as the fetus needs an advocate, there is no reason to regard the physician rather than the pregnant woman as the appropriate advocate" (Christine Overall, *Ethics and Human Reproduction,* Routledge, 1987).

4. "While electronic toys have succeeded in seducing children, much of the technology added to toys threatens to change the way children play in fundamental ways. Often, electronic toys are less creative, do not involve much imagination and encourage more passive reactions than older toys, experts say. There is a passivity that comes from having toys that entertain you" (Julian E. Barnes, "Where Did You Go, Raggedy Ann? Toys in the Age of Electronics," *The New York Times,* 10 Feb 2001).

5. "According to the most recent Nielsen ratings, the average black household watches eleven hours of television every day—about two-thirds of their waking hours. In addition, they spend at nearly five times their proportion of the population at movie theaters. Distinctions no longer exist between movies and news, television and real life" (Jacqui Jones, "The Accusatory Space," in *Black Popular Culture,* ed. Gina Dent, Bay Press, 1992).

6. "While a military attack on the West probably would have a unifying effect, a biological attack might prove divisive. Fighting battles requires mobilization and cooperation. Fighting epidemics requires quarantine and isolation. It's easy to be generous and internationalist after an event such as the tsunami, when terrible things are happening somewhere else. It's much harder when the enemy is a disease that might kill or disfigure you and your children" (Anne Applebaum, "Only a Game?" *Washington Post,* 19 Jan 2005).

Quick Quiz

1. *True or false:* The term *however* is a premise-indicator.

2. What is the *conclusion* of the following argument: "Carla is going a bit overboard with her Lakers' paraphernalia. She has Pao posters, Kobe T-shirts, and a stack of ticket stubs. Her photo album is bursting with pictures of the Staple Center, where the Lakers play at home. That must mean she'll want to buy the signed basketball at the charity auction. This is particularly true since all the team members *and* the coach signed it."

3. *True or false:* An argument can have only one conclusion, but it could have two or more premises.

4. State the *premise indicator*(s) in this argument: "Given that the pancakes were left on the griddle too long, they burned badly on the bottom. The tops don't look too bad, though."

5. *True or false:* Before locating the conclusion, it is advisable to first list as many of the premises as you can find.

6. What are any *conclusion indicators* in the following: "Although Tim studied until 4:00 A.M., he didn't finish the text. However, he did make it through the hardest chapter, the one on partial differential equations. If he gets that down, he should do okay on the exam. Consequently, Tim really shouldn't worry about passing the class."

7. *True or false:* The set of evidence offered in support of a thesis or conclusion is called the *premises.*

8. State which of these are *transition words:* therefore, consequently, because, moreover, for the reason that, to restate, in light of the fact that, although.

9. *True or false:* You can have an argument without a conclusion indicator.

10. State the *premises* in the following argument: "Tim fell asleep during his math exam. The teaching assistant tapped him on the shoulder to wake him up. When he looked at his watch, Tim realized he'd dozed through half of the exam time. As a result, Tim did not feel real good about his chances for passing the exam."

11. *True or false:* Any argument in standard form has the premises listed one by one (P_1, P_2, etc.), before the conclusion.

12. Are these premises *sufficient* for the conclusion to follow (*yes or no*)? "Some people who own parrots are computer geeks. Sean is a computer geek. Therefore, Sean probably owns a parrot."

The Range of Argument Forms

Imagine this scenario: You've been invited to be a guest on the new reality TV show *The Persuader.* It uses a game-show format with a raucous audience to set the mood, a panel of "jurors" more or less representative of the society, and contestants. The goal? To persuade the "jury" of your thesis on a topic that pops up for all to see when you select a category. Ready to play? OK, it's your turn and you pick as your category "MEDICINE." Good choice! The topic that pops up is "KIDNEY SALES." "Kidney sales?" you say to yourself, as tiny beads of sweat pop up on your forehead. Wiping your brow, you think about your position on the sale of kidneys, weighing the pros and cons and fantasizing about the fame and glory of being a winner. You decide, "Bad idea." The question is, How will you persuade your jury?

Arguments take many forms. For instance, to argue against kidney sales, you could employ a set of principles and expert opinions. You could cite statistical studies or point to studies of the exploitation of the poor by the rich. In order to present a strong argument, you want to put your evidence together so your thesis is well-supported. This is the way to go with any argument you make, whether it be in the area of selling kidneys, educating consumers about a product, persuading your friend to go camping, or anything else. Your goal should be to make a solid case, so no alternative conclusion seems as good a choice as the one being argued.

Let's go through an example of a good argument so we can see how this works. In an article in *Aviation Week & Space Technology,* David A. Fulghum noted that the supposed Iraqi invasion threat against Kuwait that followed the Persian Gulf War in October 1994 had been reassessed by the U.S. military. His argument in standard form is as follows:

P_1: Air Force officials believed that the big movement of Iraqi forces near the Kuwaiti border may have been triggered by fear and panic, caused by intense, around-the-clock allied air operations.

P_2: Iraqi troops may have dispersed south into the desert near the border with Kuwait for fear of being bombed in their garrisons.

P_3: RC-135 Rivet Joint aircraft helped determine that the Iraqi army's move south was being done without Air Force support.

P_4: U.S. officials said another sign that Iraq did not intend to invade was that neighboring Iran never put its forces on higher-military-alert status.

P_5: "I think they deployed to keep us from striking them while they were still in garrison," a senior U.S. official said.

P_6: Moreover, "Iran wasn't doing anything," the U.S. official said.

P_7: "If they were really going to attack, there would have been certain defensive measures put in place, and we didn't see them," a crewman said.

P_8: The Iraqi troop movements "had the appearance of an Army-only operation as if they were making a political statement," and not an offensive move.

C: Therefore, U.S. field commanders in Saudi Arabia now suspect Iraq never intended to invade Kuwait during October 1994's military crisis.

Our next step is to see how the premises support the conclusion:

Premise 1 lays the groundwork by giving a reason (fear, panic due to allied air operations) for the Iraqis to move troops near the Kuwaiti border.

Premise 2 links in with the first premise by explaining why (fear of being bombed) the Iraqis would move south into the desert near Kuwait.

Premise 3 by noting that the Iraqi forces that moved south did not have air support, makes it hard to think that Iraq was planning an invasion.

Premise 4 draws from the wider geographical context, by looking at Iraq's neighbor, Iran, and the fact Iran did not put its forces on high alert—which it would have done had it suspected escalated military activity on the part of Iraq.

Premise 5 offers a plausible alternative reason why Iraq moved its forces near the Kuwaiti border.

Premise 6 reinforces the point made in premise 4—that Iran would have acted if there had been evidence of a forthcoming invasion.

Premise 7 offers an overview of conditions that would have to be in place for an invasion to likely happen—and those conditions were *not* in place.

Premise 8 notes both the absence of air support (this was an army-only operation) and a possible explanation for the Iraqi army to move toward the Kuwaiti border (a political statement). This, then, provides an alternative reason for the Iraqi action not to be interpreted as an offensive one.

These premises provide solid ground for supporting the conclusion that Iraq never intended to invade Kuwait in October 1994. Why? The evidence ranges from the observations of senior officials and a U.S. crewman, plausible explanations for an alternative conclusion, and observations about the response in the region (particularly Iran's). Together they make a strong case.

Note also that the assumption that Iraqi military action was intentionally aggressive would not be unwarranted, given pre-1994 history. For this reason, it is important to examine the role assumptions play in our reasoning process.

Group or Individual Exercise

Lethal Injection

Directions: Dr. Mark Heath, an anesthesiologist, contends that Ohio's method of executing prisoners by lethal injection isn't appropriate for dogs or cats, let alone humans. Set out the argument below in standard form, and discuss the strength of the author's reasoning.

> In carrying out the death penalty, the state of Ohio administers three drugs in succession to sedate, paralyze and kill prisoners. If the executioner administers too little anesthetic or makes mistakes while injecting it, the prisoner could experience excruciating pain. In the execution, Ohio separates the prisoner from the person administering the drugs by using two rooms and a one-way mirror. This "substantially increases the risk of a major problem occurring," said anesthesiologist Dr. Mark Heath. "I would never induce general anesthesia from a different room through long tubing." He recommends administering drugs while standing next to the patient so anesthesiologists can detect if problems occur, such as a leak or a ruptured vein.
>
> The third drug is potassium chloride, which stops the heart. It is sometimes used for euthanizing animals. Heath contended that Ohio's violates the acceptable veterinary standard. He also stated that there could be other problems; for example, in two different executions, there was a struggle to find suitable veins in inmates' arms. Some contend that this method is unconstitutionally cruel and unusual. That is why Heath believes Ohio's method of lethal injection should not be used to carry out the death penalty. ("Doctor: Ohio's Lethal Injection Inhumane," *ABC News*, 7 Apr 2008)

Of course, not all arguments are good ones. Some have a few solid pieces of evidence but go off track. Some rest on dubious or questionable claims. Some depend upon unwarranted assumptions that sink the argument. And so on. Look at the argument in Figure 2.1, which represents a bad argument. Let's break it down.

FIGURE 2.1
Copy on a bag of sugar. Can you see why this is a bad argument?

> **Sugar is 100% natural simple carbohydrate.**
> **Carbohydrates are an important part of any balanced diet.**
> **Sugar contains no fat or cholesterol and has 15 calories per teaspoon.**

Example of a Bad Argument

P_1: Sugar is a 100% natural simple carbohydrate.

P_2: Carbohydrates are an important part of any balanced diet.

P_3: Sugar contains no fat or cholesterol and has 15 calories per teaspoon.

C: Therefore, a balanced diet can include sugar.

Why is this a bad argument? Examine the first two premises: P_1 states that sugar is a *simple* carbohydrate, and P_2 asserts that carbohydrates are essential for a balanced diet. However, a balanced diet requires *complex*—not simple—carbohydrates. The omission of the term "complex" changes everything here.

As you probably figured out by now, when we confront an argument, we first want to dismantle it—for example, by putting it in standard form as we did previously. Once the argument is in standard form, we can examine it and see if there are any assumptions or omissions that need to be acknowledged—and stated. We can't let these missing premises/assumptions hide in the dark—we want to pull them out into the light. We can then turn our attention to the quality of the reasoning. In the next chapter, we'll look at that next step—analysis.

Exercises

Part One

Directions: Drawing from the information presented below, set out an argument that conveys your attitude about plagiarism. Use a minimum of two of the pieces of information as part of your argument. Feel free to add other premises, as needed to bolster your argument.

For $136 [and going to one of the many websites selling term papers] a frantic high school or college student can download a 19-page paper on "Woodrow Wilson and Franklin Roosevelt." It can be faxed for $9.50 or delivered overnight for $15. Some sites, however, are free of charge. Schoolsucks.com, for example, serves as a type of portal for the disgruntled student, offering games, chats, and daily e-mails of free jokes. Visitors are encouraged to post a paper of their own when they download one from the site.

Kenny Sahr—who started the site in 1996—says it now gets 10,000 hits per day with 600,000 people signed up for the daily e-mails.

Mr. Sahr insists he has no qualms about what he does, and calls it the students' responsibility to use the papers for research only, especially because he gives no guarantee of quality. "Those papers are written by students; then we put them there. But we're not rating them, we're not telling you these are good papers. In other words, if someone turns in a bad paper, well, it's not our problem." (Kimberly Chase, "Teachers Fight against Internet Plagiarism," *Christian Science Monitor,* www.csmonitor.com, 2 Mar 2004)

Part Two

1. List the premises (P_1, P_2, etc.) and state the conclusion in the arguments about cloned food.
   a. Consumers in general are much more aware of what's in food. Consequently, burgers made from cloned cattle may make folks a little nervous. Remember, also, that people were excited about Dolly the sheep being a clone—but did you hear anyone wanting to make mutton chops out of her?
   b. In the late 1980s two companies made and sold hundreds of cattle clones. Consumers bought their meat and ate it oblivious to the fact they were gobbling down a clone. Milk from clones was also sold and no one raised an eyebrow. People now are upset about cloned animals for food, but the clones made now are created from cells from adult animals. This is different from those early clones all too many of us had for lunch or dinner way back when. Those early clones were made from embryos created by breeding a prize cow or bull and then freezing some of the embryos. Since no one complained back then, therefore, no one should complain now! A clone is a clone is a clone, regardless of the source!
   c. People are concerned about cloning now—not like in 1988 with the cloned cattle. According to Gregory Jaffe, expert in biotechnology, here's why: One is the concern over cloning humans. The other is the attention being given to genetically engineered foods and the nature of the food supply. Animal cloning gets thrown in, whether it's the same or not (Gina Kolata, "Animals Cloned for Food No Longer Draw Collective Yawn," *The New York Times,* 3 Nov 2003).

2. State the premises and conclusion in each of the following arguments:
   a. The Chinese have not got the sense of individual independence because the whole conception of life is based upon mutual help within the home . . . it is considered good luck to have children who can take care of one. One lives for nothing else in China (Lin Yutang, "Growing Old Gracefully," in *Virtuous People, Vicious Deeds,* ed. Alexander Hooke, McGraw-Hill, 1999).
   b. There is good reason for deceiving one another—it works. It works not only for the liar but also for the listener. Many of us are unprepared to speak the truth or to hear the truth, particularly about those things we

care about, such as ourselves, friends or family, or even our ideals (Hooke, *Virtuous Persons, Vicious Deeds*).

3. In your own words, explain what the author is arguing below:

TV's true violence consists not so much in the spectacle's techniques or content, but rather in the very density and speed of TV overall, the very multiplicity and pace of stimuli; for it is by overloading, overdriving both itself and us that TV disables us, making it hard to think about or even feel what TV shows us—making it hard, perhaps, to think or feel at all. (Mark Crispin Miller, "Deride and Conquer," in *Watching Television,* ed. Todd Gitlin, Pantheon Books, 1987)

4. The State Department needs your help handling a public relations nightmare around the use of depleted uranium in NATO weapons. Read the paragraph below, and then (a) set out the issues and concerns and (b) construct an argument explaining what the State Department can do.

Many Europeans suspect that depleted uranium contained in NATO weaponry has caused or contributed to numerous cases of leukemia suffered by alliance troops deployed in the Balkans. The leukemia deaths of several European soldiers who served in Kosovo or Bosnia-Herzegovina prompted the U.S. Army report . . .

On Thursday, two German arms makers reported having tested weapons containing depleted uranium during the 1970's, intensifying public concerns that some Germans may have been exposed to the low-level radiation released by such weapons. (Carol J. Williams, "U.S. Warned Germany of Uranium Leaks," *Los Angeles Times,* 20 Jan 2001)

5. North-South Airlines needs you to help them keep a problem for frequent fliers from erupting into a public relations disaster for both flight crews and customers. What will you advise them, given the information below?

On June 12, 2001, it was reported that frequent fliers—and especially flight crews—face radiation risks. The problem is the ionizing radiation emitted by the sun. When the sun is at the peak of its "storm" season, the solar wind is supplemented by bursts of protons called solar flares. These flares can expose people flying at high altitude to ionizing radiation. Occasionally airlines reroute polar flights to avoid solar storms. Though there is no evidence this exposure is dangerous, experts agree that a pregnant woman could be exposed to enough radiation on a single flight to exceed government health guidelines. Crew members who fly polar flights for years can accumulate doses that are large relative to those received by nuclear power plant workers and other "radiation workers."

Dr. Robert J. Barish, medical radiation specialist, says, "People may be hurt." Airlines don't have radiation monitors on board so that they could change altitude or reroute to avoid the solar storms. Overall, flight crews have higher rates of a variety of diseases, but it's not clear if it's connected to the radiation risk or the disruption of their biorhythms. European authorities have gone so far as to classify flight crews as radiation workers. In the U.S. the FAA does the same, but it does not require employers to track exposure.

A United Nations committee estimated that air crew members (approximately 250,000 compared to nearly four million people worldwide who are occupationally exposed to radiation) received about 24% of all the occupationally related exposure to radiation. (Matthew L. Wald, "The Frequent Flier and Radiation Risk," *The New York Times*, 12 Jun 2001)

Part Three

Directions: This op/ed piece was written by Rebecca Perez in April 2007 as part of a class assignment. Read the essay and set out the main argument. Discuss the strength of her reasoning.

American Idol: The Phenomenon behind It

My brother Paul is a seventeen-year-old boy whose favorite activities include break dancing, bonfires, and training to be an Ultimate Fighter. My Grandma, who is in her seventies, enjoys lighter fare such as yoga, gardening, and volunteering for peace movements. While they both have completely different interests and lifestyles, there are two nights a week where my brother puts down the boxing gloves, my grandma rolls up the yoga mat, and for the next hour they both do the exact same thing. They watch *American Idol*.

Around 30 million people watch *American Idol* every week. This is a television show that has propelled not only the winners of the show, but also some of the show's top contenders, to become some of the top selling artists of all time. The "Idol Alums," as they are called, have won Grammys, an Oscar, conquered Broadway, topped the Billboard charts, and held down top positions in the country, gospel, rock, R&B, and pop music industries. Even *Idol* rejects have been thrust into overnight fame; one tone deaf man from Cal State Berkeley became a sort of icon after he performed a heartfelt, albeit audibly unbearable, rendition of Ricky Martin's "She Bangs." This man even recorded an album, which I believe a few people actually bought. From this information, it seems clear that *American Idol* is a cultural phenomenon that appeals to a wide variety of people, and it looks like it is here to stay.

One of the integral parts of *American Idol*'s widespread attraction is the fact that it appeals to people of all sexes, races, and age groups. It is G-rated, but not a show aimed at children. It has a cheesy factor to it, but the brutally honest banter between the judges and the contestants gives it an edge. I think the structure of the show, and the personalities of the judges, are key factors in the show's success, but I believe it is America who keeps the show afloat by their power of vote. Every year so far America has voted the same cast of characters on the show. We have the pretty white girl, the single mother who has come so far, the black woman with the big dress size to match the even bigger voice, the girl next door, the token rocker, the token Asian, the nerdy, bespectacled white boy who turns from a caterpillar into a butterfly in front of our very eyes, the singer who is short on talent but tall on charisma, the high school student who proves age is nothing but a number, the U.S. serviceman, and the few other talented people who defy any genre, but are usually voted off quickly and go on to have careers in theatre or on the TV Guide channel.

The reason America is so glued to this show is largely because they see a part of themselves in one of the contestants, and they are drawn to them because they can relate to them. On *American Idol*, we see the contestants from their very first audition, when they are amateurs and everyday people, just like us, whom the judges see something special in. We then see them through their entire journey through the Hollywood weeks, until the top 12 are picked and we get a chance to vote for our favorites. By this time the viewers have already latched on to certain contestants, and they see them grow and transform into a performer.

In other words, America gets a chance to live vicariously through these contestants; they see them blossom from an average Joe into a confident entertainer.

Because people can see themselves in these contestants, and because they have gotten to know them throughout the audition process, the audience gets an emotional response from their performances; when they hit a bad note they feel embarrassed for them and hope they nail the next one, when they do well, they are proud of them. *American Idol* has become somewhat like a soap opera, or a drama; it is a veritable, hour long, emotional rollercoaster, where people tune in to see what will become of their favorite character. Unlike a soap opera, however, *American Idol* has characters that are real people, and I believe this is the appeal of the show. (Reprinted with the permission of Rebecca Perez)

Group or Individual Exercise

How Strict Should the "No Eating" Rule Be?

Scientist Stephanie Willett's history with the law was limited to a few speeding tickets until she had a most unfortunate encounter with a Metro transit police officer in a Washington, DC, Metro station on July 16, 2004. It seems that Willett was eating a PayDay candy bar as she was riding up the escalator. Officer Cherrail Curry-Hagler spotted her eating the candy bar and warned her to finish it, because eating and drinking in Metro stations was against the law. Willett nodded to the officer, stuffed the last of the candy bar into her mouth, threw the wrapper into the trash can, and then entered the station. Read what happened next and then answer the questions below:

[Metro transit police officer] Curry-Hagler turned around and followed Willett into the station. Moments after making a remark to the officer, Willett said, she was searched, handcuffed and arrested for chewing the last bite of her candy bar after she passed through the fare gates. She was released several hours later after paying a $10 fine, pending a hearing.

"We've been doing our best to crack down on people who are consuming food and beverages in our stations because we get so many complaints about it," said Lisa Farbstein, a Metro spokeswoman. . . . Willett said she was being unfairly punished because she made fun of the police officer after Curry-Hagler issued a second warning before the arrest. "Why don't you go and take care of some real crime?" Willett said she told the officer while still swallowing the PayDay bar as she rode a second escalator to catch her Orange Line train home.

The police officer ordered Willett to stop and produce identification. "I said, 'For what?' and kept walking," Willett said. . . . "Next thing I knew, she pushed me into the cement wall, calls for backup and puts handcuffs on me," Willett said. . . . Two other officers appeared, and the three took Willett to a waiting police cruiser. At the D.C. police 1st District headquarters, Willett said, she was locked in a cell with another person. At 9:30 P.M., after she paid a $10 fine, Willett was released. . . . "I understand the intent of them not wanting people to eat in the Metro," Willett said. "If anything, I was chewing in the Metro." Farbstein said Willett violated the rules. "Chewing is eating," she said. (Lyndsey Layton, "Mouthful Gets Metro Passenger Handcuffs and Jail," *The Washington Post,* 31 Jul 2004)

Answer the following:

1. Do you think Willett violated the "no eating" rule in the Metro station? Share your thoughts.

2. What argument should Willett make to convince a judge or jury of her innocence?

3. What argument should the prosecution make that she violated the "no eating" rule?

CASE STUDY

The Body Trade

When we draw up policy guidelines, we are generalizing from our societal attitudes and norms. We are setting out recommendations for how others should think and behave—for example, in businesses, schools, and hospitals.

In the article below, Michele Goodwin discusses a body parts scandal that occurred at UCLA. Read the article, and then summarize her argument and share your ideas for addressing the concerns she raises.

Commerce in Cadavers an Open Secret

Michele Goodwin

Are we shocked that a University of California official has been caught allegedly trading in body parts? We shouldn't be; UCLA is simply the canary in the coalmine. It's an open secret that there has long been a commercial trade in human bodies. An underground, illegal market has developed largely because of inconsistent federal policies and practices, including poor oversight of university hospitals, organ procurement organizations and biotechnology companies that engage in the exchange of body parts.

By and large, this black market serves a public good by supplying lifesaving and beneficial materials—such as heart valves and knees—to a demanding public. But without regulation and monitoring, it's not surprising that mistakes, fraud and abuse occur, as they did in the

California case of infected tissues being sold to hospitals for knee transplants in 2002, or the 1997 scandal in which the Los Angeles coroner's office was found to have sold more than 500 pairs of corneas in one year to the Doheny Eye & Tissue Transplant Bank.

In the Doheny case, more than 80% of the donors, who were unwittingly placed in the stream of commerce, were black or Latino. The coroner's office received up to $335 per pair of corneas, which Doheny resold at $3,400 per pair. The coroner was not alone in this behavior; 29 states permitted the nonconsensual removal of eye tissues from cadavers. Most of the 29 still have presumed consent laws. Currently, the Uniform Anatomical Gift Act and the National Organ Transplantation Act prohibit companies and private citizens from purchasing body parts from individuals. An individual cannot receive "payment" for donating an organ or other body part. Although hints of the existence of a market involving individual sellers are clearly apparent in sperm and ova sales, lawmakers have been slow to address this new, expanded marketplace. Such inaction drives the underground sales.

Although the laws allow "service" fees to be exchanged between hospitals and organ procurement organizations for body parts and cadavers used to promote research, those fees have come to resemble illegal payments. Hospitals, organ procurement organizations and universities have become middlemen in the human-parts supply industry, violating the spirit and legislative intent of the regulations, because they are selling body parts that will be used commercially and not for research. For-profit tissue banks and biotechnology firms engage in research, but their function is dual-purpose and, ultimately, they are beholden to shareholders who are interested in profits.

Federal oversight has been lax at best, and courts are seemingly unprepared to deal with the reality of a growing body market. State and circuit court decisions on the question of who owns the body have been inconsistent. Both individuals whose cell lines had been stolen and people who have donated family members' cadavers have sought legal remedies. State courts in Georgia and California have ruled against their claims for compensation for nonconsensual appropriation of body parts, while the federal 6th and 9th circuit courts have recognized at least a quasi property-right interest in the body.

In the UCLA case, do the sold body parts now belong to the tissue banks, UCLA or the new owners, or can they revert to the families? Can the families be compensated for their loss? Courts are stumped. Federal law proscribes individual ownership, yet a billion-dollar-a-year corporate industry thrives on buying, refashioning and selling body parts. From where, federal officials should ask, do they obtain the body parts?

Instead of ignoring the growing human-tissue industry, Congress, through the Food and Drug Administration, should regulate and monitor these exchanges. The essential elements of an informed system would include donor protections, an option for donor compensation, recourse for misrepresentation and mandatory annual reporting of donor/provider information, including race, gender and age data to prevent predatory practices. Finally, the federal government must also clarify its role in funding programs that sell body parts.

While the challenge to overhaul altruistic donations occupies lawmakers, private actors have developed a thriving black market. Thus the challenge, it seems, is whether to refashion altruism or introduce other supply alternatives with standards and regulations.

Source: Los Angeles Times op-ed 11 Mar 2004. Michele Goodwin is the director of the Health Law Institute, DePaul University College of Law. Reprinted with permission of Michele Goodwin.

CHAPTER THREE

Analysis: The Heart of Critical Thinking

Power dies, power goes under and gutters out, ungraspable. It is momentary, quick of flight and liable to deceive. As soon as you rely on the possession it is gone. Forget that it ever existed, and it returns. I never made the mistake of thinking that I owned my own strength, that was my secret.

LOUISE ERDRICH, *Tracks*

Analysis **is** not just done by scientists in a lab. It is an aspect of all of our lives, even on the most mundane or everyday level. Riding on the Metro to school, for example, you read an article in the paper about an arthritic giraffe at the National Zoo in Washington, DC, that died. Apparently, the cause was a digestive problem called tympany, which is sort of like lactose intolerance.

Because tympany is normally found in dairy cows and not giraffes, a *Washington Post* reporter asked to see the giraffe's medical records. She was stonewalled. The zoo director refused, arguing that "disclosure of the records would violate the giraffe's privacy rights." Scratching your head, you read on. Evidently, she claimed the same privacy principles that protect physician–patient relationships apply to veterinarian–giraffe relationships. Eric Glitzenstein, an animal-protection attorney whose clients have included circus elephants and polar bears, called this notion of privacy rights "mind-boggling" (Roy Rivenburg, "It's a Legal Jungle Out There," *Los Angeles Times*, 10 May 2002). You wonder what to make of all this. You haven't given much thought to animal rights and want to understand the key issues. To accomplish this, you need to develop your brainpower, gather and weigh evidence, sort relevant from irrelevant information, consider competing explanations, assess the strength of the reasoning, and arrive at some conclusion if at all possible. To say the least, these are very useful skills.

At the heart of critical thinking lies the ability to analyze. Extracting key ideas, pulling out hidden assumptions, and setting out the structure of arguments are important aspects of analysis. It also helps to have a creative, expansive side where we generate ideas and turn over alternatives in our minds. This occurs when we try to see the big picture, set goals, brainstorm ideas, and lay out a plan of action. Keep this broader view in mind as we dissect arguments, organize the various components, inspect fine details, and see how it all works together. It is not always easy to stand back and examine what we wrote, said, or thought. Think of all the times we thought of a clever retort—two hours later. It can happen to us all; but building the skills and regularly applying them helps us be able to pull them up more quickly.

In this chapter, we will look at analysis and become familiar with its various elements, including credibility, types of evidence, and the weighing of evidence. We want to be able to express our ideas clearly and set out our positions in a defensible manner. This chapter is of fundamental importance for building a wide range of analytical skills.

Assessing Credibility

Issues and problems do not exist in a vacuum, but are embedded in people's lives. Let's look at an example. In 1985, a case came to trial in Boston that centered on a police detective who struck a man suspected of soliciting a prostitute and resisting arrest. Seven people testified at the trial: Long Kuang Huang (alleged victim), Detective Francis Kelly, Bao Tang Huang (Huang's wife), Audrey Manns (prostitute), Paul Bates (construction worker–witness), Gretl Nunnemacher (defense witness), and Dr. Jane Silva (neurologist). Use the credibility grid following the article, created by Mary Anne Saul, to rate each speaker on a scale of 1 to 5 (5 being high, or very credible; 1 being low, or not credible).

Defense Witnesses Describe Chinatown Beating

John H. Kennedy

Defense witnesses in the nonjury trial of Long Kuang Huang yesterday drew a sympathetic portrait of the peasant farmer from China as perhaps a victim of mistaken identity just 10 months after he immigrated to the United States. Huang, 56, is on trial in Boston Municipal Court on charges of soliciting sex for a fee and assault and battery on Detective Francis G. Kelly Jr. last May 1 near the Combat Zone [a seedy area in Boston with strip clubs and bars]. Attorneys are scheduled to give closing arguments this morning before Judge George A. O'Toole Jr. makes his decision.

In the final day of testimony, all the witnesses were called by Huang's attorneys, and included his wife. Some described the scuffle between Kelly and Huang, although their versions differed on details. The case has become the focus of charges by some Asian-Americans of police brutality. Kelly faces police department hearings on his conduct during the May 1 incident.

Bao Tang Huang, 52, whose testimony in Chinese was translated, said her husband could write his name in English, but did not speak English. His only experience with police was in China where officers wear white uniforms and do not carry badges, she said. Both grew up and lived in a "large village" of 300 people in the People's Republic, where Huang was a farmer. They have two sons, who came with them to Boston July 1, 1984. Huang has no formal education and has worked in restaurants in the Boston area, she said.

Earlier this week, prostitute Audrey Manns identified Huang in court as the man who spoke broken English to her, and who made it clear that he would pay her $30 to have sex with him. Kelly testified he followed them for two or three blocks before arresting Manns, and then Huang after an extended struggle, in front of 35 Kneeland St.

Kelly and Manns testified that Huang kicked and hit the detective several times before Kelly connected with a single punch to Huang's face in an attempt to subdue him. The detective also testified he identified himself as a police officer, both with his badge and by speaking to Huang.

Two defense witnesses yesterday said the detective connected with two punches to Huang's face, while Manns told the detective to stop. Paul Bates, 39, was working on a renovation project at 35 Kneeland St. when he saw a woman in an "electric blue" outfit and "bright blonde" hair walk by with a man who looked Hispanic.

A short time later, Bates said he came onto the street and saw Kelly struggling with Huang. The blonde woman in the blue outfit, who he said was Manns, came over to the two. "She told him [Huang] to stop struggling, the other person was a police officer," said Bates. Bates said Manns told Kelly: "He's not the man. I wasn't with him. He was just walking down the sidewalk. I swear to God, Kelly." He said he later saw Kelly connect with two "short, chopping punches."

The version of another defense witness, Gretl Nunnemacher, differed somewhat from Bates'. She said Kelly slammed Huang against the side of the car "several" times, Kelly's fist started to come down but she said she didn't see it land. Then, said Nunnemacher, a blonde woman emerged from another car. "She said, 'Kelly, Kelly, what are you doing. Stop,' . . . she told me he was a cop." Dr. Jane Silva, a neurologist who treated Huang at the New England Medical Center, said Huang suffered a concussion with post-concussive symptoms—headaches, dizziness, listlessness.

Source: Boston Globe, 23 Aug 1985. Reprinted with permission of the *Boston Globe*.

The Saul Credibility Grid—Copy this onto a sheet of paper.

WITNESSES	CREDIBILITY RATING (1, LOW; 5, HIGH)	REASONS FOR YOUR RATING
L. Huang		
Det. Kelly		
B. Huang		
A. Manns		
P. Bates		
G. Nunnemacher		
De Silva		

When listing your reasons (criteria), think about what makes the person seem credible. Proximity to the crime, ability to observe easily, conflict of interest, background information, professional training, cultural factors, and personal characteristics may all affect a person's ability. These factors act as criteria for the credibility of witnesses. (Thanks to Ann Garry's Critical Thinking class at Cal State Los Angeles, for tracking down subsequent articles that were used in the following set of exercises.)

Exercises

1. Prosecution witness Harry Ayscough helped the defense in the Chinatown case. He testified that Audrey Manns yelled, "He's not the one, that's not him," as Detective Kelly tried to arrest Long Kuang Huang.
   a. Do you think this testimony clearly indicates that Detective Kelly may have been arresting the wrong man?
   b. Is there any other conclusion that might be drawn from the testimony?

2. Does the fact that Audrey Manns testified that it was Huang who offered to pay $30 for sex and then violently resisted arrest create any conflict with your decision about Ayscough's testimony? Discuss how you'd resolve a possible conflict in these pieces of evidence.

3. What significance should you give the fact that defense witnesses painted a sympathetic portrait of Huang and suggested that he might have been a victim of mistaken identity?

4. The case resulted in an unusual settlement. In your assessment, does this seem like a wise decision in terms of its impact on police–community relations?
   Huang received $85,000 from the city. Detective Kelly got $40,000 in back pay and overtime (he had been suspended without pay for a year), $55,000 in legal fees, and $20,000 in additional damages. In return, Kelly was to drop a suit against the police commissioner, and Huang was to drop his $1 million civil rights suit against the Boston police. Joseph Mulligan, the corporation counsel, said, "We decided to package the whole enchilada and make it all go away" (Steve Marantz, "2-Way Settlement Ends Police Suit," *Boston Globe*, 15 Jul 1989).

The Role of Assumptions

Assumptions can trip us up at any time—be on the lookout for assumptions that are questionable or unwarranted. Look back at the Chinatown case. Do you see any assumptions being made? What do we make of Bo Huang's testimony that her husband's only experience with police was in China where officers wear white uniforms and do not carry badges? The fact they had been in Boston for more than a year when the altercation with Detective Kelly occurred could be viewed as constituting sufficient time for him to be able to identify Boston police officers. Or does "experience with police" mean dealing face to face? That is unclear. Review the testimony of all the defense witnesses to see what sorts of assumptions they may hold.

Well-Reasoned Arguments

Our arguments should be well reasoned and clearly structured, so we can see how the evidence lays the foundation for the conclusion. Notice how this argument is clearly structured:

> If you want superlative sound from your audio system but don't want speakers that could do justice to Stonehenge dominating your room, this should be music to your ears: Bookshelf speakers and three-piece systems performed just as well as—and in some cases better than—floor-standing speakers in our latest tests. And some fine performers cost only $100 to $200, so you can save money as well as space.
>
> That's a switch from years past, when big-box models were considered the only way to get outstanding sound quality. . . . We tested 23 bookshelf speakers ranging in price from $100 to $650 a pair and five three-piece systems priced at $300 to $600. We compared these speakers to three floor-standing models, priced at $400 to $700. . . . The results demonstrate that smaller speakers more than hold their own. ("Small Boxes, Big Sound," *Consumer Reports,* Aug 2001)

The evidence is clearly set out, and the results of the tests are cited to demonstrate that the different units are comparable in quality. The conclusion is presented first, with the evidence offering strong support. Aim for a well-structured argument that has sufficient evidence supporting the conclusion. Rely on no unwarranted assumptions, so no alternative conclusion seems plausible. You want the evidence to point to the conclusion that you drew.

Developing Analytical Skills

Arguments may occur in a variety of forms and formats. We find them in discussions with friends, emails, newspapers, films, videos, TV programs, radio shows, and textbooks. An *effective analysis* entails recognizing the focus (and thesis), pulling out evidence, seeing the structure of the reasoning, weighing strengths and weaknesses, considering alternative explanations, examining assumptions, looking for omissions (missing pieces), and identifying potential sources of bias (e.g., prejudicial language). Once the argument is set out, the next step is to evaluate the strength of the reasoning, see if there are any key omissions or questionable assumptions, and determine whether the conclusion is well supported by the evidence.

Key Points in Analyzing an Article

Subject: What is the focus of this piece? What is it about—what's the general topic?

Territory: What is the context for exploring the ideas or issues?

Thesis: Is the author arguing a particular position? What point is the author trying to make?

Purpose: What, in a nutshell, is the purpose of the article?

Approach: How much is directed to the central idea versus side issues or tangents? How is this argument structured?

Key claims: What are the main ideas or key points offered as evidence? This is the strongest support for the conclusion.

Fine details: What examples, statistics, or other support are we given to back up the key evidence or premises? Do the details presented work to develop the central idea or vision?

Quality of support: Does the evidence work in part or in its entirety to support the thesis? Is the thesis/conclusion well supported by the evidence?

Clarity: Is the presentation clear and to the point? Are the key issues, ideas, or details of the story clearly presented?

Overall impression: What is the overall impression? Is the case convincingly made? If not, what's missing, questionable, or off-track? What are you left with; what sticks in your mind?

Exercise

Directions: Using the key points for analyzing an article, set out your analysis of the article below. In this article, Michelle Delio examines a new "toy" that allows the user to "execute" Marv, who sits in an electric chair, ready to be jolted. Then answer the questions that follow.

DEATH ROW MARV

Kids' New Rage: Executing Marv

Michelle Delio

Wired magazine, August 10, 2000

Flip the switch and a surge of electrical current slams into the figure strapped in the chair. He convulses. His hands tremble. His eyes glow red. His teeth clench. And then he utters his last words.

"That the best you can do, you pansies?"

No, it's not the nightly news from Texas. It's Death Row Marv, the latest plastic sensation from McFarlane Toys, makers of the Spawn and Austin Powers action figures. Marv is one of the main characters in the Frank Miller comic book series "Sin City." He's a big (7-plus-feet tall), ugly, dangerous, drunk, ex-con medicated into some semblance of sanity by his parole officer's psychiatrist girlfriend. But while trying to do his version of good, Marv eventually came to a bad end.

The toy, which comes complete with an electric chair, a wired helmet for Marv's head, and a switch that, when pulled, shoots the juice into the hapless Marv, had a first production run of tens of thousands, according to McFarlane Toys. No sales figures are available yet, but Marv is feeling a big buzz in more ways than one. New York's Forbidden Planet comic store and Island Comics both have waiting lists with more than 30 names on them.

"Kids really love Marv," said Island's Rick Varo. "Teen-age girls think he's cute, which terrifies me." Death Row Marv is also a big draw at Manhattan's Midtown Comics store located near Times Square. A salesman there who preferred to remain anonymous ("You never know who's looking for you," he said) noted that people have been dropping into the store on a daily basis just to jolt Marv a few times. "It's not just kids, either," he said. "We get guys in suits. We get moms. Old people. They come in looking like they had a rough day, but after they juice Marv they leave with a smile on their faces. It's a happy kind of thing."

But not everyone is having a good time playing with Marv. Dennis Golkven, a child psychologist in private practice in New Jersey, says that the toy could be dangerous. "It teaches children that it's fun to hurt people," Golkven said. Ten-year-old Jason Devors of Brooklyn, New York, disagrees. "Marv is not a person," he said. "He's just a toy."

Answer the following:

1. What do "toys" like Death Row Marv reveal about our society?

2. State the strongest argument you can for allowing Death Row Marv to be sold to children.

3. State the strongest argument you can in favor of banning or restricting toys like Death Row Marv.

Source: Copyright © 1994–2001 Wired Digital, Inc., a Lycos Network Company. All Rights Reserved. Reprinted with permission of Michelle Delio and Lycos.

Group or Individual Exercise

U.S. Government to Issue Gas Masks in Alabama

Directions: Below is an itemized list of information about the decision by the U.S. government to buy gas masks—yes, gas masks—for residents in eastern Alabama (see Associated Press, "US Will Pay for Gas Masks for Alabama," 28 Mar 2002).

Draw from 5 or 6 of these 15 facts to construct an argument. Weigh the evidence first, so your argument is strong. Make your conclusion clear and lay out your premises one by one (P_1, P_2, P_3, etc.):

1. On March 28, 2002, the federal government announced that it would pay for safety gear "that resembles a gas mask" for thousands of people living in eastern Alabama.

2. Those getting the masks live near a chemical weapons incinerator where the U.S. Army will burn deadly nerve agents.

3. Thousands of tons of the deadliest chemical weapons ever made will be destroyed.

4. As many as 35,000 Alabamians will receive the "protective hoods" and training on how to use them.

5. This is the first mass distribution of safety gear to American civilians in the history of the United States.

6. The state of Alabama will withdraw its request that a judge block the opening of the incinerator in return for the government's $7 million pledge of gear and training.

7. The hoods, "which function like gas masks but are larger and simpler to use," will go to people who live nearest the incinerator.

8. The hoods protect the wearer for six to eight hours.

9. For the hoods to be accessible, the 35,000 adults and children will have to carry the hoods with them everywhere they go in the zones near the depot—the grocery store, the movies, and school—for at least six years and possibly longer until the burning is complete.

10. The money will also be used to buy gear for as many as 500 police officers, firefighters, and emergency response workers.

11. The Army planned to begin test burning of nerve gas in September 2002.

12. A shrill "whoop-whoop" will go off on a public-address system if there is a toxic leak.

13. "Those M-55 rockets are extremely fragile munitions," said Lt. Col. Bruce E. Williams, commander of Anniston Chemical Activity. "We think we can continue to store them safely, but you can't escape the fact that if there were a one-in-a-million earthquake, or lightning strike, or a 747 [airplane] crashing on an igloo, the damage would dwarf the worst-case thing that could ever happen at the incinerator. The only real protection I can offer this community is to destroy this stockpile, and destroy it quickly."

14. On February 5, 2004, it was reported by the Associated Press that the Army had shut down the incinerator when there was a leak of a "small amount" of the deadly nerve agent sarin inside a main building. The alarms sounded. No one was reported as injured.

15. On March 3, 2004, it was reported by the Associated Press that a "trace amount" of sarin nerve agent had leaked from a weapons storage bunker at the Anniston, Alabama, Army Depot. "Sarin did not escape the area, and the concentration was not enough to hurt anyone," said Cathy Coleman, a spokeswoman for Anniston Chemical Activity, which oversees the stockpile.

Types of Evidence

Thoughts and ideas can be expressed in different ways. This needs to be noted at the outset so we can adjust our expectations and method of analysis accordingly. Whatever form an argument takes, however, fundamental issues must be addressed. We'll start with evidence. Central to an analysis is *assessing the evidence*. Once the argument is set out, we need to analyze the premises to see how well they support the conclusion. For example, when Kathleen Tuttle says, "The majority of white people in America are not racist," she is not saying "No white person in America is racist." But because the *majority* is not the same as *all*, her claim is not universal in scope. Whether her claim is actually true is another matter.

There are different types of evidence, such as facts, testimony, statistical evidence, universal and particular claims, credible sources, value claims, circumstantial evidence, conditional claims, analogies, and cause-and-effect reasoning. For the argument to be strong the premises must provide sufficient support for the conclusion, so each piece of evidence should be scrutinized.

Facts and Factual Claims

Facts are like flagstones on a path, giving us something firm to stand on. If a claim of fact were assumed to be false, it would conflict with evidence known to be true. This would create a contradiction, which means that the claim of fact must actually be true. Facts and factual claims do not permit a rival conclusion—any rival conclusion simply would lack support. Here's an example:

> The AIDS virus can be transmitted through artificial insemination. Recent cases confirmed through scientific testing that a small percentage of women have gotten AIDS through a donor sperm they used when they were artificially inseminated years ago. At that time, AIDS tests were not routinely run on potential sperm donors.

The assertion about women getting AIDS through donor sperm supports the conclusion that AIDS virus can be transmitted through artificial insemination. There is no doubt that this conclusion will follow from the evidence.

Exercises

Directions: In the following passages, note when the reasoning seems *well supported*, and explain why/why not.

1. Children's cartoons often contain acts of violence. Children are highly impressionable. We should monitor shows that may affect children. Therefore, we ought to monitor children's cartoons.

2. Many soap operas contain sexual themes and romance. Mario loves soap operas, so he must be obsessed with sex.

3. Most news programs focus on acts of violence, like murder and robbery. Therefore, Norm's suicidal tendencies must be due to the fact that he watches too much news.

4. Beth is an honest person. She recently refused to help her boyfriend get a copy of the history test, and last year she found a wallet on a bench and returned it to the owner. Not one of the $50 bills tucked behind credit cards in the wallet was touched.

5. Things are not always what they seem when it comes to politics. Facts can be twisted to suit the picture sought; speeches can be written to hide political problems and make the public feel that everything's fine when it isn't. We might be better off with a healthy dose of skepticism. That means we should be skeptical about promises made by politicians.

6. Chong must be about to quit her job. I heard her complaining about a cup of coffee spilled all over her desk by one of her co-workers. She had to retype the pesticide report she had just finished and missed happy hour with the gang. All that extra work made Chong mad as a hornet!

7. Drinking alcohol takes a heavier toll on women than on men. Their risk of liver and heart damage is greater. Their depression rates are higher. Women with a history of alcoholism report more trouble with daily functioning than men with similar histories.

8. Some children watch television more than they read. Everyone who watches too much TV is less literate than those who trade the TV for a good book. Parents need to become more assertive about their children's viewing of TV shows. Consequently, children should not be allowed unlimited viewing of TV shows.

9. Some parents spend more time watching TV than interacting with their children. Many children complain that they go to their parents with books and art materials, begging for parental attention. Parents regularly push aside their children's requests, because of their addiction to TV. Without parental help, children have more trouble reading. As a result, parental TV habits are the reason children do not read as much as in the past.

Testimony

Testimony can take a variety of forms ranging from confessionals or personal anecdotes, to eyewitness testimony, to expert testimony. We've all seen those ads with ordinary people or celebrities extolling the virtues of one thing or another.

Often we see personal anecdotes in news reports when family members share their response to a child killed by a stray bullet or hit by a train. After tragic events such as plane crashes, we hear from eyewitnesses. Lawyers often call on expert testimony to try to convince the judge or jury that their side should prevail.

All such testimony has to be evaluated—not as fact but as factual claims, informed opinion, or one's personal perspective on an issue. Generally, this involves examining the details and assertions made, along with the credibility of the one offering the testimonial. This is not always easy to do. For example, Roy Horn's tiger attacked him during the show on October 3, 2003, at the Mirage in Las Vegas. The various eyewitnesses were later interviewed to try to determine what happened. The witnesses did not agree, leaving investigators to try to piece together the story from conflicting accounts. Each account was examined in light of the proximity of the viewer to the attack and the level of detail. The credibility of the witness may also factor when evaluating testimony.

The Scope of a Claim

We need to be able to assess a body of evidence. Be attentive to the *scope* of a **claim**—what the claim is meant to cover. "*Not all* drivers are on cell phones" means that at least some are not using cell phones as they drive. "All" means more than "some," and vague generalities mean less than specific, detailed claims. We have to be careful when universal claims are used.

It's a question of scope. "*Everyone* who purchased a lottery ticket is eligible for the drawing for a new Mini" is stronger than "*Some* people who purchased a lottery ticket are eligible for the drawing for a new Mini." The term "all" covers the entire subject class, whereas "some" means "at least one." Context is also important, as there may be details about the specifics of the case that shape its interpretation. For example, if we knew that a nonsmoking lung cancer patient had a smoker for a wife, we would have a possible causal factor of the condition.

Credible Sources

Credible sources can play an important role in arguments. They can sway, if not carry, an argument. Suppose medical researchers claimed there was a causal connection between secondhand smoke and lung cancer. This would be significant if the researchers were credible sources and had no conflict of interest (e.g., if they had not been bribed by an antismoking lobby). If solid statistical data showed a pattern of health problems associated with secondhand smoke, it would provide more evidence to support a lawsuit. Assessing the credibility of witnesses and other sources is important. The outcome of a trial may turn on the credibility of the witnesses.

FIGURE 3.1 Road Sign
Not all warnings are obvious. Further
analysis may be necessary.

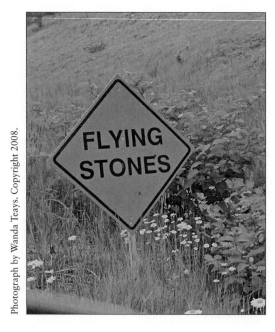

Photograph by Wanda Teays. Copyright 2008.

A credible source can be an individual (e.g., an expert) or a government agency (e.g., the Centers for Disease Control or the Census Bureau). The important thing is that the information this source provides be viewed as factually correct or at least highly likely (in the case of an expert opinion). Only strong evidence to the contrary can detract from a credible source (see Figure 3.1). Sizing up credibility is not always easy, which may account for the role of gut reactions on the part of some jurors. Assessing credibility in other aspects of our lives similarly requires us to look carefully at the various factors that weigh into the decision.

Of course, not all testimonials or "experts" should carry much weight. For example, actors and athletes are often hired to advertise a product. Look also at trials where both sides bring in "experts" to bolster their case. In high-profile trials, we often see expert pitted against expert.

Look at the case of Barney Clark, the first person to get the Jarvik-7 artificial heart. Pioneering surgeon William DeVries implanted the first Jarvik-7 artificial heart in Clark in 1982. Clark lived 112 days with the experimental device intended to make human heart transplants past history. The nurses began to question the wisdom of proceeding with the experiment but thought they lacked the credibility to challenge the surgeon:

> As the primary hands-on caretakers of the patients, they were the most continuously exposed to their physical and psychic ordeals. The nurses also developed close relations with the families of the Jarvik-7 recipients and had intimate knowledge of the painful experiences the family members underwent . . . some of the nurses became increasingly uncertain about whether the implanted devices and their patients'

reactions to them were being studied in a way that met the scientific and moral criteria of good clinical research. . . .

Despite their uneasiness about the experiment, they were inclined to assume that they did not have enough scientific training and experience to challenge the investigators' conception and execution of the research or its approval. (Renee C. Fox and Judith Swazey, *Spare Parts: Organ Replacement in American Society,* Oxford University Press, 1992)

Value Claims

Value claims may be used as evidence, but they should be handled carefully. These may relate to character references and issues of credibility. A **value claim** asserts a judgment based on a system of values, beliefs, or personal preference. It usually takes one of three forms. It may be a judgment of taste, as in "Milk should always be served warm" or an aesthetic judgment, as in "Novels are superior to movies." A value claim may be a moral judgment, as in "You ought not to watch so much TV." Value claims may be used as evidence for a thesis, but they should be handled carefully. They may relate to character assessment and issues of credibility. Personal values can shape a decision, so they warrant examination. Be aware though: As Professor Paul Green observed—and thanks to him for pointing this out—statements of personal preference are not value claims. In fact, these are statements about the individual in question (as in "I like bananas a lot more than beets") or the one(s) targeted (as in "Most children prefer ice cream to peanuts").

Moral values can weigh heavily in laws and public policies as well, as we see with such controversial issues as abortion, cloning, euthanasia, the death penalty, and other ethical issues.

Value claims are just about everywhere we turn. In a review of *Godzilla,* Ryan Harvey argued that the directors ignored the creature's soul:

So what do [directors] Emmerich and Devlin give us? A big iguana with squinty eyes, Jay Leno's chin and bad breath instead of flames. He's also a spineless wimp, dodging buildings, fleeing helicopters and hiding in the subways. The real Godzilla would never hide . . . *Godzilla* didn't let TriStar down. TriStar let *Godzilla* down. (Ryan Harvey, "Even Godzilla Movie's Gotta Have Heart," *Los Angeles Times,* 8 Jun 1998)

Statistical Evidence

Have you seen those commercials that say, "Four of five doctors surveyed prescribe Preparation K for the relief of polyps" or "Most dentists prefer Crescent mouthwash"? We need to ask ourselves, "How many doctors and dentists were actually surveyed?"

The use of statistics can be very effective, particularly when the studies are current. The key concerns in assessing statistical studies are the size, diversity, and date of the study. The sample size should be adequate and have sufficient diversity: The group sampled needs to be representative of the target population being studied. Be careful, though. If the sample size is not large enough, it may result in a **hasty generalization** (fallacious reasoning that occurs when a sample study is insufficient in terms of size, leading us to draw an incorrect conclusion). If the studies fail to be diverse enough, the result may be **biased statistics** (fallacious reasoning that occurs when a sample study is not diverse enough and, thus, fails to be representative). In Chapter 8, we will look at statistical studies.

Think of it this way: Suppose you are creating an ad campaign for cube-shaped pasta. You do a market analysis and find that 78 percent of men prefer cube-shaped to donut-shaped pasta, whereas only 45 percent of women prefer the cube-shaped pasta. If more women than men normally buy pasta, your job is to get women to change their minds. Plus, you'll try to convince the 22 percent of men who prefer donut-shaped pasta to try the cubes.

However, if the researcher found that 94 percent of children prefer cube-shaped to donut-shaped pasta, you could aim your advertising at this younger market. We know how fast-food chains target ads to children with great success. So paying attention to the role of statistics in effective reasoning can be very helpful in developing critical thinking skills.

Circumstantial Evidence

Circumstantial evidence (or indirect evidence) is any evidence not obtained from an eyewitness or a direct participant. Examples include fingerprints, DNA and other physical evidence, and business records. Circumstantial evidence has been strong enough to convict people of murder, even in the absence of a body! For example, Scott Peterson was convicted of killing his wife and unborn child, even though neither body was found. It was never determined how they were killed. Here's another example:

> This case turned on a dog hair: This is the case of the murder of Elizabeth Ballard in 1998. They tried to cleanse the world of anything linking them to Ballard's death. A single dog hair thwarted the murderers. The two men wrapped her body in plastic, vacuumed and scrubbed the room, and washed down the car trunk they used to carry her body to be dumped in the desert. But a hair of one of the murderer's dogs, Hercules, was found on the victim's socks. This one hair helped send the men to prison in 2001 for her murder. DNA analysis can now be done on pet hair, blood, feces and urine and is considered a valuable tool for prosecutors. (Bettina Boxell, "Proved Guilty by a Hair," *Los Angeles Times*, 21 Dec 2001)

Conditional Claims

Evidence may be expressed as a **conditional claim**—an "if . . . then" claim. Conditional claims have two parts: (1) the **antecedent** (the first or conditional part acting as a catalyst to something else) and (2) the **consequent** (the second or resulting part said to follow from a prior condition). The antecedent lies between the "if" and the "then," and the consequent follows the "then."

Hypotheses are often used in scientific research, statistical studies, legal reasoning, and everyday problem solving. We may start with a hypothetical condition—a "what if?"—and then see what possible effects might logically follow. Or we may start with the hypothetical condition and *predict* a specific consequent or effect. We then see how that fits with what is already known. If it does not contradict known facts or states of affairs, then it may be a fruitful lead and warrant further study.

For example, suppose we want to test a possible medical treatment for attention deficit disorder (ADD). We get together a sample group (subjects with ADD who will be participating in a trial of the drug regimen) and a control group (subjects with ADD who will be given a placebo but think they are getting the new drug). The hypothesis is that this new drug will help. The testing will either confirm or disconfirm the hypothesis "If we try drug X, then we should expect to see these results in the sample group but not in the control group."

For any given conditional claim, the antecedent is not necessarily true. Many of us have fantasized, "If I had a million bucks, then . . ." knowing the antecedent (getting $1 million) is a pipe dream. Often we are told, "If A then B," and yet A never happens. Here are two examples: (1) If he weighed 700 pounds, Will Smith could be a sumo wrestler, and (2) if foreign workers had decent working conditions and some kind of a union, they might not be as vulnerable to exploitation. In the first case, Will Smith has no shot at weighing 700 pounds regardless of how many donuts he eats. In the second example, we need more information about why the workers would not be as vulnerable to exploitation. But the lack of certainty in establishing the antecedent means that the consequent cannot be assumed.

Group or Individual Exercise

A Look at Legal Parenting Rights

Directions: Assess the reasoning in a ruling by the California Supreme Court that a man who fathers a child with a woman married to someone else may be denied all legal parental rights. Set out your response in light of the following:

1. Justice Joyce L. Kennard said that a man "who fathers a child with a woman married to another man takes the risk that the child will be raised within that marriage and that he will be excluded from participation in the child's life."

2. The court majority said that because Dawn was married at the time the baby was conceived and was living with her husband when the baby, Sam,

was born, they were bound by state law that presumes the husband to be the father of his wife's children.

3. Jerome "Jerry" Krchmar, 41, lived with a woman in 1995 while she was separated from her husband, to whom she'd been married for six years.

4. The woman, Dawn, became pregnant within a month of living with Jerry.

5. After living with Jerry for four months, Dawn moved back in with her husband.

6. Dawn insisted that Jerry was not the father of the child.

7. Jerry took a parenting class and tried to negotiate child support.

8. California law recognizes the husband as the father of a child, regardless of genetic ties.

9. Dawn was living with her husband when the baby was born.

10. Jerry filed a lawsuit before the baby was born to assert his parental rights.

11. Recognizing the importance of family stability, the law supports the married couple, even when another man is the biological father of a child.

12. Dawn and her husband refused to let Jerry see the baby, Sam.

13. Dawn's husband punched Jerry when the three people met for a blood test.

14. Jerry said, "I will never give up my son."

(Adapted from Greg La Motte, "Court Denies Unwed Dad's Parental Rights," *CNN News,* CNN.com, 8 Apr 1998; and Maura Dolan, "Court Denies Parental Rights to Unwed Father," *Los Angeles Times,* 7 Apr 1998)

Analogies

Instead of giving straightforward evidence, an argument may offer an analogy, metaphor, or comparison as evidence. An **analogy** is a comparison asserting that something true of one of the terms of the comparison will, therefore, be true of the second term. This rests on the strength of the similarities outweighing the differences between the terms of the analogy. (See Chapter 6 for a fuller discussion.) These sometimes colorful or vivid comparisons can make a great impression on an audience. See if you can find all the analogies in the excerpt from a review of a book on spirituality that was in *Shambhala Sun* magazine:

> Spirituality is like Jell-O. It comes in every imaginable flavor, it's almost impossible to pin down, and your definitions of it will only last until it morphs into another shape. That's how the eminent sociologist of religion, Wade Clark Roof, explains the difficulty of defining our culture's love affair with things spiritual. Roof, who teaches at the University of California, Santa Barbara, does come up with two clarifying categories in the slippery world of contemporary spirituality: seekers, who pursue meaning by sampling a smorgasbord of dishes, and dwellers, who feast from a single table. (Anna-Liza Kosma, "Seekers and Dwellers," *Shambhala Sun,* May 2001)

Here's another example. The term *virus* is now widely used in both medicine and technology. According to Ken Dunham, there are "valid comparisons between biological and computer viruses that support the origin of the term 'computer virus'" (Ken Dunham, "The Great Analogy," Securitydatabase.net, 2 Jul 2001).

Analogies often have persuasive power, so they warrant a detailed study. We will do this when we delve into inductive reasoning. As we'll see, the strength of the analogy rests on the strength of the relevant similarities of the two things being compared. The stronger the relevant similarities, the stronger the analogy; but if there are significant differences in what is being compared, the analogy is weakened. As we will see in Chapter 15, analogies play an important role in legal reasoning, where they take the form of legal precedent. Thus, it pays to be able to analyze the use of analogies.

Cause-and-Effect Reasoning

Cause-and-effect reasoning occurs when someone asserts that something either causes or is an effect of something else. (See Chapter 8 for a more in-depth discussion of causal reasoning.) For example, what do you do about the claim that all blue-eyed people are related? According to geneticist Hans Eiberg, every person with blue eyes may descend from an ancestor whose genes mutated between 6,000 and 10,000 years ago. Before then, Eiberg contends, all people had brown eyes. Eiberg's team traced blue eyes to one specific area "near a gene called OCA2" ("Blue-Eyed Humans Have a Single, Common Ancestor," *Science Daily,* 31 Jan 2008).

A causal claim may have merit, but it is crucial that alternative causes be dismissed first. Once they can be eliminated, a causal claim has more force. We can see this by the ways in which different theories about the origin of AIDS have been offered. Some argue that AIDS entered the human population through malaria experiments on prisoners and researchers, who injected mangabey (monkey) blood into the human subjects. Others argue that AIDS entered through oral polio vaccines given to about a million people in central Africa from 1957 to 1960, which was cultured from the cells of primates. Still others think AIDS can be traced to human consumption of primates' blood or exposure to the bodily fluids of chimpanzees. And so on. Until it is obvious what caused AIDS/HIV to enter the human population, there will be a host of theories swirling around.

We see cause-and-effect reasoning behind arguments for censorship of film and TV. There are those who insist that violence on the screen is causally linked to violent behavior. What follows from this is that to change the latter we must restrict the former. It has, for instance, been argued, "If we don't want people doing crazy things, then we shouldn't show such acts in movies like *Kill Bill.*" Such a response comes out of a belief that the causal link between movies and human behavior is strong.

Group or Individual Exercise

Botox Revulsion

Directions: TV critic Nancy McNamara has a dilemma—what to do when she realizes something has changed, but it has not been publicly acknowledged. McNamara first sets out her dilemma:

> I know we're all supposed to be watching . . . "Dancing With the Stars" to see whether professional athletics or Broadway provides a better foundation for dance. But I'm pretty sure most of us are far too preoccupied with figuring out whether Priscilla Presley has had the first successful head transplant. Whenever the woman is on screen it is virtually impossible to look anywhere else—at once puffy and yanked, her face, and its odd relationship to her neck, often takes on the dimensions of a Picasso painting. A finer mind would seize the opportunity and contemplate the larger issues of humanity—the nature of identity, our denial of mortality, the tyranny of beauty. Me, I just sit there, open-mouthed, the same questions turning like a hamster wheel in my brain: What on earth did she do to herself? And why? For a critic, this poses a dilemma—while it is appropriate, indeed necessary, to point out technical things like disruptive camera work or shoddy set design, what exactly are you supposed to say about an older actor's strange shininess, newly bee-stung lips or eyes that seem to have changed shape and placement?

McNamara then presents her argument. A shortened version is below. Locate the conclusion, and then number her premises (P_1, P_2, etc.) and place them above the conclusion, so the argument is in standard form. Once it's set out, state the types of evidence used in the argument.

> Despite a tacit understanding that actors nowadays start lifting and injecting on their 21st birthday, mentioning an inexplicably altered appearance remains strangely taboo. Let me be clear: I begrudge no woman, or man, any surgical or chemical enhancements . . . that's your business. But television is a visual art, and if people are going to significantly alter the way they look in ways not directly connected with the roles they are playing, it can affect not only their performance but the whole tone of the show. Reviewing many of the new shows for the past fall season and midseason replacements, I noticed at least three fairly famous faces that looked decidedly, and distractingly, different, frozen or tugged into almost immobility that made certain emotional scenes almost laughable.
>
> But when we see bad things happen to good faces, when cosmetic decisions interfere with performances, I think we need to speak out. For me, I wish everyone would stop not only because the sight of some ill-advised surgery or injection can wreck a perfectly OK television show, but also because I am afraid we will forget what normal looks like. (Nancy McNamara, "On TV: Botox, Face-Lifts, Reconstructive Surgery," *Los Angeles Times*, 13 Apr 2008)

Summary of Major Types of Evidence

- Facts and factual claims
- Universal claims
- Particular claims

- Testimony (personal anecdote, studied opinion, eyewitness reports, expert testimony)
- Credible sources
- Speculation or opinion
- Statistical studies/claims
- Analogies
- Value claims
- Circumstantial evidence
- Conditional claims (hypothetical propositions)
- Cause-and-effect reasoning

Exercises

Part One

Directions: Refer to the different types of evidence (universal versus particular claims, use of sources, statistical studies, value claims, circumstantial evidence, conditional claims, arguments based on analogy, cause-and-effect reasoning) covered thus far. For each statement, identify the type of evidence presented and any questions you might have about its value in assessing the box office success of the film *Titanic.*

1. International Movie Data Base (imdb.com) reports that *Titanic* made $900 million from rentals and is the top-grossing film of all time, with a dollar gross worldwide of $1.8 billion.

2. 62 percent of the men in a poll of 215 Guilford College students did not think Leonardo DiCaprio was convincingly lower class, but they still liked the movie *Titanic.*

3. Film critic Roger Ebert said the movie is "flawlessly crafted, intelligently constructed, strongly acted and spellbinding."

4. People ought to buy the DVD of *Titanic* so they can watch it over and over—plus get to see all those nifty special features.

5. *Titanic* is a lot like *Gone with the Wind* in that it looks at women of privilege who fall for rascals while being surrounded by a society tightly bound by convention.

6. If James Cameron quit making movies right now, he'd go down in history as the director of some of the most influential blockbuster films ever made.

7. Seeing *Titanic* more than five times in one week has caused men to become more romantic and women to hum Celine Dion tunes.

8. Someone called "spbethell-1" couldn't stand the movie and posted this on the imdb website: "When I saw this film, people actually cheered when the

ship went down—we would have cheered more if it went down in the first five minutes."

9. Men will probably enjoy the end of *Titanic* when Jack is so brave in the icy water.

10. Ticket stubs to *Titanic* were found on Darin's desk at work, along with a note that read, "Laura, I sure had a great time last night." Darin must have taken Laura to see the movie.

11. Everyone interviewed at the midnight showing of *Titanic* on its opening night said the sinking of the ship was awesome in terms of setting the mood.

12. An empty popcorn bag was found on the floor of Silvio's new Prius, so it's clear he went to see *Titanic* even though he said he wouldn't go without me.

Part Two

When George Edward Reynon was sentenced to be executed for the murder of Maddy Nash, he accused Bob Nash, Maddy's father, of having molested her. Reynon said that he (Reynon) had not sexually molested the little girl but that, before he killed her, Maddy said, "Don't do to me like my father did."

When he made this accusation, Maddy's grandmother burst into tears and covered her face. Bob Nash jumped to his feet and yelled, "Burn in Hell Reynon," and gestured obscenely at Reynon. Still screaming, Bob Nash was dragged out of the courtroom. Given that Nash's reaction was so immediate and so strong, it seems obvious that there is some truth to what Reynon said. It doesn't make sense that Maddy would have accused her father this way if it weren't true. Plus, Bob Nash wouldn't have gone beserk with anger if it were a lie. This suggests that Nash must have molested his own daughter at some point before Reynon murdered her.

Answer the following:

1. What is specifically being claimed in the above argument?
2. State the strongest pieces of evidence.
3. State the weakest pieces of evidence.
4. Are there any assumptions made in this argument? If so, note them.
5. Rate the strength of the argument as a whole. Explain your rating.

Independent versus Interdependent Evidence

We need to be aware of the evidence being presented and assess it for strength. It's one thing to be able to see the structure of an argument so you know what is being claimed and what the various pieces of support are. This is the crucial stage of dismantling the argument. The next stage is that of examining the evidence we have been given.

Not all evidence is of equal value. Any *one* premise is potentially much more powerful than the other premises. It may be that one or more premises independently support the conclusion. This is **independent evidence.** When one piece of evidence is sufficient in and of itself, we would say that that piece *independently,* or singly, establishes the conclusion.

Suppose, for example, that we have a confession from a suspect in a crime, as well as DNA evidence. Either the confession *or* the physical evidence may establish guilt, assuming the confession is not coerced and is made by someone who is competent. In that case, any other evidence would be extraneous. However, not all suspects confess and not all physical evidence can seal a conviction. We often need to piece together all the evidence.

If we lack definitive evidence, then we have to look at the way our evidence works together. When this occurs, we say each contributing piece of evidence is **interdependent.** With interdependent premises, the evidence operates as a package deal. This is strongest when the evidence works together like interlocking pieces, holding up the conclusion.

For example, in February 2008, the Centers for Disease Control reported an outbreak of a paralyzing condition among plant workers who used compressed air to remove pigs' brains. Here are the pieces supporting the hypothesis that the problem was caused by the compressed air: (1) The workers were exposed to splatter and aerosol droplets of pig brain tissue because of the compressed air blast; (2) the compressed air liquefied the tissue before expelling it from the pig's skull; (3) the particles of the pig brain tissue that were inhaled attacked the workers' immune systems; (4) the problem was found in several such swine slaughterhouses around the country ("Paralysis Outbreak in Meat Workers Handling Pigs' Brains," *Medical News Today,* 4 Feb 2008).

And when that evidence poses no clear conflicts or contradictions (if we assume it to be true), we have **corroborating evidence.** With corroborating evidence, it gets harder to attack a case, because the foundation gains strength. For example, because Ralph has no alibi and was known to have emailed threats to Jorge, we'd say these two pieces of evidence corroborate each other. Similarly, if we knew that Jorge got a perfect score on his SAT, had strong letters of reference, and had just received a phone call from the university's financial aid office, then we have corroborating evidence that this could be news about the scholarship he applied for shortly before his car was stolen.

CASE STUDY

SARS and Fear in the Medical Profession

When SARS, an acute respiratory infection that is contagious and potentially deadly, hit in China, people followed it with interest—and a little anxiety. When it hit North America, the fear-factor in the West jumped. Read about what happened at a Toronto hospital when assumptions around selflessness in medical caregivers crumpled.

Dr. Donald A. Henderson . . . the man in charge of the global smallpox-eradication campaign [said] "I am confident that this same selfless concern for others would prevail today should an epidemic occur." But when SARS hit in Toronto last year, . . . "It was hard at first to find doctors to cover the SARS wards," said Dr. Leslie Nickell, a family doctor who assisted the SARS control team.

. . . Nickell organized a study of the psychological impact the disease was having on the personnel at her hospital, Sunnybrook and Women's College Health Sciences Center, which ultimately admitted 71 SARS patients. Twenty-three of these were health care workers, some from Sunnybrook. The results of her survey, . . . are disturbing. Of the 2,001 respondents, 65 percent reported significant concerns about their health and that of their families. Almost 30 percent, including 45 percent of the nurses who responded, displayed significant levels of "emotional distress."

Health care workers disliked wearing the uncomfortable masks and having their temperature taken every morning as they reported to work, though they knew these measures were necessary. . . . (Gretchen Reynolds, "Who Wanted to Treat Rebecca McLester?" *The New York Times Magazine*, 18 Apr 2004)

Answer the following:

1. What do we assume about how much risk is acceptable for doctors and nurses in caring for a patient?
2. Should doctors and nurses be required to treat patients with infectious diseases? Set out your argument for or against (note any exceptions to your stand).
3. State three to four points you would say to Dr. Paul Hunter after reading this (note: monkeypox is similar to smallpox):

Dr. Paul Hunter, who lives in Milwaukee, treated one of the other monkeypox cases in late May. His patient was a meat inspector and a dealer in exotic pets . . . when the man didn't respond to antibiotics, and his rash erupted with oozing sores, "The rumor about smallpox went around the hospital fast," he said. At that point, Hunter's worry shifted from the patient's prognosis to his own. "My attitude was, I'm going to stay as far away from this guy as possible," he said later. Although Hunter was the attending physician and visited his patient in the isolation ward every day, he limited hands-on care as much as possible. "Everybody did their jobs, but they wanted to have as little direct contact with him as possible. They were all like: 'Stay away!'"

"Look," he continued, "I'm not a coward. I've had needle sticks. I've had to get H.I.V. and hepatitis tests and then wait around for the results. That's not fun. But it's part of the job." This case, he says, was different. "I have three kids, all under the age of 11. That's a big reason I didn't want to be involved if it was smallpox. I'm not going to volunteer for anything dangerous." He also declined to get a smallpox vaccination. "I said, 'You're not turning me into a first responder.' Next time, let somebody without kids handle this" (Reynolds, "Who Wanted to Treat Rebecca McLester?").

Exercise

The Three-Strikes Law in California

On June 19, 2001, a California appeals court upheld the 25-years-to-life prison sentence given to a homeless man on parole. This was handed out under the guidelines of California's so-called three-strikes law. According to this law, anyone committing a third felony is given a mandatory 25-years-to-life sentence, regardless of the severity of the crime committed (so long as it was a felony conviction). The fact of the third felony being committed independently of the circumstances results in the sentence. On the other hand . . .

1. Assume you are a member of Prisoners' Rights Now, a group that takes on cases that appear to be unjust. They ask for your position on this case. Share what you will say, after reading the following about this actual case:
   - Yes, Kevin Thomas Weber did commit a felony in breaking into a Santa Ana, California, restaurant.
   - Yes, Weber did come in through a roof vent.
   - Yes, Weber might have taken more had he not been interrupted by a blaring burglar alarm.
   - Still, Weber stole only four cookies.
2. Justice David G. Sills wrote in a unanimous opinion, "A safecracker who cracks an empty safe is nonetheless a safecracker." Respond to Judge Sills from any two of the following:
   - The perspective of the owner of the restaurant
   - The perspective of Weber's family
   - The perspective of potential burglars who have two strikes against them
   - Your own perspective

Weighing Evidence

In the process of trying to evaluate arguments, chain of arguments, and policies, and making decisions, we need to have a systematic way of dealing with the evidence. That is, we need to see how to evaluate the strength of the evidence in its support of the particular goal.

Checklist for Weighing Evidence

- **Check the scope.** Universal claims "All A is B" or "No A is B" are *stronger* than particular claims "Some A is B" or "Some A is not B."
- **Look for relevance.** Claims pertinent to the topic (focused on the issue) are stronger than general observations or vague "truisms." Set the background information concerning the context to the side, unless it is necessary to make the argument.

- **Examine the support.** The evidence must support the argument. Does any of the evidence independently support the conclusion? Are all the premises needed? Use of credible sources, properly documented, is stronger than speculation.
- **Watch for testimony.** The credibility of those giving testimony is crucial. Look out for conflicts of interest, poor grasp of relevant information, weak observation skills, emotional problems, or inattention to details that could affect credibility.
- **Ask whether facts stack up.** Relevance is the key: The more indispensable a fact is to the case, the more weight it should have. Valuable facts may seal the case.
- **Examine circumstantial evidence.** Key here is that there's no reasonable alternative explanation. Ask if a rival conclusion is feasible.
- **Examine statistical claims.** The date and size of the study are important, as is diversity in terms of relevant variables or factors. The study should be representative of the target population.
- **Watch for conditional claims (hypotheticals).** These involve "if . . . then" constructions ("If P then Q"). Can we determine if the antecedent, P, is true? Is the consequent, Q, known to be false? Is this one link in a chain of conditional propositions?
- **Scrutinize value claims.** What is the force and impact of the claim? Who holds it? What are the consequences of not believing in it? Do ethics or religion color the interpretation? Watch for personal bias that could prejudice the case.
- **Look for analogies.** Analogies can never be put forward with certainty, and they resist verifiability. Look for strength of similarities. Similarities must carry more cumulative weight than differences for the analogy (precedent) to hold. Similarities make an analogy; differences break an analogy.
- **Look for omissions.** Watch for "holes" in the reasoning. Ask if anything has been left out (whether intentionally or unintentionally).

Look, for example, at the sign in Figure 3.2. The omission leaves a lot to the imagination.

FIGURE 3.2
Some messages couldn't be any clearer—assuming you know what "HRM" stands for. Give up? It's short for "Halifax Regional Municipality." This photo was taken in Halifax, Nova Scotia, Canada.

Photograph by Wanda Teays. Copyright 2008.

Exercises

1. It seems that the estate of the Bear family was broken into, and the suspect is one Goldie Locks. Sort through the evidence. Decide if the case against Goldie is strong enough to go to trial. Choose the five strongest pieces of evidence for the prosecution and the five strongest for the defense.

   a. Goldie's alibi could not be substantiated.
   b. Goldie eats porridge every other day for breakfast, but never on Mondays.
   c. The Bears eat porridge almost every day.
   d. Porridge stains were found on Goldie's blouse.
   e. Goldie's mother served porridge yesterday but today made fried eggs.
   f. The Bears' front door was pried open, possibly with a tool.
   g. Goldie had a pocketknife in her purse.
   h. Some little girls are afraid of bears.
   i. No little girl should go wandering in the woods, where bears live.
   j. If Goldie broke into the Bears' house, she had to have had a tool or knife.
   k. Baby Bear's chair was broken.
   l. A study of robberies revealed that most robberies are committed during the day and by someone who is familiar with the victim.
   m. Goldie says she had never met the Bears.
   n. Mrs. Bear found muddy footprints on the sidewalk.
   o. Many people have mud on their feet, and little girls often have muddy feet.
   p. A piece of wood that matches that of Baby Bear's chair was found in Tom Thumb's backyard, next to Tom's truck collection.
   q. Goldie had mud on her shoes.
   r. The muddy footprints were approximately size-6 shoes.
   s. Goldie's mother said Goldie was a lovely child.
   t. Little girls are less likely to get into trouble than are boys.
   u. Dr. Zut, child psychologist, said children are innately curious.
   v. Both Tom Thumb and Goldie have size-6 shoes.
   w. Goldie has no criminal record.
   x. Goldie's kindergarten teacher said Goldie had been well behaved and helpful to the other children when she was in her class four years ago.
   y. Goldie showed no remorse and said, "I could care less about those stupid bears."
   z. The crime took place on a Monday.
   aa. Baby Bear had psychiatric treatment last year for chronic lying.
   bb. Mrs. Bear said Baby Bear's toy truck was taken during the robbery.

2. Set out your position as to whether it should be possible for Daniel Patterson to give his second kidney to his daughter, Renada, in light of the various pieces of evidence set out below. Be sure to sort through the evidence, weighing it for strengths and weaknesses.

   a. Renada, 13 years old, was born with only one kidney, an unhealthy one.
   b. For seven years, Renada was on dialysis three times a week, unable to go to school.
   c. Renada's father, Daniel, is serving 12 years in prison for burglary and drug convictions.
   d. Daniel had abandoned Renada when she was a baby but donated one of his kidneys two years ago, when he turned out to be a compatible donor.
   e. For two years, Renada lived with her father's kidney, but often skipped her medication; his kidney (now hers) began to fail.
   f. Renada needs a new kidney; her 38-year-old father wants to donate his remaining kidney (he still has three more years in prison).
   g. If Daniel gives away his last kidney, he will require dialysis; that will cost the system $40,000 a year.
   h. To take Daniel's kidney clearly puts him at risk.
   i. Over 3,100 patients are on a waiting list for a kidney in northern California.
   j. Hank Greeley of Stanford's Center for Biomedical Ethics said that a father in most situations should be allowed to make a sacrifice for his daughter, though he said this made him nervous.
   k. Arthur L. Caplan, director of the Center for Bioethics at the University of Pennsylvania, is opposed to the surgery; he says, "You don't ever want to kill a person to say you saved another's life."
   l. There has never been a live kidney transplant, says Caplan, where a person went from one kidney to none.
   m. This would be Renada's third donated kidney (her body rejected the first when she was 5).
   n. There is a question whether Renada's body would accept another kidney from her father, since, when she didn't take her medicine required for the transplant before, her face became bloated, her stomach distended, and she hunched her back and felt ill.
   o. Dr. Nancy Ascher, a professor of surgery, says, "Whether the organ was rejected because the medication wasn't taken, the body may have decided that this organ is incompatible and will do so again."

The Global Dimension

The Missing Priest in Brazil

A Roman Catholic priest who floated off under hundreds of helium balloons disappeared off the southern coast of Brazil. Reverend Adelir Antonio de Carli lifted off from the port city of Paranagua on Sunday afternoon, wearing a helmet, thermal suit, and parachute and was reported missing about eight hours later. Decide if the reasoning of church treasurer Denise Gallas is well supported. First pull out the conclusion, and then list all the premises. Once your argument is set out, assess its strength.

> The priest wanted to break a 19-hour record for the most hours flying with balloons to raise money for a spiritual rest-stop for truckers in Paranagua, Brazil. A video of Carli posted on the G1 Web site of Globo TV showed the smiling 41-year-old priest slipping into a flight suit, being strapped to a seat

attached to a huge column of green, red, white and yellow balloons, and soaring into the air to the cheers of a crowd. According to reports, the priest soared to an altitude of 20,000 feet then descended to about 8,200 feet for his planned flight to the city of Dourados, 465 miles northwest of his parish.

But winds pushed him in another direction, and Carli was some 30 miles off the coast when he last contacted Paranagua's port authority. Carli had a GPS device, a satellite phone, and a buoyant chair and is an experienced skydiver.

"We are absolutely confident he will be found alive and well, floating somewhere in the ocean," Gallas said. "He knew what he was doing and was fully prepared for any kind of mishap," she added. ("Priest Attached to Party Balloons Vanishes in Brazil," Associated Press, 21 Apr 2008).

On April 29, 2008, the search for Fr. de Carli was suspended.

Exercises

Part One

1. Assume the department store chain Nordstrom wants to tap into your critical thinking skills. Set out your position and go into detail (so you are giving an argument) as to whether this will be an effective ad campaign: "We're all shoppers. We're all neighbors. We can't wait to meet you."

2. Read about the case of the college instructor who was fired for refusing to sign a loyalty oath. State the argument for both sides, drawing from the information given.

   Wendy Gonaver was about to start a teaching job at Cal State Fullerton in Spring 2008. The day before class was to begin, she was fired because she did not sign a loyalty oath swearing to "defend" the U.S. and California constitutions "against all enemies, foreign and domestic." The loyalty oath was added to the state Constitution by voters in 1952 to root out communists in public jobs. Now, 16 years after the collapse of the Soviet Union, its main effect is to weed out religious believers, particularly Quakers and Jehovah's Witnesses.

   As a Quaker from Pennsylvania and a lifelong pacifist, Gonaver objected to the California oath as an infringement of her rights of free speech and religious freedom. She offered to sign the pledge if she could attach a brief statement expressing her views, a practice allowed by other state institutions. But Cal State Fullerton rejected her statement and insisted that she sign the oath if she wanted the job. "I wanted it on record that I am a pacifist," said Gonaver, 38.

California State University officials say they were simply following the law and did not discriminate against Gonaver because all employees are required to sign the oath. Clara Potes-Fellow, a Cal State spokeswoman, said the university does not permit employees to submit personal statements with the oath. "The position of the university is that her entire added material was against the law," Potes-Fellow said. All state, city, county, public school, community college and public university employees—about 2.3 million people—are covered by the law, although noncitizens are not required to sign.

"The way it's laid out, a noncitizen member of Al Qaeda could work for the university, but not a citizen Quaker," she said. (Richard C. Paddock, "Teacher Fired for Refusing to Sign Loyalty Oath," *Los Angeles Times*, 2 May 2008)

Part Two

In the excerpts below, decide if the author is making an argument. If so, set out the argument and state the conclusion—even if that conclusion is implied and not explicitly stated. Note also the key pieces of evidence.

1. The defense attorney in the *Sacco & Vanzetti* case (1921) insisted the eyewitness testimony was not reliable. He said, "None of the seven eyewitnesses was at all times certain of his or her identification. Andrews and Pelser had told a defense investigator that they could not make an identification. Splaine and Devlin only briefly saw a man leaning out of an automobile from a distance of over 70 feet. None of the witnesses identified Sacco until well after his arrest. The witnesses were not required to pick Sacco out of a line-up. Several of the closest witnesses to the crime were *not* able to identify Sacco" ("Sacco & Vanzetti Trial: A Summary of Key Evidence," www.law .umkc.edu/faculty/projects).

2. The prosecution insists the case is strong against Sacco: Sacco was absent from his job at the 3-K shoe factory on the day of the crime. The consulate clerk in Boston, who Sacco said he visited, could not remember him (although this is not surprising, since the clerk sees several hundred persons per day). After his arrest, Sacco told lies about his recent whereabouts, denied knowing Boda, and denied holding anarchist or radical beliefs. His explanation for carrying a gun at the time of his arrest was implausible. The prosecution suggested that these lies showed consciousness of guilt ("Sacco & Vanzetti Trial: A Summary of Key Evidence," www.law.umkc .edu/faculty/projects).

3. There are currently 70 million grandparents in the United States, one-third of all American adults. The average age of a first-time grandparent is 48, and 6 percent of American children live with their grandparents. It's not that this older generation doesn't care about its own security, it's that we also care intensely about our children's children. And we vote (Ellen Goodman, "The Granny Voters Getting Out the Vote," *Washington Post*, 11 Sep 2004).

4. A prosecutor in the trial of a software programmer, Hans Reiser, accused
    of killing his estranged wife, showed jurors a photograph of the couple's
    two young children as he summed up his case on Tuesday. Although no
    body was ever found, prosecutor Paul Hora contends Reiser killed his
    wife, Nina. He said Nina Reiser would never have left her children to
    wonder night after night where she was. She would never go back to her
    native Russia without her children. Her abandoned minivan was found
    with her purse inside, along with sacks of groceries, by that time rotting,
    that she had bought before going to Hans Reiser's house. "There's no
    doubt she's dead. That's what all this means," Hora said. The evidence
    may be circumstantial, he said, but "it's powerful. It's convincing. It's
    persuasive and it's the truth." He noted that Reiser was experienced in
    judo and that Nina Reiser's blood was found on a pillar near Reiser's
    front door ("Reiser Prosecutor: We Know Enough," *KTVU News*, www.
    ktvu.com, 16 Apr 2008).

5. Defense attorney William Du Bois Monday portrayed missing Nina Reiser
    as a woman on the run, not the victim of a heinous murder. Her husband
    Hans Reiser is accused of her murder, but Nina's body has never been
    found. Du Bois said Nina Reiser could easily run off to her native Russia
    where her two young children were with her mother. He said, "We have
    someone who has contacts across the world. . . . She's as comfortable in
    Europe as she is here." Du Bois rejected the claim that Nina would never
    abandon her children. Du Bois said, "I submit that the mantra that she
    would never leave her children does not apply because they wound up liv-
    ing with Nina's mother in St. Petersburg, Russia, so at least they're in the
    care of her family." Du Bois also told jurors not to be influenced by Hans
    Reiser's strange behavior. There was never a history of domestic violence
    involving the couple ("Defense: Nina Reiser Is in Hiding," *KTVU News*,
    7 Apr 2008).

6. In a case that appears to broaden the prosecution of women who pass
    drugs to their infants through their bodies, a woman was sentenced here
    Monday to six years in prison because her breast milk, tainted with meth-
    amphetamine, had killed her baby daughter. In recent years, 160 women
    in 24 states have been charged with delivering drugs to their babies either
    during pregnancy or through the umbilical cord immediately after child-
    birth. But the case here in this town 40 miles southeast of Los Angeles is
    apparently the first in the nation based on the passing of drugs through
    breast milk ("Mother Gets 6 Years for Drugs in Breast Milk," *The New
    York Times*, 28 Oct 1999).

7. While dining with the abductees [who claimed to be abducted by aliens],
    I found out something very revealing: not one of them recalled being
    abducted immediately after the experience. In fact, for most of them,
    many years went by before they "remembered" the experience. How was

this memory recalled? Under hypnosis. . . . Memory is a complex phenomenon involving distortions, deletions, additions, and, sometimes, complete fabrication. Psychologists call this *confabulation*—mixing fantasy with reality to such an extent that it is impossible to sort them out. . . . Every parent has stories about the fantasies their children create. My daughter once described to my wife a purple dragon we saw on our hike in the local hills that day (Michael Shermer, *Why People Believe Weird Things,* Heury Holt, 1998).

8. An appeals court said a man can press a claim for emotional distress after learning a former lover had used his sperm to have a baby. But he can't claim theft, the ruling said, because the sperm were hers to keep. [The plaintiff] Phillips accuses Dr. Sharon Irons of a "calculated, profound personal betrayal" after their affair six years ago, saying she secretly kept semen after they had oral sex, then used it to get pregnant. Phillips was ordered to pay about $800 a month in child support, said Irons' attorney, Enrico Mirabelli. Phillips sued Irons, claiming he has had trouble sleeping and eating and has been haunted by "feelings of being trapped in a nightmare," court papers state. The higher court ruled that, if Phillips' story is true, Irons "deceitfully engaged in sexual acts, which no reasonable person would expect could result in pregnancy, to use plaintiff's sperm in an unorthodox, unanticipated manner yielding extreme consequences." The judges dismissed the fraud and theft claims, agreeing with Irons that she didn't steal the sperm. "There's a 5-year-old child here," Mirabelli said. "Imagine how a child feels when your father says he feels emotionally damaged by your birth" (Carla K. Johnson, "Man Can Sue over Surprise Pregnancy," *ABC News,* abcnews.go.com, 24 Feb 2005).

9. Legal scholar Paul Butler observes that imprisonment used to be a last resort. This changed in the 1980s when its use increased, mainly against blacks and Latinos. "At the same time we had black and Latino men becoming the leaders of youth culture. We had them inventing a dominant form of popular culture," Butler said. Almost inevitably, Butler suggests, hip-hoppers began to comment on crime and punishment in their music. He writes, "Hip-hop culture makes a strong case for a transformation of American criminal justice. . . . Its message is one that we should heed" (Jabari Asim, "Crime, Punishment and Hip-Hop," *Washington Post,* 14 Jun 2004).

10. "Little girls and their big sisters are being encouraged to get dressed up [for Halloween], in many cases, like child prostitutes. Then, they wander the night judging and being judged by their friends as to how well they meet the provocative standard and begging for candy from strangers. It can be very hard for parents to find an alternative to letting them do it, short of having a war in the family or making their kids miserable. This is a continuation of what's been going on for quite a while: Halloween costumes are reflecting an increasingly sexualized childhood. They often reflect the stars and starlets and

popular culture role models that girls have, starting with Disney princesses or Hannah Montana when girls are young. But even traditional favorites, like witches and pirates, are sexier every year. And French maids are quite the thing for tweens and teens. . . . Sexy is part of that marketing to girls—just as macho and violent has become the way to market things to boys" (Diane E. Levin, as quoted by Melissa Healy, "Selling Sexy to Girls," *Los Angeles Times,* 27 Oct 2008).

Analysis of an Article or Argument

Once we feel comfortable handling evidence, we can tackle all sorts of arguments, large and small. Let's start with the title, to see if it sets the stage for any interpretation that may follow. The way things are labeled or titled may shape the way in which they are perceived.

Notice, for example, the title of the article on the Chinatown case we examined earlier. The altercation between Detective Kelly and Mr. Huang was called a "beating." However, in the article, it was called a "scuffle." There is quite a difference: A "scuffle" is generally considered fairly minor, where no one gets hurt; in contrast, a "beating" usually refers to something more severe. The judge must decide whether this was a "scuffle," a "beating," or something else. The severity of Huang's or Kelly's injuries would be a factor in coming to a decision. The language used to describe the incident shapes our understanding of the incident.

Basics

Central to an analysis is an examination of the key claims or arguments. Clarify what is being argued (the thesis), and then set out the premises. Next pull out and weigh the evidence carefully. We may be headed in the wrong direction if vital pieces of evidence are missing. Similarly, look at any assumptions. What we assume affects how we think and what we think about, so decide if the assumptions are warranted or unwarranted.

Checking for Bias

An analysis of an article involves looking at the way the article is structured; determining the author's position, frame of reference, and method of approach; examining the use of language; and checking for bias. It is important to be on the lookout for bias. There may be bias as shown through the use of language, revealing the values favored by the author. There may be bias in the very way in which evidence is presented (e.g., the author may skew the article in favor of one side). It could be that key evidence for one side is missing or distorted, ignoring or underplaying one side rather than fairly representing both sides.

Your personal reaction is generally a separate issue from an analysis. You could incorporate reactions at the end—say, right before the conclusion—to add a personal note to your essay. This is not formally part of the analysis. However, if your analysis leads to your reflections, then the personal angle could be relevant.

Group or Individual Exercise

Directions: Read the article excerpt below about Taco Bell and the use of genetically engineered corn that is not for human consumption. Then answer the questions that follow.

Genetically engineered corn that has not been approved for human consumption has found its way into Taco Bell taco shells sold in supermarkets, says a biotech watchdog group. The group, Genetically Engineered Food Alert, is calling on the Food and Drug Administration to recall the taco shells. . . . The group says the corn has characteristics that suggest it could cause allergic reactions, including nausea and shock. The FDA has had no reports of anyone becoming ill from eating the tacos and has not verified the claims. But a spokeswoman says the agency, with the Environmental Protection Agency, is "actively looking into the issue," and if the allegations are proved, the product will be pulled from the market.

Larry Bohlen of the environmental group Friends of the Earth, one of the members of the Food Alert campaign, says the group does not know of any health effects related to the tacos, but "the American public had no way of knowing whether an allergic reaction could be tied to" the biotech corn. Bohlen says only Taco Bell–brand shells sold in supermarkets have been tested, but "we're going to next test taco shells from Taco Bell restaurants." Kraft spokesman Michael Mudd says the company is having an independent lab test the taco shells. "The goal all of us share is the safest food supply possible," Mudd says. "As much progress as we've made, we have to continue to improve it."

Lisa Dry of the Biotechnology Industry Organization says the FDA is planning to do its own testing of the taco shells, and results could be available within three days. "We don't actually know whether this corn actually did make it into these Taco Bell taco shells," she says. She questioned the accuracy of lab tests conducted by Genetic Id of Fairfield, Iowa. "This lab has in the past not had accurate results. The testing process is complicated." ("Taco Bell Asked to Hold the Chalupas Biotech Corn Found in Grocery Taco Shells," *USA Today,* 19 Sep 2000)

Answer the following:

1. State the three strongest pieces of evidence *for* pulling the taco shells from Taco Bell restaurants.

2. State the three strongest pieces of evidence *against* pulling the taco shells from Taco Bell restaurants (i.e., for allowing Taco Bell to continue using them at the present time).

3. Are there any questions you would need to have answered before you'd believe the corn should be pulled from the market?

Analyzing Short Essays

In a short essay or article (less than five pages), be selective. Zero in on the most important aspects; you cannot do everything. Nevertheless, if you are writing clearly and concisely, you can do a lot in a brief analysis.

Ingredients of a Strong Analysis

1. **State what is being argued or discussed.**
   - State the thesis or focus of the essay or article.
   - Note your assessment of the article's persuasiveness.

2. **Clarify how it is being argued or discussed.**
   - Note the key points made and issues raised.
   - Include a brief statement as to how the argument or discussion is structured.

3. **Discuss the use of language.**
   - Note value-laden, biased, or prejudicial language.
   - Watch for the use of metaphors and connotations of words.
   - Note when the language is clear, concise, and accessible for the targeted audience.
   - Note the degree of clarity in the language.

4. **Set out the strengths.**
   - Note arguments that best support the author's thesis.
   - Note valuable points or insights in the exposition.
   - Point out powerful uses of language, effective use of statistics or credible sources, pertinent examples, and well-supported details.

5. **Set out the weaknesses.**
   - Note any aspects that diminish the quality of the article or eassy.
   - Note any contradictions or inconsistencies in the author's reasoning.
   - Point out when statistics are used poorly or are out of date.
   - Note any speculation or unsupported claims.
   - Watch for unfounded assumptions or references (witnesses or "experts") that are not credible.

6. **Assess the article or essay for persuasiveness.**
   - Watch for omissions.
   - See if the evidence is strong.
   - Notice if the language helps or hinders.
   - Decide if the weaknesses are too great.
   - See if the argument is fully developed.
   - See if illustrations and examples back up claims.
   - Watch for questionable assumptions.
   - Assess the strength of the reasoning.

Proceeding with Your Analysis

Even in a short analysis, include the six aspects listed above. If, however, the author's use of language is nonproblematic, then a discussion of the language may not be necessary. Carefully examine the way an article or essay is structured to see if it gives a fair presentation of the issues under consideration.

You can only evaluate the argument when you have identified the conclusion (thesis) and supporting premises (evidence). *Be careful here!* Some writers do have a thesis, but you may not find it until three, four, or five paragraphs into the paper. Such fishing expeditions may be necessary, so be ready.

Exercises

Part One

1. Set out the thesis and key claims in the following argument:

    Kimosabe must have eaten the sock. He's often a bad dog when left inside the house, and he was alone all day long. The socks were out on the table. He's been known to eat socks left on the floor. The window was wide open, but I don't think a stray cat or dog would come in and take a sock. Only a few other things are missing. So it's surely Kimosabe who ate the sock!

2. Set out the thesis and key claims in the following argument:

    Silvio lost four socks this week. Four different socks. He had done his wash and usually dumps the clothes out of the dryer onto the bed. He looked around the bed, but the four socks weren't anywhere to be found. One later turned up stuck on the inside of the washing machine. So only three are officially missing now. There is no sign of a break-in. There is no scientific explanation why socks put in washing machines should disappear. Nothing else gets lost when you wash. This goes to show, we should buy socks in multiples—never a pair at a time.

3. Set out the thesis and key claims in the following argument:

    Troy didn't do as well at the box office as expected. It "only" made around $130 million. Maybe people are tired of seeing men in skirts. On second thought, maybe the problem is that Brad Pitt is not meant to wear a toga. I know *Braveheart* did just fine, and Mel Gibson wore a kilt. And who can forget Russell Crowe in *Gladiator*? Those two seemed to be okay in their costumes—but Brad Pitt just doesn't fit the profile. He is just too contemporary. Brad's the kind of guy you expect to see at a Hollywood nightclub. But who in their right mind would look around a nightclub for Mel Gibson or Russell Crowe? Yeah, that's why *Troy* tanked.

4. Set out the thesis and key claims in the following argument; then decide if it looks like a strong case:

    Twelve hundred people are complaining of ailments since the El Al accident. The "black box" cockpit voice recorder disappeared from the evidence bin where firefighters insist they put it. Five hours into the rescue effort, after Dutch security police had cleared the crash site of emergency workers and the press, men in white-hooded fire suits were seen jumping from a helicopter into the smoldering rubble and carrying off debris in unmarked trucks. Police videotapes were erased before investigators had a chance to review them. Vital details of the cargo's hazardous contents (recently revealed to be the deadly nerve gas sarin) were kept secret for years. The disaster took 43 lives on the ground and four more on the 747 Boeing jet. This whole thing looks to be either a monumental bungle or a cover-up. (Carol J. Williams, "Dutch Probe '92 Jet Crash after News of Toxic Cargo," *Los Angeles Times,* 13 Oct 1998)

5. What are the three strongest pieces of evidence in the following argument that might be used to convince one of your friends or fellow students *not* to use steroids?

Performance-enhancing drugs and treatments have become a bigger problem than ever in international competition. Manfred Ewald, 73, oversaw the East German doping program that flourished in the 1970s and 1980s. He and his cohorts are accused of giving steroids to girls as young as 11—and intimidating those who raised objections, accusing them of "cowardice." The women suffered a wide range of health problems. Some became infertile because of the steroids. Many endured excessive body hair, deepening of their voices, and liver, kidney, and menstrual problems. One told the court that when she was 19, her liver failed—because of the mixture of steroids and contraceptive pills she had been taking. Athletes using steroids might think twice about risking liver damage and other long-term health problems. (Adapted from Steve Kettmann, "Doping Haunts E. Germany," *Wired News,* 25 May 2000.)

6. Set out the conclusion and key claims in the following argument:

Joel Myers recently learned that a collection of American Indian artifacts given by his great-uncle Cassius to the University of Nebraska may soon be on the auction block. Myers was not even aware that a small part of the collection once belonged to his relatives. Myers said he wasn't sure what to do—hire an attorney or just save his money and try to buy the items when they showed up on eBay. Once the museum was contacted by Myers, it was clear that the artifacts they were going to auction weren't just any old bunch of stuff. They have personal value to Myers. Subsequently, the Museum should hand over the artifacts to him. (Bill Donovan, "Oregon Man Questions Right of Museum to Sell Off Items Given by His Relative," *The Indian Trader,* July 2003)

7. So is this a fair decision? Read about the case of dog owners in condos and discuss the reasoning:

Paula Terifaj bought a condo in 1995. At the time, there was an unwritten no-pet rule, but she would bring along her little terrier, Lucy. When Lucy died, Terifaj got a boxer she named Rose. The condo owners association repeatedly warned and fined her for bringing Rose to the condo. In 2000, the association voted in a no-pet clause. They ended up in court. One issue was whether after-the-fact restrictions in condo covenants are valid. In June 2004 the California Supreme Court ruled that the adopted amendment was effective against all homeowners, whether or not they voted for it and irrespective of when they acquired the condo. Justice Moreno said such restrictions had to be uniformly applied and to do otherwise would undermine the stability of the community. He added that he had no quarrel about the benefits of pet ownership "but that is not the issue in this case." (John Roemer, "Condo Group Can Ban Dog, Court Decides," *Daily [Law] Journal*, 15 Jun 2004)

8. If you were hired by Paula Terifaj to write a two to three paragraph response to the decision, what would you say in defense of *her* argument (in 7.) that she should be able to bring Rose to the condo?

9. Discuss the quality of the reasoning in the following ad for Kellogg's cereal:

Kids who eat breakfast perform better in school. We all grew up hearing how breakfast is the most important meal of the day. And in fact, studies from around the world show that kids who eat breakfast perform better during their morning school hours. So how do you get them to eat breakfast every day? By serving them their favorite cereal with milk. For more information on the importance of breakfast to kids and the nutrition of cereal, call us at 1-800-468-9004. *Cereal: Eat it for life.*

Part Two

Directions: Read about surveillance cameras in New York and then answer the questions that follow.

In New York City, there are cameras lurking on the perimeter of Washington Square Park, disguised as street lamps. They dot the walls of a new building on West Fourth Street, in the form of decorative bulbs. Bill Brown, who conducts the "Surveillance Camera Outdoor Walking Tour," says the number of surveillance cameras is growing. "Like mushrooms in the forest," he says.

He says that most of the cameras are disguised to look like lamps or ornaments. By his count, the number of surveillance cameras in Manhattan has tripled in the last five years. In 1999 the New York Civil Liberties Union counted 2,397 cameras in New York—he estimates that it has jumped to 7,200 in the year 2004. He contends that this is a sign of creeping control by the authorities. They lull people into a sense of security, dulling vigilance among city residents and weakening communities.

Brown is concerned that in the not-too-distant future, the different camera systems will all be linked. As the number of cameras increase, there are virtually no laws to govern their use. This raises difficult legal questions. A privacy consultant says, "The general rule is what goes on in public has no reasonable expectation of privacy."

He continues, "I can walk in front of your house and take a picture. But suppose I put a surveillance camera in front of your house 24 hours a day? No one has addressed that in any particular way." Critics of the cameras say they do not reduce crime, that watchers get tired of staring at empty street corners and begin peeping at people. A camera at a foreign consulate was found to have been trained on a nearby apartment, Brown said. (Sabrina Tavernise, "Watching Big Brother," *The New York Times*, 17 Jan 2004)

Answer <u>one</u> *of the following:*

1. One day you come home to discover a surveillance camera is aimed at your house/apartment entranceway. Set out an argument that this violates your right to privacy.

2. You are tired of your neighbors dealing drugs. The cops come when you complain, but the drug-dealing resumes after they leave. Give an argument

that you have the right to set up a surveillance camera aimed at the street in front of your house.

3. The nice new department store in town, Blossomdale's, is afraid of being wiped out by shoplifters. They want to stick surveillance cameras *everywhere* in their store. They are willing to put up signs to notify shoppers that they are being videotaped wherever they are in Blossomdale's. Explain to them why this is—or is not—a justifiable plan.

Part Three

1. Should prisoners on death row be allowed a choice between two different forms of execution? Read the following and take a stand:

   At least 30 states, including Kentucky, use the same combination of three drugs to execute prisoners: sodium thiopental, which induces unconsciousness; pancuronium bromide, which paralyzes the muscles; and potassium chloride, which causes cardiac arrest. Arguing in a 2008 Supreme Court case on lethal injection, an attorney [for the inmates] stated that if the first drug does not work, the second induces a "terrifying, conscious paralysis" and the third causes an "excruciating burning pain as it courses through the veins." The Kentucky inmates were not asking to be spared execution or injection. Rather, they wanted the court to order Kentucky to switch to injection of a single, massive dose of barbiturates—the same method used to euthanize animals. (William Braningen, "Supreme Court Upholds Use of Lethal Injection," *The Washington Post,* 16 Apr 2008)

2. According to Kathryn Jean Lopez in "Egg Heads" (*The Human Life Review* 244), being an egg donor is no piece of cake. Read this excerpt, and construct an argument for or against ads for egg donation being allowed on college campuses and in college publications.

   Donating a human egg is much more complicated than donating a sperm. Sperm donation is over in less than an hour; egg donation takes the donor around 56 hours and includes tests, ultrasound, injections, and retrieval. Once a donor is accepted into a program, she is given hormones to stimulate the ovaries. A doctor surgically removes the eggs from the donor's ovary and fertilizes them with the designated sperm. As a result, donating eggs is not a pleasant way to make money.

3. The Famous Vegetarian: There are a number of famous vegetarians, including Albert Einstein, Alice Walker, Avril Lavigne, Franz Kafka, Gandhi, John Lennon, Mark Twain, Tracy Chapman, Brad Pitt, and Tobey Maguire. You can do a quick search and find many more. Pick a celebrity who is a vegetarian *and* who has explained why he or she is a vegetarian. Then do the following:
   a. Set out *the* famous vegetarian's argument.
   b. Give your assessment of the argument you set out, noting its strengths and weaknesses.

Analyzing Longer Articles

You may feel overwhelmed when asked to analyze an entire chapter or long article (over five pages). Don't be! Try a flow chart to block out the article or a brief summary of each paragraph. Once you get an overview, you are in a better position to do your analysis. Analyzing a long argument requires organization and detail—and involves a range of considerations.

Tips for Analyzing Long Articles

1. **Examine titles and subtitles.**
   - Try to detect the bias or implicit set of values of the author.
   - See if the title is reprehensive of the content.
   - Keep in mind the frame of reference point of view and its possible impact.
2. **Review the language.**
   - Look for loaded terms (positive and negative), false-natural terms, technical or scientific terms, connotations, descriptive language (adjectives, imagery, etc.).
   - Note the impact of race, gender, religion, age, and ethnicity on descriptions.
   - Check for bias or hidden value assumptions.
3. **Check the structure.**
   - Block out, outline, create a flowchart, or list the sequence of information (to see whose side is given first and last and whether it is a balanced presentation).
4. **Check for testimony and credible sources.**
   - Examine credibility and potential conflict of interest versus the impartiality of the person being cited.
   - Decide if the person or source in question is credible.
   - Check for bias.
5. **Examine factual reporting**
   - Focus on three things: the source, the sufficiency of information, and any bias.
   - Look at the reporter, the scope and detail of the report, and any omissions.
6. **Literary analysis.**
   - Examine themes; patterns; plot line and narrative structure; character development; diversity of perspective; connections between form and content; moral, philosophical, and social concerns; use of language; sentence style and structure; and symbols and images (mythological or metaphorical).
7. **Check for sociocultural frames.**
   - Be attentive to the treatment of social issues or moral problems, cultural baggage and biases, and societal attitudes.
   - Look for the social and cultural context of the author and work.

8. **Review the use of statistics.**
   - Look at the date of the study, the size and diversity of the sample (is it representative of the target population?), the percentage used in drawing conclusions, the relevance of the study to the topic under discussion, and any assumptions or cultural attitudes embedded in the study.
9. **Look for fallacies.**
   - Note any logical fallacies, and determine the degree to which the author's work is affected.
10. **Focus on argumentation.**
   - Define the problem or clarify the thesis.
   - Separate background information from evidence.
   - Weigh evidence.
   - Assess support (e.g., credibility of sources and documentation).
   - Assess testimony, use of facts, and factual reporting.
   - Recognize and assess circumstantial evidence.
   - Recognize and assess statistical evidence.
   - Recognize and discuss any value claims.
   - Examine the use of analogies and metaphors.
   - Examine any causal or other inductive arguments.
   - Examine any deductive arguments.
   - If deductive, test for validity, The conclusion would *have* to be true if the premises were true, and thus the argument is valid.
   - If deductive, test for soundness: the argument is valid plus the premises are actually true, so the argument is sound.

Exercises

Part One

1. Analyze the following argument on cell phones:

   Cell phones have become the digital equivalent of Hansel and Gretel's breadcrumbs. When a cell phone is turned on, it broadcasts an identification number to the closest antennas, which allow the carrier to chart its customers. It's a simple matter—known as triangulation—to track the signal as it arrives at different towers, then calculate the location of the phone based on time differences. The police have taken full advantage of this tracking trick, though—technically, at least—they need a court order to access the information. Earlier this year, Timothy Crosby, 40, was busted for raping and robbing a Brooklyn woman after the police located him by homing in on his cell phone signal. In November 2000, authorities pursued Kofi Apea Orleans-Lindsay for allegedly killing a Maryland state trooper during a buy-and-bust operation. Police used cell data to track Orleans-Lindsay to Brooklyn, where they arrested him. (Adam L. Penenberg, "The Surveillance Society," *Wired*, Dec 2000)

2. The USA Patriot Act has made it easier for law enforcement to go after suspects than in 2000. They no longer need a court order to track cell phones. And why not? On the other hand, should we be worried about eroding civil rights? Set out your three to four strongest reasons for *and* against the authorities having the right to listen in on your cell phone calls.

Part Two

Directions: The following passage concerns an oak tree whose limbs extended into a neighboring yard—and the neighbor chopped them off. Read about the case and take a stand, setting out your argument.

The action: Scott and Carolyn Scharg purchased a home in Calabasas, California. A neighbor's oak tree was growing over the walkways and onto the roof. They had the tree trimmed to avoid roof damages. They did not know they had to get the city's approval, and Carolyn Scharg said they had to cut the tree in order to get homeowner's insurance. The house had three chimneys, and trees were growing over them. Scharg argued that this created a fire hazard. The fire department requires trees to be at least 10 feet from the chimneys, she said.

The reaction: Patrick Seymour, who owned the tree, wasn't home the day the tree was framed. He said they butchered his tree and that this was a violation of the city ordinance protecting the oak trees. The Calabasas Tree Board met to resolve the situation. Carolyn Scharg said she didn't know anything about an ordinance that required permits to trim oak trees—and she even didn't know it was an oak tree, since "it didn't have acorns on it."

The city's response: The Tree Board asked the Schargs to pay $10,000 in mitigation fees. The Schargs appealed to the city council, but it upheld the board's decision. Kay Greeley, arborist for Calabasas, said the tree's recovery could take 10 years. The $10,000 is only a fraction of the cost to repair the damages that the Schargs created, Greeley said. The tree, according to Greeley, had a value of $71,400 before the Schargs cut it back and said it is not clear if the tree will survive. And if the tree doesn't survive, then Seymour's house and other dwellings below could be vulnerable to a landslide given it's on a hill side. The Schargs have said they wouldn't pay $1. Greeley expects the fight to continue (based on Michael Picarella, "Neighbors, City at Odds over What to Do," *The Acorn Hill,* 8 Aug 2002).

Group or Individual Exercise

The Global Dimension

Physicians for Human Rights (PHR) has called for Congress to investigate allegations by detainees that they have been forcibly drugged (i.e., without their consent). (Joby Warnick, "Detainees Allege Being Drugged, Questioned," *Washington*

Post, 22 Apr 2008) Read the following, state the key concerns raised, and set out their argument. Note what sort of evidence they cite as support.

> Physicians for Human Rights (PHR) urgently called on Congress and the Department of Justice, with the involvement of the FBI, to each immediately investigate allegations by detainees that they were forcibly drugged while in U.S. custody. These claims, reported today [April 22, 2008] by the *Washington Post,* also raise new and deeply troubling questions about what role health professionals may have played in violating detainees' human rights, domestic and international law, and codes of medical ethics established since World War II.
>
> The report claims that forced medication may have been used for a number of purposes including as a chemical restraint, as a facilitator of interrogation, and possibly for therapeutic purposes in the absence of informed consent. Any use in interrogation of mind-altering substances or other procedures calculated to profoundly disrupt the senses or personality is criminal under U.S. law, including the War Crimes Act and the Anti-Torture Statute. . . .
>
> Simultaneous Congressional and criminal investigations are necessary, according to PHR, to determine whether medical expertise and personnel were used to drug detainees for purposes of interrogation, sedate them for transport, and medicate them without their consent for other non-therapeutic purposes. PHR also called on the Department of Defense to investigate whether military physicians and other health professionals have violated their professional ethical standards and detainee rights, including denying detainees informed consent for therapeutic use of medication.
>
> "There is no acceptable use for mind-altering drugs in interrogation, so any use of medication to aid in interrogation of detainees in U.S. custody would be experimental. As such, it would be a clear violation of international codes and domestic law in place since the doctors' trials at Nuremberg," said Dr. Scott A. Allen, MD, a medical advisor to PHR and Co-Director of the Center for Prisoner Health and Human Rights at Brown University.
>
> "Additionally, use of medication as a restraint is unethical. Even therapeutic use of forced medication under U.S. military regulations is not ethically permissible in the absence of informed consent except for the rarest of cases, such as treatment for a highly infectious disease like tuberculosis." (Joby Warnick, "Detainees Allege Being Drugged, Questioned," *Washington Post,* 22 Apr 2008)

Wrestling Down Arguments: Dismantling Longer Articles

Real-life applications of our critical thinking skills are all around us. They pop up when we read the newspaper, turn on the TV, listen to the radio, talk to friends, look at websites, and glance up at billboards. Let's put our critical thinking tools to work by tackling longer articles. Our focus will be on articles in which someone stakes out a position and then offers a justification in an attempt to persuade us to their way of thinking. Our goal is to dismantle the argument so we can analyze it and thereby assess its worth. This can be done in a number of ways; having a few techniques to draw from can be vital. Being able to organize the argument is a key step in the assessment process.

Here are some powerful methods for breaking down longer arguments:

Method 1: The flowchart
Method 2: The highlighting of key phrases
Method 3: The standard form of the argument
Method 4: The traditional outline

We will look at each method in action, to see how to use it. After all four methods are laid out, you can select from several articles to put any or all of them to use.

Method 1: The Flowchart

The first method we'll look at is the flowchart. With a flowchart, we break down an article so we can see its structure. Once we get an overview of the structure, setting out the thesis and supporting evidence is a much less daunting task.

We will apply the method to an article that uses two parallel analogies. One analogy is between prisons and schools. The other is between what the author, Anthony Paul Farley, calls the "new slavery" (oppression of blacks today) and the "old slavery" (oppression of blacks in the past). He argues that there is a link between the "new slavery" and the dual failure of urban schools and the prison system. Read the article and try to pull out the key point(s) of *each paragraph*.

Failing Schools, Prisons Produce People Doomed to Failure

Anthony Paul Farley

Daily Journal, June 14, 2004

Two million people are imprisoned in the United States. The majority of them are black. This is slavery in a new form, as is the scandalous quality of the educational resources meted out to the heirs of *Brown v. Board of Education*. The attack on freedom and the attack on literacy are related. Among the many thousands gone the way of incarceration are few, very few, who ever had the experience of a decent school.

Far too many of our urban schools resemble prisons. Visit one of these schools, and you will see how dreams are killed at an early age by educators who do not love the children that they have promised to educate. Dreams are killed by an educational-industrial complex that creates conditions that make such love impossible to imagine, as an ever-more-color-lined nation abandons altogether the twin dreams of education and emancipation.

Many, far too many, of these dreamless children find themselves leaving their loveless schools only to land in prison. Our failing schools, like our failing prisons, are overwhelmingly and unconscionably black. The failure of the school and the failure of the prison together create the color line. The new slavery—linked to the old by the color line—is the product of this two-stranded failure.

Failing schools produce illiteracy just as surely as failing prisons produce recidivism. In the antebellum South, the dream of the literate slave was always emancipation, just as the dream of the emancipated slave was always literacy. Reading and freedom have always been connected in the minds of former slaves and former slave masters in the United States.

We cannot forget that in the United States it was illegal to educate slaves, because the same people who were prisoners of the old slavery are prisoners of the new slavery. We cannot forget, because the same people who were forcibly kept illiterate then are kept illiterate now. Slavery is present today, in the prisons and in the schools.

Our schools fail. Our prisons fail. The former produce illiteracy while the latter produce recidivism—and both kill dreams of an emancipated future in the United States. When institutions fail year after year, we must re-examine what we mean by failure. When the reformers respond to this year's failure with last year's failed solutions, we must examine what we mean by reform. All these failed yet endlessly recycled reforms continue the color line's division of the United States into two nations: black and white, separate and unequal. And there seems to be no exit. What is to be done?

This is being done in Dorchester, Mass.: Since 1994, we have conducted a literature program for women and men who have been convicted in the Dorchester District Court for various offenses. The Dorchester experiment is part of a statewide program called Changing Lives Through Literacy, founded by professor Robert Waxler of the English department of the University of Massachusetts, Dartmouth, and by Judge Robert Kane. The founding Dorchester organizers include two judges, Sydney Hanlon and Thomas May; two college English professors, Ann Murphy and Taylor Stoehr; a law professor (me); six dedicated probation officers; and a number of Boston College law students.

The program has been an outstanding success. For many of the participants, it was the first time that they ever read a book from cover to cover. Many have confessed to me their late realization that reading can be liberating and enjoyable. They look back in anger at the ways that their schools succeeded in causing them to fail themselves by producing failing grades. They realize that they can read and that they have ideas about great literature. And this causes them to look forward with hope.

At the end of each term, we hold a voluntary graduation ceremony in the District Court. The graduates invite their family and friends. Most years, one or more of the graduates gives a short valedictory speech to the audience. Each graduate is presented with a diploma. Tears and applause always accompany the graduation ceremony. Afterwards everyone joins the judges in chambers for tea.

A literature program is just the beginning. If a university-level course can be taught as probation, then anything can be taught anywhere to anyone. Probation offices all over the nation can be transformed into schools. Prisons too can be transformed, into places of elementary, secondary, university and graduate education. And with success in the transformation of our failed prisons into successful schools must come success in the transformation of our failed schools.

Because our schools have become prisons, our prisons, and the urban schools that resemble them, are hated. They are hated because they show, more than any speeches or proclamations or court rulings or acts of legislation, the true attitude of the United States toward blacks and our dreams of education and emancipation. Our prisons, whatever they may be labeled, must be transformed into schools. If this seems like a dream, it is no less real than the nightmare we will live if our nation remains half slave and half free.

One program is not enough. All of our prisons need to become schools, and all of our schools need to become limitless palaces worthy of the boundless imaginations of youth. To break the color line, to save our bodies and souls from the nightmare we have manufactured, to renounce the past and create a decent society at long last, we must fight for literacy and emancipation as for bread and roses.

Which side are you on?

Source: Anthony Paul Farley is an associate professor at Boston College Law School. Copyright 2004 *Daily Journal Corp.* Reprinted and/or posted with permission.

Setting Out the Flowchart.   Let's break down the article with a flowchart to see Farley's thesis and support. In the table below, we have numbered each paragraph and briefly labeled what's in each paragraph in the middle column. In the third column, we set out a *brief* overview. The point is to summarize, not to rewrite the paragraph. Let's take a look:

Flowchart: Anthony Paul Farley's Article, "Failing Schools"

PARAGRAPH	FOCUS	OVERVIEW OF PARAGRAPH
Paragraph 1	Thesis: Prisons are like a new form of slavery. (Analogy 1)	*Links prison rates to literacy problems*: "This is slavery in a new form, as is the scandalous quality of the educational resources. The attack on freedom and the attack on literacy are related."
Paragraph 2	Parallel to slavery continued	*Focus on schools*: Argument on the condition of urban schools and their effect on children.
Paragraph 3	Analogy between schools and prisons leads to "new slavery"	*Analogy*: Poor schools linked to prisons—both fail our children. Resulting product ("the new slavery") is stipulated.
Paragraph 4	Schools/prisons analogy continued	*Analogy continued*: Goes further on the links between schools and prisons and continues parallel to slavery ("Reading and freedom have always been connected in the minds of former slaves and former slave masters in the United States").
Paragraph 5	Illiteracy in prisons and schools (Analogy 2)	*Illiteracy and slavery*: Slavery's connection to illiteracy—parallels illiteracy in prisoners today. Posits slavery in both schools and prisons.

PARAGRAPH	FOCUS	OVERVIEW OF PARAGRAPH
Paragraph 6	Failure of prisons and schools	*Failure and failed reform*: Both schools and prisons continue to fail. Need to examine what we mean by "failure." Attempts at reform continue segregation mentality ("black and white, separate and unequal").
Paragraph 7	Solution: Introduction of Dorchester case	*Recommendation*: "Turn the prisons into schools": Start with the probation system. *Case in point*: Dorchester, MA
Paragraph 8	Dorchester: Success story	*Dorchester case continued*: "The program has been an outstanding success" and cause for hope.
Paragraph 9	Success story continued	*Dorchester case continued*: Success story continued
Paragraph 10	Application	*Applying the case*: Transforming prisons to schools/places of education. *Predicted effect*: Success in the transformation of prisons into successful schools must bring success in the transformation of schools.
Paragraph 11	Argument why schools are hated	*Argument*: Schools are hated because they show the "true attitude of the United States toward blacks." *Recommendation*: "Our prisons, whatever they may be labeled, must be transformed into schools."
Paragraph 12	Recommendations	*Recommendations continued*: Need more than one success story (the Dorchester case): "All of our prisons need to become schools, and all of our schools need to become limitless palaces worthy of the boundless imaginations of youth." *Reaffirms thesis*: We need the fight for literacy and emancipation to break the color line.
Paragraph 13	Call for action	*Challenge to the reader*: Which side are you on? [You *should* be on this side.]

We can now see the structure of Farley's argument. He starts with his thesis—prisons are parallel to schools in the "new slavery"—and then draws an analogy to the "old slavery." He then proceeds to set out his case, drawing from a successful case that he infers could work as a model for others.

Using an analogy can be very persuasive, so that warrants our attention. Farley links together two big institutions (schools and prisons) and attempts to address the problems that they share. (See Chapter 6 on analogies for a review.)

Method 2: The Highlighting of Key Words

What if you are a doctor or nurse who suspects that a patient is being abused—even tortured? Are you obligated to contact authorities (be a whistle-blower)? What if the authorities prefer that you turn a blind eye to the torture? In the article below, M. Gregg Bloche considers it a duty of doctors and nurses to report abuses and not participate—even if the patient is a suspected terrorist. Read the article, keeping your eyes peeled for key words and phrases.

Physician, Turn Thyself In

M. Gregg Bloche

The New York Times, June 10, 2004

According to press reports, military doctors and nurses who examined prisoners at Abu Ghraib treated swollen genitals, prescribed painkillers, stitched wounds, and recorded evidence of the abuses going on around them. Under international law—as well as the standards of common decency—these medical professionals had a duty to tell those in power what they saw.

Instead, too often, they returned the victims of torture to the custody of their victimizers. Rather than putting a stop to torture, they tacitly abetted it, by patching up victims and staying silent.

The duty of doctors in such circumstances is clear. They must provide needed treatment, then do all they can to keep perpetrators from committing further abuse. This includes keeping detailed records of injuries and their likely causes, performing clinical tests to gather forensic evidence and reporting abuses to those with the will and power to act.

During the 1980's and 1990's, American human rights investigators traveled to many countries with oppressive governments, assembling evidence of medical complicity in torture. A pattern emerged in rogue regimes that claimed pride in their civility: doctors both contained and abetted torture—by treating its victims, returning them to perpetrators and then remaining silent.

I was one of these investigators. I vividly remember the Uruguayan military intelligence chief who spoke to me with contempt about Argentine "barbarians" who made tens of thousands disappear. By contrast, he boasted, in Uruguay the army kept doctors nearby to keep things from getting out of hand. Fewer than 200 Uruguayans died in detention while the army ruled.

Now the American military is essentially ruling Iraq—and it is urgent that we find out what our military doctors, nurses and medics know. They are likely to have kept records.

Already, a medical assessment unearthed by investigators has given the lie to the Pentagon's claim that the former chief of Iraq's air force lost consciousness and died after saying he didn't feel well; the medical report said his death ensued from "asphyxia due to smothering and chest compression."

Congress and others investigating abuse of detainees in Iraq, Guantánamo Bay and elsewhere should quickly obtain all relevant medical records. They should ask independent experts to review these records—and to question military medical personnel about what they saw and heard. Independent doctors should also examine people who say they were abused, using state-of-the-art protocols for documentation of torture and other ill treatment. These protocols make it possible to find patterns of abuse.

Had military doctors come forward immediately with such evidence, brutal practices that have shamed us all could have been stopped at the outset. And had the perpetrators feared exposure through medical findings, they might have been dissuaded from their lawless course.

When guards and interrogators become torturers, doctors are first responders. International law demands that they act as such. In Iraq, it appears, a "don't ask, don't tell" ethic stood in the way. By staying silent for months, until an inquest began, doctors and nurses abandoned their patients. But these doctors and nurses probably saw enough to offer smoking-gun evidence of what went awry at Abu Ghraib and elsewhere. It is time for us to ask, and them to tell.

Source: M. Gregg Bloche teaches Law and Health Policy at Georgetown and Johns Hopkins Universities. Reprinted with the permission of M. Gregg Bloche.

Highlighting Key Words.   Let us now try to pin down the argument by highlighting the key words. Try these steps:

STEP 1: Number each paragraph from the first to the last. Break up long paragraphs so you have a manageable size to work with.

STEP 2: Underline or highlight key terms, concepts, names, and cases.

STEP 3: Look over what you have emphasized.

STEP 4: Summarize the article, using what you highlighted/underlined. On a computer, you can simply delete anything *not* highlighted and then shape what remains as sentences.

STEP 5: Using your summary, set out a statement of the argument.

Applying these steps to Bloche's article, we get a handle on the article's key points.

STEPS 1 AND 2: Number the paragraphs, and mark key words and phrases (in bold below).

1. According to press reports, **military doctors and nurses** who examined prisoners at **Abu Ghraib** treated swollen genitals, prescribed painkillers, stitched wounds, and recorded evidence of the abuses going on around them. **Under international law**—as well as the standards of common decency—these medical professionals **had a duty to tell those in power what they saw.**

2. **Instead,** too often, they returned the victims of torture to the custody of their victimizers. Rather than **putting a stop to torture, they tacitly abetted it,** by patching up victims and **staying silent.**

3. The **duty of doctors** in such circumstances is **clear.** They must **provide needed treatment,** then do all they can to keep perpetrators from committing further abuse. This includes **keeping detailed records** of injuries and their likely causes, performing clinical tests to gather forensic evidence and **reporting abuses** to those with the will and power to act.

4. During the **1980's and 1990's,** American **human rights** investigators traveled to many countries with oppressive governments, assembling **evidence of medical complicity** in torture. A **pattern** emerged in rogue regimes that claimed pride in their civility: **doctors both contained and abetted torture**—by treating its victims, returning them to perpetrators and then remaining silent.

5. I was one of these investigators. I vividly remember the **Uruguayan military intelligence** chief who spoke to me with contempt about Argentine "barbarians" who made tens of thousands disappear. By contrast, he **boasted,** in Uruguay the **army kept doctors nearby to keep things from getting out of** hand. Fewer than 200 Uruguayans died in detention while the army ruled.

6. Now the American military is essentially ruling **Iraq**—and it is urgent that we find out what our military **doctors, nurses and medics** know. They are **likely to have kept records.** Already, a medical assessment unearthed by investigators has given the lie to the Pentagon's claim that the **former chief of Iraq's air force** lost consciousness and **died** after saying he didn't feel well; the **medical report** said his death ensued from "**asphyxia** due to smothering and chest compression."

7. **Congress and others investigating abuse** of detainees in Iraq, Guantánamo Bay and elsewhere should quickly obtain all relevant medical records. They should **ask independent experts to review** these records—and to **question** military medical personnel about what they saw and heard. **Independent doctors should** also **examine people who say they were abused,** using state-of-the-art protocols for documentation of torture and other ill treatment. These protocols make it possible to find patterns of abuse.

8. **Had military doctors come forward** immediately with such evidence, **brutal practices** that have shamed us all **could have been stopped at the outset.** And had the perpetrators feared exposure through medical findings, they might have been dissuaded from their lawless course.

9. When guards and interrogators become torturers, **doctors are first responders.** International law demands that they act as such. **In Iraq,** it appears, a "don't ask, don't tell" ethic stood in the way. By **staying silent** for months, until an inquest began, **doctors and nurses abandoned their patients.** But these **doctors and nurses probably saw enough to offer smoking-gun evidence** of what went awry at Abu Ghraib and elsewhere. It is **time for us to ask and them to tell.**

STEPS 3 AND 4: Read and summarize what you have. Pull out the highlighted words (or delete those not highlighted using your computer). Here's what we get:

1. Military doctors and nurses who examined prisoners at Abu Ghraib under international law had duty to tell those in power what they saw.
2. Instead of putting a stop to torture, they tacitly abetted it, staying silent.

3. Duty of doctors is clear: Provide needed treatment, keeping detailed records and reporting abuses.
4. 1980s and 1990s, human rights evidence of medical complicity. Pattern: doctors both contained and abetted torture.
5. I remember Uruguayan military intelligence boasted, army kept doctors nearby to keep things from getting out of hand.
6. Iraq—doctors, nurses and medics likely to have kept records. Former chief of Iraq's air force died—medical report said "asphyxia due to smothering."
7. Congress and others investigating abuse ask independent experts to review and to question. Independent doctors should examine people who say they were abused; protocols make it possible to find patterns of abuse.
8. Had military doctors come forward, brutal practices could have been stopped at outset.
9. Doctors are first responders. In Iraq, by staying silent, doctors and nurses abandoned their patients. Doctors and nurses probably saw enough to offer smoking-gun evidence. It's time for us to ask and for them to tell.

Now shape your summary. Make only minor additions (like "the" or "and") to smooth out the passage. You do not want to change the author's intent; your goal is to pluck out a summary using the author's own words. We have:

M. Gregg Bloche, "Physician, Turn Thyself In"

Military doctors and nurses who examined prisoners at Abu Ghraib—under international law—had a duty to tell those who are in power what they saw. Instead of putting a stop to torture, they tacitly abetted it, staying silent. The duty of doctors is clear—provide needed treatment, keeping detailed records and reporting abuses. In the 1980s and 1990s, evidence of human rights abuses showed medical complicity. The pattern: Doctors both contained and abetted torture.

I remember Uruguayan military intelligence boasting that the army kept doctors nearby to keep things from getting out of hand. In Iraq doctors, nurses, and medics are likely to have kept records. For example, when the former chief of Iraq's air force died, the medical report said "asphyxia due to smothering."

Congress and others investigating abuse should ask independent experts to review—and to question. Independent doctors should examine people who say they were abused; protocols are possible to find patterns of abuse. Had military doctors come forward, brutal practices could have been stopped at the outset. Doctors are the first responders. In Iraq, by staying silent, doctors and nurses abandoned their patients. Doctors and nurses probably saw enough to offer smoking-gun evidence. It's time for us to ask and for them to tell.

STEP 5: Set out a statement of the argument. From our summary, we can see the author's thesis: Doctors and nurses at Abu Ghraib, Iraq, should come forward to report what they saw and did in the torture of detainees or prisoners. His argument can be set out as follows:

P_1: There is a duty under international law for doctors and nurses to tell those in power what they saw.

P_2: By staying silent, doctors and nurses abetted torture.

P_3: There is a clear duty to provide treatment, keep detailed records, and report abuses.

P_4: Evidence from the 1980s and 1990s showed medical complicity—the pattern of doctors both containing and abetting torture.

P_5: He saw such abuse and the role doctors played in enabling the abuse in Uruguay.

P_6: Iraq doctors likely kept records—as in the case of the Iraq air force chief who died by asphyxiation.

P_7: Congress should ask independent investigators to look into this.

P_8: Doctors are the first responders and could stop brutal practices.

P_9: By staying silent, doctors and nurses abandon their patients.

P_{10}: Doctors and nurses likely have "smoking-gun" evidence (i.e., proof of torture).

C: Doctors and nurses should step forward and tell what they know of the Abu Ghraib prison abuse.

This method has many virtues. The biggest virtue is that we end up with the argument set out by spotting key words and cutting whatever is not highlighted. This allows us to see the argument's basic form.

Any of you animals want to be a xenotransplant donor?

Reprinted with permission of Nik Scott, www.nikscott.com.

Method 3: Standard Form of an Argument

Xenotransplants—the transplanting of animal organs into humans—has elicited a range of responses and not just a little controversy. As Ben Wyld argues below, there are broader issues of global import. Read his article, and then we'll set out his argument in standard form. As you may recall, an argument is in standard form if the premises are set out P_1, P_2, P_3, and so on, like a stack of pancakes, with the conclusion at the bottom of the stack, below the last premise. Keep this form in mind as you read Wyld's argument.

Animal Organs a Risk to Humans

Ben Wyld

Sydney Morning Herald, January 13, 2004

Fears that humans may be at risk of contracting diseases through animal organ transplants have been raised after a study revealed that human and animal DNA can fuse together naturally. Researchers from the Mayo Clinic in Rochester, Minnesota, found that pigs developed human and hybrid cells in their blood and organs after they were injected with human blood stem cells.

The hybrid cells were also found to contain the porcine endogenous retrovirus, a pig virus similar to HIV, which was able to transmit to normal human cells. The finding raises the possibility that xenotransplantation, a procedure in which organs from pigs are implanted into humans, could allow animal viruses to pass to the recipient's human cells.

Jack Sparrow, the chairman of the xenotransplantation working party within the National Health and Medical Research Council, said the risk of transfer of infection was a big concern. "The public health risks of any proposed animal to human xenotransplantation trial must be minimal and must be acceptable to the community," Dr. Sparrow said.

Scientists fear the movement of viruses from animals to humans could underlie some fatal diseases, with both AIDS and SARS recent examples where scientists believe the viruses crossed over from animal populations. Dr. Sparrow said the amount of xenotransplantation research being conducted in Australia was limited. "You have to keep in mind that any actual experimental work . . . will happen at the cellular level, then the tissue level before whole organ transplantation if, indeed, we ever get to that stage," he said.

But Peter Collignon, director of microbiology and infectious diseases at Canberra Hospital, said the study, reported in the online edition of a journal published by the Federation of American Societies for Experimental Biology, reinforced the dangers of xenotransplantation. "This is the very thing we're worried about, an animal virus adapting to people and spreading . . . this isn't just some science-fiction tale," Associate Professor Collignon said.

Xenotransplantation, thought to be a possible solution to the problem of donor shortages, increased the risk of possible infection, said Professor Collignon. Recipients need to have their immune system blocked by drugs to avoid rejecting the foreign tissue. Attention, he said, should instead focus on increasing organ donor rates. "This is a major red warning flag, and we need to be very careful about going down this path," he said.

Dr. Jeffrey Platt, director of the Mayo Clinic's Transplantation Biology Program, said the finding explained how a retrovirus could jump from one species to another and might help uncover the origin of AIDS and SARS.

Source: Sydney Morning Herald, Sydney, Australia, www.smh.com.au, 13 Jan 2004. Reprinted with the permission of Ben Wyld.

Setting Out the Argument in Standard Form.   Ben Wyld thinks it unwise at the present time to proceed with xenotransplants; humans may be at risk of contracting diseases from the animal donors. His argument is as follows:

Argument: Ben Wyld, "Animal Organs a Risk to Humans"

P_1: A Mayo Clinic study found that pigs developed human and hybrid cells in their blood and organs after they were injected with human blood stem cells.

P_2: The hybrid cells were also found to contain the porcine endogenous retrovirus (PERV), a pig virus similar to HIV, which was able to transmit to normal human cells.

P_3: The finding raises the possibility that xenotransplantation could allow animal viruses to pass to the recipient's human cells.

P_4: Jack Sparrow, the chairman of the xenotransplantation working party within the National Health and Medical Research Council, said the risk of transfer of infection was a big concern.

P_5: We ought not allow xenotransplantation unless the public health risks are minimal.

P_6: Scientists fear the movement of viruses from animals to humans could underlie some fatal diseases, with both AIDS and SARS recent examples where scientists believe the viruses crossed over from animal populations.

P_7: Peter Collignon, director of microbiology and infectious diseases at Canberra Hospital, said the study, reported in the online edition of a journal published by the Federation of American Societies for Experimental Biology, reinforced the dangers of xenotransplantation. "This is the very thing we're worried about, an animal virus adapting to people and spreading . . . this isn't just some science-fiction tale," he said.

P_8: Xenotransplantation increased the risk of possible infection, said Professor Collignon. "This is a major red warning flag, and we need to be very careful about going down this path," he said.

P_9: Dr. Jeffrey Platt, director of the Mayo Clinic's Transplantation Biology Program, said the finding explained how a retrovirus could jump from one species to another and might help uncover the origin of AIDS and SARS.

C: We ought not undertake xenotransplants as long as there are such potential health risks.

Can you see how Wyld argued his case? He laid out reasons why xeno-transplants put humans at risk for disease and presented the warnings as red flags. Since these concerns are not minimal at the present time, he opposes xenotransplants.

Setting out the argument in standard form has many virtues. *The biggest virtue* is that we end up with the premises laid out neatly above the conclusion. This allows us to easily look at any one premise and weigh its value as support for the conclusion—but we must identify all the premises and not omit any evidence. Err on the side of inclusion. However, be judicious. Otherwise, you may have a much longer list of premises (or potential premises) than you need.

Method 4: The Traditional Outline

Technology has opened up a Pandora's box of ethical, legal, and social controversies. And it's not over yet. According to California's Proposition 69, which passed in 2004, collection of DNA samples will be expanded to include people convicted of any felony plus those convicted or arrested for some other offenses. Criminal penalties, such as fines for traffic tickets, will help pay for keeping track of more DNA samples. Let's look at the case of a DNA dragnet.

How would you feel if your father or brother (or you, if you are a male!) were asked to submit to DNA testing in a rape case? How would you feel if you were raped, the suspect lives in your neighborhood, and the police think a DNA test might catch him? As you might imagine, both questions raise interesting moral and social concerns. Such concerns are not academic, either, as DNA testing in crimes is now a reality. This is the focus of our next article.

The wrestling technique for pinning down this argument is a classic. Just as the Terminator was able to quickly get the basics using its programmed assessment tools, we will use a traditional outline to pare down the argument to skeletal form. This involves using headings, subheadings, supporting details, and examples—all set out in a linear fashion that packages each of the component parts of the argument.

To keep the headings, subheadings, and supporting details straight, it is important to use a conventional format. A traditional outline format is like this:

I.

II.

III. Headings

   [Use capital roman numerals I, II, III, etc. to indicate major claims.]

   A.

   B.

   C. Subheadings

      [Use capital letters A, B, C, etc. to indicate the main support under the heading/major claim in question.]

1.
2.
3. Supporting detail
   [Use numbers 1, 2, 3, etc. to indicate supporting detail for the sub-heading in question.]
   a.
   b.
   c. Examples or more specific detail
      [Use lowercase letters a, b, c, etc. to indicate examples of or specific support for the detail under the subheading in question.]
      i.
      ii.
      iii. Elaboration of examples or specific detail
          [Use lowercase roman numerals i, ii, iii, etc.]

This outline breaks down the argument according to the categories "main headings/key claims." Under each are subheadings, and under the subheadings are the detailed support and examples. The result is nested boxes, like those little Ukrainian dolls in which each doll fits inside the next larger one, and so on. Read the article, and then we'll go through a traditional outline.

DNA Dragnet in Search for Killer Raises Privacy Concerns

Jennifer L. Brown

Daily Journal, June 1, 2001

OKLAHOMA CITY—Police know who murdered Juli Busken. Not by name, but by the genetic code he left behind in the victim's car five years ago.

In their search for John Doe, police took blood from 200 men and compared their DNA to that of the man who left behind semen in Busken's car. There were no matches. Police plan to test 200 more men who either lived near the victim and have a criminal record of violence, resemble the police sketch or have been identified as a possible suspect.

There is a growing debate about whether innocent people should have to hand over their blood. Besides concern over unreasonable searches, even supporters of DNA testing say such large-scale genetic dragnets raise the possibility of police coercion.

For Busken's father, the answer is easy. Besides a rough sketch of someone who was seen with Busken before her death, a DNA match is about all he has to cling to in hopes of finding his daughter's killer. "If you don't want to give your DNA, you've got something to hide," said Bud Busken, who runs a golf course in Benton, Ark. "I'll stand by that until my dying day."

Busken, 21, had just finished her last semester at the University of Oklahoma when she was last seen on Dec. 20, 1996, and was about to drive home to Arkansas for Christmas vacation. Police believe she was abducted from the parking lot of her apartment building. Her body was found near a lake. The aspiring ballerina had been raped and shot in the head.

Cleveland County District Attorney Tim Kuykendall turned to the DNA testing last year.

Some of those tested gave DNA samples to exonerate themselves. Others were people associated with Busken, including fellow college dancers and even stagehands who worked at the university. Defense attorneys and civil libertarians call the sweeps an improper violation of the constitutional right to privacy.

A few such DNA dragnets have taken place in this country, but there's little precedent for determining their legality. Mass blood screenings are more common abroad, where the first was in 1987 in England when 5,000 people had their blood tested after two teen-agers were raped and murdered.

Fred Leatherman, chairman of the Forensic Evidence Committee of the National Association of Criminal Defense Lawyers, said he knew of no legal challenges to block mass screenings in the United States. He predicted they would be challenged, calling them "a clear violation of the right to privacy."

Critics fear what happens to DNA samples after they're collected. Some suspect they would be used in future investigations by forensic scientists who sometimes make errors, or that they might end up in the hands of health insurance companies that could see which diseases a person is predisposed to develop. "This is just horrendous, appalling," said Doug Parr, a board member of the Oklahoma Criminal Defense Lawyers Association. "It smacks of the kind of police state tactics that this country has gone to war against."

Most of the 200 men tested so far gave their blood voluntarily, but prosecutors obtained search warrants in a few cases where people declined to provide the sample. One of those was Dennis Stuermer, 23, who said his reputation has been tarnished because Oklahoma City police forced him to give a blood sample. Stuermer's photograph ran on the front page of the state's largest newspaper after a woman in jail who knew his family said he might be Busken's killer.

In the months it took to get the results of the DNA test, his landlord tried to evict him, a boss threatened to fire him and a few personal relationships deteriorated. "I was scared to death," he said. "I didn't have anything to be scared of, but people were breathing down my throat." Attorney Doug Wall said he and Stuermer, who has no criminal background, may sue the police. "Police are basically saying, 'If we pop a needle into enough arms we're bound to get lucky sooner or later,'" Wall said.

Arthur Spitzer, a lawyer with the American Civil Liberties Union in Washington, said requiring people to give DNA samples without other evidence linking them to the crime would be an unconstitutional search and seizure. Attorney Barry Scheck, who co-founded the Innocence Project, a group that helps inmates challenge convictions with DNA evidence, said there are potential problems whenever so much testing is done.

Some people might feel coerced to give blood. "It's inherently coercive when a policeman comes to your door and says 'Give us a sample of your blood and if you don't give it to us, you're a suspect,'" he said. Bud Busken believes if authorities found his daughter's killer, it might stop the emotional roller coaster he and his wife have been on since that day. "Our life is never going to go back the way it was," he said.

Source: Copyright 2001, Daily Journal Corp. Reprinted and/or posted with permission.

Setting Out the Traditional Outline.   Now we can see what the argument looks like using a traditional outline. This can be helpful whether you are writing a paper or analyzing one. Outlining works best when the article is well structured and neither rambles off topic nor jumps back and forth. Most word processing software (e.g., Microsoft Word) has an outlining layout under "Format." You may find this useful in outlining your article.

Jennifer L. Brown's article is fairly straightforward—but notice that the part of the title regarding "privacy concerns" is a clue to the dominant argument. The trickiest part involves what to do with the references to the Busken case and then later to the Stuermer case. The Busken case warrants treatment as a major claim, given that it opens the article. The Stuermer case seems best handled as a subheading under the discussion of the legality of DNA searches. But this is a judgment call. No great harm would be done in pulling it out and treating it on the level of the Busken case. The point of the outline is to pin down the argument—and there can be legitimate variations on how best to do that. With that in mind, let's look at the outline.

Outline: Jennifer L. Brown, "DNA Dragnet in Search for Killer Raises Privacy Concerns"

I. Police know who murdered Juli Busken by the genetic code he left behind in the victim's car five years ago.

   A. In their search for John Doe, police took blood from 200 men.

      1. Police compared their DNA to that of the man who left behind semen in Busken's car.

         a. There were no matches.

   B. Police plan to test 200 more men.

      1. They will test those who lived near the victim and have a criminal record of violence, resemble the police sketch, or have been identified as a possible suspect.

II. There is a growing debate about whether innocent people should have to hand over their blood.

   A. There is concern over unreasonable searches.

      1. Even supporters of DNA testing say such large-scale genetic dragnets raise the possibility of police coercion.

      2. For Busken's father, the answer is easy—do DNA searches.

         a. A DNA match is about all he has to cling to in hopes of finding his daughter's killer.

            i. All he has is a rough sketch of someone who was seen with Busken before her death.

   B. "If you don't want to give your DNA, you've got something to hide," Bud Busken said. "I'll stand by that until my dying day."

III. The Busken case.

   A. Juli Busken, 21, had just finished her last semester at the University of Oklahoma when she was last seen on Dec. 20, 1996.

      1. She was about to drive home to Arkansas for Christmas vacation.

   B. Police believe she was abducted from the parking lot of her apartment building.

      1. Her body was found near a lake.

      2. The aspiring ballerina had been raped and shot in the head.

   C. Cleveland County District Attorney Tim Kuykendall turned to the DNA testing last year.

      1. Some of those tested gave DNA samples to exonerate themselves.

      2. Others were people associated with Busken, including fellow college dancers and even stagehands who worked at the university.

      3. Defense attorneys and civil libertarians call the sweeps an improper violation of the constitutional right to privacy.

IV. A few such DNA dragnets have taken place in this country, but there's little precedent for determining their legality.

   A. Mass blood screenings are more common abroad.

      1. The first was in 1987 in England when 5,000 people had their blood tested after two teen-agers were raped and murdered.

   B. Fred Leatherman, chairman of the Forensic Evidence Committee of the National Association of Criminal Defense Lawyers, said he knew of no legal challenges to block mass screenings in the United States.

      1. He predicted they would be challenged.

         a. He called them "a clear violation of the right to privacy."

   C. Critics fear what happens to DNA samples after they're collected.

      1. Some suspect they would be used in future investigations by forensic scientists who sometimes make errors.

      2. They might end up in the hands of health insurance companies that could see which diseases a person is predisposed to develop.

      3. "This is just horrendous, appalling," said Doug Parr, a board member of the Oklahoma Criminal Defense Lawyers Association.

         a. "It smacks of the kind of police state tactics that this country has gone to war against."

   D. Most of the 200 men tested so far gave their blood voluntarily.

   E. Prosecutors obtained search warrants in a few cases where people declined to provide the sample.

V. The case of Dennis Stuermer, 23, who declined to give a DNA sample.

   A. Stuermer said his reputation has been tarnished because Oklahoma City police forced him to give a blood sample.

      1. Stuermer's photograph ran on the front page of the state's largest newspaper after a woman in jail who knew his family said he might be Busken's killer.

      2. In the months it took to get the results of the DNA test, his landlord tried to evict him, a boss threatened to fire him, and a few personal relationships deteriorated.

      3. "I was scared to death," he said. "I didn't have anything to be scared of, but people were breathing down my throat."

   B. Attorney Doug Wall said he and Stuermer, who had no criminal background, may sue the police.

      1. "Police are basically saying, 'If we pop a needle into enough arms we're bound to get lucky sooner or later,'" Wall said.

VI. Requiring people to give DNA samples raises concerns.

   A. Arthur Spitzer, a lawyer with the American Civil Liberties Union in Washington, said requiring people to give DNA samples without other evidence linking them to the crime would be an unconstitutional search and seizure.

   B. Attorney Barry Scheck, who cofounded the Innocence Project, a group that helps inmates challenge convictions with DNA evidence, said there are potential problems whenever so much testing is done.

      1. Some people might feel coerced to give blood.

      2. "It's inherently coercive when a policeman comes to your door and says 'Give us a sample of your blood and if you don't give it to us, you're a suspect,'" he said.

   C. Bud Busken brushes aside the concerns.

      1. He believes if authorities found his daughter's killer, it might stop the emotional roller coaster he and his wife have been on since that day.

Once the argument is set out in outline form, you can assess its strength. Be sure to check to see if anything is omitted. Examine the weight given to any aspect of the argument. For example, the outline shows quite a bit of attention given to the Stuermer case. It might be valuable to compare how the author treats—and links—the two cases (Busken and Stuermer). In the *first case,* the use of a DNA dragnet might reveal who the killer is—and, therefore, there would be a positive result from the DNA dragnet, even if it has a coercive element.

In the *second case,* that of Stuermer, the refusal to give a DNA sample raised suspicions that Stuermer contends have harmed him. Brown's use of expert sources reinforces Stuermer's position. This case supports the view that the use of coercion to obtain DNA samples violates any number of rights (privacy, protection against unlawful search and seizure, etc.). As a result, we see from the outline that, whereas Brown refers to the "debate" around DNA dragnets, her article presents a much more solid case *against* DNA dragnets.

By using an outline, we are able to get a better grasp of the argument. This is as true when looking at our own arguments as it is for the arguments of others.

Exercises

Directions: Using any of the methods we covered in this chapter, analyze one of the two articles below.

Article 1: Crossing the Moral Boundary

Mario Vargas Llosa

Eminent Peruvian novelist Mario Vargas Llosa looks at the issue of the global trade in women. He reflects on the French justice system, which charged one of its citizens with having sex with children while vacationing in Thailand. As discussed in the article below, the French system does not require such a crime to have taken place within its own borders. It is this moral boundary that the article reflects upon.

A model employee of the French public transport authority, according to his chiefs and workmates, the Parisian bachelor Amnon Chemouil, who is now 48, discovered one of Thailand's tourist attractions in 1992. Not its tropical landscape or its ancient civilization and Buddhist temples, but cheap and easy sex, one of the country's flourishing industries. At the resort of Pattaya, near Bangkok, he could have sex with very young prostitutes. He vacationed there again in 1993 and 1994.

On his third trip, he met in a bar at Pattaya another sex tourist, Viktor Michel, a Swiss citizen, who encouraged him to seek out even younger girls. Mr. Michel took care of everything: found the procuress and a hotel room.

The woman appeared there with a niece who was 11 years of age, and Mr. Chemouil paid $20. All the doings in the hotel room at Pattaya were recorded on video by Viktor Michel, and upon returning to Paris and his job in the public transport system, Mr. Chemouil received a copy of this cassette from his friend and added it to his collection of pornographic videos.

Some time later Viktor Michel found himself in trouble with the Swiss police, much less tolerant than the Thai ones. Searching his home for illegal pornography as part of an investigation into a pedophile ring, they found the video from Pattaya. Under interrogation, the video hobbyist revealed the circumstances in which the video had been filmed and Mr. Chemouil's identity. A report was sent to the French police, who put it in the hands of a judge.

Here I must open a parenthesis in my story, to declare my admiration for French justice. Many things function poorly in France and deserve criticism, but justice functions very well. French courts and judges act with an independence and courage that are an example for all other democracies. They have brought to light countless cases of corruption at higher economic, administrative and political levels, and have sent to trial—and in some cases, to prison—people who by their wealth and influence would in other societies be untouchable. In matters of human rights, racial discrimination, and subversion and terrorism, justice in France is usually characterized by efficacy and prompt intervention.

This was not, we may assume, the impression felt by the surprised Amnon Chemouil when he was arrested and taken before a court in Paris to pay for having violated the penal code of 1994 by sexually violating a minor. The French penal law is applicable to all offenses committed by a French citizen "within or without" French territory, and a 1998 law authorizes the courts to try "sexual aggressions committed abroad" even when the deeds are not considered crimes in the country where they were committed.

The trial of Amnon Chemouil, which took place this fall, set a precedent. It was the first time an offense of "sex tourism" had come before a court in one of the wealthy countries where this sort of tourism typically originates. Several organizations that oppose sexual exploitation of children appeared as plaintiffs, among them the United Nations Children's Fund (*Unicef*), End Child Prostitution in Asian Tourism and a group in Thailand that was able to locate in Bangkok, seven years later, the aunt and girl of the story. The girl, now 18, went to Paris and testified, in private, to the judges, who also viewed a copy of Viktor Michel's video that was found in the search of Amnon Chemouil's house.

The accused, who said that in the eight months he had spent in prison awaiting trial he had experienced a mental cataclysm, admitted he had performed the acts in the video, begged the victim's pardon and asked the court to punish him. The sentence was seven years' imprisonment, instead of the 10 called for by the prosecutor.

Many conclusions may be drawn from this story. The first is that if France's example were followed by countries like Spain, Germany, Britain, Italy and the United States, which, with their high incomes, are among the principal practitioners of "sex tourism," then it is possible that the thousands of offenses of this type committed daily in the poorer countries—especially concerning the sexual exploitation of children—might at least diminish and that some of the perpetrators might be punished.

The precedent established by France is impeccable: a modern democracy cannot allow its citizens to be exonerated of legal responsibility if they sin cheerfully outside of national borders just because a foreign country has no juridical norms that prohibit the activity or because those norms are not enforced.

Hunger, the need for money, and extensive corruption and inefficiency in many poor countries have caused child prostitution to prosper spectacularly, with the indifference or open complicity of the authorities. As *Unicef* and its allies testified at the trial of Mr. Chemouil, the dimensions of the problem are multiple and growing. We need not entertain very high hopes of its eradication, of course, because the poverty and misery that lie behind it constitute an almost insurmountable obstacle.

But the trial in Paris shows a positive side to the new bete noire of the incorrigible enemies of modernity: globalization. If frontiers had not been fading away and, in many fields, disappearing, Amnon Chemouil would never have appeared before the court that tried and sentenced him, and would surely have spent many more vacations in Pattaya. The rigid, straitjacket conception of national sovereignty is being transformed, leading to attempts at wider justice like the detention of Augusto

Pinochet in England for his crimes against humanity in Chile, and now this trial.

Globalization is not only the creation of world markets and transnational companies; it also means the extension of justice and democratic values into regions where barbarism still flourishes.

Source: Mario Vargas Llosa is a Peruvian novelist and winner of numerous awards, including the National Book Critics Circle Award, the Cervantes Prize, and the Peace Prize of the German Book Trade. This article, which also appeared in *El Pais,* Madrid, was translated by James Brander. Reprinted with the permission of Mario Vargas Llosa.

Article 2: Detainee Ethics: Terrorists as Research Subjects

Jonathan D. Moreno

The American Journal of Bioethics 3, no. 4

In our second article, Professor Jonathan D. Moreno examines the use of detainees for research in human experimentation. Using any one of our four methods, analyze the article. Note that Moreno takes a position and sets out his argument that the detainees should have the right to be treated as research subjects.

In his introduction to *The Nazi Doctors,* psychiatrist Robert Jay Lifton recalled a requirement imposed on him by the research ethics committee at Yale, where he was then on the faculty: Before beginning his interviews with the elderly physicians who had functioned in the racist bureaucracy of the Third Reich, Lifton would have to provide each of them with a consent form indicating that their participation in Lifton's research was voluntary and that they could withdraw at any time (Lifton 2000).

Though Lifton remarks on this incident almost in passing, it was for me a powerful and supremely ironic moment in his project, that some of the same individuals who contributed to the crimes that helped inspire modern research ethics should themselves be protected by the moral lessons learned. Yet consistency and principle seem to require no less than that ethical standards be applied without prejudice, in spite of the grotesqueries perpetrated by the individuals who are by virtue of their behavior objects of scientific interest. Our very humanity as moral agents is in this way affirmed, for the harder it is to apply ethical principles to persons whose conduct has violated the conditions of human decency, the more important it is to do so.

In our own time terrorism evokes its own cruel horror, and just as there is good reason to try to understand the mind of a racist thug, so there is also good reason to examine the processes that can drive an individual to wanton destruction of innocent human life. Since August 2002, behavioral scientists have been engaged in interviewing suspected al-Qaeda detainees at the U.S. Naval Base in Guantanamo Bay, Cuba. "We are trying to get more cultural knowledge and get into the minds of radical fundamentalists," one anonymous government official told the press. Sent by the FBI, the psychologists are reportedly attempting to learn about the detainees' personal lives and why they joined a terrorist organization, as well as their views of the United States (CBN News 2002; BBC News 2002; *Washington Times* 2002).

The ultimate goal of these psychological profiles is of course to gain enough knowledge of the motivations of such people so that efforts to alter their views or at least anticipate their activities can be more targeted and effective. Behavioral scientists by no means agree that these kinds of assessments can help achieve these goals, especially under the circumstances in which the detainees are being held. But putting scientific legitimacy aside for the moment, it seems a sure bet that there has been no IRB [Institutional Review Board] review within the Justice Department of the psychological profiling project, in spite of the fact that "generalizable knowledge" about Islamic militants is the aim. From one perspective this is hardly surprising: Not only do the detainees occupy a fuzzy legal status that seems to disqualify them from the rights normally ascribed to prisoners, it's hard to think of a group less likely to inspire sympathy among Americans than al-Qaeda fighters.

Nor are the detainees technically prisoners of war, because they are not associated with a state but rather with a criminal organization. Yet the Nazi war criminals were also characterized by American prosecutors as essentially a group of street toughs that happened to gain control of an important country, thereby justifying their prosecution without the immunity that was then commonly granted to national leaders. The National Socialist Party was identified by the prosecution as a "criminal organization" rather than a political party in the usual sense, which was a critical element of the case against individual party leaders (Taylor 1992). In these terms the Nazi Party and al-Qaeda analogy has some merit. Suppose, then, that the detainees should be treated as prisoners of war, as some legal commentators have argued in opposition to U.S. policy. In 1953, the Pentagon adopted the Nuremberg Code as its policy to govern human experiments, and added an eleventh rule: that prisoners of war should not be used as research subjects (Moreno 2001).

These inconvenient historical details at least suggest that, awkward as it might be, the detainees' right to be considered as human research subjects in the context of data-gathering interviews cannot easily be waved aside. Granted that the administration of a consent form at Guantanamo is about as likely an event as the current attorney general presiding over a gay marriage ceremony. Unlike the passions of the day, however, history tends to be less forgiving when governments ride roughshod over those values that are supposed to be among their most cherished. And the articulation of basic human rights following the victory over Nazi Germany is commonly taken to be one of the precious lessons of that carnage.

Finally, even the trump card of national security necessity is not so easily played. One of the findings of the President's Advisory Committee on Human Experiments in 1995 was that "for the period 1944 to 1974 [the period within the Committee's purview] there is no evidence that any government statement or policy on research involving human subjects contained a provision permitting a waiver of consent requirements for national security reasons" (Advisory Committee 1995). If the current administration has issued such a waiver, it would be without precedent.

Considering the circumstances of the detainees' incarceration not only direct ethical concerns about respect for persons, but also the indirect results of this behavioral research raise questions. It seems unlikely that these so-called interviews are benign chats over a pot of tea. Lack of cooperation could well convince authorities to extend the period of arrest and intensify the methods used to secure a more informative session. Research rules as they apply to prisoners of war or other miscreants in captivity are intended to prevent the putative scientific activity from becoming an opportunity for maltreatment.

If the war on terror continues indefinitely, as seems to be the case, this matter is sure to come up again. The Viet Cong were similarly examined during the Vietnam War, as were Communist prisoners during the Korean conflict. And then there are the unanswered questions about the very validity of such "research." Here is a radical suggestion: explaining to captives that our values include respecting their right not to be part of a scientific study might just elicit more cooperation than otherwise. In light of the stakes for both our survival and our decency it seems a hypothesis worth exploring.

References

Advisory Committee on Human Radiation Experiments. 1995. The Human Radiation Experiments, 501. New York: Oxford University Press.

BBC News. 2002. U.S. Delves into al-Qaeda Mindset. 9 August. Available from: Web (accessed August 8, 2003).

CBN News. 2002. FBI to Profile al-Qaida Detainees. 9 August. Available from: Web (accessed August 8, 2003).

Lifton, R. J. 2000. *The Nazi Doctors: Medical Killing and the Psychology of Genocide.* New York: Basic Books.

Moreno, J. D. 2001. *Undue Risk: Secret State Experiments on Humans.* New York: Routledge.

Taylor, T. 1992. *Anatomy of the Nuremberg Trials.* Boston: Little, Brown & Company.

The *Washington Times.* 2002. Psychological Profiles of al-Qaeda Suspects Sought. 10 August. Available from: Web (accessed August 8, 2003).

Source: Reprinted with the permission of Jonathan D. Moreno and Taylor Francis Publishing.

CHAPTER FOUR

Handling Claims, Drawing Inferences

DALLAS: *Something has attached itself to him. We have to get him to the infirmary right away.*

RIPLEY: *What kind of thing? I need a clear definition.*

DALLAS: *An organism. Open the hatch.*

RIPLEY: *Wait a minute. If we let it in, the ship could be infected. You know the quarantine procedure. Twenty-four hours for decontamination.*

DALLAS: *He could die in twenty-four hours. Open the hatch.*

RIPLEY: *Listen to me, if we break quarantine, we could all die.*

LAMBERT: *Could you open the god-damned hatch? We have to get him inside.*

RIPLEY: *No. I can't do that and if you were in my position, you'd do the same.*

ALIEN

Feeling feverish, you head off to the UCLA Medical Center to have some blood drawn. You pick up the consent form and begin to read it. It looks like the same old six and seven, until the next-to-last paragraph. Tucked into the paragraph labeled "Teaching and Research Institution," you find the following: "I further understand that the University of California, including UCLA Healthcare, may review and use medical information and specimens for teaching, study, and research purposes, including the development of potentially commercially useful products."

Your head bounces off the ceiling, as you leap up from your chair. You try to decide: "Do I sign away all commercial rights to my DNA—or do I forget about this blood test for now and pay for my own blood test elsewhere?" In times like these, you're glad you studied critical thinking. We need to know how to handle claims. Otherwise, we may come across an assertion and be unsure of what in the world it means. Also, we need to know what others might justifiably infer on the basis of *our* claims.

Consider two court cases. On August 10, 2000, the conviction of Sandy Murphy and Rick Tabish for the murder of Las Vegas millionaire Ted Binion was called into question. Juror 10, Joan Sanders, submitted to the court a potentially explosive sworn affidavit: "I changed my vote to guilty when it was told to me by the other jurors, 'if you are in the house when a person dies, and do nothing to assist, that is murder.'" (See "Affidavit of Joan Sanders," Court TV, www.courttv.com.)

In another case, actress Kim Basinger was sued for breaking her contract for the movie *Boxing Helena*. The court ruled that the jury instructions were simply ambiguous. Here's why: The instructions used the phrase "and/or" in asking the jury to determine whether Kim Basinger personally or her corporation, Mighty Wind, entered into the contract.

Knowing the tools of logic helps us work within systems already in place. It's sort of like x-ray vision: A firm grasp of logic gives us the ability to see how arguments are structured, to organize that reasoning, and to dismantle it so it can be evaluated. This is both useful and empowering. In this chapter, we will go deeper into analysis and critical thinking skills by examining different types of claims.

As you can see from the opening quote, the movie *Alien* shows us characters who are in a fight for survival after an alien creature is brought on board ship—attached to one of the crew member's heads. Mind you, Ripley, our hero, refuses to allow it, noting scientific protocol regarding potential contamination. But her claims are brushed aside. Their failure to give serious thought to the concerns she raises leads to disastrous results. Fortunately, this does not always happen, but there is a moral (and cognitive) tale to the story. And we certainly learn the value of drawing justifiable inferences.

Propositions

A **proposition** is a claim asserting that something is or is not the case. It is either true or false. These are all propositions: "The car rolled into the street," "Chicago is in Illinois," and "John Lennon was a Beatle." Propositions are not normally expressed as questions or exclamations, unless those are rhetorical forms of an assertion.

In classical logic, prescriptive or moral claims (like "You *ought* to eat spinach" or "Assault guns *should* be illegal") were not treated as propositions because of the difficulty in assigning them a truth value. This was also the case with aesthetic judgments, such as "Monet is the most impressive Impressionist ever!" That does not mean such claims are just opinion, since they may rest on a body of knowledge and research. But you cannot say they are true or false with the degree of certainty attached to empirical claims.

Different Kinds of Propositions

Ultimately, prescriptive and moral claims were allowed into logic, with the understanding that there may be disagreement over truth or falsity. This is also true of other value claims (such as "Redheads are sexier than blondes" or "A pear tart is a more elegant dessert than a Black Forest cake"). We proceed by *assuming* truth and then seeing the role a value claim will play in the argument.

Three Kinds of Propositions

Tautologies: propositions that are always true or true by definition.
Contradictions: propositions that are always false or false by definition.
Contingent Claims: propositions that are true or false according to the context. They are dependent on what is going on in the world to determine the truth value. This includes claims for which the truth value is unknown.

Examples of Tautologies

Either you did or you did not hear a seal bark.
If B. B. King is the king of blues, then B. B. King is the king of blues.
It is false that my car has gas but it does not have gas.

Examples of Contradictions

Adam is a baby and is not a baby.
Peaches are fruit, but peaches are not fruit.
It is false that, if my car does not have gas, then my car does not have gas.

Examples of Contingent Claims

It is raining in Portland today.
My name is Geronimo.
If that is a beautiful sunset, Kenji is taking a photograph.

Most claims are *contingent,* since the context may vary along with the parameters that determine whether the claim is true or false. For example, the claim "It's roasting outside" is contingent because it may be true on one day but not the next. We need also to be able to handle claims where the truth value is unknown. These are sentences for which the truth value simply cannot be determined—for example, "Intelligent life exists in other solar systems" or "Pig viruses will likely be even more destructive than AIDS." The evidence is not in yet on either one.

Propositions of *unknown truth value* are not useless, but there are limitations. We can use the propositions and draw inferences, but we cannot make any claims about the strength of the argument. Such propositions are relatives of contingent claims, but here we simply lack enough information to determine the truth value.

The Structure of Propositions

A proposition is either simple or compound. A **simple proposition** is one at the atomic level—that is, it does not contain any of the *logical connectives* "and," "or," "not," "if . . . then," or "if and only if." A proposition that contains any of these five logical connectives is a **compound proposition**.

Examples of Simple Propositions

Jasper chewed off some of the window sill.
Swiss cheese is awfully tasty.
85% of headache remedies have caffeine in them.

Examples of Compound Propositions

Jasper chewed off some of the window sill and then bit the computer cord.
Either Jasper popped keys off my laptop or he settled down and ate his corn.
If Jasper chewed off some of the window sill, then he's in trouble.
Jasper did not eat all the corn on his plate.
Jasper eats his corn if and only if it is warm.

The Five Types of Compound Propositions

1. Conjunctions	Propositions of the form "A and B"
2. Disjunctions	Propositions of the form "Either A or B"
3. Negations	Propositions of the form "Not A"
4. Conditional claims	Propositions of the form "If A then B" ("A is sufficient for B") or "B only if A" ("A is necessary for B")
5. Biconditional claims (equivalence)	Propositions of the form "A if and only if B" ("A is both necessary and sufficient for B")

Conjunctions

These are propositions of the form "P and Q," where P and Q are each called **conjuncts**. A **conjunction** is a proposition that asserts two things are true at the same time. This means that the conjunction is true only if *both* conjuncts are true. Otherwise, it is false.

Examples of Conjunctions

The Red Sox won the World Series and the Curse of the Bambino was lifted.
Both Jasper and Wellie are birds.
The game was called off because of the weather, but not all the players were happy about that.
Stacy's drive to Denver was great, although the cost of gas was outrageous.

Alternative Constructions of Conjunctions.   A proposition does not have to contain "and" to be a conjunction. Watch for other words or phrases that function the same as "and," such as "but" and "however." When you spy an alternative, replace it with "and." That way, you will have a uniform way of setting up propositions; otherwise, it's too easy to make mistakes.

Alternative Indicators of Conjunctions

However	Although
But	In addition
Also	As well/as well as
Moreover	Furthermore
Additionally	Plus
Along with	We might add that

Disjunctions

These are propositions of the form "P or Q," where P and Q are each called **disjuncts**. A **disjunction** is a proposition that claims either one or the other, or both. For a disjunction to be true, at least one of the two disjuncts must be true.

Examples of Disjunctions

There is Ellen or someone who looks a lot like her.
Either squirrels or burglars are in the attic making noise.

Note: Disjunctions in logic are *inclusive*. This means a disjunction is true if either *one or both* of the two disjuncts are true. You don't need both disjuncts to be true for the disjunction to be true. For example, this is true: "Either George Washington was president or Abraham Lincoln was a computer hacker." We only need the first disjunct to be true to make the disjunction true.

The "Either/or *or both*" makes the claim an "inclusive or." This contrasts with the everyday use of "either/or," which usually is treated as an exclusion not allowing both disjuncts to be true at the same time.

Negations

These are of the form "not P" (see Figure 4.1). A negated proposition has the opposite truth value of the original statement. A **negation** of a proposition is true only if the proposition itself is false.

Examples of Negations

The negation of: Galileo is the governor of Ohio.
It is not the case that Galileo is the governor of Ohio.
→ Galileo is not the governor of Ohio.

The negation of: Chocolate is not a health food.
It is not the case that chocolate is not a health food.
→ Chocolate is a health food.

If the original statement is negative, then the negation of it will be positive. In the second example, the double negative leads to a positive.

Photograph by Wanda Teays. Copyright 2004.

FIGURE 4.1
Open-ended lists leave a lot to the imagination.

Special Constructions of Negations. Two special forms of negations are the "neither/nor" and "not both." Basically, with a "neither/nor" claim, both options are eliminated (i.e., "Not this *and* not that"). With "not both," one of the two options is eliminated (i.e., "Not this *or* not that"). So if I say, "I did not eat both cheesecake and an ice cream sundae," then we know that either I did not eat the cheesecake or I did not eat the ice cream sundae. As you can see, a "neither/nor" construction ends up being a conjunction ("not this and not that"). For example, "I ate neither squid nor octopus" means "I didn't eat squid and I didn't eat octopus." We will learn how to handle these later in the chapter, along with other types of negated propositions.

Conditional Claims

Conditional claims are of the form "If P then Q" or "Q only if P," where P is called the **antecedent** and Q is called the **consequent**. Conditional claims may also be expressed as "A is sufficient for B" and "A is necessary for B." **Sufficient conditions** are those that, if met, guarantee some effect will occur. This can be expressed in the form "If A then B"—where A represents the antecedent conditions and B represents the consequent effect. **Necessary conditions** are those that, if *not* met, guarantee the effect will *not* occur. This can be expressed in the form "B only if A" or "If not A then not B." That means that if B occurs, then A has to occur as well. Consequently, "If not A then not B" is equivalent to "If B then A."

Sufficient and Necessary Conditions

A is sufficient for B:
If A occurs, B will occur as well.
→ If A then B.

Being hungry is *sufficient* for Betty Jean to eat a donut.
→ If she is hungry, then Betty Jean will eat a donut.

A is necessary for B:

If A does not occur, B will not occur either.

→ B only if A.

→ If not A then not B.

→ If B then A.

Having jelly inside is *necessary* for the donut to be tasty.

→ If there's no jelly inside, then the donut is not tasty.

→ If the donut is tasty, then there must be jelly inside.

Be careful: Sometimes the "then" is omitted, so add it for clarification. A conditional claim is true in every case except when the antecedent is true and the consequent is false. For example, this is a false proposition: "If cows are animals [true], then elephants are rodents [false]."

Examples of Conditional Claims

You'll feel stuffed if you eat too many tamales.
Rewrite as: If you eat too many tamales, then you'll feel stuffed.

Stan will go to Ottawa, if he can get plane tickets.
Rewrite as: If he can get plane tickets, then Stan will go to Ottawa.

Being able to climb Mount Hood is sufficient to make Maricela happy.
Rewrite as: If she is able to climb Mount Hood, then Maricela will be happy.

A sufficient condition of Fred's gaining weight is to eat an entire pizza.
Rewrite as: If he eats an entire pizza, then Fred will gain weight.

A necessary condition of Fred keeping his weight off is that he exercise.
Rewrite as: If he does not exercise, then Fred won't keep his weight off.
Or: If Fred keeps his weight off, then he is exercising.

Alternative Constructions of Conditional Claims.   Other forms of conditional claims include "P only if Q," "Q is necessary for P," "A necessary condition of P is Q," "P unless Q," and "Without P, then Q." We will look at the "unless" and "without" forms later in the chapter.

The "Only If" Construction.   Propositions of the form "A only if B" assert that "If B does not happen, then A won't happen either." In other words, "A only if B" can be rewritten "If not B then not A" or "If A then B." So, "A only if B" is the same as "B is necessary for A."

The "Only If" Construction

Q is necessary for P. P only if Q.

P happens only if Q does.

→ If *not* Q then *not* P.

   If you don't have Q, you won't have P.

→ If P then Q.

   So, if P occurs, so must Q.

Examples of "Only If" Claims

Jasper will go in his cage only if he's forced.
→ If he's not forced, Jasper will not go in his cage.
→ If Jasper went in his cage, then he was forced.

Watering the pear tree is necessary for it to bear fruit.
→ If we don't water the pear tree, then it won't bear fruit.
→ If it bears fruit, then we watered the pear tree.

Handy hints: Locate the "if" and the antecedent immediately follows. The consequent is what follows from the antecedent condition. It is located after the "then."

Be careful: The consequent is sometimes expressed *before* the antecedent. For example, "We will dance all night, *if* the band plays until dawn." The consequent is "we will dance all night." When this occurs, rewrite the sentence in the form of an "if . . . then" claim and locate the consequent after the "then."

Handling Alternative Constructions of Conditional Claims.   "P if Q," "Only if Q, then P," and "P only if Q" can all be rewritten in the "If . . . then" form.

The Structure of a Conditional Claim

If that is my pet bird, Jasper, then he will come down from the tree.
        ↓   ↓
      Antecedent   Consequent

Locating the Antecedent and Consequent.   If we have a conditional claim, express it in the "if . . . then" form, and then you can easily locate the antecedent and consequent. We can see how to do this in the following proposition:

We'd better call 911 *if* someone is hurt in the accident.
Rewrite as:
If someone is hurt in the accident, then we'd better call 911.
        ↓   ↓
     Antecedent   Consequent

Once we have stated it as an "if . . . then" claim, reading the antecedent and consequent becomes much easier. The antecedent then can be found between the "if" and the "then," whereas the consequent follows the "then."

Equivalence (Biconditional Propositions)

Two propositions are **equivalent** if they assert the same thing. The resulting proposition is called a **biconditional.** "P is equivalent to Q" is the same as "If P then Q, and if Q then P." When that occurs, you can say "P if and only if Q."

Any two equivalent propositions have the same truth value; they are either both true or both false. It is impossible for A to be equivalent to B when A is true and B is false (or vice versa). *Note:* The term "equivalent to" can be expressed as an "if and only if" (sometimes abbreviated as "iff") statement.

Examples of Biconditional Claims

That Robert is addicted to caffeine is equivalent to his being physiologically dependent on it.
→ Robert is addicted to caffeine *if and only* if he is physiologically dependent on it.
→ If he is physiologically dependent on it, then Robert is addicted to caffeine, and if he is addicted to caffeine, then he is physiologically dependent on it.

Maria getting married is equivalent to ending her life as a single woman.
→ Maria ends her life as a single woman *if and only if* she gets married.
→ If Maria marries, then she ends her life as a single woman, and if she ends her life as a single woman, then Maria has gotten married.

Categorical Propositions

For certain types of analysis, using categorical propositions is helpful. A **categorical proposition** begins with a quantifier ("all," "no," "some," "x%") followed by the subject, a form of the verb "to be," and then the predicate. Negative propositions that are not all-or-nothing claims will have a "not" before the predicate (e.g., "Some cats are *not* milk-drinkers").

Expressing claims in the form of categorical propositions enables us to quickly determine the strength of an argument, as we'll see in Chapters 5 and 9.

The Forms of Categorical Propositions

All P is Q.	This is called an A claim.
No P is Q.	This is called an E claim.
Some P is Q.	This is called an I claim.
Some P is not Q.	This is called an O claim.

You probably wonder where we place claims like "Charlie is a good ole boy" and "54% of toddlers prefer hot milk at bedtime." Propositions containing proper nouns as the subject are considered A or E claims, relative to being positive or negative. Propositions of the form "x% of A is B" (where x is neither 100 nor zero) are treated as I or O claims, relative to being positive or negative. So, if you have a statistical claim that is not all-or-nothing, it will function as a particular claim (I or O).

Examples of Categorical Propositions

A claim: All burnt muffins are inedible pastries.

E claim: No burnt muffin is a tasty treat.

I claim: Some burnt muffins are good breakfast food.

O claim: Some burnt muffins are not good substitutes for hockey pucks.

Quantity.   The **quantity** of a proposition answers the question "How much?" In other words, the quantity refers to how much of the subject class is said to have something predicated of it. The possible answer is "universal" or "particular" (i.e., all or some of it).

Quantity—Universal or Particular

Universal:	All P is Q.	All flies are irritating insects.
	No P is Q.	No fly is a spider.
Particular:	Some P is Q.	Some vehicles are race cars.
	Some P is not Q.	Some vehicles are not pick-ups.

A and E	→	Universal claims
I and O	→	Particular claims

Quality.   The **quality** of a proposition answers the question "Are you asserting that something *is* or *is not* the case?" You are either affirming that it is the case, so the quality of the proposition is positive, or denying it, so the quality of the proposition is negative.

Quality—Positive or Negative

Positive:	All P is Q.	All chocolate is a delicious treat.
	Some P is Q.	Some delicious treats are donuts.
Negative:	No P is Q.	No donut is a healthy snack.
	Some P is not Q.	Some healthy snacks are not vegetables.

A and I	→	Positive claims
E and O	→	Negative claims

Examples

All football players are burly men.
Anyone from Texas is a southerner.
→ A claims are universal and A claims are positive.
→ These propositions are *universal positive*.

Fish are never good ingredients to put in a custard pie.
No wind instrument has strings.
→ E claims are universal and E claims are negative.
→ These propositions are *universal negative*.

Universal Positive Propositions.   There are many ways to say "all" or "none" to indicate we are referring to all the members of the subject class. These include:

Every	Any
100%	If . . . then

Without exception	The entire
Whatever	Whenever
Whoever	Whichever
Whomever	However (when used to mean "all the ways")

Universal Negative Propositions.   Propositions that are universal negative can take a number of different forms. Replace these with "no" and treat as E claims. Universal negatives include the following:

None	0%
Not any	If . . . then not
All . . . are not	Not a one is
. . . is never	Not even one
Whatever . . . is not	Whenever . . . is not
Whoever . . . is not	Whichever . . . is not

"Not Every" Propositions.   If I say, "Not every man is over six feet tall" I mean that *some men are not* over six feet tall. I do not mean that *no man* is over six feet tall. Therefore, when we see a "not every" construction, we need to be careful. "Not every . . . is" is *not* the same as "No . . . is." "Not every" is equivalent to "Some . . . are not." For example, "Not every musician is talented" is equivalent to "Some musicians are not talented people." When we say "not every," that means we don't have all—some are not included. *Remember:* Keep the "not" when you go from "not every" to "some are not." It would *not* be correct to say "not every" is the same as "some are," so translate as "some are not."

Special Constructions of Universal Claims.   A proposition that has a proper noun as the subject is treated as a universal claim.

Examples of Universal Claims

Shawn is an artist who can operate an airbrush.
→ Treat as a universal positive claim.
→ Classify as an A claim.

The Statue of Liberty is not a monument found in Rhode Island.
→ Treat as a universal negative claim.
→ Classify as an E claim.

Treat as Universal Claims.   Propositions that point to specific individuals using "this" and "that" usually function as universals. They point to a particular subject in the same way a proper noun acts as an indicator.

This dog is an awfully strange looking beagle.
→ Treat as a universal positive claim (an A claim).

That little girl of yours is not a bashful child.
→ Treat as a universal negative claim (an E claim).

Particular Claims.   These are propositions that can be expressed in the form of "Some . . . are/are not." These include the following:

Examples of Particular Claims

Most . . . are/are not	A few . . . are/are not
Lots of . . . are/are not	Many . . . are/are not
Much of . . . are/are not	A bunch of . . . are/are not
Several . . . are/are not	Almost all . . . are/are not
Not all . . . are	More than a few of . . . are/are not
Not every . . . are	At least one of . . . are/are not

Statistical Propositions.   A special construction of universal and particular claims is the **statistical proposition.** Given a statistical proposition "x% of P is Q," the *first step* is to look at the percentage. All-or-nothing claims, where x = 0 or 100, are treated as universal propositions. If x is *between* 0 and 100, then the proposition is a particular claim.

Examples of Statistical Propositions

100% of spam is unwelcome email.
→ Classify as an A claim.

0% of text messages are handwritten letters.
→ Classify as an E claim.

59% of librarians are helpful people.
→ Classify as an I claim.

82% of phone calls are not solicitations.
→ Classify as an O claim.

Group or Individual Exercise

1. State the quantity and quality of the following propositions:
   a. No raccoon is a shy animal.
   b. Every possum is an animal that likes fruit.
   c. Robin is a person who is somewhat afraid of the dark.
   d. Quite a few animals that like fruit are parrots.
   e. No parrot is an animal to be taken for granted.
   f. Not all exotic animals are creatures found in Costa Rica.
   g. 84% of elk are animals that like to chew leaves.
   h. Batman is a person who likes to wear masks in public.
   i. Not one villain is a person who is kind to animals.
   j. Whoever is an animal lover is a patient person.

2. Identify what kind of claim (A, E, I, O) these are:
   a. Any alligator wrestler is a formidable person.
   b. A few alligator wrestlers are interested in bluegrass.
   c. All folksingers are people who enjoy train rides.
   d. Not every astronomer is a moody person.
   e. Bobby Magee was not Janice's pen pal.
   f. 65% of Southern women are people who prefer mint juleps to soda pop.
   g. No Canadian is a person who dislikes moose.
   h. Some people who photograph caribou are not tourists.
   i. A whole lot of tourists are people who are enthusiastic about scenery.

Exercises

Part One

Directions: State the quantity and quality of the categorical propositions below, and identify the proposition as A, E, I, or O.

1. All chocolate is a sinful food.
2. No dog is an animal that likes lettuce.
3. Some skunks are not animals that like mornings.
4. All fish are creatures with scales.
5. Some snakes are not poisonous reptiles.
6. Some macaws are sociable birds.
7. No leopard is a native of Baffin Island.
8. All the mammals in Ruth's backyard are deer.
9. Some radiologists are not people who are scared of dentists.
10. No Shakespearean actor is a person who needs memory lessons.
11. Some wombats are vicious beasts when angered.
12. All diners who eat their peas with a knife are folks who like cornbread.
13. Some people who sing at the top of their lungs are courteous drivers.
14. All dogs are animals capable of eating slippers.
15. Some students are people who are fond of chimichangas.
16. Aki is an awfully well-behaved pup.
17. No well-behaved pup is a dog that shreds couches.
18. Some animals that shred couches are disobedient cats.
19. Some seniors are people who like to crochet.
20. All photographers are people who like the unexpected.

Part Two

Directions: Rewrite the propositions below in categorical form, and then state the quantity and quality.

1. Not all islanders know how to swim.
2. Most fish are relaxed in the water.
3. Lots of ice-skaters have strong leg muscles.
4. A few baseball players chew tobacco.
5. Any sumo wrestler likes a back rub.
6. Not all football players are fearless people.
7. Badminton players are not bodybuilders.
8. Most hawks have powerful beaks and piercing eyes.
9. Any woman who takes up snorkeling has a good sense of humor.
10. Several karate students were injured in the park.
11. A couple of hikers got frostbitten last night.
12. Whenever you go surfing, watch out for jellyfish.
13. Much rock climbing is dangerous.
14. Almost all dancers are graceful.
15. Very few roller skaters are self-conscious.
16. Not one of the forest rangers ate the tortilla soup.
17. Nearly all of the frostbitten hikers wore slippers to bed.
18. A few of the badminton players threw tantrums on the court.
19. Not every senior tolerates rambunctious boys.
20. Just about all horror movies disturb a sensitive woman.
21. Many a sumo wrestler enjoys edamame beans and miso soup.
22. Most people who drive a car with a V8 engine put milk in their tea.
23. Not all of the dim sum was left in the dish.
24. Ginny Lou was not happy with the lumpy grits on her plate.
25. None of the snorkeling women got tangled up in the coral reefs.

Quick Quiz

1. *True or false:* "Some horses are ponies" is a particular proposition.
2. An example of a proposition in *standard form is:*
   a. Most pizzas have cheese.
   b. Not all junk food is salty.
   c. 68% of desserts have chocolate as an ingredient.
   d. Some soufflés are tasty desserts.

3. A proposition is:
   a. A claim that expresses an emotion.
   b. An offer made to someone
   c. An assertion that is either true or false.
   d. A value claim.

4. *True or false:* A proposition that is always true is called a contingent claim.

5. A proposition that is always false is called (a) a tautology, (b) a contradiction, or (c) a contingent claim.

6. An example of a *compound proposition* is:
   a. Some pets are not destructive animals.
   b. Jasper ripped the thermostat off the wall with his beak.
   c. 88% of cockatoos like to chew on wood.
   d. Both the African Grey and the cockatoo are birds that can talk.

7. A proposition that does not contain a logical connective like "and," "or," or "if . . . then" is called (a) a simple proposition or (b) a compound proposition.

8. "Either the dog ate the shoes or they have been stolen" is (a) a conjunction or (b) a disjunction.

9. *True or false*: An example of a contingent claim is "The soup was lukewarm."

10. "Having ketchup is necessary for Grandma to enjoy her eggs" would be written:
    a. If she has ketchup, then Grandma will enjoy her eggs.
    b. Grandma has ketchup and she'll enjoy her eggs.
    c. If Grandma does not have ketchup, she won't enjoy her eggs.
    d. Grandma neither had ketchup nor enjoyed her eggs.

Symbolizing Propositions

To analyze an argument, we need to see its structure. Logicians prefer a symbolic language using variables (letters of the alphabet) and logical connectives. The result is a kind of logical x-ray. It makes the structure explicit and provides a handy shorthand method so sentences and arguments can be examined easily and quickly.

Logical Connectives	Symbol	Expression	Alternatives
And	&	P & Q	$\wedge$ and •
Or	$\vee$	P $\vee$ Q	none
If . . . then	$\rightarrow$	P $\rightarrow$ Q	$\supset$
If and only if	$\equiv$	P $\equiv$ Q	$\leftrightarrow$
Not	$\sim$	P $\sim$ Q	none

Note: "P if and only if Q" could also be expressed "P is equivalent to Q," with the connective then referred to as equivalence.

Translations.   When symbolizing a sentence, mark all the *logical connectives*. Symbolize simple propositions with capital letters (A, B, C, etc.). Pick a letter that corresponds with a key word in the proposition in question; otherwise, it's going to be hard to look at the finished translation and double check it for accuracy.

Steps in Translating a Proposition

Translate the following proposition:

If I run out of gas, then my car will stop.

Step 1: Unpack the Structure.   We do this by examining the hierarchy of the connectives. This proposition's structure is straightforward because there is only one connective. The structure is:

If (I run out of gas) **then** (my car will stop).

This is a conditional claim, with the antecedent "I run out of gas" and consequent "my car will stop."

Step 2: Assign Variables to Component Propositions.   Replace the antecedent "I run out of gas" and consequent "my car will stop" with variables (A, B, C, etc.). Let the variables stand for the propositions.

Assign: R = I'll run out of gas.
          S = my car will stop.

Be careful: Assign a different variable for one and only one proposition at a time. Never use the same variable for two different propositions, or the resulting translation will be incorrect. Pick something obvious, like "R" and "S" above.

Step 3: Replace Component Propositions with the Assigned Variable

Rewrite as: If R then S.

Step 4: Put Symbols in Place of All the Logical Connectives.   In this case, the → goes in the place where the "then" is located.

Translation: R → S

Example of a Translation

Now let us translate this sentence: If we plant sunflowers and pansies, then either Mario or Debbie will pull out the weeds.

Step 1: Unpack the structure.   We have:

> **If** (we plant sunflowers <u>and</u> pansies) **then** (either Mario <u>or</u> Debbie will pull out the weeds).

Note: the main connective in bold is the "if . . . then." The antecedent is "we plant sunflowers and pansies," and the consequent is "either Mario or Debbie will pull out the weeds." Because both the antecedent and consequent are compound propositions, we have to mark those logical connectives, too. Those are underlined above.

Step 2: Assign Variables to Component Propositions.

> *Assign:* S = we plant sunflowers   P = we plant pansies
> M = Mario will pull out the weeds   D = Debbie will pull out the weeds

We are now ready to substitute the variables into the proposition:

> **If** (we plant sunflowers and pansies) **then** (either Mario or Debbie will pull out the weeds).

Step 3: Replace Component Propositions with the Assigned Variables.

> *Rewrite as:* **If** (S and P) **then** (M or D).

Step 4: Replace Connectives with Their Symbols.   We are almost done! All we have to do is put in the symbols for the connectives.

> *Translation:* $(S \ \& \ P) \rightarrow (M \lor D)$

Recap: Faced with a compound proposition, locate all the logical connectives, and look for the superstructure. Once you have the main connectives and subconnectives, you can assign variables to the individual propositions and complete the translation. Let's do another proposition:

> If boys and girls enjoy sports, then Yahaira will like either football or track.

Note the connectives: "If, and, then, either, or." The main connective is the "If/then" and between the "If" and the "then" is the conjunction "and." After the "then" is this "either/or" construction. This can be set out as follows:

> **If** (boys enjoy sports <u>and</u> girls enjoy sports) **then** (<u>either</u> Yahaira will like football <u>or</u> she'll like track).

The main connective is in bold. Symbolize the proposition:

> Put the "$\rightarrow$" under the "**then.**" Put in "&" for the "and" and the "$\lor$" for the "or."

Using variables B, G, F, and T we can write out the translation:

> *Translation:* $(B \ \& \ G) \rightarrow (F \lor T)$

Translation of an Argument

Let's symbolize an entire argument:

> The stairs creak only if the house is haunted (C, H). If the stairs do not creak, then Elmira won't be scared (C, S). If Elmira isn't scared, she'll chew her fingernails. (S, F). Either the house is not haunted or Elmira is scared. (H, S). So, either the stairs creak or Elmira will chew her fingernails. (C, F).

Premises	*Translation*
P_1: The stairs creak only if the house is haunted (C, H).	$\sim H \rightarrow \sim C$
P_2: If the stairs don't creak, Elmira won't be scared (C, S).	$\sim C \rightarrow \sim S$
P_3: If Elmira isn't scared, she will chew her fingernails. (S, F)	$\sim S \rightarrow \sim F$
P_4: Either the house is not haunted or Elmira is scared. (H, S)	$\sim H \vee S$
C: So, either the stairs creak or Elmira will chew her fingernails. (C, F)	$\therefore C \vee F$

Note: The symbol "$\therefore$" stands for "therefore."

Punctuation and Precision

Being sloppy with punctuation can lead to disaster. If we are not precise with punctuation, we may end up with a proposition that can be misinterpreted and a translation saying something different than the original proposition. Because of this, we need to learn precision.

Think of it this way: Do you want a sloppy brain surgeon cutting into your cerebellum? Do you want your car mechanic using imprecise calipers to adjust your car's brakes? Absolutely not! So we should be careful with punctuation. As a convention, start with parentheses, then use square brackets, then curly brackets. For example,

$$\{P \vee [Q \rightarrow (R \,\&\, S)]\}$$

This expresses the proposition of the form:

Either P **or,** <u>if</u> Q <u>then</u>, both R *and* S.

This is the form of the claim:

Either rats are in the walls **or,** <u>if</u> there are squirrels in the walls, <u>then</u> they are awfully large <u>and</u> make high screeching sounds.

The superstructure of this proposition is a disjunction. The first disjunct is P, and the second disjunct is "If Q then both R and S." We now have a convention that allows all of us to use the same packaging and easily read complex propositions. For example, "Either rats are on the roof or, if squirrels are in the attic, then they are awfully large and noisy" is symbolized $R \vee [S \rightarrow (L \,\&\, N)]$.

Exercises

Part One

Directions: Translate the following sentences using variables and logical connectives. Use the letters indicated as your variables.

1. Either the skunk pulled out the roses or the puppy is not yet trained. (S, P)
2. If Ryan needs to rest, then we should break for lunch. (R, B)
3. Either the FedEx guy threw the package over the fence and crushed the Australian violets or the raccoon was at fault. (F, C, R)
4. If another snail gets in my garden and chomps holes in the violets, then Anna will show no mercy. (S, C, M)
5. If Emmy Lou Harris cancels the concert, then Jody will be unhappy and listen to the Soggy Bottom Mountain Boys. (E, J, S)
6. Either the grasshoppers ate the begonia or something weird is going on. (G, W)
7. If the medfly returns and the city sprays pesticides, then we are in trouble. (M, C, T)
8. Jasper will get sick if he eats that centipede. (S, C)
9. Either the cat was stolen or it was hauled off by the coyotes last night. (S, C)
10. If the files are sent and the computer crashes, we'll be in trouble. (F, C, T)
11. Chicken soup and vitamin C help fight a cold. (S, V)
12. If mosquitoes are in the room and keep buzzing, Carlos won't be able to sleep. (M, K, C)
13. Brazilian flamethrowers and violets are in bloom, but the poppies look dead. (B, V, P)
14. Chemistry is a useful subject, if you plan to be a doctor. (C, P)
15. If Jasmine is not consistent, she won't be able to train her puppy. (C, T)
16. If Tina does more typing, her eyes will bulge and become bright red. (T, B, R)
17. If Anita sprays insecticide, the grasshoppers will die, but if she wants to avoid toxic chemicals, she'll kill them by hand. (S, G, W, K)
18. He has a great voice and wants to go on *American Idol,* but Holly forgot his name. (G, A, H)
19. Although Jamal is not a journalist, he is a good writer. (J, W)
20. If Vera does not smoke, then she won't get lung cancer, but she should watch her asthma. (V, L, A)
21. If Ernie takes either physics or statistics next semester, he'll cut back on his part-time job. (P, S, C)

22. Either Russell will work on his American lit essay or drive to the beach and hang out with Carlos. (W, D, C)

23. If Robbie takes both physics and anthropology next semester, he'll quit his raquetball lessons. (P, A, Q)

24. Either Anita will yank out the ivy and plant primroses, or she will dig up the wilted Peruvian lily and replace it with a potato vine. (I, P, D, R)

25. Only if Anita yanks out the ivy will Gary help her with the primroses. (A, G)

26. Gary helping with the primroses is necessary for Anita to be able to clear space before lunch. (G, A)

27. Ryan falling on the new potato vine was sufficient to make Anita unhappy and Gary frustrated. (R, A, G)

28. Evan planted loquat seeds in the yard, but Connolly showed no interest in gardening. (E, C)

29. If both Paul and Evan go to Chicago, then Laurel will be able to work only if she gets help with Connolly. (P, E, L, H)

30. If the morning glories spread to the fence and overtake the roses, then we'll have to cut them back; but if they don't get invasive, the morning glories will do fine in the garden. (S, O, C, I, F)

Part Two

Directions: Using the variables indicated and logical connectives, symbolize the following more complex propositions.

1. If Rachel buys a computer, she can start her own cooking blog, but so far she doesn't seem interested. (B, C, I)

2. If Sam does not wake up from his nap, then he won't be able to make little meatballs for dinner. (N, M)

3. Not just veterinarians came to the Save the Walruses concert. (V, W)

4. Unless the protestors get out of the road, there'll be a traffic jam. (P, T)

5. Reading three newspapers is time consuming; however, Omar likes getting to see the news from different points of view and being informed. (T, O, I)

6. If Sarah is not mistaken, then Carlos did not attend the speech but heard about it from Omar. (S, A, H)

7. A lot of protestors were handing out the leaflets, yet the mayor took the time to come out of his office and talk with them. (P, H, M, T)

8. Ernie and Sam will take photographs only if they have a flash; however, it may not have batteries. (E, S, F, B)

9. Whenever he takes photographs of food, Ernie sneaks some and eats it later. (P, S, E)

10. Not all the protestors wanted to go to the rally, although it is not true that Carlos fell asleep during the speeches. (P, W, C)

Quick Quiz

1. What symbol do you use for "if . . . then"?

2. How would you translate "Either the skunk pulled out the primroses or the puppy is not yet trained"? (S, P)

3. What symbol do you use for a disjunction?

4. How would you translate "Either the power steering is leaking or I'm mistaken"? (P, M)

5. What symbol do you use for a conjunction?

6. How would you translate "If Ryan needs to rest, then we should break for lunch"? (R, B)

7. What do you do to indicate that an entire proposition is false?

8. How would you translate "If it's a parrot, then it can sing and talk"? (P, S, T)

Rules of Replacement for Ordinary Language

There are seven rules of replacement for ordinary language. They are (1) "only," (2) "the only," (3) "unless," (4) "sufficient," (5) "necessary," (6) the "evers" (whatever, whenever, etc.), and (7) negation.

Rule 1: "Only." "Only" functions as an exclusion, narrowing down the territory of the predicate class. Any proposition of the form "Only P is Q" can be rewritten as "If not P, then not Q." This is also equivalent to "All Q is P." Propositions of the form "Only P is Q" are symbolized as follows:

Forms of "Only P Is Q" $(\sim P \rightarrow \sim Q) \equiv (Q \rightarrow P)$

Only P is Q
$\rightarrow$ If it's not P, then it's not Q.
$\rightarrow$ If it's a Q, then it's a P.
$\rightarrow$ All Q is P.

Examples

Only Americans eat hamburgers.
$\rightarrow$ If they are not Americans, they won't eat hamburgers.
$\rightarrow$ If they eat hamburgers, they are Americans.

→ All people who eat hamburgers are Americans.
Translation: ~A → ~H (*form 1*) or H → A (*form 2*)

Only skinny women can be models.
→ If she's not skinny, she can't be a model.
→ If she is a model, then she is skinny.
→ All models are skinny.
Translation: ~S → ~M (*form 1*) or M → S (*form 2*)

See how the exclusion works? In the first example, the use of "only" narrows down those who eat hamburgers to Americans—everyone else is excluded. In the second example, "only" limits those who can be models to skinny women; everyone else is excluded.

Rule 2: "The only." Another exclusion is "the only." Here it is the subject being restricted, *not* the predicate as above. Any proposition of the form "The only P is Q" can be rewritten "If not Q, then not P." It is also equivalent to "All P is Q." Propositions of the form "The only P is Q" are symbolized as follows:

Forms of "The Only P Is Q" (~Q → ~P) ≡ (P → Q)

The only P is Q.
→ If it's not Q, then it's not P.
→ If it's a P, then it's a Q.
→ All P is Q.

Examples

The only woman for Romeo is Juliet.
→ If she's not Juliet, then she's not the woman for Romeo.
→ If she's the woman for Romeo, then she's Juliet.
Translation: ~J → ~W (*form 1*) or W → J (*form 2*)

The only outer gear the count owns is a cape.
→ If it's not a cape, it's not outer gear the count owns.
→ If it's outer gear the count owns, then it's a cape.
→ All the outer gear the count owns are capes.
Translation: ~C → ~O (*form 1*) or O → C (*form 2*)

See how the exclusion works? In the first example, "the only" limits women for Romeo to Juliet; all other women are excluded. In the second example, "the only" limits outer gear the count owns to capes; everything else is excluded.

The Connection between "Only" and "the Only." We can change an "only" claim to one that starts with "the only." If we focus on the object, we can see how they relate. Look at this example:

The only woman for Romeo is Juliet.
This is the same as: Only Juliet is the woman for Romeo.

Do you see what happened? In both cases, the object of Romeo's affection is Juliet. This can be expressed using either "the only" or "only," but the terms are switched. In other words:

The only P is Q *is equivalent to* Only Q is P.

So we can move back and forth between them, but we need to switch the order of the terms, P and Q, in doing so.

Rule 3: "Unless."   Propositions of the form "P unless Q" can be expressed as either a conditional claim or a disjunction. As a conditional claim, it can be written, "If not Q then P." In other words, if you *don't* have Q, then P occurs. The second way to write "P unless Q" is "Either P or Q." To get to this second construction, just toss out the "unless" and replace it with "or" (or "either/or"), and you are done (see Figure 4.2).

Forms of "P unless Q" $(\sim Q \rightarrow P) \equiv (P \lor Q)$

P unless Q.
$\rightarrow$ If not Q, then P.
$\rightarrow$ Either P or Q.

Examples

We will go on a picnic unless it rains.
$\rightarrow$ If it does not rain, we will go on a picnic.
$\rightarrow$ Either we went on a picnic or it rained.
Translation: $\sim R \rightarrow P$ (*form 1*) or $R \lor P$ (*form 2*)

Unless Joe stops the car, he's going to hit the moose.
$\rightarrow$ If Joe does not stop the car, he's going to hit the moose.
$\rightarrow$ Either Joe stops the car or he's going to hit the moose.
Translation: $\sim S \rightarrow M$ (*form 1*) or $S \lor M$ (*form 2*)

FIGURE 4.2
Knowing the meaning of "unless" can be very useful!

Photograph by Wanda Teays. Copyright 2008.

Alternatives to "Unless."   An alternative to "unless" is "without." It is treated exactly the same as "unless," so it would be rewritten in either form (the conditional or the disjunction). So, you would translate "Without ice cream, pie is bland," as "If you do not have ice cream, the pie is bland."

Rule 4: "Sufficient."   "P is sufficient for Q" asserts that Q will happen whenever P occurs. In other words, "P is sufficient for Q" is equivalent to "If P then Q." This is symbolized as $P \rightarrow Q$.

Form of "P is Sufficient for Q" $(P \rightarrow Q)$

P is sufficient for Q.
$\rightarrow$ If P then Q.
Translation: $P \rightarrow Q$

Examples

Traveling to Montreal is sufficient for seeing maple leaves.
$\rightarrow$ If you travel to Montreal, then you will see maple leaves.
Translation: $T \rightarrow S$

Getting free airfare to Tokyo would be sufficient for my going there.
$\rightarrow$ If I get free airfare to Tokyo, I will go there.
Translation: $F \rightarrow G$

Alternatives to "Sufficient."   "Provided that" functions the same as "sufficient." So, you would translate "I'll take flute lessons, provided that you take up the electric guitar" as "If you take up the electric guitar, then I'll take flute lessons."

Rule 5: "Necessary."   "P is necessary for Q" asserts that Q won't happen without P. That is, if you don't have P, you won't have Q. So, if you have Q, you must also have P.

Forms of "P is Necessary for Q" $(\sim P \rightarrow \sim Q) \equiv (Q \rightarrow P)$

P is necessary for Q.
$\rightarrow$ If not P then not Q.
$\rightarrow$ If Q then P.
Translation: $Q \rightarrow P$ or the logically equivalent form: $\sim P \rightarrow \sim Q$

Examples

Oxygen is necessary to stay alive.
$\rightarrow$ If you do not have oxygen, you cannot live.
$\rightarrow$ If you live, then you had oxygen.
Translation: $\sim O \rightarrow \sim L$ *(form 1)* or $L \rightarrow O$ *(form 2)*

Gas in the tank is necessary for my car to be driven to work.
$\rightarrow$ If I don't have gas in the tank, I won't be able to drive to work.
$\rightarrow$ If I am able to drive to work, then I had gas in the tank.
Translation: $\sim G \rightarrow \sim D$ *(form 1)* or $D \rightarrow G$ *(form 2)*

The Relationship between "Necessary" and "Only." If we say something is necessary for something else, we are saying the second thing will happen *only* if the first one does. In other words, "P is necessary for Q" is the same as "Q only if P." This means that "Q only if P" can also be written "If Q then P."

Rule 6: The "Evers." The "evers" include "whenever," "whoever," "whatever," "wherever," and special constructions of "however." Any proposition with the "ever" construction should be treated as a universal claim. These propositions can be rewritten as conditional claims. This is symbolized P → Q.

Forms of the "Evers" (P → Q)

Whenever P is Q.
→ If P then Q.
Translation: P → Q

Note: This also applies to "whatever," "whoever," and "wherever" constructions. It applies to "however" constructions in the form of "whatever way," rather than functioning as a conjunction. It does not apply to "never" (see "Negations," below).

Examples

Whenever you go on your vacation, it rains.
→ If you go on your vacation, then it rains.

Whoever is hiding behind the tree is making grunting sounds.
→ If someone is hiding behind the tree, then that person is making grunting sounds.

However you tie the bow, it looks silly.
→ If you tie the bow, then it looks silly.

Rule 7: Negations. Negations take the form "P is never Q," "It is not true that P," "Not only P is Q," "Not just P is Q," and "It is false that P."

Form of a Double Negative

It is not true that P is not the case.
→ P is the case.
Translation: P

Form of "Never"

P is never Q.
→ No P is Q.
→ If P then not Q.
Translation: P → ~Q

Example

Men can never experience pregnancy.
→ If the person is a man, then he cannot experience pregnancy.
→ No man can experience pregnancy.

Form of "Not All"

Not all P is Q.
→ Some P is not Q.
Translation: P & ~Q

Examples

Not all comedians are ticklish people.
→ Some comedians are not ticklish people.

Not every joke is funny.
→ Some things are jokes and they are not funny.

Form of "Not None"

It is not the case that no P is Q.
→ Some P is Q.
Translation: P & Q

Basically this is a double negative. If there is "not none," there are "some." For example, if it's not true that no cat bites its owner, then there are some cats that bite their owners.

Examples

It is false that no sauces are fattening.
→ Some sauces are fattening.

It's not true that no one can sing the national anthem.
→ Some people can sing the national anthem.

Form of "Not Only"

Not only P is Q.
→ Some Q is not P.

Note: With "not only," the order of the P and Q switches in the translation.

Examples

Not only turnips are vegetables.
→ Some vegetables are not turnips.

Not only models are thin people.
→ Some thin people are not models.

Form of "Not Just"

Not just P is Q.
→ Some Q is not P

Note: Treat this form exactly the same as a "not only" claim.

Example

Not just sculptors are artists.
→ Some artists are not sculptors.

Form of "Not If/Then"

It's not true that if P then Q.
→ Some P are not Q.

Note: Treat this form exactly the same as a "not all" claim.

Example

It's not true that if babies are thrown in the water they will swim.
→ Some babies are thrown in the water and they do not swim.

Rules of Replacement for Ordinary Language

1. "Only"	Form 1	Only P is Q	If it's not P, then it's not Q.
	Form 2	Only P is Q	All Q is P.
2. "The only"	Form 1	The only P is Q	If it's not Q, then it's not P.
	Form 2	The only P is Q	All P is Q.
3. "Unless"	Form 1	P unless Q	If it's not Q, then P.
	Form 2	P unless Q	Either P or Q.
4. "Sufficient"		P is sufficient for Q	If P then Q.
5. "Necessary"	Form 1	P is necessary for Q	If not P then not Q.
	Form 2	P is necessary for Q	If Q then P.

6. "When/what/how/where/whoever"

Form 1	When/what/how/where/whoever P is Q.	If P then Q.
Form 2	When/what/how/where/whoever P is Q.	All P is Q.

7. Negations

P is never Q	Form 1: No P is Q.
	Form 2: If P then not Q.
Not all P is Q	Some P is not Q
Not none/not no one of P is Q	Some P is Q
Not only P is Q	Some Q is not P
Not just P is Q	Some Q is not P
It is not true that if P then Q	Some P is not Q

Formal Rules of Replacement

The remaining rules of replacement focus on logical structure. These rules provide the means to translate from one logical form to another equivalent form.

Rule 8: DeMorgan's Laws.   These are two special forms of negations. With the "not both" construction, one of the choices is being denied—either the first option or the second one. With a "neither . . . nor" construction, *both* options are being denied: the first choice *and* the second one.

DeMorgan's Law 1: Not Both ~ (P & Q) ≡ (~P v ~Q)

Not both P and Q.
→ It is not true that both P and Q is the case.
→ Either P is not the case or Q is not the case.

DeMorgan's Law 2: Neither/Nor ~ (P v Q) ≡ (~P & ~Q)

Neither P nor Q.
→ It is not true that either P or Q is the case.
→ P is not the case and Q is not the case.

Example of "Not Both"

Not both Kung Pao beef and lasagna are Chinese food.
→ Either Kung Pao beef is not Chinese food or lasagna is not Chinese food.

Jamie does not like both bluegrass and jazz.
→ Either Jamie does not like bluegrass or she does not like jazz.

Examples of "Neither/Nor"

Neither frogs nor salamanders are in the water.
→ Frogs are not in the water and salamanders are not in the water.

Ben likes neither octopus nor squid.
→ Ben does not like octopus and Ben does not like squid.

Rule 9: Transposition.   The rule of transposition allows us to flip the antecedent and consequent in a conditional claim—but doing so requires the terms to change to their opposites (positive/negative). In other words, transposing the antecedent and consequent requires us to change the quality of each one at the same time. (In short, flip and switch.)

Form of Transposition (P → Q) ≡ (~Q → ~P)

If P then Q.
→ If not Q then not P.

Examples of Transposition

If Lisa doesn't hurry, then she will be late to school.
→ If she was not late to school, then Lisa hurried.

If Homer gets muddy boots, he can't step on the rug.
→ If Homer can step on the rug, then he can't have muddy boots.

Rule 10: Material Implication.   Material implication allows us to go from a conditional claim ("if/then") to a disjunction ("either/or"), with one proviso. When we make the switch, the first term is negated. In other words, "If there's mud, we need galoshes" can change to the disjunction "Either there's *not* mud or we need galoshes." Do you see why the "not" had to be interjected?

Form of Material Implication $(P \rightarrow Q) \equiv (\sim P \vee Q)$

If P then Q → Either not P or Q.

Note: You can go from the conditional "if/then" to the disjunction "either/or" and vice versa.

Examples of Material Implication

If Casey does not stop screaming, then Christina will plug her ears.
→ Either Casey stopped screaming or Christina plugged her ears.

Either the basement flooded or the sandbags worked.
→ If the basement did not flood, then the sandbags worked.

Rule 11: Exportation.   Any conditional claim with a conjunction in the antecedent can be rewritten as an "if/then" chain (and vice versa).

Form of Exportation $[(A \ \& \ B) \rightarrow C] \equiv [A \rightarrow (B \rightarrow C)]$

If A and B, then C.
→ If A then, if B then C.

Note: Do you see how the second conjunct in the antecedent was shipped back to the consequent?

Examples of Exportation

If he spills paint and doesn't wipe it up, then there will be a mess.
→ If he spills paint, then, if he doesn't wipe it up, there will be a mess.

If the flashlight's on, then, if we aim it in the cave, the bats fly out.
→ If the flashlight's on and we aim it in the cave, the bats fly out.

Rule 12: Equivalence.   This is also known as a biconditional or an "if and only if" claim. This rule allows us to set out the two component parts of a biconditional claim in two different ways.

Forms of Biconditional Propositions

"P if and only if Q" can be written in two equivalent forms:
→ If P then Q, and if Q then P.
→ If P then Q, and if not P then not Q.
Translation of form 1: $(P \rightarrow Q) \ \& \ (Q \rightarrow P)$
Translation of form 2: $(P \rightarrow Q) \ \& \ (\sim P \rightarrow \sim Q)$

Example of Equivalence

Fish can swim if and only if they are in the water.
→ If fish are in the water then they can swim, and if fish can swim then they are in the water.
→ If fish are in the water then they can swim, and if fish are not in the water then they cannot swim.
Translation of form 1: (F → W) & (W → F)
Translation of form 2: (F → W) & (~F → ~W)

Exercises

Part One

Directions: Rewrite the following in an equivalent form using the rules of replacement.

1. Unless that's Adam, don't set out the toys.
2. Only a DVD can fit in the machine.
3. Not only maple leaves change colors in the fall.
4. Avocados are necessary to make guacamole.
5. Not both Peter and Moosh like raisin cookies.
6. Neither Moosh nor Peter like morning swims.
7. Barking puppies are sufficient to turn the pet store into chaos.
8. Unless the spare tire has air in it, we are going to need some help.
9. Not both Evan and Connolly like to wear baseball caps.
10. Taking the 8:00 A.M. plane is sufficient to get to Albuquerque for lunch.
11. Unless that's your mother watering the plants, we should call the police.
12. Marissa is not amused by either mud wrestling or snake charming.
13. Nicole is not thrilled by both bungie jumping and the luge.
14. Neither a raft nor a boat can make it over the waterfall.
15. Unless Max makes chicken pot pie, grandpa will be upset.
16. Getting into the toy box is sufficient to keep Jasper busy.
17. Li Ming will make dim sum unless she makes tamales.
18. Not only sunsets are beautiful things in nature.
19. A warm day is necessary to have a good pool party.
20. Only if we serve corn chowder will Darin come to dinner.
21. Ivana is not both a fan of watercolors and oil painting.
22. Neither watermelon nor cantaloupe is a vegetable.
23. A wet suit is necessary for surfers to keep warm in the water.

24. A noisy helicopter is sufficient to irritate King Kong.
25. Not only scary movies cause nightmares.

Part Two

Directions: Rewrite the following, without the underlined word or phrase, using the appropriate rule of replacement.

1. Only blizzards stop Kerry from working out at the gym.
2. Unless the fog rolls in, Peter is going with Linda to the movie.
3. Neither hurricanes nor floods bother Omar.
4. Only if there's an earthquake will Cubby be scared.
5. Whenever there's a tornado, Zenon sleeps downstairs.
6. The only time Grandma screams is when she sees a dead possum.
7. Not both Percy and Ubu like liver.
8. Finding a hawk feather was sufficient to please Ruth.
9. Being tall is necessary for joining the basketball team.
10. Neither football nor soccer involves swimming.
11. Only if you shout can I find you in the cave.
12. Unless there's mustard on the sandwich, the boys won't touch it.
13. Whenever the baby throws food on the floor, the pup wolfs it down.
14. Without chocolate, peanut butter isn't real tasty.
15. Candlelight is necessary for a romantic evening.
16. Squeak eats crunchies, provided that he doesn't get liver.
17. Without a friend, the little pony is sad and lonely.
18. Not both bagels and croissants are French pastries.
19. It is not the case that all enchiladas are made with meat.
20. A letter from home is sufficient to make Laura excited.
21. It is not true that if you can drive a car you can tap dance.
22. Not just oatmeal sticks to your stomach.
23. Not only a howling wind creates atmosphere.
24. It is false that if you can dance, you can swim.

Part Three

Directions: Rewrite the following using the rule of replacement as indicated.

1. Using DeMorgan's Law, rewrite: Not both Oaxaca and Toronto are in Canada.
2. Using DeMorgan's Law, rewrite: Neither Taos nor Minneapolis are in Mexico.

3. Using material implication, rewrite: Either snakes are taking over Guam or the news show exaggerated.

4. Using transposition, rewrite: If that's jello, then it's not protoplasm.

5. Using transposition, rewrite: If that's Fatso, then it's not Casper.

6. Using DeMorgan's Law, rewrite: Not both novels and poetry are on the shelf.

7. Using DeMorgan's Law, rewrite: Neither drama nor action films interest Jamal.

8. Using exportation, rewrite: If the book is stolen and she can't read the assignment, Keisha will not be able to finish her homework.

9. Using material implication, rewrite: If the tire's not flat, then we can go home.

10. Using material implication, rewrite: Either the deliveryman is sick or his car is not working again.

11. Using material implication, rewrite: If the pilots walk out, we can't make it to Lexington.

12. Using equivalence, rewrite: The workers will organize if and only if they have a leader.

13. Using equivalence, rewrite: The doctors will strike if and only if the nurses walk out.

14. Using transposition, rewrite: If Luis gets a new car, he'll sell his hot rod.

15. Using exportation, rewrite: If that's not Greg and is a burglar, then we better run out the backdoor.

16. Using material implication, rewrite: If that's a burglar, then it's not Greg.

17. Using DeMorgan's Law, rewrite: Neither Hector nor Salazar is lonely.

18. Using DeMorgan's Law, rewrite: Not both Russ and Dorothy eat shrimp.

Part Four

1. Name the rule of replacement used below:
   a. If the dog eats George's burger, George will be upset. So, if George is not upset, then the dog did not eat George's burger.
   b. Not both Lenny and Maria like poetry. So either Lenny does not like poetry or Maria does not like poetry.
   c. Either the dog ate Tori's lunch or someone stole it. So, if the dog did not eat Tori's lunch, then someone stole it.
   d. We can make it on time if and only if the bridge is down. So, if we make it on time, then the bridge is down, and if we do not make it on time, then the bridge was not down.
   e. The dog did not eat Tori's bagel and he did not eat Carl's tamale. So, the dog ate neither Tori's bagel nor Carl's tamale.

    f. If the dog ate Rose's ham salad sandwich, he might not have gone for George's burger. So either the dog did not eat Rose's ham salad sandwich or he might not have gone for George's burger.

    g. If we get lost and run out of gas, it doesn't matter if the bridge is down. So, if we get lost then, if we run out of gas, then it doesn't matter if the bridge is down.

2. Rewrite without the "only": Only sore feet keep grandpa from his morning walk.

3. Rewrite in two ways without the "unless": Unless Kineisha can handle a staple gun, she can't put up the posters.

4. Rewrite without the "whenever": Whenever Brad thinks of Malibu, he thinks of home.

5. Name the rule of replacement below:

    a. Either the creek is dry or we can dunk our toes in the water. This is equivalent to: If the creek is not dry, then we can dunk our toes in the water.

    b. If Rahma does not stop singing at the top of her lungs, she'll wake the neighbors. This is equivalent to: If Rahma did not wake the neighbors, then she stopped singing at the top of her lungs.

    c. Not both Sylvester and Tweetie are birds. This means either Sylvester is not a bird or Tweetie is not a bird.

6. Rewrite using transposition: If the painter keeps leaving lids off paint cans, his boss will be upset.

7. Rewrite without the "only if": Only if Alex learns to hold the hammer will he quit hitting his thumb.

Part Five

Directions: Rewrite the following sentences without the underlined word (and then symbolize if you can).

1. <u>Only</u> Indiana Jones and Wonder Woman know the secret code.

2. June will come to the spring dance <u>provided that</u> she gets a ride.

3. A <u>necessary condition</u> for a peace accord is that both sides must stop bio-warfare production.

4. Elizabeth will go see her parents <u>only if</u> she can go with them to the Garth Brooks concert.

5. It is <u>sufficient</u> for my cat to have fleas for me to bathe him today.

6. A <u>necessary condition</u> for giving Ubu a bath is that he is dirty.

7. <u>Unless</u> Cody leaves the skunk alone, he's going to be very sorry.

8. <u>Without</u> proper nutrition, your body will disintegrate.

9. <u>Whenever</u> Araceli stays up too late, her eyes are red and puffy.

10. <u>Only when</u> John plays racquetball does he feel in top shape.

Part Six

1. Translate the following argument using logical connectives and variables:

   If George smokes and drinks too much, then he doesn't sleep well. (S, D, W) If he doesn't sleep well or doesn't eat well, then George feels rotten. (E, R) If George feels rotten, then he does not clean his room and does not do his homework. (C, H) George drinks too much. Therefore, George does not do his homework.

2. Translate the following argument using variables and logical connectives:

   There are ghouls in my basement, but no vampires. (G, V) Only if there are vampires in my basement will I get angry. (A) If there are ghouls in my basement, then I'm not both dialing 911 and calling an exterminator. (D, E) I didn't dial 911. Therefore, I will get angry, but there are no ghouls in my basement.

3. Translate this argument:

   If I watch *Alien,* I'll be scared, but if I don't watch *Alien,* I'll be bored. (W, S, B) If I am bored, I get listless and start chopping onions. (L, C) If I start chopping onions, then my eyes water and my mascara runs. (E, M) If I'm scared, I'll pull my hair and bite my fingernails. (P, F) If I bite my fingernails, my hands won't be beautiful. (H) I watched *Alien.* Therefore, my hands won't be beautiful.

4. Translate this argument:

   There are marshmallows in the kitchen, but no chocolate. (M, C) Only if there are marshmallows and chocolate can I rest easy. (E) If either I rest easy or I do breathing exercises, then I can both sleep peacefully and not have nightmares. (B, S, N) I don't sleep peacefully if it's raining outside; however, if it's not raining, my dog barks. (R, D) Therefore, I will rest easy if I don't have nightmares, but my dog barks.

5. Translate this argument:

   If Ubu is sick, either he was chasing Jasper or he ate the meatball. (S, C, A) Ubu was chasing Jasper only if Jasper was out of his cage. (O) If Jasper was out of his cage, then Silvio was home. (S) If Silvio was home, then he wasn't working. (W) Silvio was working, but Ubu is sick. Therefore, Ubu ate the meatball.

6. Translate this argument:

   Either George ate the lemon pie or a thief broke into the house and stole it. (G, B, S) If George ate the lemon pie, then Keisha will be furious. (K) If a thief broke into the house, then we should either call the police or plan a way to trap the thief. (C, P) Keisha is not furious, but we will not plan a way to trap the thief. Therefore, we should call the police.

7. Translate this argument:

   If Jasper is out of his cage, then either the cats will start chasing him or he'll perch up on top of the cabinets. (O, C, P) If Jasper perches on top of the cabinets and is safe from the cats, then we can relax. (S, R) The cats will start chasing Jasper only if they are not napping. (N) Jasper is out of his cage and is safe from the cats, and the cats are napping. Therefore, we can relax.

8. Translate this argument:

If Bob told the truth, then the water was on; and if Gina told the truth, then the lights were out when the storm hit. (B, W, G, L) If neither Bob nor Gina is telling the truth, then an intruder got into the compound and left the kittens by the gate. (I, K) The water was not on. There were kittens by the gate. So, if there was an intruder who got into the compound, then Gina did not tell the truth.

9. Translate this argument:

There are moths in my closet, but no cockroaches. (M, C) For Steve to get upset, it is sufficient that moths are in his closet. (U) It there are either moths or cockroaches in the closet, then Steve can sleep peacefully. (S) Steve didn't sleep peacefully. Therefore, Steve will get upset, but there are no cockroaches in his closet.

10. Translate this argument:

There is a snail in Rose's patio. (S) If there is a snail in Rose's patio, then she is going to put borax around the door. (D) If she puts borax around the door, she won't have to worry about any slimy intruders. (I) If she doesn't have to worry about slimy intruders, she can relax and do email. (R, E) Therefore, Rose can relax and do email.

11. Translate this argument:

We will go on spring vacation only if Phil can spare the time. (S, P) However, if Marcie wants Phil to fix the roof, then we will change our plans and hold off until the fall. (M, C, H) Either we'll go on spring vacation or Marcie wants Phil to fix the roof and clear the woodpile from the yard. (W) So, either Phil can spare the time or we should hold off until fall.

12. Translate this argument:

If either John ("the Hand") or Tony ("the Fox") call, then tell him Rocky left for a vacation. (J, T, R) It is not true that Rocky is leaving for a vacation. Rather, he is going to stay indoors and work on a screenplay about crime. (S, W) If he works on his new screenplay about crime and Tony ("the Fox") does not call, then John ("the Hand") won't call and Rocky can leave for a vacation. Therefore, Rocky is staying indoors.

13. Translate this argument:

Mandy eats chocolate whenever she is depressed or excited. (C, D, E) Mandy had a hard day at school and is tired, but she is not depressed. (H, T) If Mandy has too much chocolate and is frenetic, then she does aerobics. (M, F, A) Either Mandy is doing aerobics or the plumbers are making noise. (P) Therefore, if either Mandy is not doing aerobics or is not tired, then she eats chocolate but is not frenetic.

14. Translate this argument:

Unless that's the wind, there must be zombies pounding on the upstairs windows. (W, Z) If there are zombies pounding on the windows, then we better call for help. (H) Only if we call for help will Dan calm down. (D) Dan did not calm down. If either Adam turns on the outdoor lights or we go outside, then we can see what's responsible for the noise. (A, O, S) We went outside. There were no zombies. Therefore, it must be the wind.

15. Translate this argument:

If Wolfie chews the door handle, then the car will be damaged and have to be fixed. (C, D, F) If Wolfie does not chew the door handle and just runs around the house, no serious problems will occur. (R, P) If the car is neither damaged nor has to be fixed, we could head out to Monterey in the morning. (M) If we head out to Monterey and the traffic is good, then we can make it to the aquarium before late afternoon. (T, A) We didn't make it to the aquarium before late afternoon, but the car was not damaged and did not have to be fixed. Therefore, the traffic was not good.

Quick Quiz

1. *True or false:* "A only if B" is the same as "B is necessary for A."

2. "Not any" is the same as (a) not all or (b) none.

3. "Neither papaya nor blueberries are vegetables" can be expressed as:
   a. Papaya and blueberries are not vegetables.
   b. Either papaya are not vegetables or blueberries are not vegetables.
   c. Not both papaya and blueberries are vegetables.
   d. Papaya are not vegetables and blueberries are not vegetables.

4. *True or false:* Transposition is the same as "unless."

5. "Not both trout and hawks are fish" can be rewritten as:
   a. Trout is not fish and hawks are not fish.
   b. Either trout are not fish or hawks are not fish.
   c. Neither trout nor hawks are fish.
   d. Not only trout and hawks are fish.

6. According to transposition, you can rewrite "If there's thunder and lightning, there'll be rain" as (a) If there's rain, then there'll be thunder and lightning, or (b) If there's not rain, then there'll not be thunder and lightning.

7. *True or false:* One way to express "Jasper will eat corn unless he goes for the eggs" is "Either Jasper ate corn or he went for the eggs."

8. According to equivalence, you can rewrite "There'll be snapplepuffs if and only if there are morks" as (a) If there are snapplepuffs, then there are morks, or (b) If there are snapplepuffs, then there are morks, and if there are morks then there are snapplepuffs.

9. *True or false:* Rules of replacement are valid argument forms.

10. "Not only cows eat grass" can be rewritten as (a) Some cows are not grass-eaters or (b) Some grass-eaters are not cows.

11. "Loud noises are sufficient to disturb Jasper" can be rewritten as (a) If Jasper is disturbed, then there are loud noises or (b) If there are loud noises, then Jasper is disturbed.

12. "Wherever you go, you make people happy" can be rewritten as:
    a. Either you go places or you make people happy.
    b. If you make people happy, then you're going places.
    c. If you go places, then you make people happy.
    d. If you don't go places, you won't make people happy.

Square of Opposition

The ability to draw inferences is not only useful but powerful as well because we go from knowing one thing to learning many other things. The square of opposition sets out vital relationships between the different categorical propositions. Once we know the truth value of one proposition, we can use these relationships to derive other truth values.

Contrary

Two propositions are contraries if they cannot both be true but could both be false. If one is true, then the other one is *necessarily* false. The truth of the A or E claim forces the contrary to be false. Only universal claims can be contraries.

Examples of Contraries

If it is true that "All drummers are musicians," then
→ "No drummer is a musician" must be false.

If it is true that "No dog has wings," then
→ "All dogs have wings" must be false.

Be careful: If an A or E claim is false, it need not mean that the corresponding E or A claim is then true. For instance, the claim "All cats are tigers" is false, but "No cats are tigers" is also false.

Subcontrary

Two propositions are subcontraries if they cannot both be false but could both be true. This is true of the two particular claims. If one is false, then the other must be true.

Examples of Subcontraries

If it is false that "Some dogs are fish," then
→ "Some dogs are not fish" is true.

If it is false that "Some mice are not rodents," thens
→ "Some mice are rodents" is true.

Remember: This only applies when the particular claim is *false*. It could very well be the case that they are *both* true. For instance, "Some dogs are not Chihuahuas" is true, and "Some dogs are Chihuahuas" is also true.

Contradictory

Two propositions are contradictories if they cannot both be true *and* they cannot both be false. All the categorical propositions have contradictories. "All P is Q" is opposite in truth value to "Some P is not Q." "No P is Q" has an opposite truth value to "Some P is Q."

Examples of Contradictories

If it is true that "All horses are mammals," then
→ "Some horses are not mammals" must be false.
If it is true that "Some birds are hawks," then
→ "No bird is a hawk" must be false.
If it is false that "No women are pilots,"
→ "Some women are pilots" must be true.

Subaltern

When a universal claim is true *and* the subject class is not empty of members, we can conclude that the corresponding particular claim is also true. This is called the **subaltern.** The process of going from the universal claim to its corresponding particular claim is called **subalternation.**

Examples of Subalterns

If it is true that "All Persians are cats" *and* we know there exist Persians, then
→ "Some Persians are cats" must be true.
If it is true that "All flying saucers are UFOs," but we don't know that flying
saucers actually exist, then
→ "Some flying saucers are UFOs" cannot be inferred as true.

We can summarize these four inferences in a diagram (see Figure 4.3):

FIGURE 4.3
The Square of Opposition

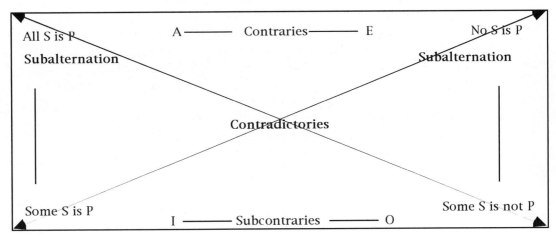

Exercises

Directions: Draw the inferences and truth values in the following (if unknown, just say so).

1. State the subaltern and its truth value of "No novels are film scripts."

2. State the subcontrary and its truth value of the false proposition "Some dinosaurs were insects."

3. State the contrary and its truth value of the false proposition "No hawks are birds."

4. State the subaltern and its truth value of the true proposition "All were-wolves are monsters."

5. State the subcontrary and its truth value of the true proposition "Some animals are ferocious."

6. State the contrary and its truth value of the true proposition "All sewer rats are rodents."

7. State the contradictory and its truth value of the false proposition "Some poisonous lizards make nice pets."

8. State the contrary and its truth value of the true proposition "No well-trained animal bites its owner."

9. State the contradictory and its truth value of the true proposition "All trapeze artists are daring people."

10. Given "All smugglers use airplanes for transport" is false:
    a. State the contrary and its truth value.
    b. State the contradictory and its truth value.

11. State the contradictory and its truth value of the true proposition "No skyscraper is a small building."

12. Given the true proposition "No cheese is a vegetable":
    a. State the contrary and its truth value.
    b. State the contradictory and its truth value.
    c. State the subaltern and its truth value.

13. Given the false proposition "Some chocolate fudge sundaes are nonfattening":
    a. State the subcontrary and its truth value.
    b. State the contradictory and its truth value.

14. Given the true proposition "All Martians are aliens":
    a. State the contrary and its truth value.
    b. State the subaltern and its truth value.
    c. State the contradictory and its truth value.

15. State everything you can infer from the true proposition "No illegal alien is a U.S. citizen."

▓ The Obverse, Converse, and Contrapositive

There are three other key moves you can make to draw inferences. These are the obverse, the converse, and the contrapositive. For these, we need to know one more thing: the complement of a class.

Complement

The **complement** of a class A is the class of those things *not* in A. So, for instance, the complement of the set of voters is the set of nonvoters. The complement of the set of noncitizens is the set of citizens. So, given any set A, the complement is the set non-A. Similarly, given any set non-B, the complement is the set B. (Think of a non-non-B as a double negative that takes us back to set B.) Examples of complements include farmworkers/nonfarmworkers, ballerina/nonballerina, and nonworkers/workers.

Obverse

The **obverse** of a proposition involves two steps: First, change the quality (from positive to negative, or vice versa); then change the predicate to its complement. For example, the obverse of "All A is B" is "No A is non-B." The result is the obverse. It has the same truth value as the original claim. If the original proposition is true, so is the obverse. If it is false, then the obverse is false. The obverse can be taken of any proposition.

Examples of the Obverse

All slugs are repulsive creatures.
→ No slug is a nonrepulsive creature.

Some men are not noncommunicative.
→ Some men are communicative people.

Converse

The **converse** of a proposition is obtained by switching the subject and the predicate, when possible. We can take a converse on an E or I claim. However, the converse of an A claim is known as *converse by limitation,* for we must step down to an I claim. So the converse of "All A is B" is "Some B is A." We can't take the converse of an O claim.

Examples of the Converse

No scuba divers are nonswimmers.
→ No nonswimmers are scuba divers.

Some ice-skaters are hockey players.
→ Some hockey players are ice-skaters.

All pilots are daredevils.
→ Some daredevils are pilots.

Some hikers are not fond of heights.
→ Does not exist (no converse of an O claim!).

Contrapositive

To take the **contrapositive** of a proposition, follow these two steps: First, replace the subject with the complement of the predicate; then replace the predicate with the complement of the subject. The contrapositive cannot be taken on an I claim; it applies only to A, E, and O claims. So the contrapositive of "No A is B" is "Some non-B are not non-A." The E claim is contrapositive by limitation: Step down to an O claim. Don't be surprised with a strange-looking result. Once you verify that the original sentence is A, O, or E, then just flip the subject and predicate, changing each one to the complement when you do the switch and, in the case of the E claim, move it down to an O claim.

Examples of Contrapositives

All trout are fish.
→ All nonfish are nontrout.

All noncitizens are nonvoters.
→ All voters are citizens.

Some citizens are not nonvoters.
→ Some voters are not noncitizens.

No FBI agent is in the CIA
→ Some nonpeople in the CIA are not non-FBI agents.

Note: Change the E claim to an O claim in contrapositives.

Neither the converse nor the contrapositive changes the quality of the original proposition. Negatives stay negative and positives stay positive. Only the obverse changes the quality: Be sure with the obverse to change positive to negative claims, and vice versa. Also, the converse is the only one of these three techniques that does not involve a complement. So be sure that you do *not* introduce it. We can summarize all this as follows:

Converse, Obverse, and Contrapositive

CONVERSE: A, E, AND I (*Note:* We can't take the converse on the O claim)

One step: Switch subject and predicate.

Note: Converse of an A goes to an I.

Forms of the Converse

All P is Q.	Converse is:	Some Q is P.
No P is Q.	Converse is:	No Q is P.
Some P is Q.	Converse is:	Some Q is P.
Some P is not Q.	No converse:	N/A

OBVERSE: A, E, I, AND O (ALL CLAIMS)

Two steps: Change quality (positive to negative and vice versa).
Change predicate to its complement.

FORMS OF THE OBVERSE

All P is Q.	Obverse is:	No P is non-Q.
No P is Q.	Obverse is:	All P is non-Q.
Some P is Q.	Obverse is:	Some P is not non-Q.
Some P is not Q.	Obverse is:	Some P is non-Q.

CONTRAPOSITIVE: A, E, AND O *(NOTE:* WE CAN'T TAKE THE CONTRAPOSITIVE ON I CLAIMS*)*

Two steps: Replace subject with complement of predicate.
Replace predicate with complement of subject.

Note: Contrapositive of an E goes to an O.

FORMS OF THE CONTRAPOSITIVE

All P is Q.	Contrapositive is:	All non-Q is non-P.
No P is Q.	Contrapositive is:	Some non-Q is not non-P.
Some P is Q.	No contrapositive:	N/A
Some P is not Q.	Contrapositive is:	Some non-Q is not non-P.

Exercises

1. What is the converse of "All dinosaurs are extinct animals"?
2. What is the obverse of "Some aliens are androids"?
3. What is the contrapositive of "No electricians are scatterbrained"?
4. What is the obverse of "No movie star is a lumberjack"?
5. What is the contradictory of "Some wild women are bodybuilders"?
6. What is the converse of the subcontrary of "Some bowlers are not over-weight"? (*Hint:* Take the subcontrary first, then take the converse of what you get.)
7. What is the contradictory of the obverse of "No circus clown is a boring person"? (*Hint:* Take the obverse first and then the contradictory of what you get.)
8. What is the contrapositive of the contrary of "All men with tattoos are adventurous"?

9. Given it is true that "All drummers are musicians," state and give the truth value of each of the following:
    a. The contrary
    b. The subaltern
    c. The contradictory
    d. The converse

10. Draw the inferences below:
    a. What is the converse of "No snakes are mammals"?
    b. What is the converse of "All mathematicians are witty people"?
    c. What is the obverse of "Some women are not citizens"?
    d. What is the obverse of the converse of "No mashed turnip is a non-vegetable"?
    e. What is the contrapositive of the obverse of "Some voters are Republicans"?
    f. Take the obverse of the contrapositive of "No apple is a watermelon."

11. Draw the inferences and then give each inference's truth value.
    a. The contrapositive of "All rodents are nonfish" (true)
    b. The obverse of "Some rodents are not mice" (true)
    c. The contrapositive of "No noninsects are grasshoppers" (true)
    d. The converse of "All non-citizens are nonvoters" (false)
    e. The subcontrary of "Some reptiles are mammals" (false)

12. Given it is true that "All robbers are thieves," draw all the inferences you can.

13. Given it is true that "No nun is a priest," draw these inferences and give the truth value of those inferences:
    a. The obverse
    b. The contradictory
    c. The converse
    d. The contrary
    e. The subaltern

14. Given it is false that "Some pit bulls are not dogs," draw these inferences and state their truth values:
    a. The obverse
    b. The contradictory
    c. The contrapositive
    d. The subcontrary

Quick Quiz

1. *True or false*: There is no obverse of an "E" claim.

2. What is the *contradictory* of "All non-Italians are movie fans"?
    a. No non-Italian is a movie fan.
    b. Some movie fans are non-Italians.
    c. Some movie fans are not Italians.
    d. Some non-Italians are not movie fans.

3. *True or false:* Two propositions that cannot both be false but could both be true are called *contraries.*

4. What is the *converse* of "All refried beans are vegetables"?
   a. Some vegetables are nonrefried beans.
   b. All refried beans are vegetables.
   c. Some vegetables are refried beans.
   d. Some vegetables are nonrefried beans.

5. The *contrapositive* of "No vegetables are chocolate" is (a) "No nonchocolate is a nonvegetable" or (b) "Some nonchocolate are not nonvegetables."

6. *True or false:* Two propositions that cannot both be true *and* cannot both be false are called *contradictories.*

7. What does it mean for two claims to be *subcontraries*? Circle all that are true.
   a. They cannot both be true.
   b. They cannot both be true.
   c. They cannot both be false.
   d. They could both be true.

8. The *obverse* of "Some nonteachers are union workers" is (a) "Some teachers are not nonunion workers" or (b) "Some nonteachers are not nonunion workers."

9. To take the *obverse of the converse* of a proposition, you (a) first take the converse and then take the obverse of that result or (b) first take the obverse and then take the converse of that result.

CHAPTER FIVE

The Logic Machine: Deductive and Inductive Reasoning

It should be apparent that the most meticulous inspection and search would not reveal the presence of poltergeists at the premises or unearth the property's ghoulish reputation in the community.

JUSTICE ISRAEL RUBIN, *ruling that a prospective buyer could recover his $32,000 down payment on a home that the owner claimed was haunted*

Suppose a real estate agent says the house you want to buy is haunted, pointing to a creaky staircase and the fact that two previous owners died accidental deaths. You go down the stairs and, sure enough, they creak. People in the neighborhood agree about the house's ghastly condition. Does this mean the house *really is* haunted? The evidence does not certainly show that the house is haunted. We would need more evidence to be convinced.

In this chapter, we will examine the two main kinds of arguments—inductive and deductive—and learn how to assess each kind. The last section of the chapter presents truth tables, one method of checking the truth of propositions and the validity of arguments. It is useful to be familiar with truth tables, though they work best on short, uncomplicated arguments. As we'll see in the second part of this book, there are other methods for assessing arguments. An acquaintance with the various tools of logic not only helps develop clear thinking but also builds confidence.

Inductive versus Deductive Arguments

In an **inductive argument,** the evidence alone is not enough for the conclusion to be certain, even if the premises are true. The evidence offers only partial support for the conclusion and consequently, you cannot be certain that the conclusion follows. So, even if the evidence is actually true (that the stairs creak and two previous owners died in accidents), the conclusion that the house is haunted might still be false. It is because of this uncertainty that the argument is considered inductive.

On the contrary, the real estate agent could say, "All the houses in Charlestown, Massachusetts, are haunted. This house at 14 Hill Street is in Charlestown, so it must also be haunted." This argument is inherently different from the inductive one. The evidence here, if true, would *force* the conclusion to be true. If all houses in Charlestown are haunted *and* the house at 14 Hill Street is in Charlestown, it would have to be true that the house is haunted. This is a **deductive** argument. The conclusion can be extracted from the premises.

Deductive and inductive arguments share an important similarity—they both require *at least one* premise and *only one* conclusion. However, a key difference involves assessing the relative strength of the arguments.

What distinguishes a deductive argument is that the conclusion is said to follow directly from the premises; no further evidence is needed to support the conclusion. At times, claims are made (e.g., in criminal trials) without the evidence *actually* being sufficient. When it is asserted or implied that this set of premises sufficiently supports the conclusion, we've got a deductive argument. If, however, a conclusion is drawn in spite of missing pieces or gaps in the set of premises, the argument is inductive. This is summarized in the following table.

DEDUCTIVE ARGUMENT	EXPLANATION	EXAMPLES
An argument is *deductive* if the conclusion is said to follow directly from the premises and nothing more need be added for that to happen.	Think of it as working with a closed set—like a puzzle that's not missing any pieces. From the pieces, you deduce that the conclusion follows. *Note:* The conclusion can be extracted from the premises—we don't need to add any more premises.	All angels have wings. Anything with wings can fly. *Therefore,* all angels can fly. If cows had wings, they'd be large birds. Cows are not large birds. *Therefore,* cows do not have wings. Charlie only eats greasy food. Charlie is eating lunch. *Therefore,* he is eating greasy food.

Inductive Argument	Explanation	Examples
An argument is *inductive* if the conclusion is said to follow with a degree of probability or likelihood from the premises—but there is always a wedge of doubt about that actually occurring.	Think of it as working with a puzzle that's missing at least one piece (sometimes more!). From the pieces, you induce that the conclusion will likely follow, but you can't be certain. *Note:* The conclusion of an inductive argument never follows with certainty. There's always at least one hole in the argument—which means we don't have all the evidence to be 100% sure.	98% of winged creatures are birds. Charlie was chased by something with wings. *Therefore,* it must have been a bird chasing Charlie. Eating greasy food can cause gallstones. Charlie eats greasy food. *Therefore,* he'll probably get a gallstone. Children are like cockatoos— they like to throw food in the air, and they love games. Cockatoos also like to flip upside down. *Therefore,* children probably like to flip upside down too!

▦ Key Terms in Arguments

An **argument** is a group of propositions, some of which (called the **premises**) act as supporting evidence for another proposition (called the **conclusion** or **thesis**) (See Chapter 2 for a review.) See if you can spot the conclusion and its supporting premises in the following argument: "Jasper must have gotten into the felt pens. First off, Jasper has a few tiny green marks on one of his wings, but cockatoos don't have green markings. Also, Jasper has green on the tip of his beak, which he didn't have when he was eating his egg this morning. Finally, the very end of his tongue has a greenish hew. Yes indeed, Jasper got hold of a felt pen!" The conclusion is in the opening and closing statements, with the premises sandwiched in between.

An **inference** is drawn on the basis of evidence, though it is not necessarily *supported* by that evidence. The terms "inference" and "conclusion" are interchangeable, as are "I infer" and "I conclude." Some people can have all the evidence in the world and still draw an incorrect conclusion. That's why we must subject arguments to careful scrutiny. In order to do this, break down the argument into its component parts—the premises (evidence) and conclusion (thesis). In a strong argument, the premises are sufficient for the conclusion.

Let's also note the difference between **sufficient** conditions and **necessary** condition (see Figure 5.1). Deductive arguments assert that the premises are

[One in a Series]

Necessary, yes.   Sufficient, no.

Does a polluter become "green" by handing out free gas masks?

Adding anti-tobacco spots to DVDs with smoking is necessary. DVDs with smoking harm children and teens every time they're watched. Proven spots from experienced health organizations can reduce the impact of films with smoking. They need to be in all distribution channels, not just DVDs.

But spots don't keep kids from being exposed in the first place.

Movies rated G, PG and (mainly) PG-13 deliver at least half of young people's exposure. The least intrusive, most effective way to keep smoking out of future youth-rated movies is to rate smoking "R."

Of course, teens will still see some R-rated movies. That's why leading health authorities endorse the R-rating for smoking *and* proven anti-tobacco spots before any film with smoking.

Spots are intended as a backstop to the "R," not a substitute for it.

Given that tobacco is the leading cause of preventable death and that films with smoking are the single biggest recruiter of new young smokers, anti-tobacco spots are the very least that media companies can do.

Spots are a start. Now, minimize the need for them.

 SMOKE FREE MOVIES

SmokeFreeMovies.ucsf.edu

SMOKING IN MOVIES KILLS IN REAL LIFE. Smoke Free Movie policies—the R-rating certification of no payoffs, anti-tobacco spots, and an end to brand display—are endorsed by the World Health Organization, American Medical Association, AMA Alliance, American Academy of Pediatrics, American Heart Association, American Legacy Foundation, American Lung Association, American Public Health Association, Campaign for Tobacco-Free Kids, L.A. County Dept. of Health Services, New York State Dept. of Health, New York State PTA, and others. To explore this critical health issue, visit our web site or write Smoke Free Movies, UCSF School of Medicine, San Francisco, CA 94143-1390.

Permission granted by Stan Lantz, www.smokefreemovies.com

FIGURE 5.1
Smoke-Free Movies Ad. Being able to tell the difference between necessary and sufficient can be vital.

sufficient for the conclusion (thesis). This is not the case with inductive arguments, where the conclusion only can be said to follow with a degree of uncertainty or probability.

A is *sufficient* for B: "If A then B" or "B if A."
If A occurs, B will occur as well.

Examples of Sufficient Conditions

An earthquake is *sufficient* to scare Alejandra.
If it's an earthquake, it will scare Alejandra.

A *sufficient* snack to relax Tony is popcorn.
If he has popcorn for a snack, then Tony will relax.

A is *necessary* for B: "B only if A" or "Only if A, B."
If A does not occur, B will not occur either.
"If not A then not B" → "If B then A."

Examples of Necessary Conditions

Having a boarding pass is *necessary* for getting on the plane.
If you don't have a boarding pass, then you won't be able to get on the plane.
If you got on the plane, then you had a boarding pass.

We can treat Adam's bronchitis *only if* he takes antibiotics.
If he doesn't take antibiotics, then Adam's bronchitis won't be treated.
If Adam's bronchitis was treated, then he took antibiotics.

In a **valid argument,** the premises are sufficient for drawing the conclusion. So, if they were assumed true, then the conclusion *must* also be true. That does *not* mean that the premises must be necessary for the conclusion, because something else might lead to the same conclusion. Once we know an argument is valid, we can test for soundness. A **sound argument** is a valid argument with premises that are *actually* true.

Propositions

A **proposition** is an assertion that is either true or false. A proposition can be expressed in the following form: *Subject* copula *predicate* (copula = a form of the verb "to be")—for example, "Grasshoppers are insects."

In other words, we are saying of something (the subject) that it has some characteristic being predicated—such as "Ice Cube is a person with many talents." The subject of the proposition is "Ice Cube" and the predicate is "a person with many talents." A proposition isn't always strictly expressed in the above form, but it can be rewritten in this format without changing the meaning of the sentence. Sentences that are not asserting that something is true or false are not propositions—for example, exclamations ("Yikes!"), nonrhetorical questions ("Where's my other sock?"), and moral claims ("You ought to vote").

Examples of Propositions

The history exam covered the Civil War.
Jelly beans are small, chewy candies.
The coyotes killed three cats in the neighborhood last month.

A proposition is **categorical** if it can be expressed starting with any of the words "all," "no," "some," or $x\%$ (where x is any number other than zero or 100). Categorical propositions are **universal** (all-or-nothing) or *particular* (at least one, not all). When the subject refers to an individual or entity (Otis Redding, the Statue of Liberty, Angie's new car, the LAPD, etc.), the claim is to be treated as universal. The forms are as follows:

Universal Propositions (all-or-nothing)

Form 1: "All A is B."   → Universal positive

Form 2: "No A is B."   → Universal negative

Form 3: "A is/is not B."   → Universal positive or negative
                                where A is a class with only
                                one member

Particular Propositions (at least one, not all)

Form 1: "Some A is B."   → Particular positive

Form 2: "Some A is not B."   → Particular negative

Form 3: "x% of A is/is not B." → Particular positive or negative
                                where $x \neq 100$ or 0

Examples of Categorical Propositions

No bat is an animal with feathers.
All Austin Minis are cars.
Some house cats are the prey of coyotes.
Some small cars are not Audis.
74% of senior citizens are people who like deviled eggs.

You often find propositions that are not in categorical form—for example, "Rabbits are small," "Rabbits are never vicious," "Some rabbits fear dogs," and "Some rabbits don't love carrots." They can be rewritten in standard form by adding the form of "to be" and turning the predicate into a noun phrase. We then have them in standard form as categorical propositions: "All rabbits are small animals," "No rabbit is a vicious beast," "Some rabbits are afraid of dogs," and "Some rabbits are not carrot lovers."

The Key to Distinguishing Propositions

A proposition asserts of some subject that it has one or more characteristics (these are being *predicated* of the *subject*). Propositions can take several forms, from sentences in the indicative to rhetorical questions. For instance, if someone says, "Did you know that skunks eat rats?" they are asserting the proposition "Skunks are animals that eat rats." Similarly, if a justice of the peace declares, "I now pronounce you, Tony and Carmela, husband and wife," the claim is that "Tony and Carmela are now married." It makes no logical difference if a proposition is expressed in the present, past, or future tense. The key thing is that something is being predicated of something else—for example, "All basketball players are people with quick reflexes." If you use "were" or "will be" instead of "are," the logical meaning is the same.

Matters of taste, opinion, and morality are often presented in the form of a proposition, such as "No dinner is memorable without a warm loaf of bread." It's fine to use these, but be aware that they are not clearly true or false. It may be wise to add the words "in my opinion" or "to me." If not, there could be a problem. For instance, contentious claims like "People with nose rings are attractive" or "Adultery is an unpardonable sin" cannot be treated as simple propositions. Similarly, expressions of emotion may not be simple propositions either (e.g., "That feels so good!"). In such cases, we tend to think in terms of *agreement* (or disagreement) with the position expressed, rather than that the claim is true or false.

A **generalization** is an inference from a smaller group (or one individual) to a larger group. When we generalize, we are asserting that what is true or false of one or more members of a group is true or false to some or all of the group. For example, we may see ducks eating snails at the park and infer that "all ducks eat snails" or "most ducks eat snails." Some generalizations are based on cause and effect or statistical studies—but not all, as the duck example illustrates. Be careful not to commit the fallacy of **hasty generalization,** where the inference is based on a sample that is too small or atypical, or the fallacy of **biased statistics,** where the sample group is not sufficiently diverse to represent the targeted population.

A **value claim** is a prescriptive statement of values—moral, aesthetic, or personal taste. Value claims cannot be treated like empirical claims that are either true or false, but they can function in arguments. We can *assume*—though not prove—that a value claim is true and use it in an argument. Consequently, we can test any argument containing value claims for validity—but not for soundness (which requires true premises, as we will see). However, as Professor Paul Green has observed, statements of personal preferences *can be* assigned a truth value (e.g., I could ascertain if the baby prefers milk to grapefruit juice) and, therefore, function differently than value claims. That means we might have sound arguments containing claims of personal preference.

A valid argument does not require that the premises *actually* be true: Our concern is only that if we assume them to be true, the conclusion must be true—it could not be false. Clearly, we can *assume* a value claim is true, even if we can't prove it. We can therefore create valid arguments involving morality, personal taste, artistic judgments, and the like. The restriction is that we won't be able to assert that any of the value claims are unquestionably true.

Examples of a Valid Argument

Any movie with live animals as stars is a work of art.

<u>*Paulie* is a movie starring a parrot (a live animal named Paulie!).</u>

Therefore, *Paulie* is a work of art.

All munchkins are snapplepuffers.

<u>No snapplepuffer is a mork.</u>

Therefore, no munchkin is a mork.

We have no idea if the premises are true, so we cannot determine soundness. However, we can assess validity. *If* we assume that the premises in the two arguments are true, the conclusion will necessarily be true. This is the case even when a premise is a value judgment (e.g., about the greatness of a film) or we don't know what the premises refer to (e.g., snapplepuffers and morks). In either case, if we presume that the premises are true, the conclusion cannot be false. Thus, the arguments are valid.

Propositions and Value Claims

Propositions are either true or false. Many use value claims *as if* they were true—but that doesn't make them empirically true. How do we *verify* that a value claim is true or false? What do we look to? If we claim, "We ought to experiment on animals," how do we show it to be true? That said, we can still use value claims in arguments and test the arguments for their strength. The key concern in analyzing arguments is the quality of the support the premises give the conclusion *if* they were presumed true. Whether they are true or false is a separate matter.

People use value claims all the time; consequently, we have to deal with them alongside propositions that can be affirmed or negated. The use of value claims presents problems of verifiability if it is asserted that they are absolutely true or false. Let's look at some examples.

Examples of Propositions

The Honda was stolen right in front of Amanda's house.
A few babies do not like vanilla pudding.
The Red Sox made history by winning the World Series in 2004.
No peanut is a dairy product.

Note: Propositions are either true or false.

Examples of Nonpropositions

Yikes!
Where's my Tweetie costume?
Congratulations!

Note: Nonpropositions cannot be assigned a truth-value and *cannot* be assumed to be either true or false for purposes of testing validity.

Examples of Value Claims

Olive Oyl is not as attractive as Betty Boop.
The Dark Knight was better than *Spider-Man 3*.
There's nothing like the South for delicious pies!
Dr. Dre is the male equivalent of Queen Latifah.

Note: Value claims cannot be assigned a truth-value, but they *can* be assumed true for purposes of testing validity (but not soundness).

Exercises

Part One

Directions: Indicate which of the following are *propositions*, which are *value claims*, and which are neither.

1. Get lost!
2. The parrot chewed a hole in the wall.
3. Chickpeas are members of the legume family.
4. A scuba mask is necessary for Nury to go underwater.
5. If sharks are in the tank, it could be dangerous to stick your hand in the water.
6. Damn you!
7. There's not a man alive who wouldn't agree that you'd look cute as a redhead.
8. Where is my calculus book?
9. Either the tire has too much air in it or it doesn't.
10. Unless the plumber can fix it, we have a sewage problem.
11. Get a load of this, Colleen!
12. Congratulations—you are now an American citizen.
13. 87% of squirrels in the University of Alberta study preferred birdseed to table scraps.
14. What in the world did you do with your sock?
15. No one with a functioning taste bud can tolerate ketchup on fried eggs.
16. Some mathematicians are not fluent in Urdu.
17. According to folklore, vampires are averse to daylight.
18. What's that—you passed your final?
19. There are Mayan pyramids in Mexico.
20. It's truly amazing to see the Northern lights.

Part Two

1. Pull out all the propositions, nonpropositions, and value claims in this paragraph:

   Gadzooks! There are three very tall men across the street! They are all wearing colored shorts and tops to match. Each has a different number on the shirt. They are dynamite! One of the guys is 7 foot 5. Men over 7 feet tall are more attractive than those shrimps a foot shorter, I'll tell you that much. Don't you agree? The taller, the better. That's what my grandma always said! But she was only 5 foot 2. Wouldn't she have been amazed to stand next to an athlete like Sun Ming Ming?

2. Pull out all the propositions, nonpropositions, and value claims in this paragraph:

The decision to settle seems sensible. In the end, the banks agreed to finance a deal that values Clear Channel at $17 billion. This was approved by shareholders in April 2008. Can you believe it! $17 billion!! That's a heck of a lot better than the offer they got a year ago. What do you think the corporation will do now that they've got the funding?

Quick Quiz

1. *True or false:* An argument must have at least two premises.
2. "All race horses are highly trained animals" is a (a) universal or (b) particular proposition.
3. *True or false:* "No birds are alligators. All hawks are birds. Therefore, no hawks are alligators" is a deductive argument.
4. An example of a *universal* proposition is (a) "Most reptiles are not poisonous" or (b) "Every rattlesnake is something to avoid."
5. *True or false:* An example of a categorical proposition in standard form is "Some cars are not Jaguars."
6. The claim "*x*% of cows are Jerseys" would be *universal* for what value(s) of *x*?
7. *True or false:* "Blues music is better than opera" is a proposition.
8. An example of a *particular* proposition is:
   a. All squid are creatures of the deep.
   b. No buffalo is a creature of the deep.
   c. Some creatures of the deep are great white sharks.
   d. 100% of Beluga whales are creatures of the deep.
9. *True or false:* "A is *sufficient* for B" is the same as saying "If B then A."
10. What are *two* ways to rewrite "A good movie is *necessary* to make Rita happy"?
    a. If Rita sees a good movie, then she is happy.
    b. If Rita is happy, then she saw a good movie.
    c. If Rita is not happy, then she did not see a good movie.
    d. If Rita did not see a good movie, then she is not happy.
11. "The Lakers are better team players than the Celtics" is a (a) proposition or (b) value claim.

12. An example of a nonproposition is:
    a. No Celtics player wears purple and yellow on the court.
    b. Go Kobe!
    c. Basketball generates more interest than football.
    d. Some basketball players are taller than 7 feet.

Deductive Reasoning

With deductive arguments, it is claimed that the conclusion comes right out of the premises. The process is a kind of extraction. A well-constructed deductive argument lays the groundwork for the conclusion to follow.

Think of all those cases in which the prosecutor tries to prove the case *beyond a reasonable doubt*. The prosecutor's task is to demonstrate that the evidence is sufficient to seal the conviction, that any reasonable judge or juror should conclude from the strength of the evidence that the conclusion follows. Their goal is to show that there can be no reasonable doubt that the defendant's guilt follows from the truth of the premises.

Attorneys may think they've sealed the case, but not all arguments are convincing. Some arguments never get off the ground. And jurors may not know if each piece of evidence is actually true. Generally, they *cannot* know if what is presented in court is *really* true. (Is that really the murder weapon? Is that really the victim's dirty T-shirt?) The task is to decide whether, *if* that evidence is assumed to be true, the conclusion follows—if so, the jury is expected to convict the defendant. Jurors are not in a position to ascertain the truth of the evidence submitted. They must focus on the reasoning and decide if it holds together under close scrutiny.

It is the *structure* of the reasoning that determines a valid argument—not the truth of the claims. The issue of truth comes later, when we look at sound arguments. This tells us *one important thing* about deductive arguments: The focus is on whether the premises make a convincing case for the conclusion. The issue of what's true or false comes up later, when we look at sound arguments.

There's a hilarious scene in the movie *My Cousin Vinny* that uses deductive reasoning to discount the testimony of one of the witnesses, Mr. Tipton. The lawyer, Vincent Gambini, proves that Mr. Tipton could not have seen the accused take off in the getaway car. Mr. Tipton had said he'd stepped away from the window to cook some grits (a ground-corn alternative to hash-browns for breakfast). He insisted that he was gone for only five minutes. Gambini knows this to be impossible and nails Mr. Tipton:

> VINCENT GAMBINI: How could it take you 5 minutes to cook your grits when it takes the entire grit-eating world 20 minutes?
> MR. TIPTON: Um . . . I'm a fast cook, I guess.

VINCENT GAMBINI: You're a fast cook? Are we to believe that boiling water soaks into a grit faster in your kitchen than any place on the face of the earth?

MR. TIPTON: I don't know.

VINCENT GAMBINI: Perhaps the laws of physics cease to exist on your stove. Were these magic grits? Did you buy them from the same guy who sold Jack his beanstalk beans?

Mr. Tipton has to concede that the laws of physics *do* exist in his kitchen, and thus, he could not have seen the accused running away from the store, as he claimed. By using deductive reasoning skills, Gambini effectively disproved Tipton's original argument.

Applications of Deductive Reasoning

In mathematics, even in arithmetic, deductive reasoning is pervasive. Think of geometry, where axioms and postulates are used to prove a theorem. You must only use those axioms and postulates; there is nowhere else you can go to get your reasons. It is a self-contained system—the conclusion comes out of the premises. Of course, if a postulate (a premise) is changed, the resulting mathematical system changes, too.

For example, if we don't follow Euclid's fifth postulate (that two parallel lines must remain equidistant and can never intersect), then we get quite distinct theoretical systems. We might draw parallel lines on a globe or orange—they converge at both ends. We might parallel lines on the inside of a trumpet, where the lines diverge and would get farther and farther apart, as if the trumpet were expanding.

Let's look at deductive reasoning in a case involving arithmetic. To solve the problem 62 minus 49, students in second grade are normally taught to borrow a "one" from the 10s place, much like borrowing sugar from a neighbor. However, as noted by Richard Rothstein, children in Shanghai are taught the reasoning behind borrowing so the process makes mathematical sense. In Shanghai schools, children are taught that 62 is the same as 60 and 2, 50 and 12, 40 and 22, and so forth. Once this is understood, the process of subtraction makes sense and isn't some magic act. Understanding the deductive reasoning involved allows students to move to more advanced mathematical topics.

Many arguments concerning moral or legal issues make use of deductive reasoning. Here's an example: "All religious people believe in a higher power. All Buddhists are religious people. Therefore, all Buddhists believe in a higher power." The focus is on Buddhists, but the form of the argument is deductive.

Example 1 of a Deductive Argument

No pilot is afraid of heights.

<u>Some football players are afraid of heights.</u>

Therefore, some football players are not pilots.

Note: The first premise asserts one characteristic of pilots—namely, not being afraid of heights. The second premise informs us that there are some people

You Tell Me Department

What about the Judge's View?

The Justice Department was demanding that at least six hospitals turn over hundreds of patient medical records on late-term abortions performed there in the last three years. They wanted to examine the medical histories of those patients to see if the abortion was medically necessary. Lawyers for the Justice Department insisted that a new law prohibiting late-term (aka partial-birth) abortions authorized this plan. Hospital administrators were worried about violating the privacy rights of their patients. The chief federal judge in Chicago tossed out the subpoena against the Northwestern University Medical Center, arguing as follows:

A woman's relationship with her doctor and her decision on whether to get an abortion "are issues indisputably of the most sensitive stripe." They should remain confidential "without the fear of public disclosure," the judge, Charles P. Kocoras, wrote in a decision first reported by *Crain's* business journal in Chicago. The subpoena for patient files is a "significant intrusion" in the patients' privacy. Consequently, the subpoena must be rejected. (Eric Lichtblau, "Justice Dept. Seeks Hospitals' Records of Some Abortions," *The New York Times,* 12 Feb 2004)

You tell me: How strong is the judge's reasoning? Share your assessment.

(football players) who do not have this characteristic. It is argued that those two premises are sufficient for the conclusion to come right out of the premises.

Example 2 of a Deductive Argument

No tiger in the zoo is a happy tiger.

<u>All happy tigers are animals that roam miles through the jungle.</u>

Therefore, no tiger in the zoo is an animal that roams miles through the jungle.

Example 3 of a Deductive Argument

If you don't know how to cook, you won't know the recipe for hollandaise sauce.

<u>Craig doesn't know how to cook.</u>

Therefore, Craig won't know the recipe for hollandaise sauce.

In all of these examples, the premises are put forward as sufficient, with no other evidence necessary for the conclusion to follow. That does not mean the arguments are actually constructed so that the conclusions really do follow. However, a deductive argument makes an implicit claim of certainty.

Main Types of Deductive Arguments

1. **Categorical syllogisms and chains of syllogisms.** These are three-line arguments (or chains of them), consisting of two premises and a conclusion,

with all of the propositions in the form of categorical propositions. These propositions can be expressed in four possible forms: "All A are B," "No A is B," "Some A is B," and "Some A is not B." For example:

All romantics cry during sad movies.

<u>No one who cries in a sad movie can eat a lot of popcorn.</u>

So, no one who eats a lot of popcorn is a romantic.

2. **Modus ponens** (Latin for mode that *affirms*). These are arguments of the form "If A then B. A is the case. Therefore, B is true also." The first premise is a conditional claim. The second premise affirms that the antecedent is true. The conclusion, then, is that the consequent must also be true. For example:

If the dentist slips while operating, Omar will need stitches.

<u>The dentist slipped while operating.</u>

So, Omar needed to get stitches.

Note: The fallacy of denying the antecedent and the fallacy of affirming the consequent are mutations of modus ponens/modus tollens and not valid argument forms. These will be discussed later in this chapter.

3. **Modus tollens** (Latin for mode that *denies*). These are arguments of the form "If A then B. B is not the case. Therefore, A is not true either." The first premise is a conditional claim. The second premise denies the consequent by saying it is not true. The inference, then, is that the antecedent could not be true either. For example:

If Bruce gets a tattoo of a dragon, his mother will go through the roof.

<u>Bruce's mother did not go through the roof.</u>

Therefore, Bruce did not get a tattoo of a dragon.

4. **Disjunctive syllogism.** These are arguments of the form "Either A or B. A is not the case. Therefore, B must be true" or "Either A or B. B is not true. Therefore, A must be true." For example:

Either that's a rainbow trout or a weird-looking salmon.

<u>That's not a rainbow trout.</u>

So, it's a weird-looking salmon.

5. **Hypothetical syllogism.** These are arguments of the form. "If A then B. If B then C. Therefore, if A then C." For example:

If Louie goes to the powwow, he'll miss the ball game.

<u>If Louie misses the ball game, he won't get a chili dog.</u>

Therefore, if Louie goes to the powwow, he won't get a chili dog.

A hypothetical syllogism could also be expressed as "All A is B. All B is C. Therefore, all A is C." For example:

Anyone who enjoys music will like my new Taylor Swift album.

Anyone who likes my new Taylor Swift album will like Loreena McKennitt.

Therefore, anyone who enjoys music will like Loreena McKennitt.

6. **Constructive dilemma.** These take the form of "If A then B, and if C then D. Either A or C. Therefore, either B or D." In other words, there's a choice between two options, each leading to some effect. You must pick between the two options. Therefore, one of two possible effects will happen. For example:

If Maricella learns to knit, she'll make a beanie; but if she takes up crochet, she'll make a scarf.

Either Maricella will learn to knit or take up crochet.

Therefore, either Maricella will make a beanie or she'll make a scarf.

7. **Variations of modus ponens and modus tollens:**
   a. **Unless.** One variation takes this form: "A unless B. B is not the case. Therefore A." or "A unless B. Not A. Therefore, B." For example:

   David will return to Omaha State unless he transfers to Reed.

   David did not transfer to Reed.

   So, David returned to Omaha State.

   b. **Application of a rule.** Another variation of modus ponens is in the form of the application of a rule according to a set of criteria: "Rule X applies to any cases with characteristics A, B, C, and D. Individual case P has characteristics A, B, C, and D. Therefore, rule X applies to case P." For example:

   People will get a fine of $270 if they are caught driving in the carpool lane without a passenger in their vehicle.

   Irene snuck into the carpool lane even though she was alone and was spotted by the Officer Williams.

   Therefore, Irene got a fine of $270.

Compounding the Terms of the Argument

Be aware that in all the examples above, A and B could each stand for a compound statement. A compound statement is one containing any of these words: "not," "and," "or," "if . . . then," or "if and only if." We can see this with the following example:

If it's either an apple or an orange, **then** it's a fruit and not a vegetable.

That's either an apple or an orange.

Thus, it's a fruit and not a vegetable.

The above argument is of the same form as:

If <u>it's an apple</u>, **then** <u>it's a fruit</u>.
That's <u>an apple</u>.
Thus, it's <u>a fruit</u>.

Although the terms of the first argument are compound, the *form* of the argument is still the same, as the terms in bold show us.

Exercise

Quick Quiz

1. The form of modus ponens is "If A then B. A. Therefore, B." So, if the first premise is "If Charlene becomes a vegan, she won't have the turkey at Thanksgiving," the second premise is (a) "Charlene had the turkey at Thanksgiving" or (b) "Charlene became a vegan."

2. The argument "Either Grandma will get some ducks or she'll forget about having more pets. Grandma did not get any ducks, so she forgot about having more pets" is an example of which deductive argument form: (a) disjunctive syllogism or (b) hypothetical syllogism?

3. An argument with two premises and a conclusion, where the premises and the conclusion are categorical propositions ("All A is B," "No A is B," "Some A is B," or "Some A is not B"), is called:
   a. Hypothetical syllogism
   b. Modus tollens
   c. Categorical syllogism
   d. Constructive dilemma

4. What form is this argument: "All people who can yodel could be auctioneers. All people who could be auctioneers would be good calling out dance numbers at the fair. Therefore, all people who can yodel would be good calling out dance numbers at the fair"?
   a. Modus ponens
   b. Hypothetical syllogism
   c. Disjunctive syllogism
   d. Modus tollens

5. The argument "If it snows, then we'll go skiing. We didn't go skiing, so it didn't snow" is an example of:
   a. Categorical syllogism
   b. Modus ponens
   c. Modus tollens
   d. Hypothetical syllogism

6. *True or false:* "All chemical engineers like to hang glide. All hang gliders are fearless. Therefore, all chemical engineers are fearless" is an example of the deductive argument hypothetical syllogism.

7. If we assume all the premises are true and the conclusion could not be false, then the argument must be (a) valid, (b) true, (c) invalid, or (d) sound.

8. According to the form of *hypothetical syllogism,* an argument that starts with "If grandma lets the children out to play, then it's not nap time" could have as its next premise:
   a. If it's nap time, then Adam will want a cup of milk.
   b. Either it's nap time or the clock stopped working.
   c. If it's not nap time, then the children could go swinging and play in the sandbox.
   d. It is nap time if and only if the children are sleepy.

9. *True or false:* An inductive argument can be valid, so long as the premises are true.

10. An example of a *disjunctive syllogism* is:
   a. Either that's the escaped convict or it's Charlie in a Halloween costume. It's not Charlie in a Halloween costume, so it must be the escaped convict.
   b. If that's the escaped convict, then Charlie better go lock the door. It is the escaped convict, so Charlie better go lock the door.
   c. If that's not the escaped convict, then it's safe to have the barbeque outside. We did not have the barbeque outside, so it must have been the escaped convict.
   d. If Charlie doesn't wear his convict costume, he'll wear the space alien suit. If Charlie wears a space alien suit, then he might be mistaken for a cyborg. Therefore, if Charlie doesn't wear his convict costume, he might be mistaken for a cyborg.

Validity

People commonly use the word "valid" to mean "good point" or "true." However, in the realm of logic, "valid" is not about that which is true; it is about the argument's construction. Logical validity concerns arguments, not propositions. It signifies a well-ordered structure in which the premises have made an airtight case for the conclusion.

Think of building blocks consisting of propositions. Propositions can be true or false. We can combine propositions to form arguments. When we do that, the focus shifts away from truth and falsity to the strength of the reasoning. In the case of deductive arguments, talking about strength means talking about validity. We cannot say of an argument that it is true or false. But if the argument is deductive, we can assess it for validity. Let's see how this is done.

A **valid argument** is an argument in which the premises provide sufficient support for drawing the conclusion. This has to do with the relationship between the premises and the conclusion.

Validity is about how the components of the argument all fit together. Validity involves whether the premises either separately or in combination sufficiently support the conclusion. This is a *structural* issue. Our goal is to see what happens if we *assume* the premises to be true. If we assume that the premises are true, do they then support the conclusion in such a way that it *has* to be true as well? If the answer is yes, then the argument is *valid*. If we could have true premises and a false conclusion, then the argument is **invalid**. An invalid argument is like a house with a rotting foundation—it cannot stand given its deficient structure.

The key is that the connection between the premises and the conclusion entails *certainty:* If true premises force the conclusion to be true, then the conclusion *certainly* follows from those premises. That means the argument is valid—and is, therefore, a strong argument in terms of its construction. For example:

No cowboy has a refined sense of humor.

Buffalo Bill was a cowboy.

Thus, Buffalo Bill did not have a refined sense of humor.

We do not have to know anything about cowboys or Buffalo Bill for this to be a valid argument. If we assume that the premises are true, the conclusion is certainly true as well. Here's another example:

No one who has a pierced belly button is inhibited.

Some Democrats are inhibited.

Therefore, some Democrats do not have pierced belly buttons.

If the two premises we true, then the conclusion must follow.

Remember: It is not important for validity whether the premises are actually true. The issue is the connection between the premises and the conclusion.

Watch for terms like "must," "necessarily," "inevitably," "certainly," "entail," and "it can be deduced." These words often indicate a deductive argument. To make sure, ask: Do the premises provide sufficient support for the conclusion?

The Juror Model of Validity

To better understand validity, imagine being a juror. There we are, sitting in the jury box, listening to the prosecution and the defense present their arguments trying to convince us to conclude one thing or another. We have to assess the evidence, witness testimony, and credibility of the experts. We have to evaluate the strength of their reasoning without leaving the room.

As jurors, we have to work with what is presented in the courtroom. We can't go look at the crime scene (unless the judge permits us to do so). And we can't go interview the neighbors to get more information. Instead, we have to determine if a solid case is being made. Our decision should be based solely on the strength of the evidence before us.

Jurors cannot know if the evidence that has been presented is *actually* true or false. We must take on faith that the legal system is working, that people are telling the truth, and that evidence is not fabricated. Obviously, these are not always true conditions. At times, serious problems force us to rethink or retry a case. As jurors we can only work with the evidence before us. Even if we know about the case—say, through news coverage—that prior knowledge should not be brought to bear upon our reasoning. The task is to decide if the prosecution has made its case.

Ask yourself: Is the evidence sufficient to convict, or is there a reasonable doubt that would allow for an alternative hypothesis? If the conclusion could be false even if the premises are true, then the argument is invalid. If the conclusion follows directly from the premises, then the argument is valid.

Examples of Valid Arguments

Either the lab destroyed the evidence or the defendant is lying.

The lab did not destroy the evidence.

Therefore, the defendant must be lying.

All alien abductions leave the victim with some memory problems.

Samantha was the victim of an alien abduction.

Thus, Samantha was left with some memory problems.

No dream about flying is a nightmare.

Levi only has flying dreams.

Therefore, Levi never has nightmares.

Did you see what form the three arguments took? In order, they are disjunctive syllogism, modus ponens, and modus ponens again. We will do more work with these valid argument forms in Chapter 10. The last two are categorical syllogisms. We will do more work with syllogisms in Chapter 9. What makes all these arguments valid is that, if the premises were true, the conclusion would *have* to be true. It is this element of certainty that marks an argument as valid.

Invalidity

An **invalid argument** is an argument in which the premises fail to adequately support the conclusion. This does not mean the premises have to be true—only *if* they are true, the conclusion cannot be false. We can tell that an argument is invalid when the premises could be true while the conclusion is false.

Example 1 of an Invalid Argument

Some men are short.

Some flight attendants are not short.

So, some flight attendants are not men.

Even if we assumed that the two premises were true, it would not follow that "Some flight attendants are not men." The conclusion could be false while the premises are true.

Example 2 of an Invalid Argument

No one with a heart condition should run the Boston marathon.

<u>Some photographers have a heart condition.</u>

Therefore, no photographer should run the Boston marathon.

Here the conclusion could be false and the premises true. The premises, therefore, fail to force the conclusion to follow.

Example 3 of an Invalid Argument

If you do not wear swim goggles, you could lose your contact lens.

<u>Rose lost her contact lens.</u>

Consequently, Rose must not have worn swim goggles.

Even if it were true that, without swim goggles, you could lose your contact lens and Rose did lose her lens, it does not follow that she wasn't wearing swim goggles. For example, she might have lost her lens down the sink when cleaning them.

A Special Case of Invalidity: Formal Fallacies

A special case of invalidity involves the two formal fallacies that relate to modus ponens and modus tollens. These fallacies occur because of an error in the very form of the reasoning.

Fallacy of Affirming the Consequent.   The **fallacy of affirming the consequent** starts with a conditional claim and then argues that, if the consequent is true, then the antecedent is also true. In other words, if the *effect* happens, this one possible cause must happen as well. This is bad reasoning because an effect can potentially have many causes, unless it is clearly stated that it has *only* the one stated in the antecedent. If it is not explicitly indicated that there is only one cause for the effect—which would be done by using "If and only if" instead of "If . . . then"— then it would be incorrect to assume from the fact that an event occurred that the antecedent had to have occurred as well. There could be another explanation.

The fallacy of affirming the consequent takes this form:

If A then B.

<u>B.</u>

Therefore A.

Here's an example: "If the rain continues, the roof will collapse. The roof collapsed. Therefore, the rain continued." But any number of things could cause a roof collapse, such as the neighbor's oak tree falling on the roof or some Halloween pranksters leaping on the roof.

An *equivalent form* of this fallacy is "All A is B. B. Therefore, A." Here's an example: "All werewolves howl at the full moon. Something is howling at the full moon. So, it must be a werewolf." Not necessarily—it could be a coyote or your neighbor's dog Cody.

Examples of the Fallacy of Affirming the Consequent

If Hassan gets another political call, he'll turn off the ringer on the phone. Hassan turned off the ringer on the phone. So, he must have gotten another political call.
[*Hold it*: Maybe he got obscene calls or he didn't want to wake up his little sister, Anna, who was napping on the couch.]

If the car has a flat tire, we'll have to call for help. We had to call for help for the car. Therefore, the car had a flat tire.
[*Hold it*: Maybe we had to call for help because we ran out of gas or because we hit a deer that ran out into the freeway.]

All women who drive convertibles are people who love the feeling of wind in their hair. Jasmine loves the feeling of wind in her hair. So, she must drive a convertible.
[*Hold it*: Maybe Jasmine likes wind in her hair and drives a Harley or rides her horse to school.]

Fallacy of Denying the Antecedent.   The **fallacy of denying the antecedent** starts with a conditional claim and then argues that, if the antecedent condition does not happen (= is not true), then the consequent effect cannot be true either. In other words, if the causal condition does not happen, then neither does the effect (consequent) occur. This is bad reasoning, because an effect may have more than one cause, unless it is so indicated by the "if and only if" condition. Thus, if one antecedent condition (cause) is eliminated, it does not mean the effect did not occur. For instance, the fact that gobbling down a jar of jelly beans will ruin your diet does not mean that *not* eating them means your diet is now safe. Not true! Instead of jelly beans, you might have wolfed down two pizzas that were *not* low carb!

The fallacy of denying the antecedent takes this form:

If A then B.

Not A.   (A is false.)

Therefore, not B.   (B is false.)

Here's an example: "If it snows through the night, we will light a fire at breakfast time. It did not snow through the night. Therefore, we did not light a fire at breakfast time." However, we may light a fire at breakfast time even if it didn't snow, perhaps to make the house look cozy for visitors.

An *equivalent form* of this fallacy is "All A is B. Not A. Therefore, not B." Here's an example: "All wolves are animals. Chickens are not wolves. So chickens are not animals." Note that the antecedent may not necessarily start the sentence—in other words, this fallacy could take the form "B if A. Not A. Therefore, not B." Here's an example: "Bill sings at the top of his lungs if he hears Otis Redding music. Bill did not hear any Otis Redding music. So, he did not sing at the top of his lungs." But perhaps Bill also sings if he hears Rihanna or Aretha Franklin.

Examples of the Fallacy of Denying the Antecedent

If we go see *The Day the Earth Stood Still,* we'll eat a large box of popcorn. We did not go see *The Day the Earth Stood Still.* So, we did not eat a large box of popcorn.
[*Hold it:* Maybe the movie was sold out, and we went to see *Slumdog Millionaire* instead and ate our popcorn then.]

If Manuel turns down his music, Alessandra will give him a neck massage. Manuel did not turn down his music. So, Alessandra did not give him a neck massage.
[*Hold it:* Maybe Manuel offered to pay her for the neck rub or he gave her a foot massage in exchange—turning down the music may be but one path to a neck massage from Alessandra.]

All cows prefer grass to lettuce. A guinea pig is not a cow. So, a guinea pig does not prefer grass to lettuce.
[*Hold it:* Just because the guinea pig is not a cow doesn't mean it eats different food.]

You'll be exhausted if you play in the volleyball tournament. Marielos was exhausted. So, she must have played in the volleyball tournament.
[*Hold it:* She could be exhausted because she shoveled snow all morning or worked in the garden planting ferns.]

Exercises

Part One

Directions: Name the formal fallacy in the following. Not all are fallacies, so be careful! If it is either modus ponens or modus tollens, note which one.

1. If the little boy eats a jar of peanut butter, he'll be thirsty. The little boy was thirsty. So, he must have eaten a jar of peanut butter.

2. All donuts are greasy and tasty. That's not a donut. So, it must not be greasy or tasty.

3. All forms of exercise are things worth thinking about when lying on the couch. Bicycling is a form of exercise. So, it is worth thinking about when lying on the couch.

4. If Zach crawls out of the living room and into the kitchen, then he may either get dirt on his knees or surprise the cats. Zach surprised the cats. So, he must have crawled out of the living room and into the kitchen.

5. All poisons are things small children should avoid. Boiling water is something small children should avoid. So, boiling water is a poison.

6. If Gabriel drinks another espresso, he'll be up all night. Gabriel did not drink another espresso. So, he was not up all night.

7. Jasper will chew up a small piece of the window if he's left on top of his cage looking out at the garden. Jasper was not left on top of his cage looking out at the garden. So, he must not have chewed up a small piece of the window.

8. If Moosh brings Turkish delights to the party and arrives early, then she'll be able to surprise Dary. Moosh was able to surprise Dary. So, she must have brought Turkish delights to the party and arrived early.

9. All college students are overworked but enthusiastic people. Amir is not a college student. So, he must not be overworked or enthusiastic.

10. Unless he studies all weekend, Lee won't be able to pass the statistics final. Lee was able to pass the statistics final. So, he must have studied all weekend.

11. If Carla goes to Iceland for her vacation, then she'll forget about going to Costa Rica. Carla did not go to Iceland. So, she didn't forget about going to Costa Rica.

12. If Russell wants to go to law school, he'll have to take symbolic logic. Russell has to take symbolic logic. So, he must want to go to law school.

13. We'll need a repairman if Jasper chews up the doorsill. Jasper did not chew up the doorsill. So, we won't need a repairman.

Part Two

1. Using the form of modus ponens, finish the valid argument that has as its first premise "If he is big and burly, then he will enjoy French literature."

2. Using the form of modus tollens, finish the valid argument that has as its first premise "If the little girl is fond of small animals, then she might like a guinea pig for a pet."

3. Give a valid argument in the form of modus ponens that has as its first premise "If you have a powerful car, you won't have trouble going over the Grapevine."

4. Give a valid argument in the form of the disjunctive syllogism that has as its second premise "A Cessna is not a four-wheel vehicle."

5. Give a valid argument in the form of modus tollens that has as its first premise "If there's meat on the sandwich, Raelynn won't touch it."

6. Complete the argument in the form of a constructive dilemma having as its first premise "If there are mosquitoes in the tent, it'll be hard to sleep, but if there are no mosquitoes, then another insect is buzzing around."

7. Explain whether this argument is valid or invalid, and why: "Either that's a poltergeist or something weird is happening in the basement. That's no poltergeist. So, something weird is happening in the basement."

8. Explain why this argument is invalid: "If Paco becomes a yoga master, he'll probably want to be a vegan. Paco is a vegan. Therefore, he must have become a yoga master."

9. Explain why this argument is invalid: "Some dogs are Labrador retrievers. Some dogs like to chase cats down the block. Therefore, some Labrador retrievers like to chase cats down the block."

10. Make up some premises to create a valid argument for the conclusion "All dentists are comfortable talking to people who are quiet." Explain why it's valid.

11. Make up some premises to create a valid *or* invalid argument for the conclusion "Some reptiles are lizards." Explain why it's valid *or* invalid.

12. Give an example of an invalid argument with all true premises for the conclusion "Abraham Lincoln was a Republican." Explain why it's invalid.

13. Give an example of an argument in the form of a hypothetical syllogism.

14. What valid argument form is this argument: "If Ray takes up swimming, he'll need goggles; but if he takes up jogging, he'll need new running shoes. Either Ray will take up swimming or he'll take up jogging. So, either Ray will need goggles or he'll need new running shoes."

15. Give an example of a categorical syllogism.

Soundness

Once validity is determined, we can assess the soundness of an argument. Now we ask whether the evidence is actually true and not just whether the conclusion would follow *if* it were true.

This moves us out of the jury box and into the world of empirical reality. Sound arguments are important—who wants to have a good argument based on questionable claims, false statements, or lies? No thanks! If we want our reasoning to be sound, then we want two things: We want the argument to be *cogent* (so our reasoning is strong, defensible, and well structured, and gives sufficient evidence for the conclusion), and we want it to be *grounded in truth*. Otherwise, we risk having a great-sounding argument that goes nowhere. Think of those cases where prosecutors have convicted innocent people on what appeared to be persuasive arguments—but it turned out that some of the evidence was simply false (e.g., as revealed later by DNA evidence).

Let's look at an example: "All men can give birth to children. We need more people living in the Arctic, and embryo implants seem to be working to produce children. Thus, we ought to implant embryos in men and boost the Arctic population." However good this idea may sound, the fact that the first premise is false means the argument has no legs. The reasoning may be strong in terms of validity, but it has no operational, functional, empirical value. The false premise ultimately sinks the argument. It is an unsound argument.

Assessing the Soundness of an Argument

We know when a deductive argument is valid or invalid. The next thing we want to consider is whether the argument is a sound one.

Criteria for a Sound Argument

→ The argument is valid.

→ The premises are actually true.

To check for soundness: First check for validity. If the premises are true, is the conclusion forced to be true (it couldn't be false)? If so, the argument is valid. Next check for the truth of the premises. If the premises really are true, the argument is **sound**. However, if either condition is not met, then the argument is **unsound**. An argument can be unsound if it is valid but doesn't have true premises. It can be unsound if it has true premises but is invalid.

Examples of Sound Arguments

All possums are small mammals.

<u>All small mammals are warm-blooded animals.</u>

So, all possums are warm-blooded animals.

Either Quebec will separate from the rest of Canada,

or it'll stay in the Confederation.

<u>Quebec has not seceded from Canada.</u>

So, it will stay in the Confederation.

These arguments are all valid because, if we assume the two premises to be true, the conclusion *must* be true—it could not be false. Since the premises *are* also true, this means that each of the arguments is sound.

Let's try another argument: "Either monkeypox was introduced into the United States by prairie dogs who got the disease from a Gambian pouch rat or the rumors were false. The rumors were not false. Therefore, monkeypox was introduced into the United States by prairie dogs that had gotten the disease from Gambian pouch rats." First, check for validity. As you probably noticed, this is in the form of a disjunctive syllogism (A or B. Not B. Therefore, A). That means it is valid. Second, check for the truth of the premises. Were the rumors true or false? As it turns out (and you can verify this!), prairie dogs in an Illinois pet store contracted monkeypox (a relative of smallpox) from Gambian pouch rats imported from Africa. So, the premises are true, and the conclusion follows as true. Thus, the argument is sound.

Unsound Arguments

An argument is *unsound* whenever either or both of these conditions are met: (1) The argument is invalid or (2) the premises are not all true. The odds are that an argument will be unsound, because many arguments are invalid, and often one or more of the premises are false.

Example 1 of an Unsound Argument

If we legalize marijuana, then alcohol consumption patterns may change.

<u>We did not legalize marijuana.</u>

So, the alcohol consumption patterns didn't change.

This argument is invalid. Even we assume the premises to be true, the conclusion could be false. There could be any number of reasons that patterns of alcohol consumption could change. Because the argument is invalid, it is unsound.

Example 2 of an Unsound Argument

All skunks are ferocious animals that can mutate into werewolves.

<u>All spotted skunks are skunks.</u>

So, all spotted skunks are ferocious animals that can mutate into werewolves.

This argument is valid, since the conclusion does follow from the premises. However, the first premise is not true, so the argument is not sound.

Group or Individual Exercise

1. Circle all *valid* arguments for the conclusion "No cockroach is capable of solving logic puzzles."
   a. Cockroaches are a lot like centipedes. They are pests and cause a lot of problems for humans. Centipedes aren't capable of solving logic puzzles. So, cockroaches are not capable of solving logic puzzles.
   b. 98% of insects are not capable of solving logic puzzles. Cockroaches are insects. So, cockroaches are not capable of solving logic puzzles.
   c. No creature from outer space is capable of solving logic puzzles. All cockroaches are creatures from outer space. So, no cockroach is capable of solving logic puzzles.

d. Having a small brain causes a creature not to be capable of solving logic puzzles. Cockroaches have small brains. So, no cockroach is capable of solving logic puzzles.

e. No insect is capable of solving a logic puzzles. All cockroaches are insects. So, no cockroach is capable of solving logic puzzles.

f. Most cockroaches are pests. No pests are capable of solving logic puzzles. So, no cockroach is capable of solving logic puzzles.

2. Are any of the valid arguments above *sound* arguments?

3. Here's the first premise: "All wasps are insects that like sweet foods." Finish the argument using modus tollens.

4. It is true that wasps like sweet foods? Is your argument in number 3 sound?

Review: Checking for Validity and Soundness

Remember, first check for validity. Assume that the premises are true, and see if the conclusion is forced to be true. If the conclusion cannot be false and if you assumed that the premises (evidence) were true, then the argument is valid. Otherwise, it's an invalid argument. Now move on to the question of soundness. Check to see if all the premises are actually true. If even one premise is false, then the argument is unsound. If both conditions are satisfied, then the argument is sound. If one condition fails, then the argument is unsound. So, if we have an invalid argument *or* a valid argument with at least one false premise, then we've got an unsound argument. We can summarize all this with a diagram (see Figure 5.2).

FIGURE 5.2
Checking for validity and soundness.

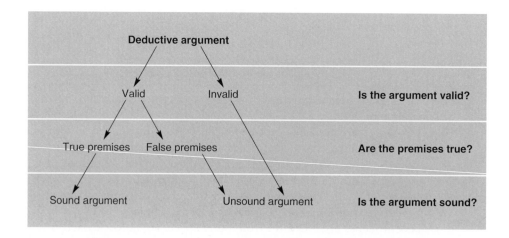

Exercises

Part One

1. Explain why this is a sound argument:

   All cows are mammals.

   <u>No mammal is a reptile.</u>

   Therefore, no cow is a reptile.

2. Explain why this is not a valid argument:

   All Olympic medal winners are athletes.

   <u>Steve is an athlete.</u>

   Therefore, Steve is an Olympic medal winner.

3. Give an example of a sound argument for the conclusion "No lizard has feathers."

4. Explain why this argument is valid but not sound:

   All gymnasts are dentists.

   <u>No dentist is over 3 feet tall.</u>

   Therefore, no gymnast is over 3 feet tall.

5. Give an example of an argument in the form of a hypothetical syllogism with this first premise: "If her goat cheese business takes off, Tina will buy a Mini convertible."

6. Give an example of a valid argument in the form of modus ponens with this conclusion: "Abraham Lincoln liked a snack before bedtime."

7. Give an example of a valid—and sound—argument in the form of modus tollens with this conclusion: "Snakes do not have legs."

8. Give an example of a sound argument in the form of the disjunctive syllogism with this conclusion: "Surfing is a demanding sport."

9. Give an example of an unsound argument in the form of modus ponens with this first premise: "If hawks can be tamed, they would make nice pets."

10. Give an example of a valid but unsound argument in the form of a hypothetical syllogism.

11. Give an example of a sound argument for this conclusion: "Therefore, grizzly bears do not make good pets." Explain why it is sound.

12. Give an example of an invalid argument using the fallacy of denying the antecedent for this conclusion: "Therefore, chocolate ice cream is not fattening."

13. Give an example of an invalid argument using the fallacy of affirming the consequent using this first premise: "If you can ride a horse, then you can do just about anything."

14. Give an example of a valid but unsound argument for this conclusion: "Therefore, all vegetables are carrots."

Part Two

Directions: Test the following arguments to see if they are valid or invalid. If they are valid and fit one of the valid argument forms, then name the form.

1. If the temperature hits 100 degrees, Chicago is miserable. The temperature hit 100 degrees in the summer of 2008. Thus, Chicago was miserable that summer.

2. Anyone who eats a hamburger for breakfast is an eccentric. Anyone who is an eccentric is unusual. It follows that anyone who eats a hamburger for breakfast is an unusual person.

3. If Pinky wears ski goggles to class, he will look mysterious. If Pinky looks mysterious, he will impress his friends. Therefore, if Pinky wears ski goggles to class, he will impress his friends.

4. Anyone who can shoot a musket while running is awfully nimble. Daniel Day Lewis is awfully nimble. Therefore, he shot a musket while running during the making of *Last of the Mohicans*.

5. Some birds are intelligent creatures. No intelligent creature should have to live in a cage. Chickens are birds. Therefore, no chickens should be kept in cages.

6. If you keep eating popcorn, you're bound to bust a tooth on a kernel, but if you don't keep eating popcorn, you'll feel deprived. Either you'll keep eating popcorn or you won't. Therefore, either you'll bust a tooth on a kernel or you'll feel deprived.

7. People who ride Harleys are trained mechanics. Tom is not a trained mechanic, so he must not ride a Harley.

8. Any man who drives a convertible in a snowstorm is desperate for attention. No one who is desperate for attention would go without a warm scarf and hat. Therefore, no one driving a convertible in a snowstorm would go without a warm scarf and hat.

9. A rat is in the basement under the washing machine. If there are rats in the basement under the washing machine, it's not okay to do your laundry barefoot. Therefore, it's not okay to do your laundry barefoot.

10. Either there are squirrels in the attic or some other animal is making noises up there. There are no squirrels in the attic. Therefore, some other animal is making noises up there.

11. Anyone who wears wraparound sunglasses is pretty darn cool. Evan wore wraparound sunglasses to school. Therefore, Evan is pretty darn cool.

12. If men in tiger suits are at the Halloween party and they get a bit too rowdy, then the neighbors will either come over or call the police. The neighbors did not either come over or call the police. So, it is not true that the men in tiger suits were at the Halloween party and they got a bit too rowdy.

13. Either he should forget about a Halloween party this year or Trent should go all out and put goony-looking gravestones in the front yard and have sound effects of moaning ghosts. Trent did not forget about a Halloween party this year. So, he went all out and put goony-looking gravestones in the front yard and had sound effects of moaning ghosts.

14. If either Pinky or Bo shows up in last year's costume, then Charlene will be disappointed. Charlene was disappointed. Therefore, either Pinky or Bo showed up in last year's costume.

15. If Trent doesn't turn down the sound effects of moaning ghosts, then either Gloria or Myron is going to go berserk and put on earmuffs. Trent did not turn down the sound effects of moaning ghosts. Therefore, either Gloria or Myron is going to go berserk and put on earmuffs.

16. Anyone who has ever gone trick-or-treating knows that boiled eggs just don't make it as treats. Grandpa does not know that boiled eggs just don't make it as treats. Therefore, Grandpa must not have gone trick-or-treating at some time in his life.

17. If Pinky wears his spider suit from last year, Bo will come in his fly suit; but if Pinky gets a tiger suit, then Bo will come as a baboon. Either Pinky will wear his spider suit from last year or he'll get a tiger suit. Therefore, either Bo will come in his fly suit or he'll come as a baboon.

Quick Quiz

1. *True or false:* A sound argument is a valid argument with true premises and a true conclusion.

2. "Some animals are tigers. All tigers are rodents. Therefore, some animals are rodents" is an example of an argument that is (a) sound or (b) unsound.

3. What would be the conclusion of a *valid* argument that has premises "All monkeys like bananas. No banana lover eats turnips"?
   a. Some monkeys do not eat turnips.
   b. No monkey eats turnips.
   c. All banana lovers are monkeys.
   d. No turnip eater is a banana lover.

4. *True or false:* An argument can be valid and have premises that are not actually true.

5. What do you know if you know an argument is unsound?
   a. Either it is valid or the premises are true—or both.
   b. It is valid but the premises are not actually true.
   c. It has true premises but is not a valid argument.
   d. Either the premises are not actually true or the argument is invalid—or both.

6. *True or false:* All deductive arguments are valid arguments.

7. The argument "No giraffes are short animals. Some short animals are in the zoo. Therefore, some animals in the zoo are not giraffes" is (a) valid or (b) invalid.

8. If you cannot determine the truth-value of the premises—so you don't know if they are actually true or false—what then follows?
   a. You cannot say the argument is deductive.
   b. You cannot say the argument is valid.
   c. You cannot say the argument is sound.
   d. You cannot say the argument is correct.

Inductive Reasoning

An inductive argument is like a puzzle with some pieces missing. So, there will always be an element of doubt in the argument. The conclusion can only be said to follow with likelihood or probability—never with certainty. In that sense, the conclusion goes beyond what is contained in the premises. For this reason, we have to be careful what applications we make of an inductive argument. Look, for example, at the cautionary note from the American Heart Association's second recommendation (the first was to eat fish oils and Omega-3 fatty acids):

> **We also recommend eating** tofu and other forms of soybeans, canola, walnut and flaxseed, and their oils. These contain **alpha-linolenic acid** (LNA), which can become omega-3 fatty acid in the body. The extent of this modification is modest and controversial, however. More studies are needed to show a cause-and-effect relationship between alpha-linolenic acid and heart disease. (American Heart Association, 31 Oct 2004)

Every so often, we come across inductive arguments that leave us scratching our heads in wonder. Think of those unusual "cures" for AIDS or mind-boggling promises about a diet drug. And then there are the curious statistics we occasionally find cited, as we see below:

> According to a study that looked at dreams, "the further your politics lean to the right, the more likely you are to have nightmares." According to researchers it's three times more likely that you will have bad dreams if you are a Republican than if you are a Democrat. The results of this study are actually coming out of the University, within a stone's throw from here—Santa Clara University in California. . . . Dream

researchers looked at more than four years of dreams dreamt by college kids from around the United States. The total number of subjects was 55; half were females, half males. Their political leanings were divided too, with half being very conservative and half being very liberal.

They found half the Republican's dreams were nightmares, compared to 18 percent of the Democrats. "What's striking is that the nightmares of people on the right were more nightmarish, they were bleaker, there was more hopelessness," says Kelly Bulkeley, the lead researcher on this study. (*New Scientist*, 11 Jul 2001, as quoted by Dr. Dean Edell)

We might question inferring from a study of 55 students to the general population. Not only is there a problem with the number of participants (too small), but these are all college students (one age and educational level). Another question is whether these were *paid* participants—if so, who paid them and could that have biased the result?

We can see from such studies that the conclusion does not follow with certainty. This is true in all inductive arguments. The fact that there are missing pieces in the argument means the premises never fully support the conclusion. Let's look at a few examples.

Example 1 of an Inductive Argument

Beyoncé is the Joan Baez of this generation. She has a voice that travels well, just like Joan Baez, who could bounce her voice off of a mountain. She is a striking physical presence—just like Joan Baez, who had big eyes, fine bones, and beautiful long hair at the peak of her beauty. She has a host of imitators, just like Joan Baez. Joan Baez was also an outspoken pacifist. So, I bet Beyoncé is against war too.

What we have here is a list of similarities between the two singers: voice, looks, and imitators. The inference is then drawn that they must also have similar political views. Even if the terms of the comparison were all true, it is unclear if the additional trait holds as well.

Example 2 of an Inductive Argument:

The hantavirus is a biological agent targeting certain groups the government is out to get. Just look at the evidence. Outbreaks of the hantavirus have not been in Beverly Hills or Boca Raton! No, they've been in New Mexico and Arizona on tribal land, killing off Native Americans. In 1993 alone, the Centers for Disease Control noted 150 cases in the Four Corners region of the Southwest (leading to the virus being nicknamed the "Navajo Virus"). Then the hantavirus showed up in South America and in rural areas where more indigenous people live. If it were just a matter of being exposed to rodent droppings, there'd be a lot more whites coming down with it! It must be a conspiracy against Native Americans.

We can see, from the reasoning in this argument, that the evidence rests on geography and victim profile. Is the evidence sufficient, though, for us to be sure of a conspiracy against indigenous peoples? Not on this evidence alone. Thus, the argument is inductive.

Major Kinds of Inductive Arguments

1. **Predictions.** In predictions, an argument is made about the future based on past or present evidence. For example:

   In light of the devastation in previous earthquakes, we can infer that an earthquake of magnitude 8.5 or greater in eastern Massachusetts will result in a large portion of Martha's Vineyard being swallowed up by the ocean.

2. **Arguments about the past based on present evidence** (also known as retrodiction). In these arguments, an inference is drawn about what happened at some earlier point in time based on current evidence. For example:

   Not all the Indians came over from Russia and Siberia. The fact that there are Native American tribes in Alaska speaking Athabascan languages found in the southwestern and the southeastern United States points to an upward migration. The Cherokee, Navajo, and Apache all share a similar language with the Athabascan tribes in Alaska. Even now, they can communicate with one another in spite of the vast geographic distance.

3. **Cause-and-effect reasoning.** Here it is claimed that an event (effect) is based on one or more causal factors. Given the existence, then, of the causal factor(s), the effect should follow. For example:

   Hepatitis C is on the rise in the prison population in the United States. It is most likely the result of inmates sharing needles, spreading the disease.

4. **Arguments based on analogy.** This argument rests on a comparison, from which it is claimed that a characteristic true of the one term in the equation will also be true of the other. In law, this usually involves the application of a precedent or legal principle. For example:

   Humans are physiologically closest to the chimpanzee. If we can use chimps to find a cure for Parkinson's disease or Alzheimer's, we'll surely be able to market the drug on humans. Therefore, this justifies using chimps in medical research.

5. **Statistical reasoning.** These arguments draw from sample studies or statistical reasoning, from which an inference then is drawn about either all or part of the targeted population. For example:

   58% of people polled by the *Westview Daily* disapprove of embryonic stem cell research. Therefore, 58% of all Americans disapprove of embryonic stem cell research.

Shifting Gears in Statistical Reasoning

Whenever we go from a sample study or poll to a larger population, as in statistical reasoning, we have shifted gears and made a move not seen in deductive reasoning. Look at the difference in these two examples:

Deductive argument: 43% of residents of Ann Arbor said they prefer rice to potatoes. Everyone who prefers rice to potatoes consumes more soy sauce than ketchup. Therefore, 43% of residents of Ann Arbor consume more soy sauce than ketchup.

Inductive argument: 76% of residents of Brush Prairie hike three to four times a week. Brush Prairie is a town in Washington State. Therefore, 76% of residents of Washington State hike three to four times a week.

Did you see the gears shift in the second argument? We went from a town to the state, much like we went from a group in a poll to all Americans in item 5 above. That's not the case in the deductive argument—even though we were using percentages there. The deductive argument has no such shift. We are still talking about the traits of the Ann Arbor residents, and the conclusion comes right out of the premises—not so in the inductive argument.

The Wedge of Doubt in Inductive Arguments

In an inductive argument the premises *could* be true, but the conclusion will never follow with certainty. Remember, there is always some *wedge of doubt* between the premises and the conclusion. We can construct inductive arguments following one of the different forms of inductive reasoning. Here are some examples of inductive arguments. Note the different forms the argument can take.

Inductive Argument 1: An Analogy (see Ben Hewitt, "Tour de Lance," Wired, Jul 2004)

Lance Armstrong is like a hummingbird.

He pedals 100–110 rpm, while his rivals tend to slow to about 70 rpm.

Therefore, Armstrong will be able to use cardiovascular strength instead of relying on muscle power.

Inductive Argument 2: A Prediction

According to the poll taken at Universal City Senior Center, the movie *The Visitor* will win "Best Picture" for 2008.

Readers' polls are pretty darn accurate most of the time.

Therefore, *The Visitor* will almost certainly win "Best Picture" 2008.

Inductive Argument 3: Statistical Reasoning

Only 6% of the 2,600 people in the Gallup Poll on June 7, 2008, said they were unsure who to vote for president.

Vashti was one of the people who was polled.

Therefore, Vashti is probably sure who she'll vote for president.

Global Dimension

Inductive Reasoning about Tsunami Relief

After the tsunami that struck South Asia on December 26, 2004, a massive relief operation was put in motion. One focus was emergency medical help. Analogies were drawn to medicine in a war zone. Read this excerpt, and discuss how this shows inductive reasoning:

> Medical specialists are comparing the emergency medical care problems that have followed the Asian tsunami with another important event in medical history—the U.S. Civil War. Conditions in field hospitals and local clinics in tsunami-wracked areas are crude at best. Electricity is unreliable, there are no antibiotics, only the simplest medical equipment is available and there are few trained medical specialists. "These descriptions are reminiscent of wartime mass casualty situations described during times like . . . the Civil War, or any pre-antibiotic era where amputation was the major treatment of extremity injuries," said Dr. Martin A. Schreiber, director of surgical critical care at Oregon Health & Science University in Portland.
>
> "Amputation is often the best choice in severely contaminated wounds and can be life saving to avoid overwhelming systemic infection," said Susan Briggs, director of the International Trauma and Disaster Institute at Massachusetts General Hospital in Boston. "If there are no antibiotics, then amputation is better than letting the patient die," said McSwain. "This reverts back to the medicine practiced during the War Between the States. Antibiotics had not been discovered. It was better to take off the infected leg than to let the patient die of generalized sepsis." Dr. John Gorczyca, chief of the Division of Musculoskeletal Trauma at the University of Rochester Medical Center in Rochester, N.Y., [says] that this represents a horrible situation, similar to Civil War–era battle treatment, with no antibiotics, horrible wounds, severe contamination, lack of surgeons and minimal technology. (Marc Lallanilla, "Tsunami Medical Care Resembles U.S. Civil War Era," *ABC News*, abcnews.go.com, 7 Jan 2005)

Group or Individual Exercise

Pesticides on produce: The Environmental Working Group cites the following list of fruits and vegetables as those most and least contaminated with pesticides (www.ewg.org, 2007). Look over the list and then answer the questions below.

Apples 89

Spinach 60

Peaches 100

Pears 65

Strawberries 82

Grapes (Domestic) 43

Potatoes 58

Mushrooms 37

Avocados 1

Cabbages 17

One thing we can *deduce* from the above is that apples are more contaminated with pesticides than cabbages. One thing we can *induce* is that eating a handful of fruit is more likely to make you sick than eating guacamole.

Answer the following:

1. Using your powers of *deductive reasoning,* draw three different conclusions from the above list.
2. Using your powers of *inductive reasoning,* draw three different conclusions from the above list.

Exercises

Part One

Directions: Name the different inductive arguments below. Explain what makes them inductive in light of the five main categories.

1. Yesterday was a lovely day for a picnic. Today is a lovely day for a picnic. It follows that tomorrow will be a lovely day for a picnic.
2. 57% of people who phoned into KBST country music station prefer LeAnn Rimes to Faith Hill. As a result, 57% of Americans prefer LeAnn Rimes to Faith Hill.
3. There is a high correlation between smoking and both emphysema and lung cancer. Therefore, anyone who smokes will probably get either lung cancer or emphysema.
4. The movie *Manhunter* is a lot like *Silence of the Lambs.* Both focus on serial killers who target women. Both have detectives who spend an inordinate amount of time trying to get into the mind of the killer. Both detectives seem to be isolated from human companionship and seem obsessed with the one case to the exclusion of anything else. *Silence of the Lambs* has a female lead in the role of the detective; therefore, *Manhunter* must feature a female detective as well.
5. Robert Alton Harris must have had a terrible childhood, because he was such a disturbed man as an adult.
6. 84% of graphic artists prefer MACs to PCs. People who prefer MACs to PCs like the ease of the MAC operating system. Therefore, Andrea, a graphic artist, will like the ease of the MAC operating system.
7. Cigarette smoking must cause people to become alcoholics, because a lot of people who are alcoholics have smoked at some point in their lives.
8. Lake Rudolph in Kenya must be the seat of human evolution, because that is where anthropologists like Richard Leakey have found some of the oldest human bones to date.

9. The pharmaceutical company tested the antinausea drug thalidomide on primates and found it had no adverse effect on either the mother or the fetus. Therefore, they should be able to put the drug on the market without worrying about what it'll do to humans.

10. Inhalers made by Schering-Plough were listed as the probable cause for the deaths of 17 people from September 1998 to June 2000, a period when the recalled inhalers were on pharmacy shelves or in the hands of asthma sufferers. As a result, there should have been a recall of the Schering-Plough inhalers.

11. "Yellowstone National Park officials announced today that—in a very rare combination of events—a concentration of toxic gases (hydrogen sulfide and carbon dioxide) along with unusually cold, dense air appear to be the most probable cause of death for five bison found at Norris Geyser Basin by Bear Management staff. . . . The bison, estimated to have been dead for approximately a week, were found lying on their sides, with their feet perpendicular to their bodies; the unusual position of the carcasses indicates the bison died very rapidly, as a group. According to the park's geologist Dr. Henry Heasler, the five bison (two adults, two calves, one yearling) were likely grazing and resting in a snow-free ground depression along the Gibbon River near multiple geothermal gas vents in the Norris area. Cold, still air from a cold front passing through the area around March 1 probably caused the geyser basin's steam and toxic gases to remain close to the ground, overwhelming the animals." (Yellowstone press release, 23 Mar 2004)

Part Two

1. Note which of the following are inductive arguments.
   a. Evidence found in Africa recently indicates that there are two more dinosaurs than previously thought. Given the type of teeth found in the skulls, it would therefore suggest that these new dinosaurs lived in a more recent period—in other words, after when scientists thought dinosaurs became extinct.
   b. All alligators are potentially vicious and disgusting beasts. Anything vicious and disgusting should be avoided at all costs. Therefore, alligators are something you should avoid.
   c. When Obi was a baby, he loved to run up to dogs—any dog—and give them a hug. One day, however, he got bit by a dog. It required six stitches. Obi, as an adult, hates dogs and has three Amazon parrots. His getting bitten as a child was probably the cause of his hating dogs as an adult.

2. Circle all the *inductive* arguments below. Try to identify which form each one is in.
   a. Sam is a lot like Carlos. He is big and crazy about the Lakers, and he has a tattoo of a snake on his neck. Sam loves to sit around the fire roasting hot dogs and drinking hot chocolate with whipped cream on top. That means Carlos probably would like to do that, too.

b. All big men with tattoos grind their teeth at night. Sam is a big man with a tattoo. Therefore, Sam grinds his teeth at night.

c. If you don't enjoy a good book, then you like to watch movies. Carlos does not like movies. So, he enjoys a good book.

d. 57% of men with tattoos name their first daughter after their mother. Sam's wife, Rose, had a baby girl. That must mean they'll name her after Sam's mother, Margie.

e. Getting snake tattoos is thought to cause men to watch nature videos in the evening. This means Sam, who got a snake tattoo, will likely watch a nature video tonight.

f. When Carlos was a little boy, he loved to hear all about dinosaurs. Therefore, he'll probably love to watch the *Jurassic Park* DVD we rented, since it's about dinosaurs!

g. Either Sam is grinding his teeth or there's a raccoon outside digging in the dog food. There's no raccoon outside. So, Sam is grinding his teeth.

h. Sam usually likes mustard and pickles with his hot dogs. Therefore, I bet he'll love this new garlic-pickle mustard I bought to put on hot dogs.

3. Indicate whether the following arguments are inductive or deductive. If it is an inductive argument, say which form it is in.

a. Sam is thinking about becoming a vegetarian. I think he should. For one thing, he's into philosophy. So is Keanu Reeves. And Keanu Reeves is a vegetarian. So, Sam should become one, too.

b. If the eclipse of the moon is tonight, Carlos will take his little sister outside to watch. The eclipse of the moon is tonight, so Carlos will take his little sister outside to watch.

c. Rosalia really would like to get a new Lexus. But I don't think it's a good idea. 73% of women who get a Lexus like the car so much, they drive all around the countryside and use up gallons of gas. Therefore, Rosalia is liable to do the same, and that will be hard on her finances!

d. Watching too much news tends to cause a person to become nervous and anxious. Rita watches an awful lot of news. I saw her watch the four-o'clock news on channel 7 and the five-o'clock news on channel 2, and then at 11:00, there she was watching channel 4 news! She better watch out—she's going to get nervous as heck and anxious too!

e. If Carlos gets a tattoo that says "I Love Mom," then he will surprise his family. If he surprises his family, the relatives will all talk. Therefore, if Carlos gets a tattoo that says "I Love Mom," the relatives will all talk.

4. Indicate which arguments are inductive and which are deductive.

a. 78% of country singers prefer grits to hash browns. Toby Keith is a country star, so be sure to serve him grits when he comes to the diner for breakfast.

b. Some Siberian huskies make great sled dogs. All great sled dogs have to work in dog teams. Therefore, some Siberian huskies have to work in dog teams.

c. At no time did Dr. Lee indicate his allegiance to the Aryan Nation Defense League (ANDL). If he had sworn allegiance to the ANDL, he would not have risked exposure meeting the reporter to share files. But he did meet with the reporter! Consequently, you're mistaken to argue that Dr. Lee is in cahoots with the ANDL.

d. Inebriation can cause a person to lose control of motor functions. Annette started drinking last night, and by 9 P.M., she was dizzy and unable to walk a straight line. It must have been due to that can of beer she drank with her peanuts.

e. No honest person would lie. All trustworthy people are honest. Therefore, no liar can be trusted.

f. Michael Horse must have been popular when he was a child, given that so many people like him now.

g. No woman who wants an easy life should be a counterterrorist. Everyone in the CIA is a counterterrorist. Therefore, no woman who wants an easy life is in the CIA.

Part Three

Directions: Set out the following arguments, listing the premises and conclusion. Name the type of inductive argument found in each passage.

1. The following argument offers reasons why it should be illegal to sell human ova (eggs):

   Prof. Jonathon Kimmelman said that allowing prospective parents to list desired traits in an egg donor will lead to "cafeteria-style child selection that turn[s] parents into the proverbial consumer." The fact that parents would use $50,000 to "buy" particular characteristics and the potentially large psychological effect on the "bought" child illustrates the need to regulate the private sector. "In our society, there are things we decided we can't sell," Kimmeman said. "It's unacceptable to sell organs or babies, and I wonder if we should consider it unacceptable to sell eggs as well." (Sydney Leavens, "Students and Professors React to Egg Donation Ad," *Yale Daily News,* www.yaledailynews.com, 10 Feb 2004)

2. The following argument seeks to explain why poor people seem to suffer more medical problems than everyone else:

   Poor people have long been known to have more medical problems than affluent people of the same age, but a new study suggests that greater inequality in the distribution of income contributes to higher overall mortality rates and deaths from heart disease, cancer, and homicide. The study found that for treatable conditions like tuberculosis, pneumonia and high blood pressure, mortality rates were higher in states where the income gap was wider. (Robert Pear, "Researchers Link Income Inequality to Higher Mortality Rates," *The New York Times,* 19 Apr 1996)

3. The following argument seeks to explain the rise in heat-related deaths in athletes:

> . . . There were 17 heatstroke deaths from 1995 to 2000, as many as were recorded in 15 previous years. Is the increasing quest for scholarships, money and superstardom—as one former NFL star thinks—pushing players beyond physical limits?
>
> Practices and procedures are being called into question in the wake of recent football-related deaths. Many trainers, coaches and former players wonder whether sports science can keep pace with players who are getting bigger and faster by the year. [Sports] author Jim Dent recounts how [University of Alabama] players, mouths frothing, literally crawled off practice fields to their Quonset huts. "[Legendary coach Bear] Bryant believed the fastest way to whip a team into shape was to deny the boys water, even in the brutal heat."
>
> Of course, players did die of heatstroke back then, but [former football player Dennis] Goehring thinks there were two reasons why more did not. First, players were carrying less body fat. Goehring was a 185-pound lineman. He played both ways. "I couldn't play today," he says. "I'd get killed." He also maintains players of his era were better equipped to handle the heat. "In those days, we didn't have air conditioning," he says. "All of us were acclimated to the heat. We worked tough, summer jobs where the heat was. . . . Today, golly bum, you never get out of the air conditioning. The body is a lot more suited to conditions that are comfortable." (Chris Dufresne, "Cruel Paradox of Camps: Old-School Training Programs Were More Rigorous Than Today's, but Heatstroke Fatalities Were Far Fewer," *Los Angeles Times,* 9 Aug 2001)

4. The following article discusses the use of blue light to address teenagers' sleep problems:

> Teenagers' morning drowsiness is often caused by out-of-tune body clocks, in a condition known as "delayed sleep phase syndrome." Scientists now say that timing exposure to blue light—avoiding it during the first two hours of being awake, then getting a good dose of it—can help restore the sleep cycle, so teens feel sleepy earlier at night and are more awake in the morning. Teenagers are notorious for staying up late, hitting the snooze button and always running late. Now, however, new research shows they can adjust to a schedule simply by sitting in front of a light—a blue light. "If you apply the light after your minimum core body temperature, you're going to advance the clock so you're going to go to bed earlier and wake up earlier the next cycle," Marianna Figueiro, lighting researcher, says. The minimum core body temperature is reached about two hours before a person naturally wakes up.
>
> "When you get the teenager up, outdoors, waiting for the school bus at seven o'clock in the morning, they may be getting light at the wrong phase," Figueiro says. This exposes teens to natural blue light too early. By wearing the goggles when teens wake up, blue light is blocked out. Then, later in the morning—after their minimum core body temperature is reached—teens can reset their internal clocks by being out in the light. An easy way schools can help is by giving students a quick mid-morning break to go outside or put blue LEDs around computer screens in classrooms. By getting enough blue light at the right time, sleep patterns can not only be changed in teens, but also in the elderly and shift workers. ("Waking Up Teens," www.sciencedaily.com, 1 Feb 2006)

5. The following argument is in opposition to the U.S. Department of Energy's proposal to lower the standard of what is allowable in terms of selling radioactive metal:

The Department of Energy [DOE] has a problem: what to do with millions of tons of radioactive metal. So the DOE has come up with an ingenious plan to dispose of its troublesome tons of nickel, copper, steel, and aluminum. It wants to let scrap companies collect the metal, try to take the radioactivity out, and sell the metal to foundries, which would in turn sell it to manufacturers who could use it for everyday household products: pots, pans, forks, spoons, even your eyeglasses.

You may not know this, but the government already permits some companies, under special licenses, to buy, reprocess, and sell radioactive metal: 7,500 tons in 1996, by one industry estimate. . . . The DOE is so eager to get radioactive metal off its hands that it has hired an arm of British Nuclear Fuels, called BNFL, to do the job. . . . The $238-million contract stipulates that the company may recycle for profit all the metals it recovers, including a large amount of formerly classified nickel. . . .

A spokesman for British Nuclear Fuels explained his philosophy to the London paper *The Independent.* "It's recycling," he said. "If you have a cup of coffee, you don't throw the cup away, you reuse it." (Anne-Marie Cusac, "Nuclear Spoons: Hot Metal May Find Its Way to Your Dinner Table; Dept. of Energy's Proposal to Recycle Radioactive Metal into Household Products," *The Progressive,* Oct 1998)

Part Four

1. Construct an inductive argument for the conclusions below, using the form indicated.
   a. Using cause-and-effect reasoning, support this conclusion: Therefore, Maureen's melanoma could be traced back to sun tanning as a teenager.
   b. Using an analogy *or* a statistical argument, support this conclusion: Therefore, *Shrek 2* will go down as one of the greatest animated films in history.
   c. Using a prediction *or* an analogy, support this conclusion: Therefore, Martin Luther King, Jr., will be recognized as one of the most influential Americans of the 20th century.
   d. Using an argument about the past based on present evidence, support this conclusion: Therefore, Fermat must have been mathematically advanced as a little boy.

2. Construct two different kinds of inductive arguments for the conclusion that is given.
   a. Watching TV over two hours a day is not good for little children.
   b. It was probably a mosquito bite that caused John's malaria.
   c. Cell phones cannot possibly be related to brain tumors.
   d. Joshua Bell, the great violinist, must have gotten a lot of encouragement as a child.

3. Indicate which arguments are inductive and which are deductive:

a. Zorro must have been a shy child, given his preference for masks as an adult.

b. Anyone who can change clothes in a phone booth and fly through the air is an impressive person. Superman can changes clothes in seconds and flies at high speed. Therefore, Superman is an impressive person.

c. Vampires can't handle bright sunlight. The longer they're in the sun, the greater the risk of second- and third-degree burns. Therefore, unless Bill gets into the dark very quickly, he will get severely burned.

d. Spider-Man usually likes oatmeal with raisins for breakfast. Consequently, he may not be happy that Mary Jane made him blueberry pancakes when he popped over after his morning swim.

e. 84% of hobbits don't wear shoes because of their thick and leathery feet. As a result, Sam inferred that Mandible, his closest hobbit friend, would not be wearing shoes on the hike.

f. If the storm hits Gotham City, Batman won't be able to make it across town in time to stop the Mafia hit. Batman did get across town in plenty of time to stop the Mafia hit. Therefore, the storm didn't hit Gotham City.

g. No self-respecting superhero fails to pay attention to the fine details. Bourne is certainly a superhero. Therefore, he's sure to pay attention to the fine details about the FBI corruption case.

Quick Quiz

1. The argument "57% of the students polled at Reed College said they did aerobic exercises at least once a week. Maricela is a student at Reed College. So, she must do aerobic exercises at least once a week" is:
   a. An inductive argument
   b. A deductive argument
   c. A valid argument
   d. An invalid argument

2. *True or false:* An inductive argument always has at least one false premise.

3. The "wedge of doubt" in an inductive arguments tells us (a) the premises are not certainly true or (b) the conclusion cannot be said to follow with certainty.

4. If an argument is *valid,* then we also know it is (a) inductive or (b) deductive.

5. *True or false:* An inductive argument cannot have a true conclusion.

6. The argument "Smoking cigars increases your chances of lung cancer. Carla smokes cigars. So, she might get lung cancer" is:
   a. A deductive argument
   b. A valid argument
   c. An invalid argument
   d. An inductive argument

7. If you *know* an argument is a *sound* argument, you also know (a) it could be inductively strong or (b) it is not an inductive argument.

8. All of the following are major kinds of inductive arguments *except*:
   a. Predictions
   b. Cause-and-effect reasoning
   c. Disjunctive syllogism
   d. Statistical reasoning

9. What kind of inductive argument is this: "Omar is really interested in politics—he reads *The Economist* and at least three newspapers every day. Therefore, he must have been a handful as a little boy, wanting to talk politics and read papers all the time!"
   a. Prediction
   b. Retrodiction
   c. Cause-and-effect reasoning
   d. Statistical reasoning

10. What kind of inductive argument is this: "78% of men polled at Zebra's Deli in San Diego said they prefer gooey pastries to toast for breakfast. Therefore, 78% of men in San Diego prefer gooey pastries to toast for breakfast"?
   a. Prediction
   b. Retrodiction
   c. Cause-and-effect reasoning
   d. Statistical reasoning

Assessing Inductive Arguments

Inductive arguments are assessed in terms of strength, not validity. Because the premises of inductive arguments never supply enough evidence to force the conclusion to be true, there is always an element of uncertainty, or probability, to inductive reasoning. An inductive argument is *neither valid nor invalid*—we can only talk about validity with deductive arguments. This is because we can't guarantee the truth of the conclusion in an inductive argument. Consider:

> 79% of high school students in Illinois admire Barack Obama.
>
> Jaime is a high school student.
>
> So, Jaime admires Barack Obama.

Even if the premises were true, the conclusion could still be false. There is too much uncertainty to conclude that Jaime must admire Barack Obama. *Think of it this way:* If I ask you to go up in my Cessna plane with me and tell you that you have a 79% chance of surviving the trip, you would not likely rush to board the plane. However, the closer my percentage gets to 100%, the better your chances of going along.

You Tell Me Department

What about Workers' Injuries and Decision Making?

Avocado picker Allen Kimball, 33, was at the last tree to be harvested and saw a bunch of avocados near the top of the tree. Grabbing his aluminum-picking pole, Kimball climbed his aluminum ladder to pick the avocados. He did not see the Southern California Edison power lines until it was too late and 12,000 volts of electricity went through his body, igniting both arms and his right leg. He's had dozens of surgeries, including the amputation of most of both arms. He faces more surgery and will likely be confined to a wheelchair within 10 years. (Donna Huffaker, "Amputee's Suit Alleges Neglect by Utility Firm," *Daily Journal,* 10 Jul 2001)

- **Kimball's Argument:** In his lawsuit against Southern California Edison, Kimball seeks $52.8 million. He says the company was responsible for the electric lines not being visible in the overgrown tree. The avocado tree was two weeks overdo for a trim when the accident occurred. Kimball's lawyer says that Kimball is 15 percent responsible for the accident, because the lines were approximately 15 percent visible from the backyard where the tree was located.

- **Edison's Argument:** Edison's attorney argued that Edison should not be held responsible for someone standing on an aluminum ladder with an aluminum pole 13 feet from the line. They said the wires cleared the branches by 6 feet (the state requires a "reasonable distance" such as 4 feet), so the wires were well within the legal guidelines. They claim Kimball was electrocuted because of his 10-foot aluminum pole hitting the wires and the fact that he didn't see the wires does not prove he *could not* see them. They argued that the only way to make power lines 100 percent visible is to chop down all the trees.

- **The Dilemma:** The question to be decided is how to assign responsibility for Kimball's injuries. Kimball's own attorney suggests a 15/85 division (where he's 15 percent and Edison 85 percent responsible). If we factor in the employer, however, this would have to change. Kimball wasn't picking avocados in his own backyard. He was doing it for his work—his employer sent him out with an aluminum ladder and an aluminum pole. A wooden pole would have protected Kimball against electrocution, but it would have been heavier. Thus, employers prefer lighter poles and ladders, so workers can go at top speed. In trying to assign responsibility, there are a number of such factors to consider.

You tell me: How should the lawsuit be resolved? State your recommendations.

There is no *one* specific method of assessing the strength of inductive arguments. Considerations vary according to the type of inductive argument. But one thing is certain: There will always be a degree of probability involved. In all inductive arguments, there exists a fundamental uncertainty about whether the conclusion follows from the premises. However, each inductive argument can be evaluated in terms of how strong or weak it is.

Inductive Arguments: Strength versus Validity

As we can see, we can assign inductive arguments a relative strength—but they do not fall in the "all-or-nothing" category found with deductive reasoning. This,

The Global Dimension

Not Lost: Searching for Buried Treasure off of Africa

On a pirate island off of Africa, people spend an awful lot of time trying to track down buried treasure. The search involves plotting, planning, and looking for a host of clues that could point the way to the gold. The quest is fueled by a belief that the pirates were aligned with members of a secret society, the Freemasons. Read about the hunt and then decide if Getler's argument is inductive or deductive—and say why.

> Warren Getler [is] a man who uses advanced sonic-imaging technology to find buried treasure. Most of the time, Getler, who works for a company called Witten Technologies in Washington, D.C., is your standard buttoned-down business type. Out here on the edge of the world, though, Getler was letting his true self show.
>
> He is a devotee of an obscure historical theory, one contending that treasure has been stashed around the world by pirates affiliated with Freemasons, the mysterious fraternal order that was started by stonemasons in medieval Europe. The handful of historians who have studied the subject believe that some pirates used elaborate Masonic symbols and signposts to record the locations of buried treasure. *Ipso facto,* if you can unravel the Masons' intricate secret language, you may be able to plot a pathway to buried booty. (Paul Perry, "X Marked the Spot," *National Geographic,* www.nationalgeographic.com, Mar 2002)

then, means an inductive argument is neither sound nor unsound—soundness requires validity, and validity does not apply to inductive arguments.

We cannot talk about validity or soundness with regard to inductive arguments. So never say an inductive argument is valid or invalid; never say it is sound or unsound. These terms simply do not apply. However, we *can* take a stand on how strong the inductive argument appears to be, and that can be instrumental when making decisions and drawing up policies.

Think of inductive arguments and deductive arguments in terms of men and women. Some of the things you can discuss about men do not apply to women and vice versa. For instance, you'd never say, "That man is (or is not) pregnant." It would be ludicrous to talk that way, and we would think you were goofy if you did. This is the same with validity, invalidity, and soundness. These terms can only be used with respect to deductive arguments. Inductive reasoning is assessed differently; with induction, we are looking for the relative strength of the argument.

Exercises

Part One

Directions: State how strong you think the following inductive arguments are. Give reasons for your decisions.

1. 36% of people who eat French fries at lunchtime skipped breakfast. Greg often eats French fries with his lunch. So, I bet he doesn't eat breakfast.

2. Queen Latifah is a lot like Serena Williams. Both are African-American females, are talented people, are famous, and have a lot of fans. Serena Williams is a great athlete. That must mean Queen Latifah would be a great athlete too.

3. Approximately 250 of the 312 people attending the wedding reception suffered food poisoning. Ed and Jack attended the reception. So, they probably suffered food poisoning too.

4. Steve usually makes barbeque chicken when the family gets together. Because we are going to his house on Thursday for Thanksgiving dinner, I bet Steve will make us barbeque chicken.

5. In a study of women who tried out for the police department, the city found that 75% of them lifted weights and did aerobics. Therefore, 75% of all American women lift weights and do aerobics.

6. Some people who get liposuction have a few problems with their skin rippling. Therefore, liposuction causes skin to ripple.

7. Lindsay Lohan got 36 months' probation for drunk driving and drug possession. She'll probably start a rehab program soon, because substance abuse can really mess up a person's life.

8. Scientists studying the pieces of pottery found in the archaeological site determined that of the 10,000 objects recovered, over 78 percent of them had some relationship to agriculture. They were either tools or receptacles for working the soil and raising crops. This suggests that the people who lived here were an agricultural, rather than a hunting, society.

9. 82% of the people attending Justin Timberlake's performance said they thought he was fantastic. Lulu attended the performance. Therefore, Lulu must have thought he was fantastic too.

10. Tom's phone number is one digit away from the pizza parlor's phone number. Last night he received 10 calls from people who wanted to order a pizza. Two nights ago he got 15 calls for pizza, and three nights ago he got 12 phone calls. I wish we didn't have to study at his house, as we are probably going to go nuts with pizza calls!

11. Circle all correct answers:
    a. A weak inductive argument is invalid.
    b. A valid argument always has true premises.
    c. An argument could be valid with false premises, provided that, if we assume the premises to be true, it would force the conclusion to be true.
    d. A sound argument is always valid.
    e. An invalid argument always has false premises.
    f. If you have true premises, you know the argument is valid.
    g. A sound argument must be valid and also have true premises.
    h. An inductive argument could be valid, so long as the premises support the conclusion.

Part Two

1. Is this a valid argument? Is it sound? State your reasons.

   Everyone who studies logic enjoys horror films.

   Everyone who enjoys horror films likes *Dawn of the Dead.*

   Therefore, everyone who studies logic likes *Dawn of the Dead*.

2. Indicate which of the arguments are inductive and which are deductive:
   a. No one who eats squid is a vegetarian. Roland eats squid. So, Roland is not a vegetarian.
   b. 68% of the listeners who responded to the November 2008 poll said that the death penalty is barbaric. So, 68% of teenagers think the death penalty is barbaric.
   c. The dinosaurs became extinct because, according to evidence found in China last year, an asteroid hit the earth during the time of the dinosaurs and sent up great dust clouds, blocking the sun and causing very cold weather.
   d. All toxic substances should be handled very carefully. Dioxin is a toxic substance. So, dioxin should be handled very carefully.
   e. Rhonda is just like her father—short, smart, and determined. Her father dreamed of becoming a pilot. Therefore, Rhonda dreams of being a pilot too.
   f. Only a mean woman could put up with him. Only mean women hang out at Reggie's Bar. Cassandra hangs out at Reggie's Bar. Therefore, Cassandra could put up with him.
   g. Reading too many computer magazines causes a person to be depressed. LaToya reads computer magazines all the time. So, she'll get depressed.

3. Set out a *deductive* argument for the conclusion "Anyone who passes the calculus final exam should be able to pass the class."

4. Set out an *inductive* argument for the conclusion "54% of Australians say the koala should be made the national animal."

5. Which of the arguments below are *inductive?*
   a. Georgia loves peach ice cream. Anyone who loves peach ice cream is a friend of mine. Therefore, Georgia is a friend of mine.
   b. 64% of women who love peach ice cream are wild and exotic. Georgia loves peach ice cream. Therefore, Georgia is wild and exotic.
   c. No woman who loves peach ice cream is cruel to puppies. Georgia loves peach ice cream. So, Georgia is not cruel to puppies.
   d. Peach ice cream usually causes women to have a warm feeling inside. Georgia just ate some peach ice cream. So, Georgia will probably have a warm feeling inside.
   e. Everyone who loves peach ice cream lives a decadent life. Anyone who lives a decadent life forgets to vote. Therefore, everyone who loves peach ice cream forgets to vote.

6. Which of the arguments below are inductive and which are deductive?
    a. All football players are big and burly. Toby Maguire is not big and burly. So, he must not be a football player.
    b. Caffeine usually causes children to behave in unpredictable ways. That little girl is drinking some of her mother's coffee. So, she'll behave in unpredictable ways.
    c. No thief is trustworthy. Marcos is trustworthy. So, Marcos is not a thief.
    d. 75% of Angelenos interviewed by NBC said they found the earthquake traumatic, but they will not leave the city. Ruth lives in Los Angeles. Consequently, she found the earthquake traumatic but won't leave the city.
    e. Mack the Knife is awfully abusive to his dog. Abusive people were often abused as children. Therefore, Mack the Knife was abused when he was a child.
    f. All munchkins are snapplepuffers. All snapplepuffer are morks. Therefore, all munchkins are morks.

7. Which of the arguments below are valid?
    a. Everyone who goes barefoot risks being made into a laughingstock. Tarzan goes barefoot. Consequently, Tarzan risks being made into a laughingstock.
    b. If he can't dodge bullets, he's not Neo. He's Neo. Therefore, he can dodge bullets.
    c. 95% of men who live in the jungle can swing from vines. Tarzan lives in the jungle. So, he can swing from vines.
    d. Spider-Man is a lot like Zorro. He wears a funny-looking outfit and helps fight evil whenever he can. Zorro can do fancy tricks with his sword. Therefore, Spider-Man can also do fancy tricks with his sword.
    e. Everyone who dresses in a gorilla suit and drives on the freeway gets a lot of attention. Anyone who gets a lot of attention becomes terribly conceited. Therefore, everyone who dresses in a gorilla suit and drives on the freeway becomes terribly conceited.
    f. Either you vote or don't complain. You didn't vote. So don't complain.

8. Explain whether this is an inductive or deductive argument:

In the early 1980s, eleven people died of cyanide poisoning. Each victim had taken a Tylenol tablet and died within a few hours. There was no evidence that the cyanide had been added at the factory. Investigators suspected the containers had been tampered with and then placed on store shelves. At the time of the deaths, there was $30 million worth of Tylenol on the shelves in stores throughout the United States. The company did not want anyone else to die of cyanide poison in Tylenol tablets. Until the source of the poisoned tablets was found, there was a risk that other people would die. Any time there is a serious risk to human life from a product, the product should be removed from the shelves and distribution stopped. Therefore, company officials concluded that the Tylenol should be removed from the shelves.

9. Select two different arguments from either the Letters to the Editor or the op-ed section of a newspaper. Tape them to a piece of paper. Lay out the arguments, stating the premises and the conclusion. Indicate if the arguments are inductive or deductive. If any are valid, note that.

10. Gather two or three different print ads (e.g., from a magazine). Tape or staple them to a piece of paper. State the arguments made in each ad. Note if they are inductive or deductive.

Part Three

1. Discuss Laker coach Phil Jackson's analogy in the following argument:

   Like life, basketball is messy and unpredictable. It has its way with you, no matter how hard you try to control it. The trick is to experience each moment with a clear mind and an open heart. When you do that, the game—and life—will take care of itself. (Phil Jackson, *Sacred Hoops,* Hyperion, 1995)

2. Read the excerpts below on the "Wendy's finger case." Note any conflicts or concerns, and then state three inductive arguments explaining how the finger got into the chili.

   A woman bit into a human finger while eating a bowl of chili at a Wendy's. Health officials said this is definitely a first for them and was not a hoax. The fingertip was about an inch and a half long, and had a manicured nail. The county medical examiner said the human finger was cooked but not decomposed. Officials counted all the fingers of the Wendy's workers—no one had a missing digit. Authorities think the finger must have come from one of Wendy's suppliers. It appears the finger was torn off, possibly by a piece of machinery at a processing plant. (See "Human Finger Found in Fast Food Chili," www.localio.com, 24 Mar 2005)
   The human finger found in a bowl of chili at a San Jose Wendy's might not have been cooked with the chili and could have been snuck in later in the preparation process, Santa Clara County officials said Friday. ("Was Finger Cooked along with Chili?" *San Francisco Chronicle,* 26 Mar 2005)
   San Jose police are investigating the case of a woman who lost part of her finger in a leopard attack. The woman, who has several exotic animals, reportedly got the finger back in a bag of ice, after doctors couldn't re-attach it. She lives about 45 miles north of Las Vegas. A month after that attack, a Las Vegas woman reported biting into a human finger while eating a bowl of Wendy's chili. Wendy's has maintained the finger allegedly found in the chili had not been cooked, and that it didn't enter the supply chain as part of its ingredients. (See "Investigators in Wendy's Finger Case Check Out Clue," www.localio.com, 13 Apr 2005)

3. Examine the argument below. Set out the conclusion and premises.

   Human organs are brokered from Pakistan to China; kidney-theft rings have swept through villages in India. People have bartered kidneys and livers to pay off debts and reinvent dreams. The poor in underdeveloped nations, such as Moldova and the Philippines, are offered "transplant tourism" packages that arrange for them to travel to another country and sell their organs to rich patients. "It's the worst kind of business in Egypt. It's worse than slavery," says Mohamed Queita, member of the Egyptian parliament, who has no comprehensive statistics but notes that one Cairo clinic had a waiting list of 1,500 people willing to sell their organs. "I don't want the poor turned into spare parts for the rich. Serious cases of poverty in this country are causing an increase in the theft and sale of organs." It is a market of desperation and ingenuity in which doctors ask few questions and donors often end up ill, and sometimes dead. As a result, Queita has proposed a bill in Egypt that transplants be limited to family members or to donors who accept no money. (Jeffrey Fleishman and Noha El-Hennawy, "Egypt's Organ Donors: Looking within for Wealth," *Los Angeles Times,* 18 Mar 2008)

4. Discuss the reasoning in the excerpt below on Lyme disease. In 1999, the Centers for Disease Control (CDC) recorded 16,273 cases. A controversy erupted.

A study to be reported on Thursday in *The New England Journal of Medicine* is fueling a running disagreement among medical researchers over the unresolved issues in Lyme disease, a tick-borne illness that is endemic in much of the Northeast and in other pockets around the nation.

The study, by Dr. Mark S. Klempner of Boston University Medical Center, showed that prolonged treatment with antibiotics was no more effective than placebos among those with persistent Lyme disease symptoms. The question is, "Why do a few patients who appear to have been treated successfully for Lyme disease have symptoms that come back strongly later?"

Both sides agree that antibiotics work in 90 percent of patients and that the disease never recurs in those patients, at least not from that tick bite. But among the other patients, symptoms either persist or come back after the standard treatment. Do the symptoms recur because the bacteria have been hiding out in the body, only to emerge again later? Or could the Lyme bacteria, even though they were wiped out by treatment, have brought on a secondary disease, a Lyme autoimmune disorder, in which the body's immune system attacks its own cells as if they were the Lyme disease organism?

Because the patients in Dr. Klempner's study were given a new round of antibiotics, the bacteria should have been killed, and the patients' symptoms should have gone away. Since that did not happen, proponents of the autoimmune theory say, the Klempner study is good evidence for their position.

The Klempner study found that extended treatment with antibiotics did not help people who believed they had persistent Lyme infection, a finding that suggested that their symptoms were unrelated to the bacteria. (Philip J. Hilts, "Certainty and Uncertainty in Treatment of Lyme Disease," *The New York Times,* 10 Jul 2001)

5. Draw three to four inferences about the Lyme controversy, in light of the following quote from microbiologist Edward McSweegan:

Protests have been organized to denounce Yale University's research meetings and Lyme clinic because, according to the protesters, Yale "ridicules people with Lyme disease, presents misleading information, minimizes the severity of the illness, endorses inadequate, outdated treatment protocols, excludes opposing viewpoints, and ignores conflicts of interest." Researchers have been harassed, threatened, and stalked. A petition circulated on the Web called for changes in the way the disease is routinely treated and the way insurance companies cover those treatments. Less radical groups have had their meetings invaded and disrupted by militant Lyme protesters. (Edward McSweegan, Ph.D., "Lyme Disease: Questionable Diagnosis and Treatment," www.quackwatch.com, 30 Jun 2001)

CASE STUDY IN CAUSE-AND-EFFECT REASONING

An issue that brings together both cause-and-effect reasoning and arguments based on analogy is the question of assigning guilt in gang killings. The dilemma is what to do when members of gangs are shooting at each other and (scenario 1) kill a bystander or (scenario 2) one gang member kills a member of a rival gang and, in retaliation, the rival gang murders a member of the gang that fired the first shot.

One issue that comes up is the question of cause. The **direct cause** *of something is that which leads to a particular effect without any intervening step. In contrast, the* **proximate cause** *of an event is the last causal factor in a chain leading to a particular effect. For instance, someone with cancer undergoing chemotherapy has a weakened immune system and then gets pneumonia and dies. The*

pneumonia is the proximate cause of the person's death but clearly not the sole cause.

Compare a child throwing a ball at a window, causing it to break (the direct cause is the throwing of the ball), to a man carrying a tuna casserole slipping on a banana peel that a prankster just threw down on the sidewalk in front of the man, causing him to send the casserole flying in the air, going through a window and breaking it (the casserole dish flying in the air is the proximate *cause of the broken window, the end of the sequence of causal factors starting with the prankster throwing down the banana peel).*

Read the following article from the legal publication the Daily Journal. *Then briefly state what was at issue and whether you think the decision in each case was a wise one in terms of addressing gang killings.*

"Provocative Act" Doctrine Rejected in Gang Killing

John Roemer

Daily Journal, August 28, 2001

SAN FRANCISCO—Gang killings in Santa Ana and Fontana led to distinctly different decisions by the California Supreme Court on Monday involving the "proximate causation" doctrine in murder cases and the state's

controversial "provocative act" rule. Both unanimous decisions were written by Justice Marvin R. Baxter.

One ruling, *People* v. *Cervantes*, appeared to be a win for defendants because it turned away an effort to expand the provocative act doctrine, which holds accountable for murder those whose non-lethal assaults lead indirectly to a killing. The other case, decided on the issue of proximate cause, was a victory for prosecutors in gang warfare cases. For the first time, in *People v. Sanchez,* the high court approved dual murder convictions for two shooters when a lone bullet from one of them—whose identity cannot be ascertained—killed a single victim.

In the first case, the court unanimously reversed the murder conviction of Highland Street gang member Israel Cervantes. The justices, in overturning a Santa Ana appellate panel, declined to broaden the provocative act theory. Cervantes was convicted of first-degree murder even though his gunshot only wounded a member of the Alley Boys gang at a street birthday party in 1994. Friends of the victim retaliated by gunning to death Hector Cabrera, a member of Cervantes' gang, and prosecutors successfully invoked the provocative act theory to win a life sentence for Cervantes.

"Given that the murder of Cabrera by other parties was itself felonious, intentional, perpetrated with malice aforethought, and directed at a victim who was not involved in the original altercation, the evidence is insufficient as a matter of law to establish the requisite proximate causation to hold defendant liable for murder," Baxter wrote.

The provocative act doctrine is most often used in cases where a defendant opens fire and someone else shoots back, killing a third party. Typically the deadly shots come from store clerks, police or other crime victims who react to a lethal emergency created by the initial shooter. But when the killers in the current case retaliated against another member of Cervantes' gang, they absolved Cervantes of responsibility for the death of their victim, Baxter wrote, citing a classic 1985 legal text, *Horn & Honoré's Causation in the Law:* "The killers 'intended to exploit the situation created by Cervantes, but were not acting in concert with him,' a circumstance that is 'normally held to relieve the first actor [Cervantes] of criminal responsibility.' In short, nobody forced the Alley Boys' murderous response in this case. The willful and malicious murder of the victim at the hands of others was an independent intervening act on which defendant's liability for the murder could not be based."

"The decision is good news for defense lawyers," said Philip M. Brooks, the Berkeley sole practitioner who wrote and argued the appeal before the high court. "Upholding this expansion of the doctrine would have completely changed the law," he said.

And in Monday's other opinion, the Supreme Court upheld the murder conviction of Julio Cesar Sanchez, a member of a Fontana gang named TDK (Diablo Klicka). That case came to the court as another provocative act case—but the justices decided it instead on the issue of *proximate cause.* The decision means that two shooters can be found guilty of a murder in which only a single bullet strikes the victim. Sanchez and codefendant Ramon Gonzalez of the rival Headhunters gang shot it out in 1996 on a Fontana street. A stray shot killed a bystander, and both shooters were convicted of murder under the provocative act theory.

Gonzalez did not appeal his conviction. The Sanchez guilty finding was overturned by a unanimous Riverside appellate panel, which concluded concurrent causation cannot be established in a single-fatal-bullet case. That was erroneous, the high court held. "The circumstance that it cannot be determined who fired the single fatal bullet, i.e., that direct or actual causation cannot be established, does not undermine defendant's first degree murder conviction if it was shown beyond a reasonable doubt that defendant's conduct was a substantial concurrent cause of [the victim's] death," Baxter wrote. He added, "It is proximate causation, not direct or actual causation, which, together with the requisite culpable *mens rea* (malice), determines defendant's liability for murder."

Defense lawyer Melvyn Douglas Sacks of Los Angeles called the decision significant. "It's a landmark for law enforcement in combating gang violence," said Sacks. "The court may regard this as a step forward for society, but it's a step backward for the defense bar," he said. "It really stretches aiding and abetting. The other guy fired first and my guy never fired his weapon until after the victim was dead." Justice Joyce L. Kennard, in a concurrence, discussed how the companion cases of *Cervantes* and *Sanchez* differ. "In both, the defendant was a gang member who discharged a firearm at someone belonging to a rival gang," Kennard wrote. "In both, defendant's conduct induced additional gunfire in which a third person died. But this court has concluded that these similarities are less significant than other circumstances distinguishing the two situations."

Proximate or legal causation was not established in *Cervantes* but was present in *Sanchez*, Kennard wrote, adding: "History sadly establishes that killings motivated by revenge may occur in cycles lasting many years and even generations. . . . Courts must try to draw appropriate lines to mark the outer limits of legal causation in these situations. The court's decisions today in these two companion cases should begin to fix this line of demarcation separating mutual combat killings from retaliatory killings in the context of urban warfare between rival street gangs." Justice Kathryn Mickle Werdegar also concurred separately.

Source: © 2001 Daily Journal Corporation. All rights reserved. Reprinted with permission of the *Daily Journal*.

▦ Truth Tables

The Basics

Propositions are either simple or compound. A compound proposition is one that contains at least one logical connective. A *logical connective* is an operator that turns simple propositions into compound propositions. There are exactly five such operators in logic—they are as follows:

CONNECTIVE	EFFECT	EXAMPLE
"not"	*Negates* a proposition	Charlie is *not* afraid of bats.
"and"	Creates a *conjunction*	Ray is afraid of bees *and* spiders.
"or"	Creates a *disjunction*	*Either* there are bees *or* there are bats in the attic.
"if/then"	Creates a *conditional*	*If* bats are in the attic, *then* Charlie won't be scared.
"if and only if"	Creates a *biconditional*	Ray will be scared *if and only if* he sees bees or spiders.

A simple proposition contains *no* logical connectives. There are five connectives, and each has a corresponding symbol. They are set out in the table below:

LOGICAL CONNECTIVES	SYMBOL
Negation	~
Conjunction (and)	& (or •)
Disjunction (or)	∨
Conditional (if . . . then/only if)	→
Biconditional (equivalence, if and only if)	≡ (or ↔)

Negation.   Negating a claim changes the truth value to its opposite. This means a proposition that was originally true becomes false when negated, and vice versa. In a truth table, this is expressed as follows:

P	~P
T	F
F	T

Conjunction.   A conjunction is the result of two (or more) propositions joined together by an "and." The conjunction of propositions P and Q (each called a "conjunct") is the proposition P and Q, symbolized as P & Q. A conjunction is true only if each conjunct is true.

P	Q	P & Q
T	T	T
T	F	F
F	T	F
F	F	F

Disjunction.   A disjunction is the result of two (or more) propositions joined together by an "or" (or "either/or"). The disjunction of propositions P and Q (each called a "disjunct") is the proposition P or Q, symbolized as P ∨ Q. A disjunction is true if at least one of the conjuncts is true. A disjunction is false only if both disjuncts are false.

P	Q	P ∨ Q
T	T	T
T	F	T
F	T	T
F	F	F

The Conditional.   A conditional is an "if . . . then" or "only if" claim. The conditionals "If P then Q" and "P only if Q" are both symbolized P → Q. In this construction, the proposition, P (on the left of the arrow), is called an **antecedent.** The proposition, Q (after the arrow, and following the "then"), is called a **consequent.** A conditional claim is false only when the antecedent P is true and the consequent Q is false. Otherwise, it is true.

P	Q	P → Q
T	T	T
T	F	F
F	T	T
F	F	T

Note: Even when the antecedent and consequent are both false, the conditional P → Q is true! It is false *only* when the antecedent is true and the consequent is false. The reason is this: When I say, "If P then Q," I am saying, "If P happens, then Q happens also." This is the same as saying, "Either not P or Q." For example, if I say, "If the dog eats four avocados, then he'll get sick," I am then saying, "Either the dog did not eat four avocados or he'll get sick" (because either he did or did not eat four avocados and if he eats four, then he's going to be sick). So, "Either he didn't eat four avocados or he'll be sick." If it is *false* that he ate four avocados, then "he didn't eat four avocados" is *true,* and so the claim "Either he didn't eat four avocados or he'll get sick" is going to be true as well.

It is false *only* when the antecedent is true and the consequent is false. So, if it is true that the dog ate four avocados, but it is false that he got sick, then it cannot be the case that "If he ate four avocados, the dog will get sick." That must be false. So, any time you have a true antecedent and a false consequent, the conditional claim has to be false.

Biconditional.   A biconditional asserts the equivalence of two propositions. This means the antecedent is both necessary and sufficient for the consequent. This is expressed as "P is equivalent to Q" or "P if and only if Q." This can be expressed as "If P then Q, and if Q then P." Two propositions are equivalent if they have the same truth-value. This means P ≡ Q is true if P and Q are both true or both false. This is expressed as follows:

P	Q	P ≡ Q
T	T	T
T	F	F
F	T	F
F	F	T

We are now ready to see what happens when we have combinations of the five logical connectives. For example, what if P and Q are both compound propositions? Let's look at some examples:

Example: Setting Out a Truth Table for the Proposition (P & Q) → ~P

Step 1: Plug in the truth-values for each one of P and Q, moving across the row. In the first row, P and Q are both true, so we'll put in T's under every occurrence of the two propositions. In the second row, P is true and Q is false, so go across the row, putting in T's wherever P appears and F's wherever Q appears. Continue until all four rows are set out with the truth values listed under each occurrence of P and Q. This is what we get:

P	Q	(P & Q) → ~P		
T	T	T	T	T
T	F	T	F	T
F	T	F	T	F
F	F	F	F	F

Step 2: We now need to go across each row and do the operations, keeping the main connective of the compound proposition in mind. The main connective here is the →. The antecedent is P & Q, and the consequent is ~P. We cannot set out the truth-value of the main connective until the last step. Always do the main connective last in the truth tables. Putting in the truth-values for the P & Q in the antecedent and the ~P in the consequent, we get:

P	Q	(P & Q)	→	~P
T	T	T T T		F T
T	F	T F F		F T
F	T	F F T		T F
F	F	F F F		T F
		⇑		⇑

Take the two operations (the "&" and the "~") as indicated above.

Step 3: Now we can get the truth-value of the main connective ("→"). This we do by working with the truth-values in bold under the "&" and those under the negation in the consequent (the ~P). Remember, the only time a conditional is false is when the antecedent is true (T) and the consequent false (F). Any other combination is true. We have:

P	Q	(P & Q)	→	~P
T	T	T T T	F	F T
T	F	T F F	T	F T
F	T	F F T	T	T F
F	F	F F F	T	T F

⇑

We can now read the main connective, as indicated.

Truth-Values of Three Types of Propositions

Tautology	All T's	A tautology is always ***true***.
Contradictory	All F's	A contradiction is always ***false***.
Contingent	Both T's and F's	A contingent claim's truth-value is dependent the truth-values of its components.

As the above table indicates, any proposition with all T's under the main connective is a tautology, any with all F's is contradictory, and any with a mixture of T's and F's is a contingent claim.

Exercises

1. Set out the truth tables for the following:
   a. A ∨ ~B
   b. A → ~C
   c. ~(A → B)
   d. A→ (~A ∨ ~B)
   e. B & (~A → ~B)
   f. A ∨ (A & B)
   g. ~(A ∨ ~B) → C
   h. (A & B) ∨ ~C
   i. C → (A & ~B)

2. Find the truth-values of the following, using the values assigned:
   a. ~[A ∨ (B → ~C)]   when A is true and B and C are false
   b. C → (A & ~B)   when A is false and B and C are true
   c. [A → (~B ∨ ~C)] & C   when A and C are true, and B is false

d. B ∨ (~A & ~C)   when A, B, and C are each true
e. A & (B → ~C)   when A is true and B and C are false
f. (A → C) & (~B → ~A)   when A and C are false, and B is true
g. ~(A & B) ∨ C   when A, B, and C are each false
h. (B ∨ ~C) → A   when A is false and B and C are true
i. (A & B) → (B ∨ C)   when A and B are true, and C is false
j. C → (B → A)   when A and C are true, and B is false

3. Determine whether the following claims are tautologies, contradictories, or contingent claims by using truth tables:
a. P ∨ ~ (P → ~P)
b. ~(P ∨ ~P)
c. P → (P → ~P)
d. ~[P & ~(P ∨ ~P)]
e. P → (P ∨ Q)
f. P & (~Q ∨ P)
g. P → (Q → ~P)
h. (P → ~Q) & (Q → ~P)
i. P → (Q & ~P)
j. (Q & R) → (P ∨ ~R)

Shortcut Method: Truth Tables

Testing the validity of an argument can be slow and laborious if you have to do a full truth table. But using the shortcut method is a quick way to determine if an argument is valid or invalid.

First, we know from conditional claims that the only time a conditional is false is when the antecedent is true and the consequent is false. An argument is parallel to a conditional claim—the premises are parallel to antecedent conditions and the conclusion is parallel to the consequent. Thus, so long as there is no case in which all the premises can be true and the conclusion false, the argument is valid. What the shortcut method does, then, is check for this one case.

In other words, we see if all the premises can be true (all T's under the main connective of each premise) and the conclusion false (an F under the main connective of the conclusion). If this can be constructed, the argument is invalid. If not, then the argument is valid.

Be careful: It's important to realize that the shortcut method is a much quicker way to establish invalidity than validity. All you need is to find *one* assignment of truth-values that will make all the premises true (all T's) and the conclusion false. To prove validity using the shortcut method, you want to show that there is no possible counterexample that would give all true premises and a false conclusion.

Example: Testing for Validity

1. A → B
2. B → D
3. A → ~C
4. E → D
5. B → D / therefore, ~C ∨ D

The first step is to set out the variables on the left, the premises in the middle, and the conclusion on the right. Assign an F to the conclusion and T's to all the premises. Our task is to see if there is at least one assignment of truth-values (and you need only one!) that permits all true premises and the false assignment for the conclusion.

A	B	C	D	E	A → B	B → E	A → ~C	E → D	B → D	/ ~C ∨ D
					T	T	T	T	T	F

Looking at this table, we can see that C must be true and D false in order to get ~C ∨ D false in the conclusion. So we put this information into our truth table and we have:

A	B	C	D	E	A → B	B → E	A → ~C	E → D	B → D	/ ~C ∨ D
		T	F		T	T	T F T	T F	T F	F T F F

The only way A → ~C can be true is if A is false, so we assign F to A. And the only way B → D can be truth when D is false is if B is false, so assign F to B. Doing this and plugging in those values in the premises, we now have:

A	B	C	D	E	A → B	B → E	A → ~C	E → D	B → D	/ ~C ∨ D
F	F	T	F		F T F	F T	F T F T	T F	F T F	F T F F

We don't need to go any further to see that we've got a problem. B → D cannot be true (as was assigned) with B true and D false. For B → E to be true, E must be false, so assign F to E. Doing so means E → D is true, as we assigned. We now have:

A	B	C	D	E	A → B	B → E	A → ~C	E → D	B → D	/ ~C ∨ D
F	F	T	F	T	F T F	F T T	F T F T	F F	F F	F T F F

⇑   ⇑

Notice that both of these are true (see arrows). As we remember, if the antecedent is true and the consequent is false, the conditional is false. Since both B and E have to be false and D has to be false, this forces the conditionals E → D and B → D to be true, as we originally assumed in order to construct the case of true premises and a false conclusion.

This means our attempt to construct a row with all true premises and a false conclusion succeeds. Consequently, this argument is invalid.

Exercises

Directions: Use the shortcut method to test for validity.

1. a. ~(A ∨ B)
   b. A → ~B
   c. B
   d. C → ~A / therefore, ~C

2. a. C → A
   b. A → B / therefore, ~C → B

3. a. (A & C)
   b. (~E → D)
   c. B
   d. ~A → B
   e. E ∨ → A / therefore, D

4. a. A ∨ C
   b. C → ~B
   c. (B & ~A) → D
   d. ~A / therefore, B ∨ D

PART TWO

Sharpening the Tools

CHAPTER SIX

The Persuasive Power of Analogies

Harvey's ghosts have mischievous or evil facial expression, [whereas] Columbia's ghost appears bewildered.

> JUDGE PETER K. LEISURE, dismissing Harvey Publication's
> suit against Columbia Pictures that the *Ghostbusters'*
> ghost looked too much like Casper's friend Fatso

If you saw either of the *Ghostbusters* movies, you remember the ghost that wreaked havoc and caused an enormous amount of destruction—so much so that a team of three men armed with an array of weapons struggled to contain it. In trying to figure out if this ghost was a rip-off of the cartoon series Casper (the Friendly Ghost) of the past, Judge Peter K. Leisure had to line them up and compare them. Exactly what similarities did they share? Were there any killer differences? The judge had to go into the thicket of analogical reasoning. Artistic integrity and an awful lot of money rested on him being able to render a decision.

Harvey Publications—the creators of Casper—claimed that the *Ghostbusters'* ghost in the movie's logo too closely resembled one of their creations, the ghost Fatso. The judge had to decide if there was too great a resemblance in the two ghosts, thus violating the rights of Fatso's creators. Stop for a minute and think: What are the generic features of a ghost? Draw up a list before reading on!

Judge Leisure decided that no company could copyright the generic outline of a ghost, but they *could* copyright facial features and certain other aspects of a drawing. To him, most ghosts had knotted foreheads and jowly cheeks, making them generic features. The question was how close the *Ghostbusters'* ghost was to the Harvey ghosts, especially Fatso, in terms of key copyrighted features. Judge Leisure found that, whereas Fatso had a mischievous or evil facial expression, the other ghost just looked bewildered. Leisure had to study ghosts (or drawings of ghosts); induce common, generic characteristics; and then decide which characteristics or features could be copyrighted. In other words, he had to have clearly articulated reasons for his decision.

As it turns out, he dismissed the suit, based on the *differences* between the two ghosts. As you no doubt remember, differences can break an analogy. There may have been similarities, but they were not sufficient to support the conclusion that the *Ghostbusters'* ghost was just a variation of the Harvey ghost. In seeing the two ghosts, you would not automatically infer that they were from the same poltergeist family.

Judge Leisure was using his powers of induction. As pointed out in Chapter 5, an **inductive argument** never offers certainty. The evidence, at best, gives but partial support for the conclusion. In this case, there were a few similarities, such as the rounded features and bulbous noses of the two ghosts. However, because of the missing pieces, there is always a wedge of doubt between the premises and the conclusion. In the "ghost wars" discussed above, the differing facial expressions raised doubt in the mind of the judge. A look of bewilderment, the judge surmised, is distinctly different from a mischievous, or even evil, expression. Because of this uncertainty—this wedge of doubt—the case against Columbia Pictures became past history as the analogy hit the dust.

In this chapter, we will focus on one of the most powerful forms of persuasion—arguments from analogy. There's something about analogies that can take hold of our imagination and carry us right along. Even the worst of analogies can seduce us into thinking the argument makes good sense, even when it is virtually groundless. That is why it is crucial to have the tools at your disposal so you can stop right there and assess the analogy.

Arguments from Analogy

Arguments based on an analogy are among the most important kinds of inductive reasoning. An **argument from analogy** consists of a comparison between two things in which, on the basis of certain similarities, a principle or characteristic of one is then applied to the other. Think, for example, of "motherboard," which suggests a human, gestating presence in computer hardware. Such an analogy affects how we see other computer operations.

Analogies can be found everywhere from politics to religion and in all aspects of our lives. For example, former Harvard University president Lawrence Summers faced on uproar over his leadership style given his comments about women's lack of success in math and science. Evidently, he took his children to see the movie *Hitch,* which is about men who are trying to improve their social skills. Like the sad sacks who need Alex "Hitch" Hitchens to help them find romance, Summers sought guidance on how to improve his leadership style (see Patrick D. Healy and Sara Rimer, "Amid Uproar, Harvard President Ponders His Style," *The New York Times,* 26 Feb 2005). Note what exactly is being compared to what, and then check out the similarities and differences.

Given their potential power, it is no wonder people turn to analogies. Look, for instance, at the 2008 federal appeals court ruling on the first case involving the government's secret evidence for holding a detainee at Guantanamo Bay. The case involved accusations against a man held for more than six years based on unverifiable claims. The government contended that its accusations against the so-called enemy combatant should be accepted as true because they had been repeated in at least three secret documents. The court drew an analogy, comparing that to "the absurd declaration of a character in the Lewis Carroll poem 'The Hunting of the Snark': 'I have said it thrice: What I tell you three times is true'." The court ruled, "This comes perilously close to suggesting that whatever the government says must be treated is true" (William Glaberson, "Evidence Faulted in Detainee Case," *The New York Times*, 2 Jul 2008).

Here's another case: In a high-profile antitrust trial against Microsoft, each side tried to find "metaphors to drive home its point in plain, even folksy language: Microsoft is a robber baron—no, Microsoft is Cyber Claus," noted journalist John Markoff.

> At the Justice Department, Joel I. Klein, head of the antitrust division, tried to speak to the common man by drawing an [unsuccessful] analogy between operating systems and computers—the focus of the Government's lawsuit—and compact disks and CD players. . . . But Microsoft had fired first in the metaphor war two days earlier [when] Mark Murray, a company spokesman, said the Government's demand that Microsoft add Netscape Navigator to its Windows 98 operating system was "like requiring *The New York Times* to wrap the front section of *The Wall Street Journal* around the newspaper." It was, he said, "like forcing Coca-Cola to add two cans of Pepsi to each six-pack of Coke." ("Analogies as Complex and Murky as the Case," *The New York Times*, 21 May 1998)

In law, these analogies take the form of **precedents**—previous cases decided by a court of law or made into law by a legislature. Think how powerful is the analogy that's drawn between obeying the law and baseball; in the "three strikes" law, the rules of a game became the model for addressing repeat offenders. In the case of criminals, however, being "out" does not mean they have return to the dugout until the next inning. It means 25 years to life in prison—a much broader sense of "out" than ever imagined in baseball.

We also see analogies in literature, poetry, mythology, and religion. Religious parables, such as in the Gospels or in a Zen koan, provide a powerful form of spiritual guidance. Here's an example of a religious parable: "It is harder for a rich man to get into heaven than for a camel to go through the eye of a needle." Religious analogies can help us think about some of life's big questions. They also help us clear our minds of distractions and trivial mental pursuits.

Analogies can be very convincing. For many, the fact that someone has drawn a comparison implies that the comparison must be correct. But this is not necessarily true, for there may be relevant *differences* that make the principle or characteristic inapplicable. Our task is to see if the combined strength of the similarities outweighs that of the differences. In that way, we can assess how strong the analogy actually is.

Form of an Argument from Analogy

A is like B in terms of characteristics p, q, and r.

<u>A also has characteristic z.</u>

So, B has characteristic z also.

Here's an example: "Education cannot prepare high school students for marriage, even with the requirement that students carry dolls to class to approximate caring for children. Educating about marriage is like teaching someone to pilot a plane without ever leaving the ground. Until you're up in the air, you have no idea what's involved in flying." In this case, an analogy is drawn between marriage and piloting a plane. To assess the analogy, first list what is similar between teaching about marriage and teaching about flying, and then list the differences. Of course, there are some significant differences.

The Fallacy of False Analogy

Occasionally, someone sets out a **false analogy.** In this fallacy, an inference rests on a comparison of two terms, but there are no similarities between the terms of the comparison other than trivial ones. For example, here's a false analogy: "Michigan minus bowling would be like Pythagoras without his theorem." It's a brain twister to think of any real similarities between Michigan without bowling and Pythagoras without his theorem. If there are no nontrivial similarities, then the analogy simply fails.

We see this in an ad comparing breast implants to diamonds. The only problem is that diamonds are meant to last forever. Breast implants, however, do not. The false analogy is made clear with the statistical realities: One-third of those getting breast implants have to get a second operation in four to five years. Problems range from leakage, to scar tissue hardening the implant and deforming the breast, to visible rippling under the skin. Given these risks, it is not surprising that an alternative analogy has appeared in an ad in *Elle* magazine comparing implants to footwear: "You know that feeling when you find the perfect pair. And we are not talking shoes" ("Do My Breast Implants Have a Warranty?" *The New York Times,* 17 Jan 2008). Both analogies warrant close examination, as there are significant differences between breast implants and diamonds *and* breast implants and shoes!

And don't assume that "experts" offer only strong analogies. For example, in a radio interview, conservative activist Grover Norquist made a comparison between the estate tax and the Holocaust (Adam Cohen, "An SAT without Analogies Is Like . . .," *The New York Times,* 13 Mar 2005). Whatever similarities you might think of, the differences between the two are significant. Adam Cohen contends that "we are living in the age of the false, and often shameless, analogy." In his estimation, intentionally misleading comparisons are becoming the dominant mode of public discourse and "nowhere are analogies more central than in politics. When Karl Marx wanted to arouse the workers of the world, he compared [their] condition to slavery." Because of this, the ability to tell true analogies from false ones has never been more important.

Be on the lookout for false analogies. And be sure you can point to some shared characteristics between the terms of the comparison when you set out an analogy. *Be careful:* There are usually *some* similarities between one thing and another, so you could think of analogies in this category as imperfect or very weak, rather than completely false.

Exercise

Bad Analogies

Directions: The *Washington Post* published winners in their "worst analogies ever written in a high school essay" contest. Among them are these:

"The little boat gently drifted across the pond exactly the way a bowling ball wouldn't" (Russell Beland, Springfield).
   "From the attic came an unearthly howl. The whole scene had an eerie, surreal quality, like when you're on vacation in another city and *Jeopardy* comes on at 7 P.M. instead of 7:30" (Roy Ashley, Washington).

Make up an analogy of your own. Compare your choice of an analogy to one of the following: doing homework, taking an exam, sitting through a boring lecture, or writing an essay (or anything connected with being in college).

The Persuasive Force of Analogies

Never underestimate the potential force of an analogy. Whether the comparison is strong or weak, an analogy can carry great persuasive power. Here are some examples that show us the importance of examining analogies. Arguments based on analogies can be clinchers. Patent attorney Jerry Dodson tells of a 12–0 jury verdict he won for Clorox Corporation against Procter & Gamble in a patent dispute. The issue turned on a Brita water treatment pitcher. To convince the jury that the Brita filter's replacement indicator relied on air pressure—in contrast to Procter & Gamble's filter's replacement indicator, which used buoyancy—he used an analogy. "I used a champagne bottle," he says. "The cork pops out because of pressure, but if you throw it into the champagne, it floats because of buoyancy. The other side could never overcome the champagne-bottle analogy."

Dodson regularly turns to an easy-to-grasp analogy to explain a complex case. "I'm always sorting through analogies, bringing new ones in and throwing old ones out" (quoted in Barb Mulligan, "Patent Attorney Jerry Dodson '69 Uses Analogies to Explain Complex Cases," Lafayette College, www.lafayette.edu/news). As Dodson demonstrates in his work as a lawyer, analogies can be powerful tools of persuasion.

Depending on how we rank the similarities and differences, the persuasive value of the analogy varies. This means there's a subjective element to any analogy. After listing similarities and differences, weighing them is not neutral. Rather, your own set of values will factor in when deciding the strengths of the different claims, especially those relating to a set of beliefs.

Note: Some analogies are highly inflammatory and offensive. It is common to see analogies used in racist, sexist, and ethnic slurs. For example, journalist Bob Herbert writes about the vitriolic language used by a radio personality, Bob Grant. Herbert asserts that Grant used the following argument from analogy:

> He would wonder aloud "if they've ever figured out how they multiply like that. It's like maggots on a hot day. You look one minute and there are so many there, and you look again and, wow, they've tripled!" (See Bob Herbert, "A Different Republican?" *The New York Times,* 29 Jun 2000.)

It is not unusual to see movies being used in an analogy. The assumption that everyone has actually seen the movie may be unwarranted, but such analogies are common. For instance, Jamal Harith, a Briton held at the Iso detention center at Guantanamo Bay, Cuba, for two years, said prisoners were beaten and sexually humiliated. Harith drew an analogy to the movie *Alien* ("In space no one can hear you scream"). He said, "It's like the *Alien* film: In 'Iso' nobody can hear you scream" (Sebastian Rotella, "Ex-Inmate Alleges U.S. Abuse at Guantanamo," *Los Angeles Times,* 25 May 2004). As you may recall, in *Alien,* a hideous monster kills off most of the crew on the spaceship. Using the analogy to a horror film, Harith sets out his view of what he experienced in prison. For us to decide if his analogy is strong, we need to break it down and evaluate it.

Be prepared: Some analogies are used to make political points. For instance, journalist Maureen Dowd used an analogy about the political use of misinformation. She wrote of "twisting facts to suit ideology, and punishing those who try to tell the truth. But they're [the Bush administration] still behaving like Cinderella's evil stepsisters, who cut their feet to fit them into the glass slipper: butchering reality to make the fairy tale come out their way" ("Bike-Deep in the Big Muddy," *The New York Times,* 27 Aug 2005). The colorful analogy is a powerful way to make a point.

Example 1: The Lifeboat Analogy

Microbiologist Garrett Hardin used a now-famous analogy in an article on world hunger. He presented this scenario: Think of our nation as a lifeboat with 50 people and 10 empty seats. There are 100 people (from underdeveloped nations) in the water, trying to get in our lifeboat. If we take them all on, we'll sink. If we take a few (how do we choose?), we lose our safety margin of the empty seats. So, we should not rescue any. This, Hardin argued, is why we are not in a position to help alleviate world hunger. We need to preserve our own resources for future use, and so should not deplete them by trying (ineffectively, given the numbers) to help.

You Tell Me Department

Is Religion like Hockey? Or Maybe Basketball or Badminton?

The Snapshots of God website includes the argument that religion is just like hockey. See if you are convinced by the reasoning:

> Many people don't like hockey because they just don't understand it. You hear whistles being blown and play stopping for no apparent reason . . . . You see people pushing each other and hitting each other with sticks . . . . In watching that one game, you might very well conclude that hockey is irrational and barbaric, and want nothing to do with it. You might not notice any real difference between a rookie and Wayne Gretsky, the best in the game.
>
>   I think that our understanding of God and religion can be much the same. You can take a distant, cursory view from the outside, observe the fighting, find all the rules confusing and conclude that there is nothing there of much sense or value. This is where the agnostics and atheists sit. You can learn enough so that it at least makes enough sense for you to get a little something out of it. This is religion for the masses . . . . You can put on a jersey, go down on the ice and try to learn a little from all the players. This is spirituality. ("Religion Is Just like Hockey," *Snapshots of God,* snapshotsofgod.com)

You tell me: Is religion like hockey? Share your response to this analogy, and explain why you did or did not find it persuasive. Be as specific as you can in setting out your reasons. Feel free to go to the website to see the analogy developed more fully.

Example 2: The Drowning Child Analogy

Another influential analogy is one philosopher James Rachels used in an article on active versus passive euthanasia (mercy killing). He presented two scenarios that he used to contrast killing (active euthanasia) to letting die (passive euthanasia—not intervening to try to save the life). In the first case, Smith stands to gain a large inheritance if anything happens to his 6-year-old cousin, and so Smith drowns the child one night in the bathtub and then makes it look like an accident.

In the second case, Jones, who also stands to gain if anything happens to his 6-year-old cousin, sneaks into the bathroom intending to drown the boy. But, before he can make his move, his cousin slips, hits his head, and falls face down in the water and dies "accidentally" as Jones watches. Rachels then compared Smith's murder of his cousin with Jones's failure to intervene to save him. As far as Rachels was concerned, both are equally morally culpable, and there is no significant moral distinction between the two scenarios. He then applied this to active versus passive euthanasia, making the same argument. He concluded that terminating the life of the seriously ill is not morally distinct from "letting them die" by not resuscitating them.

Assessing Analogies

If you allow the analogy to "get off the ground," the argument is generally successful. If, however, the weight of the differences between the two terms is greater than that of the similarities, the analogy falters. That is, the argument is not as

You Tell Me Department

Are Geese Like Slaves?

Force-feeding geese to fatten them up so they have tasty livers for the gourmet food *foie gras* (which is French for liver paté) strikes animal rights advocates as barbaric. Here's what one incensed person had to say in a letter to the editor:

> It is troubling that after such a noticeable lack of coverage of the *foie gras* issue, the *Los Angeles Times* would choose to print such a load of drivel as David Shaw's article (Matters of Taste: "They're Quacking up the Wrong Tree," May 5, 2004). First

he says that animal rights activists make "the antiabortion movement look positively passive."

Rubbish. No animal rights activist has ever shot and killed a doctor. Most animal rights activists are against harming *any* living being. Second, he argues that the suffering of ducks doesn't matter because the ducks were raised for that purpose. Many slaves were born in captivity also. That doesn't mean it was any less painful or more humane.

You tell me: Is this a good analogy? So-so analogy? Weak analogy? Explain your decision.

---

powerful if the differences outweigh the similarities. Every time you see an analogy, ask yourself, What are the similarities? What are the differences? The use of an analogy should start alarms ringing in your brain:

> That's an analogy → Hold it right there!
>
> → Stop and check it out.
>
> → Weigh the similarities and differences.

What makes an argument based on an analogy an *inductive* argument is that the evidence is partial. In an analogy, the premises provide only *some* support for the conclusion. Granted, there are differences in any comparison; there will always be holes in the argument. The result is that the conclusion does not and cannot automatically follow from the premises. If the premises are true, the conclusion following an analogy will not certainly be true—it could be false. This is why an argument from analogy is *inductive*, not deductive.

Think of it this way: No matter how similar you may be to your mother or father, there are still some differences. Even though you can draw up a long list of similarities, there will nevertheless be differences that introduce uncertainty into the comparison. For example, what do you think of this analogy: "I guess Matt [Damon] is just like us, only famous and a lot richer" (www.imnotobsessed.com, 8 Aug 2007)? We know from Chapter 4 that the use of "only" functions as a negative. Look at this analogy: "My mother is just like the Queen of England, *only* she's not British and she is neither rich nor powerful." And how about "Your jalopy is just like a Jaguar, *only* in much worse shape and ugly as sin." It's left to the imagination to decide what the two actually have in common.

Keep your antennae out and always check for similarities and differences— even with issues that move you emotionally. For example, in a July 2004 article in *USA Today,* Marilyn Adams argued that ALS (amyotrophic lateral sclerosis, or Lou Gehrig's disease) is "like a terrorist in our midst, going strong." She cited similarities: They are both random and terrifying and kill without partiality. She added that the fight against terrorism has received a lot of attention and money—and concluded that the fight against ALS should also receive a lot of attention and money. Can you think of any key differences?

Most of us have been compared to a family member (positively or negatively!). This reasoning is *inductive* because we are supposed to draw a conclusion on the basis of the asserted similarity. "Sonja, you are just like your mother! Your mother always makes delicious lemon meringue pie, so you should too!" Now Sonja may be like her mother in some respects. But that does not mean she is like her mother in *every* respect. The fact of a resemblance does not automatically mean that the two are identical.

Key Steps in Analyzing Analogies

We can tackle analogies we encounter by assessing the strengths of the comparison. Follow the steps, carefully laying out the analogy so you can then decide how strong it is.

Steps in Analyzing Analogies

1. **Clarify the terms of comparison.** Note exactly what is being compared to what.
2. **Write it out like an equation setting out the comparison.** Here's an example: Sonja/pies she bakes ≡ Sonja's mother/pies her mother bakes.
3. **State the principle or characteristic attributed to the one term that is being applied to the other term.** Here's an example: Sonja's pies should be as delicious as her mother's pies.
4. **List the similarities.**
5. **List the differences.**
6. **Survey the two lists.** Add any omissions to your lists.
7. **Weigh similarities and differences.** Determine the relative strength of the similarities compared to that of the differences. Some similarities or differences may be more important than others, so prioritize them in terms of relative importance.
8. **Assess the strength of the analogy.** Analogies, like all inductive arguments, fall along a spectrum ranging from dismal to strong. In a *strong analogy,* the similarities outweigh the differences. In a *weak analogy,* the strength of the differences outweighs the similarities. Ask yourself: Is there a killer difference? Check to see if there is a difference so great that it would outweigh any similarity. If so, the analogy fails. In a *false analogy,* there are no relevant (nontrivial) similarities at all. *Don't forget:*

Similarities MAKE an analogy.

Differences BREAK an analogy.

Analogies: Application 1

Let's examine some analogies and assess their strength. The first analogy we will look at is one often cited in the abortion debate.

Analogy 1: A Fetus Is like an Acorn.   In her article "A Defense of Abortion," philosopher Judith Jarvis Thomson used a number of analogies (see *Philosophy and Public Affairs*, vol. 1, no. 1, 1971). One of her arguments was this: "The development of a person from the moment of conception is similar to the development of an acorn into an oak tree." Let us examine this analogy using the eight steps.

Step 1: Clarify What Is Being Compared to What

In this case, the development of the fetus into a person is being compared to the development of an acorn into an oak tree.

Step 2: Set Out the Terms of the Analogy

These are *fetus/person ≡ acorn/oak*.

Step 3: State the Principle Being Asserted

The principle is: There is no clear line that separates a fetus from a person.

Step 4: List the Similarities

1. In both cases, we are talking about living things.
2. The fetus and the acorn are both early forms of the respective organisms.
3. The existence of the later organism (person/oak tree) depends upon the growth and development of the earlier form.
4. Both fetus and acorn can be destroyed or damaged by poor nutrition (soil), lack of nurturance, or other means.
5. Neither fetus nor acorn has clearly delineated stages of development.

Step 5: List the Differences

1. The fetus grows inside the mother's body, whereas the acorn grows away from and is separate from the oak tree.
2. The time it takes to develop (fetus to person, and acorn to oak) is different.
3. Quantity: An oak tree produces many more acorns than a woman does fetuses.
4. Social worth: Society values fetuses more highly than acorns and most persons more highly than most oak trees.
5. A fetus relies upon the mother's body for nurturing and sustaining its life, but an acorn has no such reliance on the oak tree.

Step 6: Survey the Two Lists

- *Look at the similarities.* We've covered the category (living things), age parallels, dependence on the "mother" organism, need for nurturance and nutrition, and lack of clear stage delineation. Is there more we could add? Well, we might add that both (barring destruction) potentially grow into the same type of organism (human/tree) from which they came.

- *Now look at the differences.* We've covered the internal versus external factor, and differences in maturation times, quantity, social worth, and source of nurturance. Could we add anything else? Well, some might point to the appearance issue (fetuses could be said to more closely resemble humans than acorns resemble oak trees).

Step 7: Weigh the Similarities and Differences

The differences seem stronger, particularly numbers 1 and 5 and maybe even 4. There are no strong similarities, though the strongest are probably numbers 2 and 5.

Step 8. Assess the Strength of the Analogy

Given this weighting, it would seem that the analogy is not very strong. Note that it is not a false analogy, where there are at best trivial similarities. In this case, there are some similarities. However, the differences loom larger, and consequently, the analogy does not appear to be very powerful. As a result, the principle being claimed that there is no clear line separating fetuses from persons has not been clearly established by using the analogy that fetuses are like acorns.

Analogies: Application 2

It may help to go through another analogy to imprint the steps firmly on our minds. The second analogy is also from Judith Jarvis Thomson, but it is more unusual than the first one.

Analogy 2: "People-Seeds."   Thomson presents the analogy as follows:

> Again, suppose it were like this: people-seeds drift about in the air like pollen, and if you open your windows, one may drift in and take root in your carpets or upholstery. You don't want children, so you fix up your windows with fine mesh screens, the very best you can buy. As can happen, however, and on very, very rare occasions does happen, one of the screens is defective; and a seed drifts in and takes root. Does the person-plant who now develops have a right to the use of your house? Surely not—despite the fact that you voluntarily opened your windows, you knowingly kept carpets and upholstered furniture, and you knew that screens were sometimes defective. ("A Defense of Abortion")

Step 1: Clarify What Is Being Compared

In this argument, Thomson is comparing the use of screens to prevent people-seeds from blowing into your house to the use of contraception to prevent pregnancy.

Step 2: Set Out the Terms of the Analogy

Defective screen/people-seed ≡ defective contraception/fetus.

Step 3: State the Principle Being Asserted

Thomson is asserting that the failure of means of contraception resulting in pregnancy ought not make us feel morally obligated to bear the child, that an abortion is morally acceptable.

Step 4: List the Similarities

1. Both contraception and screens are intentional attempts to prevent something from happening.
2. Both contraception and screens have the potential for error; neither one is foolproof.
3. Both people-seeds and fetuses are earlier stages of the person and will lead to personhood, given appropriate conditions.
4. Both have long-term consequences if allowed to go to personhood.
5. In both cases, the result is undesirable (the mother/dweller of the house did not wish to become pregnant/have a people-seed growing in the carpet).

Step 5: List the Differences

1. People-seeds float about in the air; fetuses do not.
2. In the case of a pregnancy, there is a father whose wishes may bear upon the decision; in the case of people-seeds, there is not.
3. A people-seed grows in a carpet and does not depend upon the house dweller, whereas a fetus grows inside the mother and depends upon her body for nurturance.
4. You could sell your house or move away and avoid the people-seed problem; this is not so in a normal pregnancy.
5. People-seeds require no personal risk in their development, whereas the pregnant woman undergoes risk in pregnancy.

Step 6: Survey the Two Lists

- *Look at the similarities.* We've addressed the fact that both are undesirable and that steps are being taken to prevent the people-seed/human embryo from gestating, both methods of obstruction can fail, and both have developmental and long-term consequences. Is there more we can add? Well, we could add that both might result in unforeseen difficulties for the house owner/mother and perhaps even some physical risk (the people-seed may develop into a psycho, or the pregnancy could be an ectopic or other high-risk pregnancy).
- *Now look at the differences.* We've addressed the fact that fetuses are not external to the mother, there is not necessarily a parallel to the father in the people-seed case, and escaping from the people-seed is much easier than escaping from the fetus. Is there anything else we could add? Well, we might add that there could be hundreds of people-seeds that take root in your house (say, in a big windstorm)—no pregnancy could compare in sheer numbers of developing entities.

Step 7: Weigh the Similarities and Differences

Looking over each list, the strongest similarities seem to be numbers 1, 3, and 5. The strongest differences seem to be numbers 3, 4, and 5 and maybe 2. The additional difference we noted does not necessarily mean the consequences would be worse if we had hundreds of people sprouting in the carpet compared to one fetus that becomes a child (the significance of this difference may be hard to quantify).

Step 8: Assess the Strength of the Analogy

This analogy seems stronger than our last one. That is, the similarities are not irrelevant or insignificant, and the differences are not overwhelmingly strong. The difference of the relative risk to each seems strongest, as that is a bottom-line type of difference. Given that the overall weight of the similarities is stronger than that of the differences in this analogy, we can infer that the analogy has persuasive value and may carry weight in Thomson's attempt to make her case that abortion be allowable under certain circumstances.

Group or Individual Exercise

Libraries and Counterterrorism

As of September 20, 2003, the U.S. Justice Department reported that it had not yet used its counterterrorism powers to demand records from libraries and elsewhere. Department officials asserted that they had sought access to no one's library record as of that date. That does not impress Phil Valentine, however, who sets out a blistering attack by employing an analogy ("Bogus Analogies, Libraries, and the War on Terror," *The Talent Show,* www.thetalentshow.org, 20 Sep 2003). Responding to Valentine's argument, Justice Department spokesperson Mark Corallo set out *his* analogy.

Directions: Go through both Valentine's and Corallo's arguments from analogy, and note the *strengths* of each one.

Phil Valentine's Argument: Let's pretend for a moment that I was in charge of the world and for some reason I decided to pass a law that makes it legal for the government to kidnap babies from the mall in order to grind them up and make sausages to feed people in prison. After a couple years of protests over my cruel baby-killing law, I reveal that I haven't in fact ever exercised the law. That might make people feel a bit better, but it doesn't change the fact that I can still legally kidnap and murder babies. To a much lesser extent, that's the situation that [Attorney General] Ashcroft is in right now.

Mark Corallo's Argument: The same people who would argue that, would argue that if a police officer has never had to fire his weapon in 20 years on the force, we should take his weapon away from him because he will never have to use it.

The Global Dimension

Analogies from the War on Terror

In a February 5, 2004, interview with Terrorism Monitor Special Correspondent, Mahan Abedin Saad al-Faqih of the Saudi opposition group Movement for Islamic Reform in Arabia set forth two analogies. Read them both and then select *one* to discuss. Share your reaction and indicate whether the analogy has strengths.

> **Analogy 1 (Al-Qaeda Is like a College):** Al-Qaeda is a very interesting organization. They do not believe in the party structure, they see themselves as a college where people enroll, graduate and then go their separate ways. But they are encouraged to establish their own satellite networks which ultimately link in with al-Qaeda.

This is why al-Qaeda is very resilient and can never be destroyed.

> **Analogy 2 (The American Mentality Is like a Cowboy Mentality):** Zawahiri impressed upon Bin Laden the importance of understanding the American mentality. The American mentality is a cowboy mentality—if you confront them with their identity theoretically and practically they will react in an extreme manner. In other words, America with all its resources and establishments will shrink into a cowboy when irritated successfully. They will then elevate you and this will satisfy the Muslim longing for a leader who can successfully challenge the West. (See "The Essence of al-Qaeda: An Interview with Saad al-Faqih," *The Jamestown Foundation,* www.jamestown.org, 5 Feb 2004.)

Exercise

Quick Quiz

1. An argument from analogy rests on:
   a. Statistical data
   b. A causal connection between one thing and another
   c. A comparison between two things
   d. A prediction based on what usually happens

2. An argument from analogy is always an argument that is (a) inductive or (b) deductive.

3. In assessing the strength of an analogy, you would especially want to look at:
   a. Strengths and weaknesses
   b. Assumptions and evidence
   c. Similarities and differences
   d. Induction versus deduction

4. *True or false:* In law, analogies often take the form of precedents.

5. A *strong analogy* results when (a) the weight of the similarities is clearly greater than the weight of the differences or (b) the weight of the differences is clearly greater than the weight of the similarities.

6. *True or false:* An argument from analogy can be a valid argument if the premises are true.

7. When faced with an analogy, you first want to:
   a. See if it's an inductive or deductive argument
   b. Clarify the terms of the comparison
   c. Clarify the truth of the premises
   d. Check for unwarranted assumptions
8. *True or false:* A contrast between two things is a kind of analogy.

Structuring the Analysis

We need to be able to assess the use of an analogy, a process that can be laid out as follows:

Assessing the Use of an Analogy: Steps in Structuring the Analysis

1. Ask what is at issue. What principle or conclusion is being drawn from the analogy?
2. Set out the terms of the analogy. Exactly what is being compared?
3. List the relevant similarities and differences.
4. Critically examine the lists, weighing them to see the strength of each side (assess similarities and differences).
5. Determine how you would attack the analogy. What are its weaknesses?
6. Determine how you would defend the analogy. What are its strengths?
7. If this is an analogy you intend to use, see if you can modify it to minimize weaknesses and boost strengths.
8. If this is an analogy you are evaluating, make note of the relative strengths and weaknesses, and decide if the analogy succeeds.
9. *Remember:* Similarities make the analogy; differences break the analogy.

You are now in a position to assess whether the conclusion (the principle being drawn) can be said to follow with credible support.

Exercises

Part One: Setting Out Analogies

1. Select *one* of the following analogies, and set out the comparison and list the similarities and differences.
   a. "Google is like a gigantic parasite" (Jason Pontin, ed., MIT's *Technology Review,* www.bigthink.com, 22 Jan 2008).
   b. "A beautiful woman's face is like chocolate, cash or cocaine to a young man's brain" (according to Harvard University researchers, *Neuron* 32, 2001).
   c. Pledge programs on public television are "the fund-raising equivalent of water-boarding" (Charles McGrath, "Is PBS Still Necessary?" *The New York Times,* 17 Feb 2008).

2. Set out the comparison and list the similarities and differences in the following:

Plastic surgeon Dr. Sherrell J. Aston compared cosmetic surgery patients to "the lady who gets her hair done and nails done." In his view, "People are wanting to do it as a part of personal grooming. It will become more and more common as time goes on and be programmed into people's consciousness." (As noted by Alex Kuczynski and Warren Sr. John, "Why Did They Die in Cosmetic Surgery?" *The New York Times*, 20 Jun 2004)

3. Set out the terms and list the similarities and differences in the following discussion of email spam:

"Finding a solution here is like putting socks on an octopus," FTC Commissioner Mozelle Thompson said during a break in the proceedings. "There are too many moving parts. But the clear message is that doing nothing is not acceptable. We're approaching a tipping point where consumer confidence is beginning to erode." ("Spamstrung," *The Age*, www.theage.com, 18 May 2003)

4. Set out the terms and list the similarities and differences in the following discussion:

Back in the day, a rapper playing guitar was like a nun wearing a bikini. You just didn't do it. But after I saw Wyclef (Jean) play, I knew it would be acceptable. I didn't have to be embarrassed and hide my guitar in the closet. (Edna Gundersen, "Airwaves 'High' on Afroman's Funny Funk," *USA Today*, 20 Aug 2001)

5. Focusing on his second analogy (to prisons), set out the comparison and list the similarities and differences in the following by Will Hutton:

Families are mini-civilizations; experience and research show they are the best means of rearing our young into fulfilled adulthood. But families are the prisons that can deform individuals for life and whose private arrangements generate fantastic inequality for society beyond. We hear much about the benefits of family, too little about the degree family can be bad both for children and for our wider society. ("Why Too Much Care for Your Child Can Harm Society," *The Observer (London)*, 3 Feb 2008)

6. Set out the terms of the analogy and note the similarities and differences in this comparison of cable TV to the creature in *The Predator,* noted by Eric Boehlert: "Cable TV is like the creature in *The Predator*. It's drawn to heat and conflict. It looks for things with the most edge to it" ("They Knew How to Win." Salon.com, 1 Sep 2004).

7. Set out the terms and list the similarities and differences in the following discussion of the criminal justice system:

The criminal justice system is like a mirror in which society can see the face of the evil in its midst. But because the system deals with some evil and not with others, because it treats some evils as the gravest and treats some of the gravest evils as minor, the image it throws back is distorted like the image in a carnival mirror. Thus the image cast back is false, not because it is invented out of thin air, but because the proportions of the real are distorted . . . .

If criminal justice really gives us a carnival-mirror image of "crime," we are doubly deceived. First, we are led to believe that the criminal justice system is protecting us against the gravest threats to our well-being when in fact the system is only protecting us against some threats and not necessarily the gravest ones. We are deceived about how much protection we are receiving and thus left vulnerable. But, in addition, we are deceived about what threatens us and are, therefore, unable to take appropriate defensive action. The second deception is just the other side of the first one. If people believe that the carnival mirror is a true mirror—that is, if they believe that the criminal justice system just reacts to the gravest threats to their well-being—they come to believe that whatever is the target of the criminal justice system must be the gravest threat to their well-being. (Jeffrey H. Reiman, *The Rich Get Richer and the Poor Get Poorer*, Prentice-Hall, 1994)

8. Stanley Bing sets out an analogy and a challenge: "Here are ten ways that a baby is like a chief executive officer. Tell me where I've got it wrong." Look over his list and then set out what is *different* about babies and CEOs.

1) The baby is the center of its universe, 2) The baby speaks nonsense, but nobody seems to notice, 3) The baby has a short attention span and must be entertained constantly, 4) Those who serve the baby must be attentive to its moods, which change radically from moment to moment, 5) Everything is planned around the comfort and schedule of the baby, 6) The baby is conveyed [carried] everywhere, 7) The baby has special food made for it because it can't really digest the stuff that other people eat, 8) The baby is bored by grownups, but if there is another baby in the room it perks up, 9) When the baby makes a mess, other people have to clean it up, and 10) Babies have weird hair. (Stanley Bing, "You're a CEO Baby!" *Fortune*, www.fortune.com, 21 Feb 2005)

Part Two: Analyzing Analogies

Directions: Go through the steps to assess the strength of these analogies:

1. Marriage without love is like driving a car without brakes.
2. "FaceBook is like a gossipy friend and with no interesting information" (blankisblank.com, 17 Apr 2008).
3. "*Wikipedia* is like hearing a great story in a bar: You hope it's true, but never bother confirming it." (blankislikeblank.com, 2 Jan 2008)
4. "A faith without some doubts is like a human body without any antibodies in it" (Tim Keller, *The Reason for God*, Penguin Group, 2008).
5. "A job interview is like a date" (Alison Green, www.usnews.com, 5 May 2008).
6. "Racism, like the bite of a rabid animal, can infect a victim with the deadly disease of its madness" (Lloyd L. Brown).
7. "Pennsylvania is forcing Internet providers to block Web sites that include child pornography. The Center for Democracy and Technology compared the

blocking technique to disrupting mail delivery to an entire apartment complex because of one tenant's illegal actions" ("Civil Liberties Lawyers Raise Questions about Web Filters," *The New York Times,* 20 Feb 2003).

8. "Now, in the 1990's, I see substantial similarities between the cocaine epidemic and slavery. Both are firmly grounded in economics—at the expense of a race of people. There was, and is, money to be made. It would be foolish to lose sight of this truth" (Rev. Cecil Williams, "Crack Is Genocide 1990's Style," *The New York Times,* 15 Feb 1990).

9. "To take an absurd example to illustrate why people should have a property right in their own tissues, suppose [billionaire head of Microsoft] Bill Gates' barber saves a lock of his hair and clones him, suing Gates for child support. The answer shouldn't be that Bill Gates has no recourse because he has no property rights in his tissue" (Lori Andrews, *Body Bazaar,* Random House, 2001).

10. "Most Californians view illegal immigrants as unwanted house guests. One very effective means of getting rid of such guests is to set your house on fire and burn it to the ground. This is Propositions 187's solution to illegal immigration. No decent Californian should support it" (Ron K. Unz, 1994 Republican primary challenger to Governor Pete Wilson of California).

11. "They should not allow stem cell research [that uses early human embryos]. It's no different than the experiments the Nazis did during World War II on the Jewish prisoners" (paraphrase of comment by Senator Sam Brownback, R-KS).

12. "In attempting to explain humankind's place in the timeline of evolution, Mr. [Stephen J.] Gould had this suggestion: Extend your right or left hand as far away from the body as you can—that distance would represent the beginning of earth's birth (some 5 billion years); then with the tip of either index finger extended, return either index finger and place it on the tip of your nose (which would represent the present). Now, take a file and file off the fingernail of that index finger—by filing off this fingertip, you have just eliminated humankind from its place in evolution" ("Evolution's Voyage: Assumptions," www.evoyage.com).

13. In his memoir *Parallel Time,* Brent Staples writes about the problems he ran into as an African-American man attending college in a mostly white neighborhood in Pennsylvania. Discuss how he uses an analogy to convey the experience of encountering people who were afraid of him in the excerpt below:

I'd been a fool. I'd been grinning good evening at people who were frightened to death of me. I did violence to them by just being. How had I missed this? I kept walking at night, but from then on I paid attention. I became expert in the language of fear. Couples locked arms or reached for each other's hand when they saw me. Some crossed to the other side of the street. People who were carrying on conversations went mute and stared straight ahead, as though avoiding my eyes would save them. This reminded me of an old wives' tale that rabid dogs didn't bite if you avoided their eyes.

Part Three: Constructing Analogies

Directions: Select any *two* of the following, and construct an analogy for each scenario you choose.

1. Give an analogy to argue for or against college athletes getting preferential treatment in admission to the school. Set out the terms of your analogy.

2. Give an analogy to argue for or against legalizing marijuana. Set out the terms of your analogy.

3. Give an analogy to argue for or against going with a pass/fail grading system. Set out the terms of your analogy.

4. Give an analogy to argue for or against Neo-Nazis being allowed to pass out leaflets in public high schools. Set out the terms of your analogy.

5. Give an analogy to argue for or against censoring nudity on primetime TV. Set out the terms of your analogy.

6. Give an analogy to argue for or against the use of women in combat positions in war. Set out the terms of your analogy.

Group or Individual Exercise

President Barack Obama is a man of many qualities—and comparisons. Here are just a few: "Obama thinks like a professor, inspires like a preacher" (*CNN*), "Obama is like the pilot of Flight 1589 (who landed a plane in the Hudson River, saving the lives of 155 people)" (*Slate*), Obama is "cool like a cat" (*The New York Times*), *and* Obama is like Lincoln, JFK, Roosevelt, Gandhi, Jesus . . . The analogies abound!

Directions: Read these set of comparisons of Obama to various characters from popular culture. Note three similarities and three differences in each comparison. Try to determine which comparison fits best—and *then* decide what analogy might be the best (use any here—or invent one of your own):

The New York Observer recently ran a cover story with an illustration of Obama as Spock, the science officer of "Star Trek's" spaceship Enterprise. This worked in part because Obama can appear to have a Vulcan-like reserve . . .

But maybe the better analogy is between Obama and Batman. A YouTube clip of the old 1960s "Batman" TV show shows Adam West's Batman . . . [who] doesn't flinch; he plays the Caped Crusader as a man who need never raise his voice above a whisper. He is Obama-cool.

But wait: Maybe Obama is the Road Runner . . . [who] remains unflappable. He's got the right temperament for what he needs to do. Which is move on. Keep running. (Joel Achenback, "In a Heated Race, Obama's Cool Won the Day," *The Washington Post*, 6 Nov 2008).

▦ Analogies and Hypothetical Reasoning in the Law

One of the key issues lawyers and judges face is whether a legal precedent applies. They have to decide how well the letter of the law applies to a particular case. A great deal hinges on the relevant similarities and differences of the precedent case to the case at hand. To assess this, we have to consider the amount of variation from the standard (norm or precedent-setting case) to the individual one being litigated. That is not always easy.

To help prepare students for the practice of law, one teaching technique uses a hypothetical case (alias *Hypo*). In **hypothetical law cases,** a scenario or story is presented, with the task of deciding how it is to be evaluated given the existing laws and precedents. This is an important application of analogical reasoning, requiring lawyers and law students to be both astute and imaginative in assessing the hypothetical cases.

By analyzing the specifics of the Hypo in relationship to the legal standard, students can then determine how the law should apply in the hypothetical case. Let's see how this is done. Drawing from an article "Hypothetical Rape Scenarios as a Pedagogical Device" by sociology professor Colleen Fitzpatrick in the *Journal of Criminal Justice Education,* Spring 2001, let's look at some Hypos around prosecutorial decision making in rape cases.

Group or Individual Exercise

Directions: Read the article below, which presents three of Colleen Fitzpatrick's five rape scenarios and accompanying questions. Then discuss what would be involved in answering the questions (i.e., how you would arrive at an answer of whether the district attorney should prosecute). Go into detail and elaborate on any *one* of the scenarios (pick one).

Scenario 1: Every Wednesday for the past year of her new marriage, Evelyn's husband, Paul, goes out with the "boys" for a night of bowling and drinking. Upon his return around 2 A.M., he strips off his smoky clothes and hops into bed with Evelyn. Inevitably feeling amorous toward his wife, Paul—smelling of smoke and booze—has sexual intercourse with Evelyn. On this particular Wednesday night, Evelyn decides enough is enough. When Paul comes home, gets into bed, and approaches Evelyn, she pushes him off and tells him she doesn't want to have sex tonight. Apparently not wanting to break his successive Wednesday night streak, Paul uses his strength and weight (but no hitting or striking) to have sex with Evelyn. Was Evelyn raped? Would you, as DA, prosecute?

Scenario 2: After three rapes on the Mountain University campus, the campus police have advised coeds to avoid walking a dark path between the library and a dorm. All three rapes occurred along that path after the women were dragged into the bushes lining the path. Campus police told women the path was unsafe until recently budgeted lights could be erected and operating. One half hour before the library closed, Helen realized her boyfriend would be calling her dorm room in ten minutes. This being her only chance to talk with him this week, Helen, who is fully aware of the rapes and the police warnings, decides she can only get to her room in time by taking the path. Halfway to the dorm, Helen is pulled off the path and into the bushes where she is forced to have sexual intercourse with a man wielding no weapon but strong enough to keep his hand over Helen's mouth. Was Helen raped? Would you, as DA, prosecute?

Scenario 3: Ted and Charlie were out celebrating Ted's 21st birthday. After several birthday shots at various bars in town, Charlie suggested they go visit Connie—a local prostitute. Connie answered their knock on her door, but told them she was not working this evening since she had just finished an exceptionally busy weekend. Charlie said that since it was Ted's birthday she should at least allow them to come in for a drink or to do a quick line of coke. Connie let the two in her apartment, joined them in sharing some cocaine, then told them to leave. Charlie and Ted said they would leave right after she came across with a birthday lay. Connie refused, but Charlie pushed her onto the sofa, stripped off her clothes, and despite her physical and verbal protestation, forced her to have sexual intercourse. Ted then took his turn, but at this point Connie put up no resistance and simply told them to both get out as soon as Ted had finished. Charlie tossed $50 (twice the amount Connie charged Charlie on his last visit with her) onto the table and they both left the apartment. Was Connie raped? By Ted? By Charlie? Would you, as DA, prosecute? Ted? Charlie?

Source: Reprinted with the permission of Colleen Fitzpatrick.

Legal Precedents

One of the most powerful uses of analogies is found in the law. This is in the form of a **legal precedent**—that is, a case used to apply to similar cases or claimed to be similar in some key respect. The use of a precedent can have a definitive effect on an argument, positively or negatively. Being able to convincingly argue a precedent can transform the law. Failing to do so has stymied even the best of us. A case is often applied to other, similar, cases, though there may be crucial differences. Let's see how a case can act as a precedent.

Potential Precedents

Anyone who has told their parents that they should be subjected to the same set of rules that are applied to their brothers and sisters (e.g., "Joe got to stay out until midnight, why can't I?") has argued by precedent, When we argue using a precedent, we are employing an analogy. We are implicitly asserting that there are sufficient similarities to allow for the principle of the one (the precedent-setting case) to apply to the situation at hand. The question is how this is done.

To block the use of a precedent—to break the analogy—point out the key differences between the two cases, so the earlier decision cannot be applied. If there are no significant differences, perhaps there are extenuating circumstances that should be factored in to weaken the analogy. Alternatively, you could search for *another* analogous case that would counter the analogy in question. This is something like having a battle of analogies that support different conclusions.

Earlier decisions that set precedents may be favorable or unfavorable to a later case, depending on the position argued. Lawyers often have to deal with such analogies (potential precedents). They must prove either that an earlier case is analogous or that the differences are so great that it doesn't apply. Whether or not the earlier case acts as a precedent is a matter of similarities or differences.

Steps in Analyzing Potential Legal Precedents

1. **Research.** Study the case being litigated. Seek out the details of the case and determine what legal issues exist.
2. **Examine potential precedents.** Find cases that are similar. Find potential precedents that (a) have strong similarities to show applicability and (b) have rulings favorable or useful to the current case.
3. **Show the analogy holds.** Show that the strength of similarities merits the application of the principle from the precedent to the present case. The lawyer can then assert that this new case warrants the same decision.

THE LAW AND ANALOGIES

Presenting Case	Case in Question (note key elements)
↓	↓
Analogous cases (potential precedents)	Similar earlier cases with acceptable decision
↓	↓
Legal principle	Decision from earlier cases
↓	↓
Application	Similar legal principle to presenting case
↓	↓
Assertion	**Decision Applies to Presenting Case**

Exercise

Quick Quiz

1. In the practice of the law, analogies are often used in the form of (a) precedents or (b) laws.
2. *True or false:* If there is a significant ("killer") difference, then the analogy won't likely succeed.

3. When assessing an analogy, a key concern is to look at the terms being compared and to list both:
   a. The likes and dislikes
   b. The similarities and differences
   c. The large and the small
   d. The weak and the strong

4. *True or false*: Any argument based on an analogy is a deductive argument.

5. What makes a weak or false analogy is that:
   a. There is no conclusion
   b. There are no relevant differences
   c. There are no relevant assumptions
   d. There are no relevant similarities

6. The first thing to do when assessing an analogy is to:
   a. Clarify the terms of comparison
   b. Clarify the unwarranted assumptions
   c. Clarify the differences
   d. Clarify the similarities

7. *True or false:* An argument based on analogy is sound so long as the premises are actually true.

8. What is crucial when using a precedent (analogous case) in a legal argument?
   a. To show that the precedent is a sound argument
   b. To show that the precedent has no unwarranted assumptions
   c. To show that the precedent has strong similarities to the case at hand
   d. To show that the precedent is an inductive argument

9. *True or false:* An argument from analogy is a form of a cause-and-effect argument.

10. To counter the use of a potential precedent, you should find:
    a. Key differences between the two cases, so the earlier decision cannot be applied
    b. Key similarities between the two cases, so the earlier decision cannot be applied
    c. Warranted assumptions between the two cases, so the earlier decision cannot be applied
    d. Factual claims that bolster your side

Group or Individual Exercise

The 2 Live Crew Case

Let us look at a U.S. Supreme Court case where both sides drew from legal precedents to support their arguments. *Acuff-Rose Music, Inc.* v. *Campbell* centers on the rap group 2 Live Crew's version (parody?) of Roy Orbison's song "Oh, Pretty Woman." Acuff-Rose sued 2 Live Crew (the members and its record company) for copyright infringement and interfering with potential profits. For their part, 2 Live Crew argued that their "parody" was protected under the doctrine of "fair use."

The case went all the way to the U.S. Supreme Court. Following is a key excerpt from the opinion. (You can access the entire opinion on the Internet.)

Campbell v. Acuff-Rose Music

Excerpted from the opinion of the U.S. Supreme Court

The germ of parody lies in the definition of the Greek *parodeia,* . . . as "a song sung alongside another." Modern dictionaries accordingly describe a parody as a "literary or artistic work that imitates the characteristic style of an author or a work for comic effect or ridicule," or as a "composition in prose or verse in which the characteristic turns of thought and phrase in an author or class of authors are imitated in such a way as to make them appear ridiculous." . . .

[T]he nub of the definitions, and the heart of any parodist's claim to quote from existing material, is the use of some elements of a prior author's composition to create a new one that, at least in part, comments on that author's works.

Parody needs to mimic an original to make its point, and so has some claim to use the creation of its victim's (or collective victims') imagination, whereas satire can stand on its own two feet and so requires justification for the very act of borrowing.

Here, the District Court held that 2 Live Crew's "Pretty Woman" contains parody, commenting on and criticizing the original work, whatever it may have to say about society at large.

As the District Court remarked, the words of 2 Live Crew's song copy the original's first line, but then "quickly degenerate into a play on words, substituting predictable lyrics with shocking ones . . . [that] derisively demonstrate how bland and banal the Orbison song seems to them."

That the 2 Live Crew song "was clearly intended to ridicule the white bread original" and "reminds us that sexual congress with nameless streetwalkers is not necessarily the stuff of romance and is not necessarily without its consequences. The singers (there are several) have the same thing on their minds as did the lonely man with the nasal voice, but here there is no hint of wine and roses." Although the majority below had difficulty discerning any criticism of the original in 2 Live Crew's song, it assumed for purposes of its opinion that there was some.

We have less difficulty in finding that critical element in 2 Live Crew's song than the Court of Appeals did, although having found it we will not take the further step of evaluating its quality. The threshold question when fair use is raised in defense of parody is whether a parodic character may reasonably be perceived.

Whether, going beyond that, parody is in good taste or bad does not and should not matter to fair use . . . cf. *Yankee Publishing Inc. v. News America Publishing, Inc.* ("First Amendment protections do not apply only to those who speak clearly, whose jokes are funny, and whose parodies succeed").

While we might not assign a high rank to the parodic element here, we think it fair to say that 2 Live Crew's song reasonably could be perceived as commenting on the original or criticizing it, to some degree. 2 Live Crew juxtaposes the romantic musings of a man whose fantasy comes true, with degrading taunts, a bawdy demand for sex, and a sigh of relief from paternal responsibility.

The later words can be taken as a comment on the naiveté of the original of an earlier day, as a rejection of its sentiment that ignores the ugliness of street life and the debasement that it signifies. It is this joinder of reference and ridicule that marks off the author's choice of parody from the other types of comment and criticism that traditionally have had a claim to fair use protection as transformative works.

Parody presents a difficult case. Parody's humor, or in any event its comment, necessarily springs from recognizable allusion to its object through distorted imitation. Its art lies in the tension between a known original and its parodic twin. When parody takes aim at a particular original work, the parody must be able to "conjure up" at least enough of that original to make the object of its critical wit recognizable . . . . Using some characteristic features cannot be avoided.

It is true, of course, that 2 Live Crew copied the characteristic opening bass riff (or musical phrase) of the original, and true that the words of the first line copy the Orbison lyrics. But if quotation of the opening riff and the first line may be said to go to the "heart" of the original, the heart is also what most readily conjures up the song for parody, and it is the heart at which parody takes aim.

Copying does not become excessive in relation to parodic purpose merely because the portion taken was the original's heart. If 2 Live Crew had copied a significantly less memorable part of the original, it is difficult to see how its parodic character would have come through.

This is not, of course, to say that anyone who calls himself a parodist can skim the cream and get away scot free. In parody, as in news reporting, . . . context is everything, and the question of fairness asks what else the parodist did besides go to the heart of the original.

It is significant that 2 Live Crew not only copied the first line of the original, but thereafter departed markedly from the Orbison lyrics for its own ends. 2 Live Crew not only copied the bass riff and repeated it, but also produced otherwise distinctive sounds, interposing "scraper" noise, overlaying the music with solos in different keys, and altering the drum beat.

Suffice it to say here that, as to the lyrics, we think . . . that "no more was taken than necessary," . . . [Moreover] there was no evidence that a potential rap market was harmed in any way by 2 Live Crew's parody, rap version. The fact that 2 Live Crew's parody sold as part of a collection of rap songs says very little about the parody's effect on a market for a rap version of the original, either of the music alone or of the music with its lyrics.

We therefore reverse the judgment of the Court of Appeals and remand for further proceedings consistent with this opinion.

Exercises

Part One

1. Set out Justice Souter's key argument (in the reading above) that affirmed that 2 Live Crew's version of "On Pretty Woman" was allowable as a parody under the fair-use law.

2. Discuss how the Court compared the two songs and reasoned that the 2 Live Crew song "Pretty Woman" was a parody of "Oh Pretty Woman."

3. In two to three paragraphs, respond to Dan Gilmore, who writes:

   Cultural works and inventions don't spring from an utter vacuum. They are the product of other people's ideas and works. Practically every melodic theme in music comes from older works, for example.

   Snow White was in the public domain before Disney got around to using her to make money. Victor Hugo must be spinning in his grave at the way Disney has turned the *Hunchback of Notre Dame* into a ridiculous cartoon—but Disney can do this, can create new ways to look at cultural icons, because the public domain exists. ("Copyright Tempest over '*The Wind Done Gone*,'" Siliconvalley.com, 24 Apr 2001)

4. Write two to three paragraphs on the effectiveness of comparing a mail thief's sentence of having to wear a sandwich board with a confession written on it to having to wear a red letter "A" for adultery on one's dress (in the novel *The Scarlet Letter* by Nathaniel Hawthorne):

   SAN FRANCISCO—Shaming defendants with Scarlet Letter–style punishments passed muster Monday with a federal appeals panel that upheld a mail thief's sentence to wear a sign outside a post office stating: "I stole mail. This is my punishment." One member of the 9th U.S. Circuit Court of Appeals panel, Judge Michael Daly Hawkins, dissented, stating public humiliation or shame "has no proper place in our system of justice." . . . He said the sandwich board sentence would turn the defendant into a modern day Hester Prynne, the character in Nathaniel Hawthorne's "The Scarlet Letter" who was forced to wear an "A" on her dress identifying her as an adulterer.

   In Monday's decision, a 9th Circuit panel voted 2–1 to uphold Shawn Gementera's 2003 sentence of two months in jail and eight hours of pacing in front of a post office wearing a sandwich board sign with "I stole mail" emblazoned on it.

   Judge Diarmuid O'Scannlain wrote that Gementera's punishment was not a "stand-alone condition intended solely to humiliate, but rather a comprehensive set of provisions that expose the defendant to social disapprobation, but that also then provide an opportunity for Gementera to repair his relationship with society." Visiting Judge Eugene E. Siler of the 6th Circuit in Cincinnati joined O'Scannlain in rejecting an Eighth Amendment challenge to the shaming sanction as cruel. (Pamela A. MacLean, "Mail Thief Ordered to Wear Stamp of Humiliation," *Daily Journal*, 10 Aug 2004)

5. The *Campbell* v. *Acuff-Rose Music* decision may apply to a later case. The novel *The Wind Done Gone*, a takeoff on (parody of?) *Gone with the Wind*, faced a similar challenge. The novel is a retelling of the 1936 saga *Gone with*

the Wind from the perspective of a slave, a half-sister of Scarlett O'Hara. The estate of Margaret Mitchell, author of *Gone with the Wind,* sued on the grounds that the book violated copyright protections. What aspects of the decision by the Supreme Court in the "Oh Pretty Woman" case may be useful for either the prosecution or defense in setting out their case? Share two to three ideas.

6. Think of all the Disney films using or retelling tales and myths, such as *Cinderella, Pocahontas, The Little Mermaid, Snow White, Beauty and the Beast, and Aladdin.* Do you think there are any objections to Disney drawing from ("cannibalizing"?) earlier works by others (e.g., fairy tales)? Share your thoughts.

Part Two

The case of *Cassim* v. *Allstate* centers on a couple whose troubles started with an arson fire that badly damaged their home. Things got more and more convoluted with their insurance company, Allstate, with the lawsuit dragging on for years. The use of an analogy by the Cassims' lawyer put the case into a tailspin, with an appeal by Allstate resulting in a reversal of an award from the lower court. Read about the case and then decide if the analogy sinks the case against Allstate. Set out the reasons for your decision.

Is Analogy Misconduct? 2nd DCA Thought So

Peter Blumberg
San Francisco Daily Journal, May 5, 2004

SAN FRANCISCO—Plaintiff's attorney Ian Herzog came up with just the analogy to win over jurors in a hard-fought insurance dispute when Allstate accused his clients of misrepresenting losses in a home fire. In his closing argument at the 33-day trial in 1999, the Santa Monica lawyer contended his client's behavior was no different than jurors getting permission from the judge to collect full pay from their employers on days when they were excused from the courthouse early.

Little did Herzog know that after Los Angeles Superior Court Judge Harold Cherness permitted the analogy over Allstate's objection, it would still come back to haunt him.

On appeal, Allstate persuaded the 2nd District Court of Appeal (DCA), on a 2–1 vote, to wipe out the $10 million award Herzog won from the jury, saying that his closing argument amounted to prejudicial misconduct.

But during oral argument Tuesday before the California Supreme Court, Chief Justice Ronald George put Allstate's lawyer in the hot seat, pressing him to explain exactly what Herzog did wrong. "Is this just really the sort of inventive analogy that counsel often engage in and courts countenance?" George asked. . . .

Herzog's battle with Allstate dates back more than 13 years, when clients Fareed and Rashida Cassim first filed a claim with the insurance giant after arson badly damaged the Palmdale home they bought in 1989. Allstate's refusal to pay out as much as the Cassims demanded grew into a full-fledged war, culminating in two lengthy trials and half a dozen appeals.

When it was over, Allstate accused the financially strapped Cassims of committing the arson and then inflating their losses to defraud the company. After the Cassims went into bankruptcy, lost their home and accused their insurer of bad faith, the jury came back with an award that vindicated the couple. The total judgment was $9.8 million, which included $1.7 million apiece to compensate husband and wife, $5 million in punitive damages and $1.2 million in attorney fees.

In a closing argument that covers 130 pages of the trial transcript, Herzog spent about two pages framing his analogy. Herzog likened Allstate's allegation of intentional misrepresentation on the part of the Cassims to jurors getting fired "because you misrepresented about you being on jury duty on certain days and you got paid when you really weren't."

Cherness overruled an objection by Allstate, but the 2nd DCA's majority concluded the analogy poisoned the entire trial by making jurors think that Cherness himself approved of fudging the truth as the Cassims had allegedly done. "Here, in a case where fraud in an insurance claim was a primary issue in the case, counsel for plaintiff went right to the fact that the jurors had been essentially cheating their employers," Justice Aurelio Munoz wrote. "When counsel made reference to the fact that some of the jurors might be accused of cheating there was no question he was letting jurors know that the court had no objections to the procedure."

Herzog opened Tuesday's argument by asserting that his innocent "innuendo" had been badly misunderstood. Herzog said that contrary to condoning cheating, he was pointing out that the Cassims believed it was appropriate to "reconstruct" receipts that they hadn't actually kept, just as jurors must have thought it was appropriate to do whatever the judge instructed as far as claiming credit at work for jury duty. "We want jurors to bring their experience with them, to apply their common sense," he told the high court. "I don't think jurors thought they were doing anything wrong because they were just doing what the judge told them was OK."

Allstate's attorney, Peter Abrahams, of Encino, countered that Herzog's argument put jurors in "an impossible position" because the analogy implied judicial approval for insurance fraud. "It's never pleasant to accuse opposing counsel of misconduct," he said. "I think that in this case, serious misconduct occurred."

Source: Copyright 2004 Daily Journal Corp. Reprinted with permission.

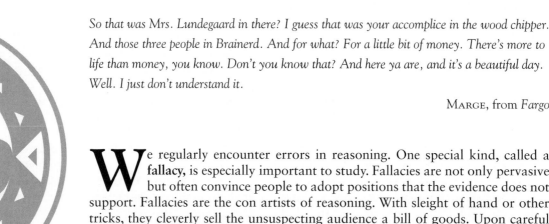

CHAPTER SEVEN

Fallacies, Fallacies: Steering Clear of Argumentative Quicksand

So that was Mrs. Lundegaard in there? I guess that was your accomplice in the wood chipper. And those three people in Brainerd. And for what? For a little bit of money. There's more to life than money, you know. Don't you know that? And here ya are, and it's a beautiful day. Well. I just don't understand it.

Marge, from *Fargo*

We regularly encounter errors in reasoning. One special kind, called a **fallacy,** is especially important to study. Fallacies are not only pervasive but often convince people to adopt positions that the evidence does not support. Fallacies are the con artists of reasoning. With sleight of hand or other tricks, they cleverly sell the unsuspecting audience a bill of goods. Upon careful scrutiny, we can see that fallacies should not be given credence. To avoid them, we have to pay attention—and not be complacent.

In a letter to the editor of *Tricycle: The Buddhist Review,* Melissa Chianta writes: "When I broke up with my first boyfriend in college, I told a friend, 'He bastardizes Eastern religions to suit his own emotional limitations.' . . . I realized that ten years later I have done the same thing!" (Summer, 2001). Chianta just experienced the flipside of the "ah-ha" effect—when we have a mental breakthrough and finally get it. Catching ourselves in a fallacy is the "uh-oh" effect—a mental sinkhole. With the tools this chapter provides, you should be able to catch yourself before plunging into a sinkhole of bad reasoning!

Fallacies: Flaws in Reasoning

Every fallacy contains a fundamental flaw in reasoning. The flaws can take any number of forms and may involve structural or linguistic errors, mistaken assumptions, or premises that are irrelevant to the conclusion. We will look at the major types of fallacies in this chapter in order to avoid making such errors and to be able to defend ourselves when others use fallacies.

Logicians disagree on the exact definition of a "fallacy" of reasoning and whether to call fallacies "invalid" or "unsound." Some fallacious arguments do appear to be failed *deductive* reasoning, because the premises are *irrelevant* to the conclusion. They are, thus, invalid and unsound by definition. Others, such as those involving statistical studies, appear to be failed *inductive* reasoning and are better considered "poor" or "faulty" than invalid. What logicians *do* agree upon is that *all fallacies are forms of incorrect reasoning* that can be highly persuasive. Nevertheless, any argument containing a fallacy is fatally flawed in its reasoning and must be rejected.

What we will learn in this chapter is how the different fallacies fall into different patterns that we can recognize—and, hopefully, how to stop the fallacy in its tracks. Being able to spot fallacies is most empowering, and friends, family, and acquaintances will be grateful that you have developed this critical thinking skill.

Look at the "reasoning" in this conversation and see if you can "bust" the fallacy:

HEATHER: Euthanasia is killing and, since it is wrong to kill, euthanasia is wrong.

LEO: You're just a woman, what could you possibly know about euthanasia? Stick to the kitchen!

HEATHER: Why should I listen to you—you are a member of the National Rifle Association. You'd certainly be biased!

LEO: Speaking of rifles, did you hear about Ruben? He bought an antique rifle used in World War II! That was a good investment. Either you know where to put your money or you just waste it.

HEATHER: That's the truth! And if you just waste your money, you won't be able to get out of the house. Then you will not have any kind of social life. Pretty soon, you'll be sitting home staring at the ceiling, your entire life rotting away in front of your eyes!

LEO: Sure thing, Heather. Hey, there's my bus. Catch you later!

Fallacy Busters. Leo dismisses Heather's argument without considering her reasons. The fact that Heather's a woman is irrelevant in this case. Her reply is just as bad, because she points to his membership in a group to discredit him. Leo then switches the topic entirely. Since there are more options than the two stated, he commits another fallacy. Finally, Heather offers the flimsy argument that wasting money will doom you to a dreary life.

There are four major kinds of fallacies:

- **Fallacies of relevance.** In fallacies of relevance, the premises simply fail to support the conclusion; they are beside the point. Here's an example: "Mickey Mouse loves Camembert cheese; therefore, you should buy some today!"
- **Fallacies of presumption.** In fallacies of presumption, the argument rests on an unwarranted assumption causing the fallacy. Here's an example: "Either you know Harry Potter or you are a cultural toad. With 400 million Harry Potter books in print worldwide, published in 67 languages, there's no excuse

Overview of the Fallacies

Fallacies of relevance are invalid and unsound because the premises are simply irrelevant to the conclusion being drawn.

Fallacies of presumption are incorrect because of unfounded or unsupportable assumptions underlying them.

Fallacies of ambiguity are incorrect because of unclear and confusing use of words, grammar, or sentence structure that leads to drawing an incorrect conclusion.

Formal fallacies are invalid and unsound because the very form or structure of the argument leads to drawing an incorrect conclusion.

Fallacies of Relevance

- Ad hominem
- Ad hominem circumstantial
- Tu quo
- Ad populum
- Ad verecundiam
- Ad baculum
- Ad misericordiam
- Ad ignorantiam

Fallacies of Presumption

- Accident
- Hasty generalization
- Biased statistics
- Bifurcation
- Complex question
- Misleading vividness
- Post hoc
- Red herring
- Slippery slope
- Straw man
- Begging the question
- False analogy

Linguistic Fallacies (Fallacies of Ambiguity)

- Equivocation
- Accent
- Amphiboly
- Composition
- Division

Formal Fallacies

- Fallacy of affirming the consequent
- Fallacy of denying the antecedent

for being a cultural toad. Thus, you should read one of the Harry Potter books."

- **Fallacies of ambiguity** (also known as **linguistic fallacies**). Fallacies of ambiguity center on the way language can mislead—focusing on emphasis, interpretation, sentence structure, and the relationship between the parts and the whole. This ambiguity results in an incorrect conclusion being drawn, causing the fallacy. Here's an example: "Popeye is fun, and so is Olive Oyl. They should get married—together they'd be dynamite!"
- **Formal fallacies.** Formal fallacies occur because of a structural error: The very form of the reasoning is incorrect. The truth of the premises will never guarantee the truth of the conclusion. Here's an example: "If Wimpy eats one more hamburger, he will have to take a nap. Wimpy had to nap. Consequently, Wimpy must have eaten one more hamburger."

We'll start with an overview and then look at each fallacy.

▨ Introduction to the Fallacies of Relevance

Fallacies of relevance rest on evidence that's beside the point and, thus, irrelevant. There is always a glaring gap between the premises and the conclusion drawn in a fallacy of relevance. For instance, you might be persuaded to hand over your shoes if someone threatens you, but that doesn't make the threat a *good reason* for surrendering them. The key is what counts as a good reason, not what counts as *persuasive*. A good reason is something that offers solid evidence for holding a position.

Fallacy Busters

We should see a direct connection between the evidence and the conclusion. If not, something is wrong. Let's look at some cases and see if we can bust the fallacy. As fallacy busters, we spot the incorrect reasoning and identify its form. Not only does this develop our critical thinking skills, but it helps others as well. It's empowering to stop bad reasoning in its tracks!

Case 1

RAY: Carl Johnson would make a great mayor: He's been active in government for 15 years. He has helped people get back on their feet. Plus, he has been instrumental in transforming the downtown so that it's not a haven for drugs.

LUCILLE: Don't you know he is gay? Would you vote for a gay man for mayor? Surely you are kidding!

You probably saw this one. Johnson is discredited because of a personal characteristic. Lucille needs to explain why sexual orientation is a relevant consideration for mayor. The candidate is dismissed without getting a fair hearing.

Case 2

ANNIE: Mommy, why do I have to go to bed? It is only seven o'clock and I am not at all sleepy. Can't I read for a while?

MOMMY: I'll tell you why you have to go to bed. If you do not go to bed right now I'll paddle your behind with a wooden spoon. Get moving!

Mommy threatens Annie—she does not give her a good reason, such as the need for sleep. She should try to persuade with evidence, not threats.

Case 3

DR. BERKOWITZ: Students, be honest throughout your entire academic career since it will make you an honorable person.

YU ZHAN: How can you say that, Dr. Berkowitz, when you plagiarized your master's thesis? Why should I pay attention to the advice of a cheater?

Here Dr. Berkowitz offers a reason for being honest, but he is dismissed for not "practicing what he preaches." We might justifiably expect someone to act on the standards by which they judge others. The unwillingness to do so points to moral weakness, but does not mean that their *reasoning* is flawed. Whether the speaker lives in accordance with those reasons (the premises) is a separate issue.

▨ Key Fallacies of Relevance

By becoming familiar with the fallacies, we'll be able to spot incorrect reasoning in ourselves and in others and, hopefully, stop ourselves from falling into any fallacious thinking.

Argumentum Ad Hominem

The **ad hominem** (or personal attack) fallacy occurs whenever there is an attack on another person (the source of an idea), instead of the person's argument (the idea itself). The attack can be on the speaker *or* someone the speaker is citing (who then is targeted in the personal attack). It is often referred to as ad hominem *abusive* because of the nature of a personal attack.

This fallacy effectively turns attention away from the issue and toward the person arguing it. This is unacceptable unless the personal characteristic under attack is demonstrably relevant to what's at issue. If not, attacking the source of the idea rather than the idea itself is fallacious. As critical thinkers, our focus should be on the quality of the reasoning—not some test of personal worth—unless personal worth *is* the issue.

Sometimes the attack on the other person is downright hostile; at other times it is subtle and less obvious. Unfortunately, abusive tactics have been known to persuade (e.g., when voters fall for them). Discrediting a plaintiff, defendant, or witness using an ad hominem attack can also occur in a trial or deposition. Here are two cases with similar tactics. In both the 1992 Mike Tyson rape trial and the 1991 William Kennedy Smith rape trial, the victim's panties were cited as indictors of her character:

> A key piece of evidence in the Michael Tyson rape trial was the victim's underwear. It was pink polka dots, little girlish, like something a mother might buy for her preteen. The prosecutor "made a sarcastic remark to the jury about this wild, sexual woman going to meet Tyson wearing her 'pajama panties.' Like something straight out of Frederick's of Hollywood, the prosecutor joked." (Dianne Klein, "Rewrite Script for Rape Trials," *Los Angeles Times,* 13 Feb 1992)

> Tyson was convicted. But William Kennedy Smith's victim wore black Victoria's Secret panties and a sheer black bra, which the defense attorney showed to the jury. [Smith was acquitted.] (Shirley A. Wiegand, "Deception and Artifice: Thelma, Louise, and the Legal Hermeneutic," *Oklahoma City University Law Review* 22, no. 1, 1997)

Ad hominem tactics can be seen in other arenas, too—as with politicians resorting to personal attacks on their opponents. People call that "mudslinging" for obvious reasons. Unfortunately, abusive tactics have been known to persuade.

Look at the case of Richard Clarke. Clarke, ex-chief of counterterrorism for the Bush administration, spoke before the congressional panel investigating events leading up to 9/11. His remarks set off a firestorm. Some thought Clarke was the victim of ad hominem attacks, as shown in the following:

> Conservatives, ever suspicious of Big Government, should love a whistle-blower—unless, of course, he's former counterterrorism czar Richard Clarke. *The Washington Times* calls Clarke "a political chameleon who is starved for attention after years of toiling anonymously in government bureaucracies." For neoconservative colum-nist Charles Krauthammer, Clarke is "a liar" and "not just a perjurer but a partisan perjurer." According to Ann Coulter, Clarke is a racist. Exiting the known world and entering into her own fantasyland, Coulter depicts Clarke musing about Condoleezza Rice: "the black chick is a dummy," whom Bush promoted from "cleaning the Old Executive Office Building at night."
>
> This ad hominem defamation is obviously intended to discredit the man in order to discredit his argument. But such low tactics aren't usually attempted against a man whose allegations are corroborated by others, including the implicated parties—and, most palpably, by events themselves. (James Pinkerton, "Conservatives Should Hail Former Counterterrorism Chief Richard Clarke, but Instead They're Smearing Him," *Salon,* www.salon.com, 29 Mar 2004)

Impeaching the testimony of witnesses through an attack on their credibil-ity may be necessary—but only when that credibility is germane to the matter at hand. For example, impeachment by felony conviction (when the person testifying has a prior conviction for a felony involving moral turpitude) is a legitimate form of impeachment. Ordinarily, the personal circumstances of a person—such as his or her social standing or choice of underwear—are irrel-evant to the logical force of the argument. As Senator Joe Biden said during the 2008 presidential campaign, "There is a difference between an ad homi-nem argument and a logical response" (quoted by Bob Herbert, *The New York Times,* 27 May 2008).

Examples of Ad Hominem

PETE: Don't you think socialized medicine is a bad idea? It seems awfully costly, and there's already a big enough burden on the ordinary citizen. Dr. Murdock was right to say that we should be talking about accessibility, not socialized medicine.

LUIS: You've got to be kidding! I can't believe you'd be swayed by a person whose healthcare needs are all met! Boy, are you duped!

KIM: El Burrito is the best Mexican restaurant in Norwalk. They use the freshest ingredients and make their own tortillas. Everything I've eaten there is delicious.

ARTHUR: Okay, but since you're Japanese, you are hardly an expert on Mexican food! Why take your advice?

PROF. QUARK: The philosophical work of Immanuel Kant is certainly exten-sive in its range. However, it's hard to take seriously the views of someone rumored to be a hypochondriac.

Argumentum Ad Hominem Circumstantial

The **ad hominem circumstantial** fallacy involves an attack on a person's credibility because of vested interests or social affiliations. Because of the circumstances or a potential conflict of interest, the person cannot possibly be impartial—or so it is implied. Here's an example: "Don't listen to what the governor of Nevada has to say about Indian casinos. He's from a state that lives and breathes gambling, so he'd certainly be biased!"

This is sometimes called "guilt by association." We see the ad hominem circumstantial fallacy when someone is criticized because of their membership in a group or professional, religious, cultural, or political associations. By shifting the focus away from the issue to the person's vested interests or associations, we go off on a tangent—and away from the question of whether their argument has merit. For instance, in the 2008 election campaign, Hillary Clinton attacked Barack Obama for supposedly having ties to 1960s radical William Ayers (= guilt by association). Robert Reich, who went to Yale Law School with the Clintons, said, "That carries guilt by association to a new level of absurdity. . . . She was a partner of Jim McDougal [of the Whitewater scandal] in the 1980s, for crying out loud" (James Grimaldi, "Clinton Quiet about Her Own Radical Ties," *The Washington Post,* 19 May 2008). On the Republican side, Sarah Palin frequently linked Obama to Ayers (now a respected professor of education), accusing him of "palling around with terrorists." After the election, Ayers called these attacks "a profoundly dishonest narrative." He said, "I don't buy the idea that guilt by association should be any part of our politics" ("Ayers Lashes Out at 'Dishonest' Attacks," Michigan Live, www.michiganlive.com, 14 Nov 2008).

Of course, people can be corrupt or corrupted. Nonetheless, when analyzing their *reasoning,* our goal is to see how it holds together—not what's going on behind the scenes. Consequently, the quality of the reasoning warrants our attention, not the person's affiliations.

The difference between ad hominem and ad hominem circumstantial is that the former is a *personal* attack, intended to demean an opponent personally and, thereby, defeat the person's argument. In contrast, an ad hominem circumstantial zeroes in on the person's circumstances, connections, or situation rather than his or her personal traits or character. An example of ad hominem circumstantial would be a *guilt-by-association* attack.

Examples of Ad Hominem Circumstantial

Of course the representative from Prince Edward Island opposes the potato surcharge—you know he's from the biggest producer of potatoes east of Ottawa. He's bound to be in their pocket! Don't listen to him.

Rosalind suggested Mother Teresa as an example of a heroic woman in the 20th century, because Mother Teresa did so much for the poor people in India. However, Rosalind is a Catholic herself and, consequently, can hardly be unbiased.

We shouldn't be surprised that Rep. Al Waxman proposed the Research Freedom Act to end the ban on fetal cell transplants. After all, he's from California, where all that high-tech fertility and fetal cell research goes on.

Tu Quo (or Tu Quoque—"You're Another One")

The fallacy of **tu quo** occurs when people are attacked because they don't follow their own advice or "practice what they preach." It is sometimes referred to as the "hypocrisy fallacy." We might refer to this as the "tu quo trap": You don't take your own advice—so your advice must be worth nothing! (See the accompanying cartoon for an example.)

Actions may speak louder than words, but the quality of our reasoning should be assessed on its own merits and not by our actions. For example, just because a politician "flip-flopped" on issues does not mean that his *arguments* were weak. If the issue is his *character,* then vacillating on issues of national interest may or may not be relevant, depending upon the situation.

Even hypocrites may exhibit strong reasoning. Personal habits and practices are generally irrelevant to the merits of an argument. The fact that a woman with emphysema smokes until her last gasp doesn't weaken her argument that smoking can kill you.

Examples of Tu Quo

> **AHMAD:** Will you please slow down, Lisa? You're driving 20 miles over the speed limit, which is dangerous in the rain. I'm scared!
>
> **LISA:** I don't have to listen to you. You got a speeding ticket last month. Point your finger at me and three point back at you!

Betty Jean has fallen into the "tu quo" trap!

Copyright 2004. Jason Karl, artist; Wanda Teays, copy. Reprinted with permission.

You Tell Me Department

Political Pundits on the Attack

In the 2008 election campaign, Governor Bill Richardson of New Mexico, longtime friend of the Clintons, came out in support of Senator Obama. James Carville, a political analyst protested. "Mr. Richardson's endorsement came right around the anniversary of the day when Judas sold out for 30 pieces of silver, so I think the timing is appropriate, if ironic," Carville told *The New York Times* (22 Mar 2008).

You tell me: Should "anything go" when it comes to politics? Do ad hominem attacks sway voters? Should they? Share your thoughts.

How can Betty Jean tell me to read classics like *Tortilla Flats,* when all she does is watch MTV?

"It's a bit ironic that California Governor Schwarzenegger is taking public stands on tightening up regulations around steroid use by professional and amateur athletes. After all, he is reported to have used anabolic steroids back in his body building days. And it wasn't so long ago that he said, 'I used steroids. It was a risky thing to do, but I have no regrets. It was what I had to do to compete' . . ." (Tom Farrey, "Conan the Politician," *ESPN News,* 17 Nov 2003).

Argumentum Ad Populum (Argument from Patriotism or Popular Appeal)

The **ad populum** fallacy attempts to persuade on the basis of popular appeal, the masses, or patriotism, rather than giving good reasons to accept the conclusion. An appeal to mass sentiment is often called the "bandwagon approach." Get on the bandwagon and join the crowd! The assumption is that the crowd or the majority knows what's best. Clearly, this is not always the case.

We also see the ad populum fallacy with "snob appeal." We are asked to join the "in-group" (the rich, famous, sexy, popular, etc.) so as not to feel like a reject, nerd, or leftover. This appeal is often used in advertising—as are the other variations on the ad populum argument.

Examples of Ad Populum

Be cool! Smoke cigars! All the cool people do!

What's wrong with you? Forget getting a Nissan. Support your country and buy an American car.

JOE: Boy, can you believe it? Over 380 *tons* of explosives disappeared in Iraq. And that includes the kind of explosives used to blow up the airplane out of Lockerbie, Scotland, way back when. You'd have thought the U.S. military would have been guarding those munitions from the get-go. That should have been a high priority—even with the troops stretched so thin.

KEISHA: I can't believe you'd say that, Joe. Your very comment denigrates the troops and is unpatriotic. I'm standing by the troops and suggest you do the same!

Note how we are asked to get behind our country, join the crowd, or jump on the bandwagon. The pressure here is to fall in line, not dissent. It is important, though, to seek good reasons for a call to conformity, rather than merely acquiescing.

References to patriotism in advertising are widespread. From images of the flag to bald eagles as logos, consumers are asked to link love of country with shopping. It is done quite dramatically at Lord & Taylor's in New York City. There, every morning at 9:30, they play the National Anthem and, presumably, expect shoppers to stand at attention, hand on heart. The response? Shopper Patty Kahr, heading back to alterations, said it was "inappropriately patriotic for a commercial setting." She added, "I think that kind of patriotism should be voluntary, not enforced. You expect it at a sporting event, but when you're going shopping for clothing?" On the other hand, another shopper, looking for a pair of pants in men's wear, said, "I didn't feel it was intrusive. It wasn't really blaring." Perhaps not—but is it a marketing ploy, however long-standing (James Barron, "A Star-Spangled Banner Yet Waves at Lord & Taylor," *The New York Times*, 26 May 2008).

Group or Individual Exercise

Directions: Gather as many ads as you can that use an ad populum fallacy—either with appeals to patriotism or popular appeal (a bandwagon argument). Gather also as many political ads as you can that use an appeal to patriotism or the bandwagon approach. Bring them in and share with the class, explaining how you see the fallacy being used.

Argumentum Ad Verecundiam (Improper Appeal to Authority)

The **ad verecundiam** fallacy occurs when an appeal is made to an "authority" to support a position, but the person is not a credible expert on the topic. Frequently, the "authority" cited is a public figure or celebrity who offers a testimonial. This is commonly seen in advertisements. It is expected that we'll be persuaded by the endorsement, rather than by good reasons for the conclusion.

Examples of Ad Verecundiam

Einstein loved to play the violin so you should too!
James Bond drives an Aston Martin. Therefore, they must be cool cars.
Oprah thinks *White Oleander* is a good book, so it should have gotten a Pulitzer Prize for literature.

We may agree with the celebrity's product choice or their endorsement. But agreement is not enough—look at the evidence.

Be careful: Expert testimony does have its place. But the person cited should be an expert in the field in question. It may be advisable to use more than one source or "expert," particularly if there is some difference of opinion about the fundamental facts or if the topic is controversial.

Argumentum Ad Baculum (Appeal to Force or Coercion)

The **ad baculum** fallacy occurs when force, threat of force, or coercion is used to persuade. This includes verbal or sexual harassment, blackmail, extortion, and threats of violence used to "persuade" someone to a position. A variation is bribery, where the coercion comes in the form of a promise, an offer, money, or position. Here's an example of an ad that points to unfortunate consequences of *not* using the product:

> Ad for Breathe Right® nasal strips [two eyes looking at each other against a pitch-black background]: **"If you really love me, you'd wear one."** You won't even know it's there. But she will. Because Breathe Right® strips can help quiet your snoring by improving your nasal breathing. And once you get used to breathing through your nose again, the less you'll get elbowed. . . .

Examples of Ad Baculum

SONCHAI: I'm sorry Tim, but I can't write you a letter of recommendation. You have been late to work many times, and you regularly have lunches two hours long!

TIM: That's up to you, Sonchai. But what goes around comes around! And don't forget: I know where you live and when I can find you home alone.

MR. SWARTHMORE: Barbara, come discuss your job promotion with me tonight. Meet me at my hotel and wear some sexy lingerie! Give a little and you'll get something back.

NURSE KRATCHIT: Good to see you back on the ward, Dr. Hernandez. I hear you've called the press about the screw-up last week in the emergency room. Please keep a lid on this. I could tell the press about that nasty medical malpractice case you had last year!

In these cases, there is a threat of physical force (the most blatant), an implied threat (coercion), fear of loss (bribery, extortion), and harassment (sexual, verbal).

Argumentum Ad Misericordiam (Appeal to Pity)

The fallacy of **ad misericordiam** occurs when an irrelevant appeal to pity or a set of sorrowful circumstances is used to support a conclusion. A sympathetic response may be called for when we become aware of someone's personal difficulties. But that does not, in itself, substitute for good reasons that directly support a conclusion.

Examples of Ad Misericordiam

He should be a senator, given his history. His wife ran off with Judge Thornton, his grandmother died of sausage poisoning, and his children are all in gangs.

Dr. Green, I deserve an A in logic. My boyfriend ran off with my cousin, Maria, and the transmission went out on my car. My life is a mess! I deserve an A for my pain.

Please officer, don't cite me for drunk driving. I know it's my second time in two years, but my parents will put me in a rehab program, and my social life will be ruined.

These sad tales are not relevant to becoming a senator, getting an A, or avoiding a charge of driving under the influence. In some cases, as in preferential treatment programs, we may want to consider such hardships as poverty or discrimination. Legitimate attempts to provide a balance could be seen in terms of justice, not pity. Weigh them carefully so you don't fall into the fallacy of ad misericordiam.

Do pro-choice advocates resort to appeal-to-pity arguments in suggesting that restricting abortion rights could lead to back-alley or coat hanger abortions? Philosopher Francis J. Beckwith thinks this is the case; see if you agree.

> Even some pro-choice advocates, who argue for their position in other ways, admit that the coat hanger/back-alley argument is fallacious. For example, pro-choice philosopher Mary Anne Warren clearly recognizes that her position on abortion cannot rest on this argument without it first being demonstrated that the unborn entity is not fully human. She writes that "the fact that restricting access to abortion has tragic side effects does not, in itself, show that the restrictions are unjustified, since murder is wrong regardless of the consequences of prohibiting it." ("Answering the Arguments for Abortion Rights," *Christian Research Journal*, Fall 1990)

Argumentum Ad Ignorantiam (Appeal to Ignorance)

The **ad ignorantiam** fallacy occurs when it is argued that something is the case (either true or false) simply because it cannot be proved otherwise. This is the "if you can't prove me wrong, then I must be right!" defense.

Examples of Ad Ignorantiam

This house is haunted. You cannot prove it's not haunted, so it must be the case!

My physics professor is an alcoholic—unless you have evidence that I'm wrong, I must be right!

Belief in reincarnation is unwarranted since no one can definitively demonstrate that the soul can enter another body and come back on earth.

A failure to disprove something does not mean the opposite is true. The fact that you cannot prove your brother is *not* dreaming of Sedna, the sea goddess, does not mean that he *is* dreaming about her. And when it comes to legal matters, a *presumption* of innocence is quite different from *proof* of innocence.

Philosopher Steven J. Naylor says this fallacy "occurs in both of the following examples: There is insufficient evidence to establish that God exists. Therefore, God does not exist. There is no proof that God does not exist. Therefore, God exists." Both arguments are fallacious, because "ignorance or lack of proof or evidence about a claim establishes neither that it is true nor that it is false" (quoted by Shandon L. Guthrie, "Atheism and the Argumentum Ad Ignorantiam," sguthrie.net).

Exercises

Directions: Identify the fallacy of relevance in the examples below. If you forget the name describe what is happening in the argument—look for the pattern, and the name may become apparent.

1. I saw an ad for Louis Vuitton luggage that featured Keith Richards of the Rolling Stones. Those suitcases must be great!

2. Smith's ketchup is all-American! Buy some!

3. Keith said it's smart to drive at a safe speed and be polite to other drivers. However, I see no reason to follow his advice, since he drives like a race car driver and has no qualms about cutting off other drivers. Who is he to talk?

4. Hundreds of people saw lights flashing on a wall, and they declared it a miracle and a sign of the Virgin Mary. Scientists cannot explain the strange phenomenon. No one has been able to prove that it's not a sign of the Blessed Virgin, so it must be!

5. CARRIE: Angelica said that people should not use ivory, because so many elephants are killed and that's wrong.
    LEN: Don't you realize she's a member of Latinas United and couldn't possibly know anything about African elephants!

6. Most women think men who recite poetry are romantic. Therefore, if Jamal wants to impress Miranda, he'd better start reciting poetry.

7. Movie star Hugh Jackman says weight-lifting and yoga keep him in shape. Maybe your parents should sign up for lessons—they are getting a tad flabby!

8. Richard Alton Harris was a victim of fetal alcohol syndrome. Plus, his mother was beaten up by his father when she was pregnant. As a result, he should not have been convicted of the murder of those two teenagers. It was too bad he was executed for the crime.

9. Hey, Professor Whitaker, I deserve an A on this exam. If you do not give me one, I will follow you home and put a mouse in your mailbox. That'll show you! So, will you give me the A or not?

10. Hey Gabriel, I hear your uncle was a sharphooter in the Army. He knew the importance of the Second Amendment—why don't you? You shouldn't support registering handguns. Any attempt to control guns means a police state is around the corner!

11. PHIL: Hey Omar—did you see the Justice Department has issued new guidelines that lets the FBI use surveillance techniques without having to link the subject to terrorism? Isn't that scary? I think we should email our legislators to protest the erosion of our civil liberties!

    OMAR: You can't be too careful, Phil. Sure, I read that John Kerry had been under surveillance after the Vietnam War, and even Senator Ted Kennedy got on some watch list—but protecting our country requires us to go the extra mile. You ought to do more to stand by your country and not be so critical.

12. Tom Cruise is underrated as a serious actor; for example, he gave a solid performance in *Valkyrie*. Rick says he would vote for him on the ZNOT radio poll of best actors, except for the fact that Cruise is into Scientology. He thinks that's creepy.

13. Since no one has proven that exorcism is not effective, we should call in a priest to examine Carrie. She needs help.

14. Dr. Johnson, I hope you can arrange to get an organ donor for my infant son. If you drag your heels, I'll make sure your wife knows about your affair with that cute nurse in ObGyn last year!

15. Charley Spengler, shortstop for the Westminster Salmonbellies, says chewing snuff is bad for your health and rots your teeth. Like we should pay attention to what he has to say? He has been chewing snuff since he turned pro.

16. URSULA: Jack, you should vote for Proposition 112—there are so many reasons it will help the homeless.

    JACK: Really? How would you know? You're from Sweden.

17. HASSAN: I can't believe you shoot deer with assault rifles. That is beyond barbaric! At least cavemen used bows and arrows and the animals had a chance.

    BRIANA: You're no vegetarian. I saw you wolfing down the flesh of a defenseless chicken just last night!

18. Professor Tregenza really should get the job at the learning center. She's really smart, plus she's not had a very easy time lately. First, she accidentally dropped a cup of coffee on her new laptop, and then her dog, Wolfie, chewed up two garden leprechauns. I'm sure she'd go the extra mile if they just gave her a chance. She deserves a break.

19. Be wary of anything that Oliver says about reproductive rights. He's active in the Defenders of the Unborn, and you know what an extreme group they are! I checked out their website, and let me tell you, the graphics turn your stomach. Speaking of stomachs, are you free for lunch?

20. MARIO: Angela, honey, what's this frozen chicken breast doing on the table instead of dinner?

    ANGELA: Mario, you big lug, if you don't get helping with dinner I'll toss the entire contents of the fridge out on the front lawn! I've had it! So, I suggest you change your ways, starting today.

21. How can you doubt the value of an American Express card when you have the testimony of Tiger Woods to vouch for it being good? Melissa said she heard that it's his main credit card.

22. Don't believe everything Mario says about Angela. He's Italian—you know how those Latin men tend to exaggerate. They can't be trusted to tell the truth.

23. Football MVP Tom Brady thinks the Movado series 800 watch is wonderful, so that may be a great watch to get your mother for her birthday.

24. Did you hear that two-thirds of American children and teens have read at least one Harry Potter book? I can't understand why your cousin, Bosco, isn't crazy about Harry Potter too. He should get with it.

25. It isn't wise of you to trust just any stockbroker, given the potential for bias. I know for a fact that your stockbroker, Alan Greenspine, is a Democrat. It'll be a cold day in Hades when a Democrat can figure out the stock market. You ought to change your stockbroker today. Give me a call and I'll get you the phone number of mine—she's a Republican and that gal knows her money.

26. Dr. Wong deserves to win the Faculty of the Year award. I know he's only been teaching at the school for two years, but he got in that snowboarding accident and sure mangled his foot. It's a wonder he can hobble into class!

27. Hey, Ralph, you should fix my car. If you don't, I will tell your wife about those photos you took of your neighbor, Alicia, when she was sunbathing in her backyard.

28. The universe must be infinite, since no one has proven it is finite.

29. Is it right to clone humans? Most people say absolutely not, that cloning whole people is immoral. That's all we need to know for us to do what's right—and that is to have a constitutional amendment prohibiting the cloning of human beings.

Quick Quiz

1. What fallacy occurs when, instead of being given reasons for coming to a decision, someone is asked to provide sexual favors in exchange for a job or raise?

2. What fallacy occurs when an advertiser uses snob appeal, such as suggesting that eating their mustard will make us feel like we own a Rolls Royce?

3. What fallacy occurs when someone makes an irrelevant appeal to a recent disaster as a reason for getting a job, raise, or better grade?

4. What fallacy occurs when someone argues that something must be true because you can't prove it is false (or vice versa)?

5. What fallacy occurs when someone argues that a position should not be accepted, even if good reasons are offered, simply because the speaker does not follow his or her own advice and the speaker's actions suggest hypocrisy?

6. What fallacy occurs when someone is discredited solely on the grounds of a characteristic like race, age, or gender?

7. What fallacy occurs when someone tries to bribe another person?

8. What fallacy occurs when someone argues for a position based solely on the basis of patriotism?

9. What fallacy occurs when someone is being discredited because of a political, religious, or social affiliation?

10. What fallacy occurs when an argument rests on the irrelevant testimony of a famous person, like a movie star or athlete?

Key Fallacies of Presumption

People make unwarranted assumptions all the time. Some of the major ways this occurs have been categorized and named, as we will see. What makes fallacies of presumption unsound arguments is that they contain an unstated assumption that causes the argument to sink. For example, what if your friend assumed that having her lucky stone in her pocket was the cause of her passing her physics final? Her success was more likely due to the fact she came prepared.

See if you can spot any shady reasoning in this conversation:

KEN: Hey! What's happening? Are you coming to the rally with me? Either you're with us or you're against us!

BERNIE: I'm with you, Ken; you know that! Have you always been a dupe?

KEN: Watch it there pal. Things have been going good for me lately. How about you? Wait, what is that I see? What's that hundred-dollar bill sticking out of your pocket?

BERNIE: Oh, Ken, you have an interesting T-shirt on. I like the idea of Tweetie Bird chasing Godzilla! What a hoot! Where do you find such things?

Did you notice all the unwarranted assumptions? In the first case, Ken sets up a false "either . . . or" choice. In the second case, Bernie asks Ken a loaded question, where he cannot answer either yes or no without implicating himself. In the third case, when Ken asks about the $100 bill, Bernie switches the topic, trying not to be caught red-handed. An unwarranted assumption leads to an incorrect conclusion being drawn.

These fallacies are like magic tricks: So long as we do not stop to think about the arguments, they look good. But they are never to be trusted. In each case, the unwarranted assumption, once uncovered, reveals how weak the argument is.

There are 12 key fallacies of presumption that we will look at below.

Accident

The fallacy of **accident** occurs when a general rule or principle is applied to a special case to which, by reason of its special or atypical characteristics, the rule simply does not apply. This fallacy might be a misapplication of a moral principle, a rule from work, or a general pronouncement made by a family member or friend.

The unwarranted assumption is that the rule applies to all cases, without exception. But most rules and principles simply fail to apply across the board. Thus, applying the rule to the exceptional or atypical case is unwarranted.

Examples of Accident

The Bible says, "Thou shalt not kill," so it is wrong to kill in self-defense.

Step 3 of the Eightfold Path of Buddhism is Right Speech. Right Speech means one must speak only truth. Therefore, I should tell my Uncle Bob he has stomach cancer.

"Be sure to return what you borrow"—that's what my father said. As a result, I should return the axe I borrowed from my roommate, even though she's been threatening the UPS deliveryman.

In each of the examples the general rule does not apply. We do consider some killing to be acceptable, including self-defense. Ordinarily, we do believe in honesty, but not without exception. And we would not likely want to return an axe to a murderous roommate. We need to watch for unwarranted assumptions in applying rules and principles. Otherwise, we may commit the fallacy of accident.

Hasty Generalization

Hasty generalization occurs when a generalization or moral principle is drawn on the basis of too small a sample or an atypical case. Stereotypes and other poor inferences have been drawn about entire groups of people on the basis of either too little information or a nonrepresentative group. Hasty generalization often occurs because the sample size is too small. Therefore, the inference drawn is an incorrect generalization. Even the FBI has fallen victim to this fallacy—for example, in the case of Oregon lawyer Brandon Mayfield. Mayfield was held for two weeks and accused of being the Madrid bomber because of a partial fingerprint match that was read off a photocopy. The error resulted in a rare public apology from the bureau.

Examples of Hasty Generalization

Inez Garcia ran through five red lights taking her sick baby to the hospital last night. Therefore, we should all be able to run red lights whenever we want.

Maya went out the other night and ate at the new Austrian Meatball Grotto down in the Village. She said the meatballs were mushy and the sauce was too salty. That just goes to show you—never, I mean, NEVER, eat at an Austrian restaurant. Those Austrians should stick to making clocks!

Physical therapy grad student–researchers proposed a study of pilates using a sample of fifteen women 20 to 50 years old. They found quite a disparity in the results. Therefore, physical therapists nationally should make a few adjustments in their treatment of women in this age group.

Here we see the two different types of hasty generalization. In the first one, the generalization is based on a special case (an exception). In the other cases, the conclusion rests on a sample that is too small—hardly a convincing study.

Biased Statistics

The fallacy of **biased statistics** occurs when an inference is drawn on the basis of a sample that is not diverse enough. That is, the sample is not representative of the target population. We see this in studies that lack the diversity found in the population in question—so the sample excludes a certain age group, gender, ethnic group, and so on—and yet draw a generalization to a population that includes the omitted group(s). The issue here is diversity, not size. For example, it is reported that women are statistically much more likely to go blind than men (www.socyberty.com). Therefore, a sample study that did not balance male versus female participants could lead to biased statistics.

Examples of Biased Statistics

Cyber Digital did a study of teenage boys in Detroit and found that 45% of them like computer games. Therefore, 45% of all Americans like computer games.
95% of toddlers prefer a bottle of warm milk at bedtime. Therefore, 95% of all children prefer a bottle of warm milk at bedtime.
A poll of KTBT FM found that 67% of community college students commute at least 10 miles from home. Therefore, 67% of all students have a commute of at least 10 miles from home.

In all of these cases, there is a shift from the sample population to the target population. That is the way to spot a case of biased statistics. Compare the sample group (teenage boys, toddlers, community college students) to the targeted population (Americans, children, students) to determine if it is sufficiently representative.

It is not a question of size, as with hasty generalization. Here the issue is *diversity*. When it comes to sample studies, there are key factors to consider, such as race or ethnicity, class, gender, age, educational level, geography, and religion. Depending on the focus of the study, some factors may be more instrumental than others in allowing inferences to the targeted group.

Bifurcation (False Dichotomy or Excluded Middle)

The fallacy of **bifurcation,** often called a *false dichotomy,* involves reducing a choice to only two options when, in fact, more options exist. This can be expressed as an "either/or," an "if/then" or an "only if" claim. Here are a few examples: "If You Vote for Hillary You're Racist" and "If You Vote for Obama You're Sexist" (www .sayanthingblog.com), and "Only if you eat a raw-vegetable diet can you be healthy." Shrinking the field to only two choices when others exist creates the fallacy.

Assuming there are other options than the two presented, a better choice may have been left out. We can't give "informed consent" if we don't know the options.

You Tell Me Department

Message from Beyond the Grave?

Advertisement for a free booklet said to be on nutritional research:

Read this or die

Nutritional Research on Heart Disease, High Blood Pressure, Elevated Cholesterol, Diabetes, Stroke and Congestive Heart Failure. Call for FREE Booklet 1 800 600 3099

You tell me: Does this ad contain a fallacy?

Let's look at bifurcation with polar extremes. Consider this case: "These events [9/11] have divided the whole world into two sides: the side of the believers and the side of the infidels" (CNN, 7 Oct 2001 quoting Osama bin Laden).

Here's another case: Linguist and social commentator Noam Chomsky said to delegates at an antiglobalism conference: "Either we will have a world without wars, or we will not have a world" (as noted by Tom Gibb, "Forum Protesters Look to Ending War," *BBC News*, www.bbc.com, 1 Feb 2002). To avoid the fallacy, we would have to make several key assumptions (e.g., that all wars have the destructive power of a nuclear war).

Examples of Bifurcation

Sean "P. Diddy" Combs's T-shirt reads "Vote or Die."

"There is a great temperamental and ideological divide between those who believe in self-defense and those who believe in surrendering and begging for mercy" (Dr. William L. Pierce).

You can go approach life with gusto. Or you can sit on your plaid couch and let life pass you by. The choice is yours.

Comedian Rob Corddry on *The Daily Show* challenged the first example, saying it was "Vote *and* die." We also see fallacies in movies. Here's an example: "There are two types of spurs: Those who come in by the door, and those who come in by the window" (Tuco Benedicto Juan Ramirez, *aka* "the Rat" from *The Good, the Bad, and the Ugly*).

Not all either/or dilemmas are fallacious. For instance, either you are pregnant or you are not. Either you have a heartbeat or you do not (assuming you haven't had an artificial heart transplant!). Either you are allergic to peanuts or you're not. Do not assume that someone who says "It's either this or that" is right, however. Check for other options. Furthermore, not all bifurcation presents polar extremes. For instance, an HMO may limit the options to two that are the least expensive, or the least risky, procedures.

Complex Question (Trick or "Loaded" Question)

The fallacy of **complex question** takes the form of a question in which two questions are rolled into one. It is impossible to answer the question without, at the same time, answering a hidden, unasked question—or affirming an assumption being made. It is often called a *loaded* question.

Remember that scene in *My Cousin Vinny* involving a trick question? Mona Lisa Vito (Marisa Tomei's character) is questioned by the prosecutor about her knowledge of auto mechanics. He asks what the ignition timing should be on a 1955 Chevy model 325. Mona Lisa responds: "A trick question! Chevy didn't make a 325 in 1955!" She goes on to point out the correct ignition timing for the 1964 model—when the 325 first came out. Not everyone is as quick as Mona Lisa to catch a trick question in action! So we need to be on the lookout.

In a February 2005 press conference with President Bush, Jeff Gannon, who passed himself off as a reporter, asked a complex—or "loaded"—question. After falsely attributing quotes to Democratic leaders, Gannon asked, "How are you going to work with people who seem to have divorced themselves from reality?" (see Suzanne Goldenberg, "Fake Reporter Unmasked at White House," *The Guardian*, 11 Feb 2005).

Logician Morris Engel asserts that complex question is a form of begging the question set in the form of an interrogative. The question itself assumes what it is trying to prove by couching the answer in the unasked question.

Examples of Complex Question

Do you usually eat junk food for breakfast?
Did you strangle Mr. Schultz before or after you took your children to the zoo?
Have you always been a liar and cheat?
Why did you cheat on the final exam?

With these, we have two questions, not one. Separate the two and examine them. For instance, we might ask if our friends usually eat chocolate before asking whether they eat junk food. At times, the use of complex, incriminating questions represents an attempt to trap the listener (like an ambush). Legislative bodies try to address complex questions by moving to "divide the question." The question is then divided into two questions, removing the unwarranted assumption.

Robert's Rules of Order Revised recommends the following guidelines for deciding whether to "divide the question." Section 6 of R. R. Rule 16 reads as follows: "On the demand of any member, before the question is put, a question shall be divided if it includes propositions so distinct in substance that one being taken away a substantive proposition shall remain" (www.bartleby.com).

Post Hoc (or Post Hoc Ergo Propter Hoc—"After This Therefore Because of This")

The **post hoc** fallacy asserts a causal connection that rests on something happening earlier in time. The fallacy goes like this: Because something precedes something else means that it must then *cause* the later thing to happen. But no evidence is given to support such a causal link. Any connection might be coincidental. It would be

You Tell Me Department

Did Red Socks Help the Red Sox?

It seems like superstition knows no bounds when it comes to sports. D. Allen Kerr tells this story:

> Former Sox hitter extraordinaire Wade Boggs used to get up at the same time every morning and eat chicken before every game. Prior to each night game he entered the batting cage right at 5:30 P.M. to take his practice swings, and he ran wind sprints at exactly 7:17 P.M. . . . He also wrote the Hebrew word chai (life) in the dirt just before stepping into the batter's box before each at-bat.
>
> Such quirks aren't limited to the playing field; folks in the bleachers and at home are almost as superstitious as the players. . . . This past Tuesday I headed out to pick up my kids in Newmarket and take them out to dinner. . . . On the way there I was listening to the Sox–Yankees game on the radio, the final game of the series at Fenway Park, when the Yanks suddenly scored three quick runs in succession in the second inning. "What the hell's going on?" I thought. Then, horrified, I realized I wasn't wearing my lucky ballcap. . . .
>
> After the Sox tied up their playoff series with the Oakland A's two weekends ago, I realized I had worn this hat while watching both Boston victories on TV. When I headed out to watch the deciding game of that series. . . . I made sure to wear it again. Sure enough, the Sox won the game and the series. So naturally, after realizing on Tuesday I had left this sacred artifact behind, I drove around the Portsmouth traffic circle in a panic, sped back home, dashed up the stairs to grab it and began my trip anew. But alas, it was too late—the baseball gods had witnessed my blasphemy and the Sox fell to the hated Yankees. ("Superstitions Curse Red Sox Fans Too," *Portsmouth Herald*, www .seacoastonline.com, 18 Oct 2003)

You tell me: Is there any harm done in thinking lucky socks or caps will bring luck? Does such post hoc reasoning have negative consequences for our thinking processes?

---

unwarranted to assume a causal connection. For example, "Matt" on the *Atheist News* blog argues that this is a post hoc fallacy: "With all these natural disasters happening how can you deny that god isn't punishing us?" (31 Aug 2007). In his view, it is fallacious to assume a causal connection between natural disasters (or natural wonders, for that matter) and God's punishing or rewarding humans.

Examples of Post Hoc

Whenever the Tigers are on a winning streak, Coach Sanders wears the same tie to each game. The Tigers won the last three games, so Coach Sanders's lucky tie must be working!

Alma's diet sure was amazing. She took OPS diet tablets every morning and then had a cup of coffee and a grapefruit for breakfast, a head of lettuce for lunch (no dressing!), and cottage cheese for dinner. In two weeks, she lost 12 pounds! Those OPS diet tabs really work miracles.

Paul had bacon, eggs, and pancakes for breakfast. Then he took the SAT. He scored in the top 20%. I am so proud of him. That just goes to show you: A good, hearty breakfast was the reason he did so well.

In these cases, the prior event is considered the cause simply because it happened earlier in time.

We also see post hoc arguments when people base their reasoning on "bad omens" or attribute success to a lucky charm or a ritual. Examine arguments carefully, watching for assumptions and omissions.

Exercises

Directions: Name the fallacy of presumption below. Draw from these choices: accident, hasty generalization, biased statistics, bifurcation, complex question, and post hoc.

1. What tool did you use to pry open the window of the lab?

2. A poll was taken of 2,000 owners of luxury cars. Of these, 82% said that the economy is doing just great and they will have an easy time when they retire. Consequently, 82% of all citizens think the economy is doing just great and they'll have an easy retirement.

3. The Bureau of Fish and Game released nine California condors into the wild. The next week the rain started coming down in buckets! That just goes to show you, the American Indians were right—the condor really *is* a bearer of rain. Those birds caused all this flooding!

4. At a conference on animal rights, two panelists said animal experimentation violates the rights of sentient beings. We can conclude that philosophers in general oppose animal experimentation because of the rights of sentient beings.

5. People should always stand up for their beliefs. Therefore, it's commendable that young people in Turkey are dying from hunger strikes to protest the conditions of Turkish prisons.

6. If we don't require a writing exit exam for college students, we might as well kiss off all our standards for a quality education.

7. Donna dated a law student she met in Ann Arbor. They went to see *Rocky Horror* and he fell asleep! That goes to show you—if you're dating a law student, you should forget about late-night movies.

8. Basically, you've got two choices: Join the Army or work on the farm until you can save money for college.

9. A poll taken of women athletes found that 68% think it's time for Americans to go on a low-carb diet. Therefore, it's clear that most Americans think it's time to knock off some weight.

10. Where did you hide the money you stole from Dr. Pettisnoot's office?

11. The policy of the Alaska Moose Bed and Breakfast is that guests must take off their shoes before entering. That means your 90-year-old grandmother better not try to sneak in with those dusty walking shoes of hers on her feet. A rule's a rule.

12. Either we should relocate the toxic waste dump to southern Nevada or we'll have to convince the taxpayers that we need a satellite station to send hazardous substances to outer space.

13. Have you always been a wild man?

14. This much is true—if you don't love hush puppies, you're not a genuine Southerner!

15. In a TV poll of 785 men in South Carolina, it was discovered that they prefer peach cobbler to hot fudge sundaes for dessert. Therefore, gals, the truth is what it is: If you want to find a way to a man's heart via his stomach, forget about a hot fudge sundae—make him a peach cobbler.

16. Have you always been so dull-witted when it comes to mathematical equations?

17. Maria came into a nice sum of money lately, if you can believe that! You know, I think it's because she's been using Feng Shui, putting her apartment in spiritual order. She put a large pile of coins in the north corner of her living room. They say that's supposed to help bring good energy to your work life. It sure must have worked! I think you should try Feng Shui, too. Maybe you can improve your finances.

18. Only if you believe money paves the road to happiness, will you be sufficiently motivated to change the world.

19. Do you realize 97% of the 240 participants at the Episcopalians' conference in Ottawa, Canada, said that prayer could bring about world peace? That suggests that 97% of adults think we can bring about world peace with prayer.

20. Kant was right to put honesty at the center of his moral theory. That means you are obligated to tell that phone solicitor your Social Security number and the list of people to whom you are financially indebted.

More Fallacies of Presumption

Red Herring

The fallacy called **red herring** occurs when an irrelevant line of reasoning is intentionally used to divert people away from the topic at hand. We see this when someone purposely shifts the subject of the conversation to avoid an incriminating line of questioning or to deceive someone. This is a form of "weaseling"—trying to escape rather than get trapped by the direction the conversation is headed. It's called a red herring because a stinking little herring (fish) is an effective way to lead hound dogs off the scent.

Examples of Red Herring

DR. GREEN: Excuse me, Jason, what are you doing text-messaging during the exam?

JASON: Oh, Dr. Green, I heard that you were invited to be program chair for the American Association of Philosophy Teachers conference. What an honor, to have your great teaching style recognized.

AMY: Honey, why is there a receipt for a Power Mac here in your pocket?

MIKE: Oh sugar, my sweet pea, you have made the most delicious pot roast I ever ate in my life—what ingredients did you put into this heavenly gravy? And how did you make such tender green beans to accompany this feast?

JOURNALIST: Governor Juarez, what do you have to say to the American people about the rising unemployment in this state?

GOVERNOR: You know, we must think positive: During my term in office, inflation has stayed constant, and I have helped keep drugs off the streets!

Most of us have seen red herring fallacies. People often jump around topics: Some families regularly communicate by going from one topic to the next and back to the first. But what marks a red herring is that the change of topic or a distraction is intended to deceive and divert attention from one thing to another. Red herrings are commonly used in mysteries to lead the viewers off the scent. In some cases, the red herring is even spelled out—as we saw in the movie *Sixth Sense*. As observed on TV Tropes,

> a red herring is a good red herring when it interweaves itself into the story's events. For example, the murder victim may have been a philanderer. His wife has no alibi. Aha! It's the wife! The wife's lack of an alibi is a red herring. It turns out [that] the deceased husband's philandering *is* what got him killed, as it turns out, by his girlfriend's jealous husband. ("Red Herring," www.tvtropes.org)

Slippery Slope

The **slippery slope** fallacy involves cause-and-effect reasoning that fails to establish the links. Someone posits a causal chain by arguing that if we allow *this* to happen, a series of other things will come about. The problem is that the causal connection is not established—there is at least one weak link in the chain.

The slippery slope fallacy can take the form of a downward spiral. The argument is that a negative chain of events will follow from something being put into effect. There is no attempt to prove these are causally related. Rather, the connection is incorrectly assumed—not proven.

Many have been victims of parental slippery slopes. This occurs, for instance, when your parents say you can't stay out late because something bad will happen and that, in turn, will lead to something even worse, and that worse thing will lead to something truly horrific.

Be aware: Not all propositions that involve causal chains are slippery slopes. If it is demonstrated that situation A will lead to situation B and so on, it does *not*

You Tell Me Department

Can You Spot the Slippery Slope?

In a speech on gun control, William L. Pierce argued as follows:

> The present campaign to disarm Americans will not abate. . . . The target now is semiautomatic rifles. Later it will be all semiautomatic pistols. Then it will be other types of handguns. After that it will be all firearms which hold more than three cartridges. "That's all a sportsman really needs," they'll say.

Then it will be all firearms except muzzle-loaders. Somewhere along the line, various types of ammunition will be banned. "Only a criminal would want a cartridge like this," they'll say. Before too many steps have been taken there will be compulsory registration of all firearms and firearm owners, in order to facilitate confiscation later.

You tell me: Can you spot the slippery slope fallacy in Pierce's argument?

involve the slippery slope fallacy. The fallacy occurs when the chain is asserted, but not proven.

An example of the slippery slope fallacy is found in a full-page ad put out by R. J. Reynolds Tobacco Company that presents a series of questions: "Some politicians want to ban cigarettes. Will alcohol be next? Will caffeine be next? Will high-fat foods be next? Today it's cigarettes. Tomorrow?" The fallacy is in presuming that banning tobacco would necessarily lead to bans on other substances. The connection should not be assumed.

Examples of Slippery Slope

I tell you, Matt, if we support the legalization of marijuana, next thing it will be the legalization of cocaine and then heroin, and pretty soon the whole society will be on hard drugs. So don't support legalizing marijuana.

DR. TAN: The college should have strict rules against cheating on exams. I'm going to take this up at the next faculty assembly.

YOLANDA: I really disagree with you, Dr. Tan. If you punish students for cheating and buying papers, next thing they'll be punished for misquotes or even spelling errors and typos. That just isn't fair. Education should not be punitive. I hope you won't push for any university policy on academic dishonesty.

My son tells me he would like to get a few rabbits as pets. But I will not allow it. If we start with a few rabbits, soon we will have a dozen everywhere, and all our money will be spent on rabbit feed. Then he will want to get other animals, too. I am not going to sacrifice my life savings to run a zoo.

Straw Man

The **straw man** fallacy involves unfairly diminishing or distorting the opposition so one can stand out in comparison. The comparison attempts to denigrate the opponent's position and suggests that the audience would be crazy not to

The Global Dimension

Britain Debates the Value of Spanking

Should the spanking of children be banned? This was being debated in England, and Brendan O'Neill argues that slippery slope reasoning was behind it. Here's the argument:

> The government is under pressure from a powerful antispanking lobby to outlaw all forms of physical punishment. Some in the antispanking lobby argue that, unless all forms of physical punishment are outlawed, the "minor tap" can easily become a "harsh strike," or something much worse. Lady Walmsley has said that all child deaths by violence "start with a smack."

But this is a slippery-slope argument, and a deeply offensive one at that. The implication is that parents who start out spanking their kids might end up murdering them. Many in the antispanking lobby blur the distinction between spanking and assault. There is an assumption that parents who spank are murderers in the making. (Brendan O'Neill, "Britain Debates: To Spank or Not to Spank," *Christian Science Monitor*, www.csmonitor.com, 19 Apr 2004)

Answer the following: Do you think O'Neill is right to label the reasoning a slippery slope fallacy?

---

select the contrasting view! It can take one of two different forms: (1) when an opponent's position is presented as so weak or extreme that it's indefensible, or (2) when an attack is made on the weakest of a variety of arguments to contrast with one's own, seemingly more defensible, position.

In the first case, when the opponent's view is presented as indefensible or hopelessly weak, we are then steered toward another, more moderate or appealing position. This is accomplished by distorting the other's view, turning it into an extreme. The image of the "straw man" (scarecrow) is of something so flimsy that it will go up in smoke if we put a match near it. In the second case, a person attempts to boost their own standing by casting doubt on the weakest of a set of arguments.

We saw the straw man fallacy in the 1994 California election when Tom Umberg, the Democratic candidate for attorney general, attacked Dan Lundgren, the Republican incumbent. He suggested that Polly Klaas, 12 years old, would not have been kidnapped and murdered if Lundgren had financed a computer tracking system for convicts. A similar attack was made on Michael Dukakis in the 1988 presidential campaign for paroling a felon, Willie Horton, who subsequently attacked again. This incident led to a later apology by Lee Atwater, campaign manager for the first President Bush.

Examples of Straw Man

Don't even think about his position. Opposing the death penalty means letting criminals walk away from crimes scot-free and giving them the green light to murder anyone they choose!

Students these days object to being searched for drugs. We must realize, however, that if we don't search them, then they will be peddling drugs at school, and drug abuse will be rampant.

Those animal rights people make me sick. If they get their way, medical advances in this country will come to a grinding halt.

With the straw man fallacy, the opposition is painted as much more extreme than it actually is. What usually happens is that the speaker's own position is offered as the preferred, reasonable alternative.

Group or Individual Exercise

Directions: Look for examples of straw man in political campaigns. Try to find as many examples of this fallacy as you can. Look at both the campaign advertising *and* the remarks of the two contenders about their opponents' views or policies.

Begging the Question (Petitio Principii)

Begging the question is a fallacy consisting of circular reasoning: This happens when someone assumes what they're trying to prove. The conclusion merely reaffirms what has already been said. For example, the speaker might reword one of the premises or use a synonym for one of the terms.

Examples of Begging the Question

People should get paid for studying for logic exams, because human beings deserve a salary for studying logic. [getting paid = getting a salary]

The belief in God is universal because everybody believes in God [universal belief = a belief everyone accepts]

The opponents of animal experimentation who are breaking into the facilities of biotech firms creating transgenic animals are justified in destroying the barns of the hybrid pigs because they have the right to tear down housing for such animals. [justified in destroying the barns = the right to tear down housing]

Don't assume what you are trying to prove. What is concluded must come out of the premises and not be a restatement of them. The evidence must provide good reasons for drawing the conclusion. If the premises and conclusion say basically the same thing, we're facing a fallacy of begging the question.

Question-Begging Epithets.   One variation of begging the question uses highly slanted language. Here, biased language stacks the deck. **Question-begging epithets** are either *eulogisms* (deck stacked by praise) or *dyslogisms* (name-calling). The result is bias expressed in either very positive or very negative terms. (See Chapter 11 on language.)

One variation of eulogisms involves **bloated claims.** Here we find exaggeration, grandiose promises, or predictions that are more pie-in-the-sky than likely. Think of those magazine covers announcing "The Sexiest Man in the World" or "The Most Beautiful Woman Alive."

In addition, we often see eulogistic or dyslogistic advertising and political campaigns, as well as those "too good to be true" offers in personal life. An example is an ad for Maybelline's Wonder Finish™ powder-finish foundation: "New Wonder Finish™ clean powder—finish foundation now liquid-perfect coverage and a weightless powder finish in one incredible makeup! Just one step. Zero flaws. Instant wow!"

Claims that are loaded in the negative (dyslogisms) are equally problematic. Suppose you called a man a "leech on society" instead of "someone down on his luck." Your listeners could be so swayed by the negative label ("leech on society") that they unfairly and incorrectly infer that the "leech" is guilty of a crime.

Examples of Question-Begging Epithets (Eulogisms)

You should listen to our legislators' comments about patriotism because they are hard-working American citizens, with an appreciation of the greatness of this country's history.

Mrs. Faridian definitely has good advice on tax reform since she is a veteran of the first Iraq war and drives the Meals on Wheels bus.

Examples of Question-Begging Epithets (Dyslogisms/Name-Calling)

Don't believe what those street thugs say about philosophy students—they are just a bunch of mealy-mouthed, pea-brained hustlers with no sense of the demands of the intellectual life.

Professor Stoll's ideas for rebuilding the downtown core seem off-base—he's a complete moron and a lush. He's too slimy for words!

The language used in the argument has either a negative or positive bias (that is why it is called "loaded"). This prejudicial slanting makes it hard to be objective in examining the evidence and suggests a relevance that doesn't exist.

Misleading Vividness

One of the fallacies connected with statistics and sample studies is the fallacy of **misleading vividness.** This fallacy occurs when strong evidence is completely overlooked because of a striking (vivid) counterexample. What causes the fallacy is that the counterexample is atypical and of little real significance next to the overwhelming statistical data or evidence that have been obtained. However, the personal anecdote or testimonial can be very persuasive.

Examples of Misleading Vividness

TINA: The American Heart Association recommends that we eat Omega-3 fatty acids and fish oil to be healthy. Check it out on their website—it's really helpful!

PINKY: Yeah? Well, my best friend, Darin, got plenty of fish oil eating salmon all the time—and he ended up with mercury in his system—and I bet it was from all that salmon! Forget those fish oils! Go for steak!

TINA: Well now I certainly won't even consider taking them. Let's go for the red meat!

CAMILLE: Given the high rates of emphysema and lung cancer among smokers, it seems pretty obvious that smoking is the root cause.

NAJI: Really? Uncle John smoked like a chimney, and he lived to 93 years of age and died of a gangrenous foot. That shows you that all those statistics mean nothing and you should smoke if you want to.

False Analogy (or Imperfect Analogy)

The fallacy of **false analogy** occurs when a comparison is drawn between two different things but there are few relevant similarities between them, thus creating the false analogy. When there are only trivial similarities, the false analogy sinks the argument. *Be careful:* There are usually *some* similarities between one thing and another, so you could think of this as an imperfect or very weak analogy rather than completely false. (See Chapter 6 on analogies for a fuller discussion.) The key here is that the similarities are minor or inconsequential—and they are significantly outmatched by the differences.

Examples of False Analogy

A good woman is just like a nice car: She is under your control and makes your life a lot easier.

A good man is like a bowl of buttered popcorn: He is comforting and doesn't talk back.

Babies are like cats: They love to sleep in the sun and don't obey orders.

From W. H. Werkmeister: "Education cannot prepare men and women for marriage. To try to educate them for marriage is like trying to teach them to swim without letting them go into the water. It cannot be done."

In the first false analogy, the "similarities" cited are trivial at best. A woman is not an object and, unless she is brainwashed, is not controlled by anyone. The second and third analogies also have only minor similarities, but the differences are significant. The last analogy sinks. Sure, people learn to swim by going in the water, as Werkmeister notes—but in marriage much depends on understanding the social, personal, and economic problems to be faced. This does not require a trial marriage. If there are no real similarities (or only trivial ones) and substantial dissimilarities, then it is a false analogy.

You Tell Me Department

When Is a Lemon like a Cat?

In an article on lemons, David Karp used an unusual analogy. He said:

> The most astonishing lemon variant, known to just a few people, is a Eureka mutant with orange skin and flesh. . . . The fruit is sort of like a cat that barks: it tastes like a lemon but has the color of an orange. (David Karp, "Lemons, Yes, but Please! Don't Squeeze," *The New York Times*, 5 Feb 2005)

You tell me: Is this a false analogy?

Exercises

Part One

Directions: Name the fallacy, drawing from *all* the fallacies of presumption.

1. Advertisement: "Only those who have seen a moose can claim to know the wilderness. Visit Alaska today!"

2. Do you always steal from your friends?

3. Most people prefer pasta to rice. A Fall 2008 poll of teachers at the Italian Educators Conference in Cincinnati, Ohio, found that nearly 87% considered pasta superior to rice for most cooking needs. Therefore, pasta, not rice, is the true alternative to bread!

4. The Constitution guarantees freedom of speech. Therefore, people should have the freedom to post pornography on high school websites.

5. Before the movie started, a message appeared asking the audience not to talk during the movie. Therefore, I'll have to wait until the credits roll to tell the woman in front of me that she put her pretty suede purse in a pool of spilled soda.

6. All you fine citizens of Philadelphia know this one truth: You must choose between security and freedom. Though you may be inclined toward freedom, don't forsake your security by outlawing assault rifles.

7. The college has a no-alcohol policy. Therefore, you probably won't be allowed to bring your rum-ball candies to the dance after the Super Bowl.

8. Birgit was on her way to discuss her new film script with her agent when a meteorite shower pelted her car with marble-sized rocks. The agent loved her script, so that meteorite shower must have been a sign of good fortune.

9. Assemblywoman Snyder said the journalist who photographed her throwing popcorn in the polar bear compound at the zoo is just a pathetic little mealybug with nothing better to do than to cause trouble for respected politicians.

10. CHONG: I deserve an A, Professor Waters.
    DR. WATERS: I'm not sure why you say this, Chong. Clue me in.
    CHONG: My work warrants the highest grade a student can get, that's why.

11. My grandma said to never tell a lie. That means I should tell the new high school principal that she needs to go on a diet. That woman has a serious weight problem—I'm going to give her a few ideas on how to knock off some of that flab of hers!

12. *Consumer Reports* said less fancy stoves have a better repair record than those new, expensive gourmet stoves with all the doodads. But I'm not sure I should listen to them, since Amanda and Dan got a new stove that wasn't high-end—and they had all kinds of problems. Maybe the expensive ones are better after all.

13. "You're a scaremonger," journalist John Stossel scolded genetic engineering critic Jeremy Rifkin. "Why should we listen to you?" (See *Fairness and Accuracy in Reporting*.)

14. Christina, if you keep drinking orange juice for breakfast, you'll get too much acid in your system. Too much acid means an ulcer can't be far behind, and next thing you know, you've destroyed your stomach lining! You'd be advised to cut back on that orange juice you've been guzzling.

15. Where did you hide the money, Janet?

16. We ought to oppose gun control. Gun control means a police state is around the corner.

17. If you don't like fried chicken and popovers, you won't want to live in Kentucky.

18. ALEX: The new X-7 turbo speedster is the most reliable three-wheel vehicle on the road. It outperformed all other three-wheelers in every single test that *Power Wheel* magazine ran! You really ought to get rid of that jalopy of yours and get an X-7, Pinky.
    PINKY: You've got to be kidding. Did you hear about Bruce's experience with the X-7? The electrical system caught fire the second week he had it—and then he never seemed to get the brakes to work well around the curve. He finally slid off the road into a cow pasture and that was that!

19. Your marriage, Gracie, is like a car with a bad transmission system—sure, it keeps going, but the price is awfully high, and you aren't really enjoying the trip!

20. It's obvious that men overwhelmingly prefer naps to exercise because, according to an August 2008 poll, 93% of male patients at nursing homes said they'd much rather nap than exercise.

21. Alma Warner has been concerned about the increasing number of abortions in this country. Be careful about voting for her for governor. A vote for her is a vote for the mentality of those who bomb abortion clinics!

22. Ticket agent to a 93-year-old woman: "I'm sorry that you were born before Social Security cards—without that or a driver's license, you won't be allowed on the plane! Too bad you stopped driving 25 years ago. A rule is a rule."

23. North Korea is thinking of building up its nuclear arsenal because they believe they need more high-tech weapons that have a nuclear capacity.

24. For the kickoff dinner for the Pre-Law Club, they served moussaka from the Greek restaurant that recently opened in Silver Lake. It was awful: It was too salty, the eggplant tasted like rubber, and there was hardly any meat in it. It just goes to show you, you can't depend on Greek food if you want a nice dinner.

25. Timothy Peppersnout couldn't possibly be guilty of financial wrongdoing. You know how nice he is to the people in his neighborhood, and he regularly gives money to charity.

26. Dr. Meek said not to respond to crying when you put the baby to bed. If you start checking every time the baby wails, then it will have the upper hand, and next thing you know, your child will become overly dependent.

27. Leonard Watkins would be good as mayor since he'd be great as the top city official.

28. PROFESSOR: Pardon me, Reinaldo. What are these test notes doing here in the exam?

    REINALDO: Oh, Professor Taheri, did I ever tell you how much I like your ties? You manage to find such colorful ones! Where do you shop?

29. If you let the little girl have a stick of gum, then she'll want gum every day, and pretty soon she'll start swallowing it. Once she starts swallowing gum, her intestines will get all clogged up, and she will have dreadful health problems. Don't give that child chewing gum.

30. Only if you have heard Pablo Neruda's poetry read in Spanish can you call yourself worldly.

31. Silvio says he loves me, and he must be telling the truth, because he would never lie to someone he loves.

32. Love is like riding on the luge—sure, someone's steering, but you're going much too fast to avoid problems, and disaster looms around every corner!

Part Two

1. Discuss whether Senator Orrin Hatch committed a fallacy (state your reasons why or why not) in the segment below:

   Raising the minimum wage causes "disemployment":
   [Some people] believe that an increase in the minimum wage is a quick, painless way to help the disadvantaged in our society. I can only wonder then why they have not offered raising the minimum wage to $15, $20, or $30 an hour. There is indeed an adverse effect on employment. For every 10% increase in the minimum wage, the

disemployment effect was between 100,000 to 300,000 jobs. Disemployment means not only jobs eliminated, but also jobs that are never created in the first place. (See Senator Orrin Hatch, www.issues2000.org.)

2. Discuss Richard Doerflinger's comment about experiments to clone human embryos:

"They're really raising the stakes here," said Richard Doerflinger of the National Conference of Catholic Bishops, which opposes federal support for any kind of embryo research. "In two days, it's amazing we've had two announcements of drops down the slippery slope. We don't think there's a stopping point once you start down this road." (Rick Weiss, "Firm Aims to Clone Embryos for Stem Cells," *Washington Post*, 12 Jul 2001)

3. Discuss the reasoning in the argument by then–Vice President Henry A. Wallace Jul 1943:

"We will not be satisfied with a peace which will merely lead us from the concentration camps and mass-murder of Fascism—into an international jungle of gangster governments operated behind the scenes by power-crazed, money-mad imperialists." (Quoted in W. H. Werkmeister, *Critical Thinking*, Johnson Publishing, 1948)

4. Can you spot the fallacies in the following?

GEORGE: Hey Julio, what's up?

JULIO: Either you've got a potato for a head or you've heard the news, George! I got a part in the new film *Temple Impossible!* You know, it's starring I.C. of the band The Blind Mice! I.C. says guys who lift weights are more likely to succeed, so I just bought a membership at Joe's Gym! You should join, too, you know! If you don't build up your biceps, girls won't find you attractive, and then you'll just be sitting around picking the dust mites out of your ears every evening! Join that gym today.

GEORGE: Have you always had menudo for brains? I joined a gym last November, you pie-head! If you don't pay more attention to what's going on in my life, I'll let the air out of your tires and we'll see how far you can drive in that new Mazda of yours! If you want to be with it, man, you'd not just join a gym, but consider taking steroids to pump up those muscles a little faster. Randy Smutts, who is trying out for the Olympics, used steroids for years! He's a monster!

JULIO: You know, that's not a bad idea, but I wouldn't listen to what Randy says. You know he's a member of the Harley Bikers Club. Plus, you know he's German—that's where Nazis came from! What a loser!

GEORGE: My mama said to never tell a lie. So I have to tell you, Julio, your new toupee looks like a possum! You really ought to just go for the glow. Forget the toupee—either you live free or you die!

JULIO: You know, my pint-sized friend, I heard two chicks on the subway say they prefer possum-heads to bald eagles! That just goes to show you, women like hairy men!

GEORGE: Don't sound like that sleazy dude I saw on TV the other night who was discussing the psychology of baldness—he couldn't tie his shoelaces if you paid him. I take it you think you need hair to be all-American. Abraham Lincoln had a beard, so why don't you?

JULIO: Yeah, I should have gotten Employee of the Year. I deserve it. Not only did I spend my life savings on lottery tickets, but that cousin of mine took my pet iguana and sold it at the flea market in Tijuana!

GEORGE: Poor you. Well, gotta go, man. Catch you.

JULIO: Later to you too! Adios.

Quick Quiz

1. What is hasty generalization?
2. What happens in a post hoc fallacy?
3. Explain the fallacy of accident.
4. What happens in a red herring?
5. Explain why the slippery slope is aptly named.
6. How does hasty generalization differ from biased statistics?
7. What's an example of a complex question?
8. Why is bifurcation a fallacy?
9. Explain how we can spot question-begging epithets.
10. What makes a fallacy a straw man?
11. How does the fallacy of misleading vividness differ from hasty generalization?
12. What is the key thing to spot in a false or imperfect analogy?

Key Fallacies of Ambiguity

You pick up a magazine and read, "Prince Philip underwent surgery in a London hospital for a hernia. After being discharged, he warned that wild pandas face extinction within 30 years" (*Auckland Sunday Star*, as noted by *The New Yorker*). This is funny because of the juxtaposition of the report on his surgery and his warning about pandas.

You've just been hit with a linguistic fallacy. Fallacies of ambiguity, also known as **linguistic fallacies,** are so named because of an unclear sentence structure, grammatical construction, or word usage. The result of the ambiguity is that an incorrect conclusion is drawn. In the case of the wild panda example, the ambiguity centers on the sentence structure—creating the humorous effect.

There are five main fallacies of ambiguity. Let's look at them.

Equivocation

The fallacy of **equivocation** occurs when different meanings of a word or phrase are used in argument. The resulting ambiguity leads to an incorrect conclusion being drawn. This is also known as a *semantic fallacy.*

We often see equivocation in puns and jokes, as the cartoons show. The equivocation is what makes the cartoons funny. Jokes—especially puns—often rest on equivocation. But when equivocation leads to an incorrect conclusion, it's not funny. A special kind of equivocation has to do with "relative terms," which have different meanings in different contexts (like "tall" or "big" or "small"). Equivocation may also occur in much more serious arguments, as noted by Drury University philosophy professor Charles Ess, who offers this example:

It is wrong to kill innocent human beings.

<u>Fetuses are innocent human beings.</u>

Therefore, it is wrong to kill fetuses.

Philosopher Mary Anne Warren argues that, in fact, this argument faces its own dilemma: Either it is guilty of equivocation, or it is guilty of question begging. It is easy enough to argue that "innocent human beings" means *two* different things in the premises—and thus the argument equivocates. For example:

innocent human being in premise 1
= "conscious of moral choice, but not guilty of committing/choosing an immoral act"
innocent human being in premise 2
= "innocent because the fetus is *not* capable of moral intentions and choices in the first place"

Betty Jean is at it again! Equivocation on the word "beat" causes the humor here.

Copyright 2004. Jason Karl, artist; Wanda Teays, copy. Reprinted with permission.

Examples of Equivocation

Title of an article in *USA Today:* "Ex-Gymnastics Stars Understand Flip Side to Expectations and Glory."

Ad for Krav Maga "Combat for a modern world": "Don't be afraid to hit on guys" (photo of woman giving an elbow-chop to a man's head).

Lamar Odom is a good basketball player, so he must be a good person, too.

Headline in *The New York Times:* "Unknown Arm of Sicilian Mafia Is Uncovered in the United States."

Examples of Equivocation Humor

The cheap eye surgeon was always cutting *corneas* [playing on corneas/corners].

Two vultures boarded an airplane, each carrying two dead raccoons. The flight attendant looked at them and said, "I'm sorry, gentlemen, only one *carrion* per passenger is allowed" [playing on carrion/carry on].

A chicken crossing the road is *poultry* in motion [playing on poultry/poetry].

Shifting definitions of "right" can cause chaos.

Nik Scott, artist, Curious Productions, Australia, Copyright 2008.

Accent

The fallacy of **accent** occurs in one of two ways: when either (1) the emphasis of a word or phrase or (2) a passage taken out of context leads to drawing an incorrect conclusion. This includes the repetition of a word or phrase to create a certain effect that leads to an incorrect conclusion. Think, for example, of ads where the word "free" is accented, but in tiny print, we are told what we have to do or buy to get the freebie. For example, the Nylon Club ad features a Chevrolet (car) as an "extra bonus" for selling an unspecified number of nylons (see Figure 7.1). Another way the fallacy of accent occurs is when someone misquotes another or takes something out of context. Taking material out of context can be very problematic, even ludicrous at times. The way individual words are emphasized can affect the meaning or the impact of a sentence. Consider the following:

> *John Connor* will be the savior of the human race in the battle against the machines.
> John Connor will be the *savior* of the human race in the battle against the machines.

FIGURE 7.1

What exactly do you get selling for the NYLON Club?

You Tell Me Department

The Second Amendment

One of the more controversial aspects of the U.S. Constitution is the Second Amendment, which focuses on the right to bear arms (weapons!). Examine the wording below, and discuss whether there is equivocation in the phrase "the right of the people." Some believe that the confusion over what exactly is intended by the Second Amendment centers upon what this phrase means.

> A well regulated Militia being necessary to the security of a free State, the right of the people to keep and bear Arms shall not be infringed.

You tell me: Does this refer to individuals who want to bear arms, or does it refer to a collective "people" in the individual states (e.g., Iowa, Alaska). In other words, could it be that it is recognizing that a state, in contrast to the federal government, could have its own "militia," such as the National Guard (which is under state governance)? Share your thoughts, and then read the Supreme Court decision on gun control that was handed down June 27, 2008 (www.supremecourtus.gov/opinions/07pdf/07-290.pdf).

John Connor will be the savior of the *human race* in the battle against the machines.

John Connor will be the savior of the human race in the battle against *the machines.*

Each of the propositions above has an impact, but the impact varies according to the emphasis. In the first case, the focus is on John Connor (versus others who could be saviors). The second proposition emphasizes what role Connor will play (savior as opposed to sacrificial lamb, cheerleader, etc.). The third proposition focuses on the group Connor will save in the battle against the machines (the human race as opposed to the chosen ones, the animal species, the children, etc.). The last proposition focuses on the opponent (the machines as opposed to the alien, the predator, the warthogs from hell, etc.). According to the emphasis, the focus and impact changes.

An example of accent is the dangling comparative. Authors Brooks Jackson and Kathleex Hall Jamieson explain that this occurs when any term meant to compare two things (like "better" or "faster") is left dangling, without stating what's being compared (*UnSpun,* 2007). For example, in the ad below, the use of "faster" creates ambiguity:

FEEL BETTER FASTER.* Take Nyquil each night & Dayquil each day for relief.

***versus no treatment**

"Faster" than what? The other products on the market? Only when we study the fine print do we learn the truth.

An example of misleading repetition is found in a Pillsbury ad once used for Hungry Jack Biscuits. The ad copy read: "*Hello **Honey!** Introducing Hungry Jack* **Honey** Tastin' Biscuits. Warm your family's heart with the golden flavor of **honey.** New Hungry Jack Biscuits have the same tender, flaky layers that Hungry Jack Biscuits are famous for, with a touch of **honey** flavor baked right in. Try our

Hungry Jack Biscuits today and treat your family to the taste of **honey**" (emphasis added). The word "honey" is repeated five times in the advertisement, leading us to think that these biscuits contain honey. However, the pictured container at the bottom of the page says "Hungry Jack *Artificial* Honey Flavor Flaky Biscuits" (emphasis added).

Examples of Accent

FREE BOX OF CHOCOLATES whenever you buy $200 worth of merchandise.
From *The Weekly World News* (14 Aug 2001): "**AMAZING DOG SPARKS RELIGIOUS REVIVAL** . . . by walking 16 miles to church every Sunday!"
Fly to France for $100—not counting tax, surcharges, fuel fees, and miscellaneous charges.

Amphiboly

The fallacy of **amphiboly** occurs when the faulty grammatical structure of a sentence creates an ambiguity. Due to the ambiguous sentence, more than one interpretation is possible, and thus, an incorrect conclusion may be drawn. This is also known as a fallacy of *syntax*. Think of an amphibian—a creature that can live in two entirely different environments. The fallacy of amphiboly occurs when the sentence structure is confusing—for example, "Soon after Sam and Ella got married they experienced food poisoning." Because of the odd sentence structure, it sounds like Sam and Ella's food poisoning was caused by their marriage!

Sometimes amphiboly results from two nouns preceding the verb or two nouns with an unclear reference afterward, as in "Baby George walked toward Grandpa, his diaper falling to his knees." Sometimes the fallacy results from a missing verb phrase—as in this twist on an example by Irving Copi: "Firefighters often burn victims." If the sentence structure seems awkward or funny, check for amphiboly.

Examples of Amphiboly

Title of an article about Superior Court Judge William R. Nevitt Jr. in the *Daily Journal:* "Former Helicopter Pilot Lands on Bench."
Marx Brothers' line: "I shot an elephant in my pajamas. (How he got in my pajamas, I'll never know.)"
Noted in the *Farmer's Almanac:* "The concert held in the Fellowship Hall was a great success. Special thanks are due to the minister's daughter, who labored the whole evening at the piano, which as usual fell upon her."

Composition

The fallacy of **composition** occurs when we infer from what is true of the parts or members of something that the same thing is true of the whole thing or organization. The fact that something is true of the members or parts of something does not mean that it will be true of the whole. Each of the parts or members may have some characteristic (say, being lightweight), but that does not mean the whole group or object will be lightweight.

The characteristics of the parts do *not* necessarily transfer to the entity as a whole. For example, there could be a football team in which every member is a great athlete, but they do not work well as a team. And we all know what it's like to buy top-quality ingredients for that oh-so-special dessert, but the crust ends up tasting like cardboard, and the filling has too many lumps for anyone to praise the resulting pie.

Examples of Composition

Beyoncé, Nora Jones, and Shania Twain are all great singers. I bet they'd be a dynamite girl group.

Since each and every one of us must one day die, that means the human race must one day come to an end.

Each of the Lakers is a great basketball player, so I can't understand why the team fell apart in game 4 of the 2008 NBA finals.

Both the fallacy of composition and the fallacy of division (the next one) are classified as fallacies of ambiguity because they turn on an ambiguity concerning class membership (the individual members of a group) and the class as an entity (class inclusion, or characteristics of the entire group). What is true of each and every member may not be true of the collective (and vice versa), and an ambiguity is created when we use the terms *as if* this were the case. W. H. Werkmeister points out the ambiguity of the word "all": This word has a collective as well as distributive meaning. The collective sense is "all together," whereas the distributive sense is "each and every one." This ambiguity is at the basis of these two fallacies.

Division

The fallacy of **division** occurs when we infer that what is true of a whole is also true of its parts. One form this fallacy takes is arguing that what is true of an organization will thus be true of its members—which is not necessarily the case. Division is the opposite of composition. There we went from what was true of each and every part and then argued that it must be true of the whole. Here we surmise that a characteristic of the whole will be a characteristic of its parts or members. But this is fallacious, too. For instance, you might have a very heavy piece of machinery that is made up of a large number of tiny, light-weight parts. So too with groups and organizations. Similarly, the fact that the Louisville Symphony Orchestra did a phenomenal job at the Kentucky Jubilee does not necessarily mean the oboe player or the cellist was in top form. And while Omar's Kenyan chicken stew may have been exquisite, it does not follow that the tomato paste that was one of the ingredients was necessarily exquisite. What is true of the whole will not automatically be true of the parts or members. And it is a mistake to think so.

Examples of Division

The school board is inefficient. So, don't expect Irene Chan, the president of the school board, to do a good job.

Housing prices have been on the increase for the past 10 years. This means we ought to be able to get a great price for our house if we put it on the market.

The American Mathematical Society is highly regarded as an organization. Therefore, Dr. Pi, a founding member, must be held in high regard.

Exercises

Directions: Name the fallacies of ambiguity below:

1. Restaurant ad: "Our omelettes are eggceptional!"

2. Airline ticket office sign: "WE TAKE YOUR BAGS AND SEND THEM IN ALL DIRECTIONS."

3. From the Bent Offerings cartoon strip: A drawing of Einstein looking in the mirror and wearing a T-shirt that says, "Just Say Know."

4. RITA (reading "For rent" ads): This house sounds good, Ernie. Just listen—it's got a big kitchen, a large dining room, and a bedroom big enough to have a rocking chair over by the window across from the bed. It must be an enormous house!

   ERNIE: That's fantastic, Rita! The twins and the baby will really like having all that space to run around in.

5. Sailors don't have to do any laundry. If they just throw their clothes overboard they'll be washed ashore!

6. The White House is not nearly as large as you'd think, given all of its functions. Therefore, the Oval Office inside the White House must not be very large either.

7. Sign in a bar: "SPECIAL COCKTAILS FOR THE LADIES WITH NUTS."

8. Ad copy for the Boston Medical Professional Corporation:

   SEX FOR LIFE!

   ERECTION PROBLEMS? PREMATURE EJACULATION?
   IMMEDIATE RESULTS (only one consultation required).
   Licensed MDs specializing in men's health. Safer and more effective treatment than Viagra. Medication exclusively formulated for premature ejaculation. Separate waiting rooms to ensure your privacy. Especially beneficial to patients with diabetes, high blood pressure, heart conditions, stress, etc., or those who would like to improve their sex lives.

   Boston Medical Professional Corporation

9. Last night I saw the movie *Nuclear Mutants*. That movie is so bad it should be punished.

10. Maria Elena had been dancing for 12 years when she broke her leg.

11. Ad copy for an airline:

    KIDS FLY FREE!
    When their parents buy first-class tickets.
    Offer valid only from February to May.

12. The Supreme Court is an honorable institution, and thus, it follows that Justice Thurgood Marshall must have been honorable, too, given that he served so long on the Court.

13. We should do what's right. What is right should be enforceable by the legal system. People have a right to die with dignity; therefore, physician-assisted suicide should be legal in this country.

14. On a restaurant menu: "OUR WINES LEAVE YOU NOTHING TO HOPE FOR."

15. Ad in a flyer: "**MAKE BIG BUCKS WITHIN A YEAR** if you participate in a fetal brain transplant study. Call today: 888-NO-BRAIN."

16. Ad for the William Bounds Ltd. pepper mill (which grinds and crushes peppercorns):

    We've got a crush on pepper!

17. Yao Ming is a big man, even for a basketball player. Therefore, he must have huge feet and hands.

18. A discussion of beautiful women cited Angelina Jolie (best lips), Julia Roberts (best smile), Andie McDowell (best hair), Drew Barrymore (best eyes), and Janet Jackson (best midriff). Can you imagine how beautiful the woman would be if she had all these traits?

19. Ad in a newspaper :"WIN FREE RENT FOR LIFE if you will be our first subject in a brain transplant."

20. Carlos had been lifting weights for 20 years when he dropped a barbell and crushed his big toe.

21. Ad for Crown Royal whiskey after the Lakers won the 2001 NBA championship: "Every Champion Deserves a Crown" (photo of a basketball next to a Crown Royal whisky bottle).

22. Ad for Crest Whitestrips teeth whitener:

    WHITEN WHILE YOU COLOR [YOUR FINGERNAILS].
    Or while you apply makeup, blow-dry your hair or even shower. Crest Whitestrips work easily into any routine. ***All it takes is 30 minutes twice a day for two weeks for a noticeably whiter smile.*** *Consider it multitasking.*

    Dramatization of typical 14-day results.

23. From the *Farmer's Almanac*: "Frequent naps prevent old age, especially if taken while driving."

24. I saw Yellowstone flying from Sacramento to Minneapolis.

25. Ad for Cointreau liqueur:

Be COINTREAUVERSIAL™
TO THE BEAT OF A DIFFERENT DRUM

26. Another ad for teeth-whitening paste:

"I woke up one morning and boom! They were whiter"
—Brooke Smith, recently engaged

So effective, you just apply it once at bedtime. *Simple White® Night* is
absorbed quickly, so there's no need to let it dry.
It whitens effortlessly as you drift off to sleep. In two weeks, you'll wake up to whiter
teeth.
Dramatically whiter teeth made even simpler. Guaranteed.
www.colgatesimplywhite.com

27. Title of a *Los Angeles Times* article: "The Lakers' Defensive Funnel Vision."

28. Don't be chicken. Try octopus for a change! It's delicious.

Formal Fallacies

Formul fallacies occur because of an error in the very form of the reasoning. Given
that a conditional proposition is true, neither denying the antecedent nor affirming
the consequent can permit us to conclude that (in the first case) the consequent is
false or (in the second case) the antecedent must be true. The fact that one cause did
not occur does not mean the effect couldn't have happened. Similarly, the fact that
an event happened does not necessarily mean that one particular causal factor had to
occur. As a result, the very form of the reasoning is incorrect. The truth of the premises will never guarantee the truth of the conclusion because of a structural error. (See
Chapter 10 on rules of inference for a discussion of the formal fallacies.)

Exercises

Part One

Directions: Name the fallacy below. These draw from *all* the fallacies we studied in
this chapter.

1. A large meal isn't fattening if you take small bites.

2. They gave my father morphine when he was dying of cancer. It was the best
   thing to do for his pain. That means everyone should be able to use morphine any time they want. Why not legalize it?

3. Mel Gibson ate dog food in *Lethal Weapon,* so it must be tasty. Try some!

4. We cannot trust juries, because anyone on a jury can make a mistake.

5. Noted by J. Casey: Al Gore argues that curbing carbon emissions is critical to reducing the impact of climate change. . . . I see what he's saying, he's saying we should get rid of all of our cars!

6. Everyone should be honest. Therefore, I should tell Amanda that she looks ridiculous in her dowdy suit.

7. Article title from *The Los Angeles Times* about hockey legend Wayne Gretzky: "Great Gretzky Deal Made Lots of Cents."

8. The decision by the Bioethics Committee was quite reasonable and fair. Therefore, Dr. Bunu, oncologist and the director of the Bioethics Committee, is a reasonable and fair-minded person.

9. We ought to allow stem cell research. Polls show that the majority of people support it.

10. Timothy McVeigh was supposedly—and I mean supposedly—executed for his part in the Oklahoma City bombing. But you know they did *no* autopsy! Without an autopsy, we cannot be sure he's actually dead. You can't prove to me he was really killed by lethal injection. I can conclude one thing and one thing only: Timothy McVeigh is still alive.

11. Frances said that eating tomatoes is bad for you: If you eat tomatoes, your diet is too acidic. An acidic diet is simply too yang! And if you have a diet that is imbalanced in terms of the yang and yin elements, you are more prone to illness and cancer. Look at those stewed tomatoes piled up on your plate! Your health is in jeopardy. Stick to seaweed treats. Here, have some nori!

12. The intricate design of nature can only be due to the existence of God because there could be no natural order and design if God did not exist.

13. No one has proven that jailing pregnant drug abusers is a societal problem; therefore, it must be morally permissible to incarcerate pregnant women who abuse drugs.

14. DIANA: Hey Frank, what's that weird mark doing on the side of your neck?
FRANK: Oh, Diana, did I ever tell you what a lovely voice you have? I bet you could get a record contract!

15. I saw Anthea out in the garden with her cat, Sophie, so I combed her matted fur.

16. I can't understand why the coach was arrested for sexual harassment. He always helps out with the Little League and drives the church school bus for the Sunday school.

17. Ad for the Olympus digital camera: "Olympus: America's Most Popular Camera Series."

18. You would be advised to think twice before voting for Jim Bradley for governor. He's a vegetarian, and someone like that will make sure the beef industry in this state is stripped of any lobbying power in the legislature!

19. VIOLET: You know, Dan, I just don't believe God exists.
    DAN: You'd better believe in God, or you'll go straight to hell!

20. Friedrich Nietzsche suffered from incurable syphilis. That means we shouldn't waste our time reading his work—it couldn't possibly have any value for us today.

21. Laura's students took a poll of patients in County General. They were all senior citizens living on a fixed income. They said that hospital food is grossly underrated. In fact, they agreed that, on the whole, most hospital food is delicious. Therefore, all American patients must think hospital food is delicious.

22. Aerobic exercise is great for your cardiovascular system. Therefore, Mr. Martinez should do it to help his recovery from his quadrupal bypass surgery last week.

23. Title of an article on fashion: "Dress Code Anarchy and the Right to Bare Arms."

24. Did you hear about Martin trying to convince Carlos to stop drinking raw eggs in beer? Martin said it's bad for your health and might even cause kidney problems. But who is he to talk? He can dish out advice, but he never takes it.

25. Why did the cow stop giving milk? Because she was an udder failure!!

26. I know you haven't had a date in months. The reality is this, Bob: Either stay in shape or no woman will find you attractive.

27. From Morris Engel: "Left-handed people have no willpower, because if they did, they wouldn't be left-handed."

28. DR. HWANG: Hey, Rita, what are you doing text messaging during the final exam?
    RITA: Oh, Dr. Hwang, did you get a new haircut? It's very flattering—sort of makes you you look like a movie star. I bet you could get a cameo in a show!

29. Where did you bury the body, Manson?

30. Ad for prayer books: "Nun Better."

31. Humans must be the products of environmental determinism since no one has proved for certain that we have free will.

32. Question asked of Diana Eck, noted in *Encountering God:* "Give me a quick yes or no: Is Christ the only way to salvation?"

33. Ad for a dentist: "Teeth extracted with the greatest pains."

34. Have you always been pig-headed?

35. I don't care if she is having an appendicitis attack. No one gets to make up the final exam—as I said on the syllabus. This policy is clearly spelled out.

36. My fellow senators, it is simply unpatriotic to oppose strict tariffs on Canadian beef. Get behind me on this one.

37. Kurt's court blog: "The trial of Joe ("the Ear") Gambino went on for seven weeks, and the jury was deadlocked. Prosecuting attorney Anthony Rialto simply could not make the case. If he's not guilty let's face it, he is innocent. He may be a bit shady, but Gambino is innocent of the accusation that he murdered Judge Rubio and stuffed him in a trashbin."

38. From the *Poor Gourmet* newsletter: "Landscape designer Anita Stebbins made the most delicious casserole with shiitake mushrooms, leeks, and truffle sauce. She was careful to follow the recipe, as a misstep could turn the delicate flavors into something like wallpaper paste. There's a truism here for all of us folks: Either you follow the recipe to a 'T' or you risk total disaster."

39. Once again, Dr. Stemp is pushing grants for biochemistry students. I'm not opposed to helping our youth in this country, but it seems a bit over the top for Stemp to ask for more science grants when he is a researcher for the International Biochemistry and Biotechnology Association. I suggest that these ties cast a shadow on any policy recommendations he makes.

40. Ambulances regularly run the red light taking people to the hospital. Therefore, we should all be able to run the red light whenever we please!

41. Hey, Heidi, why are you wearing those Nike sneakers made in a Third World country? You should wear American-made shoes! What's wrong with you—don't you love your country?

42. I was watching the Lakers game the other day—you know, when the Celtics were making the Lakers look like turnips. I realized that they have a woman down on the court interviewing players at half-time and after the game. Her questions seemed fine, but when push comes to shove, she *is* a woman and not likely to be as well versed in the sport as a man. I hope they replace her soon.

43. If Maria keeps singing in the shower, she'll ruin her vocal chords. Next thing you know, she'll lose her voice and have to get surgery. She really should not take such a risk.

44. If you want to be cool, you'll wear a ring in your belly button. So, Angelique, what are you waiting for? We could go down to the mall this afternoon after our calculus class.

Part Two

Directions: Name the fallacy below. Be on the watch: If it is *not* a fallacy, say so.

1. GWEN: Hey there, Terry, what are you doing with all those cartons of milk? Did you pay for them or what?
   TERRY: You know, Gwen, I've been meaning to tell you how much I love your Mickey Mouse padded hat! You look just darling in it! Have you thought about wearing it to class? It's sooo cute!

2. I know you didn't want to do a nude scene, Maricella. But if you get modest on me now, you can forget about trying out for the part of Rosa in the sequel to *Silence of the Sheep*. You decide, my fair one!

3. Sign on a restaurant near the football stadium: "America's favorite pizza. Come on in for an All-American meal before the game."

4. If you don't vote, you can't complain. You complained. So, you must have voted.

5. DEFENSE ATTORNEY: Tell me, Miss Raymond, you say you saw the defendant attack Mr. Busso at the Chicago Brew House at 8:00 P.M. on Saturday, July 12th?
   MARIE BUSSO: Yes, I did. He hit him with a tire iron three times.
   DEFENSE ATTORNEY: Well, tell me, Miss Busso. Isn't it a fact that you are a lesbian and that's why you were at the Brew House in the first place? Didn't you go there to pick up another woman?

6. It's a bit absurd that you, of all people, should tell me to lose weight and exercise more. I realize I'm a bit out of shape, but you are a blimp next to me. Who are you to give me advice?

7. Whenever rock 'n' roll is on the radio, Jasper yells, "Let's dance." All the times Jasper yells "Let's dance" are times that small children enjoy. Therefore, any time that rock 'n' roll is on the radio is a time small children enjoy.

8. Heredity alone makes someone into a criminal since heredity by itself determines what a person becomes.

9. OFFICER: Hey, mister, what's this foot I see sticking out of your trunk?
   SLEAZY ALBERT: Oh, officer, I hear you were given an award last night at the LAPD command center. That's really great—I bet your parents are so proud of you!

10. The Democratic Party favors strong unions. Therefore, Senator Fitzer, a Southern Democrat, will surely vote for the ballot measure to strengthen the Teachers Union.

11. Either get a decent cookbook and learn how to make quiche or simply buy a spinach quiche at the Parisian Treats bakery. I see you don't have a decent cookbook and don't know how to make quiche. Therefore, you should call the bakery and order a spinach quiche.

12. Radiated food must not be bad for your health. No one has proved it causes cancer—so it must be okay.

13. Loosely wrapped in bubble-wrap, she carried a crystal vase.

14. Robert Thurman has written a lot of books on Tibetan Buddhism, but I don't know whether to believe what he says. He's an American, you know—and that's a long way from being Tibetan.

15. Freedom of speech is a hallmark of a democracy. Therefore, neo-Nazis should be free to verbally harass the Jewish family down the street.

16. Title on an article on men who bake bread: "Men's *Rising* Obsession: They're *Loafing* and Proud of It."

17. You really ought to help John hide some of his assets from the government so he doesn't have a big tax bill this year. You know what the golden rule says about doing unto others as you'd like them to do to you. If you helped him cheat on his taxes, you can probably count on him if you ever need help in exchange.

18. Before receiving an Olympic gold medal, athletes must pass a test to show they are not on steroids. Therefore, everyone should be tested for steroids each week so we don't have a national drug problem.

19. If we teach people to think clearly and logically, our country will be stronger. This is due to the fact that a strong country requires that its citizens have well-developed reasoning skills.

20. Only those who have smelled a grizzly bear in their tent have had to come to terms with their own mortality.

21. Either you think *The Simpsons* is the most insightful social commentary today or you are simply missing out on the best philosophy going.

22. I've spent more time on this class than all my other ones, Professor Tregenza. I should get an A, not a B+. My father's in the film business and could get you a ticket to the Oscar's award ceremony. Also, I could take photos of you and your dogs Wolfie and Zsa Zsa. That should get me to an A!

23. "The universe must be infinite, my son." "How do you know, Dad?" "I know this much, son, you cannot prove it's finite—no one has found an end to it yet."

24. Why should we support the senator's proposal to end the war? You know she supported it when the president went to Congress.

25. I'm glad Darin feels better—his headache lasted hours. He tried everything and nothing seemed to work. He then decided to try the mashed-turnip cure. He ate a small serving and then took a nap. After he woke up, he felt much better. It's clear the turnips helped get rid of his headache. What good fortune.

26. The Rusty Bucket bluegrass band is fantastic! I heard them last summer when I was in Somerset for the Dutton family hoop-de-doo. The band played into the night, and we didn't even care that we were being devoured by mosquitoes—they are that good. Therefore, Dan Dutton, lead singer of the Rusty Bucket, must be fantastic too.

Part Three: Fallacy Story

Directions: Mark all the fallacies in the story below that was written by Miriam Salgado as part of a class assignment.

The Case of Mistaken Furs

MARGARIT MOUSE: Sonia, are you going to talk at all during our picnic?

SONIA SQUIRREL: Well, if you insist, have you heard the news about Willy Wolf?

MARGARIT MOUSE: Have you always been a gossip? You squirrels are all the same, always talking about everyone else!

SONIA SQUIRREL: Don't get me started on mice. They are always trying to be the big cheese!! Do you want to know or not?

MARGARIT MOUSE: Fine, tell me.

SONIA SQUIRREL: The police have arrested Willy Wolf for having attempted to kill Rosy pig and destroying her house. Rosy has picked him out of a line-up and is going to testify against him.

MARGARIT MOUSE: That awful wolf. How could he have done all those bad things to an animal as nice as Rosy? They are just wasting money having a trial for Willy; there is no way that anyone would think he is innocent. First of all, he is a wolf and wolves are notorious for picking on pigs. As if this wasn't enough, Willy is the Big Bad Wolf's nephew. Big Bad Wolf has tried to hurt many pigs: he's been arrested twice for assault with carving knife and roasting pan. That kind of hatred toward pigs runs in Willy's family!

SONIA SQUIRREL: How can you be so sure of Willy's guilt? He does have an alibi. He was with Jake the Snake the night that it happened.

MARGARIT MOUSE: Sonia Squirrel, are you nuts or something! You can't trust Jake—everyone knows that he is a low-life. Also, the movie star Arnold Armadillo says that all wolves are criminals, so it must be true! There is no doubt that Willy Wolf was the one who destroyed Rosy's house because he is one of the founders of the Tuesday Afternoon Demolition Club, whose members are destructive. Now are you convinced?

SONIA SQUIRREL: I don't care what you say—I don't think that Willy Wolf is guilty. Most of our friends also think that Willy has been falsely accused. Maybe Rosy is lying; did you ever think of that?

MARGARIT MOUSE: Gosh, how many facts do I have to give before you believe me? The majority of this town thinks that pigs are honest; therefore there is no way Rosy is fibbing. Also, you should tell everyone that Willy is guilty so the jury will be persuaded to send him to jail. This way Rosy can cash in on her insurance. She should have things go her way. After all, her house has been destroyed, two of her uncles are homeless, the third one is always mean to her, and her pet just died.

SONIA SQUIRREL: I just don't think that Willy Wolf would do something like that. I use to be good friends with him in grade school.

MARGARIT MOUSE: Either you think Willy is guilty or you're an idiot. All the signs point to him. Also, the night before it happened I had a dream in which Rosy's dead pet told me that Rosy would be attacked by a wolf. You can't prove that I didn't so it must be true!! Furthermore, the only wolf around here is Willy. Oh, I almost forgot, I asked a few pigs if they were scared of wolves and they said yes. Therefore, this whole town is scared of wolves and we should put this one away in jail right away before he hurts anyone else.

SONIA SQUIRREL: Have you always said so much trash?

MARGARIT MOUSE: You better tell all your friends Willy is guilty or I'll tell the police you went over to Rosy's house dressed in a wolf's costume!

SONIA SQUIRREL: That won't work with me, Margarit. Anyways, the only person around here that owns a wolf costume is you. I still remember that you were a wolf for my Halloween party last year.

MARGARIT MOUSE: Yeah, but what's that got to do with anything?

SONIA SQUIRREL: You and Rosy weren't real good friends, especially since she stole your boyfriend. And you always said that one day you'd get even. Also, weren't you headed toward Rosy's house yesterday carrying a big bag?

MARGARIT MOUSE: Sonia, this lunch is fantastic, you are such a talented cook. Have you ever considered becoming a caterer? I have a friend who could help you get started. Let me go see him right now!

SONIA SQUIRREL: Okay!

The next day, just as Willy Wolf was about to be transported to the courthouse, an anonymous call was made to the police to go check out Margarit Mouse's house. When the police got there, they found the wolf costume and blueprints of her plans to get revenge on Rosy pig. The police arrested the mischievous mouse and freed Willy.

The End.

Reprinted with the permission of Miriam Salgado.

CHAPTER EIGHT

Rolling the Dice: Causal and Statistical Reasoning

OTTO: *Apes don't read philosophy.*

WANDA: *Yes, they do, Otto, they just don't understand it. Now let me correct you on a couple of things here. Aristotle was not Belgian. The central message of Buddhism is not "every man for himself," and the London Underground is not a political movement. Those are all mistakes, Otto. I looked them up. Now, you have just assaulted the one man who can keep you out of jail and make you rich. What are you going to do about it huh? What would an intellectual do? What would Plato do?*

From *A Fish Called Wanda*

Between classes, you open your laptop to surf the Internet. You come across an article about the power of prayer. "Now that sounds worth reading," you think to yourself. According to the report, women receiving in vitro fertilization (IVF) who belonged to a prayer group were more successful at getting pregnant than those who had no organized group praying for them. Evidently, the women were not informed that others were praying for them, so it seems miraculous. Sounds like a bunch of hooey? Well, maybe so. But just look at the numbers:

> Women who were prayed for had a 50 percent pregnancy rate, compared with 26 percent of women with no intercessory prayer. The 50 percent pregnancy rate was significantly higher than the success rate for the entire IVF program—which was also close to 26 percent—and the previous year's rate of 32.8 percent. One hundred ninety-nine women who were IVF candidates through embryo transfer at the Cha General Hospital in Seoul, Korea, between December 1998 and March 1999 were randomly assigned into two groups for the study. One group received no prayers. (Cindy Kuzma, "Pregnant on a Prayer," *Science & Spirit*, www.science-spirit.org)

How credible is this report? Two of the researchers are Columbia University physicians—and that is certainly impressive. Nothing like solid credentials to boost a research study. Unfortunately, Daniel Wirth, the third author of the study, pleaded guilty to embezzling $2 million from Adelphia Communications (via phony invoices) as well as conspiracy to commit mail fraud. That does not mean his research is faulty—but it definitely raises concerns.

Dr. Bruce Flamm, an obstetrician-gynecologist at Kaiser Permanente and clinical professor at UC Irvine, has raised question after question about the quality of the study. He asks, "If prayer were so powerful, why did the women need to use in vitro fertilization?" and "Why were the prayers to a Christian God?" He adds, "And was God punishing the women who didn't get pregnant?" (Jeff Gottlieb, "Journal Silent after Its Article on Power of Prayer Draws Criticism," *Los Angeles Times,* 17 Aug 2004). As you can see, this controversial experiment cries out for critical thinking tools to sort it all out.

The most scientifically rigorous study yet on the power of prayer in healing found no relationship between strangers praying for those who underwent heart surgery and the outcome (Benedict Carey, "Long-Awaited Medical Study Questions the Power of Prayer," *The New York Times,* 31 Mar 2006). Of course, pregnancy and heart surgery are quite different medical conditions, so the fact that the prayers failed to work for heart patients does not necessarily mean they will fail for those seeking to get pregnant. Nevertheless, some might see this 2006 study as of some significance.

The IVF study used two important types of inductive reasoning: (1) causal reasoning and (2) statistical reasoning. You probably remember from Chapter 5 that inductive reasoning always involves an element of doubt or probability—that the premises are not sufficient to guarantee the conclusion will be true.

By claiming that prayer positively affects a woman's chance of becoming pregnant using IVF, the researchers offered a cause-and-effect argument. They brought in statistical reasoning in arguing that those in the sample group—who were prayed for—had a statistically greater chance of getting pregnant than those in the control group. They inferred that praying for women who wish to get pregnant increases the probability of the desired results. Both types of reasoning involve uncertainty and probability, even in the best of situations. However, the skepticism about both the statistical data and the causal claims in this case gives us food for thought!

In this chapter, we will look at both of these key forms of inductive reasoning. We'll start with cause-and-effect arguments and then turn to statistical reasoning. Since they can be highly persuasive, we need to use our critical thinking skills to examine both types of arguments.

▣ Cause-and-Effect Reasoning

Cause-and-effect reasoning is all around us. Cause-and-effect reasoning is common in medicine and health care, as we see with the cause-and-effect argument that "young women who took the commonly used epilepsy drug phenytoin for one year showed significant bone loss compared to women taking other epilepsy drugs" (*Neurology*, 29 Apr 2008). We also see cause-and-effect reasoning about social problems (e.g., homelessness, crime, drug use, and sexual behavior) and natural phenomena (e.g., weather conditions and environmental changes). It may be hard to think of such arguments as inductive rather than deductive because causal relationships are often presented as if they were certain. Nevertheless, there *are* uncertainties in causal reasoning. There are inherent limitations on knowing all the possible causal factors of any given event. In addition, the interaction of causal factors may affect the outcome.

CASE STUDY

Fetus May Signal the Birth Process

Around half a million babies are born prematurely every year in the United States alone. Of those, some do not survive and some suffer serious health problems. Read about a discovery by two scientists that may help change that reality and then answer the questions that follow.

Professor of biochemistry and obstetrics and gynecology Carole R. Mendelson and her colleague Jennifer Condon found that fetal lungs produce a protein called surfactant protein A, or SP-A, to signal the mother that they are ready to begin breathing air. At the same time, it activates the release of infection-fighting white blood cells into the fluid-filled womb. The white blood cells then cause an inflammation in the uterus, which leads to labor. "We believe that labor is a cascade of events and that there is an initiating signal or trigger," says Mendelson. "We believe that the fetus, through the production of SP-A at the end of pregnancy, has the capacity to signal the mother when it's ready to be born."

When Mendelson and her team injected SP-A into the amniotic fluid of pregnant mice at a stage much earlier than it normally appears, the mice started labor early—at just 17 days instead of 19 days. When they injected pregnant mice with an antibody that blocks SP-A, the mice delivered late.

Mendelson hopes this research will have clinical uses for humans down the road, perhaps even in helping prevent preterm births. "We know that the same types of signals take place in the human womb," she says. "These signals are the same signals that seem to be involved in preterm labor. If one understands what they are in normal labor, then perhaps measures can be taken to use that knowledge to prevent labor prematurely."

Answer the following:

1. Clarify what Dr. Mendelson concluded from her study.

2. What do you consider the key evidence supporting her thesis?

3. To what extent does her study of mouse fetuses apply to humans? Share any thoughts and concerns.

Source: Karen Lurie, "Triggering Birth," *ScienCentral News*, www.sciencentral.com, 15 Jun 2004.

Group or Individual Exercise

Here's a medical mystery:

> In the population of Finland in the last 25 years, levels of type 1 insulin dependent diabetes have more than doubled among children, and seems set to increase further. . . .Worldwide there has been a steady increase in the incidence of type 1 diabetes, with an average increase per year of 2.5–3.0%. This trend has been most clear in children under the age of four, and it has been highly irregular between different individual countries. Incidence of diabetes between European countries, for example, can vary up to ten-fold. The lowest incidences in the world are found in Venezuela and China, while the highest levels of diabetes are found in Finland and Sardinia. ("Type 1 Diabetes In Finnish Children Skyrockets," *Medical News Today,* 23 May 2008).

Answer the following:

1. What can you infer from this information about Finland's problem with diabetes?
2. Speculate as to possible causes of or solutions to this situation.

Basics of Cause-and-Effect Reasoning

Be careful not to confuse correlation with cause. **Correlation** is a measure of the association between two things and how they are linked. The fact of a correlation between two events does *not* mean they are causally connected. For example, one pattern that has held for a number of years is that the direction of the Dow Jones Industrial Index predicts whether the AFC or the NFC will win the Super Bowl, but there is no causal connection between them.

Cause-and-effect arguments present us with probability, not certainty. The claim is that a stated condition will result in a particular effect—that the antecedent conditions, if true, cause the supposed effect to happen. How likely it is becomes the issue. We regularly see citations of cause-and-effect arguments. At times they seem reasonable; other times they seem questionable or far-fetched.

Take the case of the 2004 Boston Red Sox, who came back to beat the Yankees in the KLCS after being three games down. Did you realize that some suspected the turnabout was influenced by the players' *hair*? Yes, hair. According to Martin Miller, the sudden change of fortune for Johnny Damon (a Red Sox player) was due to his hair. He added, "Damon's hair must have known before Game 7 on Wednesday at Yankee Stadium that it was in danger of being sheared off by angry Beantown [that is, Boston] fans who'd watched the outfielder go 3 for 29 in the playoff series" (Martin Miller, "Bosox Secret? Only Their Hairdressers Know for Sure," *Los Angeles Times*, 23 Oct 2004). Miller also considered the hair of players Kevin Miller, Manny Ramirez, and Pedro Martinez, and noted that Beverly Hills stylist Rich Ohnmacht said, "To me their hair says they are hungry, they don't have time to have their hair cut. . . . It shows they are into the game. They are cavemen." That the hair made the difference in the game is arguable—we need to examine the causal reasoning involved.

Causal Reasoning in Science and Medicine

Causal reasoning goes beyond sports. It is common in discussions of sciences, medicine, and health care. For example, the ophthalmologist looks at your beet-red eye and says, "A virus probably caused your eye to get red—most likely someone coughed or sneezed into your eye." The doctor is not absolutely certain; he is drawing an inference on the basis of the evidence before him. In eliminating other possible causes, he figures a virus is the culprit. *Prognoses* are similarly inductive. They are predictions based on the given facts of the case, along with what is known about analogous cases.

Causal reasoning is particularly important in scientific research, where empirical studies are an integral part of the research and theorizing. The fact that such reasoning is inductive does not mean it isn't taken seriously. The degree of probability may have an enormous impact on decisions people make. That is one reason doctors are required to inform you of possible risks before you consent to surgery or other kinds of medical treatment.

One way to address the uncertainty of causal reasoning is to temper the claim. Instead of saying of the stronger proposition, "This is *the cause of* that," which attributes a single cause to a given effect, we could hedge our bets by saying, "This is *a causal factor* of that." For example, consider the relationship between cigarette smoking and cancer:

> A series of authoritative reports by the U.S. Public Health Service and other international scientific organizations has conclusively documented a *causal relationship* between cigarette smoking and cancer of at least eight major sites (Shopland et al., 1991). These reports have uniformly identified smoking as a major cause of cancers of the lung, larynx, oral cavity, and esophagus—that is, cigarette smoking is responsible for a majority of the cases and deaths from cancer of these sites. These reports have also demonstrated that smoking substantially elevates the death rates for cancers of the bladder, kidney, and pancreas in both men and women, and, possibly, cervical cancer in women. A number of published reports have *suggested an association* between smoking and other cancers, including cancer of the stomach, liver, prostate, colon, and rectum. (Donald R. Shopland, "Cigarette Smoking as a Cause of Cancer," National Institutes of Health, rex.nci.nih.gov; emphasis added)

Notice the use of words like "association" and "causal relationship." An *association* between two things means they are connected in some way—but the nature of that connection may be in doubt. For example, not everyone who smokes gets cancer. Why? First, although the probability of lung cancer increases the longer you smoke, smoking may not be the sole cause of the cancer. It could be one of several causal factors, such as amount and frequency of smoking. Second, we may need to study risk factors, such as age, gender, years of exposure to smoke, density of population, environmental conditions, and previous respiratory problems like pneumonia, allergies, and asthma.

Let's look at another example. In a study of cell phones and brain cancer, we find:

> Like most research on the subject, the studies are observational, showing only an association between cellphone use and cancer, not a causal relationship . . . some of the research suggests a link between cellphone use and three types of tumors: glioma [like that of Senator Edward Kennedy]; cancer of the parotid, a salivary gland near the ear; and acoustic neuroma, a tumor that essentially occurs where the ear meets the brain. . . . Last year, *The American Journal of Epidemiology* published data from Israel finding a 58 percent higher risk of parotid gland tumors among heavy cellphone users. . . . Louis Slesin, editor of *Microwave News,* [states,] "There are some very disconcerting findings that suggest a problem, although it's much too early to reach a conclusive view."(Tara Parker-Pope, "Experts Revive Debate over Cellphones and Cancer," *The New York Times,* 3 Jun 2008)

As you can see from the report, there is "only an association and "not a causal relationship" between cell phones and brain tumors. However, the data pointing to an association do "suggest" a problem. This uncertainty is what makes this reasoning inductive, but the connections raise concerns.

Let's see what it can mean to posit a **causal relationship.** First, watch for any claims that there is a cause-and-effect relationship between two things. The word "cause" need not be present, by the way, so long as the relationship is made apparent. This can be done simply by using the word "effect" or "effect of" or the equivalent. We can see the variation in the examples below:

Causal claim 1: Gulf War vets with a host of strange symptoms "link" their ailments to vaccines intended to protect them against biochemical warfare.

Causal claim 2: Insomnia is correlated to drinking excessive amounts of caffeine, so you ought not to drink so many café lattes after dinner!

Causal claim 3: Workers at an atomic weapons factory who made uranium metal for nuclear bombs died at significantly younger ages and suffered a higher incidence of lung, intestinal, and blood cancers than the American population as a whole, according to an analysis of their medical records.

Causal claim 4: An Oxford University researcher theorized that AIDS might have entered the human population in a bizarre series of malaria experiments done between 1920 and the 1950s in which researchers inoculated themselves and prisoners with fresh blood from chimpanzees or mangabeys. Both chimpanzees and mangabeys are known to carry a virus similar to HIV2.

Notice the different ways of expressing cause-and-effect relationships. We don't want to overlook a causal argument just because we were only watching for the words "cause" and "effect." We can express causation in a number of different ways.

The Global Dimension

The SARS Epidemic in Toronto, Canada

Remember the movie *Outbreak?* There we find the story of an ebola-like epidemic that happened after an infected monkey was brought by ship to a pet store in Northern California. The monkey ended up escaping, and the chase was on. This scenario is not as far-fetched as we might think. Overnight an epidemic can strike. All it takes is one host setting things in motion. This is what happened in the movie—and it also happened in 2003 when one infected person carried SARS (severe acute respiratory syndrome) into North America.

SARS surfaced in China in December 2002 and, thanks to global travel, quickly spread to other countries. In February 2003, a single traveler introduced SARS into Toronto, Canada. By April, 249 cases had been reported and 14 people had died ("Epi-Update: Interim Report on the SARS Outbreak in the Greater Toronto Area, Ontario, Canada April 24, 2003," *Health Canada,* www.hc-sc.gc.ca). Just as the *Outbreak* monkey spread the virus to those who infected others, SARS also quickly spread. *Health Canada* reported the stages of transmission as follows:

1. Spread of SARS infection within the family of the individual case
2. Amplification of the SARS outbreak through hospital-based spread
3. Transmission within immediate household members of the health care workers, patients, and visitors to these hospitals
4. Isolated sporadic cases due to limited transmission in the workplace
5. Transmission in an extended family and associated religious group

Directions: Below is a list of individuals from each of the five categories of transmission. Put yourself in their position so you can more fully understand what they were going through. State the issues and concerns from "your" frame of reference, and make recommendations to be included in a policy statement by the government. Choose *one* as your frame of reference.

- Isabella del Rio, 25-year-old sister of SARS patient.
- Ruben Lopez, 34-year-old intern in the pediatrics ward where a baby has been checked in with SARS.
- Randy Parker, 19-year-old patient in the same hospital with a SARS patient. Rocky is in the hospital because of injuries sustained in a motorcycle accident (he lost his spleen and suffered two broken ribs and a fractured ankle).
- Mary Chung, 41-year-old lab assistant in the hospital wing where there are 14 SARS patients.
- Peter Tate, 28-year-old cousin of Nicola Tate, 23-year-old SARS patient.

Exercises

Part One

Directions: List some possible causes of the effect or event mentioned.

1. Your neighbor's burglar alarm goes off and continues for over an hour. You bang on their door but get no response, although both of their cars are on the street. Thirty minutes later it is quiet.
2. At 7:40 A.M. you go out to start your car and there is only a grating sound.

3. One evening you are sitting in your living room, watching TV, and you hear a loud sound in the direction of your backyard. You look out and realize there is a helicopter aiming a bright light at your yard and at the two neighbors' yards south of your house.

4. Over 300 people are on a flight from Halifax to Los Angeles. They stop in Detroit to refuel and bring on food. After landing, 158 people complain of dizziness, nausea, and vomiting. Upon investigating, the airline discovers that everyone who felt ill had eaten the pressed turkey sandwich.

5. Ramona lives in a working-class neighborhood and attends an urban college where most students are commuters. She works part-time at a copy shop. One day she left class and discovered a deep scratch mark the entire length of her car.

6. Windows were shattered and obscene graffiti was left at a construction site for a mosque in Milpitas, California, near San Francisco. Police were summoned to the Montague Expressway site at about 7:45 P.M. Tuesday, said Lt. Sandy Holliday. There, they found windows shattered and belongings strewn about a construction trailer and camper parked behind a large industrial building that the Al-Hilaal Islamic Charitable Foundation plans to turn into a turreted masjid, or mosque. The graffiti included references to the devil and obscene phrases about Arabs.

7. "The Health District received reports of acute gastrointestinal illness that occurred among children and staff at two jointly owned day care centers after a catered lunch. The lunch was served to 82 children age six or younger and to nine staff members; dietary histories were obtained for 80 people. Staff and all children aged four years old or older were interviewed directly; staff and parents were questioned for children younger than four years old. Of the 80 people, 67 ate the catered lunch. Fourteen people (21 percent) who ate the lunch became ill, compared with none of 13 who did not. Chicken fried rice prepared at a local restaurant was the only food significantly associated with illness; illness occurred in 14 of 48 persons (29 percent) who ate chicken fried rice, compared with none of 16 who did not; three of those who were not ill were uncertain if they had eaten the rice. Other food items (peas and apple rings) were not available for analysis" (as noted in "Bacillus Cereus Food Poisoning," www.textbookofbacteriology.net).

8. "According to the results of a very small new study (10 patients), some people may experience migraine headaches due to wheat. By limiting gluten—a protein found in wheat, oats, barley and rye—seven of nine patients reduced their symptoms of severe headache. Evidently these patients had a sensitivity to gluten, and magnetic resonance imaging (MRI) scans suggested they had inflammation in the central nervous system. Nine of the 10 patients tried a gluten-free diet, and 7 stopped having headaches. Two other patients had some, but not complete, success by switching to a gluten-free diet. One patient did not follow the diet" (Dr. Joseph Mercola, www.mercola.com).

Part Two

1. Read this passage and then complete the exercise that follows.

   Fifteen thousand banana workers who worked with pesticides and who are now sterile are suing companies (Dow Chemical, Shell Oil, Standard Fruit Co., Chiquita Brands, Inc.) that manufacture and use the pesticide DBCP. Dow and Shell developed DBCP to combat microscopic worms that attack banana plants. It was widely used in the 1960s and '70s. Banana workers who applied the chemicals had no protective clothes or gloves. Eight thousand Costa Rican workers are apparently sterilized and they blame DBCP. (*Multinational Monitor,* Jul-Aug 1990). At the 2007 trial, attorney Duane C. Miller stated that, after male farm-workers in Arkansas became sterile in 1977, Dow suspended the use of DBCP. Dow then sought to recall the pesticide. Dow responded that there was no evidence it caused sterility—even though they "hadn't checked the workers." Dole said it would indemnify Dow if anyone sued over use of DBCP, Miller said. Dow then sold 500,000 gallons of DBCP to Dole. The workers were not told that DBCP might affect their fertility. (Stephanie Hoops, "Banana Workers' Suit Goes to Trial," *Ventura County Star,* 20 Jul 2007).

   State the evidence that most supports the banana workers' lawsuit and any questions or concerns you have about the way Dow and Dole handled the case.

2. According to a February 5, 2008, report, human viruses appear to be causing respiratory problems in chimps. Researchers from the Max Planck Institute for Evolutionary Anthropology identified several pathogens in tissues from chimps that died in Tai National Park, where chimps are accustomed to people being present. Among the pathogens were strains of the human respiratory syncytial virus (HRSV) and the human metapneumovirus (HMPV), both leading causes of respiratory disease in humans. Genetic testing showed that these strains diverged from human strains less than 10 years before— indicating that the viruses, which are shed in respiration, sweat, and feces, were transmitted from humans to the apes (Henry Fountain, "Human Viruses Cause Respiratory Outbreaks in Ivory Coast Chimps," *The New York Times,* 5 Feb 2008).

   State what evidence is cited to back up the conclusion.

3. You are on the jury in the felony case involving transplant surgeon Dr. Hootan Roozrokh, accused of "dependent adult abuse, administering a harmful substance and prescribing controlled substances without a legitimate medical purpose" (*Los Angeles Times,* 31 Jul 2007). The contention is that he excessively prescribed drugs to a 25-year-old disabled man in order to hasten his death and harvest his organs. The doctor ordered a total of 200 milligrams of the narcotic morphine and 80 milligrams of the sedative Ativan for him, according to federal inspectors. This is many times the normal doses of the two drugs.

   State what more you need to know in order to decide how seriously to take the charges against Dr. Roozrokh after you read each of the following:

   a. **Chief Deputy District Attorney Stephen Brown:** The law and the facts indicated that Dr. Roozrokh "tried to accelerate Navarro's death to facilitate the harvesting of his organs."

   b. **Defense attorney M. Gerald Schwartzbach:** Dr. Navarro is an "extremely dedicated and accomplished organ transplant surgeon," and the charges filed against him were "unfounded and ill-advised."

   c. **Brown:** The central issue was the "mistreatment of a severely disabled adult." Navarro survived for hours after being given the drugs.

   d. **Schwartzbach:** "Nothing that Dr. Roozrokh did or said at the hospital that night adversely affected the quality of Mr. Navarro's life or contributed to Mr. Navarro's eventual death."

4. Read the following and then answer the questions below.

The United Nations Food and Agriculture Organization reported that our diets and, specifically, the meat in them cause more greenhouse gases than either transportation or industry. It turns out that producing half a pound of hamburger for someone's lunch releases as much greenhouse gas into the atmosphere as driving a 3,000-pound car nearly 10 miles.

[Economist Susan] Subak stated that, "producing a pound of beef in a feedlot . . . generates the equivalent of 14.8 pounds of CO2 pound for pound, more than 36 times the CO2 equivalent greenhouse gas emitted by producing asparagus. Even other common meats cannot match the impact of beef; I estimate that producing a pound of pork generates the equivalent of 3.8 pounds of CO2; a pound of chicken generates 1.1 pounds of CO2 equivalent greenhouse gases." (Nathan Fiala , "How Meat Contributes To Global Warming Producing Beef For The Table Has A Surprising Environmental Cost," *Scientific American*, 4 Feb 2009)

   a. How strong is the evidence that people should be discouraged from eating so much beef?

   b. Do wealthier, beef-eating nations owe any obligation to poor nations—all of whom experience the effects of global warming? Give a brief argument, in light of the data above.

5. Read about the experiences of some Iraq war facts, and then answer the questions that follow:

Six soldiers who have fallen ill since their return from Iraq said Friday that the Army ignored their complaints about uranium poisoning from U.S. weapons fired during combat. . . . "We were all healthy when we left home. Now, I suffer from headaches, fatigue, dizziness, blood in the urine, unexplained rashes," said Sgt. Jerry Ojeda, 28, who was stationed south of Baghdad with other National Guard members of the 442nd Military Police Company. He said symptoms also include shortness of breath, migraines and nausea. . . .

Five of the men said they also were recently tested independently by Dr. Asaf Durakovic, a former Army doctor and nuclear medicine expert, who found traces of depleted uranium in their bloodstream, with four registering high levels. . . . Since the start of the Iraq war, U.S. forces reportedly have fired at least 120 tons of shells packed with depleted uranium. . . . It is far less radioactive than natural uranium. (Associated Press, "Army Ignored Illness Complaints," 10 Apr 2004)

If you were asked to speak for the Iraq war veterans who have suffered the symptoms noted above, what argument would you make to the U.S. government?

6. Read about a surgeon who thinks music helps healing. Then answer the questions that follow.

Like many surgeons, Dr. Conrad says he works better when he listens to music. And he cites studies showing that music is helpful to patients as well—bringing relaxation and reducing blood pressure, heart rate, stress hormones, pain and the need for pain medication. He believes that music may exert healing and sedative effects partly through a paradoxical stimulation of a growth hormone generally associated with stress rather than healing. This jump in growth hormone, said Dr. John Morley, an endocrinologist not involved with the study, "is not what you'd expect, and it's not precisely clear what it means."

The study itself was fairly simple. The researchers fitted 10 postsurgical intensive-care patients with headphones, and in the hour just after the patients' sedation was lifted, 5 were treated to gentle Mozart piano music while 5 heard nothing. The patients listening to music showed several responses that Dr. Conrad expected: reduced blood pressure and heart rate, less need for pain medication and a 20 percent drop in two important stress hormones, epinephrine and interleukin-6, or IL-6. Amid these expected responses was the study's new finding: a 50 percent jump in pituitary growth hormone. Dr. Conrad argues that the growth hormone [has] a sedative effect. The growth hormone itself may reduce the interleukin-6 and epinephrine levels that produce inflammation that in turn causes pain and raises blood pressure and the heart rate. ("Scientist at Work," *The New York Times,* 20 May 2008)

a. What are all the medical benefits Dr. Conrad believes result from listening to music?
b. Does the fact that he found a jump in a growth hormone when music was played indicate that music was the cause?
c. What significance should be made of the word "may" in the last sentence?

7. Read about a case of an altercation outside a store. Then answer the questions that follow.

A white man is suing the city because police failed to respond to his seven calls to 911 (emergency). An angry crowd gathered outside his store after he ran out of stereo speakers that were on sale. It seems he had only five such items in stock. He offered to order more, but the crowd accused him of exploiting them (they were all Filipino) and started screaming. He claimed they made threats. The crowd dispersed after a half hour, and no damage was done to his store. Nevertheless, the store owner is suing the city for $1 million. He insists the police's failure to respond put him at risk, and he has suffered a nervous disorder ever since.

a. If you were on the jury, what more would you need to know before you would consider the man deserving of any settlement?
b. What more would you want to know before you would rule in favor of the city?

Quick Quiz

1. *True or false:* Cause-and-effect reasoning is a form of valid argumentation, because the conclusion cannot be false if the premises are true.

2. *True or false:* Cause-and-effect reasoning is often found in medicine and health care.

3. The term *correlation* refers to:
   a. The causal connection between inductive terms
   b. The causal connection between deductive terms
   c. The measure of the connection between the effect and its consequences
   d. The measure of the association between two things and how they are linked

4. *True or false:* Inductive arguments can never be valid or sound arguments.

5. When we look at cause-and-effect reasoning, we are looking at arguments that claim:
   a. Two or more things are causally connected—so if one happens, the other is likely to happen as well.
   b. Two or more things are certainly connected—so if one happens, the other will necessarily happen as well.
   c. Two or more things are linked together in ways that cannot be measured.
   d. Two or more things act as assumptions in a deductive argument.

6. *True or false:* If two things are correlated, then they are causally connected.

7. An example of cause-and-effect reasoning is:
   a. Saying that if you smoke, you'll probably get lung cancer
   b. Saying that if 86% of smokers have bad breath, then Josephina, who smokes, must have bad breath
   c. Saying that if all smokers are addicts, then Pablo, a cigar smoker, must be an addict
   d. Saying that if no one with pneumonia should smoke, then Lucia, who has pneumonia, should not start smoking

Correlations and False Correlations

Sometimes people draw causal connections between events that are unrelated. We see it in **post hoc reasoning**, where an inference is drawn that something causes another thing to happen just because it happened at an earlier time. (See Chapter 7 for review.) The fact that one thing precedes another does not necessarily mean they are related. To infer that they are linked without sufficient evidence is a **false correlation**. To assert such a relationship requires more evidence than the temporal sequence of when the two events happened. We need to show that there are causal—not just temporal—links between them.

Consider this unpublished study: In an attempt to explain the drop in crime in the 1990s, researchers pointed out that it could be related to the legalization

You Tell Me Department

Can We Curb Children's Exposure to Media Violence?

Three Iowa State University psychologists identified four reasons for the failure of past public policy efforts to curb children's exposure to media violence (see "Psychologists Explore Public Policy and Effects of Media Violence on Children," *ScienceDaily,* 27 Dec 2007). They found:

1. An apparent gap between what scientific findings suggest and what the U.S. courts and society understand, partially due to different conceptions of causality used by scientists and the legal system.
2. Confusion about scientific findings in court, partly due to opposing "expert" testimony—such as video game industry "experts," who would not be considered by the scientific community as real experts on media violence.

3. Different standards of causality applied by courts than by most medical and behavioral scientists—standards that change depending on the type of legal issue. In particular, U.S. courts are appropriately conservative about regulating freedom of speech because it is at the core of democracy.
4. Lack of precedent. Legislation to restrict access is unlikely to survive First Amendment challenges, because courts rely on precedent. They are unlikely to rule differently until enough time has passed for new research to be conducted and new evidence presented.

You tell me: What are the strongest points the three researchers raised? Which one could most easily be addressed? Explain how.

---

of abortion in 1973. They argued: "Many women whose children would have been most likely to commit crimes as young adults instead chose to abort their pregnancies. Because of that, a disproportionate number of would-be criminals in the 1990s were not born in the 1970s" (as cited in "Study Links Dip in Crime to Abortions," *Los Angeles Times,* 9 Aug 1999).

Look at the conclusions researchers drew. The drop in crime could relate to the fact that fewer would-be criminals were born 20 years earlier—but that could be a false correlation. Perhaps there was a drop in crime because society had changed, or perhaps because the educational system was better, or perhaps because current sentencing laws were a deterrent. It may also have been due to a rise in women breast-feeding their babies, making them more psychologically stable. And so on. Without more evidence linking abortion laws to crime statistics, the presumed correlation leaves a lot to the imagination.

Mill's Methods of Assessing Cause-and-Effect Arguments

Philosopher John Stuart Mill set forth a systematic way to look at cause-and-effect arguments. His system provides us with helpful tools for recognizing and assessing the basis for cause-and-effect reasoning. These methods are (1) the method of agreement, (2) the method of difference, (3) the joint method, and (4) the method of concomitant variation.

The Global Dimension

Finland's Impressive Literacy Model

Finland may have shockingly high diabetes rates, but it's made quite a mark with its literacy rate. Finland is rated the world's best in educating children. Should we follow their lead in putting subtitles on TV shows? Read the following report and answer the questions below.

Imagine an educational system where children do not start school until they are 7, where spending is a paltry $5,000 a year per student, where there are no gifted programs and class sizes often approach 30. A prescription for failure, no doubt, in the eyes of many experts, but in this case a description of Finnish schools, which were recently ranked the world's best. Finland topped a respected international survey last year, coming in first in literacy and placing in the top five in math and science. . . .

Children here start school late on the theory that they will learn to love learning through play. Preschool for 6-year-olds is optional, although most attend. And since most women work outside the home in Finland, children usually go to day care after they turn one. At first, the 7-year-olds lag behind their peers in other countries in reading, but they catch up almost immediately and then excel. Experts cite several reasons: reading to children, telling folk tales and going to the library are activities cherished in Finland. Lastly, children grow up watching television shows and movies (many in English) with subtitles. So they read while they watch TV.

So long as schools stick to the core national curriculum, which lays out goals and subject areas, they are free to teach the way they want. They can choose their textbooks or ditch them altogether, teach indoors or outdoors, cluster children in small or large groups. (Lizette Alvarez, "Educators Flocking to Finland, Land of Literate Children," *Suutarila Journal*, 9 Apr 2004)

Answer the following:

1. From the report, what are the key causes attributed to the high literacy rate in Finland?
2. What is the strongest case to be made for adding subtitles to American TV shows?

The Method of Agreement. Here we seek the cause of an event by examining all the cases where the event occurs and then looking for a common factor. For example, when a group of people becomes ill, we often look for a common factor, such as exposure to a toxic chemical or spoiled food. If we can find a common factor, we may think we've solved the problem. In that case, we are using the **method of agreement,** which can be set out as follows:

Method of Agreement

Cases	Antecedent Conditions	Event (or Effect)
1	A, B, E, G, P	Event happens
2	C, D, K, P, W	Event happens
3	C, B, L, P, R, S	Event happens
...		
n	A, E, L, P, W, Z	Event happens

Note: In all the above cases, a common factor, P, precedes the event. By the method of agreement, this means the probable cause of the event is P. One problem with the method of agreement is that we might overlook the real cause. Perhaps the real cause is something we ignored or didn't add to the list; so we fail to determine the most probable cause of the event.

This happened when people at a convention came down with symptoms that had the experts baffled. When those attending the conference in Philadelphia, Pennsylvania, started keeling over (some died), investigators completely overlooked the hotel ventilation system as a possible cause or causal factor of the problem. Several days passed—and things got progressively worse—until investigators asked themselves if the air the folks breathed could have contributed to their being stricken with the disease. By the time it was over, 221 people at the convention had contracted the disease, and 34 had died. Since most of those who died were Legionnaires (an association of ex-military members), they called it "Legionnaires' disease." That was in 1976—the first time the disease was encountered—and it was after that date that warnings to keep air conditioners clean were issued. Note that window units do not pose this problem because they use refrigerated air instead of evaporated water. (See "Legionnaire's Disease," *Multiline*, www.multiline.com.au.)

The Method of Difference.   With the **method of difference,** we compare two cases—one where an effect (or event) occurs and one where it doesn't occur. Next we look at the antecedent conditions for these two cases to determine what is different. In light of the differences, we then select the probable cause.

For example, suppose you buy two primroses and plant one in the sun and one in the shade. You put fertilizer on both of them and water them regularly. The primrose in the sun grows beautifully and has lots of blossoms. The primrose in the shade keels over and the leaves curl up. What do you think the problem is?

Let's see the method of difference set out in a table:

Method of Difference

CASES	ANTECEDENT CONDITIONS	EVENT
1	A, B, C, D, E	Effect occurs
2	A, B, C, E	Effect doesn't occur

Note: Only two cases are being compared—one when the event occurs and when it does not. The idea is to see what is *different* that might explain what caused the event to happen.

The problem with the method of difference is that we look at only two cases—one where the event occurs and another where it doesn't. This may not give enough data to draw a reliable conclusion. Also, we are looking only at *differences,* and the points of agreement may also be instructive in terms of what causes something to happen.

The Joint Method.   A more high-powered approach would be to combine the two methods, looking at both what is similar *and* what is different. This is what the **joint method** does. For example, suppose you plant 20 fields of corn. Fifteen

You Tell Me Department

Does Only the Mummy Know for Sure?

King Tut, mummies, and pyramids have fascinated many people for decades. Look, for instance, at the 1932 film *The Mummy*, starring Boris Karloff, and all the mummy films since. Interest in King Tut seems to be a bug that has bitten an awful lot of people! The latest theory about how Tutankhamun died fuels that interest:

> Researchers continue to investigate the cause of Tutankhamun's premature death. Bob Brier, a mummy specialist from Long Island University, has been tracking down clues that indicate

Tutankhamun may have been killed by his elderly chief advisor and successor, Ay. An X-ray of his skull revealed a calcified blood clot at its base. This could have been caused by a blow from a blunt implement, which eventually resulted in death. ("Tutankhamun, the Cause of His Death—Mysteries of Egypt," Canadian Museum of Civilization, www.civilization.ca)

You tell me: What sort of clues do you think Brier "tracked down" to arrive at his hypothesis? Do you know enough to be convinced? If not, what more do you need to conclude that Brier is probably right?

fields produce wonderful, tasty corn, and five fields only have dried, shriveled corn that even a hungry cow would reject. After wiping away your tears, you try to solve the problem. You discover that the fields with the wonderful corn are next to a pasture. Not only are the fields with crummy corn near a chemical dump, but people walking by throw their trash into them. This suggests that the common location of the successful fields figures in their yielding good-quality corn. Furthermore, both the chemical waste dump and the piles of trash landing on the struggling plants are differences that are significant enough to suggest a probable cause for these fields of corn doing so poorly. We can set out the joint method of agreement and difference like this:

Joint Method

Cases	Antecedent Conditions	Effect
1st group	A, B, D, F, P, W	Event occurs
2nd group	A, B, F, X, Y	Event doesn't occur

Note: A, B, and F are common antecedent conditions. What is different is that in the first group we find conditions D, P, and W, and in the second group conditions X and Y. Note also that there are *groups* of cases, not just two cases. This means we are more likely to discover the cause than with *either* of the first two methods and, consequently, that this is a more powerful method.

The Method of Concomitant Variation.   This last method is for cases that are not all or nothing, but where an effect occurs in degrees. With the **method of concomitant variation,** we might have increasing or decreasing amounts of some effect (like pollution in a city or disease patterns in a population). Although the effect always exists, its presence is a matter of percentage. We can set this out in this way:

Method of Concomitant Variation

CASES	ANTECEDENT CONDITIONS	EFFECT
1st group	A, B, C, D	Event occurs (E)
2nd group	A, B, C, D+	E+ (or E−)
3rd group	A, B, C, D−	E− (or E+)

Having more or less of some causal factors results in an increase or decrease of the effect (indicated by E+ and E– in the table). Note that the three different groups could be groups of individuals (say, when a disease appears in a population), or it could be groups at different times (say, when we are testing to see what happens when the air pollution goes up or down).

An example of the use of concomitant variation is the study of mosquito populations and health concerns. The West Nile virus is a potentially lethal disease transmitted by mosquitoes. The bite of an infected mosquito can be deadly for the victim. The West Nile virus appeared on the East Coast in 1999 and by January 2009 had infected humans in all but nine states. So, in ten years, the disease became a health concern beyond one state's borders. With the method of concomitant variation, researchers can study the varying rates of the spread of the disease.

Exercises

1. State the *difference* between Mill's method of agreement and method of difference (be specific).

2. Explain why the joint method of agreement and difference is considered a more powerful tool than the method of difference.

3. State when you would likely use the method of concomitant variation.

4. State which of Mill's methods to use in the following:

   On a recent trip to Kansas City, 23 bus passengers riding in the front of the bus felt itchy, broke out in hives and felt weak. The 15 passengers in the back of the bus were fine. It was found that a pesticide spray had been used in the first half of the bus, but not the second half.

5. State which of Mill's methods to use in the following:

   MIT Medical and Cambridge Hospital treated four MIT students and two members of the community for food poisoning last week. . . . "This is the worst that any food company can experience," said Tony Vo, a vendor at Goosebeary's. Last Tuesday, four MIT students and two members of the community reported cases of food poisoning after eating at the Goosebeary's food truck. All six ordered chicken teriyaki. (Jeffrey Greenbaum, "Goosebeary's Closes after Food Poisoning," *The Tech,* www-tech.mit.edu)

6. State which of Mill's methods to use in the following:

Research being conducted by JoEllen Welsh, a professor of biological sciences at Notre Dame, is offering intriguing clues about the role vitamin D might play in breast cancer treatment and prevention. Studies by Welsh have indicated that vitamin D can stop the growth of cancer cells and shrink tumors in mice. Welsh studied genetically engineered "knockout" mice that lack the vitamin D receptor to help determine the substance's function in breast tissue. "In the absence of the receptor, the mammary gland grows more than in normal mice," she said. "This suggests that when vitamin D is present, it slows down cell growth. . . . Treating cells with activators of the vitamin D receptor stops the growth of breast cancer cells and makes them undergo apoptosis, or cell death," she said. (William G. Gilroy, "Vitamin D May Help in Battle against Breast Cancer," *University of Notre Dame News,* newsinfo.nd.edu, 1 Mar 2004)

7. State which of Mill's methods to use in the following:

When Ryan had his first asthma attack, he stayed in bed, drank lots of fluids, ate lots of vitamin-rich foods, and used his inhaler. He felt better and breathed easier in five days. The second time Ryan had an asthma attack, he stayed in bed, drank lots of fluids, ate vitamin-rich foods, used his inhaler, and took prednisone. His symptoms cleared up in two days.

8. State which of Mill's methods to use in the following:

During the heat wave in the summer of 2004, there were eight smog alerts (dangerous levels of pollution) in southeastern Florida. One local hospital reported that the number of patients with breathing problems increased by 24%. By September, rates dropped back to around normal, and they decreased by 11% in November after temperatures dropped to the mid-40s.

9. State which of Mill's methods to use in the following:

Studies revealed that there were 18% more patients in the toxic hazards wing of the hospital in the first two weeks following pesticide spraying by agricultural firms in the area, but rates fell 8% after aerial spraying ceased, then another 12% when spraying on the ground was halted at the end of the growing season.

10. State which of Mill's methods to use in the following:

In an AIDS study, it was found that, of the 320 women in the study, 162 had had sexual contact with a partner who was HIV positive and used no protection. They were all found to be HIV positive. Another 138 women in the study had occasional sex with their HIV-positive partner but took precautions to protect themselves. None of them were found to be HIV positive.

Quick Quiz

1. *True or false:* The method of difference is used when the antecedent conditions differ but not the effects.

2. When cases have effects that occur in degrees, rather than all or nothing, you should use the (a) joint method or (b) method of concomitant variation.

3. The method to use when you have two groups in which there are shared but also different antecedent conditions, where in one case an event occurs and in the second case the event does not occur, is the (a) method of difference or (b) joint method.

4. *True or false*: Any argument that Mill's methods would apply to is an *inductive* argument.

5. The method to use when you compare two cases—one where the effect (or event) occurs and one where it doesn't occur—is the (a) method of agreement, (b) method of difference, or (c) joint method.

6. In the claim "If the circuits blow, the lights will go out," the antecedent condition is (a) the circuits blow or (b) the lights will go out.

7. *True or false:* In the method of agreement, all of the cases have the same effect, and you are looking at what differs among the antecedent conditions.

8. In the claim "The vandal who smashed car windows caused Katie to call the police to file a report," the effect (consequent) is (a) the vandal who smashed car windows or (b) Katie called the police to file a report.

9. If you were studying patterns of a contagious disease that struck a large city, you'd want to use the (a) method of agreement, (b) joint method, or (c) method of concomitant variation.

10 *Here's a case:* One day you went outside after a rain shower, and there were snails all over the front yard. When you saw that they had destroyed many of your lovely flowers, you vowed revenge. You spread borax on the sidewalk and in the flower beds. Three days later, it rained again. You went outside to stomp on snails and found only one small snail at the edge of the garden. Which of Mill's methods helped you crack the case?
a. Method of agreement
b. Method of difference
c. Joint method
d. Method of concomitant variation

Group or Individual Exercise

Directions: A number of lawsuits against tobacco manufacturers have been filed by consumers who were longtime smokers and ended up with either lung cancer or emphysema. Select *one* of the following to discuss:

1. If you were an advocate for the consumer suffering from lung disease, what steps would you take to strengthen your claims against the company?

2. If you were a CEO at a tobacco company, what steps would you take to strengthen the company's defense in these lawsuits?

3. If you were on a jury, what evidence would help you reach a decision about causation?

4. If you were a representative from the community on a committee reviewing the marketing of cigarettes, what sorts of warnings would you want to put on ads and packaging about the health risks of smoking?

Arguments Based on Statistical Studies

People frequently rely upon statistical data. **Arguments based on statistical studies** are inductive arguments since they draw an inference based on a sample group, where the evidence is partial at best. Statistical reasoning always entails a degree of probability—never certainty—in the relationship between the premises and the conclusion. We need to know how to properly use statistical studies to recognize strong arguments and avoid being fooled by weak ones.

For instance, suppose someone says, "A study of 150 men at a Dallas university revealed that 54% had used recreational drugs; therefore, we can conclude that 54% of Americans have used recreational drugs." Is this good reasoning?

- If you said, "No," pat yourself on the back.
- If you said, "Yes," fear not; you can be helped, so read on.

A **statistical study** has two components: (1) a **targeted population** about which we want information and (2) the **sample group** we intend to study as a microcosm of the larger group. In certain sorts of statistical studies, such as medical experiments, psychological testing, or pharmaceutical studies, research protocol may call for a control group. This group is used to compare relative responses (e.g., to a medical treatment or drug regimen) in order to eliminate other factors. In such cases, members of the control group are usually given some sort of placebo (i.e., a pill-like candy that has no medicinal value) to prevent the subjects from knowing whether they are in the control group or the experimental sample group.

Once we gather evidence from the sample study, we can *generalize* to the larger, targeted population, allowing for a certain margin of error. The **margin of error** recognizes that the inference from the smaller, sample group to the targeted population is somewhat uncertain. The study sample may or may not be representative of the whole. In statistical studies, there are always uncertainties, even in the most elaborate, well-crafted cases. For this reason, instead of concluding that x% of A is B, a margin of error is added: x plus-or-minus z% of A is B, where z recognizes the uncertainty in generalizing from the sample group to the targeted population.

Shifting Gears in Statistical Reasoning.   Whenever we go from a sample study or poll to a larger population, as in statistical reasoning, we have shifted gears. This is a move not seen in deductive reasoning. Compare these two types of arguments:

1. **Deductive argument:** 90% of the time, the Buffalo Creek banjo player plays "Hook and Line." Anyone who plays "Hook and Line" is playing an African-American tune. Therefore, the Buffalo Creek banjo player plays an African-American tune at least 90% of the time.
2. **Inductive argument:** 65% of fiddle players polled in Kentucky said they like to play solo as well as with a band. Therefore, 65% of *all* fiddle players in Kentucky like to play solo as well as with a band.

Here is how the gears shifted: We went from a polled group in Kentucky to those across the state. That's not the case in deductive arguments—even though we were using percentages there. The deductive argument has no such shift—in the example of the Buffalo Creek banjo player, the subject of the conclusion continued to be the Buffalo Creek banjo player.

A Word of Advice

If you really want to learn statistics, you need at least a semester-long course. However, we can get a general overview of statistical studies here.

Three Key Aspects of a Statistical Study

Date:	What is the date of the study? Is it still relevant?
Size:	How big was the sample group?
Diversity:	How diverse is the sample population? Is it representative of the target population?

The Importance of the Date

A statistical study conducted 10 years ago is most likely out of date. Even the results of a study conducted five years ago could be worthless. Try to find current research for your data.

Think of AIDS research. A great deal has happened in the last 10 years. Recent studies are more likely to be reliable than ones done in the past. Also, think how much has shifted in terms of DNA research. And what about media research? Or research on methods of communication? Fifty years ago, many people did not own television sets. Personal computers, DVD players, and cell phones are relatively recent additions, but they have had an impact on our lives. And think how much has changed with email access. This method of communication is far more powerful than telephones because we can ship documents, letters, essays, and the like around the world as attachments. Consequently, when examining statistical studies, pay attention to the date when they were conducted. Consider their relevance as well as their currency.

The Importance of Size

Next is the issue of **sample size.** This is the number of subjects in the sample group used as the basis for an inference about a target population. If we have only a small sample population and generalize to an entire city, our results would be of negligible value. For example, a study of 25 people in a city of 500,000 would have limited value. In fact, the fallacy of **hasty generalization** occurs when the sample size is too small. This happens, for instance, when people make generalizations about a type of ethnic food on the basis of one or two meals. A good study requires a large enough sample to avoid the problem of insufficient evidence.

The Importance of Diversity

Last is the issue of **diversity.** The sample should be representative of the population in question—namely, the one we seek information about in doing the study. This means it should have sufficient diversity, preferably comparable to the diversity of the target population. The fallacy of **biased statistics** results when the sample is not sufficiently diverse.

Two Ways to Get Sufficient Diversity in a Sample Study

1. **Representative sample.** A representative sample is obtained by matching the sample group with the target population. Try to keep a balance, among key characteristics such as gender, age, race, religion, education, class, and nationality or locality.
2. **Random sample.** A random sample is *not* obtained by carefully constructing a sample group, taking into account the relevant factors such as age, gender, nationality, and class. Rather, in a random sample, each member of the target population has an equal chance of being studied. We get a random sample by using some numerical means (like polling every third person, stopping every sixth driver, or interviewing every tenth voter) combined with a sufficient quantity. Hopefully, that process will generate enough diversity to reflect the target population.

For example, in the mid-1980s, a study of the San Pedro, California, police found that officers pulled over a disproportionate number of people of color in checking for drunk drivers. The group had a striking absence of white or wealthy drivers. Concerned about possible racism underlying who got targeted, the department instituted a change. They opted for random sampling, pulling over every sixth driver. Using this technique, *everyone* had an equal chance of being checked. The result was that those tested ranged across all racial groups, ages, and economic levels.

Group or Individual Exercise

1. In a 2008 survey by the British *Marketing Magazine,* the respondents' top five *most loved* celebrities were men. Of the five *most hated,* the top four were women—Heather Mills, Amy Winehouse, Victoria Beckham, and (ex–Atomic Kitten star) Kerry Katona. The question is, Why were men the "most loved" and why were four out of five of the "most hated" women? Before you

attempt to answer that, answer this: What questions would you like answered about the study before assuming the results should be taken seriously.

2. On April 22, 2008, the *Journal of Biology* published a study of chemotherapy. The Journal reported that "a commonly used chemotherapy drug causes healthy brain cells to die off long after treatment has ended and may be one of the underlying biological causes of the cognitive side effects—or 'chemo brain'— that many cancer patients experience." Assuming the study is solid, what more should be done (if anything) before issuing an alert to the general public and to those, like oncologists, who use chemotherapy as a medical treatment? Set out two or three suggestions.

3. Polls and the 2008 Democratic primary: What do you do when the polls give conflicted messages? Set out three recommendations for the media with regard to their handling of poll results, in light of the following situation (see "Obama by One. No, Ten. No, Five," *The Economist*, 1 Mar 2008).

   - The day before Super Tuesday, Barack Obama seemed to have the edge in delegate-rich California. One survey from John Zogby, a pollster, showed Obama leading Hillary Clinton by 13 points (49% to 36%). It was not to be. Clinton won California by 10 points—and Zogby was off by a whopping 23.
   - The average of published polls had Obama beating Clinton by 8 points in New Hampshire before the primary. The Illinois senator lost by 2. On Super Tuesday, the polls on the Democratic side were wrong in California, Missouri, Massachusetts, Georgia, and Alabama.

   The pollsters' reactions:

   - John Zogby explained his error by saying he had underestimated turnout among Hispanic voters, which was unusually high this year.
   - Robert Blendon, a Harvard professor, argued that the high turnout among some groups in the Democratic primaries confounded the screening techniques pollsters use to identify likely voters and the weighting they place on their results, which they base partly on previous years. The Democratic race saw record-breaking turnouts in several states, buoyed by young, low-income, and minority voters.
   - Andrew Kohut, president of the Pew Research Center, a polling and research organization, pointed out that everyone got New Hampshire wildly wrong. He speculated that the real problem lies in who picks up the phone. Poor voters are less likely to answer poll questions than richer ones, Kohut argues, and poor, white voters were less likely to vote for Obama. Hence the industry-wide error in New Hampshire, which has a tiny black population.

   Another factor: volatility. A quarter of California's Democratic primary voters determined their final choice within three days of the vote. Pollsters are made fools of by last-minute shifts in voters' allegiances.

Fallacious Use of Statistics

Two types of fallacies frequently show up in statistical reasoning. (See Chapter 7 for a fuller discussion.) These fallacies are:

- **Hasty generalization.** If the size is simply too small, a generalization from it could result in the fallacy of hasty generalization. This often underlies stereotypical reasoning. If the sample size is not sufficient, avoid drawing a generalization.
- **Biased statistics.** If the size is sufficient, a random sample will likely result in a sample representative of the target population. For example, in studies of human behavior, such factors as gender, race, religion, class, age, education, and nationality/locality might be factored in to fulfill the diversity quotient. The failure to do this results in the fallacy of biased statistics.

Group or Individual Exercise

Directions: The following health tips rest on research using statistical studies. Discuss the issues and concerns for each health tip and what questions you would want answered before concluding that the tip should be a guideline for good health. Which of the tips are most credible? List them from 1 (least credible) to 5 (most credible). Explain your rating. Note any reasoning you find questionable.

Health Tip 1: The use of powerful painkilling drugs during labor may have a permanent effect on the brains of babies, making them nearly five times as likely to grow up to be drug users. According to a Swedish study, exposure to multiple drug doses can lead to drug problems later. (*Daily Mail,* www.dailymail.co.uk, 30 Jan 2009).

Health Tip 2: Women who believe they are going to live for a long time are more likely than less optimistic women to give birth to sons, a new study suggests. Researchers reached the strange conclusion after completing a survey of British women who had recently become mothers. They found that for every extra year a woman thought she was going to live, the odds of her firstborn being a boy increased significantly. In the latest study, reported in the journal *Biology Letters,* 609 new mothers in Gloucestershire, southwest England, were asked, among other questions, to what age they expected to live (Ian Sample, "Optimists More Likely to Give Birth to Boys," *The Age,* www.theage.com.au, 5 Aug 2004).

Health Tip 3: Smoking is bad for your gums: Results of a new study indicated that teenage smokers are nearly three times as likely as their nonsmoking peers to have gum disease in their mid-20s. According to the authors of the study, the longer teenagers smoked, the greater the extent of gum disease (*Community Dentistry and Oral Epidemiology,* www.coloradohealthnet.org).

Health Tip 4: A survey by the National Sleep Foundation suggests that about half of American adults borrow from sleep to get more work done, watch late-night television, or surf the Internet. The amount of sleep needed varies from person to person, but the *Harvard Heart Letter* notes that for most people, eight hours seems to be about right. Over the short term, not getting enough sleep increases blood pressure and stress hormone levels. Sleep deprivation makes it difficult for the body to process blood sugar and reduces levels of leptin, an appetite-depressing hormone. These two changes could lead to diabetes and weight gain. . . . Set your internal clock by establishing a regular bedtime schedule. Avoid alcohol. . . . Regular exercise can aid a good night's sleep ("*Harvard Heart Letter* Examines the Costs of Not Getting Enough Sleep" *Harvard Health Publications,* www.health.harvard.edu, Aug 2004).

Health Tip 5: Laughter and a good sense of humor may help protect you against a heart attack, according to a recent study by cardiologists at the University of Maryland Medical Center in Baltimore. The study, the first to indicate that laughter may help prevent heart disease, found that people with heart disease were 40 percent less likely to laugh in a variety of situations compared to people of the same age without heart disease. People in the study with heart disease generally laughed less, even in positive situations, and they displayed more anger and hostility. "The ability to laugh—either naturally or as learned behavior—may have important implications in societies such as the U.S. where heart disease remains the number one killer," said Michael Miller, M.D., director of the Center for Preventive Cardiology at the University of Maryland Medical Center. (Michelle W. Murray, "Laughter is the "Best Medicine" for Your Heart," University of Maryland Medical Center, www.ummc.edu, 3 Nov 2008).

Confronting Problems in Statistical Studies

If someone who has had a heart attack is less likely to laugh, what should we infer? We may conclude, as in Health Tip 5, that the person's heart attack was the *result* of failing to laugh enough. However, it may be that the heart attack was *due* to an excessive amount of laughing, and thus, the victim has no desire to take up laughing to the degree prior to the cardiac arrest.

Alternatively, perhaps the heart attack victim finds a great deal hilarious afterward but finds a few topics (e.g., death, heart failure, doctors, hospital gowns) not at all funny, thus lowering the laugh-quotient and throwing off the statistical study. Without more information, it may be unwise to conclude that we should bring comedians into hospital cardiac wards. Statistical studies cannot always be taken at face value.

We might also question a study done of only 150 people. Was that a sufficient sample size? What race or ethnicity were the participants? Can we assume that a small size is adequate and that leaving out race and ethnicity is not a problem? These are questions we might want answered.

We may want to use a study that has some problems, in which case we need to decide what to do next. When the study is in doubt, we have two basic choices:

(1) Throw it out (in the event of serious concerns), or (2) examine its margin of error. Every study contains a margin of error. Because the inference from the sample study to the target population contains a wedge of doubt, the margin of error ought to be reflected in the conclusion—for example, "x plus or minus z% of A's are B's" (where z is some small number, usually 5 or lower).

A word of warning: The fact that you find statistical studies cited regularly does not mean you should assume they are credible or that the data are reliable. For one thing, they could be out of date, or the results of a too small or not diverse enough sample group. Or the study itself may have been flawed or fabricated. Don't assume that statistics are "facts" or that their use results in a true proposition or strong inductive argument. See Figure 8.1 for an example. This is a photograph of a burger stand in Los Angeles near a freeway off-ramp. The sign, as you can see, declares that it was "Voted Best Food in L.A." What you don't know is that this sign has been up for well over a year, so the date alone makes the claims dubious. Moreover, we definitely wonder, "Who voted? How many? And how was this vote taken? And by whom?" Perhaps it was taken of Rick's employees or by Rick's loyal, burger-loving customers. Questions abound, so be careful.

FIGURE 8.1
Some statistical claims are more dubious than others.

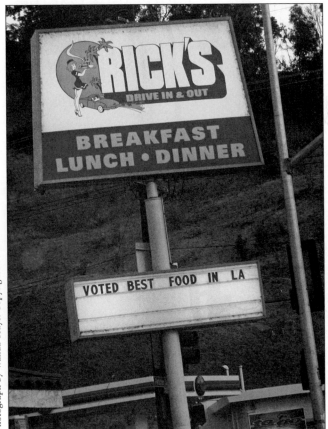

Photograph by Wanda Teays. Copyright 2008.

The Margin of Error

The smaller the margin of error is, the better. In well-orchestrated studies like those we see by the Gallup Organization, the margin of error is usually 2 or 3%. A margin of error over 5% may indicate a less reliable study. Mathematician Matthew Delaney considers a 5% margin of error hard to achieve; therefore, it may be unrealistic to think a study can achieve this level of accuracy.

Remember that the margin of error means the range goes from $-z\%$ to $+z\%$, which is a range of 2z. This means that if your margin of error is 3%, then the range is 6%, and a margin of error of 5% will give a range of 10%, which is a significant range. For example, 32% plus or minus 5% means the range goes from 27% to 37%—a range of 10 percentage points!

Group or Individual Exercise

Directions: Examine the hate crime statistics and then answer the questions that follow.

FBI Hate Crime Statistics: Victim Type by Bias Motivation, 2007

Bias Motivation	Total Incidents	Victim Type					
		Individual	Business/ Financial Institution	Government	Religious Organiza- tion	Society/ Public	Other/ Multiple/ Unknown
Total	7,624	5,974	391	253	237	11	758
Single-bias incidents	7,621	5,972	391	253	237	11	757
Race	3,870	3,158	218	167	30	5	292
Religion	1,400	665	102	56	201	0	376
Sexual orientation	1,265	1,169	30	16	2	1	47
Ethnicity national origin	1,007	911	34	14	4	3	41
Disability	79	69	7	0	0	2	1
Multiple-bias incidents*	3	2	0	0	0	0	1

*In a multiple-bias incident, two conditions must be met: (1) More than one offense type must occur in the incident, and (2) at least two offense types must be motivated by different biases.

Answer the following:

1. Which two groups have the most victims of hate crimes? Draw two inferences about victims of hate crime in the United States.

2. What are the two or three most significant types of bias, according to the table? Draw two inferences about the bias motivation of hate crimes.

3. Did you make any assumptions in answering items 1 and 2 above? If so, state them. What more would you like to know before setting out some recommendations for addressing hate crimes?

Two Forms of Statistical Arguments

Two forms of statistical arguments are prevalent: (1) statistical syllogisms and (2) inductive generalizations. Let's look at each of them.

Form of a Statistical Syllogism

x% of A is a B.

p is an A.

Therefore, p is a B.

A **statistical syllogism** has two premises. The first asserts that a percentage of the subject class (A) has some predicated characteristic (B). Then we conclude (here's the inductive aspect of the reasoning) that what was said of class A applies to a specified individual member of the class. Of course, the wedge of doubt is whether the individual member is in the x% of A with characteristic B or in the remaining 100 − x% of A that don't have the characteristic B.

(*Note:* If x = 100 or 0 in a statistical syllogism, then you no longer have an inductive argument; you have a *deductive* argument. Here's an example: "100% of apples are fruit. Snow apples are a kind of apple. Therefore, snow apples are fruit.")

Example 1

86% of women in Louisiana like shrimp creole.

Natalie is a woman living in Louisiana.

Therefore, Natalie likes shrimp creole.

Example 2

65% of cats prefer birds to mice for dinner.

Toast is a cat.

Therefore, Toast prefers birds to mice for dinner.

The strength of a statistical syllogism is directly proportional to the percentage. The closer to 100% in an affirmative claim, the better the argument. Basically,

85% and up (the higher the better) is strong. But the lower the percentage, the more questionable is the truth of the conclusion.

The second major kind of statistical argument is called an **inductive generalization.** In this case, we infer that what is true about the sample group is true in the targeted population as a whole. The wedge of doubt comes in the leap from the sample (about which we know some statistical data) to the targeted population the sample merely represents. As we know, the sample may not exactly resemble the whole group, so it is uncertain whether something true of the sample is really true of the larger group of which it is a part.

Form of an Inductive Generalization

x% of A's polled (or sampled) are B's.

Therefore, x% of all A's are B's.

In an inductive generalization we start with a sample study of the target population. We then infer that what was true of the sample group will also be true for the target population.

Example 1

73% of men polled outside the discount rug store in Obispo said they thought the president was doing a good job.

Therefore, 73% of American men think the president is doing a good job.

Example 2

49% of those in the *Investor's Business Daily* poll think the U.S. military actions in Iraq have not made the world a better place.

Therefore, 49% of the people think the U.S. military actions in Iraq have not made the world a better place.

In a strong inductive generalization, watch for date, size, and diversity. Be sure the poll is recent, the size is not too small, and the sample group is representative of the target population. The issue of diversity (that the sample represents the larger group) is crucial.

A Word of Advice

Be aware that there is a lot more to statistics than the two inductive arguments discussed here. A thorough knowledge of statistical methods is vital for anyone going into math, business, psychology, sociology, economics, or clinical studies. Moreover, not all arguments using statistics are inductive. Consider this example; "A toss of the coin will result in a 50% chance of getting heads. Joe tossed the coin. So, there's a 50% chance Joe will get heads." This argument is *deductive,* since the premises are sufficient for the conclusion and there is no wedge of doubt between the premises and the conclusion.

If you are familiar with these two inductive arguments based on statistics, you will be able to handle these two common forms: the statistical syllogism and the inductive generalization. The exercises below will help you analyze these two forms of argument when you come across them.

Exercises

1. Here is an inductive generalization:

    <u>76% of seniors in the bank poll prefer tellers to ATMs.</u>

    Therefore, 76% of seniors in the state prefer tellers to ATMs.
    a. What would you need to know to determine whether this is a good inductive generalization? (What are the criteria?)
    b. What could you do to strengthen the argument, if you cannot take the poll again?
2. Indicate which of the following are statistical syllogisms and which are inductive generalizations, and then discuss how strong the argument is.
    a. 63% of dogs are not as smart as birds. Aki is a dog. So, he must not be as smart as Jasper the cockatoo.
    b. 82% of the 75 people polled in winter 2009 by KBST radio prefer action films to documentaries. Therefore, 82% of all people prefer action films to documentaries.
    c. 72% of children 2 to 4 years old polled outside Magic Mountain said they think *Goodnight Moon* is a better bedtime story than *Curious George.* Therefore, 57% of all children 2 to 4 years old will prefer *Goodnight Moon* to *Curious George* at bedtime.
    d. 68% of action films show someone falling through a glass ceiling. *Quantum of Solace* is an action film. So, it must have someone falling through a glass ceiling!
    e. 56% of MSMC students polled outside the campus center said they are thinking of replacing their car with a scooter or motorcycle. Angie is an MSMC student. So, she'll probably want to get a scooter or motorcycle to replace her car.
3. Discuss whether the following arguments are strong statistical syllogisms:
    a. 82% of all women love sports cars.

        <u>Evangelina is a woman.</u>

        Therefore, Evangelina loves sports cars.
    b. 95% of mechanics have mood swings.

        <u>Harry is a mechanic.</u>

        So, Harry has mood swings.

c. 67% of air traffic controllers have problems with stress.

<u>Tracy is an air traffic controller.</u>

So, Tracy has problems with stress.

d. 81% of computer technicians have well-groomed hands.

<u>Yassir is a computer technician.</u>

So, Yassir has well-groomed hands.

e. 62% of electricians prefer incandescent to fluorescent lighting.

<u>Lenny is an electrician.</u>

So, Lenny prefers incandescent to fluorescent lighting.

f. 74% of gardeners prefer mulch to fertilizer.

<u>Elena is a gardener.</u>

So, Elena prefers mulch to fertilizer.

g. 46% of donuts are jellies.

<u>Big Hank is eating a donut.</u>

So he must be eating a jelly donut.

4. Give an example of a strong statistical syllogism, and explain why it is strong.

5. Give an example of a fairly strong, but not extremely strong, statistical syllogism.

6. Give an example of a weak statistical syllogism, explaining why it is weak.

7. State if this is a good inductive generalization, and explain why. Note any concerns you may have about the sample group.

A nationwide survey of actual voters reveals that Americans strongly support immigration enforcement, and that less than one-third of Obama voters favor granting amnesty to illegal aliens. The poll conducted by Zogby International on behalf of the Federation for American Immigration Reform (FAIR) on November 5 and 6 also found that a decisive majority of voters believe that an illegal alien amnesty would "further harm the interests of struggling American workers." This conclusion was based on the following poll results: 57% of voters stated that amnesty would harm American workers and further strain public resources, while only 26% believe amnesty would aid economic recovery and ease public burdens. (press release, "Zogby Post-Election Poll Reveals No Mandate for Illegal Alien Amnesty," Market Watch, 10 Nov 2008)

8. Give your assessment of the value of the poll results of this study:

Professor Whitaker wants to get out the vote of people in the under-30 age group. She took a poll of students at CSULB to see how many registered for the 2008 election and, of those, how many actually voted. Because her sample group had a disproportionately large number of Latinas in it compared to the number enrolled at the college, she calculated a margin of error of 8%.

9. What would you need to know in order to conclude an online poll is reliable? Are any concerns raised by the use of an online poll versus a phone poll? Can online polls avoid the fallacy of biased statistics? Share your thoughts after reading about the poll below.

Celebrities who win an Oscar next month should steer clear of politics during their acceptance speeches or risk alienating viewers. That's the word from 7,000 moviegoers who participated in an online poll [by online ticket seller www.fandango .com from December 27, 2008 to January 15, 2009].

The survey asked participants to name what they like most and least about Academy Awards telecasts. At 51%, the number 1 pet peeve is political speeches. "We don't care what you think about politics," one respondent wrote. Other top objections were: technical awards (34%); excessive length of the show (33%); live musical numbers (27%), and "forced" celebrity presenters' banter (26%).

The poll found that what audiences liked best are a single host for the show (65%), the "in memoriam" tribute (57%), the red carpet (fashion) pre-show (52%) and the opening monologue (48%). Plus, 27% voted for keeping the "best animated feature" category. Seventy-one per cent said they would be more likely to watch if *The Dark Knight* got a best picture nomination. ("Politics, Oscars Don't Mix: Poll," ABC News, Jan 20, 2009).

10. What can you infer from the following poll results?

Americans by a 2–1 margin support stem cell research and say it should be funded by the federal government, despite controversy over its use of human embryos. Advocates of this research say it can produce new treatments for disease, while critics oppose using embryos in research. After hearing these competing views, 58 percent of Americans support stem cell research, while 30 percent oppose it, according to a new *ABCNEWS/Beliefnet* poll. Six in 10 also say the federal government should fund it. Catholics support it personally by a margin of 54 percent to 35 percent, and favor its federal funding by a slightly wider margin, 60 percent to 32 percent. . . . One of the groups that's least supportive of stem cell research is blacks—the most solidly Democratic group in the nation. Forty-four percent of blacks personally oppose stem cell research, 15 points higher than the level of opposition among whites. . . . Among all groups examined in this poll, opposition to stem cell research is highest—58 percent—among people who think abortion should be illegal in all cases (they account for one in five Americans). More moderate abortion opponents, who think abortion should be mostly, but not always, illegal, divide about evenly on stem cell research.

Among the three in 10 adults who oppose stem cell research, 42 percent say their religious beliefs had the most influence on their opinion—making religion the most significant factor in this opposition by a wide margin. Nonetheless, that still leaves a majority of opponents who cite other chief influences, including personal nonreligious beliefs (17 percent), news accounts (13 percent) and personal experiences (9 percent).

Methodology—This *ABCNEWS/Beliefnet* poll was conducted by telephone June 20–24, 2002, among a random national sample of 1,023 adults. The results have a three-point error margin. (*ABC News,* www.abcnews.com)

Quick Quiz

1. A statistical study with a margin of error of 7% is (a) a strong study or (b) not likely to be reliable.

2. The three key aspects of a statistical study are:
   a. Date, size, diversity
   b. Date, size, control group
   c. Date, size, qualifications of person doing study
   d. Size, diversity, control group

3. *True or false:* A random sample is obtained by orchestrating a sample group so the relevant factors (like age, gender, and class) are taken into account when undertaking the study.

4. The fallacy of *hasty generalization* happens when a generalization is made based on:
   a. An old date
   b. Too large a sample
   c. A sample that is not diverse enough
   d. A sample that is too small or atypical

5. *True or false:* Arguments based on statistical studies are inductive arguments.

6. The *target population* is:
   a. The subjects in the sample group
   b. The population that is the focus of the statistical study
   c. The subjects in the control group
   d. The population outside of the sample group

7. A *representative sample* is obtained by trying to match:
   a. The target population with the sample group
   b. The random sample with the sample group
   c. The sample group with the target population
   d. The random sample with the target population

8. *True or false:* The fallacy of biased statistics occurs when the sample group is representative of the target population.

9. When assessing the quality of a statistical study, with regard to the margin of error, (a) the larger the better or (b) the smaller the better.

10. The argument "83% of large women prefer black to white shoes. Jemima is a large woman, so she'll want to buy those cute black sandals on sale at Bloomies!" is (a) an inductive generalization or (b) a statistical syllogism.

11. The argument "48% of petite women prefer high heels to platforms. Holly is a petite woman, so I bet she won't want those platforms, even though they are on sale for 50% off" is (a) an inductive generalization or (b) a hypothetical syllogism.

12. *True or false:* All inductive arguments citing statistics are inductive.

13. A statistical syllogism starts with "x% of A is a B." What is the second premise?
    a. y% of B is a C.
    b. p is a B.
    c. p is an A.
    d. B is a C.

14. If the inductive generalization has as its premise "52% of Alabama mudpies in the sample taken at Mo's Diner used whip cream instead of ice cream," what is the conclusion?
    a. 52% of all Alabama mudpies use whip cream instead of ice cream.
    b. All Alabama mudpies at Mo's Diner use whip cream instead of ice cream.
    c. 52% of desserts with whip cream are sold at Mo's Diner.
    d. I just tasted an Alabama mudpie, and therefore, it used whip cream instead of ice cream.

15. The argument "100% of motorcycles have no more than three wheels. Carlos drives a motorcycle to school, so it must not have more than three wheels" is:
    a. An inductive generalization
    b. A statistical syllogism
    c. A deductive argument
    d. An invalid argument

CHAPTER NINE

Stepping Stones of Logic: Syllogisms

When you are philosophizing you have to descend into the primeval chaos and feel at home there.

LUDWIG WITTGENSTEIN, *Culture and Value*

You are having dinner with your family when you realize that your father is serving your brother twice as many mashed potatoes as he gave your sister. You ask why. Your dad says, "Boys need to eat more than girls, that's why." Is your father's argument defensible? Let's see.

His argument is this: "All boys need to eat more than girls. Your brother is a boy. So, your brother needs to eat more than your sister." You probably have no trouble with the second premise—"Your brother is a boy." By definition, your brother is a male, and the only dispute might be whether he is young enough to warrant being called a "boy." So, you turn to the tricky premise, the first one. Is it true that "All boys need to eat more than girls"? If your sister were an Olympic athlete and your brother a receptionist, your sister would probably need more food. If, however, she is tiny and has a physically undemanding job, and he is 6 foot 7 and jogs to work, then she may need less. But it is not patently obvious that any given boy will need more food than any particular girl. We would need to know more about the individuals concerned. In that respect, the first premise is **contingent** on the specific circumstances and is neither certainly true nor certainly false. Consequently, your father's argument could not be said to be a sound one, given that the premises are not clearly true.

What your dad has done is to offer a **syllogism.** This is a three-line argument with two premises and one conclusion in which there are only three terms. In the argument above, the terms are "boys," "your brother," and "people who need more food than girls." If we replace the terms with variables, letting B = boys, Y = your brother, and P = people who need more food than girls, then the argument can be written as:

All B is P.

(All) Y is B.

Therefore, (All) Y is P.

Now we can examine the form of the argument and study the relationship between the premises and the conclusion. As we know from Chapter 5, this is a **deductive argument.** That is, the premises are claimed to provide sufficient support for the conclusion. We want to know: Is the argument valid? Is it sound? In this chapter, we will learn how to examine syllogisms in order to determine if they are valid or invalid.

Validity and Soundness

Your father's argument is well constructed. If it were true that all B is P and that all Y is B, then it would follow that all Y is P. No problem there. The concern isn't the structure of the argument, but the truth of the claims. This gives rise to two key issues—validity and soundness.

First is the issue of **validity.** The argument is structurally correct (*if* the premises are true, the conclusion cannot be false). This means the argument is valid. It does *not* mean that the premises are necessarily true. This is crucial to imprint on our brains. Validity is a structural problem, not a truth problem—contrary to how people commonly use the word "valid" to mean "good" or "true."

It helps to think of validity as similar to the concept of "beyond a reasonable doubt" in criminal trials. When you're on a jury listening to the presentation of evidence, you do not know if the claims (e.g., "Rip Long was seen lurking outside the victim's apartment") are *actually* true. As a juror, you assume the evidence presented is true. You then must decide whether the conclusion ("Rip Long beat Tony 'the Boy' Romero with a bat") is supported by the evidence. A strong case is when there is no reasonable alternative conclusion to be drawn from this set of premises.

Next is the issue of **soundness.** You may remember the two criteria for sound arguments: (1) The argument is valid, and (2) the premises are actually true. If an argument has both these characteristics, it is called a *sound* argument.

Only deductive arguments can be considered valid or invalid. Validity is an issue about the relationship between the premises and the conclusion—not about whether any statements are *actually* true. The question is: Do the premises, if they are assumed to be true, fully support the conclusion? In a valid argument, the conclusion *must* be true if we presume the premises are true; it could not be false.

With **inductive arguments,** the truth of the premises do not *necessarily* force the truth of the conclusion because there are missing pieces in the evidence. Thus, the wedge of doubt that resides with inductive reasoning. For example, this is an inductive argument: "85–90% of snakes are not venomous. Cobras are snakes. Therefore, cobras are not venomous."

In **valid deductive arguments,** however, the premises cannot be true and the conclusion false. This is slam-dunk reasoning. In a valid argument, the conclusion comes right out of the premises, leaving no doubt in our minds.

Examples of Valid Syllogisms

All reptiles are covered in feathers.

<u>All lizards are reptiles.</u>

Therefore, all lizards are covered in feathers.

If dessert is not a chocolate cake, then Nick will be disappointed.

<u>Nick was not disappointed.</u>

Therefore, dessert was a chocolate cake.

In both of these arguments, if the premises are true, the conclusion has to be true—it cannot be false. However, the first example is not a sound argument, because the premises are not both true. The second argument is not clearly sound; we need to know more about Nick's taste in desserts.

Example of a Sound Syllogism

Some convertibles are Porsches.

<u>All Porsches are cars.</u>

Therefore, some cars are convertibles.

Example of an Unsound Syllogism

All Lamborghinis are cars.

<u>All Lamborghinis are rare and exotic vehicles.</u>

Therefore, all cars are rare and exotic vehicles.

The first argument is sound because it is valid *and* the premises are actually true. In the second argument, the premises are true, but the conclusion could be false (in fact, it *is* false). Therefore, the syllogism is invalid and unsound.

Universal versus Particular Propositions

Propositions fall into one of two categories, as we saw in Chapter 4. They can be universal or particular claims. In a *universal* proposition, something is being predicated of *all* members of the subject class (i.e., that they either have or do not have some characteristic). The result is all-or-nothing claims, such as "All hawks are birds" and "No chickens are dogs." This includes propositions with subjects having only one member (e.g., a person, a city, or this particular thing). For example, "This chocolate truffle you gave me is a scrumptious treat" is a universal claim.

Basic Forms of Universal Claims

Form 1:	"All A is B."	→ Universal positive	"All parrots are birds that can talk."
Form 2:	"No A is B."	→ Universal negative	"No parrot is a duck."
Form 3:	"A is/is not B."	→ Universal positive/ negative	"Australia is a place with many parrots."
		→ *Where A has only one member*	"That baby parrot is an awfully darling bird!"

Examples of Universal (All-or-Nothing) Claims

All farmhands like a big breakfast.
That little boy is really out of control.
No weight lifter likes salad for lunch.
Any person who can drive a forklift is talented.
Every member of the film group liked *Groundhog Day*.
New Mexico is a magical place.
Ripley never liked Ash.
The U.S. Constitution is an important document.
100% of Carla's savings was spent on her trip to Scotland.

On the other hand, a proposition can be *particular*. In the case of a particular proposition, some trait is being predicated about some (but not all) of the subject class. This includes statistical propositions of the form x% of A is B, where x ≠ 100 or 0. Particular claims are about *some*, not all. Particular claims are never all-or-nothing propositions.

Basic Forms of Particular Claims

Form 1:	"Some A is B"	→ Particular positive	"Some chefs are good bakers."
Form 2:	"Some A is not B"	→ Particular negative	"Some truffles are not a chocolate candy."
Form 3:	"x% of A is/is not B"	→ Particular positive or negative	"64% of women are tea drinkers."
		→ Where x ≠ 100 or 0	"86% of soccer players are men."

Examples of Particular Claims

Some Italian food does not use tomatoes.
Many people in North Carolina are fond of lamb.
Most travelers to Nova Scotia bring digital cameras.
A few Apache at the filming of the last scene did not agree with the director.
Not all Turkish desserts contain honey.
92% of southern desserts are topped with ice cream.

▨ Categorical Propositions

Before we look at arguments, let's review how we can best express the propositions that constitute a syllogism. We will use a standardized approach, so we have
a technique for simplifying the terms of the argument. In Chapter 4, we learned
how to work with different sorts of claims. In analyzing a syllogism, it's usually
best to rewrite the premises and the conclusion in the form of categorical propositions. These are as follows:

The Four Categorical Propositions

Mood	Categorical Proposition	Example
A	All P are Q.	All basketball players are athletes.
E	No P is Q.	No violinist is a football player.
I	Some P is Q.	Some gymnasts are shy people.
O	Some P is not Q.	Some mountain climbers are not stamp collectors.

Variations of Categorical Propositions

1. **Proper nouns as subject.** When the subject is a proper noun or individual,
   then the claim is universal. Treat it as an A or E claim (A = positive, E =
   negative) (e.g., "Lisa is a wild woman" is an A claim, whereas "Kobe is not
   a short man" is an E claim).
2. **Statistical claims.** If you have statistical claims in which x% of A is B (where
   $x \neq 100$ or 0), then that claim is treated as an I or O claim (depending upon
   whether it's positive or negative). So, "82% of donuts are greasy" is an I
   claim, and "19% of chocolate is not addictive" is an O claim.

These forms (A, E, I, O) are called categorical propositions. (See Chapter 4 for
a review of categorical propositions.)

Negative Propositions

Handling negative propositions is easy once you can distinguish universal from
particular negative claims.

UNIVERSAL NEGATIVE CLAIMS	PARTICULAR NEGATIVE CLAIMS
No A is B.	Not all A is B. → Some A is not B.
A is never B. → No A is B.	Not every A is B. → Some A is not B.
Not any A is B. → No A is B.	Most A is not B. → Some A is not B.
Not a one A is B. → No A is B.	Many A is not B. → Some A is not B.
At no time is A a B. → No A is B.	x% of A is not B. → Some A is not B. (*where* $0 < x < 100$)

Examples of Negative Claims in Standard Form:

Yodeling is never acceptable in libraries.
        → No yodeling is an acceptable behavior in libraries.
Not any rotten fruit is tasty.
        → No rotten fruit is a tasty food.
Not all blues singers are women.
        → Some blues singers are not women.
Not every hiker is acquainted with Chaco Canyon.
        → Some hikers are not people acquainted with Chaco Canyon.

Categorical Syllogisms

A **categorical syllogism** is a syllogism in which the premises and the conclusion are categorical claims. The **standard form of a categorical syllogism** is what we have when we set out the syllogism in a particular order: major premise, minor premise, conclusion. We will learn how to do this, starting with the different terms of the syllogism.

The standard form of the syllogism always starts with the **major premise**. This is the premise that contains the *predicate* term (**major term**) found in the conclusion. The second premise is called the **minor premise,** and it contains the *subject* term (**minor term**) found in the conclusion. This means the premise nearest to the conclusion should contain the minor term (the subject of the conclusion). Both premises have a linking term (the middle term) that does not appear in the conclusion. The **middle term** is the term that is found only in the premises.

Here's an example:

Most cows are relatively calm.

Jerseys are cows.

Therefore, Jerseys are relatively calm animals.

Let us rewrite this argument so each proposition is in *standard form.* Express both of the premises and the conclusion in one of these four forms (abbreviated as A, E, I, O). Making things as uniform as possible helps streamline the process. The argument above in standard form is:

Some cows are relatively calm animals.

All Jerseys are cows.

Therefore, all Jerseys are relatively calm animals.

Notice that we had to change "*Most* cows are relatively calm" to "*Some* cows are relatively calm animals." Not only did we add the quantifier "some," but we also constructed a predicate class ("relatively calm animals"). Note also that "all" was added before "Jerseys" to make it explicit that the claim is universal. You need to do this to get the sentence into categorical form. It makes a big difference in a speedy assessment of arguments and makes errors less likely.

▨ The Three Terms of the Syllogism

Once we have the premises and conclusion expressed in standard form, we can take the next step. This is to locate the three terms. The major term is the predicate of the conclusion. In the example above, the major term is "relatively calm animals." The minor term is the subject of the conclusion—in this case, "Jerseys." And the middle term is the term that is only found in the two premises; here it is "cows."

Example of the Three Terms

Some easily irritated creatures are watchdogs.

All badgers are easily irritated creatures.

So, some badgers are watchdogs.

Major term   →   predicate of the conclusion, "watchdogs"
Minor term   →   subject of the conclusion, "badgers"
Middle term →   term only in the premises, "easily irritated creatures"

Exercises

Directions: Name the *major, minor,* and *middle* terms in the syllogisms below.

1. No dangerous substance is a thing that should be legal.
   All plutonium is a dangerous substance.
   Thus, no plutonium is a thing that should be legal.

2. Some snakes are poisonous animals.
   All poisonous animals are things to be avoided.
   So, some things to be avoided are snakes.

3. No good driver is a person who drives drunk.
   No drunk driver is a person worthy of respect.
   Therefore, all persons worthy of respect are good drivers.

4. No sound engineer is a person who likes blaring music.
   Trent is a sound engineer.
   So Trent is not someone who likes blaring music.

5. All attractive men are people who can wink.
   Big Mike is a person who can wink.
   So, Big Mike is an attractive man.

6. Some archaeologists are Celtics fans.
   No Celtics fan is an introvert.
   So, some introverts are not archaeologists.

7. Some music lovers are Latinos.
   All music lovers are people who sing while driving.
   So, some people who sing while driving are Latinos.

8. Some window washers are people scared of heights.
   No window washer is a person afraid to get wet.
   Therefore, some people afraid to get wet are not people scared of heights.

9. Some belly dancers are Egyptian.
   Some Egyptians are architects.
   Therefore, some architects are belly dancers.

10. All Nobel Prize winners are unusual people.
    Jorge Luis Borges is a Nobel Prize winner.
    Therefore, Jorge Luis Borges is an unusual person.

11. Some movies are things that waste money and time.
    Fargo is a movie.
    So, *Fargo* is a thing that wastes money and time.

12. Some people who sing karaoke are not neurotic people.
    All people who sing karaoke are people with a good sense of humor.
    Therefore, some people with a good sense of humor are not neurotic people.

13. Some radiologists are people who love to snorkel.
    Some people who love to snorkel are drifters.
    Therefore, some drifters are radiologists.

14. All x-ray technicians are risk takers.
    Some risk takers are mysterious people.
    Therefore, some mysterious people are x-ray technicians.

15. No weasel is a well-behaved pet.
    All guinea pigs are well-behaved pets.
    Therefore, some guinea pigs are not weasels.

16. Some birds are not falcons.
    All falcons are carnivores.
    Therefore, some carnivores are not birds.

17. All football players are big and burly people.
    <u>Some big and burly people are couch potatoes.</u>
    Therefore, some couch potatoes are football players.

18. All chefs are cooks.
    <u>No small child is a cook.</u>
    Therefore, no small child is a chef.

19. Some truck drivers are country music fans.
    <u>All country music fans are from Kentucky.</u>
    Therefore, some people from Kentucky are truck drivers.

20. Some short men are Oregonians.
    <u>Kareem is not a short man.</u>
    Therefore, Kareem is not an Oregonian.

Quick Quiz

1. *True or false:* An example of an "E" claim is "Some architects are poor swimmers."

2. Which of the following is a categorical proposition in standard form?
   a. A number of turtles were in Walden Pond.
   b. Some large mosquitos are insects loose in the tent.
   c. Several tourists got lost and took the wrong bus.
   d. Not all the lost tourists could communicate with the locals.

3. The *minor term* of a syllogism is the (a) subject or (b) predicate of the conclusion.

4. *True or false:* A syllogism can have three premises.

5. The four categorical propositions are:
   a. A, B, I, and J
   b. E, I, O and P
   c. A, E, I, and O
   d. A, B, C, and D

6. *True or false:* An example of a universal negative claim is "None of the pears were ripe."

7. What is the standard form of the proposition "Not any balloons were released at Juanita's party"?
   a. Not every balloon was something released at Juanita's party.
   b. Some balloons were not things released at Juanita's party.
   c. All balloons were things released at Juanita's party.
   d. No balloon was a thing released at Juanita's party.

8. In the syllogism "No campers are people who like hotels. Some people who like hotels are flight attendants. Therefore, some flight attendants are not campers," the *minor term* is:
   a. Campers
   b. People who like hotels
   c. Mysterious strangers
   d. People who don't like hotels

9. The proposition "Almost all of the lost tourists would eat the eel" can be written in *standard form* as (a) "Some lost tourists are not people who would eat the eel" or (b) "Some lost tourists are people who would eat the eel."

Major and Minor Premises

Order is everything in the world of syllogisms. If we are testing a syllogism, we must first set out the argument. Our first step is to locate the conclusion. If we don't know the conclusion, we won't know where the argument is headed.

Our next step is to examine the conclusion to determine which term is the major term and which is the minor term. The predicate is the major term, and once you know this, you also know the major premise. The major premise is the premise containing the major term. The subject of the conclusion is the minor term, and once you know this, you also know the minor premise. The minor premise is the premise containing the minor term. The middle term is the term found only in the premises (*not* in the conclusion).

Standard Form of a Syllogism

Major premise   →   Contains the major and middle terms

Minor premise   →   Contains the minor and middle terms

Conclusion   →   Contains the minor and major terms

Remember: Minor term = Subject of the conclusion
              Major term = Predicate of the conclusion
              Middle term = Term found in both premises

The first premise should contain the major term and the middle term. The second premise should contain the minor term and the middle term. The conclusion contains the major and minor terms. The argument must be exactly in this order to be in standard form.

Always double check: The premise *closest* to the conclusion should contain the minor term. If not, rearrange the premises. The major term should be in the first premise, and the minor term in the second premise. *Remember:* The major term is the last term of the conclusion—its predicate.

Be sure to express each proposition in *categorical form:*

Quantifier	Subject	Is/Are	Predicate
All	cats	are	animals
No	cats	are	dogs
Some	cats	are	picky eaters
Some	cats	are not	ill-mannered beasts

If the proposition does not have a quantifier such as "all" or "some," then we have to decide if it is universal or particular. For instance, "Skunks should be approached carefully" and "Scoundrels are immoral" would be rewritten as "All skunks are animals that should be approached carefully" and "All scoundrels are immoral people."

In contrast, "Muffins were eaten at breakfast" would be rewritten as "Some muffins were food eaten at breakfast," and "Nights can get cold in Alaska" would be rewritten as "Some nights are times that can get cold in Alaska." *Remember:* A universal claim is saying more than a particular claim because it has a broader scope.

Expressing Arguments in Standard Form

Let us practice working with what we know so far. Put this argument in standard form:

> Drummers are musicians
>
> <u>A lot of musicians are banjo players.</u>
>
> Therefore, all drummers play the banjo.

First, express the propositions in categorical form—in the form of A, E, I, or O claims. Then write the name of the proposition (A, E, I, O) on the left, for easy reference:

> A: All drummers are musicians.
>
> I: <u>Some musicians are banjo players.</u>
>
> A: Therefore, all drummers are banjo players.

The next step is to look at the conclusion. The predicate of the conclusion is "banjo players." That is the major term. The major premise must contain that term, so locate it in the premises. The major premise then is "Some musicians are banjo players." The major premise must be listed first. The remaining premise is the minor premise, containing the minor term "drummers." We can now put the argument in order:

> Major premise: Some musicians are banjo players.
>
> <u>Minor premise:</u>   <u>All drummers are musicians.</u>
>
> Conclusion: All drummers are banjo players.

We now have the argument in standard form.

Let's run through another one for practice. Put the following argument in standard form: "Every student enjoys a snooze. Joe enjoys a snooze. So, Joe is a student."

Always locate the conclusion first. The conclusion is "Joe is a student." In categorical form, that could be written "(All) Joe is a student" to remind you that the claim is universal positive. Adding "(All)" is optional; stick it in only if it is helpful as a reminder. Given that "a student" is the major term (the predicate of the conclusion), our major premise is "All students are people who enjoy a snooze." That leaves as our second premise the minor premise: "(All) Joe is a person who enjoys a snooze." Our argument can then be expressed in standard form as:

A: All students are people who enjoy a snooze.

A: <u>(All) Joe is a person who enjoys a snooze.</u>

A: (All) Joe is a student.

Note: The "All" was added before "Joe" to remind us that these are universal claims. The "All" is only a reminder. If you don't need it to jog your brain, leave it out.

Exercises

Directions: Put the following arguments in standard form, with each sentence expressed as a categorical proposition. Name the major, minor, and middle terms.

1. Every woman loves a challenge. All those who love a challenge are daredevils. As a result, all women are daredevils.

2. Many sports fans are men. All sports fans are people who like to discuss sports. Therefore, most sports fans are men.

3. A lot of children are afraid of the dark. Therefore, many children scream loudly, because most people afraid of the dark scream loudly.

4. No animal you can take for granted is a crocodile. Every pet is an animal you can take for granted. Consequently, no crocodile is a pet.

5. Some revolting creatures are dogs, because many dogs eat with their mouth open, and, any animal that eats with its mouth wide open is revolting.

6. All moths can fly. This is true because some insects are moths and most insects are creatures that can fly.

7. Count Dracula sucks blood. All vampires suck blood. Therefore, Count Dracula is a vampire.

8. No fruit is a vegetable. Some fruits are members of the citrus family. Therefore, some members of the citrus family are not vegetables.

9. Possums are smarter than most people think. A large number of animals that are smarter than most people think are birds. Therefore, some birds are possums.

10. Any earthquake is a scary thing to experience. Many scary things to experience are memorable. Therefore, a few earthquakes are memorable events.

11. Lots of movie stars are people who give to charity. Wimpy is not a movie star. So, Wimpy is not someone who gives to charity.

12. A few things recognized for their artistic merit are TV shows. *Jeopardy* is a TV show. Therefore, *Jeopardy* is a TV show that has been recognized for its artistic merit.

13. Most painters have a steady hand. No painter is a mean person. Therefore, some mean people don't have a steady hand.

14. All dreams about being swallowed whole are nightmares. Many dreams about sharks are dreams about being swallowed whole. Therefore, almost every dream about sharks is a nightmare.

15. Vacations are enjoyable moments. Going without sleep is not an enjoyable moment. Therefore, times you go without sleep are not vacations.

16. No hockey game is a boring sport. Many badminton games are boring. Therefore, no hockey game is a badminton game.

17. Scary movies frighten Bob. Bob avoids everything that frightens him. Therefore, all scary movies are things Bob avoids.

18. Every photographer is patient. A few cowhands are photographers. Therefore, all cowhands are patient people.

19. Every tall animal is able to look over fences. Lots of animals able to look over fences are not warthogs. Therefore, a large number of warthogs are not tall animals.

20. Not one donut is a filling snack. All popcorn is a filling snack. Therefore, not any donut is popcorn.

Quick Quiz

1. *True or false:* The minor term is the predicate of the conclusion.

2. You can find the middle term by looking at the (a) premises or (b) conclusion.

3. The major term is the (a) predicate of the conclusion or (b) subject of the conclusion.

4. *True or false:* The standard form of "Lots of balloons pop" is "Some balloons are things that pop."

5. An example of an E claim is:
   a. All yams are vegetables.
   b. No yam is a tomato.
   c. Some children are not people who love candied yams.
   d. Some seniors are people who like mashed yams.

6. *True or false:* "Some musicians are people with pet monkeys" is an O claim.

7. An example of an I claim is:
   a. Some musicians are people who wish they had a pet monkey.
   b. Some monkeys are not animals that like bananas.
   c. All fiddlers are musicians.
   d. No dancer is a person who lacks rhythm.

8. *True or false:* "Not all horses are ponies" can be rewritten "Some horses are not ponies."

9. "No racehorse is an easy animal to care for" is an example of (a) an O claim or (b) an E claim.

10. The major term in the argument "No cows are elk. All elk are large mammals. Therefore, no cows are large mammals" is (a) cows, (b) elk, or (c) large mammals.

The Mood of a Syllogism

The **mood** of a syllogism is the list of the types of claims (A, E, I, and O) of the major premise, minor premise, and conclusion (in that order). Because there are two premises and one conclusion, we will use three letters to indicate the categorical propositions that constitute the syllogism. For example, the syllogism below is in standard form:

All children are people who like marshmallows.

Some bicyclists are children.

Therefore, some bicyclists are people who like marshmallows.

The mood of this syllogism can then be read as AII (the major premise is an A claim, the minor premise is an I claim, and the conclusion is an I claim).

Handy Abbreviations

P = Predicate of the conclusion   →   Major term
S = Subject of the conclusion   →   Minor term
M = Linking term in both premises   →   Middle term

The Figure of a Syllogism

The **figure** of a syllogism is the placement of the middle term in the two premises. Let P = major term, S = minor term, and M = middle term. To determine the figure, we need to see where the middle term is located. There are four possible locations of the middle term in any syllogism.

Once the syllogism is in standard categorical form, the major term P should be in the first premise, the minor term S in the second premise, and the middle term in both premises. The arrangement of the middle term reveals the figure.

The Figures of the Syllogism

FIGURE 1	FIGURE 2	FIGURE 3	FIGURE 4
M ╲ P	P M	M P	P M
S ╲→ M	S M	M ↓ S	M S
S P	S P	S P	S P
Figure 1: M's step down right	Figure 2: M's on right	Figure 3: M's on left	Figure 4: M's step up left

Examples of the Different Figures

Mood and figure EIO—(1)
    No **M** is P.
    Some S is **M.**
So, Some S is not P.

For example:
No cars are trucks.
Some Toyotas are cars.
So, some Toyotas are not trucks.

Mood and figure AOO—(2)
    All P is **M.**
    Some S is not **M.**
So, Some S is not P.

For example:
All Corvettes are cars.
Some vehicles are not cars.
So, some vehicles are not Corvettes.

Mood and figure AEE—(3)
    All **M** is P.
    No **M** is S.
So, No S is P.

For example:
All Lexus cars are luxury vehicles.
No Lexus car is a BMW.
So, no BMW is a luxury vehicle.

Mood and figure AIA—(4)
    All P is **M.**
    Some **M** is S.
So, All S is P.

For example:
All Land Rovers are all-terrain vehicles.
Some all-terrain vehicles are jeeps.
So, all jeeps are Land Rovers.

Exercises

Directions: Put the following syllogisms in standard form, and then state the mood and figure.

1. No nurse is afraid to touch people. John is afraid to touch people. So John is not a nurse.

2. Some ice skaters love Korean barbeques. Gabriel is a person who loves Korean barbeques. So, Gabriel is an ice skater.

3. Surgeons are people with a mind for details. A number of people with a mind for details are people who love to do their taxes. Therefore, all people who love to do their taxes are surgeons.

4. No Rolls Royce mechanic is afraid to get dirty. Some Rolls Royce mechanics are not cooks. Therefore, some cooks are afraid to get dirty.

5. Many purchasing agents like to do paperwork. No person who likes to do paperwork is a hair stylist. Therefore, no hair stylist is a purchasing agent.

6. All photographers have a highly developed visual sense. All photographers are artists. Therefore, some artists have a highly developed visual sense.

7. Some welders have a talent for fine metalwork. All jewelers have a talent for fine metalwork. Therefore, some welders are jewelers.

8. All lawyers are analytical people. Some practical jokers are analytical people. Therefore, some lawyers are not fond of playing jokes on others.

9. Some people with a sardonic sense of humor are judges. All people who liked *Fargo* are people with a sardonic sense of humor. Therefore, some people who liked *Fargo* are judges.

10. A few people over 6 feet tall are not gymnasts. Most gymnasts do great back flips. Therefore, some people who do great back flips are not over 6 feet tall.

11. The vast majority of waitresses are courteous. Not any waitresses is crazy about stamp collecting. So, many courteous people are crazy about stamp collecting.

12. Anyone who loves the blues is familiar with Jelly Roll Morton. All guitar players are people who are familiar with Jelly Roll Morton. Therefore, all blues lovers are guitar players.

13. Whoever likes comedy knows about the Marx Brothers. Will Smith likes comedy, so he must know about the Marx Brothers.

14. Some people who watch MTV are computer hackers. This is because many computer hackers are people who enjoy music videos. Also, everyone who enjoys music videos likes to watch MTV.

15. Most elderly folks enjoy playing Scrabble. A few elderly folks enjoy going to the racetrack. Therefore, a lot of people who enjoy going to the racetrack will enjoy playing Scrabble.

16. Children under 10 will like *The Never-Ending Story*. Here's why: All children under 10 like tales about flying creatures. *The Never-Ending Story* is a tale about a flying creature.

17. Just about all rabbits are furry animals. Not all furry animals are nice to pet. It follows that lots of rabbits are not nice to pet.

18. Not many violinists like jelly donuts. Joshua Bell is a violinist. Consequently, Joshua Bell doesn't like jelly donuts.

⊞ Checking for Validity

Before we can test the syllogism for validity, we need to know how to tell if a term is distributed. **Distribution** involves the question of how much. If your brother asked you to distribute a stack of leaflets, you'd know that he wants you to pass them all out. Distribution of a term is similar, in the sense that a distributed term includes all its members.

When we talk distribution, we are talking about the number of members of the class in question. If the term is meant to apply to *all* members of the class it defines, then it is called *distributed*. If it applies to only an indefinite part of those members, it's called *undistributed*. To grasp this concept, it helps to see the term "distribution" in operation. We will look at the key ways to test for distribution and then run through some examples. For any given proposition there are only two terms to examine to determine distribution—the subject and the predicate. The subject is distributed in any *universal* claim and the predicate is distributed in any *negative* claim. Let's look at this in more detail.

Checking the Distribution of Terms

Checking the distribution of terms involves two steps:

Step 1: Check the location of the term (is it the *subject* or the *predicate* of the proposition?).

Step 2: According to the location, check either the quality or the quantity of the proposition. If the term is in the subject place, then check if the proposition is universal (A or E). If so, the subject is distributed. If the term is in the predicate place, then check if the proposition is negative (E or O). If so, the predicate is distributed.

Distribution Table

PROPOSITION	DISTRIBUTED TERM
All P is Q.	subject
No P is Q.	subject *and* predicate
Some P is Q.	nothing
Some P is not Q.	predicate

Subject Distributed. If the proposition is *universal,* the subject is distributed, because you are saying that all the members of the subject class either have or don't have some characteristic.

Examples

All possums are slow-moving creatures.
→ Claim is universal. The subject is distributed in universal propositions, so the subject "possums" is distributed.

Some possums are animals that like cat food.
→ The claim is particular (*not* universal). The subject is not distributed in particular propositions, so the subject "possums" is not distributed.

Note: The term "some possums" tells us nothing about *all* possums in terms of liking cat food. Thus, the term "possums" is not distributed. For instance, "All pajamas are comfortable to wear" is talking about *all* pajamas, not just some of them. Similarly, "No bathtub is a good place to fall asleep in" is talking about *all* bathtubs and saying that they are *not* places you'd want to sleep in. So, *both A and E propositions have a distributed subject.*

Checking the Subject for Distribution

Check the *quantity* of the proposition.
→ See if the proposition is *universal*. The subject is distributed in A and E claims.

Examples

No cats are dogs.
→ Check the *quantity* of the proposition. The proposition is universal (E claim). The subject is distributed in an E claim, so the subject "cats" is distributed.

Some cats are not Persians.
→ Check the *quantity* of the proposition. The proposition is particular (O claim). The subject is not distributed in an O claim, so the subject "cats" is not distributed.

Predicate Distributed.   If the claim is *negative,* the predicate is distributed. This is because a negative is excluding the subject class (some or all of it) from having the characteristic set out in the predicate.

Examples

No rattlesnake is a well-mannered animal.
→ Check the *quality* of the proposition. The proposition is negative (E claim). The predicate is distributed in an E claim, so the predicate "well-mannered animal" is distributed.

All rattlesnakes are creatures that like the sun.
→ Check the *quality* of the proposition. The proposition is positive (A claim). The predicate is not distributed in an A claim, so the predicate "creatures that like the sun" is not distributed.

Note: There are creatures that like the sun (e.g., land turtles, hummingbirds, giraffes, elephants) that are not rattlesnakes.
  For instance, "No octopus can climb a tree" asserts that the class of animals that can climb trees does not contain *any* octopi—they are all excluded from the tree-climber class. Similarly, if you heard, "Some tall people are not basketball players," you would know that the term "basketball players" does not cover all

tall people—it excludes *all* those in the subject class. Therefore, the term "basket-ball players" is distributed. So, *both E and O claims distribute the predicate.*

Determining If the Predicate Is Distributed

Check the *quality* of the proposition.
→ See if the claim is *negative*. The predicate is distributed in E and O claims.

Examples

All wolfhounds are dogs.
→ Check the *quality* of the proposition. The proposition is positive (A claim). The predicate is not distributed in an A claim, so the predicate "dogs" is not distributed.

Some dogs are not chihuahuas.
→ Check the *quality* of the proposition. The proposition is negative (O claim). The predicate is distributed in an O claim, so the predicate "chihuahuas" is distributed.

Summary of Distribution

Checking subjects: To test a subject for distribution, look at the *quantity* (universal versus particular) of the proposition.
→ If the proposition is universal, the subject *is* distributed.
→ If the proposition is particular, the subject *is not* distributed.

Checking predicates: To test a predicate for distribution, look at the *quality* (positive versus negative) of the proposition.
→ If the proposition is negative, the predicate *is* distributed.
→ If the proposition is positive, the predicate *is not* distributed.

We can see how the terms are distributed in the table below. Notice that the subject is distributed only in *universal* claims, and the predicate is distributed only in *negative* claims.

Distribution

Type of Claim	Subject Distributed?	Predicate Distributed?
A	Yes	No
E	Yes	Yes
I	No	No
O	No	Yes

So, for example, in the claim "All novels are books," the term "novels" is distributed. In the claim "No screenplay is a novel," both "screenplay" and "novel" are distributed. In the claim "Some math textbooks are not great literature," the term "great literature" is distributed. But in the claim "Some poetry is an inspiration," neither term is distributed.

▓ Testing the Validity of a Syllogism: Two Methods

You know how to put a syllogism in standard form, and you know how to find the mood and the figure. The next step is to test for validity. The quickest way is to use the rules of the syllogism. However, an alternative method is to use Venn diagrams. We'll start with the rules of the syllogism and go through the method of testing validity. Then we'll turn to Venn diagrams. You can then decide which one works best for you.

Using the Rules of the Syllogism

Any syllogism that satisfies all of the rules is valid. The rules are listed in the box on page 386. Test for validity simply by running through each rule and seeing if the syllogism checks out on each one. Let's start with a syllogism in standard form.

Example 1

All psychologists are insightful people.

Some gardeners are insightful people.

So, some gardeners are psychologists.

Look at each claim, and set out the mood and figure. It is AII—(2). Run through the rules of the syllogism to see if AII—(2) is valid.

The first rule (about the middle term) is violated: Look at the middle term ("insightful people"). In the first premise, it is in the predicate. To be distributed, the predicate must be negative—but this claim is positive. So, the term is not distributed in the major premise. Check the minor premise: The minor premise is an I claim and nothing is distributed. That means this syllogism has an undistributed middle and violates rule 1; thus, it is invalid. If we check all the other rules, we can see that they are fine (rule 2 doesn't apply because nothing is distributed in the conclusion; rules 3 and 4 have to do with negatives, and there are no negatives here; and rule 5 doesn't apply because we do not have two universal premises or a universal conclusion).

Example 2

Some dogs are Siberian huskies.

No dog can talk.

So, no Siberian husky can talk.

First, make sure that it is in standard form and that the claims are expressed as categorical propositions. Rewriting the argument, we get:

Some dogs are Siberian huskies.

No dog is a creature that can talk.

So, no Siberian husky is a creature that can talk.

Rules of the Syllogism

Rule 1: The middle term must be distributed at least once.

Rule 2: If a term is distributed in the conclusion, it must also be distributed in its corresponding premise.

- **Illicit major:** When the major term is distributed in the conclusion but is not distributed in the major premise
- **Illicit minor:** When the minor term is distributed in the conclusion but is not distributed in the minor premise

Note: A valid syllogism does not require the conclusion to have distributed terms. But *if* a term is distributed in the conclusion, then it must also be distributed in its corresponding premise.

Rule 3: At least one premise must be positive (two negative premises = invalid argument).

Rule 4: If the syllogism has a negative premise, there must be a negative conclusion, and vice versa.

Rule 5: If *both* of the premises are universal, the conclusion must also be universal, and vice versa.

Now, put it in standard form. The predicate of the conclusion (major term) is "a creature that can talk." The major premise contains the major term, and that means the major premise is "No dog is a creature that can talk." That leaves the other premise, "Some dogs are Siberian huskies," as the minor premise. Note that it contains the minor term, "Siberian husky." Putting the syllogism in order (major premise, minor premise, conclusion), we get:

No dog is a creature that can talk.

<u>Some dogs are Siberian huskies.</u>

So, no Siberian husky is a creature that can talk.

Now we can test the syllogism. Note that the mood and figure of this argument is EIE—(3). Let us go through each rule, to see if the syllogism obeys each rule. Rule 1 is okay, because the major premise is negative and the middle term ("dog") is therefore distributed. Now check rule 2. The conclusion is an E claim, and that means both the major and minor terms are distributed, so we must check each premise to see that it is distributed in its corresponding premise. The major term is okay because the major premise is a universal negative. However, the minor term "Siberian husky" is not distributed in the minor premise, because the claim is an I claim, where nothing is distributed. This means we have an illicit minor. It also violates rule 5 (the universal conclusion requires two universal premises). The other rules are fine (rules 3 and 4 are not violated). The problem is that both rule 2 and rule 5 are violated. So, the syllogism is invalid.

Not all syllogistic arguments are invalid, though. Many are valid. Let's look at some examples.

Example 3

All swimmers love summer.

<u>All people who love summer enjoy fireworks.</u>

So, all swimmers enjoy fireworks.

First, express the premises as categorical propositions and then put the argument in standard form. Expressing the propositions in categorical form, we get:

All swimmers are people who love summer.

All people who love summer are people who enjoy fireworks.

So, all swimmers are people who enjoy fireworks.

Because "people who enjoy fireworks" is the major term (predicate of the conclusion), the major premise is "All people who love summer are people who enjoy fireworks." So, we need to switch the order of the premises, and then the argument will be in standard form. Our argument is now:

All people who love summer are people who enjoy fireworks.

All swimmers are people who love summer.

So, all swimmers are people who enjoy fireworks.

Now test for validity. The mood and figure is AAA—(1). Rule 1 is satisfied, because the middle term, "people who love summer," is distributed in the first premise, the major premise. Rule 2 is fine, because the conclusion does have the minor term "swimmers" distributed, but it is also distributed in its corresponding premise (the minor premise). Rules 3 and 4 don't apply because there are no negatives. Rule 5 is satisfied because we do have two universal premises, but we also have a universal conclusion. So our argument is valid!

Remember, a valid argument isn't necessarily sound. To be sound it would have to both be valid *and* have all its premises true, which isn't clearly the case here (the premises are not obviously true).

Testing for Validity Knowing Only the Mood and Figure

If an argument is given in the form of mood and figure, just write it out using P for the major term, S for the minor term, and M for the middle term, and then test. For instance, lets test AEA—(4). This can be written:

All P is M.

No M is S.

So, all S is P.

Running through the rules, we find the following: Rule 1 is fine, because the minor premise is an E claim (and everything is distributed in an E claim). Rule 2 is satisfied because the minor term S is distributed in the conclusion and is also distributed in its corresponding premise (the minor premise, which is negative). Because P (the major term) is not distributed in the conclusion, we don't have to test it. Rule 3 is our problem. We have a negative premise and, therefore, need a negative conclusion. (Rules 4 and 5 are fine, because neither rule is violated.) The trouble is with rule 3. So, the syllogism is invalid.

We don't have to actually know the specific major, minor, and middle terms in order to assess validity. If we know the mood and figure of the syllogism, we can use the five rules of the syllogism to test the argument. Let's see how this is done.

Here is another example where we know only the mood and figure. Use S, P, and M for the minor, major, and middle terms (respectively); set it up; and then test it. For example, let's test EAE—(3). Figure 3 means the middle term is on the left, so the argument can be expressed this way:

No M is P.

All M is S.

No S is P.

Remember: P, the major term, must be in the first premise; S, the minor term, in the second premise; and M, the middle term, in both premises.

Now we can test the argument. Rule 1 is fine because the first premise is an E claim and distributes everything. Rule 2 must be checked because both the subject and predicate of the conclusion are distributed. P is also distributed in the major premise (the predicate of a negative claim is distributed), but S is not distributed in the minor premise (because S is in the predicate, the claim needs to be negative). This means we have an illicit minor, so the syllogism is invalid. Rules 3 and 4 are both okay (they don't have two negatives, and a negative premise and a negative conclusion satisfies rule 4), and so is rule 5 (because we have two universal premises and a universal conclusion). Because of the illicit minor, the argument is invalid.

Constructing Valid Arguments

Suppose we want a valid argument for the conclusion "Some vampires are blood-thirsty." Because it is an I claim, we don't have to worry about rule 2 (because nothing in the conclusion is distributed, there is no problem here).

We merely need to avoid problems with the other rules. Rule 1 means we need to have the middle term distributed. Because the conclusion is positive, we do not want any negatives in the premises (or we would violate rule 4), and with no negatives in the premises, we won't violate rule 3.

That means we need one of the premises to be a universal positive claim, distributing the middle term. This forces the middle term to be in the subject place (because if it was in the predicate, the claim would have to be negative). The other premise cannot be universal, or we'd violate rule 5. And, because it cannot be negative (or we would violate rule 4), that means it must be an I claim. Once we distribute the middle term in the A claim, it will not matter where the middle term is in the I claim. That means we have several options. Our conclusion is "Some vampires are bloodthirsty creatures." This means "vampires" is the minor term and "bloodthirsty creatures" the major term.

So, the possible valid arguments are any of these forms: AII—(1), AII—(3), IAI—(3), or IAI—(4). These distribute the middle term and violate none of our rules of the syllogism. So we can just pick one and set up our valid argument. If we pick AII—(1), our argument then is:

All M are bloodthirsty creatures.

Some vampires are M.

So, some vampires are bloodthirsty creatures.

The Cat and Trans Fat. All cats that eat trans fat are creatures that feel queasy. All creatures that feel queasy roll their eyes and say, "Agkh!" Therefore, all cats that eat trans fat roll their eyes and say, "Agkh!" Mood and figure: AAA—(1). Valid argument!

Greg Perry, artist/illustrator. Reprinted with the permission of Greg Perry, www.perryink.com.

Now all we have to do is make up an M and we are done. Let M = vampire bats. This means our valid argument is:

All vampire bats are bloodthirsty creatures.

<u>Some vampires are vampire bats.</u>

So, some vampires are bloodthirsty creatures.

Exercises

Part One

1. State the argument for each of the following if the major term is "small boys," the minor term is "boy scouts," and the middle term is "energetic people."
   a. OAO—(1)
   b. IAI—(3)
   c. EAE—(4)
2. Give an example of your own for arguments with the following mood and figure.
   a. EIO—(4)
   b. AAA—(2)
   c. OII—(1)

3. If the major term is "gardener," the minor term is "folksinger," and the middle term is "filmmaker," set out the argument for each with mood and figure.
   a. AIE—(3)
   b. OAE—(4)
   c. IEO—(1)
   d. EAO—(2)
   e. III—(2)
   f. EOO—(3)

4. State the mood and figure of the following arguments. Do not test for validity.
   a. All fly fishermen are rough-and-ready folks. Some rough-and-ready folks are people who like cornbread. Therefore, all people who like cornbread are fly fishermen.
   b. All people who like animals are energetic people. Some energetic people are tai chi masters. Therefore, some tai chi masters are people who like animals.
   c. All football players are strong people. No football player is a race car driver. So, no race car driver is a strong person.

5. Put the following argument in standard form, and then state the mood and figure: "A lot of astronauts are mathematicians. Most scientists are not astronauts. Therefore, some mathematicians are not scientists."

6. Put the following argument in standard form, and then state the mood and figure: "Several trout fishermen fell in the lake. No sumo wrestler is a person who fell in the lake. Therefore, no sumo wrestler is a trout fisherman."

7. Put in standard form and then give mood and figure: "Many cartoonists are zany people. All zany people are unpredictable. So, some cartoonists are unpredictable."

8. Test the argument in number 7 for validity and, if invalid, note any rules violated.

9. Using the rules, decide if the following arguments are valid. Note any rules violated, if invalid.
   a. AEE—(3)
   b. EIO—(2)
   c. OIO—(1)
   d. AII—(4)

10. Using the rules, decide if the following arguments are valid. Note any rules violated, if invalid.
    a. AOA—(2)
    b. IAI—(3)
    c. AEA—(4)

11. Put the following arguments in standard form; note the major, minor, and middle terms; then test for validity. If invalid, name all the rules violated.
    a. Whenever Bernie sees a rainbow, tears come to her eyes. Consequently, whenever Bernie sees a rainbow, she needs tissues. This is the case because all the times tears come to Bernie's eyes are times she needs tissues.
    b. No woman who likes dirt between her toes should garden barefoot. Every woman who likes dirt between her toes needs a pedicure. Therefore, most women who garden barefoot are people who need a pedicure.
    c. Rabid animals are dangerous. Anything dangerous should be avoided. That means we should avoid rabid animals.

12. Put the following arguments in standard form; note the major, minor, and middle terms; then test for validity. If invalid, name all the rules violated.
    a. Most donuts are exquisite morsels. All donuts are greasy. So, some exquisite morsels are greasy.
    b. Some mechanics are not good at calligraphy. All people who are good at calligraphy love handwritten letters. Therefore, some who love handwritten letters are not mechanics.
    c. A lot of tomatoes taste like cardboard. All things that taste like cardboard are bad for your health. Therefore, some tomatoes are bad for your health.
    d. No electrician is afraid of going into the cellar. Everyone who sees a horror film is afraid of going into the cellar. Therefore, some people who see horror films are not electricians.

13. Test for validity, naming any rules broken if invalid.
    a. Every marshmallow is white. Most ghosts are white. Therefore, some ghosts are marshmallows.
    b. No gorilla is a desirable pet. All gorillas like to be touched. Therefore, some animals that like to be touched are not desirable pets.
    c. Most chimpanzees enjoy bananas. Some well-behaved animals are chimpanzees. Thus, many well-behaved animals are creatures that enjoy bananas.
    d. Lots of people like to go to the movies. Everyone who likes to go to the movies eats popcorn. Therefore, almost everyone eats popcorn.

14. Put the following arguments in standard form, and then test for validity.
    a. Not all mathematicians love jokes. Not any mathematician likes boiled squid. Therefore, most joke lovers are not people who like boiled squid.
    b. Most sandwiches are not spicy. Anything with mustard is spicy. Therefore, some sandwiches do not contain mustard.
    c. All chocolate lovers are interesting people. Some interesting people are weight lifters. Therefore, all weight lifters are chocolate lovers.

15. Give an example of a syllogism that has an undistributed middle, but violates no other rule. Use "weight lifters" for the major term, "chefs" for the minor term, and "caffeine addicts" for the middle term.

16. Give an example of syllogisms in the following mood and figure.
    a. AEE—(1)
    b. EOE—(3)
    c. AOA—(4)
    d. AII—(2)

17. Give a *valid* argument for the conclusion "Therefore, no bank robber is someone to trust." Show that your argument is valid.

18. Put this argument in standard form, and then test for validity using the rules:

    All surfers like to swim.

    No person who likes to swim is afraid of the ocean.

    Therefore, no person who is afraid of the ocean is a surfer.

19. Put the following argument in standard form, and then state the mood and figure: "Paul ate way too many tamales at Marcos' party. Most people who eat way too many tamales feel like beached whales. Therefore, Paul will soon feel like a beached whale."

20. Give an invalid argument with an illicit minor for the conclusion "All music lovers are fascinating people." Show that it is invalid. (It's okay to violate other rules of the syllogism.)

21. Give an invalid argument with an illicit major for the conclusion "No pizza is a lightweight snack." Show that it is invalid. (It's okay to violate other rules of the syllogism.)

22. Give a valid argument for the conclusion "All lawyers are careful thinkers." Show that it is valid.

23. Give an invalid argument that has an undistributed middle for the conclusion "All vampires are fond of capes." (It's okay to violate other rules of the syllogism.)

24. Give an invalid argument that has an illicit major and violates rule 5 for the conclusion "Some trout fishermen are not pranksters."

25. Give an example of a syllogism with mood and figure EIO—(4). Use the major term "daredevils," the minor term "economists," and the middle term "trumpet players." Test for validity.

Part Two

1. Give a valid argument for the conclusion "No vegetarian is a meat eater." Show that it is valid.

2. Give an invalid argument that has an illicit major and an undistributed middle.

3. Why can't an argument with an A conclusion have an illicit major?

4. Try to see by inspection (look at the mood and figure, but don't yet test with the rules) if you can narrow down the arguments to what might be valid.

Pull out those you can see are invalid, note why, and then test the remainder, using the rules of the syllogism: AEE—(4), EAE—(1), III—(2), OIO—(3), EEA—(1), IEO—(2), OIE—(3), and AII—(4).

5. Why can't a syllogism with an I conclusion have an illicit minor?

6. Why can't a syllogism with an E claim in either premise have an undistributed middle?

Quick Quiz

1. Figure 2 has the *middle term* located (a) on the right or (b) on the left.

2. Figure 4 has the *middle term* located:
   a. On the right of the two premises
   b. On the left of the two premises
   c. In the subject place in the major premise and the predicate place in the minor premise
   d. In the subject place in the minor premise and the predicate place in the major premise

3. The argument is "All cartoons are animated films. No animated film is a documentary. Therefore, some documentaries are not cartoons." The *mood and figure* is (a) AOE—(4), (b) AEO—(4), or (c) AEO—(1).

4. *True or false:* If both middle terms are in the subject place, the argument has figure 2.

5. What is the *first rule* of the syllogism (rule 1)?
   a. The major term must be distributed at least once.
   b. The minor term must be distributed at least once.
   c. The middle term must be distributed at least once.
   d. If a term is distributed in the conclusion, it must also be distributed in its corresponding premise.
   e. There cannot be two negative premises in a valid syllogism.

6. *True or false:* If both premises are universal, then the conclusion must be universal, too—it cannot be particular—in a valid syllogism.

7. An example of "IAI—(1)" is:
   a. All carrots are vegetables. Some vegetables are turnips. Therefore, some turnips are carrots.
   b. Some vegetables are carrots. All turnips are vegetables. Therefore, some carrots are turnips.
   c. All vegetables are carrots. Some turnips are vegetables. Therefore, some turnips are carrots.
   d. Some carrots are vegetables. All turnips are vegetables. Therefore, some turnips are carrots.

8. *True or false:* The middle term is the *predicate* of the conclusion.

9. The argument "All tourists are people who carry maps. Yajaira is not a person with a map. Therefore, Yajaira is not a tourist" has *mood and figure* (a) AEE—(2), (b) AOO—(2), (c) AOO—(3) or AEE—3

10. The argument "No cows are vicious beasts. All Jerseys are cows. Therefore, no Jersey is a vicious beast" has *mood and figure* (a) EAE—(1), (b) OAO—(1), or EAE—(4).

11. We know that no valid syllogism has two negative premises because of (a) rule 3 or (b) rule 5.

12. *True or false:* We know the subject is distributed if the proposition is universal.

Using Venn Diagrams

An alternative approach to testing syllogisms for validity is to use Venn diagrams. These allow us to see if the conclusion follows from the premises.

Venn diagrams are intersecting circles that are used to indicate the relationship between terms of propositions. We need as many intersecting circles as the number of terms we are dealing with. If we have two terms (e.g., the subject class and the predicate class), we need two intersecting circles. If we have three terms, then we need three intersecting circles. This will be the case when testing syllogisms.

Remember: A syllogism has three terms—major, minor, and middle.

Universal Positive Claims. The A claim "All A is B" asserts that every member of A is also in B (e.g., "All tigers are cats"). With Venn diagrams, this means that the area outside the intersection of A and B is *empty.* We indicate this by shading it in (shaded = empty):

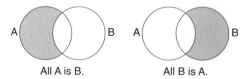

All A is B.   All B is A.

Universal Negative Claims. With the E claim "(No P is Q)," the diagram needs to indicate that there is no element in the first set that is also in the second. Since there's nothing in common between A and B, the intersection of the two will be empty (shaded):

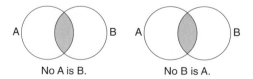

No A is B.   No B is A.

If nothing is in common between two sets, then their intersection will be empty, so shade only the intersection of the two sets in question. Be careful to shade nothing else.

Particular Positive Claims.   The I claim "Some A is B" asserts that there's at least one member of A that is also in B (e.g., "Some cats are tigers"). Because nothing is said about *all* members x of A, we cannot presume more than we know. Therefore, we cannot shade in any area like we do with universal claims. Use an X to indicate that at least one A is a B:

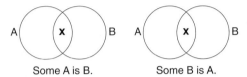

Some A is B.   Some B is A.

Remember: "Some" means "at least one." To indicate "at least one," we use an X to mark the spot. Because it is asserted that some members of the first set are in the second, we put an X in the intersection.

Particular Negative Claims.   The O claim "Some A is not B" asserts that at least one member of A is not a member of B (e.g., "Some cats are not tigers"). Here we also use an X to indicate that at least one A is not in B and thus lies outside the intersection:

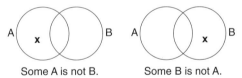

Some A is not B.   Some B is not A.

Remember: Because at least one member of the first set is not in the second, we put an X outside of the intersection.

Exercises

1. Express the following propositions using Venn diagrams.
   a. Some M is not P.
   b. All P is S.
   c. No M is S.
   d. Some M is P.
   e. All S is P.
   f. No P is M.
   g. Some P is S.
   h. Some P is not M.

    i. All P is M.
    j. No S is M.
    k. Some S is M.
    l. All M is P.
2. Express the following propositions using Venn diagrams. (*Hint:* First write them in categorical form.)
    a. Most cowboys like to nap.
    b. No animal trainer is scared of dogs.
    c. All computer technicians like puzzles.
    d. Some lion tamers are nervous people.
    e. Some rap artists are not conservative.
    f. All chefs are fond of banana bread.
    g. No janitor is a cynic.
    h. A few Italians do not like pasta.
    i. Many paramedics are fond of bingo.

Handling Three Terms. We're now ready to complicate our lives! Instead of using two intersecting circles (for the two terms), we will now use three circles (for three terms). In the four groupings that follow, we see the two universal claims (A and E) and the two particular claims (I and O) set out using Venn diagrams employing three terms.

Note: If everything in one set is contained in another set, then the area outside their intersection will be empty (shaded in):

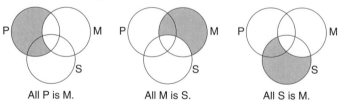

All P is M.   All M is S.   All S is M.

If nothing is in common between two sets, then their intersection will be empty (so shade the entire intersection of the two sets in question). Don't let the third circle confuse you:

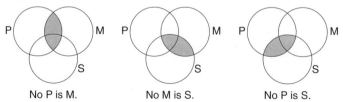

No P is M.   No M is S.   No P is S.

If there is at least one element that is common to both sets, indicate this by marking an X in the intersection of the two:

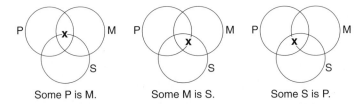

Some P is M.   Some M is S.   Some S is P.

If we do not know whether the element is in the third set and that third set is not empty, then simply straddle it on the fence:

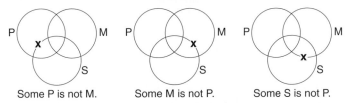

Some P is not M.   Some M is not P.   Some S is not P.

In all three cases, it is asserted that there is at least one element in the first set but not in the second one. So we have to mark that with an X outside of the intersection of the two sets. If we do not know where it lies in the big crescent, then it has to straddle the fence.

Handling Three Terms, Two Propositions.   When you have three terms to deal with, *always* do universal propositions first. Universal claims have a greater scope, and thus, they need to be placed first. If both propositions are universal, then take your pick—the order matters only if you have one universal and one particular claim.

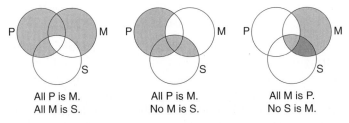

All P is M.   All P is M.   All M is P.
All M is S.   No M is S.   No S is M.

Remember: Shaded areas are empty areas. So, if *all* of one set is in another, leave the big area outside the intersection in the dark. If there's *nothing* in common between the two sets, then it is the shared area (the intersection) that is in the dark:

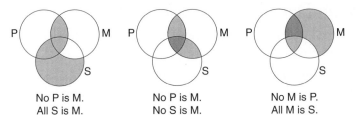

No P is M.   No P is M.   No M is P.
All S is M.   No S is M.   All M is S.

If nothing is in common between two sets, then their intersection will be empty, so shade the entire intersection of the two sets in question. For the second premise, be careful to shade only what is empty and not to shade too much:

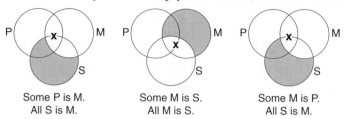

Some P is M.   Some M is S.   Some M is P.
All S is M.   All M is S.   All S is M.

Remember: Diagram universal claims first, shading in the big crescent area of the subject set that lies outside the intersection of the two sets.

For particular positive claims (I claims), X lies somewhere in the intersection of the two sets. The key is whether the X could be a member of the third set.

There are three possible placements here: The X could lie in the intersection with the third set, it could be only in the intersection area of the two sets that excludes the third set, or it could straddle the fence. If the third set is empty, the X cannot straddle the fence—leaving only the first two options open as to possible location of the X. If the X is in one set but not in the second one, the X must be placed *outside* of the intersection of the two sets.

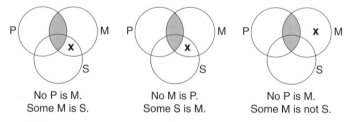

No P is M.   No M is P.   No P is M.
Some M is S.   Some S is M.   Some M is not S.

Remember: An X cannot straddle the fence of an empty (shaded) area. The reason it is sitting on the fence in the first place is that it could be on either side. But if one side is *empty,* then nothing can possibly be there. So, in the case of the Venn diagrams on the far right, first put up "No P is M." We then see that the X for "Some M is not S" cannot be on the fence between the intersection and the big crescent remaining in the P circle. That means the X has to lie in the area outside of S *and* outside P.

Using Venn Diagrams to Check Validity

We are now ready to use Venn diagrams to determine whether the argument is valid. Follow these steps:

Step 1: Identify the major, minor, and middle terms. (*Remember:* The major term is the predicate of the conclusion, the minor term is the subject of the conclusion, and the middle term appears only in the premises.)

Step 2: Put the argument in standard categorical form. This is as follows:

Major premise (the premise containing the major term)

<u>Minor premise (the premise containing the minor term)</u>

Therefore, conclusion

Step 3: Set out the premises using Venn diagrams, remembering to put up universal claims before any particular claims.

Step 4: See if you can read the conclusion without doing anything extra to the diagrams. It should be right there in front of your eyes—if not, the argument is *invalid*. In other words, the argument is *valid* only if the conclusion is expressed in the Venn diagrams of the two premises. If the conclusion can be read from the Venn diagrams of the two premises, the argument is valid. If the conclusion cannot be read from the Venn diagrams of the two premises, the argument is invalid.

If the conclusion cannot be read from the diagrams, the argument is invalid and, therefore, unsound. If you have to manipulate the diagrams to get the conclusion to appear, the argument fails.

Example 1: AEE-2 (in categorical form)

All P is M.

<u>No S is M.</u>

So, no S is P.

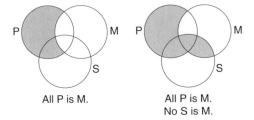

All P is M.   All P is M.
                   No S is M.

Since both premises are universal, start with either of them. The Venn diagram for "All P is M" is on the left. The Venn diagram for the universal claim "All P is M" and the minor premise "No S is M" is on the right. If the argument is valid, we can read the conclusion right from the Venn diagram. The conclusion "No S is P" would require that the entire intersection of S and P be shaded in. As we can see, this *is* the case. Therefore, the argument is *valid*.

Example 2: AII-3 (in categorical form)

All M is P.

<u>Some M is S.</u>

So, some S is P.

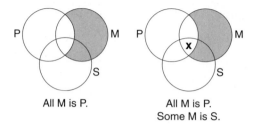

All M is P.   All M is P.
                Some M is S.

Handle the universal claim first. If we put up "All M is P," the result is shown on the diagram on the left. Now let's put up "Some M is S." Because we cannot put an X straddling the fence of an area that is shaded, we have only the very center (the intersection of all three) where the X can be. This we see on the Venn diagram on the right (above). Both premises are now diagrammed. If the argument is valid, we should be able to read the conclusion. The conclusion "Some S is P" would require that the intersection of S and P have an X in it. As we can see, this *is* the case. Therefore, the argument is *valid*.

Exercises

1. Test for validity using Venn diagrams.
   a. AEA—(1)
   b. EIO—(2)
   c. AOO—(3)
   d. IEO—(4)
   e. AAA—(3)
   f. IAI—(4)

2. Put the following arguments in standard form, and then test with Venn diagrams.
   a. All hamburgers are greasy. All donuts are greasy. Therefore, all donuts are hamburgers.
   b. No hamburger is a vegetable. All vegetables are good for your health. Therefore, no hamburger is good for your health.
   c. All anthropologists eat hamburgers. Some anthropologists are lonely people. Therefore, some lonely people eat hamburgers.
   d. No carrots are purple. Some purple things are violets. Therefore, no violet is a carrot.
   e. Every gardener is a nature lover. All nature lovers are sunbathers. Therefore, all who sunbathe are gardeners.

3. Put the following arguments in standard form, and then test with Venn diagrams.
   a. Most rude people are tired. No tired person is happy. Therefore, no rude person is happy.

    b. All happy people get a good night's rest. A lot of nurses do not get a good night's rest. Therefore, many happy people are not nurses.

    c. No puppy is ugly. All puppies are furry. Therefore, no furry thing is ugly.

    d. Most wild dogs are in the forest. No creature in the forest is an African elephant. Therefore, no African elephants are wild dogs.

4. Test the following using the rules and/or Venn diagrams.
    a. EOO—(1)
    b. AIO—(2)
    c. IAI—(3)
    d. AEA—(3)
    e. EIO—(2)
    f. AAA—(4)
    g. AEA—(1)

5. Test for validity using *both* Venn diagrams and the rules of the syllogism.
    a. OAO—(2)
    b. IOE—(4)
    c. EOE—(1)
    d. EIO—(3)
    e. AEA—(1)
    f. AII—(2)

6. Put the following arguments in standard form, and then test by both methods.
    a. The vast majority of Italians are interesting people. Some interesting people are weight lifters. Therefore, all weight lifters are Italians.

    b. A few romantics are hockey players. No pianist is a hockey player. So, many romantics are not pianists.

    c. Not any dog trainers are undisciplined people. All undisciplined people are unorganized. Therefore, not all unorganized people are dog trainers.

CHAPTER TEN

Patterns of Deductive Reasoning: Rules of Inference

When you have eliminated the impossible, whatever remains, however improbable, must be the truth.

SHERLOCK HOLMES, *The Sign of the Four*

You are driving to school when you hear a "thump, thump, thump"; suddenly, it is much harder to steer the car. "Gad," you think "another flat tire." A man in a pickup drives up and stops to help you. "Hey, you gotta flat!" he points out. Further demonstrating his reasoning skills, he says, "If you don't have good tires, you get a flat. You have a flat, so you must not have had good tires on your car. In fact, I'd say you were taken for a sucker!"

Is this an example of good thinking on his part? If you said, "No," pat yourself on the back and read on to learn the type of mistake he made. If you said, "Yes," you need help, so keep reading. Think about it: What can cause your tire to go flat? You could have old tread, you could have run over a nail, your tire could have been slashed, or you could have hit a pothole—to name just a few. Having a flat does *not* necessarily mean that you have bad tires, you are a cheapskate, or you got ripped off when you bought the tire. The existence of a flat tire does not, in itself, point to one potential cause. We need more information; we cannot eliminate possible causes in one wave of the arm.

There is a label for this fellow's faulty reasoning—namely, the **fallacy of affirming the consequent.** We will examine this and other faulty reasoning in this chapter. Most of our attention, though, will be on valid argument forms. In **valid arguments,** the premises offer sufficient support for the conclusion. That is, if we assume the premises are all true, then the conclusion *must* be true as well. (For a review, see Chapter 5.)

The most common valid argument forms have specific names and are included in the rules of inference. Knowing the correct forms will make it easier to use correct reasoning when constructing our own arguments.

Whereas rules of replacement focus on propositions, rules of inference focus on arguments. A familiarity with both the rules of replacement and the rules of inference will give us the tools to reformulate propositions and draw inferences. Once we learn the rules of inference, we can spot poorly reasoned arguments like that of the roadside helper and be able to construct well-reasoned, defensible arguments.

Advantages of Learning the Techniques of Logic

Some people question the value of these conventional ways of "doing" logic because it puts analytical tools above experience and emotion, and it requires a level of precision that forces us to be attentive to fine details.

With logic, we can hone certain argumentative skills and techniques. Perfecting the techniques acquired through a study of logic can be enormously useful—and satisfying. Logic can be used as a tool for problem solving and analysis. Having a facility with logic gives us the techniques to examine and evaluate the many kinds of arguments we confront. This does not help us develop moral fiber, but it does help us develop *mental dexterity*. Being good at logic is only part of being good at critical thinking, but it is both useful and empowering. With that in mind, let's go deeper into the terrain of logic.

Valid Argument Forms

An argument is **valid** if the conclusion follows directly from the premises and could not be false if the premises were assumed true. This does not mean the premises have to be true! *Repeat:* A valid argument does *not* have to have true premises, even if that seems counterintuitive. But it does mean that, if we assume they are true, the conclusion must necessarily be true as well.

The premises and the conclusion could be *entirely false* and yet the argument be valid. This is because the *focus in validity is on the form itself,* not the substance of the claims. For example, this is a valid argument: "All sheep can fly like a bird. Anything that can fly like a bird has wings. Therefore, all sheep have wings." However preposterous this sounds, the conclusion could not be false if the two premises were true.

Studying validity is like examining x-rays, in that the focus is on the *structure* of the argument. If there are problems with the structure (the bones), then the argument won't be able to stand on its own two feet.

The rules of inference function like patterns of good reasoning: Anything that fits the pattern, regardless of the subject matter, is a valid argument. We can assess the validity of a deductive argument by examining the structure of the argument. Nothing else is necessary at this stage.

▨ Rules of Inference

You are changing the tire when a woman comes by, walking her dog. She offers *her* argument: "If the tire only has a nail in it, then it can be repaired. Oh, look, there's a nail. Good—your tire can be repaired." What do you think of *her* reasoning?

Her argument is a *valid* one, because *if* we assume the two premises are true, then she is right to suggest the tire can be repaired. Her reasoning is, therefore, correct. That does not mean the argument is *sound,* because we do not know if the premises are actually true. *Remember:* A sound argument is a valid argument that has true premises. That is, soundness goes one step beyond validity—it requires truth, as well as a good, solid structure.

Modus Ponens

If you just have a nail in your tire, she is probably right to say the tire can be fixed—though this is not certain. Your tire may be destined for the recycling bin. However, the woman has proven that she can construct a valid argument. Her argument is called **modus ponens**—a valid argument form that asserts, "If this, then that. This; therefore, that."

The term *modus ponens* is Latin for "mode that affirms." Given a conditional claim (if *this,* then *that*), if we can affirm that *this* is true, then *that* must be true as well.

Form of Modus Ponens

If A then B.

<u>A is true.</u>

Therefore, B is true as well.

The first premise is a conditional claim. The second premise affirms that the antecedent happened. The conclusion then is that the consequent must also have happened. So, whether the antecedent is positive or negative, it gets repeated in the second premise.

Examples

If that's an alligator, you better get out of the swamp.

<u>That is an alligator.</u>

So, you better get out of the swamp.

If you've cleaned your room and you have no homework, then we can either go to a movie or try out the skates I found in the shed.

<u>You've cleaned your room and you have no homework.</u>

So, we can either go to a movie or try out the skates I found in the shed.

Note: In this last case, the antecedent was compound (a conjunction, A and B) and, therefore, the second premise has to repeat the entire conjunction. Note also that the consequent is compound (a disjunction, A or B). Nevertheless, the form of the argument is still modus ponens.

Modus Tollens

Our next valid argument form is called **modus tollens.** The term *modus tollens* is Latin for "mode that denies." The first premise is a conditional claim. The second premise denies the consequent by saying it did not happen. The conclusion then is that the antecedent could not have happened either.

Here we introduce opposites. Where modus ponens simply repeats the antecedent in the second premise, in modus tollens, the second premise is the opposite of the consequent. The form it takes is this: "If *this*, then *that*. *Not that*, therefore, *not this*."

For example, suppose a police officer stops to see how you are doing with your flat tire. He says, "If you cannot get the car lifted, then your jack is no good. Your jack looks good, so you'll be able to get the car lifted." Do you see what the officer did in his argument? Look at the first premise and then at the second. What shifted? The consequent from the first premise ("Your jack is no good") has been changed to its opposite and is now the second premise ("Your jack looks good"). What follows then is the negated antecedent (so, you *can* get the car lifted). This is a strong argument in the form of modus tollens.

Form of Modus Tollens

If A then B.

<u>B is not true.</u>

Therefore, A is not true either.

Examples

If that's not a hybrid that Louise is driving, it must be an electric car.

<u>That's not an electric car.</u>

Therefore, it must be a hybrid that Louise is driving.

Only if toxic waste or rotting sewage is stored here, should they restrict access.

<u>They restricted access.</u>

Therefore, either toxic waste or rotting sewage is stored here.

Note: Rewriting without the "only if," the first premise becomes "If *neither* toxic waste *nor* rotting sewage is stored here, then they should *not* restrict access." We can then use the second premise and the rule of modus tollens to draw the conclusion.

Hypothetical Syllogism

The valid argument form of **hypothetical syllogism** sets out a chain of conditional claims: "If *this* then *that*; and if *that* then *such-and-such*. Therefore, if *this*, then *such-and-such.*" The chain is this: The first term leads to a second term, and the second to a third; so, the first must lead to the third.

Suppose you are at home (your tire fixed!) and the phone rings. It is your mother, who has been calling all morning. She is relieved you are okay and says, "If you have another flat tire, then call me. If you call me, then I won't worry. So, if you have another flat tire, I won't worry." Your mother's reasoning is valid. Her argument is called a hypothetical syllogism. It is composed entirely of conditional (hypothetical) claims.

Form of the Hypothetical Syllogism

If A then B.

If B then C.

Therefore, if A then C.

It is crucial that the linking term, B, connecting A and C be the consequent of the first premise and the antecedent of the second one. Otherwise, there's a break in the chain, and the argument will be invalid.

Example 1

If that's a cockroach in the kitchen, then either call an exterminator or set out poison.

If we either call an exterminator or set out poison, then we can solve the problem.

Therefore, if that's a cockroach in the kitchen, then we can solve the problem.

Note: You can see that this example of a hypothetical syllogism involves a *compound term* (the consequent in the first premise is the antecedent in the second premise). It's still as valid as if it had been less complex.

Example 2

Unless he studies hard, Danny will have trouble with the GRE.

If he has trouble with the GRE, then Danny may not get into Ohio State.

Therefore, unless he studies hard, Danny may not get into Ohio State.

Note: "Unless" is the same as "If not." So "Unless he studies hard" means "If he does not study hard." We can, thus, treat this as a conditional claim.

Exercises

Part One

1. Using *modus tollens,* finish the argument that starts with "If he burns the burgers, Jason will order take-out."

2. Using *hypothetical syllogism,* finish the argument that starts with "If the take-out food does not arrive, Jason will be unhappy."

3. Using *modus ponens,* finish the argument that starts with "If there's pink fluid under the car, Vartan should check the transmission."

4. Using *hypothetical syllogism,* finish the argument that starts with "If her tooth keeps aching, Pat will go to the dentist."

5. Using *modus tollens,* finish each of the following arguments.
   a. If the children keep screaming, the dentist will not be able to concentrate.
   b. If Pat gets her tooth pulled, she won't want to go to the movies tonight.
   c. If Vartan repairs the transmission, we can go to the early show.

6. Using *modus ponens,* finish each of the following arguments.
   a. If the dentist yells at the noisy children, the patients may be alarmed.
   b. If Jason does not finish his Thai food, he'll either have the leftovers for lunch or he'll freeze them.
   c. If Vartan doesn't finish the repairs, he can't go to Yosemite this weekend.

7. Using *hypothetical syllogism,* finish the following arguments that start with.
   a. If the two truckers stop at the diner, they could get some biscuits and gravy.
   b. If the diner has no biscuits, the two truckers will go for grits.
   c. If the grits don't fill them up, Al and Carlos will order fries and onion rings.

Part Two

Directions: Name the argument forms in the following statements. Each statement involves one of the following forms: modus ponens, modus tollens, or hypothetical syllogism.

1. If it keeps snowing, the skiing will be great. The skiing was not great, so it didn't keep snowing.

2. If the sun stays out, the snow will melt and the slopes will be muddy. If the snow melts and the slopes are muddy, then we can't ski. Therefore, if the sun stays out, then we can't ski.

3. If Zenon runs for public office, he'll get a lot of votes. Zenon did not get a lot of votes. So, he must not have run for public office.

4. If we read novels and drink espresso all night long, then we won't finish our homework. We finished our homework. Therefore, we did not read novels and drink espresso all night long.

5. If you are not consistent, then you can't train a puppy. I see your puppy is trained. So, you must have been consistent.

6. If neither the police nor the fire truck arrives, we may wish we picked somewhere else to live. Neither the police nor the fire truck arrived. So, we may wish we picked somewhere else to live.

7. If the police helicopter lands in the yard, Virginia's vegetable garden will be flattened. If her vegetable garden is flattened, she will sue the city. So, if the police helicopter lands in the yard, Virginia will sue the city.

8. If the part-time job works out and you finally get some money coming in, then we can plan a weekend getaway to the desert. The part-time job worked out and you finally have money coming in. So, we can plan a weekend getaway to the desert.

9. If Sandie keeps lying in the sun, she'll get burned. Sandie did not get burned. We can conclude that Sandie did not keep lying in the sun.

10. If Steve gets everyone in the car by 3 A.M., they should be able to get to Winslow, Arizona, by evening. If they get to Winslow, Arizona, by evening, they can make it to Tulsa by Thursday afternoon. So, if Steve gets everyone in the car by 3 A.M., they can make it to Tulsa by Thursday afternoon.

Disjunctive Syllogism

There is nothing like a **disjunctive syllogism.** In this valid argument form, we start with a **disjunction** (an "either/or" claim) and then get a second premise that is a denial of one of the disjuncts. This forces the conclusion to be the remaining disjunct. Basically, it goes like this: "*This* or *that*. *Not this*. Therefore, *that*." You have a choice between two options, and one choice is eliminated—leaving you with the other choice.

For example, suppose your brother finds something weird on his plate. He picks it up and turns it over and over. He finally says, "Either that's a bit of a tooth or a piece of hard candy. It's not candy. Therefore, it's a bit of tooth." Your brother shows his potential as a logician, and you feel downright smug in telling him that his valid argument is called the disjunctive syllogism.

Form of the Disjunctive Syllogism

Either A or B.

A is not the case (or B is not the case).

Therefore, B is the case (or A is the case).

The first premise is a choice between two options. The second premise eliminates one of the options. That leaves us with the conclusion that the remaining option must then be the case. Let's look at some examples of disjunctive syllogism.

Examples

Either a wolf is howling or the wind is in the trees.

There's no wind tonight.

Therefore, it must be a wolf howling.

Either Al and Carlos will pack sandwiches and go fly-fishing or they'll hike up the gorge.

<u>They decided not to pack sandwiches and go fly-fishing.</u>

Therefore, they'll hike up the gorge.

Note: The first premise has compound disjuncts. The superstructure is still a disjunctive syllogism.

Conjunction

Conjunction is very straightforward: Two claims that are each true are true in combination. The rule of **conjunction** asserts that if we have two claims that we know to be true, then they are both true together.

Form of Conjunction

A is true.

<u>B is also true.</u>

Therefore, both A and B are true.

Examples

Omar was happy to see Lamu again when he went to Kenya.

<u>He was sorry he didn't make it to Nairobi.</u>

Therefore, Omar was happy to see Lamu again when he went to Kenya, but he was sorry he didn't make it to Nairobi.

Al ate two orders of grits and eggs.

<u>Carlos polished off a cheeseburger and fries.</u>

Therefore, Al ate two orders of grits and eggs, and Carlos polished off a cheeseburger and fries.

Simplification

Another valid form of argument starts with two things given together in conjunction. If both together are true, then it follows that each proposition is individually true. This is called **simplification**.

For example, suppose someone says that both the Democrats and the Republicans have a plan for an improved health care system. It follows that the Democrats have a plan for an improved health care system *and* that the Republicans have a plan.

Form of Simplification

<u>A and B are true together.</u>

Therefore, A is true as well (or B is also true).

In other words, knowing that the collective, A and B, is true, it follows that each conjunct individually is true as well.

Examples

The reviewer liked both *Ghost Dog* and *Wings of Desire.*

Therefore, the reviewer liked *Ghost Dog* (or the reviewer liked *Wings of Desire*).

Neither skunks nor raccoons are easy to have as pets.

Therefore, skunks are not easy to have as pets (or raccoons are not easy to have as pets).

Note: Remember from DeMorgan's Laws that you can change the "neither/nor" claim to "Skunks are not easy to have as pets and raccoons are not easy to have as pets." (See Chapter 4 for a review.)

Logical Addition

Our next rule of inference has a name that seems counterintuitive. It is called **logical addition.** This valid argument form asserts that if we know any one proposition is true, then a disjunction made up of this true proposition and any other proposition is necessarily true as well. The form it takes is "*This* is true. Therefore, *this* or *any other proposition* is also true."

The name "logical addition" is a bit misleading, because the addition here occurs by use of an "or" not an "and." Logical addition allows you to expand when you are given one thing that is true.

Form of Logical Addition

A is true.

Therefore, either A or B is true.

In this valid argument form, you can infer from anything that is true to a disjunction consisting of the true claim and any other proposition. Let's look at some examples of logical addition.

Examples

Ben's computer crashed after he downloaded the Snakepit video game.

Therefore, either Ben's computer crashed after he downloaded the Snakepit video game or it just has a dead battery.

Lynne ran into jellyfish in her Arctic swim and was not sure what to do.

Therefore, either Lynne ran into jelly fish in her Arctic swim and was not sure what to do, or she had a bad nightmare.

Note: Did you see how this example has a *compound* premise? We can still apply the rule of logical addition.

Exercises

Part One

Directions: Complete the arguments using the rule indicated.

1. *Logical addition:* Skydiving is never boring.
2. *Simplification:* Both Batman and Spider-Man wear snug-fitting clothing.
3. *Disjunctive syllogism:* Either I heard a coyote or that's the neighbor's shepherd pup.
4. *Hypothetical syllogism:* If you go barefoot, people will stare at you.
5. *Conjunction:* Jasper enjoys peas any time of the day. Jasper won't eat spaghetti.
6. *Modus tollens:* If Tony smells a rat, the game is up.
7. *Logical addition:* Canned fruit tastes slimy.
8. *Simplification:* A good slice of pie is warm and has ice cream on top.
9. *Logical addition:* The Boston marathon is not for the weak-willed.
10. *Conjunction:* The fire jumped the freeway. The houses and cars were in danger.
11. *Modus ponens:* If you take up martial arts, you'll need comfortable clothing.
12. *Simplification:* Jamal does not like small rodents and he doesn't care much for large rodents either.

Part Two

Directions: Name the rules used in the arguments below.

1. If we can find the sleeping bags, Ben and Russell will borrow them for their trip. We found the sleeping bags, so Ben and Russell borrowed them for their trip.
2. If the road is not impassible, we can make it to the cabin by morning. We did not make it to the cabin by morning. So, the road was impassible.
3. Either the jeep can make it over the ridge or Ben and Russell will just camp out until help arrives. Ben and Russell did not camp out until help arrived. So, they made it over the ridge.
4. Russell was sick of beef jerky. He wished he had a big, juicy burger with a side of fries. Therefore, Russell was sick of beef jerky and wished he had a big, juicy burger with a side of fries.
5. The jeep's brakes went out on the road back to Tucson, and Ben's cell phone battery died. Therefore, the jeep's brakes went out on the road back to Tucson.
6. If Russell quits complaining about the food, he can work on the brakes and Ben can catch a nap for a few minutes. Russell quit complaining about the food. Therefore, he can work on the brakes and Ben can catch a nap.

7. No one heard the boulder as it came crashing down the hillside. If no one hears the boulder as it comes crashing down the hillside, then they won't know to throw the ice chest out of the way. Therefore, they didn't know to throw the ice chest out of the way.

8. If there's no ice chest, there's no more ice. If there's no more ice, then the three warm sodas in the bag won't be nearly as good with the beef jerky as a nice cold drink. Therefore, if there's no ice chest, then the three warm sodas in the bag won't be nearly as good with the beef jerky as a nice cold drink.

9. The warm soda was pretty pathetic. Russell was feeling sorry for himself as the day wore on and the jeep still wasn't repaired. Therefore, the warm soda was pretty pathetic, and Russell was feeling sorry for himself as the day wore on and the jeep still wasn't repaired.

10. The brakes were finally fixed. Therefore, either the brakes were fixed or the guys will be in for a long night.

11. Ben was not too badly sunburned after the big adventure. If he was not careful, then Ben would have been badly sunburned after the big adventure. Therefore, Ben was careful.

12. Russell took off his dusty boots and crawled into bed, happy that things worked out as well as they did. Therefore, Russell crawled into bed, happy that things worked out as well as they did.

Quick Quiz

1. If the first line of *logical addition* is "The soup tasted like wallpaper paste," which could be the conclusion?
   a. If the soup doesn't taste like wallpaper paste, then go ahead and eat it.
   b. The soup doesn't taste like wallpaper paste.
   c. Either the soup tasted like wallpaper paste or Charlie got a root canal.
   d. The soup tasted like wallpaper paste and the vegie burger was inedible.

2. The argument "Charlie was unhappy about his braces and sorry he didn't get a different dentist. Therefore, Charlie is sorry he didn't get a different dentist" is in the form of (a) conjunction or (b) simplification.

3. A disjunction has a premise that is an (a) all-or-nothing or (b) either/or proposition.

4. The argument "If that's not a bluegrass player, then it must be Cousin Dan. If it's Cousin Dan, then we need to get out the guitar. Therefore, if that's not a bluegrass player, then we need to get out the guitar" is a (a) hypothetical syllogism or (b) disjunctive syllogism.

5. *True or false:* The form of *modus ponens* is "If A, then B. Not A. Therefore, not B."

6. The argument "If the nurse is careful with the stitches, then the baby won't cry. The nurse is careful with the stitches. Therefore, the baby won't cry" is in the form of (a) modus ponens or (b) logical addition.

7. What is one difference between logical addition and conjunction?
   a. Logical addition has a disjunction for the conclusion.
   b. Conjunction has a disjunction as one of the premises.
   c. Logical addition has a conjunction for the conclusion.
   d. Conjunction has one premise that is a conditional claim.

8. *True or false*: According to *conjunction,* if the premises are "The surgeon was a bit forgetful. He couldn't find a small sponge after the operation," then the conclusion would be "Therefore, the surgeon was a bit forgetful."

9. If the premise is "The fire raged all day," then a possible conclusion using *logical addition* is:
   a. The fire raged all day and the animals ran toward the river.
   b. The fire did not rage all day. Therefore, the animals did not run toward the river.
   c. Either the fire raged all day or the animals did not run toward the river.
   d. The animals did not run toward the river. Therefore, the fire did not rage all day.

10. *True or false*: According to *simplification,* a possible conclusion of the argument starting with the premises "The baby mouse fell in the big bucket and needed to be rescued" is "Therefore, the baby mouse needed to be rescued."

11. "If you can't cook, stay out of the kitchen. Annie can't cook worth a darn. So, she should stay out of the kitchen" is an example of (a) modus ponens or (b) modus tollens.

12. An example of a *disjunctive syllogism* is:
    a. The dentist was kind and not a madman. Therefore, the dentist was kind.
    b. Either the dentist was a kindly person or he was a madman. The dentist was not a kindly person, so he was a madman.
    c. If the dentist does the root canal, then Charlie won't feel very good tonight. Charlie felt good tonight, so the dentist did not do the root canal.
    d. If the dentist is a kindly person, then he'll be gentle. If the dentist is gentle, then Charlie won't be so anxious. Therefore, if the dentist is a kindly person, Charlie won't be so anxious.

Constructive Dilemma

In ancient Greece, they used to talk about being "stuck on the horns of a dilemma." This means being faced with two choices where each choice has serious consequences; yet you have to pick. So you choose one and then have to deal with the set of consequences that follow. The **constructive dilemma** is a valid argument that starts with two conditional propositions and in which one or the other antecedent is true. Consequently, either one or the other of the two consequences must also be true. Think of it as a choice between two options, where each option leads to some consequences. Either you'll pick the first choice or the second. So either you'll have to deal with the first set of consequences or the second set.

For example, what if your best friend says, "I'm in love"? You ask him what he is going to do, and he says, "If I tell my parents, they'll want me to get married, but if I don't tell them, then our relationship will really suffer." Either he's going to tell his folks or he's not. So, either of the two consequences will then follow.

Form of the Constructive Dilemma

If A then B, and if C then D.

<u>Either A or C.</u>

Therefore, either B or D.

If you look closely at the constructive dilemma, you will see that it is like a compound modus ponens, which we can show by stretching it out:

	If A then B	and	if C then D
	<u>A</u>	or	<u>C</u>
Therefore,	B	or	D

The second premise is a disjunction of the two antecedents from the first premise, and the conclusion is a disjunction of the two consequents.

Examples

If the computer crashes again, Irasema will have to reinstall the software; but if the computer quits crashing, Irasema will be able to finish her assignment for bioethics.

<u>Either the computer crashed or it quit crashing.</u>

So, either Irasema will have to reinstall the software or she'll be able to finish her assignment for bioethics.

If the band goes by bus, the concert may have to be delayed, but if the band takes the plane, the profits will be small.

<u>Either the band will go by bus or they'll take a plane.</u>

So, either the concert may be delayed or the profits will be small.

Destructive Dilemma

There is another dilemma besides the constructive dilemma. It is called the **destructive dilemma.** Here we start with two conditional claims and are told that either the first consequent is not true or the second consequent is not true. We can then conclude that either the first antecedent is not true or the second antecedent is not true. Think of it as a choice between two options, each leading to a set of consequences. Either you don't have to deal with one set of consequences or you don't have to deal with the other. So, either you did not choose the first option or you did not choose the second option.

A destructive dilemma is like a compound modus tollens. Here's an example: "If you study math, it'll help you with the sciences, but if you study literature, you'll be strong in the humanities. Either you are not going to be helped in the sciences or you won't be strong in the humanities. Therefore, either you didn't study math or you didn't study literature."

Form of the Destructive Dilemma

If A then B, and if C then D.

Either B is not the case or D is not the case.

Therefore, either A is not the case or C is not the case.

Examples

If the lotus flowers are in bloom, the crowds will come to Silver Lake, but if the flowers haven't yet opened, it'll be easy to find parking.

Either the crowds haven't come to Silver Lake or it won't be easy to find parking.

So, either the lotus flowers are not in bloom or the flowers have opened.

If his fever doesn't abate, Adam will stay indoors, but if he feels better, he'll go cycling.

Either Adam did not stay indoors or he did not go cycling.

So, either his fever abated or Adam did not feel better.

Absorption

With the rule of **absorption,** we start with a conditional claim. We then infer that the antecedent can be repeated in the consequent. The form of absorption is "If *this* then *that*; therefore, if *this* then *this* and *that*." Absorption allows us to repeat the antecedent by putting it in conjunction with the consequent.

Start with a conditional claim, such as "If it rains, the roads will be muddy." We can then infer, "If it rains, then it rains and the roads will be muddy." The antecedent gets absorbed (think *repeated*) into the consequent when we replace the consequent with the conjunction of the antecedent and the consequent.

Form of the Rule of Absorption

If A then B.

Therefore, if A, then both A and B.

Do you see how this goes? It may look like mere repetition, but it can be particularly handy for certain situations. Think of it like a Phillips head screwdriver: You don't need it very often, but when you do, nothing else works nearly as well.

Example

If the Celtics go to the play-offs, their fans will go crazy.

Therefore, if the Celtics go to the play-offs, then the Celtics go to the play-offs and their fans will go crazy.

Note: The entire antecedent has to move back to the consequent. Whatever the antecedent is—simple or compound—the whole thing has to get absorbed into (placed in conjunction with) the consequent.

> If the Celtics beat the Lakers, Phil will be depressed.

Therefore, if the Celtics beat the Lakers, then the Celtics beat the Lakers and Phil will be depressed.

Exercises

Directions: Drawing from the constructive dilemma, the destructive dilemma, and absorption, name the rule of inference in the following arguments.

1. If the hurricane moves up from Florida, Paula and Ted will hit the road. Therefore, if the hurricane moves up from Florida, then the hurricane moves up from Florida and Paula and Ted will hit the road.

2. If Amy drives the Jeep, Charlie will have to take the bus. Subsequently, if Amy drives the jeep, then she'll drive the jeep and Charlie will have to take the bus.

3. Either the billboard got blown away during the tornado or someone removed it overnight. If the billboard got blown away during the tornado, then we'll have a view of the lake, but if someone removed it overnight, then they must be planning construction on the new lot. Therefore, either we'll have a view of the lake or they must be planning construction on the new lot.

4. If the lightning hits the trees, there could be a fire. If the lightning misses the trees, then it could strike one of the cows. Either there was not a fire or none of the cows got struck by lightning. Therefore, either the lightning did not hit the trees or the lightning did not miss the trees.

5. If Steve drives through the night, he'll get out of the storm. Therefore, if Steve drives through the night, then he drove through the night and got out of the storm.

6. If the lightning hits the jeep, it could melt the steering wheel; but if it misses the jeep, Amy won't have to worry about getting a new car. Either the steering wheel was not melted or Amy did have to worry about getting a new car. Therefore, either the lightning did not hit the jeep or it did not miss it.

7. Either the weather report is wrong or the storm is going to strike. If the weather report is wrong, then Jamal and Sam can make it to the Star Trek convention. If the storm strikes, they'll have to stay home. Therefore, either Jamal and Sam made it to the Star Trek convention or they'll have to stay home.

8. If the rain doesn't stop, the roads will be flooded, but if the rain stops, we can drive to Moose Jaw. Either the rain didn't stop or it did. Therefore, either the roads will be flooded or we can drive to Moose Jaw.

9. If the cows can't find shelter from the storm, they huddle under the trees. Therefore, if the cows can't find shelter from the storm, then they can't find shelter from the storm and they huddle under the trees.

10. If the storm blows the roof off the garage, Nick's new VW convertible will get drenched; but if the storm moves on to the east, Nick can relax. Either the storm blew the roof off the garage or the storm moved on to the east. Therefore, either Nick's new VW convertible got drenched or Nick can relax.

Reminder on Validity and Soundness

All the **rules of inference** are valid argument forms. So, if we assume the premises are true, the conclusion will be forced to be true as well. The conclusion *must* be true whenever a valid argument has true premises.

Be aware that in a valid argument the evidence fully supports the conclusion. So, if we *assume* the premises to be true in any of these rules of inference, then the conclusion will follow as true. *But it doesn't mean the premises are necessarily true.* That's another issue altogether. To be *sound,* the argument must be valid, but it must also have true premises. Don't confuse validity and soundness—soundness has more stringent requirements.

We also want to have our antennae out for the formal fallacies, so we don't accidentally mistake a fallacy for either modus ponens or modus tollens, both valid argument forms.

Formal Fallacies

Fallacies are always invalid arguments, whether or not they have true premises. They are incorrect forms of reasoning, no matter how persuasive they may be. People are regularly persuaded by bad reasoning—but that doesn't change the fact that the reasoning is still bad. Our task is to spot that bad reasoning and cut it off at its knees, so to speak!

There are two key formal fallacies: the fallacy of denying the antecedent and the fallacy of affirming the consequent. They are called **formal fallacies** because the error is with a misuse of form, or structure. Even if the premises were true, the conclusion would not follow as true because of the structural problems. These two fallacies are, basically, mutations of modus ponens and modus tollens. But where both modus ponens and modus tollens are valid argument forms, the two formal fallacies are both invalid and unsound.

Valid Argument Forms versus Formal Fallacies

We know that two famous valid argument forms are modus ponens and modus tollens, as set out below:

Modus Ponens (a valid argument form, not a fallacy)
If A then B.
<u>A is true.</u>
So, B is true.

Example
If the peach pie has ice cream on it, Darin will be pleased.
<u>The peach pie did have ice cream on it.</u>
So, Darin was pleased.

Modus Tollens (a valid argument form, not a fallacy)
If A then B.
<u>B is not the case.</u>
So, A is not the case.

Example
If the shark chomps off part of Ray's new surfboard, he won't be happy.
<u>Ray is happy.</u>
Therefore, the shark did not chomp off part of Ray's new surfboard.

Note: If the two premises are true, the conclusion has to be true as well—it couldn't be false. This makes the argument valid.

If we see that an argument fits either of the valid argument patterns above, we can relax. However, that may not happen. Instead, we may be staring at a fallacy. Our job is to examine the form of the argument to make that determination.

The Fallacy of Denying the Antecedent

The **fallacy of denying the antecedent** asserts a causal relationship between the antecedent condition (A) and the consequent (B). The fallacy occurs when the person claims that, because the antecedent doesn't happen, the consequent can't happen either. However, there may be many things that cause the consequent to happen.

The conclusion does not automatically follow if the premises are true—unless a one-to-one ("if and only if") connection between the antecedent cause A and the effect B is given. The fact that one possible cause does not occur does not preclude some other factor causing the effect.

Consider this example: "If the bank robber is hiding in the college mailroom, then we had better call the FBI." The fallacy of denying the antecedent occurs when it is argued, "The bank robber is not hiding in the college mailroom; therefore, we don't need to call the FBI." The reason this is fallacious is that, even if there is not a bank robber in the college mailroom, we may still need to contact the FBI. We might, for instance, realize that, instead of a bank robber, three agents from the old KGB are camped out in the woodshed, plotting the overthrow of the Uzbekistan government. Or perhaps an escapee from the nearest prison is lurking in the back-yard. Or it may be that we've found evidence of an email scam targeting people on welfare. Simply because there's no bank robber in the college mailroom doesn't mean the consequent ("We had better call the FBI") is not the case.

Form of the Fallacy of Denying the Antecedent

If A then B.

<u>A is not the case.</u>

Therefore, B is not the case.

Note: A and B could be either positive or negative claims, and they could be com-pound propositions as well.

Examples

If another snail crawls under the door, I'm pouring salt around the house.

<u>Another snail did not crawl under the door.</u>

So, I didn't pour salt around the house.

Note: I might pour salt simply as a preventative measure or to cut down on the number of slugs and mealy bugs crawling up to the door.

<u>If George chases that skunk, he may be very sorry.</u>

George did not chase the skunk, so he was not sorry.

Note: George could be sorry for other reasons, such as losing his wallet.

The Fallacy of Affirming the Consequent

The **fallacy of affirming the consequent** is faulty reasoning of the form. "If A then B. B is true (the consequent happens). Therefore, A is true (the antecedent also happens)." As with the fallacy of denying the antecedent, having a causal connection does not make it a one-to-one ("if and only if") connection. That must be specified. If it is not stated (if A then B *and* if B then A), then the fact that B is true does not mean that A has to be true as well. There could be a number of causal factors independently causing an event.

For example, suppose someone says to you, "If the coyotes get in the backyard, the primroses will be crushed. The primroses were crushed. Therefore, there must have been coyotes in the backyard." What's wrong with this reasoning? Well, coyotes aren't the only things that can crush primroses. For example, dogs could have run through, or the maintenance men could have stomped on the primroses when they were fixing the fence in the backyard, and so forth.

Form of the Fallacy of Affirming the Consequent

If A then B.

<u>B is the case.</u>

Therefore, A is the case as well.

Note: A and B could be either positive or negative claims, and either or both could be compound propositions.

Examples

If the road is muddy, it will be hard to go hiking.

It was hard to go hiking.

Therefore, the road was muddy.

Note: **Many factors make it difficult to hike; muddy roads are only one.**

If the driver in the blue Cadillac sneaks into the carpool lane, she will get a ticket.

The driver in the blue Cadillac got a ticket.

So, she must have sneaked into the carpool lane.

Note: She could have gotten a ticket for speeding, for drunk driving, or something else besides sneaking into the carpool lane.

Exercises

Directions: Name the formal fallacy or valid argument (either modus ponens or modus tollens) below.

1. If Ray doesn't study logic, he'll go to the gym. Ray didn't study logic, so he must be at the gym.

2. If Max gets another Van Morrison album, we will get a new sound system. We got a new sound system, so Max must have gotten another Van Morrison record.

3. If Ray becomes an aerobics instructor, he won't have time to study logic. Ray didn't become an aerobics instructor, so he must have time to study logic.

4. If Pinky feels better, he can go home and take his dog Blue for a walk. Pinky did not go home or take his dog Blue for a walk. So, he must not feel better.

5. If Shannon doesn't make it to dinner, then she'll just eat takeout as she drives. Shannon made it to dinner, so she won't have to eat takeout as she drives.

6. If Amelia decides to go to law school, then she will have to take the LSAT. Amelia did not take the LSAT. Therefore, she didn't decide to go to law school.

7. If the virus comes in as an attachment and you open it, all heck will break loose. I'm glad to hear you did not open the attachment with the Melissa virus in it. Therefore, you don't have to worry about heck breaking loose on your computer!

8. If the worm gets into Mark's address book, he'll need to get an anti-virus program. The worm got into Mark's address book. So, he'll need to get an anti-virus program.

9. If you burn the potatoes and cremate the onions, the frittata won't be very tasty. Alice did not both burn the potatoes and cremate the onions. So, she must have made a tasty frittata.

10. If the virus infects your email system, you might as well erase your hard drive and start over. A virus infected Mark's email program. As a result, he might as well erase his hard drive and start over.

11. If a cook lacks the right ingredients, he won't be able to make a good soufflé. Claude wasn't able to make a good soufflé. So, he must not have had the right ingredients.

12. If Max keeps practicing his Chinese drums, he will drive Maria crazy. Max did not keep practicing his Chinese drums. So, he did not drive Maria crazy.

Quick Quiz

1. *True or false:* The form of absorption is "If A then B. Therefore, if A, then A and B."

2. The argument "If R then T, and if B then G. Either R or B. Therefore, either T or G" is (a) modus ponens or (b) constructive dilemma.

3. Destructive dilemma is like a compound version of which other rule of inference: (a) modus ponens, (b) modus tollens, or (c) constructive dilemma?

4. *True or false:* An argument in the form of constructive dilemma is a valid argument.

5. The argument form "If A then B. B. Therefore, A" is (a) the fallacy of affirming the consequent or (b) modus ponens.

6. *True or false:* An argument in the form of the constructive dilemma is like a compound modus ponens.

7. The argument "If we start early, we can make it to Tucson by dinner time, but if we want a leisurely trip, we'll spend the first night in San Diego. Either we won't make it to Tucson or we won't spend the first night in San Diego. Therefore, either we didn't start early or we don't want a leisurely trip" is an example of:
   a. Constructive dilemma
   b. Conjunction
   c. Destructive dilemma
   d. Simplification

8. Using modus ponens, if the first premise is "If the dog eats our sandwiches, we'll get some take-out," the second premise is (a) the dog ate the sandwiches or (b) we'll get some take-out.

9. The form of the argument of the fallacy of denying the antecedent is:
   a. If A then B. A. Therefore, B.
   b. If A then B. Not A. Therefore, not B.
   c. If A then B. Not B. Therefore, not A.
   d. If A then B. Therefore, if A then A and B.

10. The argument "If the dog eats three avocados, he won't feel very good. The dog didn't feel very good. So, he must have eaten three avocados" is an example of (a) modus tollens, (b) fallacy of denying the antecedent, or (c) the fallacy of affirming the consequent.

11. *True or false:* The argument "If Omar's cell phone rings, people will be angry during the movie. People were angry during the movie. So, his cell phone must have been ringing" is an example of the fallacy of affirming the consequent.

12. If the first premise is "If the jello is warm, it'll lose its shape," the second premise of the argument in a fallacy of affirming the consequent is:
   a. The jello is warm.
   b. The jello is not warm.
   c. The jello will lose its shape.
   d. The jello will not lose its shape.

Overview

At this point, we've covered a lot of territory in terms of the valid argument forms and the two formal fallacies. The following table summarizes what we've covered.

Valid Argument Forms and Formal Fallacies

RULES OF INFERENCE	
Modus ponens	If A then B. A. Therefore, B.
Modus tollens	If A then B. Not B. Therefore, not A.
Hypothetical syllogism	If A then B. If B then C. Therefore, if A then C.
Disjunctive syllogism	Either A or B. Not A. Therefore, B.
Constructive dilemma	If A then B, and if C then D. Either A or C. Thus, either B or D.
Destructive dilemma	If A then B, and if C then D. Either not B or not D. Therefore, either not A or not C.
Simplification	A and B. Therefore, A (or therefore, B).
Logical addition	A. Therefore, either A or B.
Conjunction	A. B. Therefore, A and B.
Absorption	If A then B. Therefore, if A, then both A and B.

RULES OF REPLACEMENT

DeMorgan's Laws

"Not both"   Not both A and B ≡ Not A or not B.

"Neither/nor"   Neither A nor B ≡ Not A and not B.

Material implication   "If A then B" is equivalent to "Either not A or B."

Transposition   "If A then B" is equivalent to "If not B then not A."

Exportation   "If (A and B) then C" is equivalent to
                                "If A then, if B then C."

Equivalence   "A if and only if B" is equivalent to
                                "If A then B, and if B then A."

FORMAL FALLACIES

Fallacy of affirming the consequent   If A then B. B. Therefore, A.

Fallacy of denying the antecedent   If A then B. Not A. Therefore, not B.

Exercises

Part One

Directions: Using the rule indicated, complete the argument or give an equivalent sentence.

1. *Modus ponens*: If Ryan does not get a Prius, he'll get a bicycle.
2. *Material implication*: Either Julie told the truth or she deceived her friend.
3. *Modus tollens:* If he doesn't get an Austin Mini, then Scott will buy a used Audi.
4. *Logical addition:* A deer leaped over the car.
5. *Exportation:* If the slugs get on the lilies and eat the leaves, Ruben will not be happy.
6. *Absorption:* If Ruben is happy, then his lilies must be okay.
7. *Hypothetical syllogism:* If Carla serves chili, Jamal will bring chips and salsa.
8. *Material implication:* If the band needs a sound engineer, they will call Trent.
9. *Transposition:* If Ed's fever does not break, he will go to the doctor.
10. *DeMorgan's Laws:*
    a. Neither opera nor jazz comforts a bluegrass lover.
    b. David is not guilty of both eating the tamales and gobbling up the flan.

11. *Conjunction:* Pulling weeds is good for stress. Nothing beats getting rid of deadwood.

12. *Constructive dilemma:* If they have a long talk, things will improve; but if they refuse to speak, we'd better put on some soul music.

13. *Simplification:* Omar enjoys discussing politics and is a Detroit Lions fan.

14. *Disjunctive syllogism:* Michelle is either going to swim some laps or she'll study for the chemistry exam.

15. *Modus ponens:* If the rumors spread, there will be trouble.

16. *Hypothetical syllogism:* If the Pistons win, then Anna will gloat.

17. *Disjunctive syllogism:* Either Madeleine is from Topeka or she's from Boulder.

18. *Absorption:* If that's a Harvard woman, then ask her about the Peabody Museum.

19. *Conjunction:* The photos came out wonderfully. Jamal decided to frame them.

20. *Constructive dilemma:* If he gets a digital camera, then Jamal will save money, but if he stays with his old Nikon, Jamal will take a darkroom course.

Part Two

Directions: Name the rule of inference or fallacy used below. If more than one rule is used, name both.

1. Only warm bread makes Louie happy after he loses at Scrabble. Louie lost at Scrabble. So, he'll want to have warm bread.

2. If something eats beef, it is carnivorous. John is a carnivore. So, John is a beef eater.

3. The chef quit in the middle of John's meal. He stormed out of the restaurant. Therefore, the chef quit in the middle of John's meal and stormed out of the restaurant.

4. Veronica was pleased with all the vegie options on the menu. Therefore, either Veronica was pleased with all the vegie options on the menu or she was just being polite.

5. If John orders dessert, then he won't eat all his salad. John ate all his salad. Therefore, John did not order dessert.

6. All steak eaters revolt Veronica. All those who revolt Veronica won't get invited to her party. So, all steak eaters won't get invited to Veronica's party.

7. If Steve finds mice in the cellar, he's not going to be happy. Steve is happy. Therefore, he must not have found mice in the cellar.

8. April does not like reptiles and she doesn't care much for insects either. Therefore, April does not care much for insects.

9. Bungie jumping is not good for those who are prone to squeamishness. Therefore either bungie jumping is not good for those who are prone to squeamishness or the sky is made of blue wallpaper paste.

10. Small alligators can be unpleasant. Therefore, either small alligators can be unpleasant or Steve is mistaken.

11. If the transmission goes, Ernie will get out his cell phone and sit down on the curb. The transmission did not go, so Ernie did not get out his cell phone and sat down on the curb.

12. If Leon can fix the transmission by himself, Harry will start on the radiator. Leon could fix the transmission by himself. So Harry can start on the radiator.

13. Adam ran the Boston Marathon. The Kenyans won once more. Therefore, Adam ran the Boston Marathon and the Kenyans won once more.

14. Omar decided it was time to visit Kenya and go via Amsterdam. Therefore, Omar decided to visit Kenya.

15. If Anita and Gary go to Australia, they won't go to Guatemala. They went to Australia, so Anita and Gary did not go to Guatemala.

16. If the wombat won't come out of the cave, we can't take its photograph. The wombat came out of the cave, so we could take its photograph.

17. The nature photographer gave lessons and showed tricks with Photoshop. Therefore, the nature photograph showed tricks with Photoshop.

18. The camera is either broken or it's just the battery. It wasn't just the battery. So, the camera is broken.

19. If the kangaroo quits jumping, Anita will take its picture, but if it doesn't stop jumping, she'll take a picture of the koala bear. Either the kangaroo quit jumping or it didn't stop jumping. Therefore, either Anita took a picture of the kangaroo or she took a picture of the koala bear.

20. The koala bear wouldn't stop eating leaves. Therefore, either the koala bear wouldn't stop eating leaves or he was just chewing on them for something to do.

Part Three

Directions: Name the rule of inference, rule of replacement, or formal fallacy below. *Be careful:* Not all the sentences are in standard form, so translate them first and then check for the rules.

1. Unless you come with me, I won't go to see Dr. Gutierrez. I didn't go to see Dr. Gutierrez. Therefore, you came with me.

2. I will talk with that Elvis impersonator if he stops singing. The Elvis impersonator stopped singing. Therefore, I talked with him.

3. If the operation is a success, Frankenstein won't have to put up with a plug in his neck. The operation was not a success. So, Frankenstein will have to put up with a plug in his neck.

4. If the doctor operates and leaves in a sponge, then there'll be a lawsuit. (This is equivalent to "If the doctor operates, then, if she leaves in a sponge, there'll be a lawsuit.")

5. If that's a badger, it may be wise to stay inside the car. It was wise to stay inside the car. Therefore, it must be a badger out there.

6. If the extras are stuck on the freeway and can't take the streets, they'll be late to the film shoot. This means, if the extras are stuck on the freeway, then if they can't take the streets, they'll be late to the film shoot.

7. Not any extras were on the studio set, and the director had to decide whether to wait or switch scenes. Therefore, not any extras were on the studio set.

8. Either that's an insurance salesman or it's an extra from *Dawn of the Dead*. It's not an insurance salesman. So, it's an extra from *Dawn of the Dead*.

9. Provided that that's not the electrician, it must be an insurance salesman. It's not an insurance salesman. Therefore, it's an electrician.

10. A mudslide is a sufficient condition to mess up the freeway. If the freeway is messed up, traffic will be a tad slow. So, if there's a mudslide, traffic will be a tad slow.

11. Only if the new stereo arrives will Amanda quit working on her script. Amanda quit working on her script. Therefore, the new stereo arrived.

12. Having a good sense of rhythm is necessary to do rap music. Marvin Gaye had a good sense of rhythm. So, he could have done rap music.

13. If that man on the roof is not installing cable television, Ed is phoning the police. If Ed phones the police, Jack will be alarmed. Therefore, if that man on the roof is not installing cable television, Jack will be alarmed.

14. Reading Tolstoy is sufficient to get a sense of Russian literature. The Simpsons have no sense of Russian literature. So, the Simpsons have not read Tolstoy.

15. If Jack is squeamish, he might find riding the roller coaster a bit disturbing. Jack is not squeamish. So, he shouldn't be disturbed riding the roller coaster.

16. Neither Vin Diesel nor J Lo eats at my local diner. So, Vin Diesel does not eat at my local diner and J Lo doesn't eat at my local diner.

17. LaToya will knit another afghan if she can get the right color yarn. LaToya knitted another afghan. So, she got the right color yarn.

18. If the insecticidal soap doesn't work, Anita will go after the aphids by hand. Therefore, if the insecticidal soap doesn't work, then the insecticidal soap didn't work and Anita will go after the aphids by hand.

19. If the eggs come with grits, then we won't need potatoes. This means, if we need potatoes, then the eggs did not come with grits.

20. John says, "For economic issues, I rely on logic. For political issues, I rely on logic or on gut instinct. For moral issues, I never rely on logic." What follows?
    a. If John relies on logic, he may be responding to a moral issue.
    b. If John relies on logic, he is not responding to an economic issue.
    c. If John does not rely on logic, he is responding to a political issue.
    d. If John does not rely on logic, he must be responding to an economic issue.
    e. If John does not rely on logic, he might be responding to a political issue.

Part Four

Directions: Practice with the rules and fallacies. Name the rule of inference or replacement below. If it's a fallacy, name it.

1. If Nazreen sees *The Vanishing,* she will have to sleep with the lights on. Nazreen did not sleep with the lights on. Therefore, she did not see *The Vanishing.*

2. Neither *The Eye* nor *The Host* disturbed Carlos. That means *The Eye* did not disturb Carlos and *The Host* did not disturb Carlos.

3. If the alien makes meatloaf of the predator, then the audience will cheer. (This is equivalent to "If the audience did not cheer, then the alien did not make meatloaf of the predator.")

4. If Frankenstein could get better-fitting shoes, he'd find walking easier. Frankenstein didn't find walking easier. So, he must not have gotten better-fitting shoes.

5. Either that's the Wolfman or it's Ryan in his gorilla costume. That's not Ryan in his gorilla costume. So, it must be the Wolfman.

6. Whenever the moon is full, there are strange noises in the forest near the old mill. Whenever there are strange noises in the forest near the old mill, the coyotes start to howl. Therefore, whenever the moon is full, the coyotes start to howl.

7. Waving a garlic clove is sufficient to deter a ghoul from getting within three feet of a human. The ghoul came up to the UPS deliveryman. So, he must not have waved the garlic clove.

8. If that's not an extraterrestrial, then he might work as a bouncer. Therefore, if he doesn't work as a bouncer, then he's an extraterrestrial.

9. Unless that's Dr. Lecter, your threats will mean nothing. He's not Dr. Lecter. So, your threats meant nothing.

10. Either that's an insurance salesman or it's an extra from *The Interpreter.* Thus, if it's not an insurance salesman, then it's an extra from *The Interpreter.*

11. If the new stereo arrives, Lulu won't leave her house. Lulu left her house. Therefore, the new stereo didn't arrive.

12. Not both Harry and Leon thought the problem was with the fuel pump. Therefore, either Harry did not think the problem was with the fuel pump or Leon did not think the problem was with the fuel pump.

13. If Lulu's new stereo doesn't work and she hurries, she can return it. That means, if Lulu's new stereo doesn't work, then if she hurries, she can return it.

14. If the journalist digs in the trash, she will find incriminating evidence about the mayor's brother. The journalist dug in the trash. So, she found incriminating evidence about the mayor's brother.

15. Spencer makes rich cheesecake and he spent a lot of money on the ingredients. Therefore, he makes rich cheesecake.

16. Either that's Keanu Reeves on the phone or someone is playing a trick on her. This means, if that's not Keanu Reeves on the phone, then someone's playing a trick on her.

17. If you are a cynic and only see problems, then life won't be easy for you. (This is the same as, "If you are a cynic, then, if you only see problems, life won't be easy for you.")

18. In a study of teens in South Central, it was found that 83% of them preferred rhythm and blues to country music. This means 83% of all Americans prefer rhythm and blues to country music.

19. Laura is not both a cynic and a pessimist. That means either Laura's not a cynic or she's not a pessimist.

20. If you don't like to gather pods and stones, you won't like camping. The boys liked camping. So, they must like to gather pods and stones.

21. Dr. Green, you should carry more of the load in the Philosophy Department. If you don't I will tell your son, Evan, that there's no Easter Bunny and it's you, not Santa, who gave him that bicycle last year.

22. If Jasper eats both peas and corn, he won't want zucchini. Jasper did not want any zucchini, so he must have eaten both peas and corn.

23. Nicole said never to lie, so I should tell Dr. Teays that I'm tired of all those stories about her bird and that her new hairdo makes her look like a wild woman.

24. If Prince eats another bird, we'll have to keep him indoors, but if Prince eats up his crunchies, we'll have to go get more cat food. Either Prince ate another bird or he ate up his crunchies. So, either we'll have to keep Prince indoors or we'll have to go get more cat food.

Part Five

Directions: Read the following passage, and name all the rules you see.

Zorra, the woman warrior, needs a vacation. She decided to go to Kenya. As a result, Zorra, the woman warrior, needs a vacation and decided to go to Kenya. If Zorra goes to

Kenya and wants to go on a safari, then she will go to Nairobi. This means, if Zorra goes to Kenya, then if she wants to go on a safari, she will go to Nairobi.

Zorra would like to take her pet tiger, Moo. If Zorra would like to take her tiger, Moo, then she will have to mesmerize the security personnel at the airport. Therefore, Zorra will have to mesmerize the security personnel at the airport. The security guy was pretty jerky to Zorra. Either he is going to stop Zorra from bringing Moo on the trip or he'll get distracted by that gorgeous woman with pink hair. Fortunately, the security guy did not stop Zorra from bringing Moo along on the trip. Therefore, he was distracted by that gorgeous woman with pink hair.

If Moo cannot fit under the seat on the airplane, then Zorra will have to put Moo in with the freight. Zorra did not have to put Moo in with the freight, so Moo fit under the seat. Of course, Moo was a little squashed there under the seat, but he was happy to be so close to Zorra. Therefore, Moo was happy to be close to Zorra. In fact, Moo is fond of Zorra's bright, fuschia-colored toenail polish. If Zorra wears sandals, then Moo can look at Zorra's toenails. If Moo can look at Zorra's toenails, then he will start to lick his paws. Therefore, if Zorra wears sandals, Moo will start to lick his paws!

If Moo licks his paws, then he'll calm down, but if Moo keeps his tongue in his mouth, he won't be bobbing his head up and down under the seat. Either Moo will lick his paws or he'll keep his tongue in his mouth. Therefore, either Moo will calm down or he won't be bobbing his head up and down. If Zorra orders warm milk for Moo, then he will quit licking his paws. This means, if Zorra orders warm milk for Moo, then she orders warm milk for Moo and he'll quit licking his paws. Neither Zorra nor Moo has ever been to Nairobi. This means Zorra has not been to Nairobi and Moo has not been to Nairobi. Moo is scared about the safari. Moo is afraid someone will shoot an arrow at him. Therefore, either Moo is afraid someone will shoot an arrow at him or he's just nervous about flying on such a long trip. This means, if Moo is not afraid someone will shoot an arrow at him, then he's just nervous about flying on such a long trip.

Not both Moo and Zorra are interested in the handsome man across the aisle. This means either Moo is not interested in the handsome man across the aisle or Zorra is not interested in the handsome man across the aisle. If the handsome man winks again at Zorra, Moo is going to bite his hand off. Moo did not bite off the hand of the handsome man across the aisle. Therefore, the man quit winking at Zorra. If Moo is no longer afraid of the safari, he and Zorra will have a fun vacation. This means, if Moo and Zorra do not have a fun vacation, then Moo was afraid of the safari. However, Moo finally calmed down. He was no longer afraid of the safari. Therefore, Moo and Zorra had a fun vacation! The end.

Quick Quiz

1. The form of *simplification* is (a) A. B. Therefore, A and B, or (b) A and B. Therefore, A.

2. *True or false:* The disjunctive syllogism is of the form "Either A or B. B. Therefore, not A."

3. The argument "Greg went to the *Terminator* film festival. He did not go jogging. Therefore, Greg went to the *Terminator* film festival and did not go jogging" is an example of (a) conjunction or (b) logical addition.

4. If the first premise is "If Greg watches *The Big Lebowski* again, Carla will read her new novel," the next premise, according to *modus tollens,* is (a) "Greg did not watch *The Big Lebowski* again" or (b) "Carla did not read her new novel."

5. The argument "If Jody learns Photoshop, he can make brochures, but if he takes a watercolor class, then he could try illustration. Either Jody will learn Photoshop or he'll take a watercolor class. Therefore, either he will make brochures or he could try illustration" is an example of a (a) constructive dilemma or (d) destructive dilemma.

6. "Either we will print the brochures or leave them online. We did not leave the brochures online. Therefore, we printed them" is an example of:
   a. Disjunctive syllogism
   b. Hypothetical syllogism
   c. Modus tollens
   d. Absorption

7. *True or false:* The fallacy of denying the antecedent is an unsound argument.

8. Using the fallacy of denying the antecedent, what would be the next premise if the argument started with "If the puppy chews up the couch, Ann will take him to obedience school"?
   a. The puppy chewed the couch.
   b. The puppy did not chew the couch.
   c. Ann will take him to obedience school.
   d. Ann will not take him to obedience school.

9. What is the rule of inference of the argument "The puppy didn't feel great. He regretted chewing the couch. Therefore, the puppy didn't feel great and he regretted chewing the couch"?
   a. Simplification
   b. Logical addition
   c. Conjunction
   d. Absorption

10. The argument "If the tornado hits, our vacation will be shot. The tornado did not hit. So, our vacation was not shot" is in the form of the (a) fallacy of affirming the consequent or (b) fallacy of denying the antecedent.

PART THREE

Going Out into the World

CHAPTER ELEVEN

Out of the Silence: The Power of Language

Looking at a pot, for example, or thinking of a pot, . . . it was in vain that Watt said, Pot, pot. Well, perhaps not quite in vain, but very nearly. For it was not a pot, the more he looked, the more he reflected, the more he felt sure of that, that it was not a pot at all. It resembled a pot, it was almost a pot, but it was not a pot of which one could say, Pot, pot, and be comforted. It was in vain that it answered, with unexceptionable adequacy, all the purposes, and performed all the offices, of a pot, it was not a pot. And it was just this hair-breadth departure from the nature of a true pot that so excruciated Watt.

SAMUEL BECKETT, *Watt*

Many of us empathize with Watt, the Beckett character who struggles to find words to apply to his situation. Watt wrestles with words, frustrated that they seem to work for others, but not for him. His losing battle with the word "pot" in the quote above is but one example of the struggle between words and silence played out every day in Watt's world.

On the other hand, some people believe they have the upper hand on language, that there is no real battle between words and silence. *They* are in control. They believe words cannot penetrate our exterior, that we have skulls like helmets and bodies like armor, so words can just bounce off and land in the dust. But this, we all know at heart, is just a ruse, a game of deception about the power of language. Language can have incredible power, both positively and negatively.

Language has power. The words we use shape our ideas for defining, as well as solving, problems. The very questions we ask may limit the sorts of answers we get. The very way in which an inquiry is structured can affect the results of the inquiry. Be on the lookout for the ways language can deceive, mislead, or otherwise block us from seeing clearly and evaluating the evidence.

Language can also be an instrument of liberation. Words can be used to unite us as a people, to move us to a higher moral plane, to calm, to communicate, and to achieve spiritual strength. As bell hooks says, "We are rooted in language, wedded, have our being in words. Language is also a place of struggle. The oppressed struggle in language to recover ourselves—to rewrite, to reconcile, to renew. Our words are not without meaning. They are an action—a resistance."

The Functions of Language

Language is used in a variety of ways—we will be zeroing in on the ones that have the biggest impact on our critical thinking. W. H. Werkmeister considers these to be the key functions of language:

- **Expressive function:** conveys emotions and feelings (e.g., "I had a great trip to Montreal" or "What beautiful countryside is in Colorado")
- **Evocative function:** evokes a response in others and serves as a catalyst to bring about some action or effect, as in request, commands, warning cries, and pleas (e.g., "Get a checkup every year" or "Get out the vote")
- **Poetic function:** uses rhythm, repetition, and specific words
- **Ceremonial function:** involves communion, liturgical readings, prayers, and ritualistic repetition of words
- **Logical function:** conveys firsthand reports or secondary reports not based on eyewitness testimony, and sets out connections between propositions and arguments

Werkmeister sees the logical function as the most important function of language. It is here that we speak of propositions as true or false. Such statements fall into one of the various types—including primary reports (eyewitness reports or first-person knowledge), such as "I have a toothache" and "On Tuesday, I went to the movies." Secondary reports are factual reports that are not eyewitness testimony. These include summaries, statistical studies, newspaper and textbook reports, interpretations, and analyses of primary reports, such as those made by reporters out in the field. Another logical function of language is in arguments—where we trace or derive the implications of what has been observed. The logical function is a central concern of logicians. For critical thinkers, the other functions of language may come into play and thus warrant our concern.

In this chapter, we will examine some key uses of language, focusing on a myriad of ways that it can have impact in our lives. We will see how language can function in destructive ways, persuasive ways, and inspiring, healing, and transformative ways. The range we will cover is this:

- Descriptions and asymmetry
- Denotations and connotations
- Importance of context
- Culturally defined uses of language
- Euphemisms and hedging
- Labels and categories
- Ambiguity (linguistic fallacies)
- Concepts and definitions

- Jargon, buzzwords, and technical terms
- Metaphors, images, and analogies
- The passive voice
- Loaded language

- Propaganda
- Exclusive language and hate speech
- Humor, parody, and satire
- The liberatory voice

Philosopher of language Ludwig Wittgenstein would say that this list shows how much language is like family resemblances. There are differences and yet similarities that weave in and out from one member to another, and yet we can see that they are all related. When you look at all the different kinds of uses of language discussed in this chapter, see if you can trace resemblances between them.

Descriptions

How we refer to people can have great significance. In the positive, references can instill a sense of pride and community. In the negative, they can lead to alienation, powerlessness, and despair. Have you ever read eulogies or obituaries summing up a person's life? All-too-many dead people may have rolled over in their graves because of the ways others characterized their achievements. You may chortle, not thinking ahead to what *your* obituary is going to say. But check out these from *The New York Times:*

25 Jun 2008: Arthur Galston, 88, Agent Orange Researcher

25 May 2008: J. R. Simplot, Potato and Computer Chip King

27 Feb 2008: Buddy Miles, 61, Drummer for Hendrix, Voice of California Raisins

6 Feb 2008: David Bradley, 92, Doctor and Author Warned of Atomic Threat

6 Feb 2008: Shell Kepler, 49, Actress Played Gossipy Nurse On "General Hospital"

17 Jan 2008: Richard Knerr, 82, Co-Founded Wham-O, Maker of the Hula Hoop and Frisbee

28 Dec 2007: Benazir Bhutto, 54, Aristocrat Who Championed Democracy

22 Oct 2004: Lawrence Freedman, 85, Who Peered into Killers' Psyches

27 Jun 2004: Danny Dark, 65, Whose Voice Spurned StarKist's Charlie the Tuna

8 Jun 2000: C. D. Atkins, 86, Inventor of Frozen Orange Juice Process

Descriptions and Social Attitudes

Surveying the territory, we see **descriptions** as a vehicle of values and attitudes. Look, for instance, at this description of basketball player Pau Gasol: "With his frumpy hair and delicate gait, sometimes he looked like a bird. With his long thin arms spread wide, other times he looked like a plane. In the end, though, he looked like Super-You-Know-Who, scoring 36 points." (Bill Plaschke, "After Gasol's 36 Points, the Weight Is Gone," *Los Angeles Times,* 20 Apr 2008)

Descriptions conjure up images, and images can set entire trains of thought in motion. What image pops into your brain when someone is described as "slender"? What about "skinny" or "bean-pole"? Descriptions can run the gamut. Let's look at some examples.

Description 1: Singer Patti Smith

As the foremost punk poet of our times, Patti Smith looks exactly as you would want and expect her to look. She walks in and announces, "I'm Patti Smith." As if you couldn't tell. She's dressed in jeans, boots, a loosely billowing white shirt and a long, black jacket that looks like a frock-coat. She's not wearing make-up and her unkempt black hair hangs loosely over her shoulders. She's made no attempt to disguise its rapidly multiplying grey strands. If she was serving you at the deli counter or waiting on your restaurant table, you'd have to say she looked a mess. . . . She appears stern and a little nervous and warns that she hates interviews because she's uncomfortable talking about herself. (Nigel Williamson, "Rock 'n' Roll Was Revolutionary," *Scotland on Sunday,* news.scotsman.com, 25 Apr 2004)

Description 2: Actor Angelina Jolie

When [Angelina] Jolie came into the Four Seasons, she looked around quickly, then crossed the floor like a pilgrim, with her head down, like someone used to being noticed, or bothered, like someone who does not feel safe. . . . You detect her presence not by her face, which she can obscure or render ordinary in that way of celebrities, but by how people around her react—the flurry in the water. She carries herself with strange dignity, as if she were an emissary of a secret order, a messenger from a lost kingdom. . . . She's a princess, an aristocrat. (Rich Cohen, "A Woman in Full," *Vanity Fair,* Jul 2008)

How are the moo swings?

Nik Scott, artist. www.nikscott.com. Used with permission.

Description 3: Doctor Ahmed Shafik

Dr. Ahmed Shafik wears three-piece suits with gold watch fobs and a diamond stick pin in the lapel. His glasses are the thick, black rectangular style of the Nasser era. He owns a Cairo hospital and lives in a mansion with marble walls. He was nominated for a Nobel Prize. I don't care about any of this. Shafik won my heart by publishing a paper in *European Urology* in which he investigated the effects of polyester on sexual activity. Ahmed Shafik dressed lab rats in polyester pants. (Mary Roach, posted on NPR.org, 9 Apr 2008)

Group or Individual Exercise

Directions: Answer one of the two questions below.

1. Find five to six descriptions of women and five to six descriptions of men (look in magazines, newspapers, or Internet articles). Compare the level of detail, the use of language, the positive or negative qualities, and so on.

2. Find five to six descriptions of Caucasians and five to six descriptions of members of another racial/ethnic group (look in magazines, newspapers, or Internet articles). Compare the level of detail, the use of language, the positive or negative qualities, and so on.

Asymmetrical Descriptions

When members of one group are described in ways that would not be used for a different group, the resulting description is **asymmetrical.** Such asymmetry usually indicates a **double standard,** where the rules or expectations are applied unfairly to the different groups. It can be relatively harmless, but it can also have a hurtful or inflammatory effect. The test of symmetry is if you can turn the tables.

One common double standard concerns appearance. For example, in the 2008 Democratic primary race, Chelsea Clinton was described as follows: "Her hair is long and highlighted blond. Her black flared jeans are tight, and her gray blazer nips at her small waist" (*Los Angeles Times,* 17 Apr 2008). Note also this description: "[Singer Amy] Winehouse wore a short blue spotted dress in a clear effort to look smart for her husband's trial, but the classy clothes failed to hide her alarmingly bad skin. The singer's ragged appearance shocked onlookers as she arrived at court" (*Daily Mail,* posted on *Huffington Post,* 7 Jun 2008). Thus far, men have not generally been subject to such scrutiny.

Descriptions, whether or not they are asymmetrical, reveal societal attitudes. Consider this example: "Karen Lopez, a 39-year-old Peoria resident, doesn't look the part of a pool player with her neat black tresses, makeup and collared shirt" (*The Daily Journal,* 27 Mar 2008). Look at the range: Women are "willowy," men "tall." Women are "plump," men "paunchy" or "stocky." Even slight variations can alter the force of a description. We see this with the words "fat," "obese," and "overweight." In a society fixated on weight, those who are not reed-thin are often referred to as "overweight" or "full-figured." Look at film critic James Verniere's description of Jason Segel, the male lead in *Forgetting Sarah Marshall*: "The otherwise charming Segel manages to be both pudgy and not to have a derriere at the same time. But the film, like its predecessors, also features a double standard in regard to its women, who must still be sexually attractive, if not physically perfect specimens" ("Forget 'Sarah Marshall'? Impossible!" *Boston Herald*, 18 Apr 2008).

Exercises

Part One

Directions: Supply a phrase, finding the closest match you can. Use a separate sheet of paper.

1. Men are "lone wolves," women are _____.
2. Women are "frumpy," men are _____.
3. Men are "barrel-chested," women are _____.
4. Women are "cupcakes," men are _____.
5. Men have a "beer gut," women have a _____.
6. Women are "witches," men are _____.
7. Men are "dreamboats," women are _____.
8. Women are "voluptuous," men are _____.
9. Men are "sissies," women are _____.
10. Women are "catty," men are _____.
11. Men "shoot the bull," women _____.
12. Women are "petite," men are _____.
13. Men are "hen-pecked," women are _____.
14. Women are "old maids," men are _____.
15. Men are "dudes," women are _____.

Part Two: Descriptions of Men

Directions: Discuss the following descriptions of men, and note any assumptions about gender stereotypes and societal attitudes.

1. Description of inventor Ray Kurzweil:

   Ray Kurzweil, the famous inventor, is trim, balding, and not very tall. With his perfect posture and narrow black glasses, he would look at home in an old documentary about

Cape Canaveral, but his mission is bolder than any mere voyage into space. He is attempting to travel across a frontier in time, to pass through the border between our era and a future so different as to be unrecognizable. He calls this border the singularity. Kurzweil is 60, but he intends to be no more than 40 when the singularity arrives. (Gary Wolf, "Futurist Ray Kurzweil Pulls Out All the Stops (and Pills) to Live to Witness the Singularity," *Wired* magazine, 24 Mar 2008)

2. Description of golfer Phil Mickelson:

The reality is, even if I play at the top of my game for the rest of my career and achieve my goals—I still won't get to where Tiger is right now. . . . Tiger plays a game we can only marvel at, with that perfect physique and unwavering focus. Phil, flabbier and streakier, plays one we can almost recognize—he's just like us, only better. And on a tour where the key to winning these days seems more and more to be to turn yourself into a zombie, Mickelson's occasional failings are welcome proof of humanity. He may be an idiot sometimes, but he's our idiot. (Charles McGrath, "Just Like Us—Only Better," *The New York Times,* 3 Jun 2007)

3. Description of actor Chris Tucker:

Tucker took character roles in two movies: Quentin Tarantino's *Jackie Brown* and *The Fifth Element,* in which he played a transvestite radio deejay. It wasn't too big a stretch . . . his voice is already up in that range where the genders meet, he can be campy and over-the-top, and he has beautifully fine bones that can swing either way. But believe, me, Chris Tucker is all man. Chicks dig him, of course, and he has a girlfriend and a son, but he generally keeps his private life to himself. (Rick Cohen, "Chris Tucker in Phat City," *GQ,* Aug 2001)

4. Description of pilot Captain William Lancaster:

In England one pilot bitten by the Lindbergh bug was an ex-Royal Air Force officer, Captain William Lancaster. Since leaving the service in 1926, Lancaster had struggled in civilian life, and it showed. The thinning hair and cadaverous features made a mockery of his real age—twenty-nine—giving him the appearance of someone much older. (Colin Evans, *A Question of Evidence: The Casebook of Great Forensic Controversies, from Napoleon to O.J.,* John Wiley, 2003)

Part Three: Descriptions of Women

Directions: Discuss the following descriptions, and note any assumptions about gender stereotypes and societal attitudes.

1. Description of TV personality Greta Van Susteren:

Greta Van Susteren was hailed as a path breaker for speaking openly about her facelift, which gave her a tighter, slightly Martian appearance for her new role as permanent Fox News pundette. (Christine Rosen, "The Democratization of Beauty," *The New Atlantis 5*, Spring 2005)

2. Description of actor Keira Knightley:

Licking the foam off her second cappuccino, picking at the chipped eggplant-colored polish on her bitten fingernails, and describing playing Guinevere variously as "wicked," "chronic," "crazy great," and "fab," Knightley for just a moment looks and sounds like the excitable 19-year-old she is. Her eyes ringed in black kohl, she wears two T-shirts stacked atop one another over a pair of not entirely clean jeans, and black puffy boots that she could have borrowed from Frosty the Snowman. Her hair is pulled back in a scruffy ponytail, exposing a few tiny blemishes on her forehead. As she talks, she twists escaped strands of it around her fingers. A waiflike blond in her previous films, Knightley is now curvier (thanks to the weight training she did to play Guinevere) and brunet. (Johanna Schneller, "Knightley in Shining Armor," *Premiere*, Jun 2004)

3. Description of Ene Ergma, speaker of the Estonian parliament:

Ene Ergma is a formidable woman—tough and smart. At 63, the speaker of the Estonian parliament looks like she'd be as comfortable driving a tank as playing with the grandkids. She has a PhD from Russia's Institute of Space Research, where she wrote a dissertation titled "Unstable Thermonuclear Burning at Late Stages of Stellar Evolution." ("Web War I," *Wired* magazine, Sep 2007)

4. Description of tennis player Serena Williams:

At 22, Serena is all sass and swagger, full of herself and life and apparently not willing to put it on hold so she may devote herself to being a full-time tennis drone, no matter what the critics say. (Harvey Araton, "Tennis Is Only a Game to the Williams Sisters," *The New York Times*, 27 Jun 2004)

Denotations and Connotations

The impact of a description is often linked to the connotations of words and phrases. Whereas the denotation of a word or phrase points to the most specific or literal meaning, the connotation refers to the figurative senses. The **denotation** corresponds to the dictionary definition of a term. How we define a term can have significant consequences. For example, when the Centers for Disease Control (CDC) altered its definition of SARS (severe acute respiratory syndrome) to exclude people whose lab tests turned up negative for the virus 21 days after the onset of symptoms, the number of suspected SARS cases was cut in half.

The **connotation** is the set of associations attached to the word in question, indicating a set of values. We see this with the terms "bachelor gal," "unhitched chick," and "spinster." The terms all refer to unmarried women, but they have different connotations.

Think of synonyms for the term "male": man, gentleman, guy, dude, boy, hunk, jock, stud, beefcake, dreamboat, lone wolf, sport, shark, and so on. Think, too, of synonyms for the term "female": woman, gal, girl, chick, bunny, broad, lady, fox, vixen, bombshell, bimbo, tomato, cupcake, cheesecake, honey, hen, babe, kitten, doll, witch, hag, crone, and so on (add to the list). What do you think these terms tell us about our society?

Exercises

Directions: Using a dictionary, look up the meanings of the words (what they denote), and then list the connotations of each.

1. President
2. Self-help
3. Elite
4. Disabled
5. Pacifist
6. Liberal
7. Conservative
8. Religious
9. Atheist
10. Independent
11. Maternal
12. Convict (the noun)
13. Unemployed
14. Soccer mom
15. Boy Scout
16. Cowboy

Importance of Context

Acceptable uses of language vary according to the context, such as living rooms, restaurants, classrooms, and workplaces. It also varies according to the participants—for example, talks with friends versus those with a teacher or boss. Students and patients generally are referred to on a first-name basis, while doctors and teachers are usually referred to in a more formal way. And servers (or

Language can shift according to the cultural contact.

Reprinted with the permission of Nik Scott, Curious Productions, Australia. http://www.nikscott.com.

You Tell Me Department

Why Is It Often So Hard to Apologize?

Here is a case involving an unprecedented apology on the part of the U.S. government for what the ACLU (American Civil Liberties Union) called "racial profiling" ("Detention Was Wrong, and U.S. Apologizes," *The New York Times,* 24 Aug 2007).

> **The case:** Refugee Abdulameer Habeeb, 41, had been in the United States for 10 months on April 1, 2003, when he stepped off an Amtrak train near the Canadian border in Havre, Montana, to stretch his legs. Border Patrol agents stopped him to ask if he had registered under a "special registration" system mandatory for certain foreigners (but now mostly suspended). It was not required for legal refugees, but the agents arrested Habeeb anyway. He spent three nights in the county jail, was strip-searched, and was called "Saddam" by other detainees. He was then handcuffed and flown to Seattle, where he spent four more days in detention. "I thought for a moment that this is

it, my life is done, this is the end of my life in this country," said Habeeb, who was a legal refugee because he had been jailed and tortured in Iraq under Saddam Hussein.

The government response: Jeffrey C. Sullivan, U.S. attorney for the Western District of Washington, who signed the apology, said the case was only about getting the law concerning refugees wrong—nothing else. "We all sometimes make good-faith mistakes," he said, "and that is all that was done in this case. This case was not settled because of racial profiling, but due to a legal matter according to what his status was. To say anything more than that is just wrong." Sullivan sent Habeeb a letter saying that the effort to deport him was wrong and that "the United States of America regrets the mistake."

You tell me: What would you consider a "good-faith mistake"? Do you think this incident qualifies? What do you make of the government's apology?

---

wait-persons) tell us their first name, though customers rarely share theirs. This situation creates a power dynamic that deserves our attention.

Culturally Defined Uses of Language

Our society and culture shape our use of language. There are norms around who can say what to whom and who can speak and in what order, not to mention who gets the first and last word. These are **culturally defined uses of language.** We find such norms in public gatherings and in family dynamics. Think of expressions like "Children should be seen and not heard" and "Speak when you're spoken to." Adults may also face linguistic restrictions, as, for example, in meetings with a supervisor at work, in church, and in elevators, or when stopped by the police for a traffic violation. There are many culturally defined uses of language. Let's look at three: (1) apologies, (2) bilingualism, and (3) the deaf culture.

Example 1: The apology. For some, "Love means never having to say you're sorry." For others, love means *regularly* having to say you're sorry. The very fact of caring so much for another person means we are accountable to them. Consequently, there are cultural expectations around apologies—what merits one, who is owed one, and what might follow if one is not given.

The Global Dimension

The Study of Bilinguals and Brainpower

The British Broadcasting Corporation (BBC) reported on a language study by a York (Canada) University researcher, who concluded that there is a link between bilingualism and brainpower. Here is a summary. Consider alternative explanations as you read.

> This latest study appears to back up the theory that language skills also have a protective effect. Dr. Ellen Bialystok and colleagues at York University assessed the cognitive skills of all those involved in the study using a variety of widely recognized tests. They tested their vocabulary skills, their non-verbal reasoning ability and their reaction time. Half of the volunteers came from Canada and spoke only English. The other half [of the volunteers] came from India and were fluent in both English and Tamil. The volunteers had similar backgrounds in the sense that they were all educated to degree level and were all middle class.
>
> The researchers found that the people who were fluent in English and Tamil responded faster than those who were fluent in just English. This applied to all age groups. The researchers also found that the bilingual volunteers were much less likely to suffer from the mental decline associated with old age. "The bilinguals were more efficient at all ages tested and showed a slower rate of decline for some processes with aging," they said. "It appears . . . that bilingualism helps to offset age-related losses." ("Being Bilingual Protects Brain," *BBC News World Edition*, news.bbc.co.uk, 15 Jun 2004)

Answer the following:

1. What assumptions are made in using sample groups from different countries (and, possibly, different backgrounds)?
2. Offer at least two alternative explanations for the research subjects from India having superior cognitive abilities in addition to their language skills.
3. Research the studies done on turmeric and Alzheimer's disease. As you may recall, the spice turmeric is in curry—which is often used in Indian cooking (e.g., see "Curry 'May Slow Alzheimer's,'" *BBC News*, news.bbc.co.uk, 21 Nov 2001). Studies indicate that turmeric may be a reason that Alzheimer's disease is rarely found in India. If diet may be a factor in Alzheimer's, should it be factored in when assessing this study on bilingualism's supposed benefits? Share your thoughts.

Apologies have force. Consider the decades-later apology by Prime Minister Stephen Harper of Canada to an estimated 100,000 former students of Indian Residential Schools who had been abused. Chief Gibby Jacob of the Squamish Nation stated, "It's been a long time coming, and hopefully it means something to all of those who've been traumatized spiritually, physically, emotionally and mentally. My hope is that the collective First Nations people see this as an opportunity to close a door and quit being imprisoned and victimized by the residential school trauma" (*Pique News Magazine*, 6 Jun 2008).

Not all apologies include an admission of wrongdoing. Look, for example, at the "careful apology" of former New York Yankees slugger Jason Giambi, who managed to say he was sorry without admitting to steroid use: "I feel I let down the fans, I feel I let down the media, I feel I let down the Yankees, and not only the Yankees, but my teammates." He added, "I accept full responsibility for that, and I'm sorry." He neglected to say what he was sorry for (Tyler Kepner, "A Careful Apology from Giambi," *The New York Times*, 11 Feb 2005).

Example 2: Bilingualism. In Canada, where many people are bilingual (French and English), language often reflects political allegiances and even tensions. As James Crawford notes in *Language Loyalties,* "As a practical medium and a 'marker' of ethnicity, language becomes a predictable source of tension." In the United States, many people are bilingual, but they are often expected to speak English. Bilingual students often face difficulties, and even prejudice—especially if they speak with an accent.

Example 3: Deaf culture. Using sign language instead of a spoken language creates a subculture. It often has a powerful impact on those who are linked by signing rather than using and deciphering spoken words. Those on the "outside" who don't know sign language and feel left out may feel resentful or anxious, as we see in the case below.

CASE STUDY

The Deaf Culture

Rachel Stone, superintendent for the California School for the Deaf, was fired in June 2001. State officials would not say why, but parents suspect it was because she made American Sign Language the primary form of communication at the school. Journalist Scott Gold called her "deaf and proud—a combination that doesn't sit well with the school's old guard." Stone challenged the stereotype that deaf people should model themselves after the dominant, hearing culture. She says,

There are different cultures. We are all human beings, and in the past we were told that we were not. We were told that we could not be successful. That's all I'm trying to change. For years, deaf education has been run by people who think they know what's best for deaf people, and they have failed and failed and failed. I want to put a stop to that. (Scott Gold, "Controversial Head of School for Deaf Removed," *Los Angeles Times,* 21 Jun 2001)

Stone was trying to empower deaf children to use sign language, their "native" language, instead of having teachers reciting their lecture out loud with a student translating it. She hired faculty fluent in sign language and encouraged them not to speak (voices off). Parents reported that the children swelled with pride from having their own language, their own means of communication without an intermediary. Gold quotes Stone, who says, "This is my language. Why doesn't deaf education recognize that?"

Stone's detractors say American Sign Language is not English, and students should be allowed to try to speak the language. Hearing teachers felt marginalized, some were said to feel harassed, and some resigned. State officials made Stone clarify that she was not banning speaking, only encouraging signing. Faculty seemed divided between supporting and opposing Stone's methods. One observer felt that her philosophy caught people off guard and that she moved too fast.

Answer the following:

1. Was Stone out of line to deemphasize, if not discourage, learning to speak out loud?

2. If you were a parent or family member who was part of the hearing culture, what concerns might you have about the children being taught "voices off"?

3. If you were asked to defend Stone, what would you say?

Social and Political Ramifications

Language is a carrier of values. Words can convey or connote a set of beliefs. Consequently, ideas and concepts are not isolated from the world. Culturally defined uses of language have political ramifications. We learn language at the same time that we live in the world and come to a sense of how people should interact with each other. Ask yourself whether describing an athlete as having a "Mexican bandido moustache" or comparing him to a "monkey" contributes to racist stereotyping. How we refer to one another has consequences—and reflects back on ourselves.

With non-native speakers, the possibility for miscommunication and error is always present. Similarly, those with different accents can run into barriers, even when they share their native tongue. Think of a Scot talking with a southerner, or an Australian talking with a Bostonian—they may share the same language and yet still have trouble communicating.

Exercises

1. In 2007, Andrew Speaker, an Atlanta lawyer, flew on two trans-Atlantic flights while infected with a contagious and dangerous form of drug-resistant tuberculosis. He claims his doctor never actually forbade him from flying, though he was discouraged from doing so. While in Europe, he defied instructions to turn himself in to health authorities. After he returned to the States, Speaker apologized: "I'm very sorry for any grief or pain that I've caused anyone . . . I don't expect those people to ever forgive me. I just hope they understand that I truly never meant them any harm." Doctors estimated the risk to others on the planes to be low (Lawrence K. Altman and John Holusha, "Man with TB Apologizes for Putting Others at Risk," *The New York Times,* 1 Jun 2007). Discuss Speaker's apology—should those who sat near him on the various planes "forgive" him?

2. Make a list of ways you could describe *one* of the following: a friend, a family member, or a celebrity. Try for a balance of positive, negative, and neutral descriptions. Then write two to three paragraphs discussing how description affects the way we think about people.

3. Think of all the words or phrases connected to economic status (e.g., "rich," "loaded," "fat cat," "bourgeois," "poor," "welfare bum" [or "bludger" in Australia], and "broke"). After drawing up your list, try to determine what these words indicate about our societal values regarding money and/or wealth.

4. Discuss American attitudes toward drinking by examining the words used to describe alcohol consumption, like "tipsy," "sloshed," "plastered," "pie-eyed," "soused," "potted," "three sheets to the wind," "smashed," and "tanked up."

5. Study the language used to describe *one* of the following to unpack societal attitudes: driving a car, smoking, surfing, lifting weights, eating, dieting, or cooking. List words used to describe one of these activities.

6. Give an argument for or against instituting an "English only" law for public institutions and workplaces.

7. Do a study of descriptions of *one* of the following:
   a. The different aspects of social status, such as clothes, looks, hair, professional status, and physical strength.
   b. The different ways male and female athletes are described (e.g., in newspapers and on TV and radio).
   c. The different ways skin color is described (e.g., with reference to racial and ethnic groups).
   d. Weight or height (you can narrow it to males or females).

Group or Individual Exercise

Directions: Watch two or three TV news shows (prime-time or cable) or study two or three news websites, and answer the following questions:

1. How are people referred to or described in the various news segments (leading stories, sports, human interest stories, and so on)?

2. Do the descriptions of current events reveal any bias, cultural attitudes, or values?

Euphemisms

A **euphemism** acts as a substitute for the targeted word, in order to achieve a particular end. The goal may be to defuse a controversial situation or slant an interpretation. Some euphemisms are sneaky, and their use malevolent; others are harmless. Think of euphemisms that allow us to speak of indelicate subjects, like going to "powder your nose" (go to the bathroom). Noted in the *Stouffville (Canada) Free Press* (3 Jun 2008): "I think there are probably more euphemisms for death or dying than anything else. A lot of folks don't like to say that a loved one died. They 'passed on' or 'passed away.' Depending on your relationship, you might say they 'kicked the bucket,' 'gave up the ghost,' 'joined the choir invisible,' 'shuffled off this mortal coil' or 'have gone to their reward.'"

We buy a "pre-owned" (used) car and visit our grandparents who are in "their golden years" (old age). We purchase "after-shave" (cologne for men) and "stretch the truth" (are dishonest). We call abortion of a fetus in a multiple pregnancy a "selective reduction" and refer (as does the Florida law) to surrogate mothers who do not supply the egg as "gestational carriers." We describe euthanizing (killing) a pet as "putting it to sleep." We use the terms "outsource" and "downsize" to explain subcontracting and cutbacks. Euphemisms in war-speak include "collateral damage," "friendly fire," "shock and awe," "coalition of the willing," "freedom fighters," "total information awareness," "homeland security," and "embedded journalists." And instead of saying they are "permanent bases" for the American military in Iraq, we are supposed to call them "venerable temporary facilities" (*The New York Times*, 20 Jun 2008).

The term "rendition" is a particularly striking euphemism for "transport to a country known to allow torture." Steve Hoenisch criticizes *The New York Times'* use of "security officials" to refer to SAVAK, the Iranian secret police, and the use of "some cutback on duplicate staffing" in place of the word "layoffs" or "firings" ("The Mythological Language of American Newspapers," www.criticism.com). Euphemisms should be watched carefully. Journalist Pierre Tristam argues:

> They're weedy. They're sly. They're strangely addictive. They're impossible to get rid of and, in wartime, they're more noxious than patriotic fumes. But that's what makes euphemisms language's nimblest double agents, its cheapest mercenaries, its most sought-after plastic surgeons: A euphemism does to reality what botox does to facial muscle. It croaks it. No other death brings so much life to so many. Without euphemisms every politician would have to declare bankruptcy, every priest would have a crisis of conscience; every corporation's annual report would be dangerously truthful, to its shareholders anyway. . . .
>
> Blowing a man's brains out from a distance is called "pink mist," assassination is called "regime change" and propaganda is called "public diplomacy." The sanitizing makeover disarms the truth of the original word enough to make it meaningless or enticing. The reigning king of euphemisms in the current war surplus is the word "security." (" 'Security' Tops the Plastic Heap of War's Euphemism Surplus," *Daytona Beach News-Journal*, www.news-journalonline.com, 26 Apr 2004)

▦ Hedging

Hedging effectively undercuts or raises doubt about a claim. **Hedging** can take two forms: (1) shifting from one position to a much weaker one or (2) undercutting a claim (e.g., through a negative connotation of a word or phrase). Hedging is more often found in oral communication than written expression. This may explain why we get rejection *letters* rather than phone calls telling us another applicant got the job. It also explains why it's easier to write a "Dear John" letter than to have a face-to-face meeting. In the political sphere, hedging can be dramatic. For instance, in 2001, the British Broadcasting Corporation (BBC) told its journalists the word "assassination" could no longer be used to describe the actions of Israelis murdering guerrilla opponents. Instead, BBC reporters were instructed to use Israel's own euphemism for the murders, calling them "targeted

killings" ("BBC Staff Are Told Not to Call Israeli Killings 'Assassination,'" www
.independent.co.uk 4 Aug 2001).

Exercises

1. Investigate euphemisms: Find two euphemisms, and discuss how they function and what would likely change in the context if we shifted to a less slanted or deceptive use of language.
2. Find five or six euphemisms that are part of our daily life (e.g., "complimentary" instead of "free," "previously owned" instead of "used," "task force" instead of "committee," or "insurance advisor" instead of "insurance salesman").
3. Try creating some euphemisms of your own. Focus on one area of your life—such as eating, exercising, or being a student. Create five or six of your own euphemisms. Be sure to state both the euphemism and the term ordinarily used (e.g., "smulching" for "eating fast food while driving").

Labels and Categories

Labels and categories aren't necessarily harmful. Here's a case in point: Residents of Prince Edward Island (PEI), Canada, call themselves "spud-islanders." Potatoes (spuds) are the island's main crop. What if someone "from aways" (non-spud-islander) coined the phrase to refer to the residents of PEI in a derogatory way—thinking of them as potato-heads, for example? It is unlikely that the term "spud-islander" would get a positive reception. The ownership and self-definition by the PEI residents makes all the difference.

What sounds neutral to many may seem derogatory to the one being labeled. For instance, the term "primitive peoples" won't win too many friends among the "natives." Try using the term "indigenous" or referring to groups by their tribal identity (e.g., Apache, Chumash, Blackfoot, Hopi, or Zuni) instead. The collective tribes in Canada prefer the term "First Nation" instead of "Native Canadians" or "Canadian Indians." Another phrase that grates is "developing nations." A less-loaded alternative is to name the individual nations.

Are you Latino or Hispanic? African American or black? Asian American or Chinese? Canadian or Quebecois? As we know, a label may be perfectly acceptable when members of the group in question use it with each other—but off-limits to those outside the group.

Labeling is not the same as name-calling. Not all people experience labeling as demeaning. Sometimes labels categorize people in positive or neutral ways (e.g., "married" versus "single," "gay" versus "straight," "vegetarian" versus "meat eater," or "lactovegetarian" versus "nondairy"). Name-calling, however, has little positive effect.

Consider the uproar when California governor Arnold Schwarzenegger called Democratic lawmakers blocking his budget plans "girlie men." Schwarzenegger called upon voters to "terminate" them at the polls if they didn't pass his $103 billion budget (Peter Nicholas, "Gov. Criticizes Legislators as 'Girlie Men,'" *Los Angeles Times,* 18 Jul 2004).

The use and misuse of labels can lead to surprising results. Look at some of those prosecuted under the Patriot Act—such as airline passengers charged with "terrorism" for using profanity, drunken behavior, arguing with flight attendants, or swatting their children. Over 200 passengers have been convicted of felonies. In most of the cases, there was no evidence of attempts to hijack the airplane or assault the flight crew. The *Los Angeles Times* reports that:

> Many [of convicted "terrorists"] have simply involved raised voices, foul language and drunken behavior. In one case, a couple was arrested after arguing with a flight attendant for kissing and making other passengers uncomfortable. "We have gone completely berserk on this issue," said Charles Slepian, a New York security consultant. (Ralph Vartabedian and Peter Pae, "In-Flight Confrontations Can Lead to Charges Defined as Terrorism," 20 Jan 2009)

Associations can tap into societal fears or prejudice. For example, if the terms "Asian American" and "Mexican American" are associated with foreigners, problems pop up. Peter Lew says, "I'm a fifth-generation Chinese-American, yet I'm often asked: 'How long have you lived in this country? When will you return to your country?'" (Peter Lew, letter to the editor, *The New York Times,* 19 Jun 2002)

▦ Ambiguity (Linguistic Fallacies)

When it comes to the use of language, clarity matters. **Ambiguity** is a lack of clarity in the use of language by either accident or intent, resulting in a confusion that may lead to drawing an incorrect conclusion. Problems can occur when words, grammar, or sentence structure is used in ways that create ambiguity. Ambiguity is like seeing in a fog, where a variety of interpretations can cause confusion (see Figure 11.1). Of course, some people use slippery language intentionally—twisting words to suit their purposes. Such slippery terms are sometimes called **"weasel words."** As Brooks Jackson and Kathleen Hall Jamieson note, that term refers to the way that weasels suck the contents out of an egg, leaving an empty shell (see *un.Spun,* 2007). Thus sale signs claiming "Up to 50% off" are weasely, because of the "Up to." There need only be one item that *is* 50% off for the sign to be true—all the others on the sales rack could be much less off.

Watch for ambiguity. For example, an administration spokesperson "clarified" President George W. Bush's position on stem cell research. You decide if the ambiguities are now gone:

> The president remains committed to exploring the promise of stem cell research but at the same time continues to believe strongly that we should not cross a fundamental moral line by funding or encouraging the destruction of human embryos. . . . The

Photograph by Wanda Teays. Copyright 2007.

FIGURE 11.1
This store sign plays on the *X-Files* line "The truth is out there."

president does not believe that life should be created for the sole purpose of destroying it. He does believe we can explore the promise and potential of stem cell research using the existing lines of stem cells. ("Senators Ask Bush to Ease Restrictions on Stem Cell Research," CNN, www.cnn.com, 8 Jun 2004)

It's not always easy to sort through ambiguity and determine the intent. David Harel illustrates this in *Computers, Ltd.*, with the way the following sentences differ in the relationships between their various parts:

The thieves stole the jewels, and some of them were later sold.
The thieves stole the jewels, and some of them were later caught.
The thieves stole the jewels, and some of them were later found.

When ambiguities lead to an incorrect conclusion, we are looking at fallacious reasoning. The three key linguistic fallacies are **equivocation** (where there's a shift of meaning in a word or phrase in an argument), **accent** (where the emphasis of a word or phrase leads us to an incorrect conclusion), and **amphiboly** (where faulty sentence construction leads to an ambiguity). (See Chapter 7 for a review.)

Concepts and Definitions: Meaning versus Use

The *use* of words and phrases often reveals more than any dictionary definition. There may be any number of definitions for a word—but looking at the context and the use of the word in the sentence may reveal the intended meaning. The *lexical definition* is the dictionary definition of a word. The *stipulative definition* is the one that is created or specified in a particular case—say, for an argument or discussion. For example, we might stipulate that the word "yink" describe the color that results from mixing yellow and pink. Given that it is source-specific, a stipulative definition is not normally "correct" or "incorrect," but may be controversial (e.g., if it were stipulated that the term "illegal alien" had to be used instead of "refugee").

Watch for hidden assumptions or exclusions. Ask what the term is meant to include and how it is to be applied. For example, if policies speak of employees as male, then the policy may not easily apply to females. Think of applying employment policies to pregnant women. Should pregnancy be put in the same category as illness?

Similarly, in female-dominated fields like nursing, males have had an uphill battle addressing gynocentric (female-centered) language and stereotypes. Nurse-midwife Patrick Thornton talks about his work: "I think a lot of people expected that because I was a man, they were going to be treated like a doctor treats them. When they found out that wasn't true, then that seemed to help" (see Christopher Snowbeck, "Male Nurse Midwife Adopts a Supportive Attitude," [*Pittsburgh*] *Post Gazette*, 27 Mar 2001).

Components of a Definition

There are two parts to any definition. The first is the word or phrase to define or clarify. This is called the **definiendum.** Then you have the explanation—words meaning the same thing as the word or phrase in question. This is called the **definiens. Synonyms** are words that are similar in meaning (e.g., "warm" and "toasty"), whereas **antonyms** are words that are opposite in meaning (e.g., "hot" and "cold").

Questions about **syntax** have to do with punctuation, grammar, word order, and sentence structure. Questions about **semantics** have to do with the meanings of words, with what they signify. As noted previously, the denotation of a word is the literal meaning, whereas the connotation is what the word suggests, implies, or conjures up in our minds.

Syntactical errors may seem less worrisome than semantic problems. However, grammatical or structural errors can create havoc. We may miss the point if the syntax is a mess. An example of an error syntax is "Rosa had been lifting weights for five years when she dropped a barbell on her foot." Watch also for the semantics. The use of a word or phrase in different ways in the argument may lead the reader to the wrong conclusion.

Concepts, Contexts, and Norms

Societal norms shape the scope of our concepts and definitions. If whites, the wealthy, Christians, or men set the norm, all others fall outside. If the norm is able-bodied people, the design and construction of buildings may disadvantage the disabled (through the location of light switches, the size of hallways, the height of toilets, the lack of Braille in elevators, and so on).

Definitions and concepts evolve as the need arises. Consider, for instance, the word "motorcycle." We may picture a *two*-wheel motorized vehicle, but what about those three-wheelers that you sometimes see? Legally, the three-wheelers are motorcyles—but not the four-wheelers. This led Yamaha to name them "four-wheel recreational machines" (*Gizmag*, 25 Oct 2007).

At times this causes controversy. Look at the use of the term "fetus." If the word "person" as used in the Constitution were understood to include fetuses, laws involving abortion and fetal experimentation would have to be reinterpreted. Historically, the concept "person"referred to postnatal humans, as noted in the ruling of *Roe* v. *Wade*. Recently, however, we see a shift toward greater protection for fetuses. This is shown in euphemisms "unborn child," "preborn person," and "baby."

Group or Individual Exercise

Directions: For some, a fetus is an unborn child. Others deplore the blurring of distinctions around pre- and postbirth humanity. Read about the following case and then answer the questions below:

> A U.S. district judge in Missouri has blocked temporarily the deportation of a pregnant Mexican woman who is married to a U.S. citizen, calling the fetus an "American" and citing a federal law created to protect unborn children. . . . Senior U.S. District Judge Scott O. Wright ordered that Myrna Dick, 29, of Raymore, Mo., who is accused of falsely claiming American citizenship, be allowed to remain in the United States for now and told prosecutors and the defense to prepare for a possible trial. "Isn't that child an American citizen?" he asked, according to the Kansas City Star. "If this child is an American citizen, we can't send his mother back until he is born."
>
> Judge Wright pointed to the Unborn Victims of Violence Act of 2004, which grants unborn children equal protection under the law if their mothers are targets of criminal violence. . . . (Joyce Howard Price, "Deportation Blocked; Fetus 'American,'" *Washington Times*, 29 May 2004)

Answer the following:

1. Discuss the use of language in the above excerpt. What most strikes you?

2. List all the words or terms used in the passage that suggest the author's *or* the judge's set of values.

▦ Jargon, Buzzwords, and Technical Terms

It is important to watch out for jargon and buzzwords. **Buzzwords** are newly coined terms or old words used in totally different contexts for an intended effect. **Jargon** is the terminology of a particular group or profession or the specialized technical terminology coined for a specific purpose or effect. Sometimes people consider jargon to be gibberish (without any discernible meaning). That may be due to a lack of understanding of the use of the word.

Wired magazine regularly lists the latest buzzwords and jargon associated with computers and technology. Here are some examples: "passive obesity" (flabbiness caused by physical inactivity rather than caloric excess), "social advertising" (involuntary product endorsement on Facebook by users whose online purchases are automatically broadcast to friends), and "cybrid" (a cytoplasmic hybrid—typically a cow or rabbit egg injected with human DNA—grown in an embryonic stem cell factory) (see "Jargon Watch," *Wired* magazine, www.wired.com, 18 Jan 2008 and 26 Nov 2007).

With jargon, first determine the intended meaning. "I understand this term to mean . . ." is one way to clarify your sense of a concept. Readers should not feel like they have to crack a secret code to understand how an author is using a term.

Look at the Los Angeles Unified School District's use of the term "morphosyntactic skills" in their published glossary of acronyms and terminology. The glossary doesn't define the term; it only translates it to the Spanish *conocimientos morfosintacticos.* Most just scratch their heads in befuddlement over what this phrase might mean (see Duke Helfand, "*'Edspeak'* Is in a Class by Itself," *Los Angeles Times,* 16 Aug 2001).

We need to be clear enough that our audience can grasp our meaning. If not, we may end up like Dr. Hibbert talking to Homer (from the TV show *The Simpsons,* as noted on www.imdb.com):

> DR. HIBBERT: Homer, I'm afraid you'll have to undergo a coronary bypass operation.
> HOMER: Say it in English, Doc.
> DR. HIBBERT: You're going to need open-heart surgery.
> HOMER: Spare me your medical mumbo-jumbo.
> DR. HIBBERT: We're going to cut you open and tinker with your ticker.
> HOMER: Could you dumb it down a shade?

Some people seem to use jargon to impress others. If the term is not in the dictionary (keep one nearby!), analyze the author's intent and examine the context surrounding the use of the term. Legal terms are often used quite specifically, so don't assume they have an ordinary usage. The interpretation of a legal concept can shape laws and policies. We see this with the concept of "medical treatment."

Ordinarily, when we think of medical treatment, we think of prescription drugs, special diets, and therapeutic treatments. In the case of Elizabeth Bouvia, this changed. Bouvia was a 28-year-old woman with cerebral palsy who checked

The Global Dimension

What Is a Terrorist?

Read the definition of "terrorist" set out by the U.S. State Department in Title 22 of the United States Code, Sec. 2656f(d), and list the distinct qualities that mark a person or group as a "terrorist":

> The term "terrorism" means premeditated, politically motivated violence perpetrated against noncombatant targets by subnational groups or clandestine agents, usually intended to influence an audience. . . . The U.S. Government has employed this definition of terrorism for statistical and analytical purposes since 1983. (Jon Dorbolo, "Power in Terror," *APA Newsletter of Computers*, APA Newsletters, Spring 2003)

This is not a fixed definition. The USA Patriot Act sets out a different definition of terrorism.

Compare and contrast that definition with the one set out by the State Department:

> SEC. 802. The term "domestic terrorism" means activities that involve acts dangerous to human life that are a violation of the criminal laws of the United States or any State; appear to be intended—to intimidate or coerce a civilian population; to influence the policy of a government by intimidation or coercion; or to affect the conduct of a government by mass destruction, assassination, or kidnapping; and occur primarily within the territorial jurisdiction of the United States. (HR 3162, 2001). (See "Power in Terror," *APA Newsletters*, Spring 2003.)

Answer the following:
How do *you* think we should designate someone as a "terrorist"? Can someone be a "terrorist" and not instill *terror*? What if the person just *scared* you? Share your thoughts.

---

herself into a hospital, wanting to starve herself to death. As she put it, "I'm trapped in a useless body."

In a landmark decision, the California Court of Appeals ruled that "medical treatment" included nutrition and hydration through a feeding tube. Since a competent adult has the right to refuse treatment, Bouvia could refuse the feeding tube, even if it resulted in her death. In 1993, this concept was stretched further when an ill prisoner sued for the right to refuse food and water under the umbrella of the right to refuse medical treatment. He won. By 2001, the issue was whether a severely incapacitated person who was "minimally conscious" could, at his wife's request, have his feeding tube removed and die. The California Supreme Court denied the request, but the issue remains, and the language continues to evolve.

Group or Individual Exercise

Directions: The following "User Agreement" can be found on the Kraft Foods website. Briefly state what you understand are the limits of liability, according to Kraft Foods.

> *Keep in mind that we are not liable for any damages, including . . .*
> Damages intended to compensate someone directly for a loss or injury;

Damages reasonably expected to result from a loss or injury (legally, "consequential damages");

Other miscellaneous damages and expenses resulting directly from a loss or injury (legally, "incidental damages").

Furthermore, we are not liable even if we've been negligent or if our authorized representative has been advised of the possibility of such damages—or both.

Exception: In certain states the law may not allow us to limit or exclude liability for these "incidental" or "consequential" damages, so the above limitation may not apply, and you may indeed have the right to recover these types of damages. But in any event, our liability to you for all losses, damages, injuries, and claims of every kind (whether the damages are claimed under the terms of a contract, or they're claimed to be caused by negligence or other wrongful conduct, or they're claimed under any other legal theory) will not be greater than the amount you paid to access our sites.

Metaphors, Images, and Analogies

A **metaphor** is the application of a word or phrase to draw a comparison or indicate a similarity (e.g., "She's a shrew and he's a snake"). Some we hear all the time—like "Time is money," "Her words were hollow," "I peg you as a 'glass is half empty' kind of guy," "He's a lame duck," "Things are looking up," "He's down in the dumps," "She's on cloud nine," "He's as cold as ice," and "She's a hot tamale."

Metaphors and images often become the linguistic paintbrush to convey our thoughts and feelings. They are also widely used in advertising—for example, think of Coca-Cola's "happiness factory" to call up desirable images and fantasies.

Metaphors and images can also shape an interpretation. Those that are used well can leave an impression that goes far beyond mere argumentation. Think of great movie lines that use metaphors, such as Forrest Gump's "Life is like a box of chocolates." Or think of all the memorable speeches throughout history—many used powerful metaphors and images (see Figure 11.2).

Within the context of an argument, an analogy or metaphor can be very persuasive. An **analogy** consists of a comparison between two things in which, on the basis of certain similarities, a principle or characteristic of the one term is then applied to the other term and asserted as true in that case as well. The form of an analogy is:

A is like B in terms of characteristics p, q, and r.

<u>A also has characteristic z.</u>

So, B has characteristic z as well.

For example, in an article in *USA Today,* Marilyn Adams argues that ALS (Lou Gehrig's disease) is like the act of a terrorist. The similarities noted are that they are both random and terrifying and they kill without partiality. She adds that the fight against terrorism has received a lot of attention and money. She then concludes that the fight against ALS also should receive a lot of attention and money.

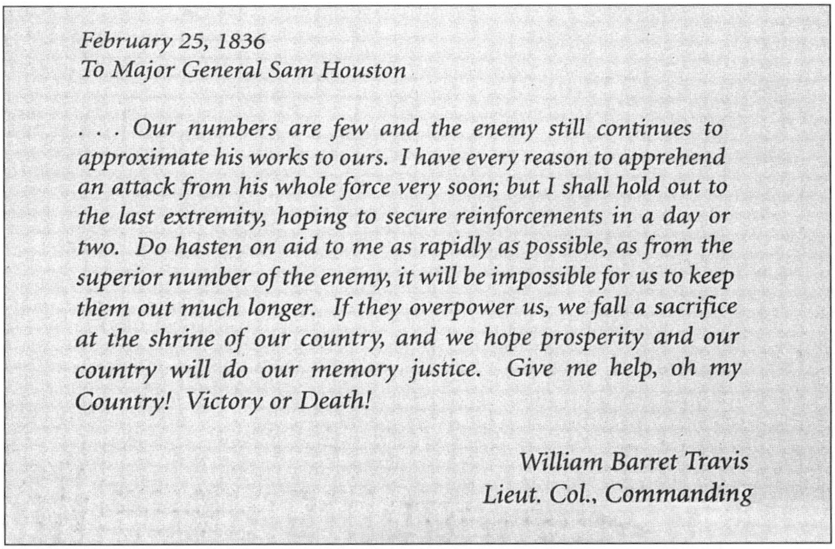

> *February 25, 1836*
> *To Major General Sam Houston*
>
> *. . . Our numbers are few and the enemy still continues to approximate his works to ours. I have every reason to apprehend an attack from his whole force very soon; but I shall hold out to the last extremity, hoping to secure reinforcements in a day or two. Do hasten on aid to me as rapidly as possible, as from the superior number of the enemy, it will be impossible for us to keep them out much longer. If they overpower us, we fall a sacrifice at the shrine of our country, and we hope prosperity and our country will do our memory justice. Give me help, oh my Country! Victory or Death!*
>
> *William Barret Travis*
> *Lieut. Col., Commanding*

Photograph by Wanda Teays. Copyright 2008.

FIGURE 11.2
A sign at the Alamo in San Antonio, Texas. Look at the eloquent use of language—despite the urgency of the message.

"If ALS were a terrorist group taking thousands of lives each year," she argues, "this country would throw people and technology and money at it until we had won. Not so with this disease. . . . It's like a terrorist in our midst, going strong" ("ALS, like a Terrorist, Kills without Partiality," *USA Today,* Jul 2004).

Analogy and metaphors should generally be used sparingly for maximum impact. As with all advice, however, there are exceptions, and each writer or speaker has to decide how to parcel out such potentially powerful uses of language.

Exercises

Part One

Directions: Pick two current events, such as a recent issue in the national news, a local story, a news item about a famous person, or an event in sports.

1. Using an analogy to a fairy tale, children's story, film character, or cartoon character, write a brief description of the event. Your goal is to be as *colorful* as you can.
2. Now write your reflections on how you used language to create an effect, why you picked the metaphor/analogy you did, and how it could shape the way we see the event being described.

Part Two

Bertrand Russell once presented a conjugation of words to illustrate how synonyms can carry a range of connotations. He offered this one: "I am firm. You are stubborn.

He is a pig-headed fool." Here are a few others: "I am svelte. You are thin. She is skinny as a green bean." "I am pleasingly plump. You are overweight. He is a blimp." "I am reserved. You have a chip on your shoulder. She is a stuck-up princess."

Answer the following:

1. Come up with four conjugations of your own.
2. Write two to three paragraphs discussing the range of the three terms and the impact of the different connotations.

CASE STUDY

Op/Ed Openings

Below are the opening paragraphs of three student papers. Each student wrote an op/ed piece on issues such as gang violence, homelessness, violence in film, and smoking in movies. Select two *and discuss their use of language. They were told to start with pizazz, to create a snappy opening to draw in the reader. You decide if they succeeded in that goal.*

1. Can I Spare You Some Change?

Opening by Thelliza Balleta, April 2004

The first time I walked down Third Street Promenade I was eighteen years old and I was amazed at how beautiful the streets were. Little did I know, L.A. was not only filled with the rich and the famous but also the hungry and the homeless. After three slices of barbeque pizza from California Pizza Kitchen, my friends and I sat at a nearby Starbucks. With caffeine in our system, we were ready to tackle our homework. Then suddenly a homeless man banged at the window. He looked straight at me, and held out his hands, asking for money. I looked straight down and tried to ignore him.

Feeling guilty for what I did, I got up and took the remains of my barbeque pizza, which was in a doggy bag, and gave it to the homeless man. I asked what his name was and he said his name was Robert and he thanked me. I sat back down in Starbucks and felt awful because I could not help Robert anymore; I could not give him money because I had none. I then asked myself, "What are we doing to help the homeless?"

2. Gang Violence Is Getting Out of Hand

Opening by Noemi Rivera, April 2004

I found myself ducked under a desk, along with the rest of my classmates, hoping a gunshot would not hit any of us. After about thirty minutes, our science teacher gave us the safety signal to get up, the drive by shooting was over. My sixth grade science class had been interrupted by gang shooting in the street near school. Gang violence is everywhere. It can happen at any time, and can hurt even those not involved in gang activity. Students should not be threatened to attend school because of gang violence. The community should not feel threatened to go about their lives because of gang violence. Society should not be menaced by gang violence. Gang violence must be put to an end; it must be stopped now.

3. Smoking and the Movies

Opening by Marissa Heilig, April 2004

Matthew McConaughey's piercing blue eyes and soft blonde curls entrance me as I fantasize in my mind that I am the object of his desire, not the gorgeous and good-willed Kate Hudson. I, like all the other girls sitting in the movie theater with overly buttered popcorn in arms and the somehow mindless action of shoving Jujubes in mouth while staring at the screen, am enthralled by his good looks and charming personality, or at least by his character Ben, in the movie *How to Lose a Guy in Ten Days.* Suddenly though, as if to no concern of his character, Matthew pulls out a cigar and begins to smoke. I am suddenly troubled with thoughts of how such a likeable character would be smoking, it can't be possible! My image of him . . . ruined.

Source: Reprinted with the permission of Thelliza Balleta, Noemi Rivera, and Marissa Heilig.

The Passive Voice

We use the **passive voice** when we make the object of an action the subject of a sentence, as in "The chicken *was eaten by* the coyote." This form avoids calling attention to the one performing the action (the coyote). Its focus is the recipient of the action (the chicken). Passive-voice constructions use a form of "to be" followed by a past participle—for instance, "The agents were contacted by Jason Bourne." The structure of this is "The agents *were* [form of the verb "to be"] *contacted by* [past participle] Jason Bourne." To make it active, change it to "Jason Bourne contacted the agents."

Using the passive voice is a way for people to avoid owning their own thoughts and ideas, observes philosopher Vance Ricks. Thanks to Professor Ricks for pointing out the importance of looking at the passive voice as part of the way language can persuade and shape how we think. The passive voice reframes the emphasis of a claim. Instead of "I think such and so," we find "It is held that such and so." This construction *makes the agent invisible*—so no one is held accountable for an action.

Ricks observes: "I've lost track of how many times I've heard or read 'It is widely believed that' or 'It is alleged that' or 'It is said to be' or other passive constructions that leave utterly unclear exactly who is doing the wide believing, alleging, saying, etc."

Using the passive voice results in a construction that is less precise and often more confusing—the *who* and *what* may be entirely left out. Look at these three constructions:

> **Active voice:** Slugs ate the plants.
> **Passive voice 1:** The plants were eaten by slugs.
> **Passive voice 2:** The plants were eaten.

In the active voice, it is clear who is eating the plants. In passive voice 1, the identification of the perpetrator (slugs) is secondary. By passive voice 2, the perpetrator (slugs) has been completely erased. There may be times when the passive voice is the best choice, but ordinarily, strive to use the active voice. And when you see others using the passive voice, decide if the construction creates problems by deemphasizing the subject or eliminating it from view.

Loaded Language

Linguistic shape shifting can transform hot words to lukewarm or cold ones (and vice versa). **Loaded language** is language that is value laden, heavy with connotation (positive or negative). It can create a bias, just as neutralized terms can defuse a controversy by making things appear innocuous or acceptable.

Loaded language should not be confused with colorful, or figurative, language. For example, "He's as subtle as a hog in heat" or "My hair feels greasier than an oil well!" may be considered *colorful* uses of language.

Each word carries a set of connotations, so watch for both the overt and covert meanings. Look out for a fallacy called **question-begging epithets.** This occurs when language is biased so that it stacks the deck in either a positive or negative direction. (See Chapter 7 for a review.)

In World War II, loaded language used by the Nazis was a powerful tool of anti-Semitism. Loathsome words such as "vermin" were used to characterize Jews. This made it easier to implement "the final solution"—the slaughter of 6 million Jews. On this side of the Atlantic, the U.S. government referred to the Japanese as "Japs." Such terminology made it easier to put Japanese Americans into "relocation" (internment) camps. And in the Iraq war, the use of the term "Hajis" affected how the people were viewed—and treated.

Exercises

It's not always easy to sort out threats from creative expression, as a California case demonstrates. Read about the case and then answer the questions below:

George approached a girl in his honors English class at Santa Teresa High School in San Jose. . . . He gave the girl a copy of a poem he had labeled "Dark Poetry" and titled "Faces." He told her the poetry described him and his feelings. . . . "Faces" began: "Who are these faces around me? Where did they come from?" It ended with these lines: "For I am Dark, Destructive & Dangerous. I slap on my face of happiness but inside I am evil!! For I can be the next kid to bring guns to kill students at school. So parents watch your children cuz I'm BACK!!" (Maura Dolan, "Teen's Poem Not a Threat, Justices Rule," *Los Angeles Times*, 23 Jul 2004)

Answer the following:

1. Do you think there is cause for concern knowing that the poem "Dark Poetry" begins in this way:

   Who are these faces around me?
   Where do they come from? . . .
   All really intelligent and ahead in their game.
   I wish I had a choice on what I want to be like they do.
   All so happy and vagrant . . .
   They make me want to puke.

2. Give your response to the ruling by the California Supreme Court on the case

> [Justice Carlos E. Moreno:] "While the protagonist in 'Faces' declares that he has the potential or capacity to kill students given his dark and hidden feelings, he does not actually threaten to do so. . . ."
>   A creative work can constitute a criminal threat, but courts must look at whether the work was really intended as a threat, he said. In George's case, there were no incriminating circumstances, Moreno said. "There was no history of animosity or conflict" between George and the classmates with whom he shared his work, and "threatening gestures or mannerisms," Moreno said. (Maura Dolan, "Teen's Poem Not a Threat, Justices Rule," *Los Angeles Times,* 23 Jul 2004)

Propaganda

Propaganda uses words to shape public consciousness and manipulate people to think, vote, and act as the propaganda machine suggests. Propaganda can come from all directions—left, right, and center. It is the *substance,* not the source, that marks propaganda. Cult specialist Margaret Thaler Singer sees propaganda in the center of a continuum:

education — advertising — propaganda — indoctrination — thought reform

Singer says propaganda centers on the political persuasion of a mass of people, whereas thought reform centers on changing people without their knowledge so they can be manipulated and controlled. Propaganda has a manipulative, controlling element as well, but it involves *persuasion.* Thought reform involves no full awareness on the part of the subject and usually has a hidden agenda. (See Margaret Singer, *Cults in Our Midst.*)

Fallacies are common in propaganda. W. H. Werkmeister cites this example: "There are two kinds of speakers, one appeals to your emotions, the other to reason. [President Franklin Delano] Roosevelt is the kind that works your emotions, the same as does [Adolf] Hitler, and the masses blindly follow to the bitter end" (*An Introduction to Critical Thinking*). Propaganda is not a relic of the past, however; examples are all around us.

Websites That Study Propaganda

- The Center for Media and Democracy at www.prwatch.org
- World War II U.S. government propaganda at www.archives.gov/exhibit (run a search for "propaganda")
- Nazi and East German propaganda at www.calvin.edu/academic/cas/gpa
- Allied World War I propaganda at www.pma.edmonton.ab.ca/vexhibit/arpost/english/home.htm

Propaganda serves important **ideological functions.** It attempts to influence the opinions or actions of others by appealing to their emotions or prejudices or by distorting facts. The goal itself may be bad (e.g., genocide) or good (e.g., peace). What marks propaganda is the *manipulation,* not the desired end. An example of propaganda is a "misinformation campaign" where the truth is stretched or disposed of in order to persuade a population to support a government's way of thinking or course of action. Werkmeister has a useful list of propaganda tricks. His list of tricks is on the left in the table below, with my examples on the right.

PROPAGANDA TRICKS	EXAMPLES
NAME-CALLING The use of invective and emotionally colored words to denigrate another or reinforce biases and prejudice	"She's a liberal; don't vote for her!" "Governor Prawn caters to pro-lifers." "Senator Thornton is a Feminazi; don't put her in charge of the school board."
GLITTERING GENERALITIES The use of abstract concepts with positive connotations, such as those appealing to truth, freedom, honor, progress, a sense of justice, pride, hope, courage, and the like—without ever being specific.	"May the sanctity of human liberty guide this campaign." "Get behind the freedom-fighters, not the terrorists." "Vote for the party that will work for a lasting peace."
TABLOID THINKING The use of hasty generalization (a fallacy) to settle a dispute or an argument.	"Every person has a price." "You can't change human nature." "It's time to clean house."
TESTIMONIALS The use of some "authority" (public figure or organization) to sell an idea. This includes planting an idea in a "news" item to sway the public (also called the fallacy of ad verecundiam).	"An unnamed source speaks of the frightening possibility of another terrorist attack over Christmas. Therefore, we need to consolidate more power in the CIA." Secretary of State Colin Powell told the UN's Security Council in 2003 (before the United States invaded Iraq): "Our sources tell us that, in some cases, the hard drives of computers at Iraqi weapons facilities were replaced. Who took the hard drives? Where did they go? What's being hidden? Why? There's only one answer to the why: to deceive,

PROPAGANDA TRICKS	EXAMPLES
	to hide, to keep from the inspectors. . . . Numerous human sources tell us that the Iraqis are moving, not just documents and hard drives, but weapons of mass destruction to keep them from being found by inspectors."
BIFURCATION The use of a simple "either/or" when actually more alternatives exist. This is a fallacy (also known as false dichotomy).	"If you want to destroy private enterprise, go ahead and support more national parks!" "America faces a choice: Either set women's rights back 100 years or support progressive reform with Senator Buchman."
ASSOCIATION The use of links drawn between an idea presented and some object, person, party, or cause that people respect or cherish—or that they fear or condemn.	"The name USA Patriot Act speaks to all that is American and needs preserving." "Osama bin Laden is the modern-day Hitler—we better fight fire with fire."
IDENTIFICATION The use of identification with those being addressed—becoming "one of the gang"—to win confidence.	"This is me in Scranton, where my father was raised, and my grandfather worked in the lace mill. Every August, we'd pile into the car and head to our cottage on Lake Winola. There was no heat, or indoor shower, just the joy of family. I was raised on pinochle and the American dream." "They're [working-class voters in Ohio] not asking for anything special. They're just asking for a fair shake. They're asking for a president who cares about them."
BAND WAGON The use of the "follow the crowd" technique to persuade (also called the fallacy of ad populum).	"All over the country, people are standing up for the family. That's why you have to vote in a constitutional amendment against gay rights." "Most of you, my fellow Americans, do support individual liberty. That means we've got to oppose banning assault weapons!!"

PROPAGANDA TRICKS	EXAMPLES
CARD-STACKINGS The use of distortion, exaggeration, forgery, deception, and misinformation to sell an idea. This is one of the most vicious tricks that can be used.	"Evidence is overwhelming that Iraq has nuclear capability. We must go to war!"

The issue of association of common propaganda techniques came up on May 15, 2008, when President Bush argued against negotiating with terrorists. He said, "We have heard this foolish delusion before. As Nazi tanks crossed into Poland in 1939, an American senator declared: 'Lord, if I could only have talked to Hitler, all this might have been avoided.' We have an obligation to call this what it is—the false comfort of appeasement, which has been repeatedly discredited by history." Who was Bush talking about?

Thinking he was the target, Senator Barack Obama fired back that this was "a false political attack" and that he never supported engagement with terrorists. The White House insisted that the *intended* reference was Senator William E. Borah, who, in 1939, said he regretted not being able to talk to Hitler before Nazi Germany invaded Poland. However, the omission at the time of Bush's speech laid the groundwork for what followed. And the "clarification" did not fully erase the perceptions that Obama *was* the intended target.

The most common form of propaganda appeals to emotions or to traditional ideals (like patriotism, religious sentiment, and group identity). It simplifies issues and offers few (but desired!) alternatives. Propaganda usually works best with little evidence or a distortion of evidence. For example, "virtually every piece of Klan propaganda from the early 1920s enjoined Klansmen to protect the virtue of white womanhood," says sociology professor Kathleen M. Blee (*Women of the Klan*).

Because it is useful to have someone else to blame, a scapegoat is often employed in propaganda. This gives a face to the problem or "enemy." It's much easier to blame someone else for our problems. More sinister forms of propaganda play into racial tension, religious conflict, and prejudice. By appealing to pride, nationalism, and group identity, propaganda can turn thoughts and actions into a team effort. This makes it harder to resist—we may want to be "one of the gang."

Group or Individual Exercise

Directions: Both exercises involve finding examples, so allow time to do so (e.g., be prepared for the next class meeting).

1. Find two examples of propaganda prior to 1975. Each example should be from distinctly different perspectives (e.g., one from the left and one from

the right, or one from one religious angle and one from another). Explain how each is an example of propaganda.

2. Find two examples of propaganda from after 1975—the more recent the better. Try to find examples from distinctly different perspectives. Explain how each is an example of propaganda.

Exclusive Language and Hate Speech

The use of demeaning or vitriolic language can ignite and sustain prejudice. All too easily this leads to disrespectful behavior and even hate crimes. **Exclusive language** posits one group (race, religion, gender, sexual orientation, etc.) as superior and another or others as inferior, lesser. For example, in 2007, talk show host Don Imus set off a firestorm when he referred to the Rutgers women's basketball team as "nappy-headed 'hos.'" This racist name-calling led to his making a public apology. He was also fired by CBS but returned to radio some months later.

Not all who call a society "primitive" or "backward" intend to demean; they may think they are being objective. However, sometimes exclusive language is devoid of any pretense of respect, as with racist language and hate speech.

Hate speech is a particular kind of loaded language. Here, words are weapons. Hate speech can be used to insult or demean a person or group because of race, ethnicity, gender, sexual orientation, nationality, religion, age, or disability. And with the expansion of the Internet, hate speech has multiplied (see Chapter 13).

Even drawing connections to hateful practices is a concern. For example, commentator Bill O'Reilly said, "I don't want to go on a lynching party against Michelle Obama unless there's evidence, hard facts, that say this is how the woman really feels. If that's how she really feels—that America is a bad country or a flawed nation, whatever—then that's legit. We'll track it down" (www.mediamatters.org, 12 Feb 2008). This elicited a strong response from MSNBC's Keith Olberman, among others. Also, President Bush publicly responded that "the noose is not a symbol of prairie justice, but of gross injustice. Displaying one is not a harmless prank. Lynching is not a word to be mentioned in jest." As a civil society, Americans should agree that noose displays and lynching jokes are "deeply offensive," Bush said ("Bush: Lynching No Joke," KNX Radio, 13 Feb 2008).

The University of Delaware publicizes one perspective, that rules that ban or punish speech based upon its content cannot be justified:

> An institution of higher learning fails to fulfill its mission if it asserts the power to proscribe ideas—and racial or ethnic slurs, sexist epithets, or homophobic insults almost always express ideas, however repugnant. . . . As the United States Supreme Court has said in the course of rejecting criminal sanctions for offensive words: Words are often chosen as much for their emotive as their cognitive force.

The line between substance and style is thus too uncertain to sustain the pressure that will inevitably be brought to bear upon disciplinary rules that attempt to regulate speech ("On Freedom of Expression and Campus Speech Codes," University of Delaware Library, www.lib.udel.edu).

Regulating hate speech without impinging on freedom of speech is not easy. A key concern is speech versus conduct. If a statute focuses on conduct—not speech—then it is less likely to be seen as violating the First Amendment. That is why a Wisconsin statute that gives stiffer penalties for racially motivated assaults than for other sorts of assaults was upheld in *Wisconsin* v. *Mitchell* (1993).

Exercises

Part One

1. What do you think should be a company or college policy regarding the use of hate speech in email or within publications, such as college newspapers or office newsletters? Set out your recommendations.

2. Do a study of contemporary music for examples of hate speech. Give an argument for or against censoring music lyrics containing hate speech.

Part Two

Directions: Select any two of the excerpts below, and make note of the ways in which racism or prejudice is expressed, stereotypes are used, and hatred and fear factor into the author's reasoning.

1. From "Dilemma of a Norwegian Immigrant," in *Annals of America,* 1862, author unknown:

> You are not safe from Indians anywhere, for they are as cunning as they are bold. The other evening we received the frightening message that they have been seen in our neighborhood; so, we hitched our horses and made ready to leave our house and all our property and escape from the savages under the cover of darkness. But it was a false alarm, God be praised, and for this time we could rest undisturbed. How terrible it is thus, every moment, to expect that you will be attacked, robbed, and perhaps murdered! We do not go to bed any night without fear, and my rifle is always loaded. . . . It is true that some cavalry have been dispatched against these hordes, but they will not avail much, for the Indians are said to be more than 10,000 strong. Besides, they are so cunning that it is not easy to get the better of them. Sometimes they disguise themselves in ordinary farmers' clothes and stalk their victims noiselessly.

2. From the Mississippi Penal Code, 1865:

> Section 1. Be it enacted by the legislature of the state of Mississippi, that no freedman, free Negro, or mulatto not in the military service of the United States government, and not licensed so to do by the board of police of his or her county, shall keep or carry firearms of any kind, or any ammunition, dirk [dagger], or Bowie knife; and, on conviction thereof in the county court, shall be punished by fine, not exceeding $10, and pay the costs of such proceedings, and all such arms or ammunition shall be forfeited to the informer; and it shall be the duty of every civil and military officer to arrest any

freedman, free Negro, or mulatto found with any such arms or ammunition, and cause him or her to be committed for trial in default of bail.

3. From *The Turner Diaries* by William L. Pierce:

I'll never forget that terrible day: November 9, 1989. They knocked on my door at five in the morning. I was completely unsuspecting as I got up to see who it was. I opened the door, and four Negroes came pushing into the apartment before I could stop them. One was carrying a baseball bat, and two had long kitchen knives thrust into their belts. The one with the bat shoved me back into a corner and stood guard over me with his bat raised in a threatening position while the other three began ransacking my apartment.

My first thought was that they were robbers. Robberies of this sort had become all too common since the Cohen Act, with groups of Blacks forcing their way into White homes to rob and rape, knowing that even if their victims had guns they probably would not dare use them. Then the one who was guarding me flashed some kind of card and informed me that he and his accomplices were "special deputies" for the Northern Virginia Human Relations Council. They were searching for firearms, he said.

Right after the Cohen Act was passed, all of us in the Organization had cached our guns and ammunition where they weren't likely to be found. Those in my unit had carefully greased our weapons, sealed them in an oil drum, and spent all of one tedious weekend burying the drum in an eight-foot-deep pit 200 miles away in the woods of western Pennsylvania.

Overcoming Linguistic Lethargy

Some people think of language as neutral and unchanging. It is neither. We can be active agents of change, so that degrading or stereotypical constructions fade away from ordinary use. One way is to make sure we avoid using language that is racist, sexist, or prejudicial.

Sexist language has its own set of problems. To say "man" and assume it includes women is to twist your brain into a linguistic pretzel. The issue is not simply one of convention. The underlying assumptions behind prejudicial language need to be rooted out. Sometimes the author does not intend to write a racist diatribe or otherwise express prejudice. We are not always in a position to confront the perpetrator; but we are not powerless, either. By recognizing and understanding the mechanisms of hate and hate speech, we can be party to social change.

Racist language creates a mind-set that makes it easier to kill "enemies." This was seen in the Vietnam War when the Viet Cong (North Vietnamese) were called "gooks." Ron Ridenhour writes: "By the time I got to Vietnam, just before Christmas 1967, everydamnbody was talking about killing gooks. Gooks this, gooks that.... How did you tell gooks from the good Vietnamese, for instance? After a while it became clear. You didn't have to. All gooks were VC [Viet Cong] when they were dead" ("Jesus Was a Gook," Part I, lists.village.virginia.edu/sixties).

We can acquire the tools to recognize racist language and thought. We can also eradicate it from our own speech and ways of thinking. Try thinking of the most disadvantaged in the equation—the butt of the joke, the object of a sexist remark, or the target of a racist diatribe. Try shifting frames of reference to obtain a more nuanced understanding of events and relationships. It's not easy to see things from the perspective of the victim or to grasp how long-lasting the effects of bigotry and hate can be.

To shift out of the mind-set of the powerful so we can achieve a more just society, philosopher of law John Rawls recommends that we try a "veil of ignorance" to distance ourselves from the race, gender, economic class, and nationality that we identify with. Think about it: If you were at the receiving end of hate speech, you might more quickly realize how deeply it can cut. Justice is not achieved by a few people in powerful places making decisions for others to follow. It comes about when everyday people bring it into each aspect of their lives. And that means change is possible.

Exercises

Part One

Directions: Read about the following case and then answer the question below.

When MIT German grad student Wilken-Jon von Appen applied for a new ID card from the Transportation Security Administration (TSA), he was turned down. He also received a warning from John M. Busch, security official: "I have determined that you pose a security threat." Von Appen is at the university doing research supported by an NSF grant of $65,000 per year. He said that getting this letter left him feeling intimidated. Another MIT student who received the letter is Sophie Clatyon from Britain. She said, "The two words 'security threat' are now in the files next to my name, my photograph and my fingerprints."

Such letters have gone out to 5,000 applicants for an ID card from the TSA. A TSA spokesperson, Ellen Howe, said the denial letters shouldn't cause problems with visa renewal or airport security, and they can enter secure ports and ships *as long as they are accompanied by someone with the new ID* [emphasis added]. (Scott Shane, "Blunt Federal Letters Tell Students They're Security Threats," *The New York Times*, 13 May 2008)

Answer the following: Is there a contradiction in stating that the label "security threat" is an "unfortunate choice of words" while refusing to reissue letters without such loaded language?

Part Two

Directions: Select *one* of the two topics below.

1. Study advertising as a kind of consumer propaganda.
   a. How is language used in ads to shape our thoughts and values?
   b. How are items made more appealing by the words used (e.g., in cigarette ads, the word "taste" is often used, though we don't normally eat cigarettes)?
2. Do a study of stereotypes (focus on one area—race, ethnicity/nationality, gender, religion, age, weight) in sports. You can find articles in newspapers and on the Internet to gather examples and issues.

Group or Individual Exercises

1. Research the ways in which racism and racist language were used by any *one* of these groups: the Ku Klux Klan, Nazis, neo-Nazis, white supremacists, or the Aryan Nation.

2. Study any recent political campaign to find examples of two or three kinds of propaganda.

Humor, Parody, and Satire

It is all too easy to fall into the stereotypical mind-set regarding issues of race, ethnicity, and gender. Humor can help jolt us out of our habitual ways of thinking. Comedy is a powerful vehicle for social commentary—and for loosening up our thought processes! As we saw in Chapter 7 on fallacies, much humor uses equivocation (playing on different meanings of a word) or amphiboly (ambiguity from faulty grammar or sentence structure).

A **satire** is a work that ridicules or pokes fun at its subject (people, groups, institutions, countries, etc.) in order to bring about a particular effect, such as social change. The original *Stepford Wives* was a biting satire on society and the institution of marriage. As Glen Lovell observes, "The word 'Stepford' entered the lexicon as shorthand for creeping regimentation. People in tract-house communities live Stepford lives; politicians who parrot safe causes are Stepford candidates, etc. etc." ("Too Good to Be True?" *San Jose Mercury News,* 11 Jan 2004). Cathryn J. Prince uses the term "Stepford" to criticize a new perk in the U.S. military: "Call it 'Stepford Soldiers.' . . . In a bizarre attempt to attract recruits, the Pentagon now offers soldiers free cosmetic surgery, from face-lifts and nose jobs to breast enlargements and liposuctions" (*Christian Science Monitor,* 30 Jul 2004).

The Liberatory Voice

Language can degrade, as we have seen. But language can also exalt, as we saw with the case of the deaf children who were proud to have "their own language." As William Raspberry says, "And, yes, words matter. They may reflect reality, but they also have the power to change reality—the power to uplift and to abase." The **liberatory voice** is language at its most inspirational—a call to social action, political transformation, spiritual healing, or the realization of our common humanity.

We've all had to deal with psychic numbing, in our own way. Humankind now has the capacity to vaporize us all, to commit mass genocide, to explode the vast nuclear arsenal. Many of us have parents or grandparents who, naïve and

The Global Dimension

Muslim Comedy Tour

Since humans first laughed out loud, comedy has been used to address prejudice, bigotry, and stereotypes. Now, Arab-American comedians are using humor to confront the public perceptions since 9/11. Read the following lines from a Muslim comedy tour and discuss what makes the lines funny or satirical (see Ahmed Khatib, "Allah Made Me Funny," press release, 17 May 2008):

- Azhar Usman, a stand-up comic with a full beard and Muslim head covering, speaks about performing in England: "In America, I'm so used to people hating me for being a Muslim. It was nice to finally be hated for just being an American."
- Tissa Hami wears the traditional hijab and jokes about praying in the back of the mosque with the other women while the men pray up front. "We're not in the back because we're oppressed," she said. "We just like the view."
- Usman points to his traditional Muslim garb and says: "Think about it. If I was a crazy Muslim fundamentalist terrorist about to hijack a plane, this is probably not the disguise I would go with."

Ahmed Khatib points to the example of Mel Brooks, who wrote *The Producers,* which has jokes about Adolf Hitler. In a TV interview, Brooks, who is Jewish and a World War II veteran, explained: "Hitler was part of this incredible idea that you could put Jews in concentration camps and kill them." He added: "There's only one way to get even. You have to bring him down with ridicule. . . . If you can make people laugh at him, then you're one up on him" (noted by Ahmed Khatib, "Allah Made Me Funny," press release, 17 May 2008).

trusting of their government, unknowingly lived downwind from nuclear weapons testing. Many of us have brothers or sisters, or aunts or uncles who took part in the war in Iraq and Afghanistan and who were exposed to nerve gas, mustard gas, biochemical agents, or uranium-tipped weapons. Many of us have neighbors who worked in agricultural fields touching pesticide-covered crops or in buildings breathing asbestos. We grieve for the cancers they now have. We are numbed by that suffering. Some of us, most of us, are numbed into silence.

Some, however, come out of their silence into speech. Think of those who have stood up against injustice and raised their voices in opposition. Think of those who have galvanized an entire community to confront oppression and work for social change. Think of those who wrote down their thoughts and ideas, even in the most repressive environments, like prisons, internment camps, boarding schools, plantations, abusive households, and violent relationships. Such acts are inspiring and even transforming. That is why the liberatory voice must be recognized—and celebrated.

As Isabel Allende says, "Writing is an act of hope." Language is a source of strength, a source of inspiration. The liberatory aspect of language moves us to organize, effect political change, address the ills of society, and take one small step to make our voices heard.

Think about some of the ways language has helped to transform society. For example, Abraham Lincoln changed this country with the Gettysburg Address. Thich Nhat Hanh helped people find spiritual wisdom. Cesar Chavez united U.S.

farmworkers, a disenfranchised group, and helped them organize to effect political and social change. The Proclamation of the Delano Grape Workers called for an international boycott of table grapes in 1969. In 1862, the prominent African-American leader John S. Rock issued his "Negro Hopes for Emancipation," a call to end slavery. Sojourner Truth spoke in New York City on May 9, 1867, at the First Annual Meeting of the American Equal Rights Association. She called for equal rights for women. Tibetan spiritual leader the Dalai Lama has been a force for peaceful change, and Israeli author Elie Wiesel a reminder that injustices, like those of the Holocaust, should prod us to work for a society free of prejudice and hate. And we can—and the liberatory aspects of language remind us of this fact.

CASE STUDY

Orhan Pamuk's Nobel Prize Acceptance Speech

Orhan Pamuk, the Turkish novelist, won the Nobel Prize for Literature in 2006. Read the following edited excerpt from his acceptance speech, where he speaks of writing as an inward journey. State his key points, and explain how he sees the power of language.

A writer is someone who spends years patiently trying to discover the second being inside him, and the world that makes him who he is: when I speak of writing, what comes first to my mind is a person who shuts himself up in a room, sits down at a table, and alone, turns inward; amid its shadows, he builds a new world with words. This man—or this woman—may use a typewriter, profit from the ease of a computer, or write with a pen on paper, as I have done for 30 years. He can write poems, plays, or novels, as I do. All these differences come after the crucial task of sitting down at the table and patiently turning inwards.

To write is to turn this inward gaze into words, to study the world into which that person passes when he retires into himself, and to do so with patience, obstinacy, and joy. As I sit at my table, for days, months, years, slowly adding new words to the empty page, I feel as if I am creating a new world, as if I am bringing into being that other person inside me, in the same way someone might build a bridge or a dome, stone by stone. The stones we writers use are words. As we hold them in our hands . . . weighing them, moving them around, year in and year out, patiently and hopefully, we create new worlds. The writer's secret is not inspiration—for it is never clear where it comes from—it is his stubbornness, his patience.

But once we shut ourselves away, we soon discover that we are not as alone as we thought. We are in the company of the words of those who came before us, of other people's stories, other people's books, other people's words, the thing we call tradition. I believe literature to be the most valuable hoard that humanity has gathered in its quest to understand itself. Societies, tribes, and peoples grow more intelligent, richer, and more advanced as they pay attention to the troubled words of their authors, and, as we all know, the burning of books and the denigration of writers are both signals that dark and improvident times are upon us. But literature is never just a national concern. The writer who shuts himself up in a room and first goes on a journey inside himself will, over the years, discover literature's eternal rule: he must have the artistry to tell his own stories as if they were other people's stories, and to tell other people's stories as if they were his own.

Source: © The Nobel Foundation 2006. Reprinted with the permission of the Nobel Foundation.

Exercises

Directions: Here are excerpts from works that have inspired social, political, and religious action. Select *one* of the passages, and read it carefully to see its power and ability to transform lives. Write a brief analysis of the use of language, focusing on one of these issues: (1) how the language is inspiring, (2) how the language could or should be changed to reflect other values or concerns, or (3) what the writer seems to assume.

Passage 1: Abraham Lincoln, "The Gettysburg Address"

Four score and seven years ago our fathers brought forth on this continent a new nation, conceived in liberty and dedicated to the proposition that all men are created equal.

Now we are engaged in a great civil war, testing whether that nation or any nation so conceived and so dedicated can long endure. We are met on a great battlefield of that war. We have come to dedicate a portion of that field as a final resting place for those who here gave their lives that that nation might live. It is altogether fitting and proper that we should do this.

But, in a larger sense, we cannot dedicate—we cannot consecrate—we cannot hallow—this ground. The brave men, living and dead, who struggled here have consecrated it far above our poor power to add or detract. The world will little note nor long remember what we say here, but it can never forget what they did here. It is for us, the living, rather, to be dedicated here to the unfinished work, which they who fought here have thus far so nobly advanced.

It is rather for us to be here dedicated to the great task remaining before us—that from these honored dead we take increased devotion to that cause for which they gave the last full measure of devotion; that we here highly resolve that these dead shall not have died in vain; that this nation, under God, shall have a new birth of freedom; and that government of the people, by the people, for the people shall not perish from the earth.

Passage 2: Thich Nhat Hanh from *The Sun My Heart* (Parallax Press, 1988)

Peace can exist only in the present moment. It is ridiculous to say, "Wait until I finish this, then I will be free to live in peace." What is "this"? A diploma, a job, a house, the payment of a debt? If you think that way, peace will never come. There is always another "this" that will follow the present one. If you are not living in peace at this moment, you will never be able to. If you truly want to be at peace, you must be at peace right now. Otherwise, there is only "the hope of peace some day." . . .

The peace we seek cannot be our personal possession. We need to find an inner peace which makes it possible for us to become one with those who suffer, and to do something to help our brothers and sisters, which is to say, ourselves. I know many young people who are aware of the real situation of the world and who are filled with compassion. They refuse to hide themselves in artificial peace, and they engage in the world in order to change the society.

They know what they want; yet after a period of involvement they become discouraged. Why? It is because they lack deep, inner peace, the kind of peace they can take with them into their life of action. Our strength is in our peace, the peace within us. This peace makes us indestructible. We must have peace while taking care of those we love and those we want to protect.

Passage 3: Proclamation of the Delano Grape Workers, 1969(Excerpt)

We have been farm workers for hundreds of years and pioneers for seven. Mexicans, Filipinos, Africans, and others, our ancestors were among those who founded this land and tamed its natural wilderness. But we are still pilgrims on this land, and we are pioneers who blaze a trail out of the wilderness of hunger and deprivation that we have suffered even as our ancestors did.

We are conscious today of the significance of our present quest. If this road we chart leads to the rights and reforms we demand, if it leads to just wages, humane working conditions, protection from the misuse of pesticides, and to the fundamental right of collective bargaining, if it changes the social order that relegates us to the bottom reaches of society, then in our wake will follow thousands of American farm workers. . . .

Our example will make them free. But if our road does not bring us to victory and social change, it will not be because our direction is mistaken or our resolve too weak, but only because our bodies are mortal and our journey hard. For we are in the midst of a great social movement, and we will not stop struggling 'til we die, or win! . . .

Grapes must remain an unenjoyed luxury for all as long as the barest human needs and basic human rights are still luxuries for farm workers. The grapes grow sweet and heavy on the vines, but they will have to wait while we reach out first for our freedom. The time is ripe for our liberation.

Passage 4: John S. Rock from "Negro Hopes for Emancipation," 1862 Speech before the Massachusetts Anti-Slavery Society

The situation of the black man in this country is far from being an enviable one. Today, our heads are in the lion's mouth, and we must get them out the best way we can. To contend against the government is as difficult as it is to sit in Rome and fight with the pope. It is probable that, if we had the malice of the Anglo-Saxon, we would watch our chances and seize the first opportunity to take our revenge. If we attempted this, the odds would be against us, and the first thing we should know would be—nothing! The most of us are capable of perceiving that the man who spits against the wind spits in his own face!

This nation is mad. In its devoted attachment to the Negro, it has run crazy after him; and now, having caught him, hangs on with a deadly grasp, and says to him, with more earnestness and pathos than Ruth expressed to Naomi, "Where thou goest, I will go; where thou lodgest, I will lodge; thy people shall be my people, and thy God, my God." . . .

This rebellion for slavery means something! Out of it emancipation must spring. I do not agree with those men who see no hope in this war. There is nothing in it but hope. Our cause is onward. As it is with the sun, the clouds often obstruct his vision, but in the end, we find there has been no standing still. It is true the government is but little more antislavery now than it was at the commencement of the war; but while fighting for its own existence, it has been obliged to take slavery by the throat and, sooner or later, must choke her to death.

Passage 5: Sojourner Truth from Her 1867 Speech to the First Annual Meeting of the American Equal Rights Association, New York City

I want women to have their rights. In the courts women have no right, no voice; nobody speaks for them. I wish woman to have her voice there among the pettifoggers [lawyers]. If it is not a fit place for women, it is unfit for men to be there.

I am above eighty years old; it is about time for me to be going. I have been forty years a slave and forty years free and would be here forty years more to have equal rights for all. I suppose I am kept here because something remains for me to do; I suppose I am yet to help to break the chain. I have done a great deal of work; as much as a man, but did not get so much pay. I used to work in the field and bind grain, keeping up with the cradler; but men doing no more, got twice as much pay; so with the German women. They work in the field and do as much work, but do not get the pay. We do as much, we eat as much, we want as much. I suppose I am about the only colored woman that goes about to speak for the rights of colored women. I want to keep the thing stirring, now that the ice is cracked.

What we want is a little money. You men know that you get as much again as women when you write, or for what you do. When we get our rights we shall not have to come to you for money, for then we shall have money enough in our own pockets; and maybe you will ask us for money. But help us now until we get it. It is a good consolation to know that when we have got this battle once fought we shall not be coming to you any more. You have been having our rights so long, that you think, like a slave-holder, that you own us. I know that is hard for one who has held the reins for so long to give up; it cuts like a knife. It will feel all the better when it closes up again. I have been in Washington about three years, seeing about these colored people. Now colored men have the right to vote. There ought to be equal rights now more than ever, since colored people have got their freedom. I am going to talk several times while I am here; so now I will do a little singing. I have not heard any singing since I came here.

Passage 6: Elie Wiesel, Winner of the Nobel Prize for Peace, 1986, in a 1999 speech at the White House, "The Perils of Indifference: Lessons Learned from a Violent Century"

Indifference is . . . a strange and unnatural state in which the lines blur between light and darkness, dusk and dawn, crime and punishment, cruelty and compassion, good and evil.

. . . We are on the threshold of a new century, a new millennium. What will the legacy of this vanishing century be?. . . So much violence, so much indifference. . . . Of course, indifference can be tempting—more than that, seductive. It is so much easier to look away from victims. It is so much easier to avoid such rude interruptions to our work, our dreams, our hopes. It is, after all, awkward, troublesome, to be involved in another person's pain and despair. Yet, for the person who is indifferent, his or her neighbors are of no consequence. And, therefore, their lives are meaningless. Their hidden or even visible anguish is of no interest. Indifference reduces the other to an abstraction.

Over there, behind the black gates of Auschwitz, the most tragic of all prisoners were the "Muselmanner," as they were called. Wrapped in their torn blankets, they would sit or lie on the ground, staring vacantly into space, unaware of who or where they were, strangers to their surroundings. They no longer felt pain, hunger, thirst. They feared nothing. They felt nothing. They were dead and did not know it.

Rooted in our tradition, some of us felt that to be abandoned by humanity then was not the ultimate. We felt that to be abandoned by God was worse than to be punished by Him. Better an unjust God than an indifferent one. For us to be ignored by God was a harsher punishment than to be a victim of His anger. Man can live far from God—not outside God. God is wherever we are. Even in suffering? Even in suffering.

In a way, to be indifferent to that suffering is what makes the human being inhuman. Indifference, after all, is more dangerous than anger and hatred. Anger can at times be creative. One writes a great poem, a great symphony, have done something special for the sake of humanity because one is angry at the injustice that one witnesses. But indifference is never creative. Even hatred at times may elicit a response. You fight it. You denounce it. You disarm it. Indifference elicits no response. Indifference is not a response.

Indifference is not a beginning; it is an end. And, therefore, indifference is always the friend of the enemy, for it benefits the aggressor—never his victim, whose pain is magnified when he or she feels forgotten. And in denying their humanity we betray our own. . . .

Source: Reprinted with the permission of Elie Wiesel.

Passage 7: Buddhist Monk and Spiritual Leader of Tibet, the Dalai Lama, from His 1989 Nobel Peace Prize Acceptance Speech in Oslo, Sweden

Your Majesty, Members of the Nobel Committee, Brothers and Sisters. I am very happy to be here with you today to receive the Nobel Prize for Peace. I feel honored, humbled and deeply moved that you should give this important prize to a simple monk from Tibet. . . . I accept the prize with profound gratitude on behalf of the oppressed everywhere and for all those who struggle for freedom and work for world peace. I accept it as a tribute to the man who founded the modern tradition of non-violent action for change, Mahatma Gandhi, whose life taught and inspired me. And, of course, I accept it on behalf of the six million Tibetan people, my brave countrymen and women inside Tibet, who have suffered and continue to suffer so much. . . .

No matter what part of the world we come from, we are all basically the same human beings. We all seek happiness and try to avoid suffering. We have the same basic human needs and concerns. All of us human beings want freedom and the right to determine our own destiny as individuals and as peoples. That is human nature. The great changes that are taking place everywhere in the world, from Eastern Europe to Africa, are a clear indication of this. . . .

As a Buddhist monk, my concern extends to all members of the human family and, indeed, to all sentient beings who suffer. I believe all suffering is caused by ignorance. People inflict pain on others in the selfish pursuit of their happiness or satisfaction. Yet true happiness comes from a sense of brotherhood and sisterhood. We need to cultivate a universal responsibility for one another and the planet we share. Although I have found my own Buddhist religion helpful in generating love and compassion, even for those we consider our enemies, I am convinced that everyone can develop a good heart and a sense of universal responsibility with or without religion.

With the ever-growing impact of science on our lives, religion and spirituality have a greater role to play reminding us of our humanity. There is no contradiction between the two. Each gives us valuable insights into the other. Both science and the teachings of the Buddha tell us of the fundamental unity of all things. This understanding is crucial if we are to take positive and decisive action on the pressing global concern with the environment. I believe all religions pursue the same goals, that of cultivating human goodness and bringing happiness to all human beings. Though the means might appear different, the ends are the same.

Source: © The Nobel Foundation 1989. Reprinted with the permission of the Nobel Foundation.

CHAPTER TWELVE

Desire and Illusion: Analyzing Advertising

And where do our sages get the idea that people must have normal, virtuous desires? What made them imagine that people must necessarily wish what is sensible and advantageous?

FYODOR DOSTOYEVSKY, *Notes from the Underground*

There is a scene in the movie *The Purple Rose of Cairo* where Cecilia, the film's protagonist, has gone to see the same movie for the third or fourth time. She seems mesmerized by it. The fantasy she is watching is much more pleasant than life with her abusive husband or her job as a waitress. Much to her surprise, Tom Baxter, one of the characters on the screen, steps out of the movie and into real life. Cecilia's life is transformed as she comes to exert much more control over the direction of her life. Sadder but wiser at the end, Cecilia comes to see both the seduction and the limitations of desire and illusion.

Advertising, like the fantasy life Cecilia found so entrancing in *The Purple Rose of Cairo*, frequently offers us an idealized world. This is a world filled with perfectly charming people having a great time. Their lives are free of disease. Their sexuality is untroubled by fear of AIDS. Their marriages are strong, not tenuous. Their relationships are loving, not indifferent or even violent. Their children are wonderful—not obnoxious or ill mannered. Their neighborhoods are a dream world of well-manicured lawns—not war zones of drugs, violence, poverty, and decay. Who wants to have the ideal character step out of the ad and into our lives? It would be far better to step out of our lives and into the ad. That's exactly what sucks us in. An ad for Princess Cruises encapsulates this desire in two words: *"Escape completely."*

It would be quite remarkable to find someone unfamiliar with advertising. Ads are on the outside and inside of buses. They are pasted on billboards, painted on buildings, written across the sky, and placed in the movies we watch. They are part of our cultural landscape. Given their ubiquity, we need tools to deal with the various aspects of advertising—such as assumptions, fallacious reasoning, power and influence, and structural components (color, symbol, images, visual and verbal messages). In this chapter, we will examine those tools. We will also look at related issues—such as the lifestyle idealized in ads, the winner/loser mentality, sexuality and gender, for-profit versus nonprofit advertising, public service ads, and political manipulation. In addition, we will look at embedded ads (product placement).

Reading the Society from the Ads

We are a society of extremes. There is a wealth of opportunities and an array of things to make our lives easier. And yet there is sorrow and need around us. This results in longing and desire. We yearn for more than we get—and what we get is not enough. Advertisers know this. Ads attempt to soothe our spiritual hunger problem and help us find a way to connect with those around us.

Ads call to us and we are soothed, like a marvelous daydream. Just think: We really can go to *"The happiest place on earth."* Don't have the time to go? But, "You deserve a break today." Come on, "Just do it." And whatever you do, "Don't leave home without it." Don't be restrained by doubts—"Because you're worth it." Okay, "Have it your way." Give me some treats! "Betcha can't eat just one." And quit being so timid—"If it doesn't get all over the place, it doesn't belong in your face." I'm so proud of you: "You've come a long way, baby." What, you aren't perfect? Sure fooled me! In fact, "I never knew you had dandruff!" Honey, you just "Be all you can be." That's certainly what I tell myself every single day. I *do* deserve that break, those indulgences; you are so right. But is it enough, is it really enough, I wonder? Could there be more in life? Well, as they say, "There are some things money can't buy. For everything else there's MasterCard." What a relief! (Ad slogans' sources in order: Disneyland, McDonald's, Nike, American Express, Loreal, Burger King, Carl's Jr., Head & Shoulders, U.S. Army, MasterCard.)

Don't buy any old soda—"Join the Pepsi Generation." Don't buy this or that brand of cigarettes—"Come to Where the Flavor Is." Don't try to figure out how one shampoo is better than another—"It's not just about the hair. It's about how you feel" (Le Metric). It certainly is about how you feel—and how to get what you want. As an ad for Toyota Solaris puts it: *Do unto you as you would have others do unto you."* This encourages us to put our wants ahead of others' needs, and self-interest above altruism.

We don't have to feel needy, desperate, or lonely—there's a community for us, if we just buy a ticket (the product) and come on in. As an ad for American Express says, "STYLE. You either have it or you apply for it." Such invitations abound. Consider this ad: "The grape varieties in Chandon require bright sun, cool mornings and Spring showers. We find these conditions are also excellent for

You Tell Me Department

Are We Driven by Greed or Altruism?

Watch how ads can bring out the worst in us—or the best in us. It's a mixed bag. And one of our tasks is to see what's there in the bag that advertising creates.

One criticism of ads is that "if you take the underlying messages of all the ads we're exposed to, they are remarkably consistent in the values they promote. And if you built a society based on those values, it would be a pretty self-centered, materialistic, live-for-the-moment, hedonistic, hyper-competitive sicko freak show society. Which is pretty much what we've got" (Jelly Helms, www.thisisdrew.com, 24 Oct 2003).

On the other hand, many ads *do* affirm noteworthy traits, as we see in the Nike ad called "Scary House." Here, two children go up to what appears to be a "haunted" house, and the boy goads the girl into pushing the doorbell. As the door literally falls open, the girl transforms into an adult runner who races home—resuming her girl-child form as she enters the door. These words remain: "You're faster than you think" (see www.methodstudios.com). Granted, you run faster thanks to Nike shoes—but the message is also that you were able to beat it out of there, that you didn't give up, or succumb to whatever scares you.

You tell me: How much of advertising plays into self-centeredness or greed—and how much recognizes and furthers positive human qualities? Can you cite examples of each?

most varieties of humans. Come to Chandon and you will see." Look also at the advertising slogan for Norwegian cruise line: "It's different out here." It's different in here, too. No longer do we need fancy cloth napkins to feel special. We may not be rich, but we can "elevate every meal" with the "everyday elegance" of a Vanity Fair paper napkin.

Assumptions about the Audience

Contemporary ads bear little resemblance to ads of the past. Those today are more subtle and sophisticated, and at an artistic level rarely achieved in earlier decades. They assume a language of discourse and engage the audience in ways that were previously unimaginable. And they routinely make assumptions about consumers' needs, desires, fears, and prejudices. We see this in an ad for Utah tourism: "Never go anywhere without your topographic map, your compass and *your restaurant guide*" (my emphasis).

One broad area of assumptions has to do with the way people want to live. As Kathleen Hall Jamieson and Karlyn Kohrs Campbell point out, "People in ads have spacious kitchens, large lawns, expensive appliances, cars; they travel worldwide. Ads take for granted that . . . the audience is not making a decision about whether to buy the product but rather is deciding which brand to buy" (*Interplay of Influence: News, Advertising, Politics, and the Mass Media,* Wadsworth, 2000). It is a world where affluence is taken for granted.

Exercises

1. What do you think is *assumed* in the following ad for Ralph Lauren? Discuss what audience is being appealed to and what is assumed about this audience's shopping tastes and fantasies.

   Ralph Lauren Presents Purple Label Made to Measure
   The Ultimate Sartorial Tradition
   A legacy of rarefied elegance continues. In the spirit of Savile Row tailoring. Purple Label offers impeccably crafted suits, dress shirts, trousers, topcoats, sport coats and formalwear: Ralph Lauren has personally selected the world's most luxurious fabrics—offered exclusively and in limited edition—and appointed some of the very few remaining artisans trained in the timeless art of hand craftsmanship.
   Experience an unparalleled dedication to excellence and service at the highest level. To schedule a private appointment please call or visit a Ralph Lauren store.

2. Discuss what is assumed about the consumer in the following two tobacco ads:

   Life is Rich. *Davidoff Cigarettes.*
   The only corners we cut are on the pack. There's no real pleasure in taking shortcuts. For Davidoff, our uncompromising attitude starts from the ground up in the fertile soils of the world, where carefully selected tobacco plants flourish under meticulous care. Only the highest-grade leaves are chosen for a deeply rich and consistently smoother, more even burn. Our filter is more luxurious in feel, while our world-renowned beveled-edge pack is made to protect the uniquely crafted cigarettes inside. Some might say this is pure indulgence. We say that's exactly the point.

   Introducing New Bandits®
   Refreshing, moist, flavorful tobacco satisfaction in a discreet pouch. The road to tobacco satisfaction is wide open. Begin your journey at SkoalBandits.com.

3. Pacy Markman of the advertising agency Zimmerman and Markman says, "Good advertising always makes the client uncomfortable. If you are completely comfortable, it is a sign you are just talking to yourself" (quoted in Gary Wolf, *Wired* magazine, Sep 2004). Find three ads that you think are examples of innovative advertising—ads that stand out from the rest.

4. John Berger argues that ads focus more on social relations than products, with envy being particularly important:

   Publicity is about social relations, not objects. Its promise is not of pleasure, but of happiness: happiness as judged from the outside by others. The happiness of being envied is glamour. The spectator-buyer is meant to envy herself as she will become if she buys the product. She is meant to imagine herself transformed by the product into an object of envy for others, an envy which will then justify her loving herself. (quoted in Robert Goldman, *Reading Ads Socially,* Taylor and Francis, 1999)

   a. Do you think Berger is right that ads promise us *happiness*, not pleasure? Can you cite some examples for or against this claim?

> b. Using a collection of ads (at least five ads), make a case for or against Berger's thesis that ads want us to become an object of envy by others.
>
> 5. In what ways does advertising play on our emotions? Illustrate your position with four to five ads to support your claims. Be sure to attach your ads.
>
> 6. How pervasive is patriotism in advertising? Find at least four ads that play on our sense of patriotism, using national symbols (like the bald eagle, national monuments, famous historical figures, military heroes, and the flag) in order to hook us. Be sure to attach your ads.

The Use of Fallacies to Persuade

Many ads honestly convey what the products can or should do for the consumer. Some ads imply that the product will transform our lives and open the door to a more desirable lifestyle or social contacts. And some involve the use of fallacies to persuade. The key fallacies found in ads are ad populum, ad verecundiam, accent, bifurcation, and equivocation. (See Chapter 7 for a review.)

Key Fallacies in Ads

1. **Ad Populum (Appeal to the Masses/Patriotism).** This fallacy occurs when an ad appeals to the masses, patriotism, or elitism (snob appeal) to sell a product. For example:

   "America's Number One Pizza." (Pizza Hut)
   "Billions and billions served." (McDonald's)
   "The world's favorite airline." (British Airlines)
   "Move ahead in luxury." (Esteem)

2. **Ad Verecundiam (Improper Appeal to Authority).** This fallacy occurs when an ad uses the testimony of a public figure or celebrity (unqualified as an expert on the subject) as a tool of persuasion, rather than citing relevant evidence. For example:

   "David Beckham" (Georgio Armani underwear)
   "What are you made of?" (TagHeuer watch; photo of Uma Thurman)
   "Roddick's Law: Fans will cheer if you give them something to cheer about." (Rolex watch)
   "Fast. Stylish. Precise. (But enough about Andre.)" (Canon camera; photo of Andre Agassi with tennis racket)
   "Where you never have to grow up." (Disney Parks; Photo of Cate Blanchett)

3. **Accent.** This fallacy occurs when the ad emphasizes a word or phrase (verbally or visually) in such a way as to distort the meaning of a passage, leading to an incorrect conclusion being drawn. For example:

You Tell Me Department

Does Mudslinging Work?

Political ads that use negative campaigning—alias "mudslinging" and "dirty tricks"—assume that smearing an opponent will turn the voters against him or her. However, this can backfire and even repel voters. And yet they often surface during elections. Take the case of what was called a "nasty" race between two incumbents in Dallas, Texas. Consider these two ads:

Ad 1 (for Martin Frost): Images of the World Trade Center in flames fill the television screen. A somber voice warns that a local Republican House member is soft on airline security. Stark words appear: "Protect America. Say No to Pete Sessions."

Ad 2 (for Pete Sessions): A plane is flying overhead and a shoulder-fired missile, presumably hoisted by a terrorist, points at it. The announcer warns of "unspeakable horror, shattered lives."

And that's not all:

From the Sessions campaign: Fliers in Dallas mailboxes accuse Frost of consorting with a former child molester and more. The child molestation issue was raised by the Sessions campaign after it learned that a Frost fundraiser was to feature singer Peter Yarrow of Peter, Paul and Mary fame. In 1970, Yarrow was convicted of indecent behavior with a 14-year-old. Frost canceled Yarrow's appearance. But he objected that a mailing by Sessions implied Frost was a child molester. Sessions denied the charge, while arguing it was "very germane" to note that Frost had asked a person with Yarrow's record for political help.

From the Frost campaign: The Frost campaign accused Sessions of "indecent exposure" because he was a streaker while in college. Justin Kitsch, Frost's spokesman, said it was legitimate to call attention to the prank because it illustrated Sessions' hypocrisy, given that he had been a vocal critic of singer Janet Jackson's exposing her breast during the 2004 Super Bowl halftime show. Sessions called it "a new low" for Frost to broach the streaking incident, but it caught voters' attention. When Sessions addressed a Lion's Club meeting in Dallas, members teased him by having someone streak through the meeting. (Janet Hook, "Slinging Mud and Whatever Else They Can Afford," *Los Angeles Times,* 29 Oct 2004)

You tell me: To what degree is negative advertising an effective technique? See if you can find examples of negative campaigning in recent elections. Point out how the "mudslinging" is used in your examples.

"Try All-Pro Protein Shake and lose weight in seven days! Results may vary." (All-Pro ad)
"FREE GIFT of a travel-size mascara when you purchase $50 worth of cosmetics." (sign in department store)
WHAT DO THE ROLLS-ROYCE PHANTOM AND THE HYUNDAI GENESIS HAVE IN COMMON? HINT: IT'S NOT THE PRICE.
For starters—they both share a Lexicon® 7.1 Discrete surround sound system.

4. **Bifurcation.** This fallacy occurs when the ad attempts to persuade by presenting only two choices when, in fact, other options could be considered in decision making. For example:

"If you're not ahead, you're out." (NIIT ad)
"Read this or die." (ad for nutritional research booklet)

5. **Equivocation.** This fallacy occurs when an ad creates ambiguity by using a word or phrase with a double meaning, resulting in an incorrect conclusion being drawn. For example:

"Canadian Club. Join it." (Canadian Club whiskey ad)
"Shake up Your Night." (Baccardi rum ad)

Group or Individual Exercise

Directions: Examine the copy for an ad *against* Kathy Angerer that was paid for by the Michigan Republican State Committee. Study this example of negative campaigning, and discuss how effective you think this ad is likely to be.

Kathy Angerer Won't Help Law Enforcement Prevent Terrorism.

Kathy Angerer is out of the mainstream . . . and she is not on our side.

Law enforcement needs information to track terrorists and prevent potential attacks in the United States.

But Kathy Angerer opposes an anti-terrorism database for our law enforcement agencies.

Kathy Angerer is a friend of the ACLU [American Civil Liberties Union], and she won't do what is needed to protect us.

A central database would allow law enforcement agencies to have instant access to critical information and assist in tracking persons that may be planning terror attacks on our homeland.

But Kathy Angerer will pull the plug on this critical effort to stop terrorism. And we just can't trust her to protect Michigan.

The Power of Advertising

Advertising does more than push a product. It also tells stories, dispenses social commentary, offers advice, and makes us laugh. More important, ads claim that our problems can be solved—if we just purchase *this* product or *that* service. They also tell us that we deserve to be indulged; we have the right to pamper ourselves, given our stressful lives. These are accomplished with four tricks.

Four Tricks of Effective Advertising

1. *Shame*   →   You've got a problem!
2. *Optimism*   →   Your problem can be solved.
3. *Solution*   →   You need *this* product.
4. *Rationale* →   You have a right to solve your problem, whatever the cost.

Example of the Fab Four in Action

How to Sell "Delirious" Perfume to a Skunk:

1. *Shame*   →   You have body odor!
2. *Optimism*   →   Perfume helps!
3. *Solution*   →   Delirious perfume works wonders!
4. *Rationale*   →   You have the right to smell nice!

Let's see these Fab Four at work in an ad for Dove Promises chocolates. The ad presents an attractive blonde woman curled up on a couch holding a chocolate egg while children are running in the grass in the background. The ad copy (text) says:

The Hunt is over.

Introducing Dove Promises for Easter, to give or get by the basketful. Eggs of rich and lingering chocolate, each wrapped in an uplifting message. An indulgence too rich to be rushed.

   You can't hurry Dove.

Off to the side is another chocolate egg beside its wrapper. The wrapper contains the "uplifting" message "Family gatherings will bring Easter joy." How very appealing! It is this dream that we buy with Dove chocolates—and the transformation is thereby achieved. By the way, did you notice the last line, "You can't hurry Dove"? This mines the depths of our collective memory, calling up the Motown classic "You Can't Hurry Love" by the Supremes. The connection between *Dove* and *Love,* is solidified. Basically, the equation is: Need → Desire. Our *need* for love is translated in the *desire* for a Dove chocolate. When wants, needs, and desires converge, it makes for the perfect advertisement.

An interesting variation of the need/desire theme is found in a two-page Jockey underwear ad featuring a beautiful lake or seaside on the left page. Superimposed over this idyllic scene are the words *"are you comfortable being."*

Group or Individual Exercise

Directions: There are two opposing views of advertising set out below. Read them both and decide which one is most defensible. Then set out your defense.

View 1: Ads Are Damaging to Society

The world of mass advertising teaches us that want and frustration are caused by our own deficiencies. The goods are within easy reach, before our very eyes in dazzling abundance, available not only to the rich but to millions of ordinary citizens. Those unable to partake of this cornucopia [wealth] have only themselves to blame. If you cannot afford to buy these things, goes the implicit message, the failure is yours and not the system's. The advertisement of consumer wares, then, is also an advertisement for a whole capitalist system. (Michael Parenti, "Advertising Has a Negative Effect on

Society," in Neal Bernard, ed., *Mass Media: Opposing Viewpoints*, Greenhaven Press, 1988)

View 2: Ads Do Not Harm Society
It is considered appropriate to attempt to persuade. This tells us something concerning our general assumptions about human nature. For why would we permit wanton persuasion to plague a helpless public? Simply because we believe that the public is not helpless, but armed with reason, guiles, and a certain savvy about how to make one's way in the market. If we are sometimes open to persuasion about frivolous products and services, it may be that we have become sufficiently jaded by affluence to let ourselves be seduced by clearly self-interested sources. (Clifford Christians, Kim Rotzoll, and Mark Fackler, "Advertising Has Little Effect on Society," in Neal Bernard, ed., *Mass Media: Opposing Viewpoints*)

Sin and Seduction in Advertising

There is a seductive quality to ads, something magical that draws us in. We hope that buying this product really *can* transform our lives, help us overcome our inadequacies, and make us feel better. The fact that envy, lust (desire), and greed are three of the Seven Deadly Sins does not escape the minds of ad agencies. Some ads play on the sinfulness of eating *those* chocolates, buying *this* car, or owning *that* sound system. For example, a Ghirardelli ad has a close-up of caramel oozing out of a chocolate, with the copy "Discover your new desire." By mixing fact and fantasy, such ads can open up a parallel universe where almost anything seems possible.

Advertising offers an *escape* from the troubles of life. Some of it is creative and inspiring, and some is amusing and entertaining. It also has power. Dr. Alan Blum, head of the antismoking group "Doctors Ought to Care," calls for more vigilance: "The problem is we think we're smarter than the cigarette industry and that's not true." With large corporations behind them, advertising agencies can do product testing and determine which images and icons have the greatest appeal. They build upon the collective belief in the folktales and myths that are part of our culture.

Advertising has complex artistic and mythological components. Look at the cast of characters. There are winners and losers, villains and heroes, knights in shining armor and damsels in distress, the flabby and the physically fit, the social nerds and the social butterflies, and so on. Ads both shape and are shaped by our cultural landscape.

Even if we don't recognize the logo, our brain files it away, ready to bring it to the surface with a little prodding. As it says on the Energizer Bunny website: "In addition to serving as one of advertising's most recognizable symbols, the Energizer Bunny® has become a cultural icon, serving as a symbol of longevity, perseverance and determination." The very fact that you can go to the website and send off friendly Energizer Bunny emails speaks volumes. (See www.energizer.com/bunny.)

You Tell Me Department

Can We Gain Perspective over Time?

Let's look at an example of an ad from 1927. The ad is for Aunt Jemima Pancake Flour. The ad shows a large stack of pancakes in the foreground with a smiling black woman looking out from the door of a cabin. The ad copy says:

American women are noted throughout the world for their constant interest in new recipes. And today an old-time recipe has won more users than any other ever recorded. Down on the old plantation, Aunt Jemima refused to reveal to a soul the secret of those light fragrant pancakes which she baked for her master and his guests.

No other cook could match their flavor. No one could learn her "knack" of mixing ingredients. Today millions of women in all parts of the United States are making tender, golden-brown cakes just like Aunt Jemima's own. Only once, long after her master's death, did Aunt Jemima reveal her recipe. It is still a secret—no cookbook gives it. Her special flours cannot be bought in stores today. But her own ingredients, proportioned just as she used them, come *ready-mixed* in Aunt Jemima Pancake Flour.

You tell me: What ads do you see today that, 40 years from now, will provoke the same kind of reaction as we have to this ad?

Exercises

1. Look at the Energizer Bunny ad in Figure 12.1, and give your analysis of why this ad campaign has been so very successful.

2. *Ad Age* posted their "top 10" list of the most powerful ads of the 20ᵗʰ century. Examine the slogans and decide what makes these memorable:

Top 10 Slogans of the Century

1. "Diamonds are forever." (DeBeers)
2. "Just do it." (Nike)
3. "The pause that refreshes." (Coca-Cola)
4. "Tastes great, less filling." (Miller Lite)
5. "We try harder." (Avis)
6. "Good to the last drop." (Maxwell House)
7. "Breakfast of champions." (Wheaties)
8. "Does she. . . or doesn't she?" (Clairol)
9. "When it rains it pours." (Morton salt)
10. "Where's the beef?" (Wendy's)

Copyright 2006. Energizer Battery. www.energizer.com. Reprinted with permission.

FIGURE 12.1
The Energizer
Bunny's energy
caught the public's
eye—and kept it.

Analyzing Ads

Most of us do not know what it would be like to live without advertising. Still, we ought not be oblivious to its power. By setting out the structural components of ads and looking at the ways ads both reflect and influence society, we can better understand what is behind that power.

When examining ads, we need to look at a range of concerns set out in the checklist on the next page.

Advertising Checklist

- **Values:** What values and beliefs does the ad convey? According to the ad, what's the best use of our time and money?
- **Story.** If you think of the ad as telling a story, what story does it tell?
- **Verbal message.** What exactly does the ad say?
- **Visual message.** How do the visual components work together? What is the visual impact of the ad?
- **Fallacies.** Does the ad contain fallacies? In particular, watch for the fallacies of accent (ambiguity due to misplaced emphasis), equivocation (ambiguity due to shift in the meaning of a word/phrase), ad populum (appeal to mass sentiment or patriotism), and ad verecundiam (false appeal to authority, as with celebrity endorsements).
- **Exaggeration.** Does the ad make false promises and exaggerated claims? What exactly does the ad claim the product will do? Does it make any guarantees? Do you see any puffery?
- **Stereotypes.** Are there stereotypes around gender, race, age, nationality, religion, economic class, and so on? Look at the various roles (such as authority figures, heroes, and villains) presented in the ad.
- **Diversity.** Who populates the ad? Does the ad reflect the society we live in? How are gender, race, age, and economic class represented? Do they typify the world we live in?
- **Power and class.** Does the ad make assumptions related to power, class, and patterns of consumption? What is the economic class of those in the ad? Who are the targeted users of the product?
- **Political agenda.** Does the ad contain political or social messages? Any hidden agendas? Ads often relay a set of attitudes in the verbal or visual message.
- **Prescriptions.** What sort of lifestyle is presented? At what cost? And what is the societal impact of this lifestyle?
- **Sexuality.** How are issues of sexuality, body images, sexual orientation, sexual violence, and intimacy handled? Does the ad turn men or women into sexual objects or use sexuality to sell the product?
- **What is left unsaid.** What is missing from this ad? Will using the product transform your life, as the ad suggests?

Ad agencies spend a lot of time and energy trying to create striking ads. Tom Egelhoff, business consultant, offers his top 10 ideas on what makes a great ad (an explication of his points is in parentheses): (1) We all like surprises (leave the ordinary behind); (2) keep it simple (idea is key); (3) get me involved (don't bore me); (4) make me curious (grab my attention); (5) great ads command answers (respond to the ad); (6) let me connect the dots (strongest conclusion is the one I draw); (7) the headline and the image tell the story (headline should tell only what I don't see); (8) great ads never brag (no one likes egomaniacs); (9) they're always well executed (good design features); and (10) they sell (show me the money!) (Tom Egelhoff, SmallMarketing.com).

Exercises

1. What are your two to three favorite ads (or ads you find appealing)? Describe each ad in as much detail as you can, explaining why you find it appealing. The ad need not be a current one.

2. What ad do you dislike the most (or find boring or nondescript)? Describe it in as much detail as you can, and then explain where it falls short of your expectations. The ad need not be a current one.

3. Below are some classic advertising slogans. Select the three or four *most powerful* and the three or four *least memorable*. Explain your choices.
   a. "You're faster than you think." (Nike)
   b. "I can't believe I ate the whole thing!" (Alka Selzer)
   c. "Our office is your office." (FedEx Kinko's)
   d. "Don't leave home without it." (American Express)
   e. "The True Definition of Luxury. Yours." (Acura)
   f. "Only your hairdresser knows for sure." (Clairol)
   g. "M'm m'm good." (Campbell's soup)
   h. "Betcha can't eat just one." (Lays potato chips)
   i. "Reach out and touch someone." (ATT)
   j. "The skin you love to touch." (Woodbury soap)
   k. "Even your best friends won't tell you." (Listerine mouthwash)
   l. "Got milk?" (California Milk Processor Board)
   m. "Be all that you can be." (U.S. Army)
   n. "Why ask why, try Bud dry." (Budweiser)
   o. "Have it your way." (Burger King)
   p. "Coke is life!" (Coca-Cola)
   q. "We try harder." (Avis)

4. Discuss the following ads and draw some inferences about their *target audience*.

   a. *American Products You Can Stake Your Life On . . .* TAPCO
   Whether defeating our enemies on the battlefield or protecting your home from an intruder, TAPCO products are designed to support you in accomplishing our mission. TAPCO manufactures and distributes only the best products for your AR-14/M16, AK, SKS, and MINI-14/30.

   b. *When You Go STAG You're Not Alone.*
   Whether you choose the world's only revolutionary factory railed lefty or our rugged righty, our factory trained customer service team will be there to support you. When your life depends on it, know that you are backed up by a lifetime warranty and over 30 years of manufacturing experience.
   When you choose STAG, you're never alone.
   STAG ARMS

   c. It's Not So Much Training
      As It Is
      GOING TO COMBAT EARLY.
      Advanced Urban Warfare Training.
      DARC1.com

5. Select *two* ads to study. Use any of the ads in this chapter or two other print ads. Answer any two of the following:
   a. State how the ads reflect the values of the dominant culture.
   b. State how the ads reflect stereotypical ways of thinking.
   c. State how the ads reflect assumptions about social roles and norms.
   d. State how the ads reflect political realities (patriotism, community ties, political allegiances).
   e. State how the ads reflect racist, sexist, or other prejudicial attitudes.

6. Jon Mandel of MediaCom, a media services agency, said of product placement: "It's got to fit and it can't be stupid. You want it to be noticeable, but not blatant. A lot of people forget that." Study any one TV show, and set out what you see in terms of product placement and its effectiveness.

7. Examine the Culinard ad in Figure 12.2. Answer the following:
   a. How does this ad work to persuade?
   b. How does this ad use humor to persuade?

FIGURE 12.2
As this ad suggests, some stacks of homework are tastier than others. Even college administrators recognize this!

FORGET THE DOG.
MAKE SURE
YOU DON'T EAT
YOUR HOMEWORK.

Come to a school where the main courses are the main courses. At Culinard, we can teach you to be a four-star chef in just 21 months. You'll dice. You'll slice. And when you get out, you'll be able to find your way around the vegetable market and the job market.

CULINARD
Develop a Taste for Success

Reprinted with permission of CULINARD, the Culinary Institute of Virginia College (www.culinard.com).

Issues of Power and Class

On the surface, ads may appear to be "just" trying to sell some product. Not so, says Robert Goldman, who thinks ads are inherently political and never ideologically impartial. In *Reading Ads Socially,* Goldman sets out these four assumptions in advertising:

Goldman's Assumptions in Advertising

Assumption 1: You should think *this* about *that:*
  → *Ads always have some political agenda.*
Assumption 2: $$ = Buy, buy:
  → *Ads assume people are paid for their labor.*
Assumption 3: Poverty doesn't exist:
  → *Ads hide class differences.*
Assumption 4: Need it? Buy it and find happiness:
  → *Ads imply we can purchase happiness, a meaningful life, and an ideal world.*

Let's look at each of these. First, Goldman contends that ads are always prescriptive (you should think *this* about *that*). In his view, ad agencies try to shape our thought processes so that consuming is a way of life. Attached to this is a worldview that favors the individual, self-interest, and excess over the community, altruism, and frugality. The second and third assumptions are that people are employed and have disposable incomes—and that there is no underclass. Ads treat us as if we were all on the same playing field—there are no tiny signs in ads warning us of the financial risks of buying products we cannot afford. The fourth assumption is the most insidious: that happiness is within our grasp—just a purchase away. Not only do we get the product, but we also get to be part of a community of others who share the same values with us. As you apply your critical thinking skills to analyzing ads, keep in mind Goldman's four assumptions, and see for yourself whether his concerns are justified.

Exercises

1. Select two or three ads and see if Goldman's points apply. Examine the ads for political agenda, assumptions, class differences, and presumptions about what money can buy. Be sure to attach the ads.

2. Focusing on *one* type of product (e.g., cars, clothes, or alcohol), compare an ad targeting the wealthy to an ad targeting the working class. Go into detail on what you find that reflects class differences in our society.

3. Find *one* ad that supports creative director Luke Sullivan's assertion that simple = good.

Sullivan explained that consumers are too busy, and sometimes too skeptical, to fall for a long, complicated, cluttered advertisement. "Go to the airport and watch somebody read a magazine," he said. "Take your client with you. The average reader will gloss over ads that are droll or complex, but simple ads will get attention," he said. "People don't have time to slow down to decode our clever ideas," he said. . . . "Simple ads are more memorable, effective, emotional and believable, and are easier for the consumer to notice," Sullivan said. And, as the old Volkswagen Beetle ads demonstrate, simple ads can be timeless. "Simple makes a good ad great," Sullivan said. (Dave Simanoff, "Tis a Gift to Be Simple in Advertising, Sullivan Says," *The Bay Business Journal*, 21 Aug 1998)

4. Discuss the text (ad copy) of the ads below, and note what audience is being targeted.
   a. Ad for Citibank:

Uprooting a tree. Putting down new roots.
After the move, I bought a new couch with my Citi card. And a new rug. 5 lamps. And a secondhand car with 4-wheel drive. But here's the thing—my daughters Jen and Sadie hadn't bought into the idea of moving to Maine. So since I had uprooted them from all their friends, I had the roots and everything else [palm tree pictured in front of Maine house] shipped 1,500 miles. Now we have a little bit of Palm Beach, right off the coast of Portland.
Whatever your story is, your Citi card can help you write it.

   b. Ad for Miraval Resorts:

[Photo of a beautiful blonde women playing a drum, with hair flying, against a background of a red sunset and, off to the right, a large cactus.]
There's life. And then there's living.
Gathered around a bonfire in the high desert of Southern Arizona is the perfect setting For Drumming Under the Stars, Zen Boot Camp or any of the 100 experiences that make every day here enlightening, invigorating and always fun. Miraval. This is living. Begin your journey to the world's favorite resort at MiravalResorts.com or 800.232.3969.
MIRAVAL Tucson.

5. Discuss the text (ad copy) of the ad for Jif™ Snack Nuts, and note what audience is being targeted.

[Upper-left-corner has a photo of a can of dry-roasted peanuts, a jar of cashews, and a can of mixed nuts. Upper right states, "Save $1.00 on any jar of Jif™ Snack Nuts coupon." Remaining lower three-fourths of the page is the ad. Background is dark blue, with a variety of nuts standing like people on a stage that resembles a turntable with "Jif" at the center.]

Every nut wants to be a star, but only a few get chosen.
Jif™ SEARCH.
We have to be choosy. We're Jif.™ Visit jif.com/snacknuts

6. Discuss the text (ad copy) of the two website ads for Harley-Davidson motorcycles, and note what audience is being targeted (and see Figure 12.3).
   a. **Ad 1** for Harley-Davidson:

   > We Don't Do Fear.
   > Neither Should You.
   > Learn How to Get a Limited-Edition Bandana
   > And Learn How to Write Your Own Rally Cry.
   > SCREW-IT. LET'S RIDE.

   b. **Ad 2** for Harley-Davidson:

   > "The richest people on earth don't necessarily have the most money."
   > The FXDF Fat Bob™, Starting at Just $14,795

7. Discuss the text (ad copy) of the ads below that target members of the upper class (you could compare them with ones aimed at those in the lower-middle or working class).
   a. **Ad 1** for International K9 Personalized Training and Sales:

   > This dog can immobilize an intruder in 2.3 seconds. He's also Jack's pony. [Photo of toddler with large German Shepherd.] Call today for free information on how to have the perfect dog. Dog Sales & Training, Executive Protection, Self Defense Education and Bodyguard Services.

FIGURE 12.3 The target audience makes all the difference.

Agency—The Richards Group. Client—Harley Davidson of North Texas. Creative Director—Todd Tilford. Art Director—Bryan Burlison. Copywriter—Todd Tilford. Reprinted with permission of Todd Tilford, The Richards Group.

b. **Ad 2** for Starwood Preferred Guest hotel chains:

A world of experiences, now enhanced. Exceptional, exceeded. [Photo of large, castle-like hotel with sunset in background and small pond and low, plush-green hills in foreground.] New sights to see. Award-winning benefits to embrace. Nine unique hotel brands in 95 countries. Discover your niche among more than 860 participating properties and nine distinctive hotel brands. . . . This year, we welcome two new brands to our expansive list of hotels emerging around the world: *aloft*™, a vision of W Hotels, is alive with energy and unexpected possibilities; and *element*™, inspired by Westin, offers smart design and lifestyle choices to help you thrive while on the road.

c. **Ad 3** for Quark Monitoring Equipment:

They may be your employees, but who do they really work for? Find out exactly where your employees' loyalties lie with one of our high-performance hidden cameras. This fully functional clock radio features a pinhole camera that records a crystal clear video image in virtually any lighting condition. Plus, it allows you to monitor office and home activities in real-time or record them for later viewing. We offer similar systems with covert faces convincingly disguised as smoke detectors, fire sprinklers, picture frames and many other home and office items. CIA tested. CEO approved.

▦ The Verbal Message

In addition to watching for assumptions, we need to be able to dismantle the ad itself. This dismantling, or deconstructing, of ads involves two steps:

1. Analyze the verbal and visual messages of ads
2. Examine the role of images, symbols, and the use of color to create an effect

Let us look at these aspects, starting with the **verbal message,** which is created by the use of words and music. This is the text of the ad—the "ad copy." Some ads rely almost completely on words to create an impact. This could center on a character (e.g., Smokey the Bear), a memorable slogan (e.g., "Just do it"), a testimonial (e.g., Nicole Kidman for Chanel), or a commentary on events or issues in the society (e.g., Benneton's ad series on global issues). When it works, the effect can be dynamite. Look, for instance, at the ad for *Time* magazine shown in Figure 12.4; note how it relies on the verbal message for its effect. One of the more striking types of use of verbal messages in ads involves the appropriation of a homily, a line from a popular song, or a political slogan. For instance, a full-page ad in the *Los Angeles Times* just three days after the 2008 presidential election made liberal use of Senator Obama's campaign slogan, "Yes we can."

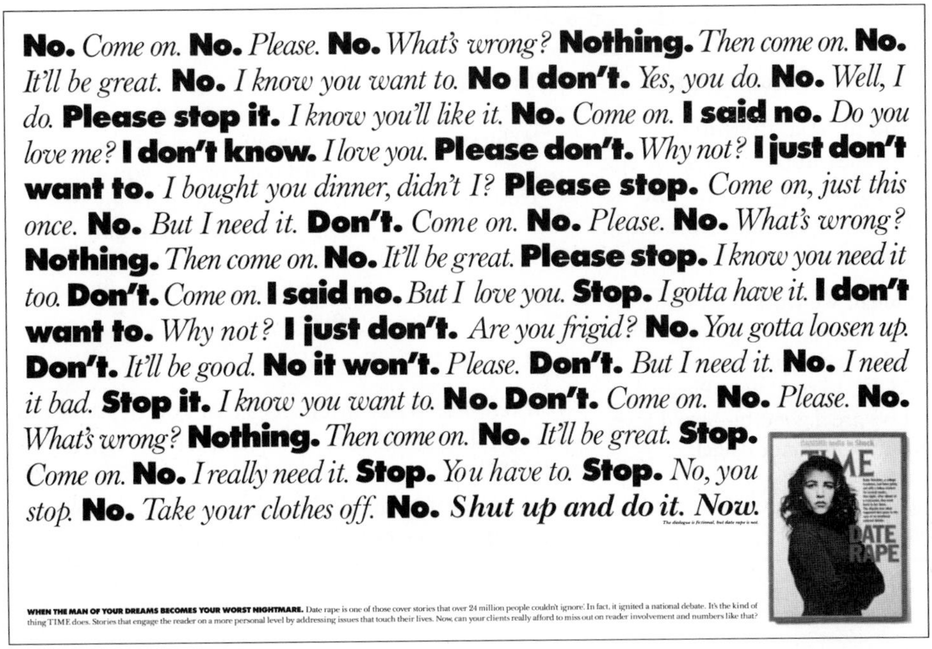

No. *Come on.* **No.** *Please.* **No.** *What's wrong?* **Nothing.** *Then come on.* **No.** *It'll be great.* **No.** *I know you want to.* **No I don't.** *Yes, you do.* **No.** *Well, I do.* **Please stop it.** *I know you'll like it.* **No.** *Come on.* **I said no.** *Do you love me?* **I don't know.** *I love you.* **Please don't.** *Why not?* **I just don't want to.** *I bought you dinner, didn't I?* **Please stop.** *Come on, just this once.* **No.** *But I need it.* **Don't.** *Come on.* **No.** *Please.* **No.** *What's wrong?* **Nothing.** *Then come on.* **No.** *It'll be great.* **Please stop.** *I know you need it too.* **Don't.** *Come on.* **I said no.** *But I love you.* **Stop.** *I gotta have it.* **I don't want to.** *Why not?* **I just don't.** *Are you frigid?* **No.** *You gotta loosen up.* **Don't.** *It'll be good.* **No it won't.** *Please.* **Don't.** *But I need it.* **No.** *I need it bad.* **Stop it.** *I know you want to.* **No. Don't.** *Come on.* **No.** *Please.* **No.** *What's wrong?* **Nothing.** *Then come on.* **No.** *It'll be great.* **Stop.** *Come on.* **No.** *I really need it.* **Stop.** *You have to.* **Stop.** *No, you stop.* **No.** *Take your clothes off.* **No.** *Shut up and do it. Now.*

The dialogue is fictional, but date rape is real.

TIME

DATE RAPE

WHEN THE MAN OF YOUR DREAMS BECOMES YOUR WORST NIGHTMARE. Date rape is one of those cover stories that over 24 million people couldn't ignore. In fact, it ignited a national debate. It's the kind of thing TIME does. Stories that engage the reader on a more personal level by addressing issues that touch their lives. Now, can your clients really afford to miss out on reader involvement and numbers like that?

FIGURE 12.4
For some ads, the verbal message is prominent.

Fallon McElligott. Art Director—Bob Brihn. Copywriter—Phil Hamft. Creative Director—Phil Hamft. Reprinted with permission.

Downtown LA Motors Mercedes-Benz. Celebrate the MBZ winter event. YES WE CAN. YES WE CAN lease you a 2009 C class as low as $429 per month. YES WE CAN make you deals with 0 down. YES WE CAN provide financing as low as 2.9% (on select models). YES WE CAN delay your first payment till Feb 2009 (purchase only). YES WE CAN pull you out of your current lease early. YES WE CAN offer you the best prices and selection of certified preowned Mercedez Benz. And YES WE CAN expand our family heritage of providing exceptional service. That is why we have sold over 60,000 cars since 1970.

It is often hard to forget advertising slogans. Just think how many you can list off the top of your head ("Coke is life," "The ultimate driving machine," etc.). These are often the heart of the verbal message. However, any part of the ad copy counts—including the promises, the discussion of the product, repetition of words or phrases, background dialogue, or buzzwords placed around the product. For example, a 2008 ad for Saturn suggests that consumers are feeling fearful or vulnerable these days:

We've rethought the SUV by designing one that helps **protect** you from every angle. Stabilitrak® **Protects** you against poor road conditions. Onstar® connects and **protects** you in an emergency. The hybrid, with limited availability, helps **protect** the environment. And six air bags **protect** you and yours from them and theirs. The Vue. The compact SUV from the company that's rethinking everything. (emphasis added)

You Tell Me Department

Are You Ready for a Market in Human Eggs?

It seems like you can find almost anything on the Web. Need extra cash? What about being an egg or sperm donor? Try an Internet search. The ad below is for human ova (www.eggdonation.com). Read the ad and then answer the questions below.

Our donors are exceptional. We work with the brightest, most beautiful women in the country. Even though the gift of donation has an immeasurable emotional reward, we'd like to spoil you! Please read on and if you feel we are a good fit—we'd love to hear from you. **Becoming a Donor Angel:**

Gorgeous	Our donors are given beautiful headshots
Reward	We offer the highest level of compensation
Achievement	We recognize you for the extraordinary person you are
Couples	You will feel the pure joy of helping a deserving family
Expensive Gifts	Our donors receive lavish presents in addition to financial compensation

Apply to Be an Egg Donor

You tell me: What inferences can you draw about potential egg donors or "recipients" from this ad? Why do you think there is no suggestion of cost? Applying Goldman's four assumptions, what might we conclude about this ad?

Group or Individual Exercise

If you go to the Harley-Davidson website (www.harley-davidson.com), you will come to a Web page inviting you to write your own "rally cry" (posted 13 May 2008). Set out your assessment of the following as part of Harley-Davidson's marketing. Note the underlined terms allow users to remove the highlighted phrase and insert their own sayings.

WRITE YOUR RALLY CRY
Before you get on the road, get it all off your chest. Click the highlighted words below to create your personal rally cry for the riding seasons.

I DON'T DO FEAR
Over the last——years in the saddle, I've seen <u>my share of conflict in the world</u>, but every time this country has come out stronger than before. Because <u>chrome and asphalt</u> put distance between me and <u>whatever the world can throw at me</u>, freedom and wind outlast hard times. And the rumble of my engine drowns out all the <u>spin on the evening news</u>. If 105 years have proved one thing, it's that <u>fear sucks and it doesn't last long</u>. So screw it, let's ride.

Testimonials

One special kind of verbal message is the **testimonial** or product endorsement. As we know from Chapter 7 on fallacies, if the testimonial is *not* that of an expert in the field in question, then the fallacy of argumentum ad verecundiam is present (false appeal to authority). Testimonials are claims about the product or service by some individual (usually a celebrity or "expert," but sometimes an ordinary person). They have an impact. Researcher Ekant Veer found that "voters who don't watch or read about politics are much more likely to be swayed into supporting a political party which is endorsed by a celebrity" (press release, www.bath.ac.uk/news, 1 Oct 2007). Examples of celebrity endorsements include Miley Cyrus for Disney and Walmart, Gwyneth Paltrow for Este Lauder (cosmetics), Roger Federer for Rolex, Andre Agassi for Longines watches and Mountain Dew, Jessica Alba for L'Oreal, Jackie Chan for Hefty trash bags, Chevy Chase for Doritos, Madonna for Pepsi, and Tiger Woods for Nike, Wheaties, Disney, American Express, and more.

One of the more striking uses of testimonials in advertising history is found in American Express's two-page ads. On the left we see the image of the celebrity, on the right handwritten answers on a form (presumably by the celebrity). The "personal" answers draw us in. For example, we learn that Beyoncé Knowles's proudest accomplishment is her *first* Grammy. Her most unusual gift? Rhinestone-studded pedicure toe spacers, of course! The last entry states that her American Express card is "there for me wherever I go, for whatever I buy." We read this "personal" slice of her life and draw the connection: If we have an American Express card, maybe wherever we go, we can use it for whatever we buy, too.

Testimonials of average folks have marketing power as well. Just think: Here's another ordinary person—just like you and me. They are on our level, and so we assume a level of trust. It's not always easy to decide where to go on vacation, what soap to use, what hair product is best for soft shiny hair, and so on. Or suppose you or someone you know has a problem with gambling. Think how powerful this testimonial might be:

Problem Gambling Helpline 1 877 MY LIMIT

Anonymous ordinary woman 1 [Photo of a middle-aged woman with short, tousled hair gazing off to the right]: "The desperation came from not being able to stop gambling. I made the call to get some help. I found people that really understood me. . ."

Anonymous ordinary woman 2 [Photo of a chubby, blonde, middle-aged woman staring at the camera, unsmiling]: "I was mesmerized. I didn't know that gambling did not affect everyone the way it affected me."

Anonymous ordinary woman 3 [Photo of a worried-looking middle-aged woman with hair pulled back in ponytail]: "The counselor made me understand that there was hope and I have not placed a bet in 6 years."

Treatment is free, confidential and it works.

The Power of Language: Analyzing the Verbal Message

If you remember the slogan, the ad scored a linguistic victory. When combined with catchy or dramatic use of music, the words can be carved onto the inside of our skulls.

In decoding an ad, the verbal message is as important as the visual elements. The ad tells a story. Some ads focus on the product's quality. Some list the key features of the product. Some contrast the competition. Some take an indirect route and focus on the benefits of ownership, such as a particular lifestyle or a membership into a desirable group. (See Figures 12.5 to 12.7.) Watch for the angle and the intended audience.

One advertising classic is the "Got Milk?" campaign (see Figures 12.5 and 12.6). The use of the simple, two-word question has few parallels. It combines a powerful visual message with a snappy, easy-to-remember line. And it has spawned a host of imitators—"Got Mulch?" "Got Termites?" "Got Land?" "Got Faith?" "Got Hope?" (2008 Obama ad). And then there's the National Enquirer's "Got Gossip? We'll pay big bucks. Call or email us." The spin-offs do not detract from the iconic status of the Got Milk ads—they just reinforce them.

FIGURE 12.5
Miley Cyrus/
Hannah Montana
for Got Milk?

Reprinted with the permission of Lowe Worldwide Inc. as Agent for National Fluid Milk Processor Promotion Board.

Pass by Steve.
Body by milk.

Off the court, milk provides the perfect assist.
Its protein helps build muscle and studies suggest teens who choose
milk over sugary drinks tend to be leaner. Staying active,
eating right and drinking three glasses of lowfat or fat free milk a day
helps you look great and stay in shape. Score three for milk.

got milk?

bodybymilk.com

Reprinted with the permission of Lowe Worldwide Inc. as agent for National Fluid Milk Processor Promotion Board.

FIGURE 12.6
Steve Nash for
Got Milk?—
athletes are now
as prominent as
movie stars.

In assessing the verbal message, try a *word study*. Carefully read the ad, watching for key words that emphasize the product's appeal or hook the consumer. Think of words like "sex," "love," "rich," "mysterious," "flavor," "fun," "pleasure," and "satisfying." When repeated over and over, the word (or phrase) acts like a drum beat, punctuating the ad's message.

Checklist for Assessing the Verbal Message—Watch for These:

- Characteristics or qualities of the product
- Consequences of owning the product
- Benefits of this product over rival products
- Comments about the lifestyle that goes with the product

- Use of humor, diversionary tactics, or insults
- Social commentary that may or may not relate to the product
- Use of statistics or statistical claims touting the benefits of the product
- The testimony of ordinary people, so-called experts, or celebrities
- Use of pseudoscientific terms to give weight to the ad's claims
- Fallacies of reasoning or questionable claims

Focusing on the product was once the norm. Just look at the Studebaker ad (Figure 12.9 on page 502). This ad is a good example of presenting the product rather than a mood, a lifestyle, or a political commentary. This ad shows *only* a car; there are no people, plants, or animals populating the ad. At that time (the 1950s), ad agencies probably thought it would be easier for consumers to put *themselves* in the picture, rather than look at someone else in that Studebaker. Using a nuts-and-bolts approach, the ad states some key specifics about the car and informs us that this is a "Common-Sense" car. The phrase "Common-Sense" is repeated five times, driving the point into readers' brains. "Gosh, it makes common sense for me to go buy a Studebaker!" This technique of repetition has continued to the present. As critical thinkers, we might ask ourselves if such repetition has the power to hook people. Things have changed. Now we not only want the car but also want what the car will bring once we own it. This is not what we see in the Studebaker ad.

Exercises

1. Examine the Studebaker ad on page 502. Why do you think it makes a reference to the Volkswagen bug?

2. Do you think it works when an ad for one product refers to a rival product (the competition)? Give the argument for *and* against this approach.

3. Create text for an ad for the car of your dreams in which *no photo or description* of the car itself appears. In the text of your ad (assume it's for the radio, then you don't have to worry about the visual message), explain (a) who your targeted audience is, (b) what you did to appeal to that audience, and (c) what verbal message you intended.

4. Create text for an ad (e.g., as part of an educational or public service campaign) using *one* of Figures 12.7 and 12.8 as your visual base.

5. Discuss how the repetition of the word "dreams" is used in this 2008 ad for Disney Parks, and note what effect Disney is trying to achieve.

   WHERE DREAMS COME TRUE.
   This year, celebrate your family's dreams in the most magical way. Join us during Disney's Year of a Million Dreams celebration. It's the most wonderful time to create the lifelong memories only Disney can. Visit disneyparks.com or call 407-W-Disney, and make your family's dreams come true.

Photograph by Wanda Teays. Copyright 2008.

FIGURE 12.7
Create a public service ad to go with this photo.

Photograph by Wanda Teays. Copyright 2008.

FIGURE 12.8
Create a public service ad to go with this photo.

6. In an ad for DNA testing (www.DNATesting.com), we see a picture of a (white) man seated in the grass, his legs crossed, with a small (white) boy on his lap. Both have very big smiles on their faces, as if they had not a care in the world. The copy, however, casts a bit of a shadow (or does it?). Discuss the verbal message here:

For Questions Only DNA Can Answer.
At home DNA Paternity Testing is easy and affordable
With **IDENTIGENE©**. The leading brand in personal DNA
Testing is now available in retail stores.
Fast. Accurate. Confidential.
1. Use cheek swabs to collect DNA samples.
2. Send samples in our postage-paid mailing envelope.
3. Results will be made available in 3 to 5 days.

7. Discuss the verbal message for this ad for Boeing aircraft:

WHERE THE SECRETS TO THE UNIVERSE ARE KEPT
The answers do not lie in technology. Technology is but a stepping stone to the next question. We are fueled by a restless imagination; and endless sense of wonder that has brought our world closer together and led us ever deeper into space. What we've discovered along the way is that all the secrets to the universe are contained in the boundless reaches of the human mind.

8. Select *one* of the following and write down your analysis of its verbal message, drawing from the elements listed above:

   a. **09 CTS**
      In today's luxury game, the real question isn't about whether
      your car has French-stitched interior accents or an available
      40-gig hard-drive... No, in today's luxury game, the real question
      is, when you turn your car on, does it return the favor?
      WHEN YOU TURN YOUR CAR ON, DOES IT RETURN THE FAVOR?
      Cadillac

   b. With zero carbs,
      Jell-O can help you
      Keep the jiggle
      Out of your wiggle.

   c. **MONT BLANC.**
      Helping others gives success true meaning.
      Encouraging future musical talent is one of the primary aims
      of Montblanc and Montblanc's brand ambassador,
      Lang Lang. Together with the world-renowned pianist,
      We support the Lang Lang International Musical Foundation.
      Lang Lang wears the Montblanc TimeWalker Chronograph Automatic,
      Featuring a self-winding mechanical movement in a 43-mm steel case
      With skeleton horns. Swiss made by Montblanc.

9. Study *one* of the following ads. Use the checklist on pages 497–498 to analyze the verbal message.
   a. Ad for Rolex watch:

   In the hearts of the truly great, PERFECTION is never achieved.

   Only endlessly pursued.
   When Haydn, Handel and Vivaldi put pen to paper, the voice they were writing to could have been none other than Cecilia Bartoli's. She's taken the most famous operas and made them national treasures. She's taken the most obscure operas and made them famous. She's taken classic arias and redefined them, building them dramatically. As she continues to top "Best of Year" lists all around the world, her voice reminds us that perfection is an endless pursuit. Oyster Perpetual Lady-Date Just Pearlmaster. **ROLEX.**

   b. Ad for Chevy Beretta GT:

   The advantage of being in control.

   Taking matters into your own hands is an idea you wholeheartedly embrace. It lets you do what you want, when you want—while having as much fun as you want. That's the idea behind rack-and-pinion steering.

   Rack-and-pinion steering acts like a two-way transmitter between you and the front wheels of your car. Turn the wheel and the pinion (a gear) at the end of the steering column moves over a bar called (you guessed it) a rack to point your wheels in the right direction. Your car responds instantly. Accurately. Almost instinctively. It also sends the feel of the road back to you, letting you fine-tune your driving. That's what makes precision handling precise.

   And, while nearly every Chevy we sell comes with the feel-good control of rack-and-pinion steering, including the Beretta GT, all of them come with the bottom-line value of a great Chevy price.

   So try one, and take a turn for the better.

▦ The Visual Message

We are a visual culture. We judge, buy, consume, or desire all sorts of things based on their visual appeal. Advertisers know this. We do not normally want to see things that are ugly or unpleasant, unless they are presented with humor. We want to see beauty and images of happiness, intimacy, and satisfaction. We like to see images of success, things working correctly, and problems being solved. Connected with these images are products. The goal is to get the consumer to link the two (the images and the products) together. This is a variation of the message in the movie *Field of Dreams:* "If you build it, they will come." In advertising, "If you buy it, they (all sorts of neat things) will come."

The desire is for much more than mere ownership. We yearn for what the product represents and the lifestyle that accompanies it. Ads used to focus almost

FIGURE 12.9
Ads of the 1950s focused on the product, rather than a mood or lifestyle.

entirely on the product, spelling out what it could do for us (see the Studebaker ad in Figure 12.9). For example, Pepsodent ads of the 1950s and 1960s ("You'll wonder where the yellow went . . .") presented images of yellow teeth that were magically transformed into gleaming white jewels. The ad implied that yellow teeth were the only things standing in the way of being adored. Attaining such popularity was directly related to the use of the product.

One of the most powerful ad campaigns, with strong visual and verbal components, is that of the Energizer Bunny (see Figure 12.1). The pink, drum-playing bunny—now an icon—that keeps going and going caught the public's eye when it first appeared in 1989, and it has since carved a niche in our cultural landscape. These ads are classics because of their wit, aesthetic impact, and endearing qualities. In comparing the bunny's endurance to that of the Energizer batteries, we are directed to the product's merits. This alone is striking. In addition, the ad has a metaphysical component in linking the bunny to the viewer and offering words of wisdom. Like the bunny, we, too, should never give up. The sheer optimism and vision resonates with the audience.

Permission granted by Perrier Group of America.

FIGURE 12.10
Can you see how this ad for Perrier demonstrates the power of a visual message?

Look also at the Perrier ad in Figure 12.10. This advertisement is effective because it is both visually striking and thought provoking. It plays with social stereotypes by showing a couple in an old pickup with empty Perrier bottles in the truck bed, suggesting that Perrier is something an ordinary guy and gal from the back roads of Texas would enjoy. The Perrier ad is clever but not shocking.

In contrast, some ads use in-your-face approaches to take consumers by surprise and create a kind of disequilibrium in their brains. For example, Benetton (the clothing manufacturer) created an international furor with ads depicting illness, suffering, and even death. These ads included such images as a bird drenched with oil, a dying AIDS patient, and a prisoner on death row. The images have nothing to do with the product (clothes). But they do make a political statement, calling up Robert Goldman's first assumption about the ideological aspect of ads.

The Cast of Characters

One aspect of the visual message is the use of characters identified with the product (e.g., the Energizer Bunny, the Blue Man Group, the Pillsbury Doughboy, Mr. Clean, Joe Camel, the Jolly Green Giant, Mr. Peanut, and Aunt Jemima). Over time the characters take on mythic status and become cultural markers. More

You Tell Me Department

Let's face it, only an arsonist would not be moved by Smokey's warnings about the danger of forest fires and steps to take to help prevent wildfires. At this point, Smokey the Bear is as much a cultural icon as an advertising legend. Look at the two images of Smokey and the campaign messages on these few pages. For more on the ad campaign, visit the website.

Answer the following:

1. Which ad do you consider most effective? List your reasons why.
2. Assume you have been hired by the Forestry Service to target teenagers and college-age adults so they will be drawn to Smokey and his message. What would you do with the Smokey ads to reach this audience?

recent Energizer ads don't even have to show the bunny himself—just the shadow of the bunny carries the "Keep Going" message onward. It is assumed that the audience knows the character so well that a shadow can trigger a response.

Companies run risks when they attempt to update the characters, changing their appearance or "personalities." Will the consumer-public take kindly to the Pillsbury Doughboy losing his chubby form, Aunt Jemima flipping crepes instead of pancakes, or the Jolly Green Giant yearning to wear a red tie? Not necessarily.

> Someone thinks about such questions. For instance, someone decided that Mr. Peanut needed a transformation. . . . "After decades of presenting Mr. Peanut, its venerable brand character, as a dignified dandy, meant to be timeless in his appeal, Planters is giving him a far more contemporary persona intended to better connect with consumers," reports popular culture scholar, Stuart Elliot. For that reason, we may be seeing Mr. Peanut shooting some hoops and showing off some moves on the dance floor instead of crossing his legs while holding a nice cane. It may sound minor, but Elliot notes that "much is at stake if shoppers reject the personality transplant. Disapproval could diminish the value of the character." ("Thoroughly Modern Mr. Peanut," *The New York Times,* 19 Mar 2004)

Evolution of an Ad Campaign

Who doesn't know the refrain "Only you can prevent forest fires"? The voice of Smokey the Bear is embedded in the heads of millions. He appeared on the scene in the early 1950s and has been going strong since. This is the longest public service campaign in U.S. history. (See Figures 12.11 and 12.12.)

Smokey was created in 1944 by the U.S. Forestry Service. The "the" in "Smokey the Bear" evidently traces back to the songwriters of Smokey's anthem, who needed a "the" to maintain the rhythm. The ad campaign's message remained unchanged until 2001, when the increasing number of wildfires in the nation's wild lands spurred a new focus. For other interesting historical tidbits, go to the website (www.smokeybear.com).

Smokey the Bear is not the only long-term ad icon. There is also Snap, Crackle, and Pop (www.Kelloggs.com); Aunt Jemima (www.auntjemima.com); and the

Copyright U.S. Forestry Service. Reprinted with permission.

FIGURE **12.11**
Smokey is our friend—not a vicious bear (1954)!

Jolly Green Giant (www.bettycrocker.com), among others. After a point, such characters enter the cultural lexicon.

The Use of Color and Symbols

Some ads are in black and white, and the strong lines are part of the visual message. Other ads rely on color to create a mood or call up associations. Many ads use patriotic symbols, such as flag motifs, eagles flying majestically across the page, and the Statue of Liberty, national memorials, or other historical monuments. Such symbols often reinforce the copy—for example, "America's number one pizza" or "The motor oil that Americans trust"—linking loyalty to what we consume. They also make us feel safe, at home in a world that is not always safe or homey. However, appeals to patriotism in ads often exhibit the ad populum fallacy (see Chapter 7).

Vivid colors and images can create unique and eye-catching ads, as with the ads for Absolut Vodka shown in Figures 12.13 and 12.14. These ads are not aimed at minors, and the company has taken a strong stand against targeting those who

FIGURE 12.12
After five-plus decades, Smokey has become part of the cultural fabric. A hat or mask jogs the brain. At this point, Smokey has achieved iconic status.

Copyright U.S. Forestry Service. Reprinted with permission.

are underage. The Absolut ads succeed because of their sophisticated, and at times even abstract, nature. They are closer to mental puzzles than sales pitches, as they challenge the limits of minimalism.

(In granting permission for including these ads in this text, Seagram & Sons intends that they be used in conjunction with exercises for developing critical thinking skills. They are not presented here to condone, or even tolerate, the consumption of alcoholic beverages by minors. Rather, Seagram & Sons takes seriously the social responsibility to restrict Absolut advertising to people over 21 years of age.)

Embedded Advertising: Product Placement

Whereas ads of 20 or 30 years ago raved about the product, recent ads tend to be more contextual. The product may be embedded within the lifestyle presented

You Tell Me Department

Move Over, Marlboro Man?

Given the impact of anime on the West, perhaps the time of the samurai has come. Or maybe it's neither cowboy nor samurai—could today's hero be a warrior from *Lord of the Rings*? Or perhaps a mythic hybrid, like *Bat*man or *Spider*-Man or *Wolf*man? Over a decade ago, the president of Tech Marketing Inc. said of the power of the Marlboro Man in cigarette advertising: "The mythical fighting man in our culture *is* a cowboy. He's our samurai. . . . You have to understand what smoking's all about. We as a society have abandoned tribal initiation rites, and cigarettes are a substitute" ("Uncle Sam Is No Match for the Marlboro Man," *The New York Times,* 27 Aug 1995).

You tell me: Is that still true? If you were targeting the under-30 market, what would you use as the "mythical fighting man"?

FIGURE 12.13
Absolut country of Sweden vodka and logo, Absolut, Absolut bottle design, and Absolut calligraphy are trademarks owned by V&S Vin & Sprit AB. © V&S Vin & Sprit AB.

Under permission by V&S Vin & Sprit AB.

FIGURE 12.14
Absolutely one of
the Seven Deadly
Sins.

Under permission by V&S Vin & Sprit AB

rather than subject to a hard sell. **Embedded advertising** is advertising incorporated into broadcast programming, such as a TV show, movie trailer, YouTube video, or video game, rather than into a stand-alone advertisement ("Advertising Issues on Washington's Agenda for 2008," Broadcast Law Blog, 14 Jan 2008). When they work, these ads can be very effective. No mention is explicitly made about the product: We connect the dots. We "read" the copy and view the images with a sense of familiarity and acceptance. The logo or the slogan sparks a chain of associations between the product and a parallel universe we'd like to inhabit.

It's hard to see a movie these days without being subjected to product placement—the product is incorporated into the lives of the characters on screen. Take one example—jello. In the Jell-O website's history section, we discover the following:

JELL-O® gelatin and pudding have been featured and/or mentioned in many Hollywood movies, including *Some Like It Hot* with Marilyn Monroe [and] Steven Spielberg's *Jurassic Park* and teamed up with the video release of *Mighty Morphin*

Power Rangers: The Movie. In addition, they have played parts in *Kindergarten Cop, Corrina, Corrina, My Best Friend's Wedding, The Muse,* and *Reindeer Games.* (Kraft Foods, www.kraftfoods.com)

In 2007, British movie trailers had embedded advertising—as, for example, for the movie *The Bourne Ultimatum.* Now embedded ads are also found in the virtual world, as product placement has shown up in Second Life. Embedded advertising's appeal is that it comes much closer to guaranteeing an audience than do traditional TV ads (which are often a catalyst for a break).

The result is a sort of *covert advertising*—in contrast to overt advertising of a product or service. YouTube, among others, is also experimenting with overlaid advertisements. Overlaid advertising is a form of microadvertising at the bottom or bottom corner of the video. For example, overlaid ads sometimes use a text or text-plus image to promote the next episode of a TV show.

Embedded advertising sounds like a dream come true for ad agencies. In fact, one such company, MirriAd, has declared that they embed the brand "into the heart of the content. The presentation of the brand is flawless, and it cannot be missed. Yet it is unobtrusive" (www.mirriad.com). However, digital ad producer Andy Kinsella says, "I'm not sure I like the idea of advertising mixed with content in such a way, especially when the viewer doesn't know or understand what's happening" ("Advertising Blended with Content—Welcome 'Embedded Advertising,'" Andykinsella.com 3 Mar 2008).

Should there be some form of accountability with regard to embedded advertising? A 2003 episode of the TV show *House* did just that. At the end of the credits was the following: "Rioux Vision, Inc. promotional consideration furnished by GE Healthcare, Humanscale, Artromick International, Inc., Sota Turntables, Hewlett-Packard, Dell, Saeco, USA." Is this one of those "gotcha" moments? Is this a tiny invasion of privacy? Such issues arise for consumers.

Group or Individual Exercise

Directions: Read about product placement in video games, and then answer the questions that follow.

Crouched in military fatigues, you peer through night-vision goggles and brandish a semiautomatic gun as you hunt down terrorists who've overtaken Las Vegas. . . . While patrolling a neon-decorated side street in the video game "Rainbow Six Vegas," you spot a jar of body wash. You spray the container with bullets, and voila! A 60-second video of whimsical bloopers pops up, and billboard advertisements of scantily clad women hawk Unilever Corp.'s Axe shower gel: "Score with Axe."

Welcome to the new world of video gaming, where software companies are becoming more imaginative in wringing money from gamers. In-game advertising has been going on for years as marketers try to reach people who've largely stopped watching television. . . . Veterans of the $7 billion U.S. video game market defend the corporate co-option of the techniques once solely the realm of techies: If Hollywood has been employing product placement and other unconventional marketing tricks for years, why not the game industry? (Rachel Konrad, "Software Companies Find Revenue Outlet with Embedded Advertising," *Lubbock [Texas] News*, 6 Jan 2007)

Answer the following:

1. Do you agree with the view that, if Hollywood uses product placement "and other unconventional marketing tricks," then the video game industry should be able to do the same? Set out an argument with three or four reasons for or against allowing embedded ads in video games.
2. The comparison of video games to Hollywood movies requires us to consider both similarities and differences. (See Chapter 6 for a review of analogies.) Can you think of *key differences* when evaluating the argument that embedded ads in video games should be acceptable?

Winners and Losers in Advertising

Some ads suggest that we "deserve" the product being advertised by being cool or attractive. This approach assumes we want to enter that parallel universe where people are having such a nice life—but is this assumption unwarranted? The ads make the winner–loser demarcation clear, as a memorable ad campaign for Foster Farm chickens illustrates. Two chickens try to pass themselves off as Foster Farm chickens, but telltale evidence (such as a half-eaten bag of French fries) gives them away. They are failures, rejects trying to be members of a club they can never join. We laugh—but our laughter masks the fear that, like the second-class chickens masquerading as the real thing, we too, might be pretending to be more than we are.

Ads sometimes exploit this fear by presenting "winners" or "losers" who may or may not succeed in spite of our assumptions. Consider the mythology of the ad—its story and the images and symbols it employs to tell it. Assess the ad's overall effectiveness in relaying messages not only about the product but also about how we ought to live. For example, some ads show "losers" who turn the tables and get the upper hand—"loser" no more. We see this in the Diet Coke ad in Figure 12.15. The figure contains only one of a series of frames, which reads: "I can't believe he dumped me. Well, he wasn't exactly Prince Charming. Imagine dating a guy who belches the national anthem. And he did kiss like a mackerel. Maybe my next boyfriend won't give me an I.O.U. for my birthday. And if he's this hairy now, what's he gonna look like in five years? I can't believe he dumped me." Look also at the success story presented in Figure 12.16 on page 512.

Reprinted with the permission of the Coca-Cola Company.

FIGURE 12.15
Drinking Diet
Coke can help
us get over life's
indignities.

Exercises

1. Focusing on color, find three ads: (a) one that is particularly striking or appealing in terms of the use of color or visual images, (b) one that is visually disturbing or unappealing, and (c) one that is boring or visually ineffective. Briefly explain why you judged them as you did.

2. Collect five to six print ads for the same type of product (e.g., cigarettes, perfume, cars, or watches). Be sure your ads are in color, not black and white. State (a) which ad is most effective in its use of color, (b) what symbols, images, and themes are used, and (c) what the collection reveal about us as a society.

3. Suppose you want to study contemporary North American society but all you can use in your study are advertisements. Gather at least 10 ads across a range of products. On the basis of your study, what can you infer about this society?

4. Given the same batch of ads you collected in question 3 (or a new batch, if you are ambitious), what can you infer about societal attitudes toward men?

5. Given the same batch of ads that you collected in question 3 (or a new batch, if you are ambitious), what can you infer about societal attitudes toward women?

6. Gather five print ads on one theme (e.g., cosmetics, cars, cigarettes, shoes, or toys). What patterns emerge from studying these ads? What overall message is there? Are there any aspects or messages that cause you concern? Go into detail.

7. Do a study of ads or product websites targeting children. Gather five print ads aimed at children or teenagers (specify which). What patterns emerge in these ads? Are there any aspects or messages that cause you concern? Go into detail.

Ads with a Social or Political Theme

Given the potential to reach a wide audience, nonprofit groups often turn to ads. Politicians figured this out long ago, as we see in carefully orchestrated political campaigns. If we can sell people on a particular car or cell phone, we ought to be able to sell them on one aspiring politician over another. There are websites

FIGURE 12.16
Sheer
exuberance—a
winning trait.

Reprinted with the permission of Lowe Worldwide, Inc., as agent for National Fluid Milk Processor Promotion Board.

that provide surveys of political advertising over the years. See, for example, the Museum of the Moving Images website (livingroomcandidate.org) for political campaign ads going back to 1952 and the Presidents USA site (www.president-susa.net) for presidential candidates' slogans.

Organized groups can reach the general public with a public service campaign. Let us look at ads that carry a social message. Groups concerned about social, political, or environmental causes regularly use ad campaigns to get their message to a wide audience. For example, Smoke Free Movies, the American Cancer Society, and the American Lung Association all present strong health-related messages. Antismoking ad campaigns have been effective in persuading people either to stop or to avoid starting smoking. It would be valuable to compare antismoking ads to ads put out by the tobacco industry. R. J. Reynolds refused permission for inclusion of their ads in this textbook, given that the primary audience of this book is under the age of 21. Consequently, you won't see their ads in this book, but you can readily find cigarette advertising online. (See, for example, the Philip Morris Ad Archive, www.pmadarchive.com, *Adland,* www.ad-rag.com, and the Smithsonian Ad Archives, www.americanhistory .si.edu/archives/d-7.htm.)

Exercises

1. Looking at the American Lung Association ad shown in Figure 12.17, discuss how effective you think it is, including its verbal and visual message.

2. Pick a political or social issue that you care deeply about. Assume you are creating an ad for your side of the issue and your audience is radio listeners (so you do not need to do any visuals). Write (or create) an ad that would present your position and motivate a listener to act.

3. Study the following public service radio commercial:

   PATRICK REYNOLDS: Do you know what's in cigarettes? I can tell you right now the answer is no. Because the last thing tobacco companies want is for you to know how many poisonous chemicals there are in cigarettes. And there are plenty. Stuff like formaldehyde, cyanide, in fact, some of the chemicals in cigarettes are so poisonous that it's illegal to dump them into landfills.

   But apparently, tobacco companies think it's okay to dump them into our lungs. The worst thing is, they do it without telling you. Because you won't find a list of the chemicals anywhere on the pack or in their ads. I'm Patrick Reynolds. My grandfather founded the R. J. Reynolds tobacco company. That means my family's name is on the side of more than seven billion cigarette packs a year. Why am I telling you this? I want my family to be on the right side for a change.

   ANNOUNCER: A message from the Massachusetts Department of Public Health.

4. Create a public service *radio* ad on any *one* of the following: Gang violence, substance abuse, animal rights, get out the vote, eating a balanced diet,

FIGURE 12.17
This public service ad from the American Lung Association dramatically raises concerns about air pollution.

Permission granted by the American Lung Association of Los Angeles County.

ODDS ARE THAT LOS ANGELES WILL SOON BE SETTING ANOTHER FASHION TREND.

It isn't so farfetched. The air in Los Angeles isn't only the dirtiest in the nation, it's the deadliest. Long-term exposure can lead to asthma, bronchitis and emphysema. As well as increasing the risk of death from lung and heart disease. But together, we can turn things around. For more information, call 1-800-LUNG-USA or visit www.lalung.org. And help us put air pollution out of style.

✝ AMERICAN LUNG ASSOCIATION. of Los Angeles County

Photo: Jim Fett

LET'S CLEAR THE AIR.

helping children learn to read, being a companion to an elderly person, planting gardens to fight urban decay, sexual harassment, or date rape. Be sure to include a brief statement explaining what you hope to achieve in your ad. (This means you only have to create a text—suggesting musical accompaniment is optional.)

Political Messages and Manipulation

The government also uses public service advertising. For example, it provided warnings about terrorism (see examples on the Ad Council website, www.adcouncil.org). There were also warnings during the Cold War. In the 1950s, schools had students doing bomb drills and hiding under school desks, as if by doing so they'd survive a nuclear attack. The U.S. Civil Defense Agency put out posters to "educate" (cynics would say "brainwash") citizens to prepare them for an atomic war.

Reprinted with permission of the Still Pictures Unit of the National Archives.

FIGURE **12.18**
"Misinformation" campaigns are not new—just look at this public "service" ad from the 1950s.

One such example is a poster that pictured a little girl sitting at a desk with her head resting on her hands, as if she were thinking to herself (see Figure 12.18). The question is: "What happens to us if the bomb drops?" The ad is directed to "Mummy," who is told that an atomic war bears some resemblance to natural phenomena. Specifically, "An atomic blast is something like a tornado, a fire and an explosion all rolled into one." Posted clearly in a boxed area is a list of "official disaster first-aid items," such as four triangular bandages, 12 sterile gauze pads, Castor oil eye drops, and two large emergency dressings, among other minor items to help address the (obviously minor!) wounds you'd get in an atomic blast.

This "public service" ad contains a number of unwarranted assumptions, and it rates as a form of misinformation intended to manipulate the audience. Perhaps most egregious is the implication that atomic war is survivable—the wounds will just need a little field dressing.

Exercises

1. Study the attempts to make the idea of atomic war palatable in the U.S. Civil Service ad "Mummy." Examine the visual message of the ad, discuss how the child is used to "sell" the message.

2. Study recent government public service ads related to terrorism or national security, and note similarities and differences to the "Mummy" ad.

3. Create a public service ad campaign (you can create a radio spot if you want to just write the copy). You might focus on driving energy—efficient vehicles, promoting environmentally conscious farming, becoming a big brother or big sister for a child in need, or doing volunteer work (e.g., at schools, hospitals, or old folks' homes), or lending a helping hand to victims of natural disasters.

4. Thinking in terms of a radio program as the vehicle of communication, create a public service warning for any *one* of these:
   a. A hantavirus outbreak in New Mexico and Arizona
   b. E. coli in drinking water at Kendall Elementary School in Sumas, Washington
   c. Risks of pesticide exposure from aerial spraying of crops outside Bakersfield
   d. Salmonella-contaminated peanut butter traced back to The Peanut Corp. plant in Georgia
   e. Ashes and smoke from a major fire in San Diego County, California

5. Create a public service radio ad for *one* of the following:
   a. An outbreak of SARS (highly contagious, potentially fatal respiratory disease) in Toronto, Canada
   b. A botched batch of designer heroin that can paralyze its users
   c. An allergy alert for undeclared peanuts or almonds in Neighbors Coffee of Oklahoma City
   d. Anthrax scares at abortion clinics

6. Looking over your public service ad, state your targeted audience, your intended goal, and how your ad will be able to reach the intended audience.

The Global Dimension

Fighting Big Tobacco

Cigarette companies are seeking to expand their markets. Read over some of the consequences of their "progress," and then answer the questions that follow.

While smoking rates in developed countries have slowly declined, they have shot up dramatically in some developing counties, where Philip Morris International (PMI) is a major player. These include Pakistan (up 42% since 2001), Ukraine (up 36%), and Argentina (up 18%). PMI stands to rank as the world's largest nongovernment tobacco company, with sales volume totaling more than four times that of its U.S. sibling. In 2006, PMI had revenue of $48.26 billion, compared with $18.47 billion at Philip Morris USA. ("Philip Morris Readies Aggressive Global Push," *Wall Street Journal,* 29 Jan 2008)

Given the fast-changing legislative climate around the globe, "manufacturers are needing to spot potential first, act rapidly on a national level rather than on a regional level," says Zora Milenkovic, head tobacco analyst for the research firm Euromonitor International. ("Philip Morris Readies Aggressive Global Push," *Wall Street Journal,* 29 Jan 2008)

In the United States, more than 21 million adult women and 1.8 million girls [in the year 2007] smoke cigarettes, putting them at risk for heart attacks, strokes, lung cancer, emphysema and other life-threatening illnesses. As a result, more than 178,400 women die of smoking-caused disease each year, with additional deaths caused by the use of other tobacco products such as smokeless tobacco. Since 1987, lung cancer has been the leading cancer killer among women, surpassing breast cancer. In the United States, smoking rates among males and females in high school are almost equal (22.9 for males and 23.0 for females), and 18.1 percent of adult women

are current smokers. (Quit Smoking Pro, 30 Sep 2007)

China has long been identified as the most important international cigarette market, now and in the future—O'Sullivan and Chapman called China the "ultimate prize" among the world's emerging tobacco markets. Almost two-thirds of Chinese men (63%), and 3.8% of Chinese women, are smokers, giving a total of 350 million smokers in China, with more on the way. Young Chinese women are likely to be an important target group for growth for Big Tobacco. (Thomas E. Novotny, *Plos Medicine,* 18 Jul 2006)

Tobacco advertising that targets teens is putting half-a-billion young Asians at risk for tobacco-related diseases, says the Asia-Pacific director of the World Health Organization [WHO]. In a statement issued on the eve of the WHO-designated "World No Tobacco Day," Shigeru Omi said the tobacco industry's marketing efforts aim to persuade half-a-billion young people in the Western Pacific to try their first cigarette, Agence France-Presse reported. "Youngsters are led to believe that certain types of cigarettes do not contain nicotine, when in fact they do," Omi said. He accused tobacco companies of "falsely associating use of their products with desirable qualities such as glamour, energy and sex appeal, as well as exciting outdoor activities and adventure." ("Health Highlights," *U.S. News and World Report,* 30 May 2008)

Answer the following:

1. Find two or three tobacco ads aimed at any of the targeted groups mentioned (women, children, Asian teens, etc.). Note the ways in which the ads appeal to the group in question.

2. Can you think of a way to counter this sort of advertising? Offer some suggestions.

CASE STUDY

The Pizza Wars

The Pizza Wars have finally ended. They started with Pizza Hut declaring "war" on poor-quality pizza and daring anyone to come up with a better pizza. Papa John's ad, "Better Ingredients. Better Pizza," hit Pizza Hut like a torpedo. Pizza Hut sued Papa John's, arguing that this constituted false advertising.

The excerpt below is from Donald M. Gindy's "True Lies" (*Daily (Law) Journal*, 26 Jun 2001). Papa John's claimed that its "vine ripened tomatoes" were superior to the "remanufactured tomato sauce" used by Pizza Hut. Plus, its fresh dough and filtered water created a better-tasting pizza.

True Lies

Donald M. Gindy

With a resounding thud, the pizza wars ended March 19, when the U.S. Supreme Court refused to review the decision of the 5th U.S. Circuit Court of Appeals in *Pizza Hut Inc. v. Papa John's International Inc.* (2001). The nature of the lawsuit was a claim of false advertising under the Lanham Act allegedly committed by Papa John's when it claimed "Better Ingredients. Better Pizza."

Pizza Hut threw down the gauntlet as its president, from the deck of a World War II aircraft carrier, declared "war" on poor-quality pizza. Pizza Hut "dared" anyone to come up with a better pizza. At about the same time, Papa John's was launching a new advertising campaign proclaiming that it sold a better pizza because it used better ingredients. The matter went to trial in Dallas, resulting in a verdict in favor of Pizza Hut. Under the Lanham Act, "a plaintiff must demonstrate that the commercial advertisement or promotion is either literally false, or that it is likely to mislead and confuse consumers." Pizza Hut relied on a theory that Papa John's ads were deceptive and were intended to mislead purchasers of pizza. . . .

But was Papa John's ad mere "puffery"? That is to say, was the claim an expression of opinion or a type of boasting on which no reasonable person would rely? The court concluded that "Better ingredients. Better Pizza," standing alone, would not mislead consumers. But Papa John's lost its bragging rights when it coupled the slogan with misleading statements of specific differences in the ingredients used.

Pizza Hut asserted that its competitor had placed before the public "a measurable claim, capable of being proved false or of being reasonably interpreted as a statement of objective fact." Papa John's claimed that its "vine ripened tomatoes" were superior to the "remanufactured tomato sauce" used by Pizza Hut and that its fresh dough and filtered water created a better-tasting pizza. By pointing to specific differences between itself and Pizza Hut and by failing to present at trial any scientific support or the results of independent surveys to substantiate its claims (such as taste tests), Papa John's had, in fact, left the arena of opinion and entered the realm of quantifiable fact. As a result, it subjected itself to a claim that it misled consumers.

However, the burden of proving false advertising falls on the shoulders of Pizza Hut. It is essential [for Pizza Hut] to prove not how consumers would react but how they actually do react. The test thus becomes, assuming that the ads were misleading, whether they actually influence a reasonable consumer in his or her purchasing decision. Since the court found that Pizza Hut had neglected to present such evidence, it had failed to satisfy the element of the cause of action relating to the "materiality" of Papa John's ads. In the absence of such a survey, Pizza Hut's entire action had to fail.

Answer the following:

1. Do you have enough information to conclude that Papa John's ad was false advertising?

2. If not, what would you need to know—what questions would you want answered—before you could decide who won the war?

3. State the strongest points of both sides (indicate which is which!).

Source: Donald M. Gindy practices intellectual-property law in Century City. © 2000 Daily Journal Corporation. All rights reserved. Reprinted with the permission of the Daily Journal Corporation.

CHAPTER THIRTEEN

Web Sight: Critical Thinking and the Internet

Knowledge and information are key drivers of human freedom, growth, well-being and progress. The Internet and other networked information technologies are capable of delivering this potential widely and effectively. They can help people listen, but can also help them speak and be heard.

BERKMAN CENTER FOR INTERNET & SOCIETY, Harvard University

A mythic being central to the Laguna Pueblo culture is Spiderwoman, who is so powerful that she can *think* things into being. She spins a web of stories that can transform the world. Language becomes prayer, ceremony, and ritual as she weaves the web linking people to ceremonies and to the earth. This is a positive force: "Their evil is mighty but it can't stand up to our stories."

We reaffirm this powerful link between people every time we access the Internet. We reach out into the universe when we use email, go online for technical support, access a database or a library catalog, or use a **URL** (uniform resource locator) to call up a website. Each **www** we type reminds us that we are inextricably bound to one another in the **World Wide Web**. We are globally as one, tied by a web that allows us to traverse thousands of miles in a matter of seconds or minutes. It is truly an astonishing resource.

The Internet has fundamentally changed our lives. It has the potential to democratize knowledge by making available a seemingly limitless range of possibilities for investigation and the communication of ideas and information. It has no geographical boundaries: It doesn't matter if you live in a penthouse or a shack, a fleabag motel or a swanky suite, a yurt on top of Mount Tamalpais or the backseat of your car in Fresno. It truly is a *worldwide* web. Whether you are in New

York City or Montreal, Tijuana or Taiwan, Cape Dorset or Guadalajara, you can go online and access products and services, and obtain phone numbers, addresses, and directions from one place to another, along with a wealth of information.

The Internet has the potential to level the playing field by allowing us to expand our knowledge base and communicate across virtually all borders and boundaries. The exponential growth of its use is staggering as we see:

- In 1994, there were approximately 10,000 Web servers.
- In 1999, there were an estimated 10 million Web servers and 146 million people connected to the Internet (see James Gillies and Robert Cailliau, *How the Web Was Born*).
- In 2005, an estimated 218.4 million North Americans and 816.4 million people worldwide were Internet users (according to Nielson Net ratings).
- In 2009, there were 199 million Internet users in the United States, according to the Pew Research Center.

This resource requires either a wireless hub or a reliable telephone line and electricity—and access to a computer. This means the Internet is not available to everyone. Witness the low Internet use by Africans and Appalachians alike. Once we provide global access to the Internet, the resulting resource will be revolutionary.

Think of all we can access through the Internet. We can locate people and businesses, do library research, access professional journals, take a virtual tour of an art museum, and create a map from point A to point B. We can research photos at the National Archives, access military records, read the entire first edition of Marx's *Das Kapital* in either German or English, and check out the worldwide reaction to the Super Bowl. We can converse with specialists on health issues, compare film scripts, examine political commentaries on virtually any topic you can name, and delve into newspaper archives. If it's communication we desire, we can enter a chat room. We can read reviews on movies and concerts, local blues artists, or virtually any topic under the sun. We can participate with online communities via Facebook and YouTube, among others.

Within our reach is a vast network linking us to religious organizations, political and social action groups, job opportunities, and medical services. Of course, there are links to the Aryan Nation, white supremacists, and other extremist groups as well. There are also links to quacks offering a range of health remedies and to hucksters selling worthless products, not to mention pornographers and dubious characters eager to meet some nice young person to molest. Even gang members and taggers have turned to the Internet. The explosion in graffiti in the Los Angeles area in recent years has been driven in no small part by the Internet: "Now, by taking pictures or video, their homies don't have to walk, drive or take the bus to see their tags. They go online" (*Los Angeles Times*, 29 May 2008).

Group or Individual Exercise

The Worldwide Encyclopedia

In its March 2005 edition, *Wired* magazine ran an article on Jimmy Wales, who gathered together an army of contributors to create a "library of the future," a Web encyclopedia called "Wikipedia." Read about his efforts, and share your response and any ideas you have for other ways to democratize knowledge via the Internet.

> Four years ago (2001), a wealthy options trader named Jimmy Wales set out to build a massive online encyclopedia ambitious in purpose and unique in design. This encyclopedia would be freely available to anyone. And it would be created not by paid experts and editors, but by whoever wanted to contribute. With software called Wiki—which allows anybody with Web access to go to a site and edit, delete, or add to what's there—Wales and his volunteer crew would construct a repository of knowledge to rival the ancient library of Alexandria. [As of] 2005, the nonprofit venture is the largest encyclopedia on the planet. Wikipedia offers 500,000 articles in English . . . and the total Wikipedia article count tops 1.3 million. (Daniel H. Pink, "The Book Stops Here," *Wired* magazine, Mar 2005)

Imaging the Internet

The language used to describe this resource is very revealing. Think of terms like "World Wide Web," "Internet," and "cyberspace." All three (webs, nets, and spaces) have *physical correlates* that are instructive to contemplate. The Web may seem fragile, but it is a well-constructed series of links with almost limitless possibilities.

The **Internet** really *is* a kind of net. Just like fishing nets that pull in battered old shoes as well as rainbow trout, the Internet offers useless junk as well as valuable information. Much of the Internet is wide open territory.

In that sense, **cyberspace** really is a kind of space. People, as well as corporations, have staked out territory, set down guidelines, and enforced rules of conduct. Some have made claims about who owns what in cyberspace. Given the vastness of the enterprise, it is virtually impossible to control its growth, regardless of any attempts to rein it in. The result is a universe of ideas, information, products, services, texts, contacts, commentaries, speeches, images, audiovisual aides, movies, music, historical documents, personal bios, family albums, and more.

The Internet resembles the Wild West, with few laws and almost no way to enforce them. It's so easy to erect a website or sign up for an email address that keeping some semblance of order is difficult. Plus, there is no central authority. No one has to "certify" our page. There are neither Internet publishing bodies nor Web police, comparable to those in "real life."

The sheer glut of what's out there is staggering. But navigating the Web can be frustrating and difficult. To a great extent, we are on our own. The host of search engines and techniques may or may not get us to where we want to go. As T. Matthew Ciolek notes in his article "The Six Quests for the Electronic Grail":

> [The Web] can be said to resemble a hall of mirrors, each reflecting a subset of the larger configuration. It is a spectacular place indeed, with some mirrors being more luminous, more innovative or more sensitive to the reflected lights and imagery than others. The result is a breathless and ever changing "information swamp" of visionary solutions, pigheaded stupidity and blunders, dedication and amateurishness, naivety as well as professionalism and chaos. (T. Matthew Ciolek, "The Six Quests for the Electronic Grail," www.ciolek.com)

True, there is often a sense of being in an "information swamp." Also, rarely are there guides or guidelines to orchestrate order in the chaos or lead us through the mazes we encounter.

Given the inherent untidiness of the Internet—indeed, a kind of anarchy—we need to acquire tools to navigate the system. Librarians can help steer the way, but there is no *one* source we can access that will put things in order for us. Rather, we have to rely on our own problem-solving skills and ability to follow leads (and links) to find what we are looking for.

Other issues related to the Internet are important as well. As critical thinkers, we want to examine Internet-related issues of freedom of speech, privacy rights, intellectual property, and accessibility.

Exercises

1. Does email force us into a frantic state, thinking we have to respond immediately? Read the following and state whether you agree:

    The unhindered and massive flow of information in our time is about to fill all the gaps [in time], leading as a consequence to a situation where everything threatens to become a hysterical series of saturated moments, without a before-and-after, a here-and-there to separate them. Indeed, even the here-and-now is threatened since the next moment comes so quickly that it becomes difficult to live in the present. . . . The consequences of this extreme hurriedness are overwhelming; both the past and the future as mental categories are threatened by the tyranny of the moment. (Thomas Hylland Eriksen, *Tyranny of the Moment: Fast and Slow Time in the Information Age,* www.studentaffairs.com)

2. Set out directions to someone who has never used the Internet on how to search for the following:
   a. A particular professor at a specific university (e.g., Dr. Alfred E. Newman at Mad University)
   b. An essay written by a particular author (e.g., "Still Crazy after All These Years" by Zooey Wild)
   c. The website of a newspaper (e.g., the *Chicago Tribune*)
   d. The requirements for a philosophy major at a particular university (e.g., at Oxford University in England, the University of Texas at Austin, or Santa Monica College)
   e. Directions from an airport to your university (e.g., from the Detroit Metro Airport to the University of Michigan Law Library in Ann Arbor)
   f. The latest edition of *Wired* magazine
   g. Five different reviews of a movie

3. Explain to a beginning Internet user how to find articles on a complex topic with three to four terms (e.g., *Marines* who refused *anthrax vaccinations* and faced a *court-martial*; the first term is "Marines," the second is "anthrax," the third is "vaccination," and the fourth is "court-martial"). *Hint:* Don't forget the usefulness of plus and minus signs in running a search. Be aware, however, that different search engines and databases use different mechanisms. Some include all terms automatically, for example.

4. *Know thyself.* Do an Internet search on *one* of the following: your family name, one grandparent or godparent, your birthplace, your birth date (day in history), your dream getaway, or your favorite music. Try several search engines (such as www.google.com or www.metacrawler.com) and several search terms (e.g., type in your last name and your dream place). Summarize what you learned (and what you were *not* able to learn) in your study. Note also what you learned about Internet searches from your study.

▦ Web Hoaxes

The Web lends itself to practical jokes and hoaxes, given the ease of constructing and dismantling sites—real and bogus. For examples, see the Gallery of Hoax Websites (www.museumofhoaxes.com) or Hoaxbusters (hoaxbusters.ciac.org). Some websites play on people's gullibility and curiosity but are otherwise quite innocent. Some are actually pornography sites. Others try to manipulate users so they are forced to see alternative viewpoints from the one they were seeking.

Web Hoaxes, Parodies, and Spoofs

- www.martinlutherking.org (professional-looking, but a white supremacy site).
- www.onion.com (a parody site with silly articles—some have thought them real and cited them).

- www.funnycrap.com (a spoof site that creates fake sites).
- www.whitehouse.net (cartoon). Other URLs that include "white house" lead to porn sites; the real thing can be found at www.whitehouse.gov (see the link to "kids").
- www.whirledbank.org (an alternative version of www.worldbank.org that has the motto "Our Dream is a World Full of Poverty").
- www.gatt.org (a counterfeit version of www.wpo.org [the World Presidents' Organization is a global organization of more than 3,300 individuals who are or have been chief executive officers of major business enterprises]— www.gatt.org is highly critical of the World Trade Organization).
- www.adbusters.org/spoofads (spoofs of advertising).
- www.improb.com (publishes the parody "The Annals of Improbable Research").
- www.buydehydratedwater.com (Buy dehydrated water).
- www.ihr.org (historical review—a front for Holocaust revisionism).
- www.globalwarming.org (says global warming is a hoax).

Deceit and Trickery with Domain Names

Web hoaxes and parodies aren't the only potholes on the Internet. What about the debate over domain names? A person, business, or organization may have the same name as a much more famous person or organization or a similar name— thus leading to confusion on a user's part.

For example, People for the Ethical Treatment of Animals didn't like it that People Eating Tasty Animals had the domain name peta.org—and the original PETA sued to get it! Here's another example: The Islamic Society of North America, one of the biggest Islamic groups, does *not* own www.isna.org. This website is run by the Intersex Society of North America! And Southwest Airlines' URL is *not* swa.com (the home of Simpson Weather Associates). In addition, some have purchased domain names of celebrities and corporations—frustrating both those whose names have been used and those who look for information using the obvious URLs (to no avail).

This phenomenon is related to **cybersquatting**—where someone buys the name of a well-known company and then demands money to give it up. For example, in a case filed with the U.S. District Court for Southern Florida in October 2007, Dell took aim at companies licensed to register and sell new domain names to the public. Dell claimed that these cybersquatters were responsible for registering and profiting off nearly 1,100 domains that were "confusingly similar" to Dell's various trademarks by using "typosquatting"—close misspellings of the website name. The complaint further charged that the registrants created and controlled a series of shell corporations in the Bahamas to act as the entities registering the domains (Brian Krebs, "Dell Takes Cybersquatters to Court," *The Washington Post*, 28 Nov 2007). As noted by Susan Thea Posnock:

> Though the Internet presents a powerful new channel, it also enables individuals to encroach upon magazine brands, by registering domain names with the intent to sell the URL back to the publishers at a high cost or lure customers to their own sites.

Publishers say the best way to avoid cybersquatters is to strike first by registering domain names early. ("Conquering Cybersquatters," *Folio: The Magazine for Magazine Management,* Spring 2001)

Cybersquatting has created havoc for companies, groups, and individuals. In recognition of the greedy or malevolent acts of some cybersquatters, Congress enacted the Anti-cybersquatting Consumer Protection Act (ACPA) in 1999. This act allows publishers to take civil action against anyone with bad-faith intent to profit from use of an identical or confusingly similar domain name. Those who don't want to sue can seek an international arbitration through the Internet Corporation of Assigned Names and Numbers.

According to the World Intellectual Property Organization (WIPO), in the years immediately following the enactment of ACPA, they were flooded with filings against cybersquatters. For example, the World Intellectual Property Association's Arbitration and Mediation Center reviewed cybersquatting cases ranging from authors and books (jrrtolkien.com, thecatinthehat.com), to pop stars (nsyncfilm.com), to TV shows (oscartv.com), to movie stars (piercebrosnan.com), to sports personalities (terrellowens.com) and sporting events (torino2006.net, madrid2012.org) ("WIPO Continues Efforts to Stamp Out Cybersquatting," World Intellectual Property Organization, 27 Jan 2004).

The ACPA law targeted those who sought to profit using the domain name of another. The trouble is, not every cybersquatter wants to make a profit. Some just want to make a political statement, parody a corporation or individual, or wreak a little havoc in the system. This appeared to be the case for the lawyer who opened verizonsucks.com back in 2000. Verizon's lawyers were not amused and took legal action.

Group or Individual Exercises

1. Select a few spoof or hoax sites from the list above and study them. Try to figure out the source (author or group) of the site, its purpose, and any links that take you to the "mother site," and reveal the agenda behind the site—the issues and concerns it raises.

2. Using your Internet search skills, find out what you can about how to avoid a Web hoax (fake websites that look like the real thing—for example, martinlutherking.org was created by a white supremacy group). Write a summary of what you find on Web hoaxes, and give three suggestions to avoid getting trapped by them.

3. Find two to three examples of cybersquatting websites—sites that use the name of a company, group, or individual although they are not affiliated with that group or person. List the URL and explain what the site is really about (as opposed to its misleading name).

Hoax Busters

Hoax-buster and scam-buster sites can be helpful resources. Paul Piper notes a number of such sites, including these:

- www.nonprofit.net/hoax/hoax.html
- www.fraud.org/welmes.htm (a consumer fraud center, including Internet fraud)
- www.ciac.org/ciac/index.html (U.S. Department of Energy)
- www.scambusters.org

Of help when confronting problems with hoax sites are the American Library Association (www.ala.org) and the U.S. Department of Energy (ciac.energy.gov). Websites that offer advice on how to avoid fake sites include these:

- www.virtualchase.com (a guide to legal research on the Internet)
- www.library.cornell.edu/olinuris/ref/research/webeval.html (links and references on evaluating websites)

Web Research

You've procrastinated as long as possible, but you are running out of time and that essay deadline is looming. It's too late to go to the library; all you have is your computer for a research tool. Ask yourself:

"Will I access good information?" This is a *search* question.
"Can I distinguish higher-level from lower-quality websites and documents?"
  This is an *evaluation* question.

We need to look at both of these questions. The first one involves being able to search the Web. For that, you need to know how to use search engines, when to try more than one search engine, and other ways to access reference material. That can take time, which needs to be factored in as well. Also, you need to apply problem-solving and questioning techniques to optimize searches. The second question brings in the range of critical thinking skills set out in this chapter.

Whether you are a seasoned veteran of Internet research or a novice, there's still a lot to learn and, as more and more websites are developed, the number of sites out there in the cyber galaxy is increasing. Below are 10 pearls of wisdom of Web research to keep in mind as we navigate cyberspace.

Ten Pearls of Wisdom of Web Research

1. **Research takes time.** Allow time to follow links and links within links to investigate the resources out there. If you do, you may find far more than you ever imagined possible.
2. **Think like a fox.** Maybe you'll win the lottery, maybe not. Maybe you'll find great stuff after your first search, maybe not. Try different search engines and different ways of formulating questions or search terms.

3. **Be imaginative.** Be crafty when phrasing search terms. If one doesn't work, try another. Try different search engines and electronic databases, approach the topic through various avenues, and consider different perspectives. You may hit the jackpot with one of them.

4. **Remember that libraries are good things. Librarians are your friends.** Try local library resources (e.g., lapl.org), university library sites, the Library of Congress, and so on. These have a wide range of tools, links, and databases for accessing a wide variety of sites including online dictionaries. And don't forget the Librarian's Index to the Internet (www.lii.org) and the American Library Association website (www.ala.org).

5. **Don't try to reinvent the wheel.** Investigate professional organizations. Remember, laws and legal decisions are available online (e.g., the U.S. Supreme Court site, www.supremecourtus.gov; the U.S. Supreme Court multimedia database, www.oyez.com; and the legal database, findlaw.com), as well as statistics, government documents, photo archives, historical papers, music and film reviews, and other hard-to-find resources.

6. **Know your friends.** Publishers' websites are good places to scout for documents; government sites can be a treasure trove, as can national archives, newspapers online, online journals, and metasearch engines.

7. **Consider unlikely suspects.** Go to sites that seem tangential. These may not directly relate to your search, but they can provide a back door to the topic or to links and resources that take you where you want to go.

8. **Network.** Communicate with those who are in the know: Email professionals, organizations, or other online contacts if you have questions or concerns. Be as precise as you can in your request. Many experts are generous with their time and will answer questions or offer leads.

9. **Ask questions.** Formulating your search as a question helps in navigating search engines and using search tools. Clarify the focus of your search and how you might be able to narrow down the topic should the need arise. Contacting reference persons or giving feedback to a site may require good, clear questions.

10. **Keep an open mind.** Be receptive to new ideas and fresh perspectives. Try a variety of approaches. Think of your research as tackling an intellectual puzzle. The answer to your prayers may be staring you in the face, but you need to be perceptive and receptive to different ways of seeing the world.

Exercises

1. Choose any *two* government websites, such as the FBI site, www.fbi.gov; the NASA site, www.nasa.gov; the Internal Revenue Service site, www.irs.gov; the Centers for Disease Control site, www.cdc.gov; or the U.S. Postal Service site, www.usps.gov.

   a. Compare and contrast the quality of the resources.

   b. Compare and contrast the relative ease of navigating the sites.

2. Pick any *two* celebrities (e.g., movie stars, athletes, famous authors), and then compare and contrast the best website you found for each of your two figures.

3. How are people honored? Select *one* area (Grammy Awards, Pulitzer Prize, Booker Prize, Nobel Prize, Caldecott Medal, Academy Awards, Juno Awards, Gemini Awards, Emmy Awards, Nammy Awards, NBA Hall of Fame, the Olympics, Boston marathon, etc.), and then evaluate the awarding organization's website.

Problem-Solving Skills Are Vital

You know those sci-fi films where the ship lands (or crashes) on an alien planet? Sometimes, as in *Contact*, the alien planet is wonderful to behold and a great place to visit. Other times, as in *Alien* and *Aliens*, the alien planet is a place to escape from, and the sooner the better! So it is with travel in cyberspace.

There are a lot of helpful, even fantastic, websites out there. But, as we travel to the outer reaches of the cyber galaxy, we may land in hostile territory. We could land on a website graveyard filled with dead links, dead ends, and nonexistent "contacts." Or we could land on a website junkyard, piled up with useless trivia, outdated relics, or once-valuable treasures that are no longer relevant. Fortunately, our critical thinking skills can help steer us to a website that either meets our objective or provides valuable leads so we can continue our quest. As we navigate, we need to keep in mind the pearls of Web research noted above. Fundamental to our success are problem-solving and questioning techniques.

Internet Problem-Solving Skills

- Being able to define the problem or issue to begin the search
- Deciding upon the appropriate terms to launch the search
- Being able to redefine terms to throw a wider net
- Being able to narrow down the search by combining search terms
- Knowing when to mention names or use quotes to narrow down a search
- Turning to alternative search engines and databases to widen the search

Problem-solving skills are a must for Internet use. Be prepared to experiment with search engines, search techniques, and search terms; to navigate through poorly constructed websites; and to deal with hoaxes and dirty tricks. The Internet is in many ways more complicated than the traditional library—the organizational system starts with a search. The results depend to a great extent on the wording of the search itself.

Search results are often organized by frequency of visitation (a sort of popularity contest). While having some benefits in research, we can't depend on the numbers of visitors to a site as a guarantee that the material posted there is of superior quality. Furthermore, there are those who have a stake in their site coming up in the top five and who may resort to Google-bombing or other tricks to make the site pop into view as you search. Be prepared to dig through the search results to make sure you've found the best material to explore.

Results involving news searches are generally organized in descending order by date. This can be extremely useful, particularly if we are searching for information that is timely. However, if our quest is for specific sorts of information, regardless of the date, we may have some fishing to do. Fishing takes time. Allow for that.

Question techniques are also important. Being able to formulate different types of questions is crucial in using the Web. We also need to be able to ask questions to help access information, ideas, images, and Web documents. Just being able to ask ourselves exactly what it is we are looking for—and for what purpose and level of detail—can make all the difference in the terms we use to commence the search and where we go from there.

Group or Individual Exercises

1. Find the best website you can for those who study or collect *one* of the following: stamps, sports cars, insects, antique dolls, soccer jerseys, feathers, baseball cards, or beads.

2. What is the ideal university website? Set out your ideas about what should and should not be on a university website (e.g., phone numbers of offices and staff, cafeteria menus, course schedules, courses required for each major, average SAT score, retention rate, and campus safety).

3. Find a website in one academic area (e.g., sociology, psychology, history, or chemistry), and note how easy it is to navigate and access information and documents.

Web Analysis

Let's assume we've arrived at a Web page that looks promising. There are two key components in **web analysis:**

1. **Assessing the Web page to determine credibility.** This focuses on the source of the information—the site itself and its legitimacy.
2. **Assessing the quality of the article(s) found on the Web page.** This focuses on the content of the Web page—the quality of the reasoning found there.

The first issue is to get to a legitimate *source* of information and ideas—one where the authors have the appropriate qualifications or credentials and where the site itself is subject to review. The second issue is one of *content*. Here we are concerned with the quality of the reasoning set out in the articles and other material found at the site.

The Global Dimension

FBI and CIA "Editing" of Wikipedia

Directions: Read the following from Randall Mikkelsen's August 2007 report and then answer the questions below.

People using CIA and FBI computers have edited entries in the online encyclopedia Wikipedia on topics including the Iraq war and the Guantanamo Bay prison, according to a new tracing program. The changes may violate Wikipedia's conflict-of-interest guidelines, says a spokesperson for the site.

The program, WikiScanner, was developed by Virgil Griffith of the Santa Fe Institute in New Mexico and posted this month on a website that was quickly overwhelmed with searches. The program allows users to track the source of computers used to make changes to the popular internet encyclopedia where anyone can submit and edit entries. WikiScanner revealed that CIA computers were used to edit an entry on the U.S.-led invasion of Iraq in 2003. (Randall Mikkelsen, "CIA, FBI Computers Used to Edit Wikipedia," Reuters, www.abc.net.au, 17 Aug 2007)

Answer the following:

1. Draw up a list of the factual claims and points raised.
2. State three to four good reasons for the FBI and CIA being able to "edit" Wikipedia or any other website other than their own.
3. State three to four good reasons for the FBI and CIA *not* to be permitted to "edit" Wikipedia or any other website other than their own.

In addition to tapping our own reasoning powers, we can consult the American Library Association's (ALA) guidelines for evaluating the credibility of websites. As we know, anyone can publish almost anything on the Web. There is no Internet editor or cybercop to weed out the oddities, the fringe, the threatening, the unpopular, and the cheesy. That has both advantages and disadvantages.

One advantage is that it makes it less likely that tyrannical governments can exist without a channel for opposition. The Internet not only provides access to information, but also allows networks to form and alliances to build. Anyone with Internet access is fairly free to search for a wide range of documents. We can also go through archives that might otherwise be eliminated because they are narrow in scope or of interest to only a small number of people.

Be warned: Are you one of those people who think that Wikipedia is *always* a reliable source? Well, watch what you assume. The very nature of an instrument that allows input leaves it open to some degree of manipulation. For example, it has been alleged that some Wikipedia entries could be traced to FBI and CIA computers.

Assessing the Source: Credible Web Pages

We cannot assume that everything we find on the Web is legitimate, well researched, or credible. Most documents have not been subject to a peer review, a professional organization, or an editorial staff. In addition, most are not held to any standard of excellence. This means we have to learn to evaluate sites and determine the value and legitimacy of the material we find.

A handy guide to locate credible websites is available from the American Library Association. The ALA sets out five criteria for evaluating the credibility of websites: (1) accuracy, (2) authority, (3) objectivity, (4) currency, and (5) coverage. These criteria are useful for navigating the Internet to ensure that the websites you use are credible and up to date.

ALA Tips for Assessing the Credibilty of a Web Page

1. **Accuracy:** Who wrote the page and how can you contact them? What is the purpose of the document and why was it produced? Is this person or group qualified to write this document?
2. **Authority:** Who published the document? What is the domain of the document? Is an institutional affiliation listed?
3. **Objectivity:** What goals or objectives does this page have? Who is the intended audience? How detailed is the information? Does the author express any opinions? Is the page a mask for advertising? Do you detect any bias?
4. **Currency:** When was the document produced? When was it updated? How up to date are the links (if any)? Are there any dead links on the page? Is any of the information out of date?
5. **Coverage:** Is the information presented cited correctly? Are there links to more detailed documents or related resources? What function do the visual images (or sound/videos) serve?

Exercises

Directions: In the questions below, focus on the legitimacy of the website itself, drawing from the ALA guidelines (above).

1. Select any controversial moral or social problem (e.g., animal rights, abortion, stem cell research, or gay rights) and find *one* website whose *legitimacy* can be called into question and *one* website that appears credible.
2. Find a website whose author lacks the appropriate *authority* to be taken seriously or that is clearly self-serving.
3. Find a website that completely fails the *objectivity* test. Be sure to explain how it fails.
4. Find a website that passes the *objectivity* test. Be sure to explain how it succeeds in presenting balanced and objective material.
5. Find two examples with respect to *currency*—one website that is verifiably up to date and another that is hopelessly outdated.
6. Find a website that provides an excellent example of *coverage* on a current topic (such as prison reform, teens and alcohol abuse, choosing a college, good nutrition, or child obesity).
7. Find a website with good *coverage* on any *one* of the following how-to topics: house-training a puppy, repairing a banjo, cooking shellfish, ostrich

farming, painting with glazes, caring for an exotic pet, polishing an antique car, training for marathons, or teaching a parrot to talk.

8. Apply any *two* of the ALA guidelines to a website on *one* of the following: animal rights (e.g., peta.org or an anti-PETA site), prisoners' rights (e.g., aclu.org/prison or hrw.org/prisons), surrogate parenting (e.g., www .creatingfamilies.com, www.spcsurrogates.co, or www.surrogateparenting .com), or civil rights (e.g., www.splcenter.org or www.civilrights.org).

Quick Quiz

1. "Will you access good information?" is (a) a search or (b) an evaluation question.

2. When someone buys the name of a well-known company and then demands money to give the name up, it is called:
   a. Cyberbribery
   b. Cyberpiracy
   c. Cybersquatting
   d. Cybercapitalism

3. *True or false:* One pearl of wisdom of Internet research is "Don't try to reinvent the wheel."

4. "Can you distinguish higher-level from lower-quality websites" is:
   a. An evaluation question
   b. A search question
   c. A metacognitive question
   d. An organizational question

5. "URL" stands for:
   a. Uniform Research Language
   b. Universal Resource Locator
   c. Unilateral Resource Latitude
   d. Unidimensional Resource Linguistics

6. *True or false:* An "authority question" focuses on information and links.

7. Who wrote a Web document and how to contact them are issues of:
   a. Accuracy
   b. Objectivity
   c. Currency
   d. Coverage

8. *True or false:* www.yahoo.com and www.google.com are examples of search terms.

9. Assessing a Web page to determine its credibility is an issue of:
   a. The popularity of the site
   b. Cybersquatting
   c. The legitimacy of the site
   d. The quality of the reasoning

Assessing the Content

Whether we surf the Web or dog-paddle our way through a few websites, we need to be able to think critically about what we see and read. Not only do we have to deal with images, symbols, and text, but we also have to deal with advertising, dirty tricks, hoaxes, spoofs, manipulation, or pornographic hinterlands, and advertising strangleholds that trap us until we shut down. And that's not even considering computer viruses that arrive through email attachments or email advertising that pops up out of nowhere.

One interesting aspect of the Internet is the longevity of content—and users' tracks. This appears to be the case even with documents that individuals, groups, and organizations try to remove from public access. Gary Bass of OMB Watch, an organization opposed to government secrecy, sums it up with an analogy: "The Internet is not like a faucet you can turn off and on. It's like a leaky faucet that keeps dripping long after it's turned off" ("The Web Never Forgets," *Los Angeles Times,* 27 Nov 2001). Even if the document is removed from one site, it might be embedded on another site or blog. Furthermore, it may be retrievable through Internet archives.

For example, on the website of "Wayback Machine" (www.archive.org), we find this: "Thanks to a generous grant from the Mellon Foundation, the Internet Archive completed a 2 billion page web crawl in 2007. This is the largest web crawl attempted by the Internet Archive. The project was designed to take a global snapshot of the Web." Also posted there is this: "Browse through 85 billion web pages archived from 1996 to a few months ago." The website also directs browsers to archive.bibalex.org, the Internet archive at the New Library of Alexandria, Egypt, that mirrors Wayback Machine.

The legitimacy of the website itself cannot be assumed—thus the guidelines above. Once we've arrived at a credible website, we are ready for the second stage of Web analysis—that of examining the content and assessing the quality of the reasoning. For these tasks, the tools acquired in the first part of this book are crucial.

Critical thinking skills are not just handy—they are essential to accessing information, evaluating websites, and analyzing the material on the sites. The range of critical thinking skills that apply to use of the Internet can be summarized as follows:

Checklist for Assessing Content

- **Assess thoroughness.** Ask yourself if the website does what it's supposed to do in terms of providing information and resources, as well as links and hyperlinks when appropriate.
- **Determine the frame of reference.** Consider other perspectives that might be taken on the situation and how things would change if other voices were heard.
- **Examine the reasoning.** Zero in on arguments and assess the strength of evidence cited in support of the conclusion. Pull out key claims and examine

the structure of any arguments set out on the Web page or associated articles. Be aware of inductive and deductive arguments. Watch especially for the use of analogies, reliance on statistical studies, and cause-and-effect reasoning.

- **Analyze and evaluate.** Look at the quality of the arguments and assess their strengths and weaknesses. Check for warranted versus unwarranted assumptions, stereotypical or prejudicial thinking, and the use of images and symbols.
- **Check the use of language.** Watch for loaded terms, biased language, asymmetrical descriptions, repetition, metaphors, and poetic expressions to convey an idea.
- **Watch for fallacies.** The Internet is not immune from fallacious reasoning, so watch for some common fallacies: ad populum (appeal to the masses or to patriotism), ad verecundiam (irrelevant testimonial or improper appeal to authority), ad hominem (personal attack), ad hominem circumstantial (attack due to vested interests or affiliation), and question-begging epithets (slanted language biasing an interpretation). (See Chapter 7 for a review.)
- **Watch for diverse perspectives.** Examine the values and worldview implicitly presented. How narrow or broad is the website's understanding of the people or issues involved? See how inclusive the author is of alternative positions.
- **Assess visual and verbal messages.** Check the presentation of information and the use of images/photographs. See if they are relevant to the topic—or if they are gratuitous.
- **Assess ads.** Figure out the ads' purpose and likely connection to the material on the Web page and the website in general. The ads may not just be helping pay the rent—they may be an indicator of a vested interest by the author(s) of the material.
- **Check references and links.** Examine the use of references, documentation, citation, and associated links. The links can be as revealing as footnotes in terms of the quality of the research.

Exercises

1. Discuss the content of any *one* of these websites:
   a. American Nursing Association (www.ana.org)
   b. American Medical Association (www.ama.org)
   c. American Philosophical Association (www.apa.udel.edu)
   d. Revlon (www.revlon.com)
   e. Barbie (www.barbie.com)
   f. Porsche (www.porsche.com)
   g. Kelloggs U.K. (www.kelloggs.co.uk)
   h. Coca-Cola Company (www.cocacola.com)

2. Discuss the content of any *one* of these museum sites:
   a. Getty Museum (www.getty.edu/museum)
   b. National Museum of the American Indian (www.nmai.si.edu)
   c. California African American Museum (www.caam.ca.gov)
   d. Canada Technology and Science Museum (www.sciencetech.technomuses.ca/english)
   e. NASA Museum (www.hightechscience.org/nasa_museum)

3. Analyze *one* news site (e.g., pbs.org, www.abcnews.com, www.cnn.com, www.atimes.com, www.theglobeandmail.com, or www.nbc.com).

4. Compare the website for the president of the United States with the corresponding website in another country (e.g., the prime minister of Canada).

5. Analyze *one* website on any topic in medicine (such as smallpox, AIDS advances, lasik eye surgery, or treatments for teenage acne) or law (such as legal services for the poor or legal research). Focus especially on the site's use of graphics, and assess the overall organization of the site.

6. Analyze a website of *one* of the following hate groups noted by the Southern Poverty Law Center (www.splcenter.org/intel/map/hate.jsp): Christian Identity, Racist Skinhead, Ku Klux Klan, Neo Nazis, Neo-Confederate Movement, American Front.

7. Compare and contrast the website of the Democratic National Committee with that of the Republican National Committee or the websites of Canadian political parties: the Conservatives, the Liberals, and the N.D.P.

8. Compare and contrast a small-town newspaper website with that of a large urban newspaper, such as the *Globe and Mail* (www.globeandmail.com), *The New York Times* (www.nytimes.com), *The Washington Post* (www.washingtonpost.com), the *Atlanta Journal-Constitution* (www.ajc.com), *The Oregonian* (www.oregonian.com), or the *Edmonton Journal* (www.edmontonjournal.com).

9. Compare and contrast any *two* websites for a car manufacturer (e.g., VW vs. BMW, Jaguar vs. Lexus, or Prius vs. Mini USA).

Booby Traps on the Web

Spam

Spam is *not* something tasty to snack on while working on the computer. It is unwanted email that is sent—usually on a mass scale—to email accounts of people who neither directly nor indirectly requested such email. As anyone knows who has ever been spammed, such emails waste time and effort. In the early years of spam, recipients had the illusion that a "do not subscribe" reply would suffice to end the unsolicited communication. If anything, replies made the situation *worse*—for then companies knew that *you existed and you opened their email!* In some cases, that signaled unscrupulous agencies to send you more spam. Why? Well, if you read enough of the email to find the response button, who knows? Maybe you would read the next one and be interested.

Unfortunately, spam artists have become very clever about finding ways to send out their unwanted emails. They appear to have no qualms about using others' names and email addresses as a mask for their underhanded, deceptive practices. This causes the recipient of an email that appears to be from an actual person to open it.

Dirty Tricks

Yes, there are hoax sites. And then there are dirty tricks. As anyone who uses the Web regularly knows, sometimes you click on a link and end up at a pornography site. This is an example of what's been called "user manipulation." J. D. Biersdorfer cites a case in September 1999 in which people trying to get to 25 million popular Web pages were intentionally rerouted to pornography sites that trapped them—they could escape only by shutting down their computers. In that case, the FTC (Federal Trade Commission—www.ftc.gov) filed an injunction against those who were responsible.

But that's not the only dirty trick. Manipulators of the Web have also been known to disable the "back" button, keeping you stuck at the site in hopes that you'll look at its content and ads. Then there's metatagging.

Metatagging

A **metatag** is a place in the HTML code where information about the site is listed. Putting popular terms (like "sex") in the metatag guarantees more surfers to that website (see J. D. Biersdorfer, "Trapped in the Web without an Exit," *The New York Times,* 7 Oct 1999). Metatags are certainly not inherently evil. They were designed to better match computer users with the sites they seek. Some search engines rely on metatags to offer a description of the site. It is when Web designers include irrelevant words that users are deceived. Metatagging can be used for deceptive and sneaky purposes. Note, for instance, the observation by "De Novo" about law schools using metatags:

> Having previously mocked Harvard Law's website for putting a metatag on their website to describe the school as "The world's premier center for legal education and research," I should be fair and spread my contempt to Penn Law, which has an almost-but-not-quite as pathetic tag: meta name = "Description," content = "The University of Pennsylvania Law School, or Penn Law, provides a superior legal education through cross-disciplinary studies and our deserved reputation as a congenial and stimulating environment." (www.blogdenovo.org/archives/1913.html, 20 Dec 2007)

Biersdorfer notes that companies could embed names of the rival so that if someone searches for the rival company, they get the manipulator as well. If you've ever hunted for sites on controversial issues like abortion, you've also encountered metatagging. Searches for pro-choice sites bring up pro-life sites. Of course, some supposedly "pro-choice" sites turn out to be sites where the woman's choice should be to not get the abortion at all.

Computer Viruses

Life can be funny. Even when it comes to computer viruses, things can take a humorous turn. Take the example of the "naked wife" virus that evidently ran amok in March 2001. While the worm was chomping its way through victims' computer files, governmental officials were gnashing their teeth trying to find a way to warn people. Evidently, they became victims of their own forethought. The very warnings they tried to send bounced back—censored, censored, censored. Here's the scoop:

> A recent example [of literal meanings that are frequently wrong or confusing] is the "naked wife" virus that spread rapidly through cyberspace a few months ago. The Department of Energy found it couldn't send out a warning about the virus because its prudish computer software interpreted "naked wife" literally—and censored the warning. (K. C. Cole, "Moving beyond the Boundaries of a Literal Meaning," *Los Angeles Times,* 14 May 2001)

According to CNN, the bug masqueraded as a Macromedia Flash movie, using the subject line "Fw: Naked Wife." The email message stated: "My wife never looks like that! :-) Best Regards," and then added the name of the sender. The worm spread by emailing itself to addresses listed in the user's Microsoft Outlook address book, clearly wreaking havoc.

The Internet has brought the world that much closer.

Nik Scott, www.nikscott.com. Copyright 2008.

You Tell Me Department

What about the "Naked Wife" Warning?

If the Department of Energy (DOE) could not use the term "naked wife" to send a warning, how might we alert the public about this virus? We may need to know whether it was the word "naked" that was objectionable, the word "wife" that caused the glitch, or the complex phrase "naked wife." It may be interesting to know if "naked husband" would have caused a similar reaction in the government's software.

You tell me: So what could the Department of Energy have done to get around the software censorship? Offer some ideas and suggestions.

Children's and Teens' Internet Use

Considerable effort has gone into studying the impact of the Internet. Look, for instance, at its effectiveness in the 2008 presidential election. Furthermore, according to David Pogue, tech wizard of *The New York Times,* 90% of teenagers are online every single day. He notes, "They are absolutely immersed in chat, Facebook, MySpace and the rest of the Web; it's part of their ordinary social fabric to an extent that previous generations can't even imagine." Pogue also asserts that "the threat of online predators is misunderstood and overblown. The data show that giving out personal information over the Internet makes absolutely no difference when it comes to a child's vulnerability to predation." He notes that cyberbullies pose a more realistic threat than sexual predators (David Pogue, "How Dangerous Is the Internet for Children?" *The New York Times,* 28 Feb 2008).

Henry Jenkins, director of the Program in Comparative Media Studies at the Massachusetts Institute of Technology (MIT), thinks the public dialogue about the Internet has become *bifurcated*—split into a false dichotomy. One school of thought holds that there are two ways of looking at the Internet: that it breeds violence and social anarchy or that it liberates children from the confines of home and limitations of narrow-minded parents. Jenkins expresses this polarization in terms of myths. The Myth of the Columbine Generation links school shootings to children's unfettered access to Internet pornography and violence. This myth is characterized by despair. The Myth of the Digital Generation, in contrast, links online accessibility to developing children's creative potential and making them better informed, socially connected individuals (see Henry Jenkins, "The Myths of Growing Up Online," *Technology Review,* www.technologyreview.com, 3 Sep 2004). Jenkins believes that the truth lies somewhere between these two extremes.

Many children *do* have access to potentially disturbing, graphic images and text via the Internet—that much is true. However, children also have access to information and ideas that can transform their lives in terms of their education and personal growth. For this reason, being able to apply critical thinking skills to use of the Internet is a necessity for even the youngest of users.

The Global Dimension

Growing Up Online

In a conference held at the University of London, participants from 40 countries looked at the impact of new media on children.

A highlight of the conference was London School of Economics professor Sonia Livingstone's announcement of the preliminary findings of a major research initiative called UK Children Go Online.

According to the study, children were neither as powerful nor as powerless as the two competing myths might suggest. As the Myth of the Digital Generation suggests, children and youth were using the Internet effectively as a resource for doing homework, connecting with friends, and seeking out news and entertainment. At the same time, as the Myth of the Columbine Generation might imply, the adults in these kids' lives tended to underestimate the problems their children encountered online, including the percentage who had unwanted access to pornography, had received harassing messages, or had given out personal information. (Henry Jenkins, "The Myths of Growing Up Online," *Technology Review,* www.technologyreview.com, 3 Sep 2004)

Answer the following:

1. Jenkins thinks the truth lies between these two extremes. Do you agree? What do *you* think of the influence of the Internet on children?
2. How can either parents or schools help children use the Internet? (For example, should all schools install software to block certain types of websites?)

Blogs and More Blogs

Web logs, or **blogs,** are websites that function as online journals. Blogs can be about anything—and bloggers can be anyone. No one checks credentials for bloggers to get online. Consider this example of a blogger's entry:

Alaska dog owners, it is time to unite. We have moose in our yards. We have frozen water bowls. We have wolves, doggone it, walking off with cute little pugs at our state capital! Mushers have their own network of resources, but the time has come for ordinary pet owners to come together and discuss our only-in-Alaska issues. (*Anchorage Daily News,* www.adn.com/blogs, 6 Feb 2008)

Some blogs are narrowly focused (e.g., on recent advances in technology), while others are basically wide open. Many include links to commentary, news items, or other websites, making it easy for the audience to access the material the blogger cites (for instance, see the Drudge Retort, www.drudge.com). Other blogs more closely resemble a journal, with topics wide open. We might say of these: The personal *is* political.

Just about any field you can name has a blogger or two sharing ideas or opinions. Some blogs are great resources, with succinct summaries of what has been written on a topic. According to Lev Grossman, blogs existed under the radar until 2002. Then things changed:

You Tell Me Department

Forget Blogs—What about Text Messaging?

TxtMob was introduced at the 2004 Democratic National Convention. It allowed more than 260 subscribers to automatically blast text messages to the mobile phones of every other subscriber. An article in *Wired* magazine about this new device reported:

> "There were . . . a number of interesting uses that the system got put to" at the DNC, said John Henry, TxtMob's developer. "Police did arrest one protester, and there were not a lot of people around. Someone saw it happen (sent a TxtMob message), and a hundred of that kid's friends were on the scene in minutes . . . to make sure" the police acted correctly. And because of concerns that police at the convention would run roughshod over them, some protesters found that TxtMob was useful for keeping each other apprised of police movements.
>
> For now, TxtMob is being used exclusively for political organizing. But Henry said . . . he envisions it in any number of environments, . . . According to Emily Turrettini, author of Textually

.org, a blog about advances in text messaging, TxtMob could well prove to be a crucial tool for anyone trying to organize groups of people amid rapidly evolving circumstances. (Daniel Terdiman, "Text Messages for Critical Masses," *Wired* magazine, 12 Aug 2004)

You tell me:

1. Should TxtMob be available to those outside of law enforcement?
2. Does the potential benefit outweigh the risks?
3. *Update:* Four years later, the TxtMob messaging in the 2004 case became an issue in a lawsuit. The attorney for New York City issued a subpoena to the MIT student who created TxtMob: The city wanted the records of all the messages that were exchanged through the TxtMob service, as well as information about who sent them. The search for digital footprints is on ("TxtMob Subpoena Shows the Hazards of Using Technology to Protest," www.privacydigest.com, 1 Apr 2008). Do you think this should be permitted?

The occasion was [Senator] Strom Thurmond's 100th birthday party, during which [Senator] Trent Lott made what sounded like a nostalgic reference to Thurmond's past segregationist leanings. The mainstream press largely glossed over the incident, . . . "That story got ignored for three, four, five days by big papers and the TV networks while blogs kept it alive," says Joshua Micah Marshall, creator of talkingpointsmemo.com.

Mainstream America wasn't listening, but Washington insiders and media honchos read blogs. Three days after the party, the story was on Meet the Press. Four days afterward, Lott made an official apology. (See Lev Grossman, "Meet Joe Blog," *Time* magazine, 21 Jun 2004.)

Blogger Emily Gould speaks of the appeal of blogging: "One of the strangest and most enthralling aspects of personal blogs is just how intensely personal they can be." She adds, "Long before I had a blog, I found ways to broadcast my thoughts— to gossip about myself, tell my own secrets, tell myself and others the ongoing story of my life." However, "The big difference between these youthful indiscretions and my more recent ones is that you can Google my more recent ones" ("Blog-Post Confidential," *The New York Times,* 28 May 2008). This much wider potential audience changes everything. Once the blog is sent out into cyberspace, it's virtually impossible to pull it back.

Blogs are more Wild West than high society. As a result, some aspects of blogs are problematic—their anonymity means little or no accountability. According to graphic designer Steven Heller, blogs allow anonymous potshots that can be posted according to whim. The absence of accountability is the blog's great flaw ("Blog Me, Blog Me Not," *Print*, May–Jun 2004).

Grossman agrees, saying, "In a way, blogs represent everything the Web was always supposed to be: a mass medium controlled by the masses, in which getting heard depends solely on having something to say and the moxie to say it. Unfortunately, there's a downside to this populist sentiment—that is, innocent casualties bloodied by a medium that trades in rumor, gossip and speculation without accountability." On the other hand, not all blogs have accountability problems; they may never go beyond the level of the personal. Of course, that standard may be hard to obtain without considerable self-control in naming others (even by pseudonyms).

Blogs can be great resources, especially for current events or specialized topics. They have certainly had an enormous impact on mainstream media. But the lack of accountability or qualifications on the part of the blogger tells us this: Blogs must be viewed with care and occasionally caution. Watch for credibility on the part of the source, and have your critical thinking tools at your disposal.

▦ Wikis

Blogs are not the only aspect of the Internet that signifies a dramatic departure from traditional means of mass communication. Wikis have also changed everything, by providing a means for collaboration without ever meeting the other participants—who can be as far apart as Vancouver and Sydney, Hollywood and Mombasa, or Greenland and Antarctica. What distinguishes a **wiki** is that it is a website allowing collaborative editing of its content and structure by its users. The foremost example is Wikipedia, an online collaborative "encyclopedia" that has considerable fluidity, as many can input, edit, or comment on entries (barring restrictions by the website).

There are many other wikis. For instance, Wiki How (www.wikihow.com) is a wiki "How-to Manual" that can be edited. Topics range from "Enjoy a Car Trip," to "Do Razor Scooter Tricks," to "Live with a Moluccan Cockatoo," to "How to Get into Your House When You Lock Yourself Out." As evidence that wikis are not always reliable, let's see what to do if we are locked out of our house. The steps are listed below, with assumptions added:

1. Borrow a screwdriver from a neighbor.
   → *Assumes:* You have a neighbor nearby, who is home, has a screwdriver, and is willing to loan you tools.
2. Take off the screws on your letterbox. Lift up the flap and you should see them.
   → *Assumes:* You have a letterbox mailbox, and your mailbox is located *on* your house and not elsewhere.

3. Pull off the letterbox, trying not to damage the door frame that much.
   → *Assumes:* You have the strength to do this and the ability to do it without yanking off part of your door.
4. Put your hand through the hole in your door, and try to reach either a set of keys or the handle to open the door.
   → *Assumes:* You have small hands, your letterbox is located near the door and/or you have keys inside within reach, and you don't have a vicious dog inside that will bite your groping hand.
5. If this doesn't work, try to find an open window that you might be able to get through.
   → *Assumes:* You didn't think of that already and any open window is within reach, rather than three stories up.
6. If you have a tiled roof and a ladder, you may be able to climb onto the roof, and gain access by removing tiles.
   → *Assumes:* You have a ladder nearby, you are willing to risk your life by climbing onto a tiled roof, removing tiles will not damage the roof, you won't have a 15-foot drop to get inside, and so on.

Theoretically, wikis can be an amazing resource for information and collaboration. However, the very openness of wikis can lead to credibility problems. Examine Wikipedia entries to see the range of quality. Use this rule of thumb: Before assuming anything obtained from a wiki site is a "fact," double-check it. Here are five wiki tips:

The Fab-Five Wiki Tips

1. Check the editors' credentials and/or personal bio to determine their qualifications.
2. Try to determine if anyone can edit the wiki or if there are restrictions (e.g., use of offensive language or negative remarks about a person or group) or controls as to who can post or edit their material.
3. Check out at least three or four of the wiki entries randomly chosen. Draw some inferences about the quality, and note if it falls short of what you might expect.
4. Pick one or two of the entries you examined and run a verifiability check—see if a known reputable site either collaborates the information or at least does not contradict it.
5. Don't get hooked—if it smells fishy or looks shoddy, look elsewhere or double-check the credibility of the author(s) and/or reliability of the site.

▦ The Internet and Intellectual Freedom

One good thing about the exposure to ideas is that it makes us think! Of course, not all ideas that we come across are noble or worth preserving. Some ideas are disturbing, disgusting, or detestable. On the other hand, some ideas are cathartic, inspiring, or groundbreaking. Some ideas have truly changed the world.

Of course, access to information is not a given. Some put obstacles in the way. For example, "Johns Hopkins University said Friday that it had programmed its computers to ignore the word 'abortion' in searches of a large, publicly financed database of information on reproductive health after federal officials raised questions about two articles in the database. The dean of the Public Health School lifted the restrictions after learning of them" (Robert Pear, "Health Database Was Set Up to Ignore 'Abortion,'" *The New York Times*, 4 Apr 2008).

Access to ideas and information is necessary for a democracy to flourish—and we cannot take this for granted. Indeed, "Restriction of free thought and free speech is the most dangerous of all subversions. It is the one un-American act that could most easily defeat us," asserted Supreme Court Justice William O. Douglas ("The One Un-American Act," *Nieman Reports* 7, no. 1, Jan 1953). The American Library Association (ALA) seconds this view:

> The free expression of ideas as embodied in the First Amendment is a basic human right. As American citizens, we have the right to read what we want to read, hear what we want to hear, watch what we want to watch and think what we want to think. Intellectual freedom is the right to seek and receive information from all points of view, without restriction, even those ideas that might be highly controversial or offensive to others.
>
> As a personal liberty, intellectual freedom forms the foundation of our democracy. It is an essential part of government by the people. The right to vote is not enough—we also must be able to take part in forming public opinion by engaging in open and vigorous debate on controversial matters. Libraries allow people to be well-informed so they can make the decisions our Constitution says are ours to make. (See American Library Association, www.ala.org.)

Incidentally, not all librarians agree with this position. One side of the controversy goes like this: What about the fact that libraries "discriminate" in what books and videos they purchase? One criterion for selecting what to buy is *quality*. Does the filtering process that libraries use in purchasing materials for the library have no parallel in the cyberworld? Some contend that the use of filtering software violates the right to access information and ideas. They consider that any form of censorship has the potential to take us down a slippery slope, leading to the censorship of literature or ideas. That is why the ALA is fighting attempts to "protect" children by requiring filtering software in library computers.

On the other hand, many librarians and others argue that human filters have been in place since public libraries first opened. They note that we ordinarily set limits around what is socially permissible and have had no problem ejecting people from libraries if they cross the boundary of decency or acceptable behavior. It is important for us to look at both sides of this issue and apply our critical thinking skills.

Censorship of the Internet

It's interesting to consider the censorship of the Internet alongside that of books. There are many similarities, but one key difference is how easy it is to access

Internet sites in the privacy of your own room. Thus, unsupervised children may come upon (or seek out) material that parents would not normally allow them to access and libraries would not likely contain (e.g., pornography and hate speech). The question is what sort of policy is optimal.

Harry S. Truman remarked in 1950 that "once a government is committed to the principle of silencing the voice of opposition, it has only one way to go, and that is down the path of increasingly repressive measures, until it becomes a source of terror to all its citizens and creates a country where everyone lives in fear" ("Special Message to the Congress on the Internal Security of the United States," www.trumanlibrary.org, 8 Aug 1950).

Group Exercise

Directions: Taking into consideration the proliferation of pornography, hate sites, and potentially offensive documents, answer the following:

1. State the three to four strongest arguments for and against censorship of the Internet.

2. Assume a mediation model. You can't have all or nothing when it comes to censorship, so what would you agree to let on the Internet? And what would you consider essential to be banned?

3. State the strongest justification you can for what should be *included* or what should be *excluded* from the Internet. Focus on *one* group of users: private users, adults at public sites (cybercafes, libraries, colleges, and universities), or minors at public sites (schools, libraries, cybercafes, etc.).

Exercises

1. Assume you don't know much about a particular topic (e.g., politics, social justice, or networking opportunities) *or* place (e.g., the United States, Canada, Mexico, France, or Kenya) *or* group of people (e.g., Democrats, Republicans, Christians, Muslims, or Jews). Assume also that the *only* source of information available is the Internet—particularly blogs. Pick *one* topic, place, or group (state what it is), and see what you can find. Summarize your findings in three to four paragraphs.

2. Suppose you are hired by a swanky company to work on their Internet "library." They have specialists in all areas *except* wikis. You have been asked to survey the territory and summarize your results (the range of types of wikis, the quality, and so on). Prepare a brief report.

3. Using the Fab-Five Wiki Tips, test *one* wiki that targets a specific audience (e.g., lawyers) or a narrow topic (e.g., house repairs). Do not put "Wikipedia" or any megawiki to the test. Share the results of your study.

Conflicting Views of the Internet

Many worry about the gap between the rich and the poor and the ways in which the Internet may be fueling that division. This concern is expressed by *The Vatican* in the following:

> One of the most important of these involves what today is called the digital divide—a form of discrimination dividing the rich from the poor, both within and among nations, on the basis of access, or lack of access, to the new information technology. . . . Individuals, groups, and nations must have access to the new technology in order to share in the promised benefits of globalization and development and not fall further behind. . . . Cyberspace ought to be a resource of comprehensive information and services available without charge to all, and in a wide range of languages. (Pontifical Council on Social Communications, *The Vatican*, www.vatican.va)

This raises important questions about economic and social justice and educational equity. The Internet, however, can also be used to fortify resistance, strengthen channels of communication, and share information—and it can do all this quickly and efficiently. And, although it provides channels for mega-corporations to expand their horizons, the Internet also permits websites allowing those in faraway places to survive.

Think of Benedictine monks illuminating manuscripts on Web pages (see the Vatican website at www.vatican.va). Think of Tibetans trying to sustain their culture, religion, and language (see the government of Tibet in exile at www.tibet.com). Think of all the Native American tribes whose websites are hubs of information (see, for example, www.cherokee-nc.com, www.tlingit-haida.org, and www.navajo.org). Think of all the indigenous artists trying to sustain traditional

Somebody knows that you're a dog.

Nik Scott, artist, www.nikscott.com. Reprinted with the permission of Nik Scott.

arts and crafts by selling beadwork, weaving, and sculpture through websites. Such groups often lacked the resources, contacts, financial backing, and channels to reach others. The Internet opens up a host of opportunities that can be transformative.

The Internet and Individual Privacy

This section could be called *Big Brother is watching you!* Finding a way to balance the competing concerns of computer privacy versus national security is not easy. The trend seems to be "less is more"—individuals should be willing to give up privacy rights in order to have a more secure society. Between the USA Patriot Act and changes allowing the FBI to access email from "public" servers, the concept of a right to privacy is being chipped away. This may be for the collective good, but it does have a price in terms of individual liberties. We need to find a way to balance the competing interests.

In October 2004, the United States funded a chatroom study to see if terrorists using the Internet to communicate could be monitored (and presumably stopped). Given the ongoing war on terror, the surveillance of email and Internet activity seems to be locked into place. According to CNET, "In January [2004], President Bush signed a pair of secret orders—National Security Presidential Directive 54/ Homeland Security Presidential Directive 23—that apparently deal with detecting and preventing Internet disruptions" (23 Apr 2008). This was part of the president's "Cyber Initiative" to combat terror.

When they are focusing on chatrooms, authorities are not violating constitutional rights to privacy, experts say. However, Johnathan Zittrain, Internet scholar at Harvard Law School, said, "It's the ability to gather and analyze massive amounts of data that creates the privacy problem, even though no individual bit of data is particularly private" (as quoted by Michael Hill, "U.S. Funds Chat-Room Study to Thwart Terrorist Plotters," *Daily [Law] Journal,* 12 Oct 2004). FBI director Robert Mueller thinks we need legislation that balances the privacy rights of individuals with the necessity of having some omnibus search capability to detect illegal activity and preempt it where it comes through a choke point (firewall) ("FBI Wants Widespread Monitoring of 'Illegal' Internet Activity," CNET .com, 23 Apr 2008).

There are broader concerns about individual privacy, given the high value of personal information and the many avenues for identify theft (e.g., the buying patterns of consumers and the interests of groups with considerable economic power).

Have you ever opened your "preferences" on your Internet server to examine your list of "cookies" that enable access to websites? This can be an eye-opening experience, as it reveals how open your window is to the world. Attached to the cookies for the particular site are almost always a host of cookies enabling companies to track your use of the Internet (i.e., what websites you navigate to). This is of great interest to advertising agencies because it helps companies figure out where to invest their marketing dollars. That the practice comes at a price to your privacy does not cause the twinge of the corporate conscience that some would like to see. Consequently, consumers and privacy watchdog groups seek to address this.

Our use of the Internet involves a range of applications—from purchasing books, to banking, to social networking—that leaves us open for our personal information being used without our knowledge or consent (and sometimes with grievous results):

> The data-sharing issues grow as more companies take a page from popular social-networking sites like MySpace and Facebook that let their users create pages full of details like where they live and work, who they are dating, and what their weekend plans are. People can share that information with other people by adding them as "friends," a term usually taken to describe anyone they know. As that idea has caught on, Internet companies have taken it further. If people like sharing basic information, the thinking goes, they'll love sharing even more particulars—like their shopping and reading habits. ("Web Sites Let Others See Users' Personal Data," *The Wall Street Journal,* 10 Feb 2008)

Basically, as Internet users, we are vulnerable, and until there is more regulation in place to protect us, we will have to take steps on our own. As *The Wall Street Journal* points out, "For consumers, there is no silver bullet to solving these privacy issues because each Web site shares information differently. So right now the onus is on individuals to protect themselves by painstakingly visiting each site to change their settings." As law clerk William McGeveran observes:

> First, there is rising concern in nearly every other area of the law about information privacy. Scholars engage in lively discussion about its possible social, legal, and constitutional dimensions. Congress has enacted new protection for the confidentiality of records about an individual's health care, finances, and even video rentals.
>
> Some of these initiatives encountered difficulties in implementation, but the trajectory of policy concern points consistently toward privacy. Information about campaign contributions is more easily available to the public than any of these other types of data, and perhaps more sensitive, yet there is little sign of commensurate concern about its privacy. ("Mrs. McIntyre's Checkbook: Privacy Costs of Political Contribution Disclosure," as noted by Rich Hasen, electionlawblog.org, 17 Mar 2004)

Group or Individual Exercise

Following the Money Trail

You have awakened from your political slumber and decided to donate money to a worthy political cause. Feeling very strongly about who should win the election, you dip into your life savings and give $200 to the League of Disaffected Voters. Your act of civic involvement, unbeknownst to you, gets your name on a fundraising tracking list. William McGeveran, as we know from the above quote, has concerns about such electronic forays into your once-private affairs. Read the following comments by Rick Hasen and then answer the questions below:

> I'm all for disclosure of major contributors and spenders in federal campaigns, but every once in a while I'm reminded of the privacy costs that come from disclosing the identity of small contributors. The last time was when I read William McGeveran's fine article on the topic. Now comes a link from the excellent website Political Wire (www.politicalwire.com) to Fundrace 2004's Neighbor Search (www.fundrace.org/ huffingtonpost.com). Just plug in your home address and find all of your neighbors who have given as little as $200 to a presidential candidate. I found out a number of interesting things about my neighbors through this simple search. ("The Anonymity Costs of Disclosing Small Donations," electionlawblog.org, 17 Mar 2004)

Answer the following:

1. Try out Fundrace's Neighbor Search to see how it posts the names and addresses of contributors. State three to four possible uses that might be made of this information by political campaign organizers and/or advertising agencies.

2. Is this information that could be used in ways that violate individual liberties in general or that you in particular would find offensive? Share your thoughts.

The Internet and Community

The Internet has become a channel for communication on a vast scale. News is sent around the world in a millisecond. In a flash, people can send out to the world their thoughts on politics, world events, neighborhood conflicts, and the like. The Internet allows people to communicate without ever hearing other people's voices or seeing their handwriting.

The potential for the "noble community" that librarian Nancy Pearl sees possible with books is also there with the Internet. We saw this in 2004 when the biggest evacuation in Florida history was under way. Hurricane Frances was heading straight toward Florida, and she was big (the size of Texas). Thanks to the Internet, the state of Florida was able to post information on services, emergency shelters, weather updates, the status of roads, Red Cross aid locations, and the like. Similarly, the cyclone that hit Myanmar (Burma) and the 7.8-magnitude earthquake in China in 2008 brought considerable devastation and many deaths and injuries. The Internet became a crucial source of information and action on a global scale.

A good example of a community network site is the Three Rivers Free-Net (TRFN) in Pittsburgh. There we find a public recognition of its goals:

> Author Paul Bowles once wrote that "the only effort worth making is the one it takes to learn the geography of one's own nature." In a sense, by working to link in cyberspace non-profits that don't easily meet in real space, TRFN does just that; it creates an internal geography to counter Pittsburgh's segmented physical geography.

The potential for transcending physical geography to allow networking can bring significant benefits. When you don't have to drive through sleet or snow or find a

The Global Dimension

Landmine Victims in Central America

The U.S. State Department estimates that there are 60–70 million landmines in nearly 80 countries. Equally mind-boggling is that one kills or maims victims an average of every 22 minutes. According to the United Nations, 30–40% of these victims are children. More than 52 million stockpiled antipersonnel mines have been destroyed by 69 countries, including 4 million in 2003 ("Global Landmine Use Decreases, but Mine Ban Campaign Cautions against Complacency," www.icbl.org/news, 9 Sep 2003). In an article on innovative uses of online courses, Bonnie Rothman Morris tells the following story. Read it and then answer the questions that follow:

> A medical worker in San Miguel, a city in eastern El Salvador, Mrs. Monge de Quintanilla toils daily . . . making and fitting prosthetic limbs for up to eight amputees daily, most of whom are victims of land mines. She acquired her skills as a prosthetist a decade ago through a military program during the war in El Salvador. In June she started an eight-month distance-education course intended to train her in the latest prosthetic techniques. She is one of 23 prosthetists in El Salvador, Nicaragua and Guatemala who are taking the pilot program, which was developed by the Center for International Rehabilitation, a three-year-old organization in Chicago that works to help victims of landmines. (Bonnie Rothman Morris, "Online Course Lets the Isolated Bring Their Medical Skills Up to Date," *The New York Times,* 30 Aug 2001)

The lessons for the prosthetics course were developed at the Northwestern University Prosthetic Orthotic Center.

Answer the following:

1. Discuss the potential for using the Internet to help address other societal problems.
2. Suggest ways of disseminating medical or other expertise and ideas to help those who are short on money, resources, or personnel and yet face serious problems like the one Mrs. Monge de Quintanilla is trying to alleviate.

common meeting time in order to network, everything shifts. And the structure of written, as opposed to oral, communication can bring a multiplicity of voices—and *new* voices—into the dialogue, and new ideas can take shape.

Exercises

1. What do you think will be the impact of such tools as YouTube and Facebook on (pick *one*) dating patterns, community or job networking, advertising, TV, or political campaigning? Set out some predictions and ideas.
2. Select *one* issue, such as homelessness, poverty, access to health care, gang violence, battered women and children trying to rebuild their lives, teenagers struggling with substance abuse or alcohol, or children with learning disabilities trying to make it through public schools.
   a. Write down all you think is being done to address this issue in our society.
   b. Are you optimistic or pessimistic about how much we are doing to try to make a difference? Set down your thoughts.
   c. Using *only* the Internet, see what is being done to address the issue you selected. Summarize your findings.

3. Select *one* of the following groups: the police, the fire department, local church groups, doctors/nurses, social workers, psychologists, lawyers, teachers, actors, musicians, airline employees, members of the military, Mothers Against Drunk Driving, or Al Anon.

   a. Set out your ideas about what the group you selected is doing for community outreach or other ways it provides services for the community.

   b. Try several searches (e.g., police and community outreach) to find information about the group you picked. Summarize the results and discuss whether you were surprised at your findings.

   c. See what you can find on your group using community-networking websites such as Seattle Community Network (www.scn.org) or Blacksburg Electronic Network (www.bev.net). Note that you can read about public libraries' role in providing community information at databases such as si.umich.edu/cfdocs/community/index/cfm.

4. In light of the excerpt below, set out your three strongest arguments for or against allowing prisoners to use the Internet for online dating.

   Online dating is the Web's largest trackable source of consumer dollars. . . . Prisons, one of America's largest industries, are worth an estimated $40 billion. . . . Convict matchmaking giants like prisonpenpals.com and jailbabes.com claim between 7,000 and 10,000 ads, and scores of competitors: from the straightforward (inmate .com) to the suggestive (ladiesofthepen.com). . . . Notoriety seems to almost guarantee mail—and proposals. . . .

   Penpal sites make their money by charging inmates roughly $40 to $75) to post their ads and print and forward any responses, or by charging pen pals (usually around $20) for inmate addresses. Few US prisoners are allowed access to e-mail or the internet, so most never see their listings. Some sites boast pages of testimonials: from soon-to-be-released convicts who've found love to death-row inmates who say letter-writing has given them a way to come to peace with dying.

   Some states take an active stand against the sites. The Oklahoma Department of Corrections issued "misconduct" citations to 51 inmates for violating the department's policy that "inmates may not directly or indirectly use any Internet services." [In fall 2002, however] a California judge overturned that state's DOC prohibition against inmates receiving mailed printouts from the Web, calling the policy "arbitrary." (from Mary Wiltenburg, "Web's Largest Business Pairs Up with Another Huge Industry: Prisons," *Christian Science Monitor*, www.csmonitor.com, 7 Aug 2003)

5. *You decide:* Convicted murderer Mumia Abu-Jamal (who says he was framed) has a number of websites supporting his release from prison (his legal appeals have thus far been denied). Convicted murderer Leonard Peltier (who asserts his innocence as well) also has websites presenting the case for his release. Examine at least one of the pro-Abu-Jamal websites *or* the pro Peltier websites, and then share your thoughts on how the Internet can (and should?) be used for political and personal causes.

6. What should be done to protect young people from sexual predators on the Internet? We keep reading about teenagers and children who are lured by a sexual predator posing as a "friend" in online chat rooms. There are more than 40 million users on MySpace, where you can create "friendships." Read the following, and then offer your suggestions about how to stop Internet predators.

"There is no silver bullet," said Bob Weaver, the assistant special agent in charge of the New York Electronic Crimes Task Force, which is run by the Secret Service and harnesses the efforts of 45 law enforcement agencies. "Traditionally, law enforcement in general has a stovepipe approach," he said. "The primary focus is on arrests, prosecutions and convictions. Now you're getting into education. Now you make a difference." (Elissa Gootman, "Stepping Up Protection for Youths on the Internet," *The New York Times,* 21 Aug 2001)

Facebook, the world's largest social networking site claims to have more than 175 million active members. From May 2000 to January 2009, it removed over 5,000 convicted sex offenders from the site ("Facebook Gives Sex Offenders the Boot," www.msnbc.com, 19 Feb 2009).

Hate Speech on the Web

The Web is no more immune from hate speech than any other vehicle of communication that does not have strict controls. The very existence of hate-filled websites creates a controversy around issues of freedom of speech and freedom of information. Many think we should err on the side of freedom, letting the audience decide for themselves. On the other hand, some are alarmed at the rise of hate sites.

The white supremacy (alias "White Nationalist") website called Stormfront is said to be the Web's first hate site, as well as the most-visited white supremacist site on the Internet. It even has children's pages, called "White Pride for Kids" (see Tara McKelvey, "Father and Son Team on Hate Site," USAToday.com, 10 Aug 2001). Stormfront describes itself in this manner: "Racialist discussion board for pro-White activists and anyone else interested in White survival" (www.google.com). Note the terms "racialists," "pro-White activists," and "White survival." The latter suggests that the authors believe whites are under some sort of imminent threat and thus need to take proactive "racialist" steps. Some infer that "racialist" and "racist" are closely linked.

Other countries are starting to take action against Internet hate speech. For example, the Council of Europe has adopted a measure that would criminalize Internet hate speech, including hyperlinks to pages that contain offensive content. It bans "any written material, any image or any other representation of ideas or theories, which advocates, promotes or incites hatred, discrimination or violence, against any individual or group of individuals, based on race, colour, descent or national or ethnic origin, as well as religion if used as pretext for any of these factors" (Julia Scheeres, "Europeans Outlaw Net Hate Speech," *Wired* magazine, 9 Nov 2002).

Reaction on this side of the Atlantic has not been very positive. American civil rights groups concerned about freedom of speech have condemned the European ban as "chilling" and/or "terrifying." The U.S. Justice Department has indicated it will not support broader restrictions because of potential incompatibility with First Amendment rights to free speech. "It's a terrifying prospect," says James Gattuso, a research fellow for the Heritage Foundation, a conservative think tank. "It's inherently dangerous for governments to define what appropriate speech is. You can't define or limit speech without chilling speech" (Michelle Madigan, "Internet Hate-Speech Ban Called 'Chilling,'" *PC World*, 2 Dec 2002).

Exercises

Part One

On February 28, 2005, the husband and the mother of a federal judge, Joan Humphrey Lefkow, were murdered execution-style. Speculation was that the murders were tied to a decision unfavorable to a white supremacist, Matt Hale. After the ruling, some websites evidently targeted Lefkow. Although the perpetrator appeared to have no ties to Matt Hale or to white supremacists, the case had a chilling effect on judges across the country. Here's why:

> The judge was once the target of a murder plot by a white nationalist, and postings praising the slayings on supremacist Web sites were accompanied by "RAHOWA!," meaning "racial holy war."... In a discussion on a white nationalist Web site in 2003, members had talked about the case against Hale and posted the Lefkows' home address. Anti-Defamation League official Mark Pitcavage said another white supremacist's short wave radio show last April had discussed killing the judge.... Judge Lefkow had been threatened by white supremacists since she ruled against them in a trademark case. ("Hate Groups Eyed in Judge Kin Slay," *CBS News*, www.cbsnews.com, 2 Mar 2005)

Answer the following:

1. List the key concerns for judges and lawyers prosecuting hate groups.
2. Make the strongest case you can for or against censoring websites that condone acts of violence in the name of a cause or political ideology.

Part Two

1. What should be done about racist websites that focus on a particular group or groups (e.g., blacks, Jews, Muslims, gays and lesbians, or abortion rights groups)? Should there be any restrictions, so long as they do not advocate violent acts? Would you impose restrictions if the website advocated threats or violence against members of the targeted group? Set out your recommendations, stating your reasons for each.

2. Read about the case below, and then share your thoughts as to whether you would amend any of your recommendations in question 1:

The FBI is reviewing a white supremacist Web site that purports to list the addresses of five of the six black teenagers accused of beating a white student in the small town of Jena and "essentially called for their lynching," an agency spokeswoman said. The Web site features a swastika, frequent use of racial slurs, a mailing address in Roanoke, Virginia, and phone numbers purportedly for some of the teens' families "in case anyone wants to deliver justice" ("Authorities Probe White Supremacist Web Site Calling for Lynching of 'Jena Six,'" FoxNews.com, 23 Sep 2007)

Group or Individual Exercise

Poisoning the Web: Hate Speech

Directions: Read the article below and summarize the argument by stating the thesis and key claims offered as support. Then state your response to the article and any recommendations you have about how to address hate speech.

Poisoning the Web: The Internet as a Hate Tool

The Anti-Defamation League

For years hate groups have created written materials of every kind to spread their propaganda, including books, glossy magazines, newspapers, flyers and even graffiti. As communication technologies advanced, these groups have kept up. First, they used standard broadcast-band and short wave radio, audiotape, videotape and public access cable TV. More recently, bigots of all kinds recognized the Internet's power and rushed to use it to rally their supporters, preach to the unconverted, and intimidate those whom they perceive as their enemies.

Even before *Stormfront* appeared on the Web, extremists had begun exploiting other ways to use the Internet, and these practices continue today. Lively conversations take place on numerous extremist Internet Relay Chat channels, such as #Nazi and #Klan. The USENET, a collection of thousands of public discussion groups (or newsgroups) on which people write, read and respond to messages, attracts hundreds of thousands of participants each day, both active (those who write) and passive (those who simply read or "lurk"). Newsgroups have been compared to community bulletin boards. Haters of all sorts debate, rant, and insult their opponents on newsgroups with titles such as *alt.politics.white-power* and *alt.revisionism.*

Electronic mailing lists (or "listservs") flourish as well. Such lists are like private "bulletin boards" available only to subscribers. While some lists keep their subscription information confidential, most are easy to join. Postings to some of these lists are moderated (i.e., monitored by the list operator who applies certain standards of acceptability), but others are entirely unregulated. . . .

Extremists also use E-mail, which allows them to communicate with one another directly, their missives ostensibly hidden from public view. In fact, E-mail is not truly private: computer-savvy individuals can intercept and read private messages. Some users, nervous about eavesdroppers, now use cryptographic programs. Cryptography converts written material using a secret code, rendering it unreadable by anyone who does not have the means to decode it. With encrypted E-mail, extremists have found a secure forum in which to exchange ideas and plans. . . .

Though purveyors of hate make use of all the communication tools the Internet provides, the World Wide Web is their forum of choice. In addition to its multimedia capabilities and popularity with Internet users, the Web allows bigots to control their message. Organized haters complain about civil rights activists who critique their manifestoes in USENET newsgroups and other interactive forums. In contrast, haters can refuse to publish critical messages on their Websites, just as a TV station can refuse to broadcast another station's opinions over its airwaves.

Furthermore, it is impossible for someone surfing the Web to know if any particular organization, other than one with a national reputation, is credible. Both the reputable and the disreputable are on the Web, and many Web users lack the experience and knowledge to distinguish between them. Increasingly, Web development tools have made it simple for bigots to create sites that visually resemble those of reputable organizations. Consequently, hate groups using the Web can more easily portray themselves as legitimate voices of authority.

Source: Reprinted with the permission of the Anti-Defamation League

CHAPTER FOURTEEN

Voices and Visions: The Media

In a speech at the United Nations in 1987, President Ronald Reagan said, "I occasionally think how quickly our differences worldwide would vanish if we were facing an alien threat from outside this world." He thought an extraterrestrial invasion would trump national differences. Then-national security advisor Colin L. Powell was convinced Reagan had been inspired by the movie The Day the Earth Stood Still.

NOTED BY J. HOBERMAN, *"The Day the Earth Stood Still:* A Message to
Earth From Another Time, Another Place," *The New York Times,*
December 6, 2008

In the great existential comedy *Groundhog Day,* a TV weatherman is locked in a time warp—a real-life Mobius strip—where he must relive the same day, Groundhog Day, over and over again. He comes to realize that, if nothing else can change, he can change himself. And so dawns his awareness that he, Phil Connors, is free to make something of his life. We watch his transformation from a sarcastic and self-centered person to someone who is compassionate, generous, and thoughtful. He starts to identify with the townspeople; his perception of the community tradition has much greater significance than mere filler on the nightly news. Once Phil becomes a participant, rather than a disinterested observer, he changes, and his work as a reporter changes as well.

The media can be a powerful force in presenting and interpreting current events and reflecting upon society. As critical thinkers, we benefit from seeing how ideas, issues, and arguments are treated. Both the news media and the entertainment media wield considerable power in terms of shaping perceptions and policies. In this chapter, we will first look at the news media and then turn to film and popular culture.

The News Media

Journalists provide an important antidote to social chaos by reporting and analyzing newsworthy events and placing them in historical and political context. They play a vital role in our society. As journalist Frank Rich says, "A public estranged from the press is also disengaged from the institutions and newsmakers that journalists cover—and will understandably look outside the system for both information and leadership." The very fact, for instance, that we can experience world events via live coverage shows us how powerful the news media can be.

This power is not exercised in a vacuum, however. We cannot take the media for granted. Being able to freely inquire into events, express concerns, and raise questions is vital to our democratic society. If the media use their power wisely, we can be an informed citizenry, and institutions can be held in check.

The media subvert their own power, however, when they succumb to corporate interests or political double-dealing. Laurie Garrett argues that "what suffers in the atmosphere of immediacy is analysis. What suffers in this search for speed is depth. The media in the wealthy world are becoming increasingly simplistic, superficial, and celebrity-focused" (Anu Shah, "Corporate Influence in the Media," *Human Rights Issues,* www.globalissues.org). We can't assume that all the news that's fit to print will actually reach us. By developing our analytical skills around how the news media both select and package the news, we can be a more discerning audience.

Tabloid-Style Journalism

Of course, you aren't one of those people who pick up a tabloid and flip through it. You probably missed the latest on the Batboy ("Batboy Nearly Killed in Serious Accident! Breaks Both Legs and Sprayed with Pesticides!!!"). And you weren't privy to the top stories in the *Weekly World News,* like "Half of Pentagon Generals Speak with a Lisp" and "Aliens Using Email to Seduce Earth Women." Hopefully you caught *The National Enquirer's* shocker "Hitler's Ghost Haunts [Tom] Cruise."

It's best not to fool oneself. Periodically, mainstream ("legitimate") news media have been known to succumb to tabloid-style journalism, too. Look, for instance, at the CNN website for May 15, 2008. There we find an article titled "Girl's Twin Found inside Her Stomach." It sounds like something out of a Grimms' fairy tales—until you read it:

> A nine-year-old girl who went to the hospital suffering from stomach pains was found to be carrying her embryonic twin, doctors in central Greece said Thursday. Doctors at Larissa General Hospital examined the girl and surgically removed a growth they later discovered was an embryo about six centimeters [2.4 inches] long. . . . The girl has made a full recovery.

That this was on the front page indicates that the line between "hard news" and "human interest" stories has blurred. Such stories are "hooks," drawing us in so we will stick around for less flashy "news."

Be on the watch for such **tabloidism.** The time devoted to the sensational or titillating is time lost on other, more significant, issues.

Exercises

1. Do a study of the ways in which one of your local TV stations covers *one* of the following. Note how the coverage of the topic you selected reflects on our society.
   a. Crime stories
   b. Human interest stories (ordinary people)
   c. National news
   d. International news
2. Find an example of the news media at their *best,* showing how the press presents an issue in a fair and balanced manner or uses investigative journalism to unveil hypocrisy or corruption.
3. Find an example of the news media at their *worst,* showing how the press fails to give a well-rounded account of an event or forsakes professional integrity for shallow entertainment purposes.
4. Do a study of a newspaper or news station over two to three days, and see if you can find any instances of *tabloidism.* Determine if the attention to the sensational or celebrity-driven news is to the detriment of more pressing stories.

Group or Individual Exercise

1. List 10 functions or types of coverage of news media (e.g., national news, sports, and weather reports).
2. What is *one* area not currently included that might be newsworthy?
3. List three to four ways the news media could better serve the community.

The Watchdog Role of the Media

By turning a spotlight on an event, public figure, political issue, societal problem, or moral controversy, the news media can relay relevant details and information to help us draw inferences as to what direction or policy would be preferable. This power is not to be underestimated.

One important function of a newspaper is to serve as a watchdog over the institutions in our society. This is not without controversy. Consider this example from 2004: When CBS's *60 Minutes* scheduled a program showing photos of abuse at Abu Ghraib prison in Iraq, Defense Department officials asked them to hold the story back for a few weeks. They consented, bringing the scandal to the public eye on May 6, 2004. Around the same time, Seymour Hirsh's article on Abu Ghraib came out in *The New Yorker*. This, effectively, created a double-whammy. More recently, journalists Dana Priest of *The Washington Post* and Richard Serrano have been instrumental in bringing human rights abuses to the public eye.

The news media are potentially watchdogs in all areas—not just politics. For example, Eileen Welsome of the *Albuquerque Tribune* received the Pulitzer Prize in 1994 for her series on radiation experiments during the 1940s on unsuspecting American citizens by government scientists and doctors. One consequence of these studies coming to light was that a federal bioethics committee was set up to study the experiments, and a presidential apology was issued to the research subjects.

Analyzing the Newspaper

First, get an overview. Look at a newspaper (or news website) as a whole document, and then look at the specific elements, so you get a sense of how it works.

Do a survey of the news articles. Determine how many columns in the front section were written by the staff reporters and how many were obtained from news syndicates like the Associated Press, Reuters, *The Los Angeles Times*, and *The New York Times*. This shows us how many sources supply the news. Watch for the emphasis (local, regional, national, international) and the range (hard news, entertainment, human interest, self-help, community services, etc.). Watch what dominates the news, and what has been shoved to the back burner or omitted.

Sharpening Our Antennae

Suppose you pick up *The New York Times*, and there on the front page is a photo of the Dalai Lama, the Buddhist spiritual leader from Tibet. You see his face quite clearly. It is in profile, with his right hand on the arm of a woman facing him. You see her less clearly, given that little more than the cheek of Rigoberta Menchu, Guatemalan Nobel laureate, is shown. The article's title is "Nobel Winner Accused of Stretching the Truth." You may not know that the Dalai Lama received the Nobel Prize in 1989 and that Rigoberta Menchu received it in 1992. But you do recognize *his* face in the photo. As you read the article, you discover that it is *she*, not he, who was accused of stretching the truth. The choice of the photograph, however, leaves a different impression.

Thanks to our heightened critical thinking powers, we are watching for such "errors," slips, misleading photos, and juxtapositions of image and text. This allows us to spot things that can go astray and lead to the wrong conclusion on the part of the reader.

Watching for Style and Content

What makes something newsworthy? How do newspapers inform us while keeping us interested? There is a delicate balance: If the newspaper is dull or dry, the audience will be limited. But if we see a newspaper that neglects newsworthy events in favor of the unusual, celebrity news, or wrenching human interest stories, it edges closer to a tabloid.

Read the news article for both style and content, and study the way the material is presented. *Style* refers to the presentation, including graphics and images, layout, type size, and font. *Content* refers to the substance of what is written—the text (unless the graphics or charts are referenced and germaine). Have your antennae out: News articles are rarely neutral or without a point of view, so look for the frame of reference.

Group or Individual Exercise

Where's the Beef in McDonald's French Fries?

Just when you thought you could eat a French fry without eating an animal by-product, the oil hit the fan. Examine the news item below and then answer the questions that follow.

SEATTLE—Facing a class-action lawsuit from angry vegetarians, McDonald's this week confirmed that its French fries are prepared with beef extract. . . . Although the fast-food giant has been saying since 1990 that its fries are cooked in pure vegetable oil, company spokesman Walt Riker said Wednesday that McDonald's never said its fries were appropriate for vegetarians and always told customers that their flavor comes partly from beef. A class action suit has been filed for "emotional distress" caused to vegetarians, some of them vegetarian for religious reasons, who thought McDonald's fries were in line with their strong feelings about not eating meat.

The list of French-fry ingredients that McDonald's offers at its franchises and on its Web site includes potatoes, partially hydrogenated soybean oil and "natural flavor." The list does not mention that the "natural flavor" comes from beef. . . . Harish Bharti, the Seattle lawyer who filed the suit against McDonald's Tuesday, said the confirmation that the company uses beef extract to flavor its fries validates his case. Bharti argues that a reasonable person who heard that McDonald's fries are prepared in "100 percent vegetable oil" and read the list of ingredients would assume the food is suitable for vegetarians. (Eli Sanders, "McDonald's Confirms Its French Fries Are Made with Beef Extract," *Boston Globe*, 4 May 2001)

Answer the following:

1. Would you say the author is sympathetic to the concerns of vegetarians? Explain.

2. The article later notes that Walt Riker, a McDonald's spokesperson, was asked why they did not specify that beef extract was used. He replied, "It's a good question. We'll review it. We'll take a look at it." He added that using "natural flavor" as a synonym for beef extract is within federal Food and Drug Administration guidelines. If *you* were the reporter, what questions might you then have asked Riker about this comment?

3. How would the article likely differ if the author were a press agent for McDonald's? Set out your ideas.

4. The McDonald's website lists the ingredients of its french fries (see below). How might vegetarians who want to eat McDonald's fries express their concerns?

French fries: Potatoes, vegetable oil (canola oil, hydrogenated soybean oil, natural beef flavor [wheat and milk derivatives]*), citric acid (preservative), dextrose, sodium acid pyrophosphate (maintain color), salt. Prepared in vegetable oil (may contain one of the following: Canola oil, corn oil, soybean oil, hydrogenated soybean oil with TBHQ and citric acid added to preserve freshness), dimethylpolysiloxane added as an antifoaming agent. *CONTAINS: Wheat and milk (**natural beef flavor** contains hydrolyzed wheat and hydrolyzed milk as starting ingredients).

Try to discern the author's thesis. Note the types of evidence cited. Watch for the use of quotes or expert testimony. Survey the front page, reading each heading and subheading. Get an overview by seeing how much is world news versus state or local news and how much is timely news (watch the date) versus attention-getting "non-news" (filler or human interest).

Checklist for Analyzing Style and Content

1. **Review the structure.** How is the article set out? Note where the thesis is presented and the way in which the author makes his or her case.

2. **Check the language.** Does the author use any loaded terms, technical terms, or prejudicial language? Does the title reflect the focus of the article?

3. **Watch for symbols and images.** What sort of picture do you get from this article? Is the style forceful and hard-hitting, or is it subtle—even folksy? Try to characterize the approach.

4. **Note any analogies and metaphors.** Does the author use a comparison to make a point? Analogies and metaphors can carry a great deal of weight, so watch for them.

5. **Watch for the use of testimony or expert witnesses.** Is there any reliance on what others had to say about the issue? Are those who give testimony or expert "advice" well qualified to be doing so? Note the credentials of those who are cited.

6. **Check the frame of reference.** From what point of view is the article written? Does the author write from a personal, or subjective, perspective? Is it written in the first person, or from a neutral stance?

7. **Check for descriptive/prescriptive language.** How much time does the author spend describing a state of affairs, going into detail on the specifics of the case? Does the author set out a position on what course of action *ought* to be taken?

8. **Note any photographs, graphs, and visual aides.** Do any photographs or visual aides accompany the article? What sort of impact do they have? How do they add to the article's appeal?

9. **Watch for recognition of audience.** Does the author write for a specialized, or learned, audience? Or is the article geared to anyone who can read? How much is presumed on the part of the reader by the author?

10. **Review for balance and fairness.** What does the author include and/or exclude? Do we get both sides (when it would be appropriate for the author to provide them)? Is anything either included *or* omitted that shows short-sightedness or bias?

Exercises

1. Discuss any *two* of these headlines, using the checklist. Draw an inference about the main focus or "angle" of the article so titled.
   a. "'Sexercise' Yourself into Shape" (*BBC News*, 11 Feb 2008)
   b. "Middle Ground is Shaky" (*The Washington Post*, 20 Feb 2009)
   c. "Illinois Man Designs Beer Can Coffin" (*USA Today*, 7 May 2008)
   d. "Napping Secret Out of the Bag" (*Denver Post*, 5 May 2008)
   e. "Dr. Jekyll and Mr. Hybrid" (*Boston Globe*, 7 May 2008)

2. Discuss any *two* of these headlines, using the checklist. Draw an inference about the main focus or "angle" of the article so titled.
   a. "Why Do So Many Pro Baseball Players Have August Birthdays?" (Slate.com, 16 Apr 2008)
   b. "Strangers Bring Us Closer to God" (NPR, 5 May 2008)
   c. "The Racehorse's Extraordinary Peeing Power" (Slate.com, 1 May 2008).
   d. "Canadian Shoppers Aren't Lazy, Just Busy" (*Globe and Mail,* 7 May 2008)
   e. "Empires Crumble, but Giant Robots Are Forever" (*Wired* magazine, 7 May 2008)
   f. "Peter Rabbit Must Die" (*The New York Times*, 5 June 2008)

3. Read the article on the border patrol's new weapon against smugglers, and then answer the questions below.

   The border patrol has decided to go nuclear against those who want to sneak barrels of mustard gas, bales of marijuana or bundles of bucks into the country. Starting early next week, U.S. Customs and Border Protection, or CBP, agents will start testing a nuclear scanning device, called a Pulsed Fast Neutron Analysis system (PDF), that will show a border agent the molecular construction of all materials in an 18-wheeler without the agent having to open the truck.

The $10 million system, which CBP installed in an old cotton field next to the Ysleta border crossing near El Paso, Texas, shoots pulsed neutrons through a cargo container's walls. Items in the trailer react to the mini-bombardment by emitting gamma rays. The machine then reads the gamma ray signature to create a three-dimensional rendering of the inside of the container. (Ryan Singel, Wired.com, 27 Aug 2004)

a. Suggest three possible titles for such an article.
b. Share your thoughts on the *actual* title of the article and what it suggests concerning what the article is about: "New Nukes at U.S. Border."

4. Using the checklist analyze the excerpt below on athletes who are *not* Olympic medal winners. Share what you inferred about the author's position on the subject.

ATHENS—Some bow gracefully to the inevitable as they approach the finish line; others grimace with fury and frustration. Some go home happy simply to have taken part; others wonder why they wasted four years of blood, sweat, and tears. . . .

But with the right approach, [says] Andrew Walton, who advised the British Olympic team in 1984, "Losing itself is a valuable experience." Obviously, the top athletes go to Athens intent on winning. But, . . . "We try to stay away from talking about winning and losing," he explains, "because if you don't win you are automatically a loser, and things aren't that black and white in sports. . . . The key question is, 'Are you satisfied with your performance?'" The sporting world was not always so forgiving. ("Losing Is an Art for Most Olympians," *Christian Science Monitor,* 27 Aug 2004)

5. When the racehorse Eight Belles was euthanized (put to sleep) in May 2008 after it shattered both its front ankles in a freak fall at the end of a race, the people at the racetrack and in the TV audience were not able to see the euthanasia being performed. Since they had special screens for such a contingency, it is clear that this decision (to censor what could be seen in such cases) had been put in place as policy at an earlier time. Where should a news editor (of a newspaper *or* a news website *or* TV news) draw the line when it comes to running disturbing images or photographs? Be as precise as you can in setting out your recommendations (e.g., torture of animals cannot be shown, but images of injured animals are okay).

6. Do you think newspapers and online news sources should have to operate by the same set of rules when it comes to the use of language (e.g., profanity, colorful descriptions, jokes, and anecdotes)? Briefly set out your position.

7. Some newspapers (e.g., *The New York Times*) have put in place what they call a "public editor" who is empowered to observe and to discuss with readers, reporters, and editors how well the newspaper is covering the news. (See the "Week in Review" section of *The New York Times*' Sunday edition for an example.) The goal is to have an independent eye watching and assessing how fair and balanced their coverage is. State what *three* duties a public editor should have.

Quick Quiz

1. *True or false:* The term "media" includes newspapers as well as TV and film.
2. The term "frame of reference" refers to:
   a. The point of view or perspective from which something is presented
   b. Bias or prejudice as indicated by the use of language or symbols
   c. The images and photographs accompanying the text
   d. The theoretical model used in an analysis
3. *True or false:* The first step when analyzing a newspaper is to look at the photographs on the front page to see how they are trying to appeal to the audience.
4. The key concern when an article refers to the testimony or comments of an "expert" is (a) that the expert keeps comments brief and clear or (b) that the expert is well qualified and the comments are relevant to the topic discussed.
5. Whether the writing style is "folksy" or more sophisticated is an issue of:
   a. The author's background
   b. The approach of the article
   c. The credibility of the newspaper itself
   d. The use of images and symbols
6. *True or false:* The way graphics are used on a news website is an issue of *content*.
7. The type size and font used is an issue of (a) style or (b) content.
8. *True or false:* A writer who assumes the reader is college educated has a particular *audience* in mind.

Watching for Professional Standards

People tend to trust news media. They are seen as a good source of information and, with blogs and letters to the editor, a way to discuss current events with others. However, to be a legitimate source of information, the news media must adhere to fundamental values centered around integrity.

Occasionally, integrity falls by the wayside, as when there is a misrepresentation of the facts or biased coverage. Everyone suffers when journalists fabricate or omit vital details. It is bad enough if it's a reporter—like Jack Kelly and Jason Blair—who fabricates stories. It's even worse when the news media themselves are complicit. For example, the failure to closely examine the evidence used to justify the Iraq war led to a public apology in 2004 from *The New York Times*. *The Times*' editor said, "Looking back, we wish we had been more aggressive in re-examining the claims as new evidence emerged—or failed to emerge." Similarly, *The Washington Post*'s Bob Woodward said, "We did our job, but we didn't do enough" (Howard Kurz, "The Post on WMDs: An Inside Story," *The Washington Post,* 12 Aug 2004).

Another example is a *Los Angeles Times* retraction of a March 17, 2008, story on rap artist Tupac Shakur due to evidence now seen as not "credible." The problem was that "the Times has since concluded that the FBI reports on a 1994 assault were fabricated and that some of the other sources relied on" do not support major elements of the story ("The Times Retracts Tupac Shakur Story," 7 Apr 2008).

Don't take things at face value. We need to have our antennae out and hold those in the news media to high standards. As an empowered audience, we have a role in sustaining professional ethics. By developing our analytical skills, we can then assess the issues and possible solutions or policy recommendations.

Checking the Use of Language

Watch the use of language. A word or phrase can shape the meaning of an entire passage. For example, all of these refer to the same person: Eleanor Roosevelt, Mrs. Roosevelt, the First Lady, the president's wife, Franklin's wife, Sara's daughter-in-law, and Anna's mother. However, they do not all *function* the same way in a sentence. Calling the First Lady by her first name suggests familiarity or informality. Using terms like "the president's wife" or "Franklin's wife" define her in terms of her husband. And so on. Depending upon the context, any one of the references to Eleanor Roosevelt may be appropriate, but each term has different connotations.

The way we use words can shade an interpretation or slant the piece from one extreme to another. This is apparent when racist or sexist language is used, because such language is loaded and can have an explosive effect on readers. As noted above, newspapers issue apologies for problems such as misrepresentation, sloppy reporting, and plagiarism.

The way language is used warrants our consideration. Arriving at good decisions about what words (and images) to use to avoid conflict or bias is not always easy.

A Free Press

It is not easy to find a balance between informing the public and disclosing personal details or graphic, disturbing images. On what side should we err if we want to ensure freedom of the press? The answer may vary according to our criteria (e.g., who the audience is, what our goals or intentions are, and how we preserve respect for human dignity). For example, many people think the news media should publish disturbing (if not grisly) photos to fully convey the cost of war, gang killing, or drug abuse.

We can only succeed as a free country if we are informed citizens and have the ability and right to think for ourselves. This means the right to access information and to have the critical thinking skills to reason about what we see and hear. A free press is an important source of information, ideas, and insights.

The Global Dimension

Free Press versus the Iranian Government

Stephen Kinzer writes about his attempt to go to Iran and the problems he ran into. He reflects on the consequences for freedom of the press in his article "Red Lines and Deadlines" (www.pbs .org). He sets the stage by noting:

As the time for my January [2004] trip to Iran approached, I began contacting people there to arrange interviews. Among them were powerful figures in the religious regime, some of whom seemed alarmed to learn that a journalist who had written favorably about [Prime Minister Mohammed] Mossadeq was being allowed into the country. A few hours before I was to leave, I received a startling message from the Iranian diplomatic mission in New York: Stay home or risk arrest at the Tehran airport. I will probably never know what led to this sudden change in the regime's attitude toward me, but I have a theory: Probably I was caught in the same power struggle that envelops all of Iranian public life. Those who promoted my trip and obtained my visa so quickly did so because they hoped I would help propagate their ideals in Iran. Their conservative rivals also suspected I would do that, and when they learned I was coming, they stepped in to cancel my trip.

Freedom of the press is necessary for an informed public, as the case of Iran shows. In the summer of 2001, there was an outcry against repressive actions against the press in Iran:

An unprecedented attack has started against the press in Iran. Some 43 newspapers, weeklies, and other publications have been ordered shut by the judiciary. We condemn the closing of the newspapers and the jailing of their editors and writers. We support freedom of expression for all. We condemn suppression of the people's rights and voices in all shapes and forms. (*Iran News*, www.payvand.com)

In response to the government's action, a letter campaign was launched. Form letters were distributed in hopes that people would fill out the letter and mail it in protest to the Iranian president. Read the letter (also from *Iran News*, www.payvand .com) and then answer the questions that follow.

His Excellency
Hojjatoleslam Seyed Mohammad Khatami,
President of the Islamic Republic of Iran
The Presidency
Palestine Avenue
Azerbaijan Intersection
Tehran, Islamic Republic of Iran

Your Excellency:

As you are well aware, an unprecedented attack has started against the press in Iran. Some seventeen newspapers, weeklies, and other publications have been ordered shut by the judiciary. Unfortunately, as you also know, such actions run contrary to the Constitution and civil legal code of the Islamic Republic of Iran in more than one area.

Overwhelming legal backing for the press, their rights, and freedoms, has been enshrined in the Constitution of the Islamic Republic of Iran, and its laws—a Constitution which is the fruit of the struggles of the Iranian people against dictatorship during the Islamic revolution of [1979].

As concerned Iranians abroad, who maintain no affiliations with groups seeking the overthrow of the current system of government of Iran, and respect the choice of the people of Iran as exemplified in countless popular elections over the past 20 years, we respectfully call upon your excellency to safeguard the Constitution and laws of this ancient land. We are extremely concerned about the future course and fate of the free press in Iran, and urge you to take action on their behalf.

Answer the following:

1. Note that the frame of reference is *Iranians abroad*. Do you think the letter would have more impact if it were modified to include "concerned citizens of the world" or other groups? Share your thoughts and ideas.

2. What are the potential benefits of a letter campaign such as this one?

3. It is usually easier to criticize the policies of other countries than those that shape our own society. Do an Internet search and see what national or local issues around freedom of the press society today faces. State those issues and concerns, citing the sources you find.

Ownership and Control

We need only watch the movie *The Manchurian Candidate* or read a futuristic novel like *1984* or *The Handmaid's Tale* to get a sense of what tyrannical control of information entails. This includes what information is released and what is withheld.

The exposure to contrasting opinions and points of view helps us become less dogmatic and more open-minded. We gain mental flexibility by being able to look at issues from a variety of perspectives, as we saw in the discussion in Chapter 1. Newspapers and news programs can provide valuable information and ideas. To do this effectively, however, journalists must be able to go beneath the surface and examine different facets of issues. Journalist John Balzar takes this up in his discussion of editorial cartoons. He observes:

> The very thing that makes editorial cartoonists stand out in journalism may also account for their being targets now: their skill at penetrating the skin and jabbing raw nerves. Editorial cartoonists are famed for bringing in bags of scalding letters to the editor. Publishers and editors sometimes wince, but the good ones are expected to honor covenants that hold this interchange to be part of a newspaper's role in a community—stirring the civic kettle. (John Balzar, "Biting the Bullet," *Los Angeles Times*, 24 Aug 2004)

The value of freedom of expression should not be underestimated. Exposure to ideas helps us develop our intellectual and creative potential. It also helps us be more tolerant of other worldviews. This was illustrated in the documentary *Control Room* which looks at Al Jazeera, the leading TV news source in the Arab world. The documentary shows how political ideologies can affect decision making at all levels of news broadcasting. It also shows how important it is to strive for balanced news coverage and for an open dialogue about the issues the news media cover.

The free expression of ideas, however, is not an unbridled outpouring devoid of a sense of morality. There is no justification for racist diatribes and hate speech. We need not lose sight of justice, but we need to expose ourselves to a range of ideas. Without an open inquiry that allows for the expression of diverse perspectives, we condemn ourselves to tunnel vision. It is crucial that the news media present balanced coverage and offer a range of perspectives on the issues we face as a society.

Images and the Public Consciousness

Editorial cartoons, photographs, and even comic strips have the capacity to become etched in our collective memory. Think of the photos of the planes hitting the Twin Towers on 9/11. Think of the little girl running naked and screaming after being

Group or Individual Exercise

Talk Radio in Iraq

Some think of talk radio as a venue for people to rant about politics. But that's not the only model a talk radio station could follow. Read about Radio Dijla in Baghdad:

BAGHDAD—A housewife calls to talk about a broken sewer pipe. A student calls to talk about a lost love. . . . The station is one of the most listened-to in Baghdad, according to its employees, a claim that appears to have merit, judging by its broad following. . . . The station receives an average of 185 calls an hour. Most calls are about the nuts and bolts of life. "Iraqi citizens have big problems but nobody listens to them," said Haidar al-Ameen. . . . The station forces the government to make time. Local and federal officials come as guests and are grilled by listeners.

Beyond easing the frustrations of daily life, the station provides a chance for Iraqis to talk publicly about politics for the first time in decades. Their calls open a window onto the lives of ordinary Iraqis, whose opinions often go unheard in the frantic pace of bombings, kidnappings and armed uprisings. . . .

On the station's first day, Salim simply sat at the microphone and asked listeners what they wanted to talk about. Now, in addition to the government official call-in shows, the station has programs on which lawyers answer questions. (Sabrina Tavernise, "Talk Radio Gives Iraqis a Powerful New Voice," *International Herald Tribune*, www.iht.com, 31 Aug 2004)

Answer the following:

1. How might talk radio be used to strengthen free expression?
2. Listen to a talk radio show for at least 30 minutes and then discuss the format and the range of topics that were discussed. Note any concerns you might have. What can you infer from what you heard?
3. State two or three ways talk radio could provide a public service, focusing on one group (e.g., college students, sports fans, single men/women).

---

napalmed in the Vietnam War. Think of that photo of Marilyn Monroe with her dress blowing up around her waist, showing her legs. You can probably think of some of your own family photos that have their tentacles in your brain!

Images can create dilemmas for news editors—whether the images are cartoons, drawings, or photographs. We know images can have an impact. Just think of those ghastly photos of celebrities looking tired, overweight, or drunk, or with botched botox treatments that we see on tabloids at grocery store checkout stands. Staring at such photos reminds us why *not* being famous has its virtues.

Generally, mainstream sources (print or online) have restrictions about what sorts of photographs can be printed (e.g., no nudity and no photographs of the faces of dead people)—and yet the rules are not carved in marble. There are serious questions about what kinds of images are appropriate for a newspaper to publish on the front page and what should be consigned to page 18 (or left out entirely). And then there are the photos that do not get published—such as those of coffins of dead soldiers or close-up photos of dead people.

The Dangers of Controls

In any tense political climate, it is not surprising that editors clamp down on comic strips and political cartoons. Photographs and articles are also subject to being sanitized to remove any "offensive" or politically volatile sections. One influence on the decision making around such editorial "management" is media conglomerates, such as Time Warner, that own media outlets, cable companies, TV stations, newspapers, and so on. They are a force unto themselves. More and more news sources are being bought out by a shrinking number of corporations, restricting the range and diversity of news coverage.

Of course, whatever counts as "news" reaches the public only if there are outlets. As Robert M. McChesney observes, "The global commercial-media system is . . . politically conservative, because the media giants are significant beneficiaries of the current social structure around the world, and any upheaval in property or social relations—particularly to the extent that it reduces the power of business—is not in their interest" (Quoted in Anup Shah, "Media Conglomerates, Mergers, Concentration of Ownership," *Human Rights Issues,* www.globalissues.org, 29 Apr 2007). This cuts both ways. If the global media system showed a liberal bias and we had little or no access to a more conservative approach, we would similarly suffer.

"Newspapers are, more and more, being run by corporations, by people who don't always understand the value of generating dialogue," said Bruce Plante, cartoonist for the *Chattanooga Times* editorial page ("Biting the Bullet," *Los Angeles Times,* 24 Aug 2004). Corporate interests can't help but want some attention paid to increasing revenue. This concern is not necessarily in sync with the concerns of informing the community, opening up a dialogue on social issues, and providing diverse perspectives on current events.

Linguist and social commentator Noam Chomsky warns of the danger of the media falling under the power of the government or corporate interests. His advice? We need to be vigilant about being an attentive and critical audience. In other words, our critical thinking skills should be operating at full speed. Chomsky comments on his interest: "I am interested in the whole intellectual culture, and the part of it that is easiest to study is the media. It comes out every day. You can do a systematic investigation. You can compare yesterday's version to today's version. There is a lot of evidence about what's played up and what isn't and the way things are structured" (Noam Chomsky, "What Makes the Mainstream Media Mainstream," *Z Magazine,* www.zmag.org, Jun 1997).

Chomsky's Guiding Questions

Question 1: How do the media relate to other systems of power and authority? This asks about the *internal structure* of the media and their setting in the *broader society.*

Question 2: What can we infer about the *media product* itself, in light of what we observe about the structure? This asks about *mass* media (entertainment, Hollywood, soap operas, etc.) and about the *elite* media.

You Tell Me Department

Are Cartoonists Dangerous?

Political cartoonist Michael Ramirez is no stranger to controversy. On July 21, 2003, the U.S. Secret Service arrived at the *Los Angeles Times* newsroom to "visit" the Pulitzer Prize–winning political cartoonist regarding a recent cartoon. Agent Peter Damos was turned away after meeting with an attorney for the newspaper. But the incident sent shockwaves through the small world of political cartoonists.

The cartoon in question was based on an award-winning photograph from the Vietnam War in which General Nguyen Ngoc Loan executes a Viet Cong prisoner by shooting him point-blank in the head. Ramirez's cartoon plays off that photo—it depicts President Bush with his hands behind his back as a man labeled "Politics" prepares to shoot Bush in the head. The background of the drawing is a cityscape labeled "Iraq." You can see the cartoon at cagle.slate.msn.com. Evidently, the Secret Service thought the cartoon represented a threat to the president. The agency's actions caused U.S. Rep. Christopher Cox (R–Newport Beach), chair of the House Committee on Homeland Security, to speak out on Ramirez's behalf. (cox.house.gov, 21 Jul 2003). Here is the letter he wrote:

The Honorable Ralph Basham, Director, U.S. Secret Service, 950 H Street, NW Washington, D.C. 20223

Dear Ralph:

I am writing regarding the recent interrogation of editorial cartoonist Michael Ramirez by the Secret Service.

I am pleased to learn that the decision to question Michael Ramirez was neither made nor approved by Washington headquarters of either the Secret Service or the Homeland Security Department. However, the use of federal power to attempt to influence the work of an editorial cartoonist for the *Los Angeles Times* reflects profoundly bad judgment.

Not only is the work of this individual well known (he is a winner of the Pulitzer Prize whose work is syndicated in more than 900 newspapers), but the published work on its face was well within the ample bounds of any federal law which the Secret Service is charged with enforcing. The reported suggestion by the Secret Service that Mr. Ramirez should take into account the possible reaction of unstable people to editorial opinion expressed in graphics implies a standard that would render adult discussion of serious issues impossible.

It is legally irrelevant, but further embarrassing to the federal government, that the editorial cartoon in question—far from constituting an incitement to violence against President Bush—expressed support for President Bush's policies. I take a back seat to no one when it comes to support for the federal responsibility to protect the life of the President. As a White House lawyer for President Reagan, I sat in court next to Sarah Brady during legal proceedings to determine whether John Hinckley [who shot Reagan and is now in prison] could be released.

Mr. Ramirez is owed an apology, and the public is owed an explanation both of how this happened and why it will not happen again.

Sincerely, Christopher Cox, Chairman

You tell me: Do you think Ramirez was out of line depicting the execution of the president? Do you think the *Los Angeles Times* was out of line to publish this political cartoon? Do you agree with Rep. Cox that an apology was owed?

The elite media are the agenda-setting media that set a framework within which others operate. *New York Times* sends notices to editors, even in the middle of the country, about what the top news stories will be the next day. Chomsky asserts that the little newspapers that lack the resources to research the big news events are pressured to fall in step with the elite media. He argues, "If you get off line, if you're producing stories that the big press doesn't like, you'll hear about it pretty soon" (Noam Chomsky, "What Makes the Mainstream Media Mainstream," *Z Magazine*, www.zmag.org, Jun 1997).

Shaping Public Opinion

At times, the news media have been used to shape public opinion by inflating one event to the detriment of others. We saw this with the coverage of Paris Hilton's brief jail sentence, Britney Spears' hair-cutting incident, and Joe the plumber's comments on the economy. Discussions of media coverage characterized these stories with such terms as "media circus," "media zoo," and "feeding frenzy."

One concern of media analysts is the question of *influence*. The very idea of the "fourth estate" is that an educated citizenry depends upon a free press. We must, therefore, ensure that journalists are not coerced to manipulate information.

Although the overwhelming majority of news organizations worldwide and nationally are privately or stockholder-owned, there are public news sources, like NPR and PBS (the United States), the BBC (Britain), the NHK (Japan), and the CBC (Canada). These public media help protect us from corporate or governmental interests controlling news coverage—both in the choice of focus and in the depth of analysis.

Exercises

1. On February 17, 2009, *The New York Post* ran a cartoon by Sean Delonas showing two police officers (one with a smoking gun) looking down at a dead chimp. The caption was, "They'll have to find someone else to write the next stimulus bill." Public outrage led to a *Post* apology and insistence that it was not intended as a depiction of President Obama, [or] as a thinly veiled expression of racism. Examine the cartoon (at www.nypost.com/delonas/delonas.htm) and share your thoughts about what the *Post* editor should have done.

2. See if you can find an article in a nontabloid newspaper (print or online) that you consider balanced, fair, and without any obvious bias. Cite the evidence, drawing from your article, that this is the case.

3. See if you can find an article in a nontabloid newspaper (print or online) that you consider unbalanced, unfair, and indicative of a clear bias. Cite the evidence, drawing from your article, that this is the case.

4. See if you can find an example of how corporate ownership affects the style or content of what is covered as news (e.g., of a major political event, such as the last presidential election). Note if the coverage was balanced and fair to both major parties. Did you detect any bias toward one political view?

Balanced News Coverage

Seek a range of perspectives. Read newspapers of different political, social, and religious persuasions. Expose yourself to a wide variety of commentaries on world events. Keep an open mind. And watch for discrepancies. What's front-page news in one area may be relegated to page 24 in another city's newspaper.

It's important to seek sources presenting the interests of different cultural groups and social organizations. Watch for the potential influence of gender, age, class, sexual orientation, race, and ethnicity on topics and coverage. And be on the lookout for author bias, editorial bias, or assumptions about audience bias.

Thanks to the Internet, we now have newspapers from all over the world at our fingertips. This fact radically alters the ways in which we can become informed about current events, offering resources on a scale unthinkable 5 or 10 years ago.

Six Factors for Balanced News Reading

1. **Political:** Seek diversity of political viewpoints. (Look at the range of voices and ideas in the discussion.)
2. **Economic:** Seek diversity in terms of financial or class interests. (Look at who stands to gain or lose.)
3. **Frame of reference:** Seek diversity of perspectives. (Look at gender, race, class, and so on.)
4. **Conceptual:** Seek diversity in ways problems are defined and solved. (Look at the approach taken, the use of language, assumptions, and alternative interpretations.)
5. **Ethical:** Seek diversity of ethical and religious viewpoints. (Look at values and beliefs.)
6. **Cultural:** Seek diversity of opposing viewpoints. (Look at the worldview, social traditions, and group identification.)

Exercises

1. According to a report by journalist David Barstow, a Pentagon "information apparatus . . . has used [a group of military] analysts in a campaign to generate favorable news coverage of the administration's wartime performance." Read the following and state the main pieces of evidence he cites to support his view.

Records and interviews show how the Bush administration has used its control over access and information in an effort to transform the analysts into a kind of media Trojan horse—an instrument intended to shape terrorism coverage from inside the major TV and radio networks. Analysts have been wooed in hundreds of private briefings with senior military leaders, including officials with significant influence over contracting and budget matters, records show. They have been taken on tours of Iraq and given access to classified intelligence. They have been briefed by officials from the White House, State Department and Justice Department, including Mr. Cheney, Alberto R. Gonzales and Stephen J. Hadley.

In turn, members of this group have echoed administration talking points, sometimes even when they suspected the information was false or inflated. Some analysts acknowledge they suppressed doubts because they feared jeopardizing their access. A few expressed regret for participating in what they regarded as an effort to dupe the American public with propaganda dressed as independent military analysis.

Kenneth Allard, a former NBC military analyst who has taught information warfare at the National Defense University, said the campaign amounted to a sophisticated information operation. "This was a coherent, active policy," he said. As conditions in Iraq deteriorated, Mr. Allard recalled, he saw a yawning gap between what analysts were told in private briefings and what subsequent inquiries and books later revealed. "Night and day," Mr. Allard said, "I felt we'd been hosed." . . .

Over time, the Pentagon recruited more than 75 retired officers, although some participated only briefly or sporadically. The largest contingent was affiliated with Fox News, followed by NBC and CNN, the other networks with 24-hour cable outlets. But analysts from CBS and ABC were included, too. Some recruits, though not on any network payroll, were influential in other ways—either because they were sought out by radio hosts, or because they often published op-ed articles or were quoted in magazines, Web sites and newspapers. At least nine of them have written op-ed articles for *The Times.* The group was heavily represented by men involved in the business of helping companies win military contracts. Several held senior positions with contractors that gave them direct responsibility for winning new Pentagon business. ("Behind TV Analysts, Pentagon's Hidden Hand," *The New York Times,* 20 Apr 2008)

2. State what Noam Chomsky might say about the Pentagon exerting such influence (apply one or both of his key questions).

3. What criteria would you use to determine when the news media are doing a good job of deciding what is newsworthy and presenting it in a fair and balanced way? State three or four of *your* criteria for excellence in reporting—either in general or in a specific area (e.g., entertainment news or sports). Find an example of the news media at its *best,* showing how the press presents an issue in a fair and balanced manner or uses investigative journalism to unveil hypocrisy or corruption.

4. What are indicators (red flags) that the news media are doing a poor job of deciding what is newsworthy and presenting it in a fair and balanced way? State three or four. Find an example of the news media at its *worst,*

showing how the press fails to give a well-rounded account of an event or forsakes professional integrity for entertainment value.

5. Examine the front section of two different nontabloid newspapers or news websites, from different geographic regions.
   a. Studying the two newspapers, how do they rate on the six factors of balanced coverage (see list above)? Compare and contrast the papers.
   b. Assume that the news articles are selected to interest the targeted audience. From the articles in the two newspapers, what can you infer about the different audiences (the readers for each of the papers)?
   c. What are possible reasons for the overlap (if any) between the two newspapers? Note similarities and differences (e.g., the same lead story, on national vs. international news).
   d. Looking at a list of articles in the two newspapers, draw some inferences about the journalistic goals or guidelines set for individual staff writers.
   e. What are the pros and cons of a local newspaper using news services as a major source of articles?

Individual Responsibility

As members of the audience, we are often put in the position of having to evaluate the relative importance of news items. Keeping informed and maintaining sharp critical thinking skills helps us accomplish that goal. We also need to read in-depth news coverage and commentaries—and expose ourselves to a range of perspectives. In this way, we may obtain a broader understanding of events and their impact on people's lives.

A reader can use newspapers as *vehicles for social action* in three major ways. One is through letters to the editor. Another is through a commentary (e.g., an op/ed piece in the editorial section of the paper). The third is through press releases (usually sent out by an institution or an organization). In the case of a letter to the editor, the reader can express a point of view on a current issue or a reaction to news coverage of a particular event. With op/ed articles, the author sets out a position, with the goal of persuading others to his or her way of thinking. With a press release, an organization can bring events and news to the public eye by sending a prepackaged article, in hopes the newspaper will publish it. By working in community, we can let our collective concerns be expressed and have a voice in the direction our society takes.

The Distinct Role of Sports in the News Media

Sports coverage plays a unique role in the news media and remains a staple of print, radio, and TV. Although sports is male-dominated, it attracts both males and females as participants and viewers. The language, images and descriptions,

Great for dunking.

My friends told me, "T-Mac, you're gonna be big some day." Must've been the milk. About 15% of your height is added as a teen and the calcium and vitamin D can help. Will drinking a cool glass of milk make you the hottest scorer in town? Hey, it couldn't hurt.

got milk?

Reprinted with the permission of Lowe Worldwide Inc. as agent for the National Fluid Milk Processor Promotion Board.

FIGURE 14.1
Stars like Tracy McGrady are at the crossroads of sports and culture.

and outpouring of emotion give sports coverage a narrative power that other news typically lacks, for a number of reasons. One is the unique role of athletes in our society. With strength and finesse, and with actions magnified for all to see and each move subject to instant replays, the athlete is a cultural icon.

Sports and sports coverage form an integral part of our culture (see Figure 14.1). Consequently, when we apply our critical reasoning skills to this area, we discover a window on society. With such fertile ground for digging, we need the right tools. These are set out in the checklist below.

Sports Coverage Checklist

1. **Examine the reasoning.** Zero in on arguments; assess the strength of evidence cited in support of the conclusion. Check for facts, opinions, and ideas.
2. **Analyze and evaluate.** Check for warranted versus unwarranted assumptions, potential sources of bias or prejudice, stereotypical thinking, and the use of images and symbols.

3. **Watch for visual and verbal messages.** Check the presentation of information and the use of images and photographs.
4. **Check the use of language.** Watch for loaded terms, biased language, asymmetrical descriptions, repetition, metaphors, and poetic expressions to convey an idea.
5. **Notice inductive and deductive lines of reasoning.** Watch especially for use of analogies, reliance on statistical studies, and cause-and-effect reasoning.
6. **Be on the alert for fallacious reasoning.** Check especially for the fallacies of ad populum (appeal to the masses), ad verecundiam (irrelevant testimonials of famous figures), ad hominem (personal attack), ad hominem circumstantial (discrediting by social or political affiliation), question-begging epithets (slanted language biasing an interpretation), and bifurcation (false dichotomy). (See Chapter 7 for a review.)
7. **Be aware of the frame of reference.** Consider other perspectives on the situation and how things would change if other voices were heard.
8. **Watch for cultural or ethnic sensitivity.** Examine the values and worldview implicitly presented, narrowing or broadening our understanding of the people or issues involved.

Values and Language of Sports Coverage

Sports coverage is often flashy and opinionated, with values and beliefs threaded throughout both articles and advertising. Examine the different elements—the athletes, teams, coaches, fans, sponsors, owners, support staff, mascots, cheerleaders, bands, and other team enhancers.

- Try to determine what does or doesn't count.
- Notice how much attention is given to individual players, teams, winning and losing, competition, sportsmanship, brushes with the law, violence in sports, the fans, and so on.
- Study the way people are described and look at the narrative dimension.
- Think of athletes as characters in a story.
- In the hierarchy of the different sports, consider who is on top and what societal (and corporate) interests are at play.
- Examine the use of language, colorful descriptions, nicknames, and other ways of referring to athletes.
- Watch for both overt and subtle differences in the coverage of sports figures and events.

Sports coverage is often presented in a lively and colorful narrative style—a story with powerful images and metaphors to convey ideas. Study how it presents moral issues, such as baseball's three time MVP winner Alex Rodriguez's admission to using steroids. Watch for uses of language that are eulogistic (euphemistic) or dyslogistic (i.e., that create either a positive or negative slant to the story). Watch also for language that plays on our emotions and appeals to team loyalties.

You Tell Me Department

Should Athletes Take Political Stands at the Olympics?

Most athletes had no interest in anything other than their performance at the 2008 Summer Games of the Olympics [held in Beijing], but some wanted to make political statements.

> Athletes who display Tibetan flags at Olympic venues—including in their own rooms—could be expelled from [the 2008] summer's Games in Beijing under anti-propaganda rules. Jacques Rogge, the president of the International Olympic Committee (IOC), said that competitors were free to express their political views but faced sanctions if they indulged in propaganda.
>
> Unfurling Free Tibet banners or wearing Save Darfur T-shirts at Olympic venues are acts likely to be regarded as a breach of the charter. . . . But there are still many grey areas and concerns among human rights campaigners that athletes' right to free speech will be curtailed . . .
>
> The British Athletes' Commission (BAC) is seeking a tighter definition of propaganda under the charter. They would also like more guidance on the writing of personal blogs during the Games. "There is a difference between propaganda and opinion and I would expect most of our athletes to know it. Wearing a Free Tibet T-shirt is going to be seen as propaganda," said Pete Gardner, the BAC's chief executive. "We want the IOC to clarify that." (Ashling O'Connor, "Athletes Who Take Tibet Stand 'Face Olympic Cut,'" *The (London) Times,* timesonline, 11 Apr 2008)

You tell me: What, if anything, should be permissible in terms of expressing a political opinion at the Olympics *and* having it covered by the media?

▦ Visions of the Real: Popular Culture

If the real world reflected the world we see and hear in popular culture, here's what we'd find: There would be many more males than females; vastly more whites than people of color; more people who were rich than poor; far fewer mothers, more attentive fathers, and children who seemed to have no homework; many prostitutes and nearly nude dancers; a plethora of serial rapists and murderers; a scattering of gorgeous women and almost no one who was old, frail, or had disabilities. The society would be ridden with conflicts resulting in a vast amount of gun-related violence, bombs, explosions, men leaping across rooftops, people falling through glass ceilings, phones that didn't work, lots of car accidents and high-speed chases, and lone heroes who prevailed in the face of extraordinary odds.

Of course, the "reel" world and the "real" world are not one and the same. The images and the stories found in popular culture—particularly TV and film—are so much a part of our lives that it may be hard to imagine ordinary life without them. And in a society where celebrities attempt to use their status to influence voters, political dialogue, and global policy decision making, the "reel" and the "real" move together like platelets on the San Andreas Fault. That is, when one moves and shifts, the other reacts and adjusts. Thus, we have TV stars like Oprah endorsing Obama, movie stars like Angelina Jolie serving as a UN spokesperson,

You Tell Me Department

What Do Video Games Reveal about Us?

Are boys and men primarily brutes wanting to act out on the plane of violent imagery? Are girls and women primarily interested in sorting out social relationships and cracking puzzles? Here's one view:

> "In a game, there's really a problem, or set of problems, that we're selling," says Will Wright, one of the founding figures in the video game industry. "One way I think of games, as a designer, is the possibility space. What are the different states I can get into in that game, what are all the worlds I can experience?" Technological advances have greatly extended those possibilities. "Now these games are becoming more of a system through which people play out their own personalities,"

says Wright. Wright discusses male versus female consumers (players) of video games. He says: "Men are happy to sit there shooting the target over and over and over, blowing shit up," says Mr. Wright. "They have simple goal structures." Women, though, want more—not necessarily something different, just better. "They are more creatively driving the experience. They want a higher standard in interactive games," he says. "It doubles your market if you can start appealing to the other half of the people on the planet." ("Gamers Learn to Grow Up," *The Financial Times,* 1 Sep 2004)

You tell me: Do you think Will Wright is right—that men want to blow up things, while women "want more" and have a higher standard? Share your thoughts.

---

musicians like Bono advocating for economic change in Africa, and so on. Not only do they speak—others listen.

Looking at the Big Picture

We can apply critical thinking to the different areas of popular culture and look at the underlying meaning, patterns, stereotypes, and both implicit and explicit messages about how to live and think. Philosopher Jean Beaudrillard, who influenced *The Matrix,* thinks we need to pay close attention to reality and images—and images of reality and images of images. These are not always easy to separate, so look at both content and context. For example, was Saddam Hussein found in a hole? Or was his capture staged to make us think well of the war effort? (See "Ex-Marine Says Public Version of Saddam Capture Fiction," United Press International, 9 Mar 2005.) There are economic and political interests that may weigh in.

Analyzing Popular Culture

We commonly find all types of arguments about aspects of popular culture. Here are key navigational tools to keep in mind:

- **Have your antennae out.** Pay close attention to arguments and examples.
- **Check the reasoning.** The fact that the topic is interesting does not mean the reasoning is sound.

got milk?

Metamorphosis.
What's changed since "The Amanda Show"?
Me. Thanks to milk. Some studies suggest teens
who choose milk over sugary drinks tend to be
leaner, plus the protein helps build muscle.
Grow beautiful, inside and out.

body <small>by</small> milk.
www.bodybymilk.com

Reprinted with permission of Lowe Worldwide, Inc., as agent for the National Fluid Milk Processor Promotion Board.

FIGURE 14.2
The "Got Milk?" ads became part of popular culture, and imitators sprang up everywhere—as Figures 14.3 and 14.4 show.

- **Review the evidence.** The fact that you agree with the author's thesis does not mean the evidence is in place.
- **Watch for details.** Backing up claims with relevant examples, statistics, and other forms of justification is crucial.
- **Be on the lookout for unwarranted assumptions, fallacies, and bias.** You've got the tools to sniff out problems—so put them to work.
- **Set out arguments in standard form to help see what's what.** There's nothing like a systematic approach to keep things organized.
- **Watch for omissions or "holes" in the reasoning.** Don't fill in missing premises or make any assumptions that whitewash defective reasoning.
- **Watch for facts, opinions or speculation, and ideas.**
- **Watch for images and symbols.** (See Figure 14.2.)
- **Watch for inferences.** Check to see if they are well founded.
- **Decide if arguments are inductive or deductive.** Proceed to determine the quality.

FIGURE 14.3
The "Got . . . ?" is
now part of our
cultural lexicon.

Photograph by Wanda Teays. Copyright 2008.

FIGURE 14.4
The catchy "Got . . . ?"
even made it to the
presidential campaign!

Obama for President campaign. Used with permission.

Media literacy is the study of the media, its messages, and impact on the public. As Justin Lewis and Sut Jhally point out, media literacy should be about helping people become sophisticated *citizens* rather than sophisticated consumers:

> Media literacy, in short, is about more than the analysis of messages, it is about an awareness of why those messages are there. It is not enough to know that they are produced, or even how, in a technical sense, they are produced. To appreciate the significance of contemporary media, we need to know why they are produced, under what constraints and conditions, and by whom. (Justin Lewis and Sut Jhally, "The Struggle over Media Literacy," in Horace Newcomb, ed., *Television: A Critical View,* 6th ed.)

With the exception of music, popular culture tends to ignore economic class—white, black, Asian, Latino, Native American, or otherwise. We may be interested to learn why this is the case in our quest for media literacy. Also of concern are the frame of reference, the intended audience, and the social context.

Putting the Navigational Tools to Work—
Drawing Inferences

We are often put in the situation of observing, sorting and weighing perceptions or drawing inferences about different aspects of popular culture. This is especially true given the many awards and rating systems: "thumbs up/thumbs down," "four out of five stars," and so on. From these various signals, we draw inferences. Sometimes those inferences are well supported; other times, not. Consider alternative inferences that could be drawn, and watch what you assume.

Group or Individual Exercise

Directions: Look over the list of the top-20-grossing films in the United States as of February 20, 2009 (www.imdb.com), and then answer the questions below.

1. *Titanic*
2. *The Dark Knight*
3. *Star Wars*
4. *Shrek 2*
5. *E.T.: The Extra-Terrestrial*
6. *Star Wars: Episode I—The Phantom Menace*
7. *Pirates of the Caribbean: Dead Man's Chest*
8. *Spider-Man*
9. *Star Wars: Episode III—Revenge of the Sith*
10. *The Lord of the Rings: Return of the King*
11. *Spider-Man 2*
12. *The Passion of the Christ*
13. *Jurassic Park*
14. *The Lord of the Rings: The Two Towers*
15. *Finding Nemo*
16. *Spider-Man 3*
17. *Forrest Gump*
18. *The Lion King*
19. *Shrek the Third*
20. *Transformers*
21. *Iron Man*

Answer the following:

1. What strikes you most about this list?
2. Draw two to three inferences about the audience (or the audience's interests) given this list of profitable films.

CASE STUDY

Women in Film

How are women faring these days in film? Not so good, if we are to believe *Los Angeles Times* movie critic Rachel Abramowitz. Read her argument and then assess its strength.

So far, my search for intelligent chicks in the summer movies is proving to be a bust. Here's the range of female characters: slut, nasty slut, stupid slut, mean slut and fat friend. Is it me or is it a little depressing to see Oscar winner Gwyneth Paltrow slumming it as pretty Pepper Potts in the "Iron Man" juggernaut? At 35, the svelte Paltrow is playing what some directors call the handbag part, the accessory, the girlfriend role, a warm-body-type role usually assigned to the likes of Jessica Alba, Katie Holmes or a legion of interchangeable Bond girls.

Ditto for Cameron Diaz, another pretty 35-year-old who rocketed to success 10 years ago wearing sperm in her hair in "There's Something about Mary." She also played second banana to [Julia] Roberts in "My Best Friend's Wedding," donning the role of the threatening fiancée, and almost stealing the movie when she responds to Roberts' challenge to sing karaoke by croaking horrifically but with the gusto of the eternally plucky. Now she's taking the Brittany Murphy role opposite Ashton Kutcher in "What Happens in Vegas." ("When the Box Office Fire Cools, What Are Actresses like Gwyneth Paltrow and Cameron Diaz to Do?" *Los Angeles Times,* 13 May 2008)

CASE STUDY

Drawing Inferences from Music Reviews

If you've ever read any reviews, you know one thing if you know anything: Reviewers may agree in commending or criticizing a work, but it is more likely that they'll be all over the map. It's not as subjective as evaluating a culinary experiment (e.g., shrimp stir-fried with fruit or apple pie with hot chocolate sauce), but the assessment can vary widely. The perspective and criteria of evaluation are crucial. With a music or film review, we expect to see an assessment with some detailed explanation of the rating. Here are summary reviews and ratings of Tom Waits' *Real Gone* (see Figure 14.5) (see *Metacritic,* www.metacritic.com).

Review 1: *Playlouder*

In *Real Gone's* fearsome complexity of rhythm, lyric and device, Tom Waits appropriates like a shoplifter without much time, and creates something entirely his own. A new music. RATING: 100.

Review 2: *Pitchfork*

It lurches along like a junk-heap jalopy, unsteady and unsafe, bits flying off in every direction, stopping, starting, and bouncing in pain. RATING: 80.

Review 3: *PopMatters*

Real Gone leans on nail-bending percussion and swagger in a manner that recalls Bone Machine's metallic binge more than the recent theatrics of Alice or Blood Money. RATING: 80.

Review 4: *The New York Times*

Like an altar built of barbed wire, scrap metal and broken glass, *Real Gone* hammers ungraceful materials into something like beauty. RATING: 70.

Photograph by Wanda Teays. Copyright 2004.

FIGURE 14.5
Waits for the bus in Hollywood, CA.

Review 5: *Drowned in Sound*

Tough going and very samey, both in sonics and lyricism. Even if you enjoy the basic template, you may well run out of steam before the end. RATING: 50.

What do you see? The top rating mentions lyrics ("fearsome complexity"), as does the lowest rating ("tough going and very samey"). Are these contradictory? It may be that the qualities are similar (complex and fearsome vs. tough going), but the value placed on that aspect is at issue. Except for the last review, the other five overlap ("gangsta" with "unsteady and unsafe," "metallic binge" and "barbed wire . . . ungraceful," "bouncing in pain" and "broken glass"). Compare Review 2 and Review 5: "lurches along like a junk-heap jalopy," which gets a rating of "80," versus "tough going," with a rating of 50.

Behind Review 2: Tom Waits is channeling frequencies that the rest of us cannot hear. . . . *Real Gone,* like most of Tom Waits' records, is teeming with all kinds of mysterious noises: clangs and spits, faceless hollers, squawks, irrational toots, not-quite-human coughs, vicious bangs, apologetic whispers.

Behind Review 5: He certainly deserves a chunk of respect . . . Waits assiduously avoids compromise. . . . [But] the album peaks, way too early, on the awe-inspiring, enormous, ten-minute "Sins of the Father." This monster takes that blueprint to its limit, enveloping you in an extreme world of love and death and sin in one massive phlump. Sadly, Waits can't follow it. He's come too soon.

What this indicates: Going behind the review summary fleshes out the differences. The 50 rating in Review 5 rests on the view of an early peak, leaving the rest of the CD hanging. In contrast, Review 2 seems to have no problems with the lurching and "mysterious noises." This is at the crux of the disagreement. Consequently, seeing what lies behind the rating gives us a sense of the evaluation.

Applying the Navigational Tools to an Argument

When faced with an argument, stop and check out the reasoning. Set out the argument—state the conclusion and number each premise P_1, P_2, and so on. Then stack the premises, with the conclusion at the bottom. That makes the argument easy to read. We can then see how the premises work together to support the argument. If they don't offer sufficient support, we need to determine if there is a way to bolster the argument.

Exercises

1. State the key claims in the following argument, which concludes that a TV cartoon show could be a hit.

   Just as "The Simpsons" essentially saved Fox Network [20] years ago, animated cartoons could become the small screen's pinch hitters, even if they've been benched for a while. "To a large degree, network programming has quit taking risks and is becoming the same thing over and over again," says Mike Lazzo, a senior vice president at Cartoon Network. "And I think that animation is just something different." While different, cartoons have also become more accepted, no longer sandwiched between Lucky Charms and Barbie advertisements on Saturday mornings. That generation has grown up—and they constitute a large chunk of the prime-time audience . . . an animated version of Aaron McGruder's subversive comic strip could spark interest. (Marie Ewald, "TV Gets Animated," *Christian Science Monitor,* 14 May 2004)

2. State the thesis and key claims in this discussion of hip-hop.

   [H]ip-hop has a few things going for it after all. While a common complaint is that the industry is ruined because of a lack of support from "true hip-hop," the tastes of the average consumer are actually evolving: underground artists are actually eating now, gaining mainstream acceptance. . . . Kanye West, with the success of singles like "Jesus Walks" and "All Falls Down," has shown that rap artists don't have to talk about pimping and hoes to be successful. DJ Danger Mouse has had an underground name for years, but shook the world when he merged a capellas from Jay-Z's *Black Album* with the Beatles' *White Album.* . . . Artists can make fun songs—songs to dance to, songs to ride to, songs to get drunk to—without compromising their art. . . . If you don't like certain types of music, just don't support them. . . . (William Ketchum III, "Is Hip-Hop Too Commercial?" *Ballerstatus,* www. ballerstatus.net, 10 Sep 2004)

3. State the key claims in the discussion below about the public's fascination with Paris Hilton.

   Sick and tired of hearing about Paris Hilton? Then pack your suitcase and head for a desert island because America's most famous celebrity inmate is about to be a free woman again. . . . Hilton, a one-woman pop-culture phenomenon, said she will emerge from incarceration for violating her probation on drunk-driving charges a changed woman. "In a way, I'm really glad this happened because it changed my life forever," said Hilton. "I just realize that the media used me to make fun of and be mean about. Frankly, I'm sick of it. I want to use my fame in a good way."

But whether Hilton's desire for a more simple life will lead to fewer appearances in the media spotlight remains doubtful, experts say. . . . Robert Thompson, a professor in pop-culture at the University of Syracuse, said, "On one level the amount of coverage Hilton gets is absolutely absurd in that it is not news of any kind. But there is always a vacancy in society for frivolous nonsense. Is this as important as 50,000 other things going on in the world that news resources could be used for? Clearly the answer is 'No.' But at any given time there are 20 or so mega-celebrities who transcend everything, and at the moment she is playing a starring role in that bubble. . . . If she starts reading a book for an hour before retiring to bed at 9 p.m. every night, stories about her will dry up because she'll cease to be interesting to us," Thompson said. (Rob Wollard, "Media Circus 2.0 as Paris Hilton Awaits Release," Inquirer.net, 24 Jun 2007)

4. Set out Henry Jenkins' argument *against* the claim that "scientific evidence links violent game play with youth aggression."

Claims like this are based on the work of researchers who represent one relatively narrow school of research. . . . But most of those studies are inconclusive. . . . In these studies, media images are removed from any narrative context. Subjects are asked to engage with content that they would not normally consume and may not understand. Finally, the laboratory context is radically different from the environments where games would normally be played. Most studies found a correlation, not a causal relationship, which means the research could simply show that aggressive people like aggressive entertainment.

That's why the vague term "links" is used here. If there is a consensus emerging around this research, it is that violent video games may be one risk factor . . . which can contribute to anti-social behavior. But no research has found that video games are a primary factor or that violent video game play could turn an otherwise normal person into a killer. (Henry Jenkins, "Reality Bytes: Myths about Video Games Debunked," www.pbs.org)

Analyzing Reviews and Assessing Arguments

Reviewers have a tricky job: They need to make their judgment clear to the reader, give a sense of the story line, and set out reasons for their rating. This must be done succinctly and in a readable and engaging way. Because the review presents the critic's assessment of the film, we need tools of analysis to see what the critic is saying and why.

Reviews are an interesting form of argument: They have to tell a story so as not to lose the audience, and they have to present a position that is backed up by evidence and examples. (See Chapter 2 for a review of argumentation.)

Our task is to evaluate the strength of that evidence. To do a good job, reviewers need to make their case. So, in analyzing the review, examine it as an argument and evaluate it. See if the evidence offered lends sufficient support for the conclusion the reviewer has drawn.

Key Elements of a Film Review

- A brief plot summary
- An assessment of the acting
- An evaluation or rating
- A presentation of key evidence and assumptions
- The details of the argument
- Concluding remarks reiterating the rating

Note that you can easily access film reviews and film criticism through websites like www.metacritic.com, www.imdb.com, filmlinc.com, www.filmcriticism.com, www.lib.berkeley.edu/MRC, and allmovie.com.

Exercises

1. A plot summary must be concise and clear—as with this one for *Steamboy:* "Ray Steam is a cheeky young lad who receives a strange metal ball, which is dubbed a 'steamball,' from his grandfather, who must go into hiding. It contains a power that can preserve or destroy the human race, and he must protect it from an evil villain who has built an elaborate machine that will dominate London" (G. Allen Johnson, *San Francisco Chronicle,* www.sfgate .com, 18 Mar 2005). Write a plot summary of any TV episode *or* a film you've seen recently.

2. Compare and contrast these two reviews of *The Dark Knight*

   Reviewer 1 (Scott Foundas of *The Village Voice*):

   What a brooding pleasure it is to return to Christopher Nolan's Gotham City—if "pleasure" is the right word for a movie that gazes so deeply and sometimes despairingly into the souls of restless men. . . . And like the rival illusionists of Nolan's 2006 film *The Prestige,* the longer Batman and the Joker engage in their battle of wills—the one confident in the inherent goodness of mankind, the other equally certain that man is but a savage beast—the more the distance collapses between them. . . . *The Dark Knight* will give your adrenal glands their desired workout, but it will occupy your mind, too, and even lead it down some dim alleyways where most Hollywood movies fear to tread.

   Reviewer 2 (Michael Sragow of the *Baltimore Sun*):

   The Dark Knight is a handsome, accomplished piece of work, but it drove me from absorption to excruciation within 20 minutes, and then it went on for two hours more. It's the standard-bearer for the school of comic-book movies that confuses pompousness with seriousness and popular mechanics for drama. It's scaled to be an urban epic about the deterioration of hope and possibility in Batman's hometown, Gotham City (standing in for all Western cities), but there isn't a single stirring or inspired moment in it. . . . [Director Christophor] Nolan's use of incessant tension music and gun-to-the-head jeopardy cheapens even the classiest bits. True believers may buy into the gloom and doom of *The Dark Knight,* but many of us will ask, with the Joker, "Why so serious?"

3. Study Desson Howe's review of *Fargo,* and then set out your assessment of his argument.

The Coen Brothers' *Fargo,* a satirical, macabre saga set on the frigid plains of the American Midwest, works like a charm. . . . And throughout the hypnotized Midwestern atmosphere of this movie—picture a cross between Garrison Keillor's *A Prairie Home Companion* and George A. Romero's *Night of the Living Dead*—Frances McDormand enjoys the comedic role of her career.

In the story, which is loosely based on real events, Minnesota car salesman Jerry Lundegaard (William H. Macy) travels to Fargo, N.D., where he hires thugs Carl (Steve Buscemi) and Gaear (Peter Stormare) to have his wife (Kristin Rudrud) kidnapped. . . . The abductors get away with their hostage, but leave a bloody scene behind them. This brings in Police Chief Marge Gunderson. . . . Gunderson conducts her first murder investigation with remarkable, and comic, aplomb. At the crime scene, with bodies littered around an upturned car on the snowy plains, she performs her job with the chirrupy nature of a crossing guard. . . .

There's a nutty regionalism at work: A surrealistic statue of Paul Bunyan, for instance, greets visitors to Gunderson's little town; the goofy locals never seem to blink and pepper every sentence with a "Yaaaah." Into this, the Coens expertly weave the grotesque, as the kidnappers' desperate plight forces them to take bloodier measures.

But after watching this . . . I couldn't help wondering about Joel (the co-writer/director) and Ethan (the co-writer/producer) Coen. . . . Do these guys ever step outside themselves? Do they have a worldview, a feel for humanity?. . . It's worth seeing *Fargo* if you have the taste for this kind of irony, but please, also mutter a short prayer for the filmmakers to step outside once in a while and breathe a little oxygen. (Desson Howe, "*Fargo*: In Cold Blood and in Cold Climes," *The Washington Post,* 8 Mar 1996)

4. Study two different reviews of any one current blockbuster movie (either out in theaters or just out on DVD). Go into detail comparing and contrasting the two reviews of your movie. *Note:* You can find movie (and music and DVD) reviews at www.metacritic.com and www.imdb.com, as well as other places on the Internet.

Group or Individual Exercise

Assessing Arguments in Film Reviews: *The American President*

Let's take an argument and set it out in standard form. Our focus will be a (negative) review of *The American President* by John J. Pitney Jr. He argues that movies such as *The American President* show us that Hollywood thinks voters are stupid. Pitney's argument is as follows:

Premise 1: *The American President* concerns a chief executive (Michael Douglas) who is progressive yet practical. He says that gun control is hard to pass because people do not understand the link between guns and gun-related crime.

Premise 2: After the president falls in love with an environmental lobbyist (Annette Bening), an evil senator (Richard Dreyfuss) turns the unthinking masses against the good president by making nasty comments about his new lady friend.

Premise 3: The president's approval ratings tumble, and the White House staff bemoans the people's willingness to believe anyone with a microphone.

Premise 4: At a climactic moment, the domestic policy advisor (Michael J. Fox) compares Americans to nomads who need a drink of water but get a glass of sand.

Premise 5: The president bitterly replies: "They drink the sand because they don't know the difference."

Premise 6: The image of a dumb, deluded electorate is hardly original with this movie; it is one of the film industry's moldiest clichés.

Premise 7: Many other films treat the electorate like idiots; for instance, in *Mr. Smith Goes to Washington* (1939), ruthless thugs smash the young Smith with false charges and vicious news stories, and the gullible public goes along.

Premise 8: In *Citizen Kane* (1941), Orson Welles plays a legendary newspaper publisher who can whip his readers into a war frenzy with far-fetched stories about Spanish galleons off the Jersey coast and thinks he can tell people what to think.

Premise 9: In *The Candidate* (1972), an idealistic Senate contender runs an issue-based campaign against a stodgy incumbent (with the stereotypical dark suit and short white hair) and seems doomed to lose until he starts speaking in platitudes and wins over the voters with mushy statements.

Premise 10: Political films show contempt for the people.

Conclusion: Hollywood thinks the voters are stupid.

Answer the following:

1. What are the strengths of Pitney's argument?

2. What would an opponent need to do to disprove his claims?

3. Is his sample of four political films sufficient to draw inferences about Hollywood attitude toward voters? Why or why not?

In assessing an argument it helps to have some guidelines to keep in mind. (See Chapter 3 for a review of tools on assessing arguments.)

Tips for Assessing Arguments

- **Check the factual claims.** Are the claims made actually true? Do not assume the speaker is necessarily correct.
- **Check any assumptions.** Determine if they are warranted or unwarranted. Unwarranted assumptions should be recognized and carefully examined.
- **Check for exaggeration.** Are the claims made inflated or slanted to one side or another, when in fact another interpretation is possible?

- **Check for omissions.** Were relevant details omitted that would offer another perspective or lead us to a different conclusion than the one being drawn?
- **Check for fallacious reasoning.** If a sample is used, is it sufficient in number and representative? *Note:* If the sample group is too small, the speaker may have committed the fallacy of hasty generalization. If the sample group is biased toward one point of view or group, the speaker may have committed the fallacy of biased statistics.
- **Check for details.** Examples and illustrations can bring home a point and show how the work makes ideas concrete.
- **Check the strength of the reasoning.** Decide if the conclusion is sufficiently supported by the evidence given. The evidence lays the foundation for the conclusion, and it is important that this foundation is a solid one.

With these guidelines in mind, let's return to Pitney's argument. First, consider the claims of fact. He says that *The American President* presents voters as dumb and deluded, that they "believe anyone with a microphone." Pitney ignores the end of the movie, and what happens after the president expresses his bitterness about the gullibility of the public. We need to know: Did the "unthinking masses" come to see that the "good president" was *really* a good president and that they were wrong to believe his critics?

Second, examine Pitney's assumptions. He assumes a familiarity with the other films he cites. However, this assumption may or may not be warranted.

Third, watch for exaggeration. It's a temptation to inflate key points for an extra boost. Assuming the public initially fell for the nasty comments about the president's new lady friend, does that mean they are "unthinking masses" or "a dumb, deluded electorate"?

Fourth, watch for omissions. Pitney stops at the president's bitter reply to his domestic policy advisor's comment about nomads getting sand instead of water to drink. Consider what happens after this. Decide if Pitney develops the implication that the public is deluded.

Fifth, watch for fallacious reasoning. Given all the films coming out of Hollywood, it is unlikely that only four of them make or imply judgments about voters. Pitney's collection ought to be a *representative* sample if we are going to draw conclusions from it. If not, his reasoning is not well founded.

Lastly, evaluate the strength of his reasoning. Examine the connection between the premises and the conclusion. Consider whether Pitney's citation of four films made between 1939 and 1995 warrants the conclusion "Hollywood thinks voters are stupid." The conclusion should not say more than is warranted by the evidence. Does he make that case?

Placing a Work of Popular Culture in Context

As you know from audience surveys at movie premieres, a great deal turns on the response of the target audience. And works that succeed in one context (e.g., urban areas) may fall flat in another. If we simply focus on the content and do what might be called a "textual analysis," we may not be able to grasp the bigger

The Global Dimension

Examining the *Pan's Labyrinth* Review

Examine Wesley Morris's review of *Pan's Labyrinth,* set out in standard form below. Morris (*The Boston Globe*, 12 Jan 2007) rates the film as a transcendent work of art. Assess his reasoning.

P₁: **Director Guillermo Del Toro's early promise:** "While his earlier movies had whiffs of soul, they looked like classic horror pictures—the Mexican director was a cult taste with a cultish following. As it turns out, the geeks were on to something."

P₂: **Director Guillermo evolved and refined storytelling in a voluptuously realized film:** "Del Toro's gratifying surreal and fantastical instincts now have an unstinting moral eye on the world. Saying a filmmaker has matured suggests that he's forgone what made him so entertaining in the first place. But in evolving with this voluptuously realized film, with its omnipresent dangers, Del Toro has simply refined the deftness of his storytelling."

P₃: **A beautiful film about ugliness, told through a grim historical lens:** "A beautiful film about ugliness, *Pan's Labyrinth* is still pure del Toro (the insects and slime, for instance, are still here), but he gazes through a grim historical lens."

P₄: **Context:** The film is set in 1944 after the Spanish Civil War, centering on a girl (Ofelia), her sicky mother (Carmen), and the nasty fascist (Captain Vidal) her mother married. "Set in 1944, after the Spanish Civil War, just as Franco begins his terrible domination, this fractured fairy tale introduces us to a girl named Ofelia (Ivana Baquero) whose father died in the Spanish Civil War and whose sickly mother, Carmen (Ariadna Gil), has recently wed the nasty fascist Captain Vidal (Sergi López)."

P₅: **Plot:** Ofelia and Carmen have moved to the Captain's military outpost; one evening, Ofelia follows a dragonfly into a netherworld. There Ofelia meets a faun who insists that she's a princess who must accomplish three tasks relating to a magical book he shows her.

P₆: **Plot details:** The book becomes a kind of instruction manual whose demands keep her busy above ground and below—the faun is as forboding as her stepfather.

P₇: **The greater context:** "Del Toro masterfully intercuts Ofelia's quests with scenes of the guerrillas who hide in the hills and launch random attacks." The men survive with the surreptitious dedication of the Captain's physician and his formidable housekeeper.

P₈: **Emotional force:** "In so many ways, *Pan's Labyrinth* is about pain, real human pain."

P₉: **His other films:** "The new movie's clarity of vision is far more robust, making similar ghosts flesh and blood."

P₁₀: **High-quality acting:** "The brilliance of López's performance as the Captain is how he conflates the dream state and the fascist state, giving us a monster with a seductively human face, but never too human."

P₁₁: **Piercing insights:** "*Pan's Labyrinth* questions the limits of fantasy, how complete devotion to allegory can be blinding."

P₁₂: **Aesthetic dimension:** "Del Toro is still interested in the physical surrealism of David Cronenberg and the social critiques of Luis Buñuel. But unlike, say, fellow fantasist Tim Burton, whose movies can prize the saccharine while peddling bogus pathos, Del Toro has made a film rich in both visual audacity and moral consequence."

P₁₃: **Complete package of film mastery:** "*Pan's Labyrinth* is a feat of unique cinematic alchemy: A master of horror-movie schlock has made a stunning magic-realist masterpiece."

Conclusion: "*Pan's Labyrinth* is a transcendent work of art."

picture of how the work shapes or is descriptive of society. What may speak to a segment of the society at *this* time or *that* place could land like lead on another group or at another time.

Content is to context like an egg is to the circumstances in which the egg is laid—for example, which hen laid the egg, whether the setting was a barnyard or an agribusiness, and where this egg was one of hundreds gathered that day. When we look at content, we consider the various aspects of the work itself (e.g., plot or story line, characters, themes, and visual and audio components). The context includes the time and place the work was created, the audience response, the social and political setting, the target audience of any marketing, and the corporate backing.

Context and content are not always distinct. For example, reality TV not only has members of the audience moving into the show as characters but also shows products that were advertised separately in the past, embedded via product placement into the shows.

Context

We can think of the relationship of context to content as similar to that of background to foreground. Context provides us with the cultural roots, the audience and its receptivity, the sociotemporal framework, and the economic and/or ideological thrust behind the work. It is the obverse of the work. A *contextual* analysis, therefore, takes us outside the work so we can see the other factors involved in how a piece of popular culture makes its mark.

Checklist for Examining Context

1. **Identify the audience.** Who is the audience? Does it have broad appeal? Has it generated a narrow fan base?
2. **Identify the sponsor(s).** Who are the work's sponsors? Private corporations? Public funding? Nonprofits?
3. **Examine the marketing.** How is the work marketed—and to whom? What do the ads convey?
4. **Assess the sociotemporal framework.** When and where was the work produced (time/place)? Are there any relevant political or social factors or cultural currents?
5. **Trace the "money trail."** Are economic interests at work? Any product placements?
6. **Check for response and reverberations.** What is or was the audience response? Have there been any continuing effects? Any critical acclaim?
7. **Note any political agendas.** Is there a political agenda at work? Conservative? Liberal? Religious? Marxist? For or against the status quo? And so on.
8. **Identify the frame of reference.** From whose perspective—and values—is the work presented?

9. **Look for any missing pieces.** Whose voices are in—and whose are out? Whose *should* be in, given the work?

10. **Check for symmetry/asymmetry.** How do the society and/or relationships presented correspond to those of the audience? Is diversity represented? Is there a bias or imbalance when the work is compared to the "real" world?

Content

When we examine content, we undertake a *textual* analysis, deconstructing the work to see how it is structured, how its components work together, and how to interpret it through different lenses (e.g., social, political, ethical, spiritual, and mythological).

Checklist for Examining Content

1. **Identify the genre.** What genre best fits the work? Drama? Comedy? Action? Horror? Documentaries? Animation? Rap? Determine what genre seems most fitting as a label.

2. **Check for originality.** Is it a spin-off or a retread of an earlier work? Is it imitating or borrowing from another work? Is it unique or derivative?

3. **Examine the focus or plot.** What is the work about? How could it be summarized in a few sentences?

4. **Review characterization.** If there are characters, what is their significance? What role do the main characters play in the work as a whole?

5. **Examine the narrative.** What is the impact—the power of the story, script, or lyrics? What stands out when looking at the level of the language? What is memorable—for example, movie lines or quotes?

6. **Identify the frame of reference.** What "voice" carries the work? From whose frame of reference or point of view is the work being presented? Does that perspective shift, or is it consistent?

7. **Determine levels of interpretation.** What are different ways of "reading" or interpreting the work? Does it have political or social aspects? Does it have an ethical or spiritual message? Could it be understood in terms of justice versus injustice?

8. **Assess the lasting value.** Does the work stand out above the rest? Does it speak to the audience beyond mere entertainment? What stands out artistically?

9. **Determine the total impact.** What is the verbal and/or visual message? Do they reinforce one another? Is music or sound effects a factor?

10. **Identify prescriptive versus descriptive aspects.** Does the work try to shape us, to tell us what we ought to think about one thing or another, or to influence us? Does it reflect the society or aspects of society? Can we see ourselves in the work? Does it mirror the world we live in—or does it offer an alternative, a parallel world different from our own?

You Tell Me Department

Does Barbie Have a Sense of Humor?

Just when you thought Barbie was going to retire and live in a gated community, with or without Ken, we find that an artist has used the doll in a satire. Read about this case and then answer the questions below.

> SAN FRANCISCO—Mattel Inc. should have known it didn't have a shapely leg to stand on when it sued a Utah artist for his parody of the voluptuous cultural icon, Barbie. Now Barbie's corporate parent must pay artist Tom Forsythe's lawyer $1.8 million in fees and costs incurred defending against a copyright violation claim over his use of the doll to lambaste the "conventional beauty myth." U.S. District Judge Ronald S. W. Lew held that Mattel forced Forsythe "into costly litigation to discourage him from using Barbie's image in his artwork." Lew earlier dismissed the copyright, trademark and trade-dress violation claims against Forsythe.
>
> Forsythe, a self-taught photographer from Kanab, Utah, produced a series of 78 photographs in 1997 that parodied Barbie dolls in various absurd and sexualized positions, often nude and being menaced by vintage kitchen appliances. "Malted Barbie" depicted the nude doll inside a vintage Hamilton Beach malt machine. "Barbie Enchiladas" portrayed the dolls wrapped in tortillas and covered with salsa in a casserole dish. (Pamela A. MacLean, "$1.8M Fees in Barbie Case," *Daily Journal*, 25 Jun 2004)

You tell me: Barbie is still a powerhouse in the toy world. The Fall 2009 line at Mattel's website features "Wedding Day" Barbie and Ken in traditional wedding attire (at last!). (www.barbiecollector.com/news/news/FALL2009line.aspx). Is Barbie's image tarnished by such satirical treatments as wrapping the doll in a tortilla like she's an enchilada? What are the strongest claims in support of Tom Forsythe's right to create satires on Barbie? If you were the judge, would you rule for Tom Forsythe (the artist) or Mattel (the corporation)?

11. **Check for diversity.** Are the inhabitants—the characters—representative of the real world? Is there a balance of different voices and diverse perspectives? Whose view is dominant?

12. **Assess the power and influence.** Where do we see power and influence manifested in the work? Who are the leaders, the bosses, those who take control? Who are the followers?

Exercises

1. Michael Eric Dyson says, "Rap music grew from its origins in New York's inner city over a decade ago as a musical outlet to creative cultural energies and to contest the invisibility of the ghetto in mainstream American society . . . [Rap tapped] into the cultural virtues and vices of the so-called underclass . . . " ("The Politics of Black Masculinity and the Ghetto in Black Film," in Carol Becker, ed., *The Subversive Imagination*). If film and TV ignore or downplay economic strife, rap music does not. Why do you think rap is the main medium to examine class issues—particularly poverty and ghetto life?

2. Answer *one* of the following:
   a. Find the lyrics to any rap song that demonstrates rap's ability to examine the gulf between the rich and the poor and the consequences of entrenched poverty on its victims.
   b. Find the lyrics to any rap song that demonstrates rap's ability to examine the collective despair or rage of those who are disenfranchised—that is, ignored or marginalized by a capitalistic society.

3. How has terrorism and the resulting fear it evokes impacted popular culture? And what do you make of films like *Eagle Eye* and TV shows like *24* that feature governmental agencies with expanding powers of surveillance?

4. In *Understanding Media*, Marshall McLuhan says of movies that they offer "the most magical of consumer commodities, namely dreams." One such dream, as shown in *Gran Torino* and *Slumdog Millionaire*, is to be lifted out of poverty. Cite three examples of films that show we *can* (or, alternatively, *cannot*) escape from class roles or gender and ethnic stereotypes.

5. What is the social significance of horror films with their mutants, zombies, flesh-eating ghouls, vampires, and other undead? Set out three to four reasons why audiences flock to horror films like *The Exorcist, Alien, 28 Days Later,* and *Night of the Living Dead*.

6. What factors help create a surprise hit either on TV or in film? State what you see as the key factors. (Think of films like *Shrek 2, The Bourne Supremacy,* and *Slumdog Millionaire,* and hit TV shows like the various *CSI* series, *30 Rock* and *The Sopranos*.)

7. Why are some films box office duds? If a film executive asked for your advice on why some films are total failures, what would you say? Share your thoughts.

8. Give your assessment of the following explanation for the popularity of Spider-Man:

   He [Spider-Man] really could be any one of us. To be Superman, you had to come from another planet. To be Wonder Woman you had to be born a mythological Amazon princess. But to be Spider-Man, you just had to be bitten by a radioactive spider. (Hey, it could happen.) You didn't have to be from a superhuman race. You just had to have it happen to you, and we all have things happen to us. (Danny Fingeroth, "Look Within: You'll Find a Spidey There," *Los Angeles Times,* 1 Jul 2004)

9. Danny Fingeroth thinks Spider-Man's appeal is tied to his being more "realistic" than other superheroes, since being bitten by a radioactive spider doesn't seem that unlikely. He also considers Spider-Man's symbolic value. Respond to this claim:

   If the Hulk represents rage, Superman optimism, and Batman revenge, Spider-Man, more than any other superhero, represents heart. And that's the key, I think, to his ever-growing popularity. He's not embarrassed by it or ashamed of it, nor should we be of our own striving to be better than we are, to get up again and again no matter how many times we get knocked down. It's Spider-Man's greatest super-power. And ours. ("Look Within: You'll Find a Spidey There," *Los Angeles Times,* 1 Jul 2004)

Group or Individual Exercise

Directions: Give your assessment of these famous movie lines—what makes them *memorable*?

1. "I'll be back."
2. "Life is like a box of chocolates."
3. "I'll make him an offer he can't refuse."
4. "Frankly my dear, I don't give a damn."
5. "Go ahead, make my day."
6. "I'm as mad as hell, and I'm not going to take this anymore!"
7. "Greed, for lack of a better word, is good."
8. "I'll have what she's having."
9. "Here's looking at you, kid."
10. "Show me the money!"
11. "You want answers?" "*I want the truth!*" "You can't handle the truth!"

Note: Did you guess the movies these lines come from? They are (1) *The Terminator*, (2) *Forrest Gump*, (3) *The Godfather*, (4) *Gone with the Wind*, (5) *Sudden Impact*, (6) *Network*, (7) *Wall Street*, (8) *When Harry Met Sally*, (9) *Casablanca*, (10) *Jerry Maguire*, and (11) *A Few Good Men*.

CHAPTER FIFTEEN

Clearing the Path: Legal Reasoning

What is required of us is moral ambition. Until our composite sketch becomes a true portrait of humanity, we must live with our uncertainty; we will grope, we will struggle, and our compassion may be our only guide and comfort.

A. STONE, *as quoted by Justice Harry Blackmun, dissent,* DeShaney v. Winnebago
County Department of Social Services *(1989)*

J ust when you thought mad cow disease was past history, it's back on the map. Korea shut the door on American beef some time ago, and when Korea's president tried to reopen it, demonstrators by the tens of thousands hit the streets in protest. "Why are they picking on American cows?" you ask, suspecting some conspiracy. As it turns out, it's not a conspiracy at all; the issue is health concerns about mad cow disease. What's to stop mad cow disease being brought into Korea by American beef?

The solution smacks us over the head: Why not test each cow as it heads to slaughter? The "rapid test" for mad cow disease takes a few hours, costs just $20 a cow, and can identify any animal with this brain-wasting disease that is potentially fatal to humans. It is at this juncture that such an idea gets tied up in legal knots: The U.S. Department of Agriculture bars use of such testing. Here's the scoop:

> In 2004 Creekstone Farms in Arkansas City, Kan., wanted to test the cattle it slaughters to comply with the wishes of its Korean and Japanese customers. But the department ruled that the rapid test could only be used as part of its own mad cow surveillance program, which randomly checks about 1 in 1,000 dead and slaughtered cattle in the United States every year. The sale of the kits to private companies is prohibited under an obscure 1913 law that allows the department to prohibit veterinary products that it considers "worthless." Creekstone sued the government in

2006, arguing in court that the Agriculture Department could not deem worthless a test that it used in its own surveillance program. The court agreed, but the department appealed. A decision is expected soon. (Michael Hansen, "Stop the Madness," *The New York Times,* 20 Jun 2008)

At times, lawyers get a bad rap and are the butt of jokes (e.g., "What's the difference between a lawyer and a catfish? One is a scum-sucking bottom feeder, and the other is a catfish"). However many chuckles this may elicit, when Creekstone Farms wanted to fight back against an outdated 1913 law, they didn't go to a catfish for help!

Good lawyers are well grounded in analytical skills. They regularly have to "think on their feet" and set out arguments under time pressure. They are expected to write clearly and defensibly and to be able to spot unwarranted assumptions, weaknesses, and omissions in their opponent's reasoning. In short, they employ a broad range of critical thinking skills in virtually all aspects of their work. The techniques we learned in the first two parts of this book are the tools of the trade in the practice of law.

We will see the application of critical thinking in this chapter. First, we will look at the range of legal reasoning skills and see how decisions reach expression. Next, we will take up fundamentals of LSAT logic and get an overview of the four areas covered. Whether or not you plan to be a lawyer, being able to think like one can be very useful. In this way, you can develop mental dexterity and sharpen your analytical skills. Finally, we will turn to logic puzzles, which are a fun way to develop deductive thinking skills. They also help you become more organized and systematic in your thinking—which is clearly beneficial for studying for the LSAT or just being better at critical reasoning.

⧉ The Range of Legal Reasoning

Legal reasoning has a considerable range in terms of applications and skills. This includes being able to construct and unpack arguments, spot unwarranted assumptions, examine analogies, apply legal precedents, argue cases, weigh evidence, evaluate arguments, respond to criticism, counter an opponent's reasoning, assess the credibility of witnesses, spot fallacious reasoning, and write and speak clearly and defensibly. Depending upon the area of law you intend to practice, one or more of these skills may be more important—but all come into play over time.

We can see this range with the following example: A 2008 California Supreme Court case examined the potential liability of "good Samaritans" who give nonmedical assistance. Let's see how our critical thinking skills are called to action. Start by looking at the key details of the case involving plaintiff Alexandra Van Horn (accident victim) and defendant Lisa Torti (good Samaritan). See if you can clarify the issues and concerns (e.g., by highlighting them or jotting down notes as you read):

1. In 2004 co-workers went out to a bar on Halloween for dancing and drinking, leaving in two cars at 1:30 A.M.

2. Van Horn was a passenger in the first car and Torti rode in the second car (both were passengers).
3. After the first car (going an estimated 45 miles per hour) hit a light pole, the second car stopped, and Torti and driver of the second car rushed to help.
4. Torti testified that she saw smoke and liquid coming from the wrecked car, thought it was about to explode, and inferred that she had to act quickly.
5. No one else thought the car was about to explode.
6. Torti took Van Horn's arm and pulled her out of the car.
7. Van Horn claimed Torti yanked her "like a rag doll," aggravating her injuries and causing permanent damage to her spinal cord.
8. Torti left Van Horn by the wreckage—an act that Van Horn's attorney later called "irrational" and inconsistent with Torti's claim that she thought an imminent explosion likely.
9. Van Horn is now a paraplegic.
10. Torti has been accused of negligence in aggravating Van Horn's injury.

What are the issues and concerns? Principally, the issue is whether Torti bears any responsibility for Van Horn's injuries. The facts indicate that Van Horn ended up a paraplegic; the question is what caused this to happen. Either Torti's rescue attempts were a factor in the injuries or they were not. If they were, then we must determine the degree to which her actions harmed Van Horn and whether Torti bears any subsequent legal responsibility (the court would then assess her share of fault). There is also the issue of Torti's good intentions (i.e., to pull the crash victim out of the car) and whether those intentions partially or completely excuse the harm those actions may have caused.

Let's see what details stand out from the perspectives of the two litigants. Van Horn's case rests on items 5–9; Torti's on items 3, 4, and 6. As you can see by comparing the two sets of items, Van Horn's case focuses on Torti's *actions* at the scene of the accident, while Torti's focuses on her *state of mind*—her intentions (presumably to help Van Horn get out of the car as soon as possible), and her assessment of the danger. From Van Horn's perspective, what stands out is that she was pulled ("yanked") out of the car in such a way as to cause or to exacerbate a spinal injury. From Torti's perspective, she felt a sense of urgency to get Van Horn out of the car before there was a fire or explosion.

Where are we thus far? We have a sense of the issues and concerns of the case and what the two key players would likely highlight in presenting their arguments. Before proceeding, we should ask if there is anything that stands out or is problematic—and, therefore, pivotal in arriving at a decision? What more would we want to know? Well, two questions pop up: (1) Why would Torti rush to pull the victim out because of a possible explosion and then leave her "near" the wrecked car? and (2) How close *was* Van Horn to the wreckage after Torti pulled her to safety? This takes us to items 5 (that no one else thought an explosion was imminent) and 8 (Torti left Van Horn "near" the wreckage). If Torti did think that an explosion was imminent, was she inconsistent or "irrational" in where she left the injured Van Horn? Surely, knowing these additional facts would give us firmer ground for our analysis.

Before we turn to the ruling, let's look at the issue of altruism. If we give Torti the benefit of the doubt, should she be blamed if her attempt to help Van Horn may have worsened the injuries? The very fact that she rushed to pull Van Horn to safety while expecting a fire or explosion could be construed as an act of considerable bravery on Torti's part. And here she is being sued! That can't help but trouble some who examine this lawsuit. Let's see if it troubled the California Supreme Court justices.

The seven justices were split 4 to 3, with the majority ruling for Van Horn, seeing Torti as potentially liable for the other woman's injuries. They said that only those giving medical care qualify as good Samaritans, and therefore Torti was not immune from civil liability because the care she rendered wasn't medical. The dissenting justices asserted that such a narrow view amounted to "arbitrary and unreasonable" limitation of the protection for those trying to help (Carol J. Williams, "California Supreme Court Allows Good Samaritans to Be Sued for Nonmedical Care," *Los Angeles Times,* 18 Dec 2008).

As you can see from this case, legal reasoning draws from all areas of critical thinking, and thus, the work you did in the previous chapters of this textbook helped lay a foundation for the work you would do if you pursued a career in law or otherwise tried to develop your legal reasoning skills.

Legal Precedent

One of the most powerful uses of analogies is in the law. A previous analogous case that has become law is called a *precedent*. A case is often applied to other, similar cases, even in the face of crucial differences. Precedents can carry—or sink—a case.

A precedent may be favorable or unfavorable to a later case, depending on the particulars. Lawyers often have to demonstrate that an earlier case (the potential precedent) is analogous or that the differences are simply too great for the precedent to apply. The analogy turns on similarities and differences. (See Chapter 6 for a review.)

We see precedents in daily life (e.g., "Josie gets to stay out until 2:00 A.M. Why can't I?"). There must be sufficient similarities for the principle of the precedent-setting case to apply to the situation at hand. Of course, a killer difference (e.g., Josie is 21 years old and "you" are only 12 years old) can deflate the analogy, and the precedent then fails. In law, applying a precedent is as follows:

Steps in Applying a Legal Precedent

1. Posit a potential precedent favorable to your case.
2. State the legal principle or decision of the precedent case.
3. Show that the legal precedent has sufficient similarities to *your* case.
4. Conclude that the earlier decision applies here as well.

The use of a precedent can have a definitive effect on an argument, positively or negatively. In fact, using a precedent in novel ways has transformed the law. For example, in *Roe* v. *Wade* (on abortion rights), the Supreme Court ruled that there were "zones of privacy" guaranteed by the Constitution. This interpretation led to wide-ranging applications, including decisions on euthanasia, the right to refuse medical treatment, and gay rights.

To block the use of a precedent, point out key *differences* between the two cases, so that the earlier decision does not apply. The precedent sinks without any relevant similarities. The greater the differences, the less effective is the asserted precedent. If there are no significant differences, however, perhaps there are extenuating circumstances such that the precedent should be rejected. One way to do this is to find another precedent (analogous case) to counter the one proposed. If nothing else, it diminishes its force by offering an alternative that leads to a different conclusion.

The Power of Assumptions

As we know from the first part of this text, assumptions can make or break an argument. Pay close attention and keep your antennae out, watching for any omissions and unwarranted assumptions. It's advisable to watch your own reasoning as well. You don't want to be bamboozled by unwarranted assumptions lurking behind your own argument.

Group or Individual Exercise

The Skateboarder's Lawsuit

This is a case about a teenager, Angelo Seaver, who had been smoking marijuana and went skateboarding on a dark, moonless night. He went into a public park after closing time and hopped on his skateboard, but crashed into a locked gate, injuring himself.

Directions: Before reading the passage below, briefly state how you picture the accident and any assumptions you may have. List two or three questions you would like to ask Seaver or park officials. Do you think Seaver bears any responsibility for the accident? Now read the article and answer the questions that follow.

> A teenager stoned on marijuana enters a public park after closing, rides his skateboard down a driveway on a moonless night and crashes into a locked gate. And then he sues Santa Cruz County for his injuries because he didn't see the gate coming. Seventeen-year-old Angelo Seaver's blame-the-government strategy didn't go far with a trial judge. But it did win over a three-judge appellate panel.
>
> On Friday [30 Apr 2004], the 6th District Court of Appeal in San Jose, CA ruled that because Seaver was riding his skateboard for transportation, not to perform stunts, he was not engaged in a "hazardous recreational activity." The panel found that because there were no signs, reflectors or lighting to help Seaver see the gate, the county created a

"dangerous condition of public property." Justice Eugene Premo concluded that it was a mistake for the trial judge to toss out Seaver's suit based on the primary assumption of risk doctrine that normally holds people responsible for their own sporting accidents. . . .

Court records show that on the night in question in January 2002, Seaver and his friend had ridden their skateboards all over town. They became tired by about 10 P.M. While waiting to catch a bus home, they smoked some pot at Anna Jean Cummings Park. Seaver then launched himself down the park's driveway, gaining speed, and slammed into a three-foot high metal gate. Seaver's injuries were not described in the ruling.

Santa Cruz Superior Court Judge Robert Atack dismissed Seaver's suit on the grounds that he acted recklessly. "Based on the undisputed facts of this case, this metal gate did not create a substantial risk of harm when the park was used with due care in a reasonably foreseeable manner," he stated. But the [Court of Appeal] found that the accident could have happened to *anyone* because they could have entered the upper section of the park after dark and not known it was closed.

"These users would have no notice that the gate would be closed because the gate was at the bottom of the driveway and the only sign indicating park hours was posted at the main entrance on the lower level," Premo wrote, adding that the gate was difficult to see. The appellate court also faulted [Judge] Atack for suggesting that the dangers inherent in skateboarding make it more like skiing than bicycling.

Premo said it all depends on what the rider is trying to do with the skateboard. It's one thing to test one's limits by performing tricks, and quite another to use a "long board" strictly for transportation. Because there was no evidence that Seaver was doing stunts, Premo wrote, a jury rather than the judge should decide the county's liability for his injuries. . . ." (Peter Blumberg, "Panel Revives Skateboarder's Injury Lawsuit," *Los Angeles Daily [Law] Journal,* 4 May 2004. Copyright 2004 Daily Journal Corp. Reprinted with permission)

Answer the following:

1. Looking back at your assumptions and any stereotypes that surfaced, what stands out now that you know more about the case?

2. What were the key issues in the appellate court's assessment of the case? Which of Judge Atack's assumptions did the three justices in the appeal question?

3. Was the Court of Appeals right to overturn the lower court ruling? Explain.

Exercises

Part One

1. In *Hudson* v. *McMillian* (1992), the Supreme Court ruled that prisoners who are beaten, however minor, without provocation or without a reasonable cause can be considered the victims of "cruel and unusual punishment." The presenting case involved a prisoner, Keith Hudson, who was handcuffed and beaten by two guards while their supervisor watched, warning the guards

only against having "too much fun." Hudson suffered a split lip, loosened teeth, a broken dental plate, and bruises, but no life-threatening or serious health problems. The Supreme Court ruled that this was a violation of the 8th Amendment and turned on "contemporary standards of decency." Justices Thomas and Scalia dissented, seeing the prisoner's complaint on the level of his being given unappetizing food. They expressed concern that we are in danger of prisons becoming too lenient.

   a. State what are the key concerns in the case.

   b. State whether Scalia and Thomas's analogy holds.

2. Here is a set of jury instructions for the state of Michigan (posted on www .umich.edu). Read and summarize the key points, and then discuss any problems you have with the list below.

Use of Deadly Force in Self-Defense

1) The defendant claims that [he/she] acted in lawful self-defense. A person has the right to use force or even take a life to defend [himself/herself] under certain circumstances. If a person acts in lawful self-defense, [his/her] actions are excused and [he/she] is not guilty of any crime.

2) You should consider all the evidence and use the following rules to decide whether the defendant acted in lawful self-defense. Remember to judge the defendant's conduct according to how the circumstances appeared to [him/her] at the time [he/she] acted.

3) First, at the time [he/she] acted, the defendant must have honestly and reasonably believed that [he/she] was in danger of being [killed/seriously injured/forcibly sexually penetrated]. If [his/her] belief was honest and reasonable, [he/she] could act immediately to defend [himself/herself] even if it turned out later that [he/she] was wrong about how much danger [he/she] was in. In deciding if the defendant's belief was honest and reasonable, you should consider all the circumstances as they appeared to the defendant at the time.

4) Second, a person may not kill or seriously injure another person just to protect [himself/herself] against what seems like a threat of only minor injury. The defendant must have been afraid of [death/serious physical injury/forcible sexual penetration]. When you decide if the defendant was afraid of one or more of these, you should consider all the circumstances: [the condition of the people involved, including their relative strength/ whether the other person was armed with a dangerous weapon or had some other means of injuring the defendant/the nature of the other person's attack or threat/whether the defendant knew about any previous violent acts or threats made by the other person].

5) Third, at the time [he/she] acted, the defendant must have honestly and reasonably believed that what [he/she] did was immediately necessary. Under the law, a person may only use as much force as [he/she] thinks is necessary at the time to protect [himself/herself], but you may also consider how the excitement of the moment affected the choice the defendant made.

Part Two

The Imperfect Self-Defense: In this California case, a man referred to as "Christian S" killed another man because he believed he was in imminent danger of death. His defense, called the imperfect self-defense, was accepted by the California Supreme Court. It was later used in the Menendez case (where two brothers, Eric and Lyle, were accused of murdering their parents, who they said were abusive to them). This defense has other ramifications, particularly in the case of battered women who kill their abusers. The passage is from the California Supreme Court ruling in *re: Christian S.* (1994), 7 Cal.4th 768. Read this selection and then answer the questions that follow.

"Murder is the unlawful killing of a human being, or a fetus, *with malice aforethought.*" By contrast, "Manslaughter is the unlawful killing of a human being *without malice.*" The vice is the element of malice; in its absence the level of guilt must decline (*People v. Flannel*). The doctrines of imperfect self-defense and diminished capacity arose from this principle.

(2) We explained imperfect self-defense in *Flannel.* "It is the honest belief of imminent peril that negates malice in a case of complete self-defense; the reasonableness of the belief simply goes to the justification for the killing." We concluded that, "An *honest but unreasonable* belief that it is necessary to defend oneself from imminent peril to life or great bodily injury negates malice aforethought, the mental element necessary for murder, so that the chargeable offense is reduced to manslaughter."

[*Note:* It is well established that the ordinary self-defense doctrine—applicable when a defendant *reasonably* believes that his safety is endangered—may not be invoked by a defendant who, through his own wrongful conduct. It does not apply when the other's attack or pursuit is legally justified. It follows, that the imperfect self-defense doctrine cannot be invoked in such circumstances. For example, the imperfect self-defense doctrine would not permit a fleeing felon who shoots a pursuing police officer to escape a murder conviction even if the felon killed his pursuer with an actual belief in the need for self-defense.]

Answer the following:

1. What constitutes an imperfect self-defense? State the key aspects of the definition. Compare it to other concepts of self-defense you can think of.

2. Would this be a legitimate defense for killing someone you suspect is stalking you?

Quick Quiz

1. In the practice of the law, analogies are often used in the form of
   (a) a precedent or (b) an assumption.

2. *True or false:* If there is a significant ("killer") difference, an analogy will succeed.

3. When assessing a potential precedent, look at the terms being compared and list:
   a. Warranted and unwarranted assumptions
   b. Similarities and differences
   c. The laws the analogy has influenced
   d. The statistical data behind the analogy

4. What is crucial when using a precedent in a legal argument (circle *all* that are true)?
   a. To show that the precedent is recent
   b. To show that the precedent draws from federal, not state or local, law
   c. To show that the precedent has strong similarities to the case at hand
   d. To show that the precedent has an opinion that is favorable to the case at hand
   e. To show that the precedent is an inductive argument

5. A potential precedent sinks if:
   a. There is no conclusion
   b. There are no relevant differences
   c. There are no relevant assumptions
   d. There are no relevant similarities

6. *True or false*: An argument from analogy is a form of a cause-and-effect argument.

7. To *counter* the use of a potential precedent you would focus on (a) differences or (b) similarities between the two cases.

8. *True or false:* The use of a precedent to argue a case is a form of inductive reasoning.

Controversial Cases and the Law

In addressing legal issues, keep in mind the broader social context within which law plays a key role. Laws that ignore the needs and wishes of the people risk being overturned by voters (via proposals on a ballot), courts (via challenges to a case), or legislators (via amendments or new laws to override or refine an earlier law).

There have been laws that, in retrospect, were clearly unjust (e.g., laws barring interracial marriage, laws permitting slavery, and laws that did not consider marital or date rape a crime). As society evolves, laws and customs must adapt, although this is not always easy. Some issues are highly contentious (e.g., abortion, animal rights, euthanasia, and the death penalty) and thus not easily resolved.

Two recent court decisions deal with controversial issues. One is same-sex marriage; the other is the legal status of detainees in Guantanamo Bay, Cuba. The first case went to the California Supreme Court, resulting in a May 15, 2008, decision to permit same-sex marriage. There, the chief justice considered the treatment of gays to be analogous to the treatment of slaves in the old South. The second case went to the U.S. Supreme Court, resulting in a June 12, 2008, decision permitting detainees at Guantanamo Bay to appeal decisions to civil courts. Subsequent to the decision on same-sex marriage, an initiative to define marriage as only between a man and woman was adopted by popular vote in California's November 2008 election. Further legal challenges are pending before the California Supreme Court.

Group or Individual Exercise

Controversial Court Decisions

Directions: Unless your instructor tells you otherwise (e.g., by dividing the class into groups and assigning the two cases), select *one* of the cases below.

Case 1: Same-Sex Marriage. On May 15, 2008, the California Supreme Court issued its ruling that there was no compelling state interest to prohibit same-sex marriages. Read about the decision and what Chief Justice Ronald M. George was thinking about before he issued the ruling. Set out his key points and discuss his comparison to civil rights cases of the past. Then state at least two or three points that opponents might raise regarding this decision.

The Ruling: An Outline

1. Marriage is a fundamental right, and that right includes having the relationship accorded dignity and respect by society at large.

2. Sexual orientation is a "suspect classification," in the same way that race, gender, and religion are suspect bases for imposing differential treatment under the law.

3. Because marriage is a fundamental right, and sexual orientation is a suspect classification, the court looks at the marriage laws using a "strict scrutiny" standard. This means the state must show that the statutory scheme is *required* to serve a *compelling* state interest. In other words, the court will not simply allow the Legislature to choose the best means to serve a particular policy; the Legislature is required to show that the statutory scheme is essential to serve a compelling interest.

4. The different treatment of opposite-sex and same-sex couples does not serve a compelling interest. Allowing same-sex couples to marry does not deprive opposite-sex couples of any right. Forbidding same-sex marriages causes significant harm to the couples and their children. Because of historical "disparagement" of gays, excluding them from marriage is likely to be seen as official policy that their relationships are of lesser value. Perpetuating the current marriage scheme would perpetuate a "premise" that gays are "second-class citizens."

Chief Justice Ronald M. George Discusses the Ruling: Before the California Supreme Court's historic decision, moderate Republican Chief Justice Ronald M. George said the decision "weighed most heavily" on him—more than any previous case in his nearly 17 years on the court. As he read the legal arguments, the 68-year-old moderate Republican was drawn by memory to a long-ago trip he made with his European immigrant parents through the American South. In an interview, he said the signs warning "No Negro" or "No colored" left quite an indelible impression on him. (All the quotes and references here and below are from the *Los Angeles Times,* 18 May 2008.) "I think there are times when doing the right thing means not playing it safe. I am very fatalistic about these things," he said. "If you worry, always looking over your shoulders, then maybe it's time to hang up your robe." In his opinion, the fight for same-sex marriage was a civil rights case similar to the battle to ban laws against interracial marriage. He noted that the California Supreme Court moved ahead of public sentiment 60 years ago when it became the first in the country to strike down the anti-miscegenation laws.

As for the basis for his decision, he said, "What you are doing is applying the Constitution, the ultimate expression of the people's will." Justice George added, "When is it that a court should act? When is it that a court is shirking its responsibility by not acting, and when is a court overreaching? That's a real conundrum. I have respect for people coming out on different sides of this issue."

Law Professor Gerald Uleman Reacts to the Ruling: The "very carefully written opinion is very sensitive to how this will be perceived. He [Justice George] realized that this more than any other thing he does as chief justice will define his legacy. He'll certainly take a good deal of political heat over this."

Case 2: Detainees Right to Appeal.

Arguing that "the laws and Constitution are designed to survive, and remain in force, in extraordinary times," U.S. Supreme Court Justice Anthony Kennedy wrote the majority opinion in *Boumediene et al. v. Bush, President of the United States, et al.* The Court ruled that Guantanamo detainees have a constitutional right to go to federal court to challenge their continued detention. Thus, the Court affirmed that the Constitution's reach included the territory of Guantanamo and the "aliens" detained there under U.S. control. The view was that the truncated review procedure available to detainees at Guantanamo Bay failed to provide "the fundamental procedural protections of habeas corpus." Read about the ruling, and then set out the key points and discuss the way in which the justices are seeing the reach of the Constitution.

The Ruling: An Overview

The decision rested on habeas corpus and rejected the view that the Constitution has no effect in Guantanamo (which has been under control of the U.S. government for over 100 years). The Constitution holds there, the Court ruled. Furthermore, "The Constitution grants Congress and the President the power to acquire, dispose of, and govern territory, not the power to decide when and where its terms apply. To hold that the political branches may switch the Constitution on or off at will would lead to a regime in which they, not this Court, say 'what the law is.' These concerns have particular bearing upon the Suspension Clause question here, for the habeas writ is itself an indispensable mechanism for monitoring the separation of powers."

The Court ruled, "In considering both the procedural and substantive standards used to impose detention to prevent acts of terrorism, the courts must accord proper deference to the political branches. However, security subsists, too, in fidelity to freedom's first principles, chief among them being freedom from arbitrary and unlawful restraint and the personal liberty that is secured by adherence to the separation of powers."

▦ LSAT Skills: Preparing for the Law School Admissions Test

The LSAT requires skills in both logic and critical thinking. You have been preparing as you worked your way through this text! The exam contains four sections: reading comprehension, analytical reasoning ("the games"), logical reasoning ("the arguments"), and writing (an essay). The reading comprehension section tests your ability to read a passage, pull out key points, watch for author bias, and so on. The writing section presents two options and criteria for decision making. You choose one option and set out your argument. The analytical reasoning section draws on your ability to organize information quickly and rewrite it using techniques such as the rules of replacement and square of opposition. The logical reasoning section focuses on argumentation, including the rules of inference and replacement, argument structure, and syllogistic reasoning. A solid grounding in Chapters 4 and 10 are especially helpful in these two reasoning sections.

For the analytical and logical reasoning sections, Chapters 3, 5, and 9 help ground you in the basics, since both of these sections focus on deductive reasoning. Occasionally, you'll see inductive reasoning (particularly analogies) and fallacies. Remember the difference between modus ponens and the fallacy of affirming the consequent, and between modus tollens and the fallacy of denying the antecedent; see Chapter 10 for a review.

Being able to symbolize sentences helps you organize information and quickly assess arguments—see Chapter 4. The LSAT generally contains a few fallacies, so you may want to review Chapter 7. The analytic reasoning section tests your skill at puzzles, an area you might find difficult under the time constraints.

Overall, give yourself plenty of time to become comfortable with the sections of the LSAT and the sorts of questions you'll be asked. Then practice, practice, practice. Since these are timed tests, speed and accuracy are crucial.

Reading Comprehension

The LSAT demands good skills in reading comprehension and the ability to quickly pick out key details and obtain a sense of the whole, as well as vital parts. You need to get a sense of the main ideas, the use of concepts, the structure of the excerpt, the author's point of view, and any assumptions made.

Reading Comprehension Hints

- **Do aerial surveillance.** Glance over the passage to get an idea of what it is about. Get a general sense of the topic being discussed, any specifics that jump out at you, and the way the author lays out the discussion.
- **Know what's being asked of you.** Look at the questions *first*. This is your guide to what to look for as you read. Questions may focus on the author's purpose, thesis, key arguments, assumptions, and applications. Notice what is included or excluded and the range of terms and concepts used in the questions.

- **Organize the material.** Look at the opening and closing sentences—and see if there is a summary (usually at the end of the passage). The selection may be out of context, with no introduction or conclusion, so try to get a sense of how the passage is organized. Mark key points. Watch for propositions and judgments, along with any evidence (premises) offered.
- **Block out the structure.** Underline premise-indicators, conclusion-indicators, and key terms and concepts. See how the selection is organized (e.g., with sequences or lists). Look for conditional claims and see if an antecedent condition is given. Watch for the application of ideas and concepts, comparisons, contrasts, similarities, and differences. *Remember:* Examples are supplementary and *not* points in themselves. Think of an example as an example *of* some point—so look for the point being illustrated.
- **Use all and only what is given.** Do not add anything—not your own knowledge, facts, or assumptions—when answering questions. Work with what is given, and draw any inferences solely from that. Watch for any assumptions, omissions, and biases in the passage. And avoid tangents.
- **Draw inferences from what you have read.** See where the author is heading in the passage. Locate the conclusion first. The "purpose" of a passage is the reason for it. Why did the author write this in the first place? What was the goal? Watch for the support (evidence) underlying the inferences you (or the author) have drawn.
- **Work on speed.** Give yourself as much lead time as you can to develop reading comprehension skills. A year isn't too long. Get copies of old LSATs, which are available online or at the library. You can also find them in LSAT prep books. These give good hints and lots of practice. Read as much as you can, and then go over what you've read, looking for key points and direction.

A review of the range of LSAT reading comprehension questions shows us several categories of questions you may be asked.

Typical LSAT Questions

1. **Questions about what is actually said.** "What best summarizes the passage," "state the author's intent," "the author's attitude can best be described," "what is the purpose," "the primary purpose is," "what is assumed," and "which one is an assumption the speaker relies upon."
2. **Questions about structure, strengths, and weaknesses.** "Which, if true, would most seriously weaken the proponent's" (= one in favor, the author's), "which best describes the organization," "which one points out a flaw in the argument," and "the proponent's reply proceeds by."
3. **Questions about what we can conclude from the passage.** "What could be inferred," "if all the statements above are true, what must also be true," "according to the passage . . . *except,*" and "the author implies."

We can see from this list that techniques covered in this textbook have laid the foundation for you. These include being able to pull out key points, summarize a passage, highlight key words, spot the frame of reference, discern the personal slant (i.e., author's attitude), watch for assumptions (both warranted and unwarranted), draw inferences (i.e., implications), and assess the argument for strengths and weaknesses.

Of course, the LSAT exam is under time pressure, so develop speed applying your critical thinking skills. But we have covered the bases, so you want to develop the techniques and practice, practice, practice, so you can answer the questions.

Group or Individual Exercise

The Personal Injury Lawsuit

1. This case centers on a suicidal woman ("Miss Daniell") who locked herself in the trunk of a car and then couldn't get out. She sued the car manufacturer (Ford Motor Co.) (*Daniell v. Ford Motor Co.,* 581 F. Supp. 728,731 [D. N.M. 1984]). Read about the case and then unpack the argument—set out the conclusion and the premises in standard form. Assess the strength of the reasoning.

In 1980, Miss Daniell became locked inside the trunk of a 1973 Ford LTD automobile, where she remained for some nine days. She now seeks to recover for psychological and physical injuries she suffered as a result. She contends that the automobile had a design defect in that the trunk lock or latch did not have an internal release or opening mechanism. She also maintains that the manufacturer is liable based on a failure to warn of this condition.

[Three facts bring down her case] First, she ended up in the trunk compartment of the automobile because she felt "overburdened" and was attempting to commit suicide. Second, the purposes of an automobile trunk are to transport, stow and protect items from elements of the weather. Third, she never considered the possibility of exit from the inside of the trunk when the automobile was purchased.

She intentionally sought to end her life by crawling into an automobile trunk from which she could not escape. This is not a case where a person inadvertently became trapped inside an automobile trunk. She was aware of the natural and probable consequences of her perilous conduct. Not only that, Miss Daniell, at least initially, sought those dreadful consequences. She, not the manufacturer of the vehicle, is responsible for this unfortunate occurrence.

As a general principle, a design defect is actionable only where the condition of the product is unreasonably dangerous to the user or consumer. A manufacturer has a duty to consider only those risks of injury which are foreseeable. A risk is not foreseeable by a manufacturer where a product is used in a manner that could not reasonably be anticipated by the manufacturer, and that use is the cause of the plaintiff's injury.

The purposes of an automobile trunk are to transport, stow and secure the automobile spare tire, luggage and other goods and to protect those items from elements of the weather. The design features of an automobile trunk make it well near impossible that an adult intentionally would enter the trunk and close the lid. The court holds that the plaintiff's use of the trunk compartment as a means to attempt suicide was an unforeseeable use. Therefore, the manufacturer had no duty to design an internal release or opening mechanism that might have prevented this occurrence. (*Daniell v. Ford Motor Co., Inc.* [1984], as noted in Julie Van Camp, *Ethical Issues in the Courts;* Wadsworth 2000)

2. Philosopher Julie Van Camp asks, "If the plaintiff were a 10-year-old child who suffered severe and permanent physical injury after accidentally locking herself in the trunk, should Ford Motor be held liable for damages?"

   a. State your answer to Van Camp's question. *Note:* She asks us to do some analogical reasoning and determine what—if anything—should change in the decision, if we change a key detail of the case.

   b. Do you think the shift to "accidental" creates a crucial difference in the case? Discuss.

3. What if, instead of the adult (Daniell) trying to commit suicide by locking herself in the trunk of the car, we had a woman who jumped in the trunk and closed the door (thus locking herself in) to hide from a serial killer known to be roaming her neighborhood? She could not have foreseen such a use when she purchased the car. Does the decision above still apply in this case?

Exercises

Prisoners Trade Kidneys for Shorter Sentences

Under a proposal being considered in South Carolina, prison inmates could get up to six months shaved off their sentences if they donate a kidney or bone marrow. According to the Organ Procurement and Transplantation Network, more than 95,300 Americans are awaiting an organ transplant, and about 6,700 die every year before an appropriate organ is found. Under South Carolina's program, the state's Department of Corrections would decide which inmates could donate. Money for medical procedures, and any prison guard overtime, would be paid by the organ recipient and charitable organizations (Jenny Jarvie, "Inmates Could Trade an Organ for an Early Out," *Los Angeles Times*, 9 Mar 2007). Read the arguments for each side and then answer the questions that follow.

(Pro) **Senator Ralph Anderson:** "We have a lot of people dying as they wait for organs, so I thought about the prison population. I believe we have to do something to motivate them. If they get some good time off, if they get out early, that's motivation. We would check that this was voluntary and they had all the information. It would not be forced upon them. America has a major healthcare crisis; I believe this would save money, improve the quality of healthcare and save a whole bunch of lives."

(Con) **Law Professor Lawrence Gostin:** "For a prisoner to actually have a benefit for giving up an organ violates every ethical value I'm aware of. It's grossly unethical, if not unlawful. Getting out of prison early is more valuable than money. That's your freedom."

Answer the following:

1. Set out Anderson's argument in standard form for his thesis that inmates ought to be able to trade an organ for an early release. Note which of his premises are the strongest support for *his* thesis.

2. Set out Gostin's argument in standard form for his thesis that inmates ought to be able to trade an organ for an early release. Note which of his premises are the strongest support for *his* thesis.

3. Which of the two arguments (Anderson's or Gostin's) do you think is strongest? State your reasons.

Analytical Reasoning

We might think of the reading comprehension and writing sections of the LSAT as the bookends. In between are the two applications sections. One is the analytical reasoning section (alias "the games"), and the other is the logical reasoning section (alias "the arguments"). Analytical reasoning requires you be able to quickly organize criteria, set up the given information, simplify, and draw inferences (e.g., using the rules of replacement) that you can apply to the answer set. We'll look at this first and then turn to the logical reasoning section.

To work on the analytical sections of the LSAT or other standardized exams, you need strong deductive reasoning. For an overview, see Chapter 5; to review the rules of replacement and rules of inference, see Chapters 4 and 10; to review the rules of the syllogism, see Chapter 9; and to review the major fallacies, see Chapter 7.

Analytical reasoning draws from deductive reasoning with regard to both argumentation and claims and inferences. Of help here are the rules of replacement and translations of ordinary language—for example, "only," "unless," "not only," "neither/nor," and "not both" (see Chapter 4).

Tips on Analytical Reasoning (The Games)

- **Jump Around.** It doesn't matter where you start. Jump around as much as you want or plow on through. Just don't allow yourself to get stuck, or you may miss out on the questions ahead that you might find much easier.
- **Do the familiar first.** Look for the types of games that you feel most comfortable with. The familiar ones are likely the easiest to do. In turn, this builds confidence, which helps you in tackling the least familiar questions.
- **Diagram, diagram.** As fast as you can, diagram the set of criteria (translate them) so you have them in skeletal form. A key issue is whether you understand the specs of the rule. If not, move on and return to this question later.
- **Think like a fox.** There are three main parts—the introduction (setting out the context), the criteria (setting out relationships), and the questions (applying the criteria). Get the first two in place and then turn to the questions.
- **Use the rules.** Think in terms of the handy abbreviations you've learned in critical thinking (e.g., "neither A nor B" = ~A & ~B). Your goal is to get hold of the structure using some shorthand form to set out the rules and expand your knowledge base. Using the rules of inference and replacement (e.g., DeMorgan's, transposition, or "only if"), write out all the equivalent claims.

- **Draw inferences and combine rules.** Look at what you have with your rules—do any work together? Can you infer more rules from the ones you've been given? The more you can pull out of the rules, the faster you'll go. Cross out answers that you eliminate, so you narrow down the answer choices.
- **Map out a strategy.** If you are a visual person, picture the scenario and the way the rules/criteria are shaping how you will proceed. If you think in terms of categories, you can focus on the rules and plug in the information from your introduction.
- **Don't carry over.** Each question is a distinct and separate unit—the information that is added to particular question does *not* carry over to the next. Neither the added information in one question nor the results you obtain can be brought forward to the next question. Nothing carries over except the base information of the root question.
- **Read carefully.** If the question asks for a choice that "must be true," then it cannot be false—so if you can think of an exception, you can eliminate that choice. If it asks for "all but" or "all that are true *except*," you should look for the choice that *has* to be false (it contradicts what you know to be true).
- **Don't do more than you need to.** The questions often give another (distinct) condition as an additional *temporary* criteria—it doesn't carry over to the other questions. The added piece of information allows you to draw more inferences and then proceed to the answer set (if you don't see the correct answer directly, proceed via elimination).

We are now ready to tackle some games typical of those found on the analytical reasoning section of the LSAT. All the examples and exercises here and in the logical reasoning section are amended from or variations of actual LSAT questions (from old exams), so these will give you an idea of what you'll be asked.

An Example of Analytical Reasoning

The Blue Nose Diner has a staff of five employees—Chefs Maria and Orlando, baker Philomena, and waiters Ruben and Sissela. The International Gourmet (IG) has five reality shows, which all the employees attend, according to the following criteria:

> If Maria goes to one of the reality shows, then Ruben does not go.
> If Orlando goes, then either Philomena or Ruben, but not both, goes along too.
> If Philomena goes, then Sissela does not go.
> If Sissela goes to one of the shows, then either Maria or Orlando, but not both, goes with her.

Question: If Orlando goes to one of the reality shows, then which of the following would be a complete and accurate list of the other employees of the Blue Diner who also went with Orlando?

    a. Mario and Ruben
    b. Mario and Sissela
    c. Philomena and Ruben

d. Ruben

e. Sissela

Step 1: Set up what you know, translating the criteria so it can be quickly read. Use all the techniques we've studied to draw inferences of equivalent propositions. Doing so we get:

Criteria	Expressed as Pairs
1. M → ~R	(M, ~R) ≡ (R, ~M) (*Transposition*)
2. (O → P) v (O → R) and O → ~(P & R)	(O, P) or (O, R), (*DeMorgan's*) not both
3. P → ~S	(P, ~S) ≡ (S, ~P) (*Transposition*)
4. S → (M v O) and S → ~(M & S)	(S, M) or (S, O), (*DeMorgan's*) not both

Step 2: Turn now to the question to see what additional criteria are given and what you are then asked to do. Looking at the question above, we see that we are given the additional piece of information that Orlando is going (= O), so now we can use our critical thinking skills to crack the case. Let's eliminate what we can. Let's go through each answer (unless you can pick out the correct answer by inspection).

Answer (a): M & R. We have O, which means that by criterion 2 we have P or R (not both). According to criterion 1, if we have R, then we don't have M, so this knocks out this answer.

Answer (b): M & S. We have O, so we also have either P or R (not both). Since this choice has neither of them, this knocks out this answer.

Answer (c): P & R. We have O, which means we have P or R (not both). This answer is both, so it can be eliminated.

Answer (d): R. We have O, which means we have P or R (not both). This answer would work. Confirm by trying the last answer choice.

Answer (e): S. No problem with S going, but we have O, which means we have P or R (not both). This answer has neither P nor R, so is eliminated.

That leaves answer (d): R is the correct answer.

Exercises

Part One

Zorra and Moo are off to the circus—they want to see the animals in the ring. There are eight animals: Hyena, Iguana, Jaguar, Kangaroo, Lion, Monkey, Orangutan, and Rhino. The animals come in one by one (*no two together*). The rules are:

Lion enters before both Orangutan and Hyena.

Hyena enters after Rhino.

Kangaroo enters before Lion but after Iguana.

Jaguar enters after Lion.

Iguana enters before Monkey.

1. What could be *true*?
   a. Orangutan is the second animal to enter.
   b. Iguana is the third animal to enter.
   c. Hyena is the fourth animal to enter.
   d. Jaguar is the fifth animal to enter.
   e. Lion is the sixth animal to enter.

2. If Rhino is the seventh animal to enter, what could be *true*?
   a. Iguana is the second animal to enter.
   b. Kangaroo is the fourth animal to enter.
   c. Monkey is the fifth animal to enter.
   d. Lion is the sixth animal to enter.
   e. Orangutan is the eighth animal to enter.

3. If Hyena is the fifth animal to enter, what must be *false*?
   a. Rhino is the first animal to enter.
   b. Kangaroo is the second animal to enter.
   c. Lion is the third animal to enter.
   d. Monkey is the fourth animal to enter.
   e. Orangutan is the sixth animal to enter.

Part Two

In the Snapplepuff Museum, there are eight shelves, numbered from left to right (consecutively). Exactly six platinum records—B, C, D, F, G, and H—are to be placed on the shelves. No more than one record can be placed on any shelf. The conditions are below:

B must be on a lower-numbered shelf than G.

C and H (not necessarily in that order) must be placed on shelves immediately next to each other.

Any shelf to the left or right of the shelf on which F is placed must be empty.

State the set-up using variables (letters) and symbols.

1. If shelves 1–4 all hold records, which one of the following could be the four platinum records, in order from shelf 1 to shelf 4, on those four shelves?
   a. C, B, G, D
   b. C, H, B, F
   c. D, B, G, H
   d. D, G, H, C
   e. F, B, G, C

2. If D is on shelf 2 and F is on shelf 5, then G must be on shelf:
    a. 3
    b. 4
    c. 5
    d. 6
    e. 7

3. If shelves 3 and 7 are empty and G is on shelf 5, what must be *true*?
    a. B is on shelf 1.
    b. C is on shelf 1.
    c. D is on shelf 6.
    d. D is on shelf 8.
    e. F is on shelf 2.

Part Three

Eight spices—F, G, H, J, K, L, M, and N—are used in three cakes—Chocolate Cake, Parisian Torte, and Tiramesu. There are exactly three spices in the Chocolate Cake, three spices in the Parisian Torte, and two spices in the Tiramesu. The criteria are as follows:

J cannot be in the same cake as N.

G must be added to Tiramesu.

If H is added to Chocolate Cake, N must also be added to Chocolate Cake.

F must be added to Chocolate Cake.

Neither G nor K can be added to the same cake as M.

State the set-up using variables and symbols.

1. What is a possible assignment of spices to the cakes?

	Chocolate	Parisian	Tiramesu
a.	F, H, M	J, K, L	G, N
b.	F, H, N	G, J, M	K, L
c.	F, K, L	J, M, N	G, H
d.	F, L, N	H, J, M	G, K
e.	F, L, N	J, K, M	G, H

2. If L is added to Chocolate Cake, what spice must be added to Parisian Torte?
    a. H
    b. J
    c. K
    d. M
    e. N

3. If J and L are added to Chocolate Cake, what spice must be added to Tiramisu?
    a. L
    b. H

    c. M
    d. K
    e. N

Part Four

Jody just got seven paintings donated to the Biada Art gallery—T, U, V, W, X, Y, and Z—from which he must choose exactly five for the exhibit. Any combination is okay if it fits the following conditions:

If T is chosen, X cannot be chosen.

If U is chosen, Y must also be chosen.

If V is chosen, X must also be chosen.

State the set-up using variables and symbols.

1. Which one is acceptable to include in Jody's exhibit?
    a. T, U, V, X, Y
    b. T, U, V, Y, Z
    c. T, W, X, Y, Z
    d. U, V, W, Y, Z
    e. U, V, W, X, Y

2. If painting T is chosen, what painting *cannot* then be chosen for the exhibit?
    a. U
    b. V
    c. W
    d. Y
    e. Z

3. If Jody chooses V for the exhibit, what must be true?
    a. T is not chosen.
    b. Y is not chosen.
    c. U is chosen.
    d. W is chosen.
    e. Z is chosen.

Logical Reasoning

In the logical reasoning section of the LSAT, the focus is on examining and analyzing arguments and then drawing inferences. Question types include (1) matching the principle or form of an argument with one of the answer choices, (2) matching the argument with one of the answer choices in terms of parallel structure, (3) specifying what error is committed in the argument, (4) sorting out the paradox in seemingly conflicted claims in an argument, (5) pinpointing the source of a disagreement, and (6) clarifying the function or role of a particular fact in the argument. These all require that you pay close attention to the reasoning (in terms of both structure and content). From that, apply your logical skills, drawing on the rules of inference and replacement, formal fallacies, and rules of the syllogism.

There is usually one question per argument, with 1.5 minutes the average time per question. Order does not matter, so jump around, trying to do as many as you can and not getting bogged down by one question. *Remember:* The questions are of equal value, so move on rather than getting stuck.

Let's look at questions and skill that you might find in this section of the LSAT. As you work your way through them, use the rules of inference (modus ponens, modus tollens, etc.), the rules of the syllogism (to test validity), the rules of replacement (DeMorgan's Laws, transposition, material implication, etc.), the rules for ordinary language ("only," "not only," "unless," etc.), and the formal fallacies.

Exercises

1. A dog whisperer who studied pets in Silver Lake found that dogs that were never beaten never bit a pizza delivery man. She concluded that the best way to keep dogs from biting a pizza delivery man is not to punish them for bad behavior. The dog whisperer's conclusion is based on which of the following *assumptions*?

   i.   The dogs she studied never bit a pizza delivery man.
   ii. Dogs should not be beaten.
   iii. There were no instances of a dog that was not beaten biting a pizza delivery man that she had failed to observe.

      a. i only
      b. ii only
      c. iii only
      d. ii and iii only
      e. i, ii, and iii

2. Jasmine said, "It requires strong arms to be an Olympic swimmer. Developing strong arms requires practice. Therefore, it requires practice to be an Olympic swimmer." Which of the following most closely parallels this argument?
   a. Ryan can be a good soccer player if he wants to. Ryan did a good job playing soccer at Friday's match. Therefore, Ryan must have wanted to be a good soccer player.
   b. It is important to be attentive when you are driving. If you aren't sleepy, you will be attentive. Therefore, you should not be sleepy while you are driving.
   c. A vote for Nazneen is a vote for quality education. Dan voted for Nazneen. Therefore, Dan wants quality education.

d. It costs $250 to fix the stereo. It costs $75 to fix the TV. Therefore, the stereo cost more to fix than the TV.

e. You must exercise to lose weight. You need to lose weight to wear the size-12 skirt that you bought. Therefore, you must exercise to wear the size-12 skirt that you bought.

3. How do you symbolize "Dogs that are not vicious, never bite pizza delivery men" (V, B)?

a. $V \rightarrow B$

b. $\sim B \rightarrow V$

c. $\sim V \rightarrow \sim B$

d. $\sim B \rightarrow \sim V$

e. $\sim(B \rightarrow V)$

4. According to *modus tollens,* what follows from "Only dogs that are never trained will bite a pizza delivery man"?

a. That dog has never been trained. So it bites pizza delivery men.

b. That dog has never been trained. So it does not bite pizza delivery men.

c. That dog bites pizza delivery men. So it has never been trained.

d. That dog does not bite pizza delivery men. So it has been trained.

5. According to *modus ponens,* what follows from "Biting pizza delivery men is sufficient for a dog to be vicious"?

a. That dog is vicious. So it bites pizza delivery men.

b. That dog is not vicious. So it does not bite pizza delivery men.

c. That dog bites pizza delivery men. So it is vicious.

d. That dog does not bite pizza delivery men. So it is not vicious.

6. According to the *disjunctive syllogism,* what follows from "Either that is a dog or it's a large possum"?

a. That's not a dog, so it must be a large possum.

b. That's a dog, so it must not be a large possum.

c. If that's not a dog, then it's a large possum.

d. If that's not a large possum, then it's a dog.

e. That's a dog only if it's not a large possum.

7. If each of the following claims is true, what must also be true?

i. All books from the Yavitz collection are stored in the Dockstader Room.

ii. All books found in the Dockstader Room are logic texts.

iii. No book written by Gordon Gecko is kept in the Dockstader Room.

iv. Every book stored in the Dockstader Room is listed in the computer.

a. All logic texts are stored in the Dockstader Room.

b. No book from the Yavitz collection listed in the computer is a logic text.

c. No book by Gordon Gecko is a logic text.

d. The Yavitz collection contains no books by Gordon Gecko.

e. Every book listed in the computer is stored in the Dockstader Room.

8. "Whenever some of the cooks are grilling salmon and all of the bakers are making pies, all of the waiters are setting up. Some of the cooks are grilling salmon, but some of the waiters are not setting up the tables." Which of the following can be deduced from these two statements?
   a. Some of the cooks are not grilling salmon.
   b. Some of the waiters are setting up.
   c. None of the bakers are making pies.
   d. All of the bakers are making pies.
   e. Some of the bakers are not making pies.

9. Since all the lamps George has repaired have brass parts, it follows that all lamps must have brass parts. The author argues on the basis of:
   a. Special training
   b. Generalization
   c. Syllogism
   d. Ambiguity
   e. Deduction

10. "It makes no sense to pay high prices for French wine when there is lower-priced wine made right in California. Neither you nor your friends can tell the difference in quality. If you don't think they'll be impressed by California wine, try serving it in crystal goblets with a nice cheese." This advertisement rests on which of the following *assumptions?*

    i. It is difficult if not impossible to distinguish French wine from California wine.
    ii. Most wine is not packaged at the place where wine is made.
    iii. Some people may purchase French wine over California wine as a status symbol.

       a. i only
       b. ii only
       c. iii only
       d. i and ii only
       e. i and iii only

Let's go over a few of the questions. Hopefully, you have tried them yourself first! Question 4 asks us to apply modus tollens to "Only dogs that are never trained will bite a delivery man."

First, translate the proposition with the "only". As you may recall, "Only P is Q" is the same as "If it's not P, then it's not Q" ($\sim$P $\rightarrow$ $\sim$Q). Using transposition, we have "If Q, then P" (Q $\rightarrow$ P). So, the claim "Only dogs that are never trained will bite a deliveryman" can be rewritten, "If it's not a dog that has never been trained, then it will not bite a deliveryman." Using transposition, we get, "If it bites a delivery-man, then the dog has never been trained." Now apply modus tollens (P $\rightarrow$ Q. $\sim$Q. Therefore, $\sim$P). We then get, "If it bites a deliveryman, then the dog has never been trained. That dog *has* been trained. Therefore, it won't bite a deliveryman."

Question 7 asks what we can conclude if these are true: "All books from the Yavitz collection are stored in the Dockstader Room. All books found in the Dockstader Room are logic texts. No book written by Gordon Gecko is kept in the Dockstader Room. Every book kept in the Dockstader Room is listed in the computer." Let's set this up.

1. Y → D
2. D → T
3. G → ~D by *transposition* = D→ ~G
4. D → L

So what can we conclude? From 1 and 2 (using hypothetical syllogism), we get Y → T. From 1 and 4 (using hypothetical syllogism), we get Y → L. Using 1 and 3, we get Y → ~G. Our answer choices are (a) T → D, (b) Y → ~T, (c) G → ~T, (d) Y → ~G, and (e) L → D. You can see that (d) is a match! *If you find the right answer, stop there. There is only one right answer!* However, we can run through the others so you can see that none of them are correct. None of (a), (b), (c) and (e) can be inferred from what we have—they all contradict what is given or inferred from when we use hypothetical syllogism. That leaves (d). As you see, that was what we got when we used 1 and 3 and hypothetical syllogism.

Let us now set up question 8: "Whenever some of the cooks are grilling salmon and all of the bakers are making pies, all of the waiters are setting up. Some of the cooks are grilling salmon, but some of the waiters are not setting up the tables."

Tackle this in two stages. First, simplify. Let S = "Some of the cooks are grilling salmon," B = "All of the bakers are making pies," and W = "All of the waiters are setting up." The second sentence is S ("Some of the cooks are grilling salmon") and ~W ("Some waiters are not setting up tables" = "Not all waiters are setting up"). S → W. B → W. But ~W. That means if we use modus tollens on the first two, we can deduce both ~S and ~B. Plugging in what "S" and "B" stand for we get ~S = ~("Some of the cooks are grilling salmon") and ~B = ~("All of the bakers are making pies").

We know from the square of opposition (see Chapter 5) that the negation (contradictory) of an I claim (such as "Some of the cooks are grilling salmon") is an E claim ("None of the cooks are grilling salmon"). But that's *not* one of the answer choices, so turn to ~B = ~(All of the bakers are making pies). By the square of opposition, the negation (contradictory) of an A claim is the O claim ("Some bakers are not making pies"). (*Note:* We can also figure this out using "not all" ["Not all P is Q" = "Some P is not Q"].) So "Not all bakers are making pies" = "Some bakers are not making pies." This is answer choice (e), the correct answer.

LSAT Writing: Exams with a Choice of Two Options

In some essay exams, such as the LSAT, you are given a choice of two options and have 30 minutes to set out your argument. This entails defending your choice and arguing against the other option. Generally, the idea is not that one option is the "right answer" and the other is "wrong." The issue is how well you make your case; you need to clearly state your choice, set out both the affirmative and negative arguments (the first for your choice, the second against the rejected choice), and use all and only the criteria. This means that you made no unwarranted assumptions and did not introduce *your own* criteria.

The goal is to make a decision and defend it using only and all the conditions stated and showing why the alternative choice should be rejected. Here are some guidelines for those taking—or grading—the writing portion of the exam.

Guidelines for Defending a Choice between Options

1. **Organize your answer in terms of the given criteria.** Announce the decision first, then support with evidence and argument. *Evidence* is the facts given in the sketch. *Argument* is the conclusion or inferences you can reasonably derive from the facts.

2. **Remember that arguments can be both positive and negative.** Positive arguments support the conclusion you reach. Negative ones point out the flaws or weaknesses in the opposing conclusion.

3. **The best arguments have both positive and negative elements.** Make the case for your choice and show why the other option should be rejected.

4. **Don't forget that criteria may not have equal weight.** Thus, you may assign them different weight in your answer. In doing so, be explicit (e.g., "the most important aspect of this job is . . ."). Use only the criteria stated: Any added or invented criteria that you bring in are extraneous and may be used against you. Minimally, you need to justify why you added some criteria. It's best to work with the criteria given to make your case. *Remember:* The criteria operate as a *closed set,* so all and only the criteria should be used in arriving at a decision.

5. **Stay focused and be precise.** In stating and defending your conclusion, stick to the question. Avoid going off on a tangent or stating the obvious (e.g., the candidate you selected is deserving—they both are!). Support your conclusion by building a strong case with the facts provided.

6. **End your essay by restating your conclusion.** Summarize the one or two (or even three) strongest points that support it so your final paragraph presents the essentials of your argument.

7. **Use outlining techniques in your argument.** It helps to itemize points, as in "The three most important considerations are (1) _____, (2) _____, and (3) _____." Then show how your candidate meets these criteria more closely than the other candidate does. This technique helps the reader follow the argument and thus makes the argument more persuasive.

8. **Synthesize material; don't just repeat it.** In writing a good answer, show not only that you have read the facts carefully and can repeat them but, more important, that you can combine related facts to address the criteria.

9. **Remember grammar and spelling matter.** Written expression is a primary tool, and if your tool is dull, then you won't have the same impact.

10. **Have an introduction that states your position and how you will proceed.** Then elaborate (in the body of your essay), and end with a conclusion that shows how your elaboration got you there.

⊞ Logic Puzzles

HOW TO SOLVE LOGIC PROBLEMS

Solving Logic Problems is entertaining and challenging. All the information you need to solve a Logic Problem is given in the introduction and clues, and in illustrations, when provided. If you've never solved a Logic Problem before, our sample should help you get started. Fill in the Sample Solving Chart as you follow our explanation. We use a "•" to signify "Yes" and an "X" to signify "No."

SAMPLE LOGIC PROBLEM

Five couples were married last week, each on a different weekday. From the information provided, determine the woman (one is Cathy) and man (one is Paul) who make up each couple, as well as the day on which each couple was married.

1. Anne was married on Monday, but not to Wally.
2. Stan's wedding was on Wednesday. Rob was married on Friday, but not to Ida.
3. Vern (who married Fran) was married the day after Eve.

EXPLANATION

Anne was married Mon. (1), so put a "•" at the intersection of Anne and Mon. Put "X"s in all the other days in Anne's row and all the other names in the Mon. column. (Whenever you establish a relationship, as we did here, be sure to place "X"s at the intersections of all relationships that become impossible as a result.) Anne wasn't married to Wally (1), so put an "X" at the intersection of Anne and Wally. Stan's wedding was Wed. (2), so put a "•" at the intersection of Stan and Wed. (don't forget the "X"s). Stan didn't marry Anne, who was married Mon., so put an "X" at the intersection of Anne and Stan. Rob was married Fri., but not to Ida (2), so put a "•" at the intersection of Rob and Fri., and "X"s at the intersections of Rob and Ida and Ida and Fri. Rob also didn't marry Anne, who was married Mon., so put an "X" at the intersection of Anne and Rob. Now your chart should look like chart 1.

Vern married Fran (3), so put a "•" at the intersection of Vern and Fran. This leaves Anne's only possible husband as Paul, so put a "•" at the intersection of Anne and Paul and Paul and Mon. Vern and Fran's wedding was the day after Eve's (3), which wasn't Mon. [Anne], so Vern's wasn't Tue. It must have been Thu. [see chart], so Eve's was Wed. (3). Put "•"s at the intersections of Vern and Thu., Fran and Thu., and Eve and Wed. Now your chart should look like chart 2.

The chart shows that Cathy was married Fri., Ida was married Tue., and Wally was married Tue. Ida married Wally, and Cathy's wedding was Fri., so she married Rob. After this information is filled in, Eve could only have married Stan. You've completed the puzzle, and your chart should now look like chart 3.

In summary: Anne and Paul, Mon.; Cathy and Rob, Fri.; Eve and Stan, Wed.; Fran and Vern, Thu.; Ida and Wally, Tue.

In some problems, it may be necessary to make a logical guess based on facts you've established. When you do, always look for clues or other facts that disprove it. If you find that your guess is incorrect, eliminate it as a possibility.

The solution for each problem is provided and contains an explanation of the puzzle, as well as a summary of the answer.

Welcome to the world of Logic Problems, where many hours of puzzle pleasure await you!

SAMPLE SOLVING CHART:

WILD ABOUT WRESTLING   BY KAREN VALENCIA   ★★★

Every Saturday afternoon, *Wild, Wild, Wonderful World of Wrestling* features six exhibition matches that pair off twelve wild wrestlers. The fans roar for the good guys, hiss and boo at the bad guys, and have a great time. Can you identify the good guy (each has a one-word name) and the bad guy (each has a three-word name; one is Anak The Great) in each of the six matches in last week's show?

1. The Savage Scourge, Troglodyte, and Samson The Strangler fought in that order in three consecutive matches.

2. Gog The Gargantua, Mammoth, and Barbarius fought in that order in three consecutive matches.

3. Scorpio's match and Cyclops's match weren't consecutive.

4. Titan The Terrible wasn't in the third match.

5. Cyclops wasn't in the fourth match.

6. The Magnificent Bulk wasn't in the fifth match.

7. Barbarius didn't wrestle The Savage Scourge.

8. Colosso (who wasn't in the fourth match) didn't wrestle Samson The Strangler.

9. Troglodyte didn't wrestle either Gog The Gargantua or Titan The Terrible.

	Barbarius	Colosso	Cyclops	Mammoth	Scorpio	Troglodyte	Anak The Great	Gog The Gargantua	The Magnificent Bulk	Samson The Strangler	The Savage Scourge	Titan The Terrible
First												
Second												
Third												
Fourth												
Fifth												
Sixth												
Anak The Great												
Gog The Gargantua												
The Magnificent Bulk												
Samson The Strangler												
The Savage Scourge												
Titan The Terrible												

"Wild about Wrestling." Copyright © 2008 Dell Magazines, A Division of Crosstown Publications. Used with permission of the publisher.

SHOW BUSINESS

Five television companies have produced new series to be networked on different days of the week. From the information given below, can you name the star of each show, say which company has produced it, and on which day of the week it will be screened?

CLUES

1. Marjorie Woodstock is to have her own regular program called *It's a Dog's Life*; this is not the Isis program, which will be shown on Wednesday.

2. Midland TV is not responsible for either the Sunday production or *On the Trail*, which does not star Andy Wilson.

3. Felix Finlay's contract is with Eastern TV.

4. *The Choice Is Yours* will be screened two days before the Highland program.

5. *Cabaret Time* is the Friday night feature.

6. Jenny Simpson's program, which is not produced by Western TV, will be seen at the weekend; Sandy McTavish's show will appear the day before *Penny Dreadful*.

	Andy Wilson	Felix Finlay	Jenny Simpson	Marjorie Woodstock	Sandy McTavish	Eastern	Highland	Isis	Midland	Western	Tuesday	Wednesday	Friday	Saturday	Sunday
Cabaret Time															
It's a Dog's Life															
On the Trail															
Penny Dreadful															
The Choice Is Yours															
Tuesday															
Wednesday															
Friday															
Saturday															
Sunday															
Eastern															
Highland															
Isis															
Midland															
Western															

Program	Star	Company	Day

Logic puzzles directions and puzzles "Show Business," "Whodunit," and "Wash-Day Blues" are from *Original Logic Problems*, September 1990 issue. Copyright 1990 by Penny Press, Inc., 6 Prowitt Street, Norwalk, CT 06855. Used with permission.

WHODUNIT?

Superintendent Keene was investigating a break-in at the local drugstore next door to the cinema. From the modus operandi he quickly narrowed the field down to five suspects. From their statements recorded below, can you give the true identity of the five men and say where each *claimed* to be and whom he claimed to be with at the time the crime was committed? Remember that the four innocent men consistently told the truth and that the guilty party lied throughout and *made up* his alibi.

STATEMENTS

1. Tommy said, "My name is Spratt and I spent the evening with my fiancée. Whilst we were out, we saw the Chaplin brothers go into the pub."

2. Jack said, "My name is Piper. I did not visit the cinema, and I spent the evening with a female companion."

3. Charlie said, "My name is neither Chaplin nor Duck and I went out with my girlfriend that night. We did not go to the cinema."

4. Peter said, "My name is Spratt. I went to the greyhound track with a male friend. On the way there we saw Jack going into the cinema."

5. Donald said, "I am not Mr. Duck and I went out for the evening with a companion who can prove my alibi."

	Chaplin	Duck	Piper	Spratt	Tucker	Cinema	Disco	Greyhounds	Home	Pub	Brother	Fiancée	Girlfriend	Male friend	Wife	False alibi
False alibi																
Charlie																
Donald																
Jack																
Peter																
Tommy																
Brother																
Fiancée																
Girlfriend																
Male friend																
Wife																
Cinema																
Disco																
Greyhounds																
Home																
Pub																

First name	Surname	Location claimed	Companion claimed

WASH-DAY BLUES

Based on idea by E. A. Pursell of Newcastle

The husbands of five women in the maternity ward of the local hospital made valiant attempts to cope with the family wash in their wives' absence. However, each man had one unfortunate mishap. From the information given below, can you match the couples, say which garment each husband ruined and in what manner?

CLUES

1. Paul and Sandra are a couple, but it was not their daughter's skirt which was blown off the clothesline.

2. It was Neil who had the mishap with the ironing.

3. Christine's husband managed to shrink one garment in the wash.

4. John was responsible for the ruined tee-shirt; "a" is the only one of the five vowels contained in his wife's name.

5. David's wife is not Brenda and he did not damage the nightdress, which was not the garment whose color ran.

6. Ann's daughter's dress suffered in one incident.

	Ann	Brenda	Christine	Mary	Sandra	Dress	Nightdress	Jumper	Skirt	Tee-shirt	Blown off line	Color ran	Scorched	Shrank	Torn in wash
David															
John															
Neil															
Paul															
Simon															
Blown off line															
Color ran															
Scorched															
Shrank															
Torn in wash															
Dress															
Nightdress															
Jumper															
Skirt															
Tee-shirt															

Husband	Wife	Garment	Accident

Exercise

Here is an example of a writing question from the LSAT. Using the guidelines above and a 30-minute time limit, make a selection and set out your argument.

"Twiga," a toy store and puppet theatre in Santa Monica owned by Basma Adams, has been doing booming business for the last six years. Adams had an idea to start an animation studio using stuffed animals from Kenya. Write an argument for one of the two following choices. Three criteria should influence your decision:

- Adams needs a larger space than her current facility.
- Adams seeks enough financial stability to allow her to handle the expenses the new venture would require.
- Adams would like to strengthen her ties to the film industry.

Adams is considering moving to Silver Lake, where there is a thriving film community. The new location would allow more networking and a chance to meet other animators. It is a bustling neighborhood, with public transportation and magnet schools that draw young families to the area. There are no other toy stores comparable to Twiga within 4 to 5 miles. The building is quite a bit larger than the Santa Monica store, so Adams could keep the toy store and theater going and wall off an area for her animation studio. It would only require minor repairs to move right in.

Adams is also considering a location in a once-classic section of Hollywood that is being renovated after years of neglect. The area is well known in film circles for the many scenes filmed there in the 1940s and 50s. The space is positioned between a movie studio seeking to develop its independent film division and a condo development that should be ready for sales and leasing within 18 months. The studio has grants that new filmmakers can apply for, providing solid funding for those who are approved. The Hollywood location is approximately 30% larger than the one in Silver Lake, with the rent twice the amount. It is in move-in condition, so there would be no delay getting set up.

Glossary

Absorption. One of the rules of inference and thus a valid form of argument. It is of the form: "If A then B. Therefore, if A then (A and B)."

Accent. One of the fallacies of ambiguity. This fallacy occurs when accent (the emphasis of a word or phrase) leads us to draw an incorrect conclusion.

Accident. Fallacy that occurs when a general rule or principle is applied to a special case in which, by reason of its special or atypical characteristics, the rule simply does not apply. This fallacy might be a misapplication of a moral principle, a rule from work, or a general pronouncement made by a family member or friend. The unwarranted assumption is that the rule applies to all cases, without exception.

Accountability. The extent to which an individual or institution could be held responsible for a decision, policy, or action.

Ad Baculum. Fallacy that occurs when force, the threat of force, or coercion is used to persuade someone to a conclusion. This includes verbal or sexual harassment, blackmail, extortion, and threat of violence used to "persuade" someone to a position. A variation is bribery, where the coercion comes in the form of a promise, offer, money, or position.

Ad Hominem. Fallacy that involves an attack on the character or traits of the person making an argument, rather than their ideas or argument. We see ad hominem when someone is discredited because of such traits as race, gender, nationality, or age.

Ad Hominem Circumstantial. Fallacy that involves an attack on an opponent because of their special circumstances or vested interests, rather than focusing on their ideas or arguments. We see ad hominem circumstantial fallacy when someone is criticized because of the person's membership in a group or professional, religious, cultural, or political associations.

Ad Ignorantiam. Fallacy that occurs when someone argues that something must be the case true or false) because you cannot prove otherwise. This is the "if you can't prove me wrong, then I must be right!" defense. The person argues on the basis of a lack of proof to the contrary. However, a failure to disprove something does not mean the opposite is true. And when it comes to legal matters, a *presumption* of innocence is quite different than *proof* of innocence.

Ad Misericordiam. One of the fallacies of relevance; this fallacy occurs when there is an attempt to persuade on the basis of an appeal to pity or someone's unfortunate circumstances rather than on the basis of evidence.

Ad Populum. One of the fallacies of relevance in which there is an attempt to persuade on the basis of an appeal to the majority, snob appeal, mass sentiment or patriotism.

Ad Verecundiam. One of the fallacies of relevance; this fallacy occurs when there is an attempt to persuade on the basis of the testimony or appeal to a public figure or celebrity who is not an expert in the field in question.

Addition.   Addition is one of the rules of inference and thus a valid form of argument. It is of the form: "A. Therefore, either A or B."

Ah-ha effect.   A mental breakthrough—when we finally get something.

Ambiguity.   A lack of clarity in the use of language either by accident or intent, resulting in a confusion that may lead to an incorrect conclusion being drawn. Problems can occur when words, grammar, or sentence structure create an ambiguity or a variety of interpretations.

Amphiboly.   Fallacy that occurs when the sentence structure or use of grammar creates an ambiguity, leading to an incorrect conclusion being drawn.

Analysis.   The process of gathering evidence, weighing premises, sorting out warranted from unwarranted assumptions, structuring arguments, evaluating the strength of an inductive argument, and assessing the validity and soundness of deductive arguments. The central task of analysis is the evaluation of an argument to determine its strength.

Analytical Tools.   Ways to weigh evidence, construct or dismantle arguments, analyze the various aspects of reasoning, acquire a facility for both inductive and deductive reasoning, and determine the strength of the reasoning holding the argument together.

Antecedent.   The condition that is claimed to lead to a certain effect (known as the "consequent"). The antecedent lies between the "if" and the "then" in a conditional claim.

Antonyms.   Words that are opposite in meaning (e.g., hot and cold, tall and short).

Application of a Rule.   Using a set of criteria to draw a conclusion, as with: "Rule X applies to any cases with characteristics A, B, C, and D. Individual case P has characteristics A, B, C, and D. Therefore, rule X applies to case P."

Argument.   A set of propositions that consists of a conclusion and the premises (evidence). The premises act as supporting evidence for the conclusion. An argument consists of *only one* conclusion and *at least one* premise.

Argument based on statistical studies.   An inductive argument consisting of one or more inferences about a targeted population drawn on the basis of a sample group. There are two components to a statistical study: The targeted population about which we want information and the sample group to be studied as a microcosm of the larger group.

Argument from Analogy.   An inductive argument that rests on a comparison that claims a characteristic true of the one term in the equation will also be true of the other. In law this usually involves the application of a precedent or legal principle.

Assessment Tools.   Ways to gather information, consider options, organize data using a set of criteria, sort warranted from unwarranted assumptions, sort into relevant categories, and break down an argument in order to evaluate the quality of the reasoning.

Assumption.   Something that is taken for granted or supposed to be the case without proof. An assumption is usually unstated.

Asymmetrical Descriptions.   When members of one group are referred to, valued, or described in ways that would not be used for a different group. An asymmetry usually indicates a double standard—generally resulting in one group being treated with more leniency or given higher status.

Asymmetry.   When a set of criteria applied to one group results in distinctly different results than when applied to a parallel (seemingly similar) group. In other words, two asymmetrical things simply do not match up. For example, newspaper descriptions of one ethnic group or gender are often dissimilar from descriptions of the dominant ethnic group or gender.

Attitudes and Dispositions of a Critical Thinker.   The key attitudes and dispositions of a clear thinker—such as being receptive, flexible, open-minded, a careful listener, attentive to detail, observant, questioning, and willing to persevere. Personal traits include being willing to take risks and able to look at problems from different vantage points.

Authenticity.   That which forms the basis for personal integrity and self-respect, including being true to oneself.

Authority (of a Web Page).   The source of a document or Web page. Concerns around authority center on legitimacy and credibility.

Begging the Question (Petitio Principii). Fallacy that involves circular reasoning, whereby the speaker assumes what she or he is trying to prove. The conclusion is drawn on the basis of evidence containing a restatement of the conclusion itself. What is concluded must come out of the premises and not be a restatement of them.

Beyond a Reasonable Doubt.   The standard of proof in criminal trials—that the evidence offers sufficient support for the conclusion so an alternative explanation is highly unlikely or impossible. This is a higher standard than that of civil trials, which rests on the preponderance of the evidence.

Bias.   Functions as a kind of blinder or filter, slanting our thinking one way or another. It must be set aside if we want to think clearly, formulate strong arguments, and act out of a sense of justice. Prejudice and bias have to do with attitudes and states of mind—oppression involves action.

Biased Statistics.   Fallacy that occurs when a statistical study is used to draw an inference about a target population, but the sample group is not diverse enough.

Biconditional.   A proposition in the form "A if and only if B" or "A is equivalent to B." These

can be expressed in either form: "If A then B, and if B then A" and "If A then B, and if not A then not B."

Bifurcation (Also Known as "False Dichotomy" or "Excluded Middle").   Fallacy that involves the presentation of an either/or situation having more than two options. This occurs when two choices are presented as complete and absolute (i.e., uncompromising contrasts).

Bloated Claims.   A variation of eulogisms that includes exaggeration, grandiose promises, or predictions to offer possibilities that are too good to be true.

Blogs.   Web logs; that is, web sites that function as online journals usually compromised of links and postings in reverse chronological order (most recent is first).

Bubble outline.   Method of organizing a text or laying out an argument using circles ("bubbles") of varying size. The larger circles indicate key ideas or concepts and the smaller ones related concepts or examples of the key idea to which they are joined.

Buzzwords   (See Jargon). A newly coined word or an old word used in a new way or used in a totally different context for an intended effect.

Categorical Proposition.   Propositions that are expressed in one of four forms: "All A is B," "No A is B," "Some (or x% of) A is B" and "Some (or x% of) A is not B," where $x \neq 0$ or 100. For example, "All cockatoos are birds" and "75% of cockatoos are animals that enjoy cantaloupe."

Categorical Syllogisms.   Three-line arguments (or chains of them), consisting of two premises and a conclusion, with all the propositions in the form of categorical propositions. The resulting argument consists of three terms that make up the subjects and predicates. These terms are called the major term (predicate of the conclusion), the minor term (subject of the conclusion), and the middle term (the remaining term found in each of the premises).

Categories (See Labels).   Words used to characterize something or someone. Categories can be neutral or imbued with meaning (positive or negative).

Causal Claim.   A proposition of the form "A causes B," "A is caused by B," or "B is the effect of A."

Cause-and-Effect Reasoning.   A kind of inductive argument that argues that a particular event or effect occurs on the basis of specific antecedent conditions said to be the causal factor or factors.

Censorship.   Editing of a creation or performance or prohibiting any part of it to be seen or otherwise exhibited—presumably because of aspects deemed offensive to the public taste or morality.

Circumstantial Evidence.   Evidence that does not singularly or collectively definitively support a particular conclusion, but alternative explanations seem unlikely. This occurs when we have no hard evidence one way or the other, but the evidence points to the one conclusion. No amount of circumstantial evidence can provide certainty. What gives circumstantial evidence its weight is the lack of an alternative explanation.

Cogent.   Synonymous with "clear and convincing." A cogent argument is convincing because of the quality and persuasive force of the evidence supporting the conclusion. A cogent argument is well reasoned and clearly structured so we can follow the argument, seeing how the evidence lays the foundation for the conclusion.

Complement.   The set of all elements that are not contained in a given set. The complement of a set A is non-A. For example, the complement of "voters" is "non-voters."

Complex Question.   Fallacy that consists of two questions rolled into one, so the complex

question cannot be answered without answering the previous, unasked question. The result is that the person is asked to give a simple answer to a multi-part (a complex) question, where the hidden question is potentially incriminating.

Composition.   Fallacy that occurs when it is argued that what is true of the parts or members must then be true of the whole or organization. Each of the parts or members may have some characteristic (say being lightweight), but that does not mean the whole group or object will be lightweight. The characteristics of the parts do *not* necessarily transfer to the entity as a whole.

Compound Proposition.   A proposition that contains at least one logical connective (i.e., "not," "and," "or," "if . . . then," and "if and only if"). For example, "Jasper loves corn and pine nuts."

Conceptual.   A type of question that draws upon knowledge of key terms and concepts and asks students to think on a more abstract level.

Conceptual framework.   A worldview or way of thinking that shapes an interpretation. The conceptual framework acts as a way to define the terms of an inquiry, arrive at a set of criteria for evaluating evidence and slants the ways in which decisions are made and justified.

Conclusion.   The proposition said to follow from at least one piece of evidence. Arguments consist of a set of premises (evidence) and one conclusion.

Conclusion-indicator.   A word or phrase that often precedes a conclusion. If you can replace the term with "therefore" without changing the argument, the term is a conclusion-indicator (for example: "thus," "hence," "consequently," "it follows that," and so on).

Conditional Claim.   A proposition that can be expressed in the form "If A then B." It is sometimes referred to as a hypothetical proposition, since we may not know whether the antecedent, A, is actually true in order to assert "If A then B."

Conjunct.   A term found in a conjunction. The terms "A" and "B" are both conjuncts for the conjunction "A and B."

Conjunction.   Any proposition that can be written in the form "A and B." Note: conjunctions could have terms that are equivalent to "and," such as "plus," "also," "moreover," and "but." The rule of conjunction asserts that if A is true and if B is also true, then the claim "A and B" is then true.

Connotation.   An issue of semantics that has to do with what words signify. The *connotation* is what the word suggests, implies, or conjures up in our minds, whereas the *denotation* of a word is the literal meaning.

Consequent.   What is said to follow if some antecedent condition is assumed true. In an "if . . . then" claim, the consequent follows the "then."

Constructive Dilemma.   A valid deductive argument of the form: If A then B, and if C then D. Either A or C. Therefore, either B or D. In other words, there's a choice between two options, where each option leads to some effect and you have to pick between either of the two options. The constructive dilemma is often referred to as a compound modus pouens.

Context.   The time and place in which a work was created, including audience response, the social and political setting, the target audience, and corporate backing.

Contingent Claim.   A proposition that is either true or false, depending upon its component variables. In other words, contingent claims are neither tautologies (always true) nor contradictions (always false). For example, "Today is Sunday" is a contingent claim.

Contradiction.   A proposition that is always false, or false by definition (for example, any proposition of the form "A and not A," such as "The sky is blue but it is not blue").

Contrapositive.   The resulting proposition after the subject is replaced by the complement of the predicate and the predicate is replaced by the complement of the subject. The contrapositive cannot be taken on an I claim such as "Some A is B." The contrapositive of the E claim "No A is B" is the O claim "Some non-B is not non-A." For example, the contrapositive of "All painters are artists" is "All nonartists are nonpainters."

Contraries.   Propositions that cannot both be true, but could both be false. For example, A (universal positive) and E (universal negative) propositions are contraries since they cannot both be true, but could both be false.

Converse.   The resulting proposition after the subject and predicate are interchanged. The converse cannot be taken on an O claim. No change in the quality is required, except in the case of the A claim ("All A is B," which requires the converse to be changed to the I claim "Some B is A"). For example, the converse of "No cowhands are lonely people" is "No lonely people are cowhands."

Correlation.   A measure of the association between two things and how they are linked.

Corroborating Evidence.   A form of reinforcement, in the sense that the corroborating evidence strengthens the case by mutually supporting other evidence. When evidence poses no clear conflicts or contradictions if we assume it is actually true, we have *corroborating* evidence.

Credible Sources.   Sources considered to be legitimate, authentic, reliable, genuine, respectable. Jurors (and judges!) are regularly put in the position of having to assess the credibility of expert witnesses. Sizing up credibility is not always easy.

Critical Thinking Tools.   The means by which we accomplish the various tasks of critical thinking. There are four basic kinds of tools. (1) surveillance tools; (2) analytical tools; (3) assessment tools; and (4) synthesis tools.

Culturally Defined Uses of Language.   Norms around who can say what to whom, who can speak and in what order, and who gets the first and last word. We find these norms in public gatherings or in family dynamics. Our society and culture shape our use of language.

Currency.   The time a web page was last updated. Concerns around currency center on whether the page is up-to-date or outdated.

Cybersquatting.   When someone buys up the name of a well-known company and then demands money or simply refuses to give it up.

Deadly Triad.   The status quo *plus* habit *plus* stereotypical thinking. This triad is formed by the mindset of the dominant culture, the habitual ways of doing things, and belief systems that lock attitudes and stereotypical ways of thinking into place. Think of this deadly triad as conceptual snow goggles.

Deconstruction of an Ad.   Assessing its verbal message and visual message and the role of symbols and images in an attempt to analyze the various elements making up the ad.

Deductive Argument.   An argument in which the premises are claimed to be sufficient for drawing the conclusion. This assumes there are no missing pieces. In that sense, a deductive argument is a closed set. Examples of valid deductive arguments are modus ponens, modus tollens, disjunctive syllogism, and the hypothetical syllogism.

Definiendum.   The word or phrase that is being clarified or the meaning being sought.

Definiens.   The words meaning the same as the word or phrase in question (the explanation, the definition).

Definition.   A two-part explanation: first, the word or phrase to define or clarify. This is called

the *definiendum*. Second is the explanation—words meaning the same as the word or phrase in question. This is called the *definiens*. *Synonyms* are words that are similar in meaning (e.g., warm and toasty), whereas *antonyms* are words that are opposite in meaning (e.g., hot and cold).

Denotation.   An issue of semantics. The *denotation* of a word is the literal meaning, whereas the *connotation* is what the word suggests, implies, or conjures up in our minds.

Description.   A statement about what is or is not the case pertaining to something or someone. Generally, each item in a description is either true or false and could be verified by examination.

Destructive Dilemma.   One of the rules of inference and thus a valid form of argument. It is of the form "If A then B, and if C then D. Either not B or not D. Therefore, either not A or not C." It is often referred to as a compound modus tollens.

Disjunction.   A proposition in the form of "Either A or B." The terms A and B are called *disjuncts*. For example, "Either pudding is a vegetable or it is a creamy dessert."

Disjunctive Syllogism.   A valid deductive argument of the form: "Either A or B. Not A (or not B). Therefore, B (or therefore, A)."

Distribution.   When all the members of a class have a certain predicated characteristic. Determining distribution rests on two things: the location of the term (subject or predicate) and (2) the proposition's quality (in the case of the subject) or quantity (in the case of the predicate). Only universal propositions have a distributed subject and only negative propositions have a distributed predicate. In universal negative propositions, both terms are distributed.

Diversity of the sample.   The extent to which a sample group in a statistical study is representative of the targeted population in terms of key factors such as race or ethnicity, age, gender, education-level, and so on.

Double Standard.   When rules are applied unfairly to different groups, resulting in one group being treated with higher or lower status than the other.

Dyslogism.   A variation of begging the question that uses highly slanted language such as name-calling to bias an argument against someone or something.

Embedded advertising   Product placement. This is a form of marketing that places products in scenes, art, or scenarios that are not ostensibly advertising. For example, the movie *ET* has the protagonist using a particular brand of candy in various scenes.

Equivocation.   Fallacy that occurs when there is a shift of meaning in a word or phrase leading to an incorrect conclusion being drawn.

Ethical and Spiritual Dimension of Popular Culture.   The aspects of popular culture that relate to religion, faith, values, and morality.

Evaluation Question.   Referring to the Internet, a question that focuses on distinguishing the quality of the Web page or Web site and checking for any of the following: accuracy, authority, coverage, currency, and objectivity.

Exaggeration.   Inflating or distorting something (e.g., stretching the truth) in order to achieve a desired effect.

Euphemism.   A variation of begging the question that uses highly slanted language to bias an argument in favor of someone or something.

Equivalent.   Two propositions that have the same logical meaning, even if their form may differ. "A is equivalent to B" entails "If A then B" and "If B than A."

Fact.   Something known to be true or that could be confirmed by empirical or other means. Facts are actually the case, known by observation or reliable testimony, rather than inferred or surmised. Statements of fact include all that we can say is "true" or are true by definition.

Factual Judgments.   An inference generally drawn from earlier observations (the factual picture). A factual judgment is made on the basis of a set of facts about the issue in question. Because the judgment is one step removed from the fact, this means that the inference drawn on the basis of the fact is not necessarily true—it must be scrutinized so we are not misled. For example, to assess the impact of a new law on your economic interests as a student, you would arrive at a factual judgment by seeing how those interests fit into the entire factual picture surrounding the new law.

Fallacies of Ambiguity.   (Also known as Linguistic Fallacies). Fallacies that center on the use of language in terms of emphasis, interpretation, sentence structure, or the relationship between the parts and the whole. The ambiguity results in an incorrect conclusion being drawn, causing the fallacy. The names of the fallacies relate to the form the flawed reasoning takes.

Fallacies of Presumption.   Fallacies that rest upon an unwarranted assumption, that leads to an incorrect conclusion being drawn. The names of the fallacies relate to the form the flawed reasoning takes.

Fallacies of Relevance.   Fallacies in which the premises simply fail to support the conclusion. So they are irrelevant. The names of the fallacies relate to the form the flawed reasoning takes.

Fallacy.   A deceptive or misleading argument that may persuade us, but is nevertheless unsound. A fallacy may take many different forms, but they all share a common trait—namely, they are poorly reasoned arguments, however persuasive they seem on the surface.

Every fallacy contains a fundamental flaw in reasoning.

Fallacy of Affirming the Consequent.   One of the formal fallacies. It takes the form: "If A then B. B. Therefore, A."

Fallacy of Complex Question.   Fallacy that consists of two questions rolled into one, so the complex question cannot be answered without answering the previous, unasked question. The result is that the person is asked to give a simple answer to a multi-part (a complex) question. It is this first, hidden, question that is incriminating and carries a presumption of guilt that is then attached to the second, stated, question. For example, "Have you still a slob?" assumes that "you" are guilty of having been a slob in the past.

Fallacy of Denying the Antecedent.   One of the formal fallacies. It takes the form: "If A then B. A is not the case. Therefore, B is not the case either."

Fallacy of Misleading Vividness.   A fallacy of presumption that occurs when strong evidence is overlooked because of a striking counter example.

False Analogy.   Fallacy that draws an inference resting on a comparison between two terms having no real similarities, other than trivial ones. The form it takes is this: "A is like B and A has property P. Therefore, B has property P as well." The problem is the comparison of A and B is seriously flawed.

False correlation.   Inference that one thing that precedes another is causally related to it despite insufficient evidence.

Figure.   In a syllogism, determined by the location of the middle term. There are four possible figures. Knowing the figure is crucial for assessing the validity of a syllogism.

Film review.   A commentary on a film that includes some or all of the following: plot, character development, evaluation or rating, justification for assessing the film or its components (such as the acting), and a detailed argument about the film.

First Amendment   (of the U.S. Constitution). Guarantees freedom of speech.

Flowchart.   Method of organizing a text or laying out an argument using numbered labels (or boxes). Each label has a description of the numbered paragraph in the text or argument.

Formal Fallacies.   Fallacies that occur because of a structural error. As a result, the very form of the reasoning is incorrect. The different names of the formal fallacies refer to the pattern of that flawed reasoning, such as the fallacy of denying the antecedent and the fallacy of affirming the consequent.

Forms of argument.   Two categories of arguments (as determined by logicians): deductive and inductive.

Frame of reference   A particular vantage point (point of view) that could be used to examine a given issue. The frame of reference influences the ways issues are presented and potentially "stacks the deck." This framework is shaped by our prior knowledge, assumptions, values, language or notation, among others.

Functions of language.   The major functions of language are (1) *expressive* (e.g., in conveying emotions and feelings, (2) *evocative* (e.g., in trying to evoke response in others and as a catalyst to bringing about some action or effect), (3) *poetic* (e.g., in using rhythm, repetition, and a specific choice of words), (4) *ceremonial function* (e.g., in establishing communion, liturgical readings, prayers, ritualistic repetition of words), and (5) logical (e.g., to convey first-hand primary reports or secondary reports not based on eyewitness testimony).

Habit.   Routines that may act as blinders or restrictions on perceiving the world and evaluating what is seen and that therefore should be scrutinized as a potential obstacle to clear thinking.

Hasty Generalization.   Fallacy in which a statistical study is used as the basis for an inference, but the sample size is too small or atypical. This fallacy is commonly seen in stereotypical reasoning based on a sample of one or two. If the sample size is not sufficient, avoid drawing a generalization.

Hate Crimes.   One of the most odious expressions of prejudice. The American Psychological Association says of hate crime that not only is it an attack on one's physical self, but it is also an attack on one's very identity.

Hedging.   Undercutting a claim or raising doubts about it by the use of language. Hedging can take two forms: (1) it can indicate a shift from one position to a much weaker one; or (2) it can suggest a negative connotation of a phrase or claim.

Higher-Order Thinking Skills.   Comprehension skills, that include application, synthesis, drawing inferences, comparison or contrast, justification, analysis, evaluation, moral reasoning, and using inductive and deductive reasoning.

Hoax-Buster.   A resource or Web site intended to help users identify Web sites that are hoaxes or spoofs.

Human Interest Story.   A news story intended to appeal to the general reader because of its focus on a particular case (such as a moving story about an individual or group of individuals).

Hypothetical Case (Alias Hypo).   A law case that presents a scenario or story with the task of deciding how it is to be evaluated given existing laws and precedents. This is an important application of analogical reasoning, requiring lawyers and law students to be both astute and imaginative in assessing the hypothetical cases.

Hypothetical Syllogism.   A valid deductive argument of the form: "If A then B. If B then C. Therefore, if A then C."

Ideas.   Solutions, intentions, plans of action, or theories. The ancient roots of the word go back to a general or ideal form, pattern, or standard by which things are measured. More commonly now, we use it to refer to insights, purposes, or recommendations.

Independent Evidence.   One piece of evidence that is sufficient in and of itself (singularly) to establish the conclusion.

Inductive.   An argument in which the conclusion can only be said to follow with probability or likelihood even if the premises are assumed to be true. The conclusion of an inductive never follows with certainty. Examples include predictions, cause and effect arguments, statistical reasoning, and arguments from analogy.

Inductive Generalization.   An argument of the form: "x% of As polled (or sampled) are Bs. Therefore, x% of all As are Bs."

Inference.   A conclusion drawn on the basis of some evidence or observations. An inference is an answer to the question, "What's it about? What story does this tell?"

Interdependent Evidence.   When a conclusion could not be established by any one of the premises but the premises together support the conclusion. In other words, the evidence works as a unit, not singularly, to establish the conclusion.

Invalid.   An argument in which the assumed truth of the premises does not guarantee that the conclusion is also true. In other words, if the premises could be true while the conclusion was false, the argument would be invalid. Invalid arguments are always unsound.

Jargon.   The language of a particular group or profession or the specialized technical terminology coined for a specific purpose or effect.

Joint Method.   Combining the method of agreement and the method of difference to determine the cause of an event. This method, then, looks both at what was the same *and* what was different in the event's antecedent conditions.

Labels.   Words used to characterize something or someone—such as a person, group, or set of objects. Labels can be neutral or imbued with meaning (positive or negative).

Legal Precedent.   A previous legal case used as an analogy to draw an inference to another case. We are implicitly asserting that the similarities allow for the ruling of the precedent-setting case to apply to the case at hand.

Lexical definition.   The dictionary definition of a word.

Liberatory voice.   Works of inspiration that have a transformative effect on the audience. Think of those who have stood up against injustice and raised their voices in opposition.

Linguistic fallacy.   Also known as a fallacy of ambiguity (because of the lack of clarity leading to a mistaken conclusion due to the use of language). The three key linguistic fallacies are equivocation (where there's a shift of meaning in a word or phrase leading to an incorrect conclusion), accent (where the emphasis of a word or phrase leads us to an incorrect conclusion), and amphiboly (where the sentence structure or use of grammar creates an ambiguity, leading to an incorrect conclusion).

Loaded Language.   Value-laden language that creates either a positive or negative bias. The use of loaded terms tends to unfairly prejudge the case. Loaded language is to be distinguished from colorful, or figurative, language. With the latter, striking images (from ugly to funny to beautiful) are evoked because of the vivid use of language, but it does not function as a means of persuasion for a particular conclusion.

Logical Addition (a.k.a. Addition).   One of the rules of inference and thus a valid form of argument. It is of the form "A. Therefore, either A or B."

Lower-Order Thinking Skills.   Thinking skills that are at a more basic, rather than advanced level. This includes observation, gathering data, comparison, and contrast.

Major Premise.   The premise of a syllogism containing the major term (the predicate of the conclusion).

Major Term.   The predicate of the conclusion in a syllogism.

Margin of Error.   Recognizes that the inference from the smaller, sample group to the targeted population contains a degree of probability, which is indicated by the range of the margin of error plus-or-minus z. The margin of error means the range goes from $-z\%$ to $+z\%$, which is a range of 2z. This means that if your margin of error is 3%, then the range is 6%, and a margin of error of 5% will give a range of 10%, which is a significant range. The smaller the margin of error z, the better.

Metaphor.   The application of a word or phrase to draw a comparison or indicate a similarity (e.g., "she is a shrew and he's a snake").

Metatag.   A metatag is a place in the HTML code where information about the site is listed.

Method of Agreement.   A way to determine the cause of an event by examining all the cases where the event occurs and then looking for a common factor among the antecedent conditions.

Mood of a syllogism.   The list of types of proposition (A, E, I, O) of the major premise, minor premise, and conclusion (as expressed in standard form). Since there are three propositions to a syllogism, the mood consists of some combination of A's, E's, I's, and O's. Typically, the mood is stated before the figure, as we see with mood and figure OAO-(3).

Method of Concomitant Variation   A way to determine the cause of an event by examining situations in which more or less of some causal factor(s) result in an increase or decrease of the effect.

Method of Difference.   A way to determine the cause of an event by examining all the cases where the event occurs and where it doesn't in order to determine what was different and therefore identify the cause.

Middle Term.   The term that only appears in the two premises of a syllogism.

Minor Premise.   The premise of a syllogism containing the minor term.

Minor Term.   The subject of the conclusion in a syllogism.

Modus Ponens.   A valid deductive argument of the form "If A then B. A. Therefore B."

Modus Tollens.   A valid deductive argument of the form "If A then B. Not B. Therefore not A."

Necessary.   A condition P is necessary for Q if Q could not occur without P. This means, if Q is true, then P is also true. "P is necessary for Q" is the same as "If not P then not Q," or the equivalent proposition, "If Q then P."

Netspeak.   A mode of communication over the Internet that uses abbreviations (e.g., CUL8R, RUOK).

News Media.   The institutions in charge of producing news and commentary, including both print media (newspapers or newsletters), electronic media (online news sources), and TV news.

Objectivity.   Being fair and balanced in an assessment or presentation. The contrast is subjectivity, which points to a vested interest or possible bias.

Obverse.   Proposition that results after two steps: (1) change the quality of the proposition to its opposite (positive to negative or vice versa) and then (2) replace the predicate by its complement. The obverse can be taken of any categorical proposition. For example, the obverse of "No snakes are lizards" is "All snakes are nonlizards" and the obverse of "Some cows are Jerseys" is "Some cows are not non-Jerseys."

Opinions.   (1) Statements of belief or conjecture, for example, "The best music is rhythm and blues" and "Practicing verb drills is a drag." (2) Statement of perception, individual taste, or emotion. This gives rise to the refrain, "Well, that's just a matter of opinion." (3) Legal opinion. In a legal context, opinions may be expressed as a formal statement, a ruling, or considered advice. Court opinions, for example, function as an explanation for a decision that becomes law.

Particular Claim.   A proposition that could be expressed in the form "Some A are (or are not) B." This includes statistical claims of the form "x% of A is/is not B," where x is neither 100% nor zero. A particular claim is to be contrasted with a universal claim, which is an all-or-nothing claim.

Passive Voice.   Making the object of an action into the subject of a sentence, as in "The chicken was eaten by the coyote." Passive constructions can be spotted by looking for a form of "to be" followed by a past participle. One effect of the passive voice is that it avoids calling attention to the one performing an action (the coyote); rather, its focus is upon the recipient of the action (the chicken).

Post Hoc Fallacy.   Fallacious argument in which it is claimed "A causes B" on the basis of "A" happening before "B." The fact are event occurs before another does not reson they are causally related.

Predictions.   An argument about the future based on past or present evidence. A prediction is an inductive argument.

Premise.   A proposition offered or assumed as evidence in support of a particular conclusion. Unstated assumptions may function as premises, so it is important for all premises to be articulated when analyzing an argument.

Premise-Indicator.   A word or phrase that precedes a premise. If a word can be replaced with "because," (for example: "given that," "in light of the fact that," "whereas," and so on) it is a premise-indicator.

Prescription.   A recommendation. Prescriptions can be written in the form of "This *ought to* be done" or "This *ought not* to be done" or related claims (such as "X ought or ought not do Y").

Problem-solving skills.   The analytical skills required to guide an investigation, arrive at an answer, or come to a resolution (e.g., of a dilemma). The include questioning-skills, observation-skills, the ability to sort and weigh evidence, the ability to use a framework or shift information into categories, and the ability to draw inferences on the strength of available evidence.

Prognoses.   Predictions based on the given facts of the case, along with what is known about analogous cases. Prognoses entail inductive reasoning because of the lack of certainty.

Propaganda.   Use of words and images to shape public consciousness, to predispose people to certain ideas, policies and actions—and to manipulate them to think, vote, and act in ways in sync with the propaganda machine. Propaganda can come from all directions—left, right, and center—it is the substance, not the source that marks propaganda.

Proposition.   An assertion that is either true or false. Declarations and rhetorical questions may operate as propositions, in order to clarify what's being asserted. A proposition can always be expressed in the form in which something (called the predicate) is either affirmed or denied about something else (called the subject).

Quality.   Answers, "Are you asserting something *is* or *is not* the case?" You are either affirming that it is the case (the quality is positive) or denying it (the quality is negative); therefore, the quality of a proposition is always either *positive* or *negative*.

Quantifier.   A term that indicates "how much"; such as the universal quantifiers "all" or "no" and the particular quantifier "some." Statistical propositions of the form x percent of A is B (x is neither 0 nor 100) are treated as particular propositions.

Quantity.   Answers the question, "How much?" In other words, the quantity refers to how much of the subject class is said to have something predicated of it. The possible answer, are "universal" or "particular" (i.e., all or some of it).

Propaganda.   Material (words or images) used deceptively in order to persuade an audience to a particular way of thinking (e.g., about politics, society, the government, or the like). Propaganda can take a number of forms.

Question-Begging Epithet.   Fallacy that occurs when language is biased so that it stacks the deck in either a positive or negative direction and leads to an incorrect conclusion. This results from the slanted language causing us to unfairly prejudge the case.

Question Techniques.   Methods that focus the inquiry, narrow down the territory under consideration to eliminate false leads or irrelevant material.

Red Herring.   Fallacy that occurs when an irrelevant line of reasoning is intentionally used to divert people away from the topic at hand. We see this when someone purposely shifts the subject of the conversation to avoid an incriminating line of questioning or to deceive someone. It's called a red herring, because a stinking little herring (fish) is an effective way to lead the hound dogs off the scent.

Retrodiction.   An inductive argument about the past based on present evidence.

Rule of Inference.   A valid deductive argument form that allows us to draw an inference on the basis of the structure of the argument. Examples include modus ponens, modus tollens, disjunctive syllogism, hypothetical syllogism, constructive dilemma, simplification, and conjunction.

Rule of Replacement.   Rule that allows us to restate a proposition into an equivalent form. Examples include DeMorgan's Laws, material implication, transposition, and exportation.

Rules of the Syllogism.   Conditions that must be met in order for the syllogism to be valid. There are 5 rules of the syllogism.

Sample Group.   A microcosm of a larger group, the targeted population, that we study in order to generalize about the larger group.

Search Question.   Keywords or description in order to obtain a list of links on a particular topic using Internet software.

Sample Size.   The number of subjects in the sample group used as the basis for an inference about a target population. The fallacy of hasty generalization occurs when the sample size is too small and the fallacy of biased statistics occurs when the sample size is not diverse enough.

Semantics.   The meaning of words, what they signify in contrast to syntax, which focuses on the use of grammar, sentence structure, and punctuation, which are structural issues.

Simple Proposition.   An assertion that does not contain any logical connectives ("and," "or,"

"not," "if . . . then," and "if and only if"). For example, "Pudding is a tasty dessert" is a simple proposition; whereas "Pudding is not good for your diet" is a compound proposition.

Simplification.   One of the rules of inference and thus a valid form of argument. It is of the form: "A and B. Therefore, A (or: Therefore, B)."

Slippery Slope.   Fallacy that involves an argument against something on the basis that, if it is allowed, it will lead to something worse, which in turn leads to something even worse and so on (down the slippery slope). The unstated assumption is that the first in the causal chain leads to the second and that leads to the third, and so on. The connection is incorrectly assumed and not proven. *Note:* Not all propositions that involve causal chains are slippery slopes. The fallacy occurs when the chain is asserted, but not proven.

Slogan.   The jingle or sales line that is meant to be memorable and identify that product with this manufacturer.

Sound.   A valid argument with true premises. Only deductive arguments can be sound (inductive arguments can't be sound because they could never be valid).

Spam.   Unsolicited email—the web equivalent of junk mail.

Speculation.   A form of guesswork. We normally use the term "speculation" to apply to hypotheses that have little, if any, evidence to back them up. There may be a kernel of evidence, but not enough to draw a solid conclusion.

Square of Opposition.   Diagram indicating the relationship between categorical propositions: universal claims are contraries, particular claims are subcontraries, universal positive claims are contradictories of particular negative claims, universal negative claims are contradictories of particular positive claims, the two particular claims are subalterns of the two universal claims that are of the same quality (positive or negative).

Standard Form of a Proposition.   A proposition expressed as one of these forms: "All A is B," "No A is B," "Some A areare not B," or "x% of A are/are not B."

Standard Form of a Categorical Syllogism.   A syllogism in which the propositions are all expressed in the form of an A, E, I, or O claim ("All A is B," "No A is B," "Some A is B," Some A is not B," and the syllogism is ordered: major premises, minor premise, conclusion.

Standard Outline.   Method of organizing a text or laying out an argument using traditional outline form consisting of alphabetical letters, roman numerals, and numbers to indicate main themes, sub-themes, explanations, and examples.

Statistical Reasoning.   When an inference is drawn about a target population on the basis of what is said to be true of a sample group. Key factors in statistical reasoning are the size of the sample, the diversity of the sample, and the date the study is done.

Statistical Syllogism.   An inductive argument in the form: "X% of A is B. p is an A. Therefore, p is a B" and where x is neither 100 nor zero. For example, "85% of women like men with a good sense of humor. Ursula is a woman. Therefore, Ursula will like men with a good sense of humor."

Stipulative definition.   A definition of a word is one that is created or specified, e.g., in a particular case, say for an argument or discussion.

Strategy for Setting out Arguments.   (1) State the conclusion (thesis/hypothesis); (2) List the premises (reasons/evidence) one by one; (3) Examine the premises (reasons/evidence) to see if it is sufficient to support the conclusion.

Straw Man Fallacy.   Fallacy that presents an opponent's position as so extreme that it's indefensible. We are then steered toward another, more moderate or appealing position which is offered as the alternative. The image of the "straw man" (scarecrow) is that of something so flimsy that it will go up in smoke if we put a match near it. With the straw man fallacy, the opposition is usually painted as much more extreme than it actually is and the speaker's own position is offered as the better alternative.

Subaltern.   A particular proposition that can be inferred from the truth of the universal proposition, where we know the subject class is not empty. For example, the subaltern of "All tigers are cats" is "Some tigers are cats."

Subalternation.   The process of inferring from the universal claim to its corresponding particular claim.

Subcontraries.   Propositions that cannot both be false, but could both be true. For example, I (particular positive) and O (particular negative) propositions are subcontraries, since they cannot both be false, but could both be true.

Sufficient.   The minimal conditions for the truth of a proposition. This is expressed as follows: "P is sufficient for Q" is equivalent to "If P then Q" or "If not Q then not P." All three expressions are equivalent.

Surveillance Tools.   Perceive problems; recognize unsupported opinions versus facts and supported claims; spot prejudicial or biased modes of thinking, recognize the different uses of language; and watch for what is not said, omitted, downplayed or discarded.

Syllogism.   Three-line argument with two premises and one conclusion in which there are only three terms (called the major term, the minor term, and the middle term). The major term is the predicate of the conclusion, the minor term is the subject of the conclusion, and the middle term is the remaining term found only in the premises.

Synonyms. Words that are similar in meaning (e.g., warm and toasty).

Syntax. Sentence structure, grammar, and punctuation, in contrast to semantics, which focuses on the meaning, or significance, of words.

Synthesis Tools. Articulate goals and decisions using a defensible set of criteria; resolve personal conflicts and professional dilemmas; recognize the role of ideas and creativity in problemsolving; evaluate decisions, plans, and policies; summarize arguments and synthesize information; and examine our own thinking processes and decision-making strategies.

Systemic Violence. Violence that is found throughout a work or performance, as opposed to being present in one scene or aspect of the work.

Tabloidism. Journalism that uses titillation, exaggeration, shock, disgust, or graphic photographs or details to attract an audience.

Targeted Population: The group about which we seek information in a statistical study by generalizing from the characteristics of a sample group.

Tautology. A tautology is a proposition that is always true, or true by definition (for example, "Either that's a bowl of pudding or it's not a bowl of pudding").

Thematic Approach. Presents an analysis of a film of TV program within a particular framework or theme (such as justice versus injustice, good versus evil, psychology, existentialism, etc.). When doing a thematic approach, our goal is to be single-mindedly focused on the central theme and to go into depth, citing examples to back up points.

Thesis. The position being argued by an author. In an argument it functions as the conclusion for which the premises (evidence) are offered as support.

Transition Words. Act to amplify, emphasize, introduce, illustrate, or contrast. Examples are "moreover," "to restate," "primarily," "in simpler terms," "notably," "in fact," alternatively," "on the other hand," and so on. Transition words are neither premise-indicators nor conclusion-indicators.

Tu Quo. Fallacy that occurs when there's an attempt to discredit those whose actions are not in keeping with their words or who don't "practice what they preach."

Universal Claim. A claim that can be expressed in the form "All A is B" or "No A is B." In contrast, particular claims assert or deny a predicated characteristic of only some (neither all nor none) of the subject class.

Unsound Argument. An argument that has one or both of these traits: (1) it is not valid, (2) it does not have true premises.

URL. A Web address. For example the URL of the *Washington Post* is http:www.washingtonpost.com.

Valid. An argument in which the premises certainly support the conclusion. This means that, if we assume the premises are true, the conclusion would be forced to be true as well. The conclusion cannot be false and the premises true in a valid argument. A valid argument is not necessarily sound; soundness requires that the argument be valid *and* the premises actually true. Validity does not apply to inductive arguments—only to deductive ones.

Value Claims. Express some kind of moral, social, or aesthetic judgment and, thus, are not normally presented as either true or false. They may be used as evidence, but they should be handled carefully. Value claims are usually expressed in sentences that assert a judgment or a recommendation.

Variable. A letter (A, B, C, or p, q, r) used to stand for propositions. For example, "If pudding is on the menu, then George will order it" could be rewritten using variables P = pudding is on the menu and G = George will order it. The proposition then would be written: "If P then G."

Venn Diagrams.   Intersecting circles that are used to indicate the relationship between terms of propositions or to assess validity. The diagram must contain as many intersecting circles as the number of terms involved.

Verbal message.   What is being said in ads in terms of the text (or copy).

Visual Message.   The use of color or black and white, symbols, images, "characters," and the layout of an ad.

Watchdog.   An individual, group of individuals, or association whose job or duty it is to observe and report on someone or something for the welfare of the general public.

Weasel Words.   Slippery terms that are used in manipulative ways, twisting the meaning of words or phrases to create a certain effect.

Web Analysis.   Analysis of a Web page or document on a Web site. The American Library Association sets out five aspects to Web analysis: authority, accuracy, coverage, currency, and objectivity.

Wiki.   A web site allowing collaborative editing of its content and structure by its users (barring some restrictions by the website).

w.w.w.   Abbreviation for "World Wide Web."

Index